D0983207

THE NOBEL PRIZE WINNERS

Physiology or Medicine

THE NOBEL PRIZE WINNERS

Physiology or Medicine

Volume 2
1944-1969

Edited by
FRANK N. MAGILL

SALEM PRESS
Pasadena, California   Englewood Cliffs, New Jersey

∞ The paper used in these volumes conforms to the American National Standard for Permanence of Paper for Printed Library Materials, Z39.48-1984.

Library of Congress Cataloging-in-Publication Data
The Nobel Prize winners: physiology or medicine/edited by Frank N. Magill. p. cm.
Includes bibliographical references and index.
Contents: v. 1. 1901-1944—v. 2. 1944-1969—v. 3. 1969-1990.
1. Medical scientists—Biography. 2. Nobel prizes.
I. Magill, Frank Northen, 1907-
R134.N63 1991 91-12143
610'.92'2—dc20 CIP
ISBN 0-89356-571-7 (set)
ISBN 0-89356-573-3 (volume 2)

PRINTED IN THE UNITED STATES OF AMERICA

CONTENTS

THE NOBEL PRIZE WINNERS

ALPHABETICAL LIST OF PRIZE WINNERS

ALPHABETICAL LIST OF PRIZE WINNERS

ALPHABETICAL LIST OF PRIZE WINNERS

THE NOBEL PRIZE WINNERS

Physiology or Medicine

1944

Physiology or Medicine
Joseph Erlanger, United States
Herbert Spencer Gasser, United States

Chemistry
Otto Hahn, Germany

Physics
Isidor Isaac Rabi, United States

Literature
Johannes V. Jensen, Denmark

Peace
International Red Cross Committee

HERBERT SPENCER GASSER
1944

Born: Platteville, Wisconsin; July 5, 1888
Died: New York, New York; May 11, 1963
Nationality: American
Area of concentration: Neurophysiology

Gasser and his colleague Joseph Erlanger demonstrated that the speed of nerve impulses varies with the diameter of the nerve fiber and thus inaugurated the study of differentiated function of nerve fibers

The Award

Presentation

Professor Ragnar Granit, head of the Department of Neurophysiology of the Nobel Institute of the Royal Caroline Institute in Sweden, made the presentation address at the ceremony awarding the Nobel medal to Herbert Spencer Gasser and his colleague, Joseph Erlanger, on December 10, 1944. Granit cited their work as the third great milestone to date in understanding of nerve physiology. First, in the mid-nineteenth century, Emil Du Bois-Reymond had shown that the nerve impulse consisted of a wave of electrical energy transmitted along the nerve cell. Second, Edgar D. Adrian had demonstrated that a single stimulus could produce not one but a rapid series of such impulses. (Adrian was awarded the Nobel Prize in Physiology or Medicine in 1932 for this work.) The discoveries of Gasser and Erlanger were said to represent the third great advance in this tradition.

In sketching the background for Gasser and Erlanger's work, Granit noted that the Swedish physiologist Gustaf Göthlin had suggested in 1907 that thick nerve cells probably conducted electricity at a greater velocity than thinner ones, since electrical current travels faster through thicker cables than thinner ones. If true, this variability in speed would help explain why nerve cells vary in thickness. More important, it could help explain how the human nervous system processes sensory experience and organizes our responses to it.

By applying the cathode-ray tube and the oscillograph to the task of measuring electrical impulses in the nerve fiber, Gasser and Erlanger recorded more sensitive measurements than had been made previously of impulse speed. They demonstrated conclusively that this speed did in fact vary according to the diameter of the nerve fiber.

Nobel lecture

In his Nobel lecture, entitled "Mammalian Nerve Fibers," delivered on December 12, 1945, Gasser discussed the significance of his and Erlanger's findings regarding the different functions of the various fibers making up a nerve cell. He also conveyed the dynamic quality of a discipline in rapid transition, as new discoveries challenged and modified older ideas.

Gasser referred to his long and happy collaboration with Erlanger and indicated that his talk was based largely on experiments the two had conducted together. The early focus of their work was the nerve's action potential, a change in electrical charge along the nerve cell caused by an initial stimulus. By measuring changes in electrical polarity at various points among the nerve's long axon, scientists had earlier established that the nerve signal consisted of a single electrical impulse which traveled along the axon. This signal consisted in a change in electrical polarity that moved rapidly down the length of the cell. Immediately afterward, the original polarity reestablished itself, so the nerve could be ready for another signal. These signals were all-or-nothing phenomena. A nerve fired or it did not fire; the strength of a single impulse did not vary.

Building on these findings, Gasser and Erlanger began to examine more closely the nature of the electrical signals transmitted along the axon. In particular, they wanted to examine a series of after-potentials—smaller and more rapid changes in polarity that typically followed the spike potential, or original response to a stimulus. Gasser said that a thorough understanding of how the individual elements of the nervous system operated would lead to a better understanding of how the animal functioned. It was also important to study the nerve in conditions which, as closely as possible, duplicated the environment within the living organism, since living nerve cells reacted sensitively to minor changes in oxygen content, pH changes, and other factors.

Gasser and Erlanger classified nerve fibers into three groups, based on thickness. Those with the smallest diameters they called A fibers, those of intermediate thickness were B fibers, and the thickest fibers of all were called the C fibers. By isolating single fibers and making sensitive electrical measurements, Gasser and Erlanger established that the speed with which the electrical impulse traveled along the fiber varied directly with the diameter of the fiber. The larger the diameter of the fiber, the faster the signal traveled along it. Since each nerve cell consisted of fibers of various types, and since all types of fibers in the cell responded to a stimulus, it followed that the nerve was carrying several kinds of information about each stimulus. This finding opened a broad vista of possibilities for examining the ways in which the nervous system processed sensory information and transmitted it to the brain and the spinal cord.

Gasser noted that discoveries in neurophysiology were proceeding so rapidly that terminology was in constant need of revision. For example, the simple classification of nerve fibers into the A, B, and C categories was already being challenged by new findings regarding the complexity of the fibers. Gasser relied on this preliminary system of classification since this was the vocabulary most familiar to his fellow scientists. This tension between rapid change and the need to establish stable terms characterized neurophysiology during this period of revolutionary discoveries regarding the functions of the nervous system.

Gasser closed with an expression of the scientist's excitement about what his investigations reveal: "The more one sees of the exquisite precision with which events take place in the central nervous system the more one is impressed by it." He predicted that the different speeds with which impulses traveled along the axon would lead to a greater appreciation of the role of timing in the nervous system's integration of sensory information.

Critical reception

In 1944, for the first time since the presentation of the first Nobel awards in 1901, the award ceremony was held at a place other than Stockholm with someone other than the King of Sweden making the presentations. World War II had disrupted the work of the Nobel Committee, and no awards had been made since 1938. In 1944, the committee announced awards for that year and for 1943. Presentations could not be made in German-occupied Sweden, however, so the ceremony to honor the winners for 1943 and 1944 was held in New York at the Waldorf-Astoria Hotel.

Crown Prince Gustaf Adolf of Sweden made a radio address to the assembled party, noting the four American winners being honored at the ceremony. (Besides Gasser and Erlanger, Henrik Dam and Edward A. Doisy, the 1943 winners for their work on vitamin K, received their awards at the ceremony.) President Franklin Delano Roosevelt also addressed the group by radio. Saying that science should be a servant of the people, he looked forward to the time when scientists of all countries could again work together. The Swedish minister to the United States, Wollmar F. Bostroem, acting as the king's representative, presented the awards.

The effect of the war was also evident in Gasser's remarks. Stressing the need to educate for peace, he suggested that students should be exposed to noble thoughts not as dogmas, but as the best that humanity had achieved to that point. A strong education in the evolution of human thought, he believed, would inculcate in students a strong desire for peace. While the collaborative nature of scientific activity provided a strong model for peaceful cooperation, this structure could not alone withstand stress without a comparable commitment to peaceful accommodation in other aspects of human life.

Gasser and Erlanger's achievement was widely recognized among scientists as providing a necessary foundation for any further examination of nerve function. Ralph Waldo Gerard, a prominent American neurophysiologist and professor at the University of Chicago, commenting on the Nobel award, traced the importance of electrical measurements of nerve impulses over the preceding hundred years. By use of the galvanometer, changes in the electrical potential along the nerve cell had first been detected in the mid-nineteenth century. Around 1900, a more sensitive galvanometer made finer measurements possible (the electrocardiogram resulted from other researches with this instrument). In the early 1920's, the signals from still more sensitive instruments were intensified with amplifiers. The advance in technique that Gasser and Erlanger had made was to apply the cathode-ray oscillograph to the task of detecting minute fluctuations in electrical signal. The exquisite sensitivity of this device made possible observations that had eluded all previous investigators.

Edgar Adrian, whose discovery that the nerve signal was a single all-or-nothing electrical impulse laid the foundation for Gasser and Erlanger's work, also cited the significance of their findings. He noted that the understanding of pain transmission had already been significantly increased by charting the different speeds at which pain messages were conducted along the nerve.

Biography

Herbert Spencer Gasser was born on July 5, 1888, in Platteville, Wisconsin. His father, Herman, was a country doctor and his mother, Jane Elizabeth Griswold, was a teacher. Herman Gasser read widely among the philosophers of the day, including Charles Darwin and Herbert Spencer; he thought enough of Spencer to name his son after him. Young Herbert read avidly in his father's collection as a boy. He enrolled at the University of Wisconsin as a zoology major and completed college in two years. Gasser next took courses at the University of Wisconsin medical school, studying physiology under Joseph Erlanger, who later was Gasser's collaborator. Since at that time the University of Wisconsin offered only preclinical training, Gasser transferred to The Johns Hopkins University, where he earned the M.D. in 1915. He returned to the University of Wisconsin as instructor of pharmacology. In 1916, his former teacher, Erlanger, who had moved to Washington University in St. Louis, invited Gasser to join him there.

Following some research into the effects of wounds on blood composition during World War I, Gasser began the work in neurophysiology that would make him one of the world's best-respected investigators of nerve function. Working with H. Sidney Newcomer, he devised a vacuum tube amplifier to intensify electrical signals. In the late 1920's, he and Erlanger conducted their groundbreaking experiments on the transmission of signals along the axon. Throughout this period, he held an appointment as professor of pharmacology at Washington University.

An invitation to join the physiology faculty at Cornell Medical College in New York in 1931 finally made it possible for Gasser to teach in his principal field of interest. In 1935, he was appointed director of the Rockefeller Foundation, and he held this position until his retirement in 1953. He continued his researches on nerve function after retirement.

Gasser maintained a lifelong interest in music. He also enjoyed carpentry, literature, and travel. His health was often poor, and he suffered from migraine headaches. He died in New York on May 11, 1963.

Scientific Career

Although his career included diverse appointments, Gasser's scientific work followed a single, devoted path. After a brief early period spent studying the effects of injury on blood composition, Gasser the researcher focused his energies, his rigorous standards, and his commitment to meticulous detail on the problem of how electrical impulses were transmitted along nerve cells.

Gasser first met Joseph Erlanger, with whom he would share the Nobel Prize, as a student in Erlanger's physiology class at the medical school of the University of Wisconsin. Gasser's ability in this field was immediately recognized when he was appointed an instructor in physiology in 1907, while he was still a student in the medical school. At Wisconsin, he also studied pharmacology under Arthur S. Loevenhart, and much of his teaching career was spent in this field.

After completing his medical education at The Johns Hopkins University (he received the M.D. in 1915), Gasser was invited to join Erlanger in St. Louis, where the latter was organizing a department of physiology at Washington University. Erlanger had been granted lavish funds to build one of the country's largest and best-equipped physiology laboratories. With the outbreak of World War I, research priorities shifted in the direction of wound effects and healing, and Gasser and Erlanger began investigating the relationship between shock and blood loss following injury. In 1918, at the invitation of his former teacher Loevenhart, Gasser joined the Armed Forces Chemical Warfare Service to aid in investigation of gas agents for military use. When the war was over, he returned to Washington University.

Another physiologist, Alexander Forbes, had worked in electronic surveillance during the war. Back at his Harvard laboratory after the war, Forbes began applying what he had learned about electrical instruments to the problem of measuring electrical events in the nerve cell. Gasser learned of this work and was inspired to take a similar approach. Working with a classmate from Johns Hopkins, H. Sidney Newcomer, he developed a vacuum tube amplifier and joined it to a string galvanometer to measure the course of an electrical impulse traveling along a nerve cell. They published their results in a paper in 1921, but Gasser was not satisfied. He realized that the instrument was partially distorting their results, and he began the search for a more sensitive method of recording the electrical events in the nerve cell. Gasser persuaded Erlanger to join him in applying the latest in electrical technology in the laboratory. Erlanger had not worked on nerves but had investigated electrical events in the control of the heartbeat.

Meanwhile, in 1921, Gasser accepted a position as professor of pharmacology at Washington University. Shortly thereafter, Gasser received a grant from the Rockefeller Foundation to study at various European centers of physiological research. At this time, Europe was still considered the leader in scientific medical research, but following the influential Flexner Report in 1910, American medical schools and research laboratories had begun modeling themselves on the scientific laboratories of the European medical schools, and the United States soon became a leading source of medical research. The generous support of Erlanger's laboratory had resulted from this wave of reform in American medical education.

Gasser spent two years abroad, studying at London, Paris, and Munich. When he visited the physiology laboratory at Cambridge, long considered one of the world's preeminent research centers in physiology, Gasser wrote joyfully to Erlanger that their laboratory in St. Louis was larger and better equipped. He returned to St. Louis in 1925.

A series of exacting experiments conducted throughout the 1920's catapulted Gasser and Erlanger to the forefront in neurophysiological research. They separated nerve cells to isolate individual fibers—a task so exacting that an error of one micron (one-thousandth of a milligram) could ruin a result. Gasser and Erlanger classified the fibers into three groups, A, B, and C, based on the speed with which they transmitted electrical impulses. They then set out to test a proposition first made by Gustaf Göthlin in 1907: that the diameter of the nerve fiber would affect the speed with which it transmitted an electrical impulse.

Gasser and Erlanger's technical innovation was to use the cathode-ray tube and the oscillograph to make their recordings. Each cathode-ray tube lasted only a few hours, and hundreds of repetitions were required to produce a visible photographic image. Gasser built and maintained the equipment himself, although by the 1930's the devices became complex enough that electronics assistants had to be hired.

By recording in meticulous detail the electrical events in the nerve cell, they established that, as expected, the thickest fibers, the A group, transmitted the fastest messages; the B group, of intermediate thickness, was next fastest; and the C fibers, the most slender, were also the slowest to pass along the electrical current. This work made it possible to examine the differing functions of each type of fiber in carrying information to the central nervous system (the brain and spinal cord). Fibers in the fast A group carried sensory impulses into the central nervous system and carried back messages to the voluntary muscles. The B fibers were found in nerves of the digestive organs, while C fibers, the slowest of all, carried pain sensations.

In 1922, Gasser and Erlanger published the first distinct recordings of nerve-action potentials—the changes in electrical charge that represented the nerve's response to a stimulus. Their continued experiments revealed that what had been thought of as a single event was actually a cluster of individual action potentials, each representing a single signal traveling along the long portion of the nerve cell, or axon.

Gasser and Erlanger demonstrated their findings at the Eleventh-International Physiological Congress at Boston in 1929. Their work led physiologists to conceptualize the workings of the nervous system in a new way. From the analogy of engineering communication systems, it had been assumed that a nerve fiber could carry different kinds of messages. Gasser and Erlanger, by demonstrating the different functions of fibers, showed the nervous system to consist of differentiated fibers, each dedicated to carrying a single kind of message. Integrating these different messages into a coordinated response was the job of the central nervous system.

The 1930's were a dynamic time in the study of nerve function, and many of the country's leading neurophysiologists were engaged in studying the problem of electrical transmission in the nerve cell. Gasser was a founding member of the Axonologists, an informal group of neurophysiologists formed in 1930 at the time of the annual meeting of American Physiological Society in Chicago. Meeting annually, these scientists kept one another up to date on their findings and contributed to the fertile atmosphere for research that characterized this period in the United States.

In 1931, Gasser finally obtained an appointment as professor of physiology at Cornell Medical College in New York City. There, he continued his research into the transmission of nerve impulses. He and Erlanger had discovered, through their sensitive recording devices, that a single impulse typically gave rise to a single, sharp impulse followed almost immediately by a flurry of smaller impulses. Gasser's careful work in identifying the separate phases of these events (the signal prompted by the stimulus; a brief period in which the cell was hyperexcitable; and a refractory period in which it could not be stimulated) laid further groundwork for the study of nerve function. Always a meticulous technician, Gasser was frequently consulted by other scientists on matters of technique as well as for theoretical guidance.

In 1935, Simon Flexner retired as director of the prestigious Rockefeller Institute, and he recommended Gasser as his replacement. Flexner, a pathologist and brother of Abraham Flexner, the influential reformer of medical education, had been the Rockefeller Institute's first director. Under his leadership, the institute had emphasized research into infectious diseases. It was expected that the appointment of a physiologist would lead to greater emphasis on basic research on physiology. In fact, Gasser, though he made no dramatic changes, shifted the institute's priorities in a slightly different direction. Noting that substantial progress had been made in treating and preventing infectious diseases, Gasser believed that chronic degenerative diseases would become increasingly important to study. In this view, he joined a few prescient observers who could see that medicine in the ensuing decades would be concerned more with chronic illnesses such as heart disease and cancer than with short-term bacterial infections.

Gasser stayed at the Rockefeller Institute until his retirement in 1953. Retirement as an administrator did not mean the end of his research career: Gasser continued his private researches on nerve cell function using the latest equipment—the electron microscope.

During his career, Gasser published hundreds of scientific papers. He was a member of the National Academy of Sciences, the American Physiological Society, and the American Society for Pharmacology and Experimental Therapeutics. In the 1930's, he served on the editorial board of the *American Journal of Physiology*, and in 1945, he was awarded the Kober Medal by the Association of American Physicians.

Bibliography

Primary

PHYSIOLOGY: "Physiological Action Currents in the Phrenic Nerve: An Application of the Thermionic Vacuum Tube to Nerve Physiology," *American Journal of Physiology*, vol. 57, 1921, pp. 1-26 (with H. S. Newcomer); "A Study of the Action Currents of Nerve with the Cathode Ray Oscillograph," *American Journal of Physiology*, vol. 62, 1922, pp. 496-524 (with Joseph Erlanger); "The Compound Nature of the Action Current of Nerve as Disclosed by the Cathode Ray Oscillograph," *American Journal of Physiology*, vol. 70, 1924, pp. 624-666 (with Joseph Erlanger); *Electrical Signs of Nervous Activity*, 1937 (with Joseph Erlanger); "Axons as Samples of Nervous Tissue," *Journal of Neurophysiology*, vol. 2, 1939, pp. 361-369.

AUTOBIOGRAPHY: "Herbert Spencer Gasser," *Experimental Neurology*, supplement 1, 1964.

Secondary

Bergland, Richard. *The Fabric of Mind*. Ringwood, Australia: Penguin Books Australia, 1985. This provocative book, by a Harvard neurosurgeon, argues that the mind is best understood as a gland in which information is carried by hormones rather than as a computerlike electrical system. Bergland discusses the importance of Gasser's work in understanding communication within the neuron.

Ganong, W. F. *The Nervous System*. 2d ed. Los Altos, Calif.: Lange Medical Publications. This book-length examination of the physiology of the nervous system is intended for medical students but starts by discussing basic physiological principles. It is suitable for readers who have read the chapter on the nervous system in a physiology text and want a more detailed explanation of how the nervous system works.

Marshall, Louise H. "Instruments, Techniques, and Social Units in American Neurophysiology, 1870-1950." In *Physiology in the American Context, 1850-1940*, edited by Gerald L. Geison. Bethesda, Md.: American Physiological Society, 1987. This essay by a historian compares Gasser and Erlanger's neurophysiology laboratory at Washington University to similar laboraties at Harvard, Johns Hopkins, and other universities. Marshall discusses the importance of close communication within the discipline and of state-of-the-art instruments in bringing the United States to the forefront of neurophysiological research in the 1930's.

Martini, Frederic. *Fundamentals of Anatomy and Physiology*. Englewood Cliffs, N.J.: Prentice-Hall, 1989. This introductory physiology text starts with definitions of basic terms and moves from the cellular chemistry through a discussion of tissues, organs, and organ systems. Chapter 12, "The Nervous System: Neural Tissue," discusses transmission of electrical impulses along the axon. Later chapters focus on the brain, the spinal cord, and the integrative functions of the nervous system.

Smith, Anthony. *Physiology*. New York: Viking Press, 1984. This set of essays is a good introduction to human physiology. Chapter 6 covers the nervous system. The book is suitable for a reader with only a general background.

Caroline J. Acker

1945

Physiology or Medicine

Baron Florey, Great Britain
Sir Alexander Fleming, Great Britain
Ernst Boris Chain, Germany and Great Britain

Chemistry

Artturi Ilmari Virtanen, Finland

Physics

Wolfgang Pauli, Austria and United States

Literature

Gabriela Mistral, Chile

Peace

Cordell Hull, United States

BARON FLOREY
1945

Born: Adelaide, Australia; September 24, 1898
Died: Oxford, England; February 21, 1968
Nationality: British
Areas of concentration: Biochemistry, microbiology, and pathology

Florey was instrumental in the development of methodology that made penicillin available for widespread medical use. He also identified practical procedures for the discovery of other antibiotics and therapeutic drugs; his work spanned biochemistry, bacteriology, and medicine

The Award

Presentation

Göran Liljestrand, professor at the Royal Caroline Institute and representative of the Nobel Awards Committee, delivered the Nobel presentation address about the three cowinners, Alexander Fleming, Ernst Chain, and Baron Florey, on December 10, 1945. He pointed out that "attempts have been made to reach the goal of the medical art—the prevention and cure of disease—by many different paths." He went on to note that once Louis Pasteur and Robert Koch had laid bare the nature of infectious disease "a generation ago," vaccines that used the "capacity of human and animal bodies to fight the invaders" were developed and people began to seek other kinds of remedies.

Next, Liljestrand reminisced about Alexander Fleming's 1928 discovery of penicillin, arising from the observation that contamination by a mold (*Penicillium notatum*) killed bacteria in laboratory cultures. He noted that though the possibility that penicillin "might be used as a remedy" for infectious diseases was then within reach, penicillin would have stayed "a fairly unknown substance, interesting to the bacteriologist, but of no great practical importance," had it not been for Howard Florey.

Florey, of the University of Oxford's Pathological Institute, and Ernst Chain planned and carried out the purification of penicillin. Liljestrand next described the complex purification and pointed out that the first human tests (after great success with animals) were disappointing because the drug caused fever. Happily, he noted, it was soon found that the fever was attributable to a minor impurity that was ultimately removed.

Florey convinced the United States to finance large-scale preparation of penicillin. Once penicillin was widely available, it produced miraculous cures of patients who had been considered doomed. Diseases cited as curable by penicillin were blood poisoning, cerebral meningitis, gas gangrene, pneumonia, and venereal disease. Thus, Liljestrand said, there is no doubt that the work with penicillin "is of the greatest importance for medical science."

The conclusion of the talk noted that the penicillin story is "a splendid example of different scientific methods combining for a great common purpose" and that it "has shown the fundamental importance of basic research." Liljestrand also noted that "the work demanded assistance from many different quarters, an unusual amount of scientific enthusiasm, and the firm belief in an idea."

Nobel lecture

Florey's Nobel lecture, entitled "Penicillin" and delivered on December 11, 1945, was designated by Florey as an attempt to "show how the present great activity in the investigation of antibacterial substances is due to the development of appropriate methods and their coordination." He first pointed out that, since 1895, an immense amount of antibiotic research had been done with fungi, bacteria, and plants, via bacteriological techniques that differed very little from those used with penicillin.

No antibiotic of medical value had developed from that work, Florey noted, saying that this was because the researchers had made little effort to understand the chemistry of the antibiotics. Florey then pointed out that his own successful study of penicillin—and recent, nearly successful work of others, with gliotoxin, gramicidin, and tyrocidine—was attributable to the fact that such chemical study was carried out. Regrettably, he stated, gliotoxin, gramicidin, and tyrocidine were of limited medical value because they were too toxic for human use.

All these recent efforts pointed to the best general method for finding chemotherapeutic substances. This was, in a stepwise fashion, to identify production of an antibacterial substance in a test organism; determine the best method for growing the organism under conditions wherein it produces the substance; isolate the antibacterial chemical by use of chemical methods; determine the kinds of disease bacteria against which it is effective; examine its toxicity to test animals and to human tissue cultures, to be assured that it is probably medically usable; find a means to produce very large amounts of the pure chemical; and test it on human victims of infectious diseases. This methodology, changed slightly, is still the classic procedure.

Efforts such as the discovery of streptomycin by Selman Waksman's group, said Florey, seemed likely to develop valuable antibiotics. He noted that streptomycin could be used to fight bacterial diseases (such as tuberculosis) that were unaffected by penicillin. The confidence in this methodology was justified because Waksman and others identified tetracyclines and other antibiotics in a similar fashion.

Florey ended by noting that antibacterial antibiotics were only one kind of antibiotics that could be identified. (He was correct here, too—there are, for example, fungicides and chemicals that kill protozoa.) Finally, Florey supported the importance of identification of the mechanisms by which antibiotics carry out their antimicrobial actions, suggesting that such efforts would be valuable.

Critical reception

The world greeted the announcement that Florey and his colaureates were to be awarded the 1945 Nobel Prize with great enthusiasm. The ability of the drug penicillin to cure disease was astounding; furthermore, it had saved thousands of lives on the battlefields of World War II. Public commentary about Florey, Fleming, and penicillin may be typified by the highly literate article, written by Daniel Schwartz, in *The New York Times Magazine* (January 2, 1944). Schwartz hailed penicillin as a "wonder drug," which he said "came at exactly the right time." Schwartz pointed out that it had many advantages over the sulfa drugs and that penicillin "cleared out infected wounds that defied all of the usual treatments."

Schwartz also stated that it was not until 1939, "eleven years after Fleming's original discovery" of penicillin, that Florey's group of scientists at the University of Oxford "began work with penicillin in earnest." He noted that the problems involved in their efforts to purify the drug were very complex, that from "all this work the advantages of penicillin became obvious," and that the work was exceptionally valuable to the world. Similar comments were made in *Liberty Magazine* (July 24, 1943) and many other periodicals.

The point of view of the scientific world can be exemplified by comments in the Nobel address of Liljestrand. He stated that penicillin would have had "no great practical importance" had it not been for Florey, who, with Chain, "planned and carried out its purification and convinced the United States to finance its large-scale manufacture." He also noted that the penicillin story was "a splendid example of different scientific methods combining for a great common purpose" and that "the work demanded assistance from many different quarters, an unusual amount of scientific enthusiasm, and the firm belief in an idea."

Other indications of the great respect given to Florey's work by the scientific community were the many other honors and awards he received, which included the presidency of the Royal Society (the highest office in British science).

Biography

Howard Walter Florey was born in Adelaide, Australia, on September 24, 1898. He was the only son of Joseph Florey (a boot manufacturer) and Bertha (Wadham) Florey. His early education took place at Saint Peter's Collegiate school in Adelaide. He then attended medical school at the University of Adelaide. The university awarded Florey his medical degree in 1921. At that time, he won a Rhodes scholarship to England's University of Oxford. Arriving in England, he enrolled in Oxford's Magdalen College, which awarded him the B.Sc., then an M.A. in physiology, by 1924.

Florey became a John Lucas Waller student at the University of Cambridge and, in 1925, he spent a year abroad as a Rockefeller Fellow in the United States. Next, Florey returned to Cambridge, where he completed his Ph.D. in 1927. Florey married Mary Ethel Reed, a fellow medical student, in 1926. They would have two children, Charles and Paquita. Mary Florey died in 1966, and Baron Florey married Margaret Jennings, a former Oxford colleague, in 1967. Florey was appointed as the Huddersfield Lecturer in Special Pathology at Cambridge. In 1931, he became the Joseph Hunter Professor of Pathology at the University of Sheffield.

Florey left Sheffield in 1935 to become director of Oxford's William Dunn School of Pathology. In that capacity he moved the study of pathology at Oxford away from a single-minded study of anatomy and morphology to science that included (and emphasized) study of physiology and biochemistry.

Florey is best known for his work on penicillin, in collaboration with Ernst Chain. This effort, beginning in 1938, was a component of a systematic examination of naturally occurring antibiotic substances. The purification and manufacture of penicillin by Florey, Chain, and their collaborators was a milestone in medicine and won the 1945 Nobel Prize in Physiology or Medicine. Florey had many other interests, however, including the study of other antibiotics, endocrinology, examination of the structure and function of the smaller blood vessels, and demonstration of the protective role of mucus in both the respiratory tract and the digestive tract. Florey's efforts produced a large number of papers in physiology and pathology.

Florey received many honors for his remarkable talents; he was knighted (1944), and he became Baron Florey of Adelaide and Marston in 1965. He was president of the Royal Society of London for five years. Many view Howard Florey as the most effective medical scientist of his generation. He maintained active participation in medical research until February, 1968, when he died of a heart attack.

Scientific Career

Howard Florey's scientific career may be described as a lifelong effort to understand the basis for disease processes and to learn how to cure them. It began in 1917, when he began a Rhodes scholarship at the Honors Physiology School of the University of Oxford. There he studied the interactions between the nervous system and the muscles that line blood vessels that enable them to circulate the blood throughout the body. Florey's mentor at Oxford was Charles Sherrington, a famous neurophysiologist of the time.

Working with Sherrington converted Florey to Sherrington's conviction that understanding the biochemistry and physiology of normal tissues was an essential aspect of success in deciphering disease processes. Both men agreed that comparison of the phenomena that occurred in normal tissues and those seen in the disease state was essential to solving the enigmas of disease processes. This conviction remained with Florey throughout his life. It helped make him stand out from most of his professional contemporaries, who limited their endeavors to descriptions of the anatomy and morphology of diseased tissues.

After earning the B.Sc. and an M.A. at Oxford, Florey went on to doctoral studies at the University of Cambridge under the direction of internationally reputed biochemist Frederick G. Hopkins. His Ph.D. research dealt with capillary action in blood circulation. Florey's interaction with Hopkins strengthened his belief in the importance of biochemistry to medical research. Because of this, Florey insisted—all through his career—that his students and collaborators become cognizant of the physiological and pathological approach to studying disease processes.

Florey received his Ph.D. from Cambridge in 1927 and became a lecturer in special pathology at that university. During this period at Cambridge, Florey studied mucus secretion and became very interested in understanding the basis for the resistance of the digestive tract to bacterial infection. This interest led him to read about the discovery, by Alexander Fleming, of the antibacterial enzyme lysozyme. Florey soon began to study this protein biological catalyst himself.

In 1932 Florey was appointed to the chair in pathology at the University of Sheffield, and four years later he became the director of Oxford's Sir William Dunn School of Pathology. At this time Florey began his long association with Ernst Chain, who was to be an essential collaborator in many research efforts and a cowinner of the 1945 Nobel Prize. As an offshoot of their mutual interest in the antibacterial chemicals produced by various microbes, Florey and Chain began to study penicillin, which had been discovered by Alexander Fleming in 1928.

Fleming had shown that a crude form of penicillin could be isolated from the culture medium in which the mold *Penicillium notatum* was grown. At the time when Florey and Chain began their effort, penicillin was a bacteriological curiosity, viewed by Fleming as a possible antiseptic suitable for local application. No one had realized that this chemical would be a potent systemic antibacterial drug or that it would become the "wonder drug" that opened up the scientific use of antibiotics in modern medicine.

Fortuitous study of crude penicillin soon provided Florey and his coworkers with the exciting observation, reported in "Penicillin as a Chemotheraputic Agent" (1940), that its injection into mice killed disease-causing staphylcocci and bacteria that caused gangrene. In these experiments, all the untreated mice injected with the disease bacteria died; however, virtually all the penicillin-treated animals survived. Furthermore, penicillin possessed only minor toxicity. This was exceptionally important, because all the other known antibiotics—such as tyrocidine and the gramicidin of René Dubois's group—were too toxic for such use.

Consequently, Florey began to direct the great scientific resources of Oxford's School of Pathology toward full-scale study of the drug. By virtue of much work, carried out by numerous gifted Oxford scientists, the basic project proceeded quickly. First, the wide range of microbes killed by penicillin was identified. Then the pharmacology and the toxicology of the drug were delineated in animals and in humans.

A major initial stumbling block to human studies was the fact that successful treatment of a single human being required administration of the entire "yield" of penicillin, isolated from hundreds of gallons of culture medium. The efforts of another of Florey's colleagues, Norman Heatley, led to development of the laboratory equipment that allowed the production of enough penicillin for wider human testing. Thanks to all these efforts, production of penicillin was soon increased enough to allow successful treatment of ten cases of human bacterial infection, reported in "Further Observations on Penicillin" (1941).

Exciting though this was, Britain—in the throes of World War II—did not have the resources to produce enough penicillin for widespread use. Therefore, Florey traveled to the United States and convinced the American Office of Scientific Research to fund the effort. Thanks to this massive American funding and to collaborative efforts by American industry, enough penicillin was soon produced to allow its widespread use in treatment of war casualties which resulted from the 1944 Normandy invasion.

With large-scale production of penicillin now well in hand, Florey next identified the best methods for testing the efficacy of the drug and effecting the most appropriate ways to administer it to patients. In 1945, Florey shared the Nobel Prize in Physiology or Medicine with Fleming and Chain "for the discovery of penicillin and its curative effect in various infectious diseases." He went on to study several other antibiotic substances. Florey's most successful endeavor in this area was participation in the early aspects of the discovery of the cephalosporins. The overall methodology that Florey utilized in these efforts was the same procedure that he had directed in the penicillin research; he discussed the procedure in his Nobel lecture. It involved a step-by-step process beginning with the identification of production of an antibacterial substance in a test organism and ending, finally, with tests on human victims of infectious diseases.

After 1955, Florey turned his efforts back to research in experimental pathology. His best-known endeavors in this field involved the study of the structure and function of the capillaries and other small blood vessels via electron microscopy. Important aspects of Florey's research during this period also include clarification of the protective role of mucus in the respiratory and digestive tracts, investigation of the nature of atherosclerosis, study of human reproduction, and examination of other aspects of endocrinology (the study of the actions of hormones). Florey's research endeavors did not cease until his death of a heart attack in 1968.

Another of Florey's contributions to science was accomplished during his term as president of the Royal Society of London (1960-1965). During his tenure in the highest office in British science, Florey expanded the membership of the society, moved the society into an active role in government, and established the Royal Society Population Study Group. In 1965, Florey was made a baron and given the Order of Merit for these efforts.

In addition to these honors, and to the receipt of the Nobel Prize, Florey won awards that included the Lister Memorial Award of the Royal College of Surgeons (1945), the Copley Medal of the Royal Society (1957), and the Lomosonov Medal of the Soviet Academy of Sciences (1965). He belonged to many prestigious medical societies, including the Royal College of Physicians and the Royal Australian College of Physicians. Florey received honorary degrees from seventeen British and Australian universities.

Another aspect of Florey's well-rounded intellectualism was his efforts as an educator. Florey was instrumental in the development of the Australian National University, an endeavor that began in 1946 and continued almost until his death. In honor of his contribution to development of the university, Florey was named its chancellor in 1965. He was also Provost of the Queen's College of Oxford University, a position he had held since 1962.

Florey is viewed as one of the most effective medical scientists of his time. He exerted a profound influence on both medicine and basic science. He helped educate and mold many excellent physicians and basic scientists; he possessed great organizational ability, exceptional common sense, and a strong sense of responsibility toward colleagues. Furthermore, Florey was an exceptional educator and a superb pragmatic scientist. He led by example and believed that experiments should be designed carefully to produce the most well-defined results possible.

Bibliography

Primary

MEDICINE: "Penicillin as a Chemotheraputic Agent," *Lancet*, August 24, 1940, pp. 226-233 (with E. Chain, A. D. Gardner, N. G. Heatley, M. A. Jennings, J. Orr-Ewing, and A. G. Sanders); "Further Observations on Penicillin," *Lancet*, August 16, 1941, pp. 177-185 (with E. P. Abraham, E. Chain, C. M. Fletcher, A. D. Gardner, N. G. Heatley, and M. A. Jennings); "Penicillin," *Endeavor*, vol. 3, 1944, pp. 3-11 (with E. Chain); "An Antibiotic from Penicillium Tardum," *British Journal of Experimental Pathology*, vol. 28, 1947, pp. 31-38 (with N. Borodin and F. J. Philpot); *Antibiotics*, 1949 (with E. Chain, A. D. Gardner, N. G. Heatley, M. A. Jennings, A. G. Sanders, E. P. Abraham, and M. E. Florey); *Lectures on General Pathology*, 1954.

Secondary

Abraham, Edward P. "Howard Walter Florey." *Biographical Memoirs of Fellows of the Royal Society* 17 (1971): 255-302. This account of Florey's life was meticulously prepared by Abraham, one of his close Oxford colleagues. It describes Florey's role in penicillin development clearly and fairly, giving insight into Florey's character and into several aspects of his career. Scientific areas of endeavor are described particularly well.

Elder, Albert E. *The History of Penicillin Production*. Vol. 66 in *Chemical Engineering Progress Symposium Series*. New York: American Institute of Chemical Engineers, 1970. The book contains eleven articles describing industrial development of Florey's penicillin. Included issues are the role of government, design of manufacturing processes, preparation of stable penicillin, and methodology used to prepare some different penicillins used today. Necessary integration of efforts of biologists, chemists, and engineers is stressed and described.

Evans, R. M. *The Chemistry of the Antibiotics Used in Medicine*. Oxford: Pergamon Press, 1965. This small volume briefly and succinctly describes the main types of antibiotics known in the 1960's. Of special interest are penicillins, cephalosporins, and streptomycin. Useful coverage of most antibiotics that a reader will encounter is included in the text.

Florey, Howard W., E. Chain, A. D. Gardner, N. G. Heatley, M. A. Jennings, H. G. Sanders, E. P. Abraham, and M. E. Florey. *Antibiotics*. 2 vols. London: Oxford University Press, 1949. This two-volume compendium is an excellent review of the field of antibiotics from its beginnings at the end of the nineteenth century to the 1940's. A very valuable source on the history of the antimicrobial substances; contains 3,600 references.

Flynn, Edwin H. *Cephalosporins and Penicillins: Chemistry and Biology.* New York: Academic Press, 1972. This detailed book covers the chemistry and biology of closely related cephalosporins and penicillins thoroughly, dealing with history, structure, chemistry synthesis, and interconversions. It is quite technical; however, careful reading identifies basic issues that are of use to nontechnical readers.

Mac Farlane, Gwyn. *Howard Florey: The Making of a Great Scientist*. London: Oxford University Press, 1979. This biography deals mostly with Florey's life up to 1942. It contains insight into his early life and to the forces that molded him. The development of penicillin is dealt with, as are other aspects also mentioned in Williams' book.

Williams, Trevor I. *Howard Florey: Penicillin and After.* London: Oxford University Press, 1984. This detailed biography describes many aspects of Florey's career, including development of penicillin as a therapeutic drug, his academic career, his role in the Australian National University, and modernization of the Royal Society. Important insight is given about the controversy over whether Florey or Fleming was primarily responsible for penicillin.

Sanford S. Singer

1945

Physiology or Medicine

Baron Florey, Great Britain
Sir Alexander Fleming, Great Britain
Ernst Boris Chain, Germany and Great Britain

Chemistry

Artturi Ilmari Virtanen, Finland

Physics

Wolfgang Pauli, Austria and United States

Literature

Gabriela Mistral, Chile

Peace

Cordell Hull, United States

SIR ALEXANDER FLEMING
1945

Born: Lochfield, Scotland; August 6, 1881
Died: London, England; March 11, 1955
Nationality: British
Area of concentration: Bacteriology

By his discovery of penicillin and his research into its properties, Fleming effected a revolution in the treatment of disease and thereby saved millions of lives around the world

The Award

Presentation

On December 10, 1945, Göran Liljestrand, a member of the professional staff of the Royal Caroline Institute, presented the Nobel Prize in Physiology or Medicine to Alexander Fleming, Ernst Boris Chain, and Sir Howard Walter Florey. Liljestrand began his address with a brief survey of earlier efforts to combat disease-causing bacteria. In 1877, Louis Pasteur had noted that anthrax bacilli were susceptible to other airborne germs, but subsequent efforts to apply that observation to the war against disease proved disappointing. Fleming's 1928 observation that a mold, *Penicillium notatum*, inhibited the growth of staphylococci was, therefore, not the first to suggest that microorganisms will attack each other. His research, however, indicated that the mold produced a substance, which Fleming named penicillin, that might at last destroy such harmful bacteria as those causing diphtheria, pneumonia, meningitis, anthrax, and gas gangrene. Penicillin does not cause a toxic reaction in human white blood cells.

Neither Fleming nor a team of biochemists was able to produce a stable form of the substance, and by 1931 research into its therapeutic possibilities had ceased. Then, in 1938, Florey and Chain took up the study of the drug and succeeded in preparing a dry form that retained its potency. Animal and then clinical tests indicated that penicillin "led to recoveries which not infrequently proved miraculous." Liljestrand conceded that not all disease-causing organisms yielded to it: Tuberculosis, typhoid fever, and polio, for example, remained the scourges they had been for centuries. Yet penicillin encouraged the hope of discovering new drugs that would eradicate these illnesses, too.

Liljestrand concluded his speech by noting that the discovery of penicillin once more showed the importance of basic research, for Fleming was studying the behavior of bacteria when he made his initial observation. The development of the drug also demonstrated the need for scientific cooperation, since many people with varying areas of expertise contributed to the production of penicillin. This achievement showed that the human mind, which had so recently contrived the deaths of millions in World War II, could equally apply itself to saving millions of lives.

Nobel lecture

Because Fleming's work was concerned with the initial stages of penicillin's development, his lecture, entitled "Penicillin" and delivered on December 11, 1945, focused on its discovery and early research into its properties; he left to Florey and Chain the discussion of its use as a drug to fight disease. Always modest, Fleming at once dismissed the notion that he had been trying to find antibacterial substances through a systematic, well-researched investigation. A mold, later identified as *Penicillium notatum*, contaminated a culture plate on which he was growing staphylococci, and the mold inhibited the development of bacterial colonies.

Fleming realized that this phenomenon merited further study. He therefore cultured the mold. After it had grown for several days on a plate, he spread various bacteria across the surface of the agar gel and found that staphylococci, streptococci, and *Corynebacterium diphtheriae* would not grow near the mold, though other bacilli did. Next, he grew the mold in broth to determine whether the liquid might contain an antibacterial substance. By embedding the broth in agar and again spreading bacteria across a culture plate, he noted that indeed the liquid inhibited bacterial growth.

A bacteriologist rather than a clinician, Fleming first used these discoveries to isolate bacilli that generally are overwhelmed by penicillin-sensitive organisms. For example, the whooping cough bacillus (*Bordetella pertusis*) was hard to grow in the laboratory because a throat swab or cough plate would contain far more streptococci and staphylococci bacteria that overwhelmed the whooping cough bacteria. If, however, the agar were impregnated with penicillin, only the whooping cough bacillus, insensitive to the drug, would survive and flourish.

Fleming continued to examine the properties of his new substance and found that penicillin remained effective even if diluted a thousand times, making it a very potent antiseptic. In contrast, phenol loses its potency when it is diluted three hundred times. Fleming also observed that penicillin did not merely inhibit bacterial growth; it actually killed germs by destroying their cell walls. It also could diffuse through agar and so could spread through the body to reach infections not treatable by topical applications.

Many drugs can inhibit or kill bacteria, but they also destroy healthy cells, especially white blood cells, one of the body's chief means of warding off disease. From his earliest work Fleming had concentrated on natural immunity and resistance, and over the years he had found that every antiseptic that killed bacteria in a test tube actually helped them in the body because it was more deadly to white blood cells than to germs. In his address Fleming briefly described an experiment in which he placed a small dose of staphylococci in a capillary tube with serum. If he added normal saline, 5 percent of the bacteria survived; the white blood cells destroyed the rest. If he placed a very dilute solution of phenol (1 part to 2,500) in the capillary tube along with the serum and bacteria, more colonies formed. At a concentration of 1 to 600, phenol totally destroyed the natural resistance of the body. (White blood cells were not effective.) Yet bacteria thrived, because the phenol was too dilute to harm them. Penicillin, on the other hand, revealed no such toxicity to white blood cells.

These encouraging results might have prompted Fleming to pursue therapeutic applications, but he was neither a clinician nor a chemist. He could not find a way to manufacture the drug in large quantities or preserve it in a form that remained effective for more than a short time. Therefore, he used the drug to grow bacteria selectively and kept the unusual mold strain alive. He published papers predicting that one day penicillin would play an important role in the treatment of disease, but no one showed much interest.

After sulfa drugs appeared in the mid-1930's, confidence increased in the possibilities of chemotherapy, and technological advances permitted the freeze-drying of penicillin to render it stable. Using mold obtained from Fleming, Florey and Chain succeeded in tapping penicillin's great potential. Fleming ended his speech with both hope and caution. On the one hand, he suggested that other, better drugs would be discovered or synthesized. At the same time he warned that bacteria could soon become resistant to penicillin, especially if one used inadequate doses. He therefore urged, "If you use penicillin, use enough."

Critical reception

As Gwyn Macfarlane points out in *Alexander Fleming: The Man and the Myth* (1984), Fleming was not the first to observe the antibacterial effects of penicillin. As early as 1871, Joseph Burdon-Sanderson reported that *Penicillium* mold could inhibit bacterial growth. In 1884, Joseph Lister treated an infected wound with a *Penicillium* culture, and in Naples in 1895 Vincenzo Tiberio used extracts of the mold to treat diseased animals. Four years later, it was observed in France that animals injected with a lethal dose of pathogenic bacteria did not die if they also received *Penicillium glaucum*.

The day after the Nobel Prize Committee announced its decision to split the 1945 award in physiology or medicine equally among Fleming, Florey, and Chain, *The New York Times* carried Chain's remark that "Dr. Fleming's report had been forgotten completely in the vast mass of scientific literature" until he and Florey had resurrected it (October 26, 1945). The next day, the newspaper's editorial sympathized with this view, noting that the Nobel Prize Committee appreciated "the fact that there is only a tenuous connection between the discovery of penicillin and its isolation and study by Florey and Chain." Fleming's fellow scientists had not been impressed with his work on penicillin: He was regularly rejected for membership in the Royal Society until 1943. According to W. F. van Heyningen, secretary of the Society of General Microbiology when Fleming was president of that body, Fleming did not think he deserved to win the Nobel Prize.

For more than a decade after he had discovered penicillin, Fleming did little to publicize or investigate the drug. Between 1929 and 1931, he produced two papers dealing with it; thereafter, he seems to have abandoned all interest in its therapeutic possibilities. His notebooks show that in June, 1931, he found that the drug inhibits the growth of *Claustridium*, the organism that causes gas gangrene, but he never published this finding. It was Sir Almroth Wright, Fleming's mentor, who in 1942 described Fleming as the discoverer of penicillin. Though journalists also sought out Florey, he refused to grant interviews. While Fleming always credited the researchers at the University of Oxford, the press did not. When Fleming and Florey were knighted in July, 1944, only Fleming's name appeared in the newspaper headlines. *The New York Times* for December 19, 1945, carried a picture of King Gustav presenting the Nobel Prize to Fleming; Florey and Chain were not photographed.

If Wright and the press thrust greatness upon Fleming, though, he was not undeserving. He had observed the activity of the mold, had been curious enough to undertake research into its properties, and had kept the unusual *Penicillium* strain alive. It was mold from Fleming's lab that Florey and Chain used at Oxford, as it was Fleming's 1929 paper that prompted them to study penicillin rather than some other antibacterial agent. The Nobel Committee had considered giving half the prize to Fleming, then decided to divide the award equally among the three recipients. Florey and Chain deserve the majority of the credit for developing penicillin therapy, but if not for Fleming they would have lacked the information and material that led to their achievement.

Biography

The youngest child of Hugh and Grace (Morton) Fleming, Alexander Fleming was born on his father's farm, Lochfield, in Ayrshire, Scotland, on August 6, 1881. After attending local schools, he joined his half brother Tom and his brother John in London. For two years, he attended the Regent Street Polytechnic; then, at sixteen, he became a shipping clerk. Four years later, he received a £250 legacy from an uncle. Encouraged by Tom, an ophthalmologist, Fleming decided to enroll in medical school, and because he had recently played a water polo match against St. Mary's, that was the institution he chose.

The school was not prepossessing. David Cormalt Jones described it as "shabby, squalid . . . ill-lighted and coarsely furnished." Yet Fleming chose better than he could have imagined, because in 1902 Almroth Wright joined the faculty. Wright had developed the technique of inoculating against typhoid by using heat-killed bacteria, and he believed that vaccination could prevent or cure virtually all diseases. His views form the basis of playwright George Bernard Shaw's *The Doctor's Dilemma* (1906); Wright maintained that in the future physicians would be immunizers.

Fleming was a brilliant student, capturing virtually every prize that the school offered. Charles Pannett, Fleming's schoolmate, later recalled that Fleming's "instinctive sense of observation was most acute even in those days." In 1906 he received his license to practice, and on his twenty-fifth birthday he joined Wright's laboratory, which would become the Wright-Fleming Institute (1948).

During World War I, Wright and Fleming moved to Boulogne, where they undertook important work on the treatment of wounds. On one of his leaves, Fleming married Sarah Marion McElroy (1915). After the war, he returned to St. Mary's, becoming assistant director of the Inoculation Department with the responsibility of supervising the production of the vaccines that financed the lab. In the course of his work, he discovered lysozyme, an enzyme important in natural immunity, and he found penicillin.

After he received the Nobel Prize, Fleming was much in demand as a speaker (though he was by all accounts a poor lecturer) and had little time for research. He did, however, publish a number of papers on such matters as the effect of penicillin on blood coagulation and on bacterial growth. His first wife died in 1949; four years later he married a former coworker, Dr. Amelia Coutsouris-Voureka. Two months after retiring from the Wright-Fleming Institute (January, 1955) he died of a heart attack (March 11, 1955) at his Chelsea home. He is buried in St. Paul's Cathedral in London.

Scientific Career

Fleming's interest in bacteriological research stemmed from the investigations of his mentor, Sir Almroth Wright (1861-1947), who studied vaccination therapy. To measure the effectiveness of this treatment (to determine a person's resistance to a particular infection), Wright created the "Opsonic index," from the Greek for "I prepare food." Wright believed that inoculations worked by making bacteria more palatable to the cells that destroyed these invaders. The view that the physician's chief role is to encourage the body's natural defenses would also be Fleming's for most of his life, and it may help explain his apparent indifference in the 1930's to the possibilities of penicillin as a therapeutic agent.

In addition to some early publications on the accuracy of the Opsonic index, Fleming extended Wright's laboratory microtechniques. In an era when researchers made their own equipment, Fleming's dexterity in the manufacture and use of small tubes and pipettes was most valuable. In 1909, he perfected a means of testing for syphilis by using only a few drops of blood rather than the 5 milliliters previously needed. A simple fingerstick therefore would suffice; no longer would one need to rely on the difficult and painful method of venopuncture.

Wright's laboratory was the first in England to use Salvarsan (dioxy-diamino-arsenobenzene dihydrochloride), also known as formula 606 because it took that number of attempts to find the treatment to cure syphilis, securing the drug from Paul Ehrlich, its discoverer. With Leonard Colebrook, Fleming published his results with the drug. Primitive and dangerous as the remedy was, it heralded a new age in medicine: For the first time, a drug could destroy a pathogenic organism. By introducing Salvarsan to England, Fleming was playing a supporting role in the opening scene of the drama of chemotherapy. Decades later, he would assume center stage.

With the outbreak of World War I, Fleming and Wright were sent to France to study infected wounds. Fleming would publish a dozen papers on the subject. He claimed that the best piece of research he ever did dealt with the question of how best to cope with this problem, and he described this work in his Nobel Prize lecture in comparing penicillin to earlier antiseptics such as phenol. He and Wright quickly saw that the standard method for treating wounds—applying some antiseptic such as iodine or carbolic acid to destroy germs—did not work. Using his skill with glassware, Fleming created an ingenious "artificial wound" that demonstrated the inability of topical applications to reach the interstices of an infected area. Antiseptics are quickly diluted to ineffectiveness by the influx of bodily fluids, so the chemicals cannot destroy bacteria, but they remain sufficiently potent to destroy the white blood cells that might have fought off the infection. Wright and Fleming therefore urged that wounds be irrigated with normal saline solution to promote the flow of white blood cells into the area. Despite these recommendations, official practice did not change until World War II. Fleming also demonstrated that anaerobic bacteria (such as those responsible for tetanus and gas gangrene) can thrive in a wound exposed to air if aerobic bacteria such as staphylococci or streptococci are present to use up the oxygen.

With the end of the war, Fleming returned to St. Mary's to direct the production of vaccines and to study natural immunity. Fleming was a skillful but messy laboratory worker, stacking old culture plates on his bench until there was no room for more. Touring a meticulously clean facility after World War II, Fleming stated that had he kept his laboratory in that condition he never would have discovered lysozyme or penicillin.

The first of these substances he observed in 1921 while looking at a two-week-old plate that showed no growth of bacteria near a bit of nasal mucus that he had attempted to culture. Wright named the bacteria *Micrococcus lysodeikticus*, and the substance that destroyed the germ he called "lysozyme." Fleming hoped that this naturally occurring substance (present, as he discovered, in virtually all bodily fluids—hair, nails, and even plants) would attack disease-causing organisms, but his investigations showed that it killed only nonpathogenic bacteria (germs that were not harmful because the body destroyed them naturally). Although lysozyme did not prove of clinical value, Fleming remained fascinated by it. He published eight papers on the subject, and his 1932 address to the Section of Pathology of the Royal Society of Medicine dealt with lysozyme rather than with his more recent discovery of penicillin.

This choice is not as bizarre as it might seem, for lysozyme does play an important role in natural immunity. The discovery of the substance in white blood cells explained how they destroyed bacteria after engulfing them, and it settled an outstanding controversy over the function of such fluids as tears. Élie Metchnikoff claimed that their role was merely to wash away bacteria, but Fleming showed that the body actually destroys many organisms. Tears, saliva, and skin provide a chemical as well as physical barrier. Fleming's work on lysozyme was important also because here he developed techniques that he copied in his research into penicillin. Interestingly, Florey and Chain studied lysozyme before they turned to penicillin.

Like his discovery of lysozyme, Fleming's more famous find came about by accident. In the spring of 1928, he was asked to contribute the section on staphylococci to the encyclopedic *A System of Bacteriology in Relation to Medicine* (Fleming's piece appeared in 1929). He was growing various strains of the bacteria to study the shapes and colors of various colonies; on the floor below, C. J. Latouche was examining the allergenic properties of molds. In late July or early August, Fleming prepared some culture plates but did not incubate them. He left these on his bench when he went away for vacation; returning in September, he was throwing away old plates when he noticed that one was contaminated with a mold and that around the mold no bacteria were growing. He showed this plate to several colleagues, none of whom found it especially interesting, but Fleming recognized that this was something unusual. He photographed the plate and preserved it in formalin.

In his Nobel lecture, he described the research that followed. In 1929, he published his initial findings in an article entitled "On the Antibacterial Actions of Cultures of a *Penicillium* . . . " that appeared in the *British Journal of Experimental Pathology*; in the eighth of the summary's ten points, he wrote, "It is suggested that [penicillin] may be an efficient antiseptic for application to, or injection into, areas infected with penicillin-sensitive microbes." The title of the article reveals Fleming's chief interest, though: It emphasizes the study of the mold *Penicillium*. In contrast, the first paper on penicillin by Florey and Chain was entitled "Penicillin as a Chemotherapeutic Agent" (1940). Fleming used the drug throughout the 1930's for the purpose of preparing pure strains of bacteria for vaccines. Most of the interest in Fleming's discovery came from other bacteriologists seeking to isolate organisms that were normally hard to grow because of contamination from penicillin-sensitive organisms. Fleming published little about penicillin during the 1930's.

Ronald Hare offers four reasons for Fleming's apparent indifference to the clinical use of penicillin. Hare notes that no other chemical had proved effective against bacteria; Fleming found that staphylococci quickly develop immunity to the drug in the laboratory; in the impure state of the drug that Fleming produced, large doses were necessary to treat a single patient; and penicillin was so unstable that he could not keep enough on hand for use as a practical therapeutic agent. To these explanations one might add that limited clinical trials were not impressive. As his continued fascination with lysozyme attests, Fleming was more interested in natural immunity than in chemotherapy. He may well have agreed with Wright's 1912 judgment that "the chemotherapy of human bacterial infections will never be possible."

Even the introduction of sulfa drugs in the mid-1930's did not change Fleming's mind on this matter. He studied these new medicines and demonstrated that they did not kill bacteria; they only prevented the germs from multiplying. Again, it was the white blood cells that actually destroyed the invaders, so Fleming continued to advocate vaccine therapy, though in conjunction with chemotherapy, to enhance natural immunity in the battle against infection. As late as 1941, he still clung to this view.

By 1942, the work of Florey, Chain, and their colleagues at Oxford had shown the effectiveness of penicillin as a therapeutic agent. Fleming, too, helped promote the drug when, in August of that year, he was the first to inject it into the spinal column of a man dying of meningitis. The patient recovered in a week. *The Times* of London published the story of this medical miracle. Together with Almroth Wright's letter to the editor published there, it launched Fleming's ascent to world fame. The success itself prompted Fleming to persuade Sir Andrew Duncan, Great Britain's minister of supply, to involve the government in the production of penicillin, so that by 1944 enough of the drug was available for all soldiers.

Election to the Royal Society came in 1943, knighthood in 1944, the Nobel Prize in 1945. The last ten years of Fleming's life were filled with honors: twenty-five honorary doctorates and more than a hundred fifty other awards. He was much in demand as a speaker, and wherever he went he was revered. In Spain, crowds lining the streets kneeled to kiss the hem of his coat. Such popularity left little time for research, but he did publish a number of papers dealing with penicillin's effect on blood clotting and on bacterial growth. He also showed that bacteria use flagella to propel themselves, thus disproving the theory that they move by rotating their bodies.

In 1911, when Fleming was introducing chemotherapy to Great Britain, Ronald Gray drew a cartoon showing him as "Private 606," holding a syringe almost as tall as he was. When Fleming died in 1955, Manuel Laviada sculpted a reverential bust for the Gijón monument. In the intervening decades, Fleming produced more than a hundred papers on such significant subjects as the treatment of wounds and natural immunity. Penicillin was thus not his only contribution to medicine, though it was his greatest. Delivering his eulogy, C. A. Pannett stated that Fleming had "saved more lives and relieved more suffering than any other living man, perhaps more than any man who has ever lived." People previously condemned to death by infected scratches, not to mention pneumonia, recovered because of penicillin, and this success led to the search for and discovery of even more powerful antibiotics. Florey and Chain deserve much credit for this revolution, but Fleming's observation on that September day in 1928, and his recognition that here was something worth investigating, prepared the way for their work.

Bibliography

Primary

MEDICINE: "A Simple Method of Serum Diagnosis of Syphilis," *Lancet*, vol. 1, 1909, p. 1512; "On the Bacteriology of Septic Wounds," *Lancet*, vol. 2, 1915, p. 638; "The Action of Chemical and Physiological Antiseptics in a Septic Wound," *British Journal of Surgery*, vol. 7, 1919, p. 99; "On a Remarkable Bacteriolytic Substance Found in Secretions and Tissues," *Proceedings of the Royal Society*, vol. *B*93, 1922, p. 306; "Observations on a Bacteriolytic Substance (Lysozyme) Found in Secretions and Tissues," *British Journal of Experimental Pathology*, vol. 3, 1922, p. 252; "A Comparison of the Activities of Antiseptics on Bacteria and Leucocytes," *Proceedings of the Royal Society*, vol. *B*96, 1924, p. 171; "On the Antibacterial Actions of Cultures of a *Penicillium*, with Special Reference to Their Use in the Isolation of *B. Influenzae*," *British Journal of Experimental Pathology*, vol. 10, 1929, p. 226.

Secondary

Allison, V. D. "Sir Alexander Fleming, 1881-1955." *Journal of General Microbiology* 14 (1956): 1-13. In this obituary, Allison, who knew Fleming for thirty-four years, first as his student and then as a colleague, provides an excellent summary of the Nobel laureate's work. He is sometimes wrong on dates, however, and the bibliography is limited.

Colebrook, Leonard. "Alexander Fleming." *Biographical Memoirs of the Royal Society* 2 (1956): 117-127. A colleague, Colebrook observed Fleming's work at first hand. He claims that Fleming was more the technician than the intellectual, that research was his sport rather than his vocation. In addition to providing a good summary of Fleming's life, this article contains a comprehensive bibliography of Fleming's publications.

Hare, Ronald. *The Birth of Penicillin and the Disarming of Microbes*. London: Allen & Unwin, 1970. Hare entered St. Mary's as a student in 1919, and he worked with Fleming in the Inoculation Department from 1925 to 1931, the years in which Fleming discovered and studied penicillin. Hence, although the book is autobiographical, Hare was in the right place at the right time to observe Fleming's most important work. Hare gives an excellent picture of medical and research methods of the 1920's and 1930's, and he was the first to explain exactly how Fleming discovered penicillin, Fleming's own account being very sketchy. Includes bibliographical footnotes.

Ludovici, L. J. *Fleming: Discoverer of Penicillin*. London: Andrew Dakers, 1952. Because he wrote while Fleming was still alive, Ludovici could consult with his subject. The work offers a good nontechnical introduction to Fleming's life and work; its tone reveals the reverence accorded Fleming in the early 1950's.

Macfarlane, Gwyn. *Alexander Fleming: The Man and the Myth*. Cambridge, Mass.: Harvard University Press, 1984. Revisionist but authoritative, Macfarlane's biography draws on a manuscript life by Fleming's brother Robert, on interviews, and a reading of Fleming's notebooks. Macfarlane says that he "tried to convey . . . an objective and impartial account of the events of Fleming's life and the details of his scientific work" in a manner accessible to the nonscientist. Includes lists of Fleming's honors from 1902 to 1955 and his major publications.

Maurois, André. *The Life of Sir Alexander Fleming, Discoverer of Penicillin*. Translated by Gerard Hopkins. New York: E. P. Dutton, 1959. Fleming's widow asked Maurois to write this book, which has the strengths and weaknesses of any authorized biography. Lady Fleming made her late husband's papers available to Maurois and introduced him to those who had known and worked with the Nobel laureate. His information, presented in a manner readily understandable by the layman, is therefore reliable. Interpretations, though, are occasionally marred by partiality and a lack of scientific training. Still, a good introduction, with many fascinating photographs.

Joseph Rosenblum

1945

Physiology or Medicine

Baron Florey, Great Britain
Sir Alexander Fleming, Great Britain
Ernst Boris Chain, Germany and Great Britain

Chemistry

Artturi Ilmari Virtanen, Finland

Physics

Wolfgang Pauli, Austria and United States

Literature

Gabriela Mistral, Chile

Peace

Cordell Hull, United States

ERNST BORIS CHAIN 1945

Born: Berlin, Germany; June 19, 1906
Died: Ireland; August 12, 1979
Nationality: German; later, British
Areas of concentration: Biochemistry and chemical pathology

Chain, in collaboration with Howard W. Florey and other workers at the University of Oxford, carried out basic research on the purification and therapeutic use of penicillin. Chain was primarily responsible for the chemical characterization of penicillin, which made it easier to design methods of purification and synthesis

The Award

Presentation

In a ceremony on December 10, 1945, Professor Göran Liljestrand of the Royal Caroline Institute in Stockholm, Sweden, delivered the presentation speech outlining the accomplishments of Ernst Boris Chain. Later in the ceremony, Chain received from the hands of King Gustav IV the 1945 Nobel Prize in Physiology or Medicine jointly with Alexander Fleming and Howard W. Florey.

After mentioning the work of Louis Pasteur and Robert Koch, Liljestrand told how Alexander Fleming, in 1928, had accidentally contaminated a culture of staphylococcus bacteria with mold and noticed that the bacteria had been killed in a region around each moldspot. Fleming went on to identify the mold as *Penicillium notatum* and to conduct various experiments on the cultivation of this mold in broths of nutrients. The active substance from the mold passed into the broth, and Fleming tested these crude penicillin-containing preparations on many bacterial cultures, discovering which bacteria were killed and which were not. He also found that, where the bacteria were killed, the penicillin preparation used was effective even at high dilutions, such as 1 part penicillin to 500 parts of inert substance. Mice could be injected with these penicillin preparations without serious side effects.

The biochemist Harold Raistrick, assisted by Percival W. Clutterbuck and Reginald Lovell, took up chemical studies of Fleming-type preparations. They established that penicillin was easily rendered inactive during purification schemes but did not succeed in preparing any pure samples of penicillin; indeed, their results tended to indicate that such samples might be very difficult to obtain.

Together with Florey, Chain took up the study of penicillin in 1938 at the Pathological Institute of the University of Oxford. Methods of assay were developed so that the relative strengths of different penicillin preparations could be determined. Mold cultures were grown in large numbers of individual glass bottles, and the penicillin was extracted from the broth by solvents which were applied in the cold to delay deactivation of the penicillin. Eventually, by 1941, enough material had been produced to allow some clinical trials on human patients. Florey traveled to the United States and succeeded in arousing interest in penicillin. Major advances in the culture of penicillin mold were later to be made in the United States. Clinical trials became more widespread as the purity and available supply of penicillin increased. Many serious infections that had been considered incurable were easily controlled with penicillin. By the mid-1940's, penicillin was being used to treat wounds suffered by soldiers in World War II and was widely regarded as a miracle drug.

Nobel lecture

On March 20, 1946, Ernst Boris Chain delivered a Nobel Prize lecture entitled "The Chemical Structure of the Penicillins." He began with remarks on the historical development of the chemical work on penicillin in which he mentioned the contributions made by others. He outlined the wartime arrangements for formalized cooperation between American and British researchers and paid tribute to the American workers. Enormous collaborative effort, largely conducted under awkward wartime conditions of secrecy, had recently produced more than seven hundred research reports.

"Penicillin," as originally conceived, was an impure mold-broth extract with germ-killing properties. As studies continued, it turned out that there were in reality not one, but many, penicillins—the term itself, derived from the name of the molds of the *Penicillium* genus, can apply to a number of mold species within the genus that can be used to make the antibiotic. Four separate, pure penicillins were obtained. They possess a common core of chemical structure but differ in the side-chain structures. These compounds are acids, soluble in water and easily decomposed by heat or extremes of acid or basic conditions. Many chemicals cause penicillins to lose their biological activity, and activity may also be lost by the action of an enzyme, penicillinase, secreted by some penicillin-resistant bacterial strains.

Much of the research on penicillin was conducted under difficulties imposed by wartime conditions. Because of security considerations, exchange of information and material between workers in the United States and in Great Britain was hampered; thus, much of the structural work by Chain and others at Oxford was done with very small samples of material of dubious purity. Eventually, the penicillin research was reported to a joint Anglo-American committee, which circulated the results to all workers in both countries.

The first pure crystalline penicillin (called "penicillin II") was prepared in 1943 in the form of its sodium salt. Three other penicillins (I, III, and IV) were also discovered as products of mold. All these compounds are composed of carbon, hydrogen, nitrogen, oxygen, and sulfur, and possessed a carboxyl group—a particular arrangement of carbon, hydrogen, and oxygen atoms that made the penicillins act as acids. The presence of the carboxyl group was shown experimentally by exposing the penicillin to a chemical reagent that converted the group to a derivative compound called an ester. In addition to the carboxyl group, two of the penicillins (I and IV) were shown to have a well-known component in their chemical makeup—a benzene ring. This is a group of six carbons and five hydrogens arranged in a hexagon-shaped ring.

Structure determination of the penicillins depended heavily on degradative studies. Penicillin was broken down by acids or other chemicals, under controlled conditions, to form simpler compounds. These "degradation products" were fragments of the original structure. The study of the degradation products and their structures resulted in information that allowed chemists to deduce the structure of the original penicillin. Once the structures of all the degradation products were known, the structure deduction resembled what a person might do to assemble a jigsaw puzzle from its many pieces.

Chain described the degradative studies in great detail and showed that the preponderance of evidence favored a structure known to chemists at the time as the beta-lactam structure. The beta-lactam structure could not be unambiguously proved by chemical methods alone but was considered a hypothesis until X-ray studies of penicillin crystals proved the existence of this form.

Chain pointed out that penicillin can be considered to be built up from two amino acids in much the same way as peptides, but with the novel beta-lactam structure. He speculated that the antibiotic properties of penicillin seemed to depend on the presence of this structure and that other useful medicinals might be discovered among proteins or other natural substances that contain a beta-lactam unit.

In his concluding remarks, Chain discussed the difficult problem of chemical synthesis of penicillin. All feasible routes had been explored, and in spite of tremendous efforts, no success had been forthcoming. At the end of his lecture, he remained pessimistic as to the chances of the discovery of any synthesis that could compete economically with the fermentation process; indeed, Chain proved correct. Although a successful synthesis of penicillin was eventually reported in 1956-1957 by John C. Sheehan and coworkers at Massachusetts Institute of Technology, it was too expensive for commercial use.

Critical reception

When the 1945 Nobel Prizes were announced in October, months of speculation came to an end. Everyone was sure that the discovery of penicillin and the development of its use were prizeworthy, but opinion was divided as to exactly which individual or individuals deserved the prize. Fleming had certainly discovered penicillin long before Florey or Chain became interested in it, but the latter two had taken it up and pursued it with such vigor as to bring about its widespread clinical use.

Chain was in New York when word of his award reached him. When *The New York Times* contacted him at the home of a friend and informed him of the award, he was "amazed, incredulous, and beaming like a schoolboy," as reported in the October 26, 1945, edition of the newspaper. He told the reporters that the Nobel Committee had obviously considered all the facts carefully and reached a fair decision. He then took the opportunity to give an account of his version of the penicillin story, including his views on profits being made by drug companies from the sale of the drug. Chain had probably tended to feel somewhat slighted by the scientific establishment and the bureaucracy in Great Britain. He had been fearful that all the credit for penicillin would go to Fleming. Now, with the prestige of the Nobel Prize, he was assured of his share of the credit, and of great respect in the academic world.

Biography

Ernst Chain was born in Berlin, Germany, on June 19, 1906. He was the son of Michael Chain, an immigrant from White Russia, and his German wife, Margarete. The boy grew up in an atmosphere in which intellectual activity was encouraged and where science was important, since his father ran a business producing metal salts in a chemical factory he owned.

In the Chain household, both Russian and German were spoken, and the family had many artistic friends. Music was important, and Ernst became a talented pianist, entertaining visitors and accompanying friends who were singers. The Chains were of the Jewish faith, and Ernst was aware of his faith and influenced by it all his life.

Ernst received a good education, attending first the Luisen-gymnasium and then the Friedrich-Wilhelm University. He was awarded his degree in 1930 in chemistry and physiology and then worked for a short time at the Kaiser-Wilhelm Institute in Berlin-Dahlem, where he became acquainted with its director, Fritz Haber, as well as various other famous or soon-to-be famous scientists. He then moved on to a post at the Charité Hospital in Berlin, where he did biochemical research.

With the rise of Nazism in Germany, Chain emigrated to Britain, where he worked under the direction of Sir Frederick G. Hopkins at Cambridge during 1933 to 1935. (Hopkins won the Nobel Prize in Physiology or Medicine in 1929.) Subsequently, he moved to Oxford to the Sir William Dunn School of Pathology, where he became a lecturer in chemical pathology. At Oxford, Chain became interested in penicillin, and with Howard Florey and other scientists there, made the discoveries for which he is most famous. He remained at Oxford until 1948, when he went to Italy to take up a post as scientific director of the International Research Center for Chemical Microbiology at the Instituto Superiore di Sanita, in Rome.

After returning to Great Britain in 1961, Chain became professor of biochemistry at Imperial College of the University of London, where he stayed until his retirement in 1973. In 1969, he was knighted by Queen Elizabeth. Following his retirement, Chain continued to travel and lecture, despite failing health, until his death in Ireland in August, 1979. He was survived by his wife, the former Anne Beloff, whom he had married in 1948, and three children, Benjamin, Daniel, and Judith.

Scientific Career

Throughout his career, Ernst Chain was interested not only in the academic aspects of biochemistry but also in its practical, even industrial, aspects. He wanted to harness what was known about enzymes and life processes for the good of humanity. He was concerned with changing the attitude of government toward the support of research and with educating young scientists who would carry these ideas into the future.

After his graduation from the university, Chain began work at the Charité Hospital in Berlin, where he did enzyme research, but he soon emigrated to Great Britain, and after brief periods at University College Hospital Medical School in London and the University of Cambridge, he joined the faculty of the Sir William Dunn School of Pathology at Oxford in 1935. Here, Chain pursued research that he had started in Cambridge on the action of snake venom and began new work on an enzyme, lysozyme, that had been investigated previously by Alexander Fleming. Chain established that the toxic effect of snake venom resulted from the ability of one of its components to destroy a vital respiratory enzyme in the body of the snake's victim. In studying lysozyme, Chain discovered that it catalyzed the breakdown of carbohydrates. Still another project on which Chain worked at this time was spreading factor, which could break down a connective material in skin, allowing the rapid spreading of anything injected.

Howard Florey, who directed the William Dunn Laboratory, and Chain began to work on penicillin, along with others there, in 1939. Alexander Fleming, who had made his famous accidental discovery of penicillin in 1928, had researched it to some extent but did not foresee the use of purified penicillin as an injectable or ingestible drug as it is known today. He saw it mainly as a sort of antiseptic for treating wounds or other lesions. It was not clear to Fleming, or to Chain at the start, that penicillin would turn out to be a relatively simple organic compound, as opposed to an enzyme. Progress was slow at first and hampered by lack of adequate funding. Eventually, Chain obtained support from the Rockefeller Foundation. While his coworkers struggled with the problem of growing mold cultures and extracting crude penicillin from the broth, Chain studied the fundamental chemical properties and structure of the new antibiotic. By 1940, it was clear that penicillin could safely be given by injection.

Interest in penicillin became widespread in the United States as well as Great Britain. Various drug companies in the United States began research programs and also began to take out patents on some of their discoveries, such as an improved form of fermentation that resulted in greater yields of penicillin. Chain was dismayed at the thought that profits would be made for drug companies at the expense of patients. Also, he resented the idea of paying royalties in order to get more penicillin for experimental purposes. He approached the Medical Research Council in Great Britain to protest these developments, but obtained little encouragement.

Penicillin research proceeded both in the United States and in Great Britain, with Chain and the others in the group at Oxford making major contributions. One of the penicillins was eventually purified to the extent that it could be converted to a crystalline sodium salt suitable for single crystal X-ray structure determination. This breakthrough occurred in 1943. The crystals were examined by British crystallographer Dorothy Crowfoot, and their diffraction patterns revealed the relative positions of the atoms. The data analysis involved was very lengthy and time-consuming (there were no digital computers). By early 1945, the structure of penicillin was finally known with certainty to be the long-speculated beta-lactam.

From 1945, Chain became increasingly interested in the industrial-scale production of penicillin and other antibiotics by fermentation or other processes involving enzymes. He believed that the government should set up a central laboratory and plant where practical studies could be made and where training could take place. The projected costs of these plans were very great; little support was forthcoming from government sources in Great Britain. Chain consulted industrial concerns and various national governments in Europe, as well as the government of Israel and the Weizmann Institute. Eventually, he decided to take up the directorship of a new laboratory in Rome, and left Oxford in 1948. The institute at which Chain worked in Italy was housed in an eight-story building and was home to many distinguished scientists. There was also the opportunity for Chain to take over a penicillin factory owned by the Italian government and use it for research purposes. In this facility, after extensive modifications were made, basic studies were carried out on the manufacture of antibiotics and other useful products of enzymatic reactions. A device was developed for aeration of fermentation mixtures by a vortex process. Also, a process for making lysergic acid derivatives was discovered.

A second line of research in Rome was more academic and small-scale and grew out of some studies that Chain's wife Anne had done during her Ph.D. research. The goal was to understand the details of glucose metabolism in muscle and the role of insulin. An elaborate series of experiments was done, involving the use of radioactively labeled glucose, and Chain was eventually able to propose a new theory of insulin action.

Chain also continued to make contacts with industry around Europe and to discuss various plans for commercial production of penicillin or other products. One such contact was with Beecham Group of England, where there was interest in producing penicillin products for consumer use and also in production of tartaric acid, a component of grape juice used in food products that can be made cheaply by fermentation.

The Beecham researchers in consultation with Chain discovered a process for production of a crucial penicillin derivative called 6-aminopenicillanic acid (6-APA). All the known penicillins could be derived from 6-APA by simple reactions, and the potential existed for making new, tailor-made penicillins from 6-APA that would be adaptable to the many varied demands of therapy. One outgrowth of this development was the creation of orally administered penicillin, a great improvement over massive, painful injections.

In 1961, Chain returned to Great Britain to Imperial College, University of London, where he had accepted the chair of biochemistry. He was able to attract considerable funding from both industrial and governmental sources, and he planned to develop a biochemistry department that could help British industry take discoveries from the laboratory through pilot-plant stage and into production. There he remained until his retirement in 1973, while he continued to direct significant research and contribute to the intellectual life of the university by organizing conferences and lectures.

Chain served extensively as a consultant to the food industry and became interested in the growth of microorganisms that could be used as food. A result of this interest was the discovery of a species of fungus that could be cultured in large amounts and was of sufficiently high protein content to be successfully used as feed for poultry. Extensive studies of fungal viruses were also carried out, with the aim of producing a means of immunization against viral diseases. New antibiotics were discovered and means of production developed.

At Imperial College, there also took place the development of new instruments and equipment, for example, an automated instrument for determining the amino acid content of proteins. With this instrument, identification and study of proteins was greatly facilitated and accelerated.

Chain and his coworkers were innovators who pioneered a new blend of basic science, technology, and medicine. Penicillin was the first antibiotic to be produced by large-scale growth of microorganisms. Chain contributed extensively to the development of penicillin and sought to take what had been learned and apply it in related areas. Food science and agriculture have benefited from Chain's research as well as medicine. Applications of biotechnology, of which he was a founder and practitioner, are of ever-increasing importance. One need only consider genetic engineering, gene-implantation, and the development of monoclonal antibodies to appreciate the continuing potential of this field.

Bibliography

Primary

BIOCHEMISTRY: *Enzymatische Esterbildung und Esterspaltung*, 1932; *Landmarks and Perspectives in Biochemical Research*, 1964; *The Chemical Structure of the Penicillins*, 1966; "Thirty Years of Penicillin Therapy," *Proceedings of the Royal Society of London*, vol. 179, 1971, pp. 293-319; *Food Technology in the 1980's: A Royal Society Discussion*, 1975 (with others); *Biologically Active Substances: Exploration and Exploitation*, 1977; "A Short History of the Penicillin Discovery from Fleming's Early Observations in 1929 to the Present Time," in *The History of Antibiotics: A Symposium*, 1980.

MEDICINE: "Penicillin as a Chemotherapeutic Agent," *Lancet*, vol. 2, 1940, pp. 226-228 (with H. W. Florey); "The Development of Penicillin in Medicine," in *The Smithsonian Institution Annual Report for 1944*, 1945; *Antibiotics: A Survey of Penicillin, Streptomycin, and Other Antimicrobial Substances from Fungi, Actinomycetes, Bacteria, and Plants*, 1949.

PUBLIC POLICY: *Drug Research in Academic Laboratories and the Pharmaceutical Industry*, 1964.

Secondary

Clark, Ronald W. *The Life of Ernst Chain: Penicillin and Beyond*. New York: St. Martin's Press, 1985. Clark, a biographer of various scientists (such as Albert Einstein, Charles Darwin, and Thomas Huxley), here turns his attention to Ernst

Chain, from whose widow Clark obtained access to original correspondence and papers. The author has also obtained recollections of Chain from many of his acquaintances and friends. There are five pages of photographs and a bibliography.

Hobby, Gladys L. *Penicillin: Meeting the Challenge*. New Haven, Conn.: Yale University Press, 1985. The author worked with Dr. Karl Meyer at the College of Physicians and Surgeons in New York on some of the earliest clinical studies of penicillin in the United States in 1940. There are photographs of most of the major figures in the penicillin story, of production equipment, of samples of penicillin, and of laboratory results, such as chromatograms. Much space is devoted to the development of mass production of penicillin. Contains notes, references, and statistical material.

Holmstedt, B., and G. Liljestrand, eds. *Readings in Pharmacology*. New York: Macmillan, 1963. There is an extensive quotation from a paper in the British Medical journal, *Lancet*, on pages 304-315, in which Chain describes the status of the penicillin work at Oxford in 1940. Also quotes from Alexander Fleming's first paper on penicillin.

John R. Phillips

1946

Physiology or Medicine

Hermann Joseph Muller, United States

Chemistry

James Batcheller Sumner, United States
John Howard Northrop, United States
Wendell Meredith Stanley, United States

Physics

Percy Williams Bridgman, United States

Literature

Hermann Hesse, Switzerland

Peace

Emily Greene Balch, United States
John R. Mott, United States

HERMANN JOSEPH MULLER
1946

Born: New York, New York; December 21, 1890
Died: Indianapolis, Indiana; April 5, 1967
Nationality: American
Areas of concentration: Genetics, evolutionary biology, and public health

Muller is widely recognized for his research on mutations induced by X rays, especially in fruit flies, which led to his concern about the radiation hazard to people from medical X rays and radioactive fallout, as well as its possible effects on the long-range evolution of the human race

The Award

Presentation

At the Nobel Award ceremony on December 10, 1946, Professor T. Caspersson from the Swedish Royal Caroline Institute recognized Hermann Joseph Muller for his notable contributions to the study of genetics. Muller had first become interested in biology at Columbia University in the early 1900's. The famous experiments by Gregor Mendel on heredity in plants had been published in 1866; new questions were now being asked about how genetic information is transmitted from one generation to the next. The cell nucleus contains chromosomes, which could be seen with a microscope; however, the genes, which form the substructure of chromosomes, as well as the whole process of cell division, were understood only vaguely.

Muller and his colleagues focused their attention on mutations as a way to make progress in understanding heredity. Mutations cause changes in the offspring, which may then persist for many generations. Spontaneous mutations occur naturally but are relatively rare. The principle of evolution, by which new species of organisms have evolved, depends on favorable mutations which occur occasionally. Muller developed experimental procedures to measure the natural mutation rate in fruit flies. He showed that the mutation rate could be increased by artificial means: temperature, chemical processes, and especially by X-ray irradiations. The discovery of mutations induced by X rays aroused a great sensation in 1927 and stimulated similar work on other organisms. The rapid development of experimental genetics has led to practical results such as plant improvements and an understanding of birth defects and diseases in general. Muller is recognized as one of the pioneers of modern cellular biology.

Nobel lecture

The title of Muller's lecture, given on December 12, 1946, was "The Production of Mutations." The offspring of plants and animals breed true most of the time. The traits inherited from one generation to the next are extremely stable, but occasionally mutations do arise. These mutations are very diverse; they are most often harmful or lethal but are occasionally beneficial. Muller's lecture focused on the progress that had been made during the past thirty years in trying to understand what causes mutations.

Starting in graduate school, Muller and various coworkers had been studying mutations in fruit flies. It is well known that chemical reactions go faster at higher temperatures. Similarly, they found that the mutation frequency in fruit flies increases with temperature. They theorized that thermal vibrations at the molecular level caused "submicroscopic accidents" in the genetic material of a cell.

Since natural mutations resulting from heat are relatively rare, Muller developed the idea of using X rays as a way to increase the mutation frequency. This proved to be a successful method of study. In a thirty-minute treatment, the number of mutations could be increased greatly. A number of interesting results were obtained in the 1920's which formed the basis for modern thinking about radiation damage in cells. For example, the frequency of mutations was shown to be directly proportional to the dose—that is, more X rays caused more mutations. This suggested that there is no minimum dose below which radiation is harmless. It was also found that genes are more sensitive to radiation damage during cell division than in the resting stage; therefore, radiation is very effective in killing rapidly dividing cancer cells compared to the surrounding healthy tissue.

Muller considered whether beneficial changes in genetic material could be produced by radiation. It is impossible to change genes "to order," but a selection of favorable mutations can be made the same way a biologist could propagate only the best plants or cull out the superior producers in a herd. Muller's lecture in 1946 foreshadowed some of the remarkable developments in biotechnology that would take place forty years later.

Muller tried to understand how more complex species could have evolved from simpler life-forms. The X-ray irradiation experiments had shown that breakage and rearrangement of chromosome fragments took place. Muller suggested that the number of genes could have increased during evolution by the duplication of small parts of chromosomes. Muller gave a warning to radiologists and others who use radiation. First, it produces a somatic effect, which means that radiation can result in skin burns, sterility, growth inhibition, or malignancy to the irradiated individual. Second, there will be a genetic effect on succeeding generations. Radiation should therefore be used with proper precautions; care should be taken to shield the gonads. Humanity has an obligation to future generations, he said, to avoid the production of undesirable mutations in the human germ plasm.

Critical reception

Muller's Nobel award was announced on October 31, 1946, and three days later *The New York Times* gave him an enthusiastic endorsement in a Sunday editorial. "Professor Muller did as much as any single man to raise genetics, the science of heredity, from its humble beginnings to its present position. Biologists will rejoice that such brilliant work has been fittingly recognized." The editorial recalled the work of Thomas H. Morgan, who had started the study of fruit flies in 1910 and whose maximum observed mutation rate was 400 mutants in 20 million flies. By comparison, Muller, with X-ray irradiation, obtained 150 times that rate. The editorial went on to describe some extreme examples of "monstrosities," such as fruit flies with three wings, bulging eyes, or no legs. They also pointed out that fruit flies propagate rapidly and can breed within a day after being hatched. In humans, physical changes caused by mutations (such as anemia, for example) may not become evident for a thousand years.

Science News on November 9, 1946, also cited Muller for "twenty years of solid devotion to research on genes." In the biographical section of their article, they noted that Muller had worked in "various European countries" during the 1930's. It is interesting that the editors did not explicitly mention the four years that he had lived in the Soviet Union. The Committee on Un-American Activities of the U.S. House of Representatives was starting to hold hearings to identify "Communist sympathizers" among writers, educators, and others. It would have been harmful to Muller's reputation to bring up the Russian connection at this time.

A much more negative evaluation was given by *Time* magazine in its issue of November 11, 1946. Muller's pessimistic view that "most mutations are bad" was stated; however, the writer of the article felt the need to defend the opposing point of view in the rest of the report. "Some geneticists believe the next Hiroshima generation may show many bad mutations. But most of these would be eliminated by the law of the survival of the fittest. The few superior mutations would survive to improve the race." The writer claimed that the additional mutations that could result from the atomic age may be good rather than bad, and the outcome is not clear. The article is a mixture of editorializing and factual reporting. Apparently, the editors of *Time* were anxious to maintain a positive public image for the future prospects of atomic energy.

With the prestige of the Nobel Prize, Muller continued to speak in public about the genetic hazards of radiation. In 1955, he prepared an article entitled "How Radiation Changes the Genetic Constitution" that was to be delivered at the first Atoms for Peace Conference in Geneva, Switzerland, but Muller was denied permission to present it by the U.S. Atomic Energy Commission. Subsequent publicity of this incident brought about an apology from the AEC chairman Lewis Strauss. As Muller's name became more widely known to the general public, he wrote numerous articles addressed to nonscientists on the implications of science for society.

Biography

Hermann Joseph Muller was born on December 21, 1890, in New York City. He developed an early interest in biology and evolution, stimulated by youthful visits to the American Museum of Natural History. He was graduated from Morris High School in the Bronx. Since his father had died when Hermann was nine years old, the family could not afford college expenses, but he was fortunate to receive a scholarship to Columbia College (now University) in the fall of 1907. From his course work and individual reading, he became fascinated by new ideas in physiology and heredity, especially the role of chromosomes. He received his B.A. in 1910. Continuing his education at Columbia, he wrote a master's thesis on the transmission of nerve impulses, and he started a Ph.D. program there under the guidance of Thomas H. Morgan, who was awarded the Nobel Prize in Physiology or Medicine in 1933. Muller received the Ph.D. in 1916, whereupon he was invited by Julian Huxley to teach at Rice Institute in Houston, Texas. In 1918, he returned to Columbia as a faculty member for two years, continuing his research on genes and inherited characteristics. From 1921 to 1932, he was a professor at the University of Texas at Austin, where he used fruit flies to observe induced mutations caused by X-ray irradiation. In 1927, he published his most famous article, entitled "Artificial Transmutation of the Gene," which gave him an international reputation.

In 1932, Muller was awarded a Guggenheim Fellowship for a year of research in Berlin. He saw at first hand how intellectual freedom was being restricted by the authoritarian Nazi regime. For the next four years, he went to Russia as a geneticist at Moscow and Leningrad. He became involved in the unfortunate controversy with Trofim D. Lysenko, whose unusual theory of inheritance was supported not by experimental evidence but by personal friendship with Joseph Stalin. In 1937, Muller volunteered to go to Spain, where he served in the medical corps. From 1938 to 1940, he was at the University of Edinburgh, then returned to the United States, where he taught at Amherst College. In 1945, he became a professor of zoology at Indiana University in Bloomington, where he remained until his death in 1967.

The Nobel Prize awarded in 1946 gave Muller an opportunity to speak out on a number of social issues. He was greatly concerned about the radiation hazard to humans resulting from the excessive use of X rays by doctors, as well as nuclear fallout from military weapons testing in the atmosphere. In 1955, when anti-Soviet feeling was high in the United States, he was denied permission to attend the first Atoms for Peace Conference in Geneva. He was a member of several conferences which tried to promote international cooperation by scientists. Muller was also concerned about biology textbooks for high school students, where he advocated greater emphasis on genetics and evolution. He was the recipient of numerous honorary degrees and awards, including Humanist of the Year in 1963.

Muller was married to Jessie M. Jacobs in 1923, and one son was born the following year. They were divorced in 1935. He married again in 1939, to Thea Kantorowicz; a daughter was born in 1944.

Scientific Career

Muller's education in the biological sciences spanned the years from 1907 to 1916, all at Columbia College, where he successively received the B.A., M.A., and Ph.D. degrees. His undergraduate courses in heredity and evolution and in cell structure particularly stimulated his interest. As a beginning graduate student, he came under the influence of Professor Thomas H. Morgan, who was starting his work in genetics with the common fruit fly, *Drosophila melanogaster*. The goal was to understand how the chromosomes and their substructure of genes transmit inherited characteristics to the next generation. The experimental method was to follow observable mutations, such as red or white eyes, or wings that were bent, truncated, or serrated, through several generations to see if they followed the normal Mendelian laws of inheritance.

When a mutation has occurred in the organism, it is possible to see the chromosomal changes that will take place in succeeding generations even before the organism reproduces. With a high-power light microscope, it is possible to see individual chromosomes (genes are too small to see). A chromosome may become broken and then the two fragments may become reunited. A chromosome could also break at two locations and the broken segment can undergo a total rotation to the other direction before rejoining the remaining fragments. If such a mutation is not lethal, it will be transmitted in its mutated form to the offspring. The key concept that emerged from the experimental work was that genes are very stable, but occasional spontaneous mutations occur in nature. The cell copies mutational errors. Natural selection then determines if the organism can survive.

After Muller moved to Texas, he began a series of experiments to measure the natural mutation rate in fruit flies. He found that raising the temperature increases the mutation rate. This suggested that chromosome breakages may be the result of thermal agitation of the molecules. The number of natural mutations is quite rare, however, so Muller began to work with X rays in 1924. In 1927, he published his famous article in *Science*, "Artificial Transmutation of the Gene," reporting spectacular success in producing a huge increase of mutations. With the dose that he was using, the number of mutations increased by a factor of 150. He also reported that the type of mutations occurring artificially were usually the same as the natural ones, although some new ones were also observed. He suggested that X-ray irradiation provided a new tool for biologists to investigate the gene structure of chromosomes.

Muller anticipated the future development of genetic research during a talk addressed to a meeting of chemists and physicists in 1936. He challenged the physical scientists in his audience to use their expertise to explore the substructure of the gene, what is now called molecular biology. "When, through some micro-chemical accident or chance quantum absorption, a sudden change in the composition of the gene takes place . . . then the gene of the new type reproduces itself according to the new pattern. This shows that the copying property depends upon some more fundamental feature of gene structure." It is interesting that James Watson, who developed the double-helix model of deoxyribonucleic acid (DNA), attributed his interest in genetics to a course he took under Muller while he was a graduate student at Indiana University.

Based on his observations of mutations in irradiated fruit flies as well as other animal studies, Muller became very concerned about the careless exposure of humans to X rays. In the 1930's, a medical procedure to induce ovulation in sterile women was to give a massive dose of radiation to the ovaries. Many physicians believed that this therapy was safe because no unusual number of abnormalities were found among their children. Similarly, irradiation of male testes produced temporary sterility, but the sperm count later recovered to a normal level. Muller pointed out the fallacy of looking only at the first generation of offspring. Gene mutations may remain hidden for many generations before they give rise to a lethal birth defect. An individual who has inherited a mutant gene from one parent and a corresponding normal gene from the other parent may exhibit no noticeable effect. The popular idea that a mutation immediately results in a monster or a freak is a gross distortion of the facts.

After the atomic bombs were used over Japan in 1945, scientists started to collect data from the offspring of survivors who had received large radiation doses. Muller predicted that hardly any increase in abnormalities would be observed. His prediction was contrary to popular opinion but has been confirmed. As was shown by the experiments with irradiated fruit flies, harmful or lethal mutations show up as a slight increase spread over many generations, not a dramatic increase in the first generation.

In the 1950's, both the United States and the Soviet Union were testing nuclear weapons, with the release of large amounts of radioactive fallout into the atmosphere. Muller joined with other scientists to publicize the hazards of fallout. It was a time of intense antagonism and even hysteria toward the Soviet Union, and any public statement criticizing U.S. military policy was viewed with great suspicion.

A persistent theme in Muller's scientific career was the ideal of intellectual freedom as well as the freedom to express what may be unpopular views at the time. The Scopes "monkey" trial of 1921 had led to legislative restrictions on teaching evolution, especially in the South. Since the principle of evolution is a key concept in the study of genetics and heredity, a direct conflict of viewpoints existed between scientists and popular opinion. A more direct confrontation with University of Texas administrators arose because Muller gave financial support to a student newspaper that had been banned by the university, presumably for publishing Communist propaganda. Tension increased further at this time because Muller invited and hosted a visit to the campus by two Russian geneticists. In 1933, Muller decided to leave Texas and obtained a Guggenheim Fellowship to go to Berlin to do research at the prestigious Kaiser Wilhelm Institute.

Historical circumstances unfortunately were antagonistic to intellectual freedom. Adolf Hitler and the Nazi Party had come to power in 1933, and the situation at the institute was tense. A surge of emigration by scientists of Jewish heritage had started. Books by Jewish authors were collected from libraries and bookstores and burned in the public square in front of the opera house. After spending only a few months in Berlin, Muller decided to move to the Institute of Genetics in Moscow, where he hoped to find the ideal Marxist society, where "power belongs to the people." This was the time when the agronomist Trofim D. Lysenko was on the rise in the Soviet hierarchy with his controversial antigenetic viewpoint. Lysenko promised great improvements for growing potatoes in southern Russia by using summer planting; he soon developed a personal friendship with Joseph Stalin. Other agronomists were fearful to criticize Lysenko, even though his results had not been confirmed by independent field trials. When potato yield did not increase, it was blamed on lazy farmers or failure to follow proper planting procedure. Muller became disillusioned and left the Soviet Union in 1937. Lysenko continued to have a great influence on Soviet agriculture even after Stalin's death in 1953. "Lysenkoism" became a symbol for political power that stifles free scientific inquiry. After Muller returned to the United States, he wrote a number of articles that showed how genetics research had deteriorated in Russia because of the political dominance of one man.

Just as plant and animal species can be improved by genetic selection, Muller believed that the human race could do much more to control its own evolution. Eugenics is the scientific field of study whose goal is to improve the hereditary qualities of humankind. Certain diseases such as diabetes and mongoloidism are recognized as being inherited. A couple whose recent family history shows a genetically transmitted illness may prefer to adopt a child rather than to take the chance of becoming biological parents. This kind of negative eugenics seeks to prevent the continuation of harmful mutations.

Muller had a utopian vision of positive eugenics that tries to improve the world's population through germinal choice. With cryogenic techniques, prospective parents could select human sperm from donors who possessed the human qualities that they valued most highly, and freeze it with liquid nitrogen. Needless to say, this was a very controversial viewpoint that raised the specter of Nazi experimentation to create a master race. In his writings on eugenics, Muller tried to identify the most desirable qualities for humankind: health, intelligence, creativity, and cooperativeness. He recognized that the environment has an important role in developing these qualities through better education and improved social conditions. Nevertheless, he believed that even an abstract quality such as cooperativeness, in contrast to aggressiveness, could be developed through voluntary eugenic choice. The process of evolution had shown that "there is no permanent status quo in nature." Muller challenged his readers and listeners to rethink traditional human values, to consider whether the world's population could be improved through deliberate choices in genetics. Muller will be remembered both for his scientific contributions and for his advocacy of far-reaching social concerns.

Bibliography

Primary

GENETICS: *The Mechanism of Mendelian Heredity*, 1915 (with Thomas H. Morgan, Alfred H. Sturtevant, and Calvin B. Bridges); "Artificial Transmutation of the Gene," *Science*, vol. 66 (July 27, 1927), pp. 84-87; *Out of the Night: A Biologist's View of the Future*, 1935; *Genetics, Medicine, and Man*, 1947 (with Clarence C. Little and Lawrence H. Snyder); "The Destruction of Science in the USSR," *Saturday Review of Literature*, vol. 31, 1948, pp. 13-15; "Radiation and Human

Mutation," *Scientific American*, vol. 193, 1955, pp. 58-68; *Studies in Genetics: The Selected Papers of H. J. Muller*, 1962.

Secondary

Carlson, Elof A. "H. J. Muller." *Genetics* 70 (January, 1972): 1-30. The most complete biography of Muller's life and professional career, written in a chronological narrative form. Anecdotes about his working habits and his relationships with colleagues and critics provide interesting glimpses into his life-style. Some background in basic genetics is needed to follow the more technical aspects of his scientific contributions.

Joravsky, David. "The Lysenko Affair." *Scientific American* 207 (November, 1962): 41-49. Lysenko was a Russian agronomist with an unorthodox theory of planting potatoes in mid-summer to increase yield. His ideas were adopted by the State in the 1930's based not on objective field trials, but because of his personal friendship with Stalin. "Lysenkoism" became a symbol for situations in which political power dominates over scientific testing.

Muller, Hermann Joseph. *Man's Future Birthright: Essays on Science and Humanity*, edited by Elof Axel Carlson. Albany: State University of New York, 1973. Nine essays on a wide range of subjects have been reprinted with an introduction by Muller's friend and coworker, Dr. Bently Glass. The articles deal with broad themes such as eugenics, radiation hazards, science fiction, and the search for world peace. No special background in biology is needed to appreciate these stimulating essays.

____________. *The Modern Concept of Nature: Essays on Theoretical Biology and Evolution*, edited by Elof Axel Carlson. Albany: State University of New York Press, 1973. Ten articles and public lectures on general themes in biology by Muller are reprinted here. Introductory comments by the editor help the reader to identify key concepts and to appreciate the historical setting for each selection. A glossary of technical terms is given in the appendix.

Sigurbjornsson, Bjorn. "Induced Mutations in Plants." *Scientific American* 224 (January, 1971): 86-95. Plants or seeds can be irradiated with gamma rays to produce mutations. As Muller had shown in 1927, most mutations are harmful, but a few may be beneficial. This article describes how plant breeders can select favorable mutations for increased yield or disease resistance in crop varieties that have been important for the green revolution.

Sonneborn, T. M. "H. J. Muller, Crusader for Human Betterment." *Science* 162 (November 15, 1968): 772-776. This article was written shortly after Muller's death by a colleague in the Department of Zoology at Indiana University. It gives an overview of Muller's education, scientific contributions, and vision for a better society, written by someone who knew him personally and admired him.

Hans G. Graetzer

1947

Physiology or Medicine

Carl F. Cori, Czechoslovakia and United States
Gerty T. Cori, Czechoslovakia and United States
Bernardo Alberto Houssay, Argentina

Chemistry

Sir Robert Robinson, Great Britain

Physics

Sir Edward Victor Appleton, Great Britain

Literature

André Gide, France

Peace

American Friends Service Committee, United States
Friends Service Council, Great Britain

CARL F. CORI

GERTY T. CORI

CARL F. CORI and GERTY T. CORI
1947

Carl F. Cori

Born: Prague, Austro-Hungarian Empire (now Czechoslovakia); December 5, 1896
Died: Cambridge, Massachusetts; October 20, 1984
Nationality: Czechoslovak; after 1928, American
Areas of concentration: Biochemistry, enzymology, and endocrinology

Gerty T. Cori

Born: Prague, Austro-Hungarian Empire (now Czechoslovakia); August 15, 1896
Died: St. Louis, Missouri; October 26, 1957
Nationality: Czechoslovak: after 1928, American
Areas of concentration: Biochemistry, enzymology, and endocrinology

The Coris determined the important metabolic relationship between glucose and glycogen in the body; they crystallized the enzyme physphorylase, synthesized glucose, and discovered the Cori ester

The Award

Presentation

Professor A. Hugo Theorell, head of the Biochemical Nobel Department of the Royal Caroline Institute, made the presentation address in Stockholm on December 10, 1947, on behalf of the teaching body of the Institute. The 1947 prize was awarded jointly to the Coris and Bernardo Houssay for their separate achievements in the study of the metabolism of sugars. Theorell emphasized the importance of carbohydrates to the body in supplying energy for its functions and the devastating effect of faulty sugar metabolism, which leads to diabetes. He reminded the audience that Claude Bernard, ninety years before, had discovered glycogen in muscles and the liver and had found that this substance was made of many glucose molecules bound together and stored so that they could be used when needed to keep the sugar content of the blood relatively constant.

It had also been shown earlier that glucose, in the body, often formed a phosphate, a molecule in which phosphoric acid was attached to the sixth position of the sugar. The Coris isolated a second phosphate (the "Cori ester") in which the bonding occurred at the one position. This new compound, which plays an important part in the interconversion of glycogen and glucose, was isolated from muscle tissue that had been washed with water. The washing removed an enzyme (a biological catalyst which enables a reaction to occur) that normally changes the Cori ester to glucose-6-phosphate. The Coris discovered this enzyme and another, phosphorylase, which, in the presence of phosphate, causes the glycogen to break up into glucose-1-phosphate, the first step to returning the stored glucose to the blood. They also found that this was a reversible reaction: The Cori ester could become glycogen when certain amounts of reactants were present. Using the correct enzymes and esters, the Coris were able to carry out the synthesis of glycogen in a test tube.

Continuing their study of glucose, Theorell noted, now in the blood and tissues, the Coris and coworkers showed that hormones react chemically in metabolic processes; they discovered that insulin promotes a reaction in the body catalyzed by the enzyme hexokinase and that this reaction can be prevented by another hormone found in the pituitary gland.

Nobel lecture

Carl and Gerty Cori delivered their lecture, entitled "Polysaccharide Phosphorylase," on December 11, 1947, with each laureate describing part of their joint research. Carl began by explaining how the enzyme phosphorylase can make or break a bond at the end of a chain of glycogen or starch. These natural polymers consist of glucose (grape sugar) units and serve to store this sugar in animals and plants. The phosphorylase either causes a phosphate to attach to a glucose unit in the glycogen and remove it from the polymer chain or causes a sugar to add to the chain, releasing a phosphate (a reversible reaction). The combination of glucose with phosphate in the reaction results in the compound glucose-1-phosphate, or Cori ester, which occurs in extremely small quantities in resting muscle. This ester was discovered when the Coris were investigating whether the splitting of glycogen gave glucose-6-phosphate. They found that if they washed minced frog muscle with water to remove the phosphates but not the glycogen and then incubated the extract, an ester was formed that had different properties from glucose-6-phosphate. They postulated that a precursor had been discovered. This precursor was glucose-1-phosphate, an ester which has the phosphate attached at a different place on the glucose part of the molecule. The 1-ester could be changed to the 6-ester by an enzyme, phosphoglucomutase, and, because this enzyme was soluble in water and had been removed by the washing, the Cori ester could be isolated. A chemical synthesis of glucose-1-phosphate produced a compound identical to the natural ester, thus proving its structure.

The Coris' investigation of the reversible reaction (glycogen + phosphate = glucose-1-phosphate) could only go forward when the enzymes phosphorylase and phosphoglucomutase could be isolated and purified. Gerty Cori, in the second part of the lecture, described the isolation of phosphorylase from muscle tissue. It was then discovered that some glycogen was necessary for either the forward reaction, glycogen to glucose-1-phosphate, or the reverse reaction, the formation of glycogen, to occur. Two forms of phosphorylase were found, one active (a) and one inactive (b) in the presence of adenylic acid, which could be converted from one to another by another enzyme. The Coris showed that the a form predominates in resting muscle but that a large quantity of b form is produced on contraction of the muscle. This conversion could be considered as a regulatory mechanism to assure that the body always has some stored glycogen. With the discovery of phosphorylase, the mechanism of glucose and glycogen conversion could be understood.

In the final part of the lecture, Carl Cori discussed plant and animal phosphorylases and the reactions they catalyze. Some form polymeric compounds from glucose that have straight chains (starch), while others (glycogen) form polymers that are branched like the branches of a tree growing out of the trunk. He suggested that another enzyme is needed to produce the branched configuration. The lecture concluded with the presentation of a theory of the action of phosphorylase, the reactants being inorganic phosphate and the end (terminal) glucose unit of the polymer chain. The glycogen or starch is reduced one unit at a time, and the chain can be built up by adding one glucose-1-phosphate each time. A certain amount of the polymer must be present for the reaction to occur, and, because branched chain polymers have more end units, they are more activating.

Critical reception

Because the Coris were considered by their students and peers to be extraordinary scientific pioneers, the award of the Nobel Prize in 1947 was greeted with enthusiasm. *Nature* commented primarily on their studies of carbohydrate metabolism and the in vitro synthesis of glycogen. The Coris' current work on hexokinase, the article said, was expected to lead to an explanation of how adenosine phosphates were involved in bioreactions. *Science* emphasized the importance of the glycogen synthesis and noted that the Coris were the third husband and wife team to be awarded a Nobel Prize.

Although *The Times* of London simply announced the recipients, *The New York Times* (October 24, 1947) informed its readers of the new laureates on the front page. The article noted that this was a husband-wife team of naturalized American citizens, and the writer included details about their son and his interests. Carl was described as shy, Gerty as vivacious, and they were identified as physicians who had never practiced. The reporter confused glycogen with the enzyme phosphorylase and credited the Coris with being the first to synthesize an "enzyme" in a test tube. Carl is misquoted as saying that this was the first time such a large molecule had been built in a test tube, all other studies of "enzymes" involving the breakdown of the compounds. The relationship of the research to insulin and diabetes and the possibility of its leading to a cure was emphasized in an editorial in *The New York Times* on October 24. Again, the writer reported that the Coris had not only isolated but also synthesized phosphorylase. On December 4, the newspaper ran a photograph of the Coris leaving for Stockholm, saying that they would lecture in Vienna. When asked about curing cancer using radiation, Carl indicated that he could not predict this and that to do so might give false hope to those affected.

Time magazine, on November 3, included a long article on the Coris, also emphasizing the possibility of a diabetes cure arising from their work. The writer recognized the fundamental importance of their research on the step-by-step transformation of carbohydrates and sugars into other substances in blood and tissue. Their discovery and "synthesis" of an enzyme which began the process of converting glycogen into sugar was noted, as well as their recent discovery of a "mysterious substance" in pituitary extract that regulates the body's absorption of sugar.

In the February, 1948, issue of *Science Illustrated*, an excellent article appeared on the Coris and their prize. The well-illustrated piece explained the interconversion of glucose and glycogen and identified the relationship between the metabolism of glucose and the production of energy in the body. Noting that laymen were often impatient with the kind of pure research done by the Coris, the writer described the requests which had been sent to the couple for cures and samples of all the compounds mentioned in the press releases about the prize. By emphasizing that the work was done "jointly" and detailing the cooperative way the couple did research, the article gave Gerty due credit for her accomplishments. It concluded with the statement that although the Coris had not invented any "cures," the future development of medicine would depend on a knowledge of how the body functions.

Biographies

Carl Ferdinand Cori and Gerty Theresa Radnitz Cori were both born in Prague, then a part of the Austro-Hungarian Empire, in 1896, she on August 15, he on December 5. Gerty was the eldest of three daughters of Otto Radnitz, a businessman and manager of sugar refineries, and Martha Neustadt Radnitz. Gerty was educated by tutors at home and then entered a private girls' school. Because she wished to study chemistry and was not prepared for entrance to the university, she studied at the Tetschen *Realgymnasium* and began her medical studies at the German University of Prague (Carl Ferdinand University) in 1914.

Carl's parents were Carl I. Cori, who had earned an M.D. at Prague and a Ph.D. in zoology at Leipzig, and Maria Lippich Cori, daughter of a professor of mathematical physics. In 1898, the family moved to Trieste, where the father became director of the Marine Biological Station. Carl studied at the classical *Gymnasium* from 1906 to 1914 and participated in the expeditions and research at the station. His interest in biology led him to enter the medical school at the German University of Prague, where he met his future wife and collaborator.

In his third year, Carl was drafted. He served in the ski troops, at a bacteriological laboratory, and at a hospital for infectious diseases. In 1918, he returned to his studies, and after graduation the Coris moved to Vienna and were married. Carl worked at both the university clinic and the pharmacological institute, while Gerty joined the staff of the Carolinen Children's Hospital, where she remained while Carl spent six months at the University of Graz with Otto Loewi. Discouraged by the social and economic conditions in Europe, he accepted an offer to move to Buffalo, New York, in 1922 to become a biochemist at the Institute for the Study of Malignant Diseases. Gerty followed him in a few months and was appointed assistant pathologist at the institute (now Roswell Park Memorial Institute), later becoming assistant biochemist. The Coris were now able to continue the successful collaboration that they began in medical school. Others often tried to discourage them from working together because joint research would have an adverse effect on Carl's career.

In 1928, the Coris became United States citizens; in 1931, they moved to Washington University School of Medicine in St. Louis, where Carl served as chair of the department of pharmacology and Gerty became a research assistant at a token salary. Their son, Carl Thomas, was born in 1936. During World War II, Carl was appointed professor of biological chemistry as well as pharmacology and was responsible for a laboratory under contract to the Office of Scientific Research and Development, studying the effect of toxic gases on enzyme systems. In 1946, Carl became head of the department of biological chemistry and Gerty was appointed associate professor of research biology. In 1947, the year they received the Nobel Prize, Gerty became professor. In this same year, Gerty was diagnosed as suffering from myelofibrosis, a disease of the bone marrow, which required many blood transfusions. In spite of her illness, she continued her laboratory research and was appointed by President Truman to sit on the first board of the National Science Foundation. She died of kidney failure in October, 1957.

Carl married Anne Fitz-Gerald Jones in 1960 and remained at Washington University until his retirement in 1966. He then moved to Boston to become visiting professor of biochemistry at the Massachusetts General Hospital and Harvard University School of Medicine. He died in his home in Cambridge in October, 1984.

Although the Coris shared a common bibliography until her death and identified themselves as equal collaborators, the honors they received varied. Carl was elected to the National Academy of Sciences in 1940, Gerty in 1948. He alone became a foreign member of the Royal Society. Carl was awarded the prestigious Lasker Award of the American Public Health Association and the Willard Gibbs Medal of the American Chemical Society; Gerty received the Garvan Medal for women chemists of the American Chemical Society. Together they were honored with the Adler Prize, the Midwest Award of the American Chemical Society, the St. Louis Award, the Squibb Award of the American Society of Endocrinology, and the Sugar Research Foundation Award. In addition, the Coris were recipients of many honorary degrees.

Scientific Careers

Both Gerty and Carl Cori chose to study medicine because they were interested in doing scientific research. During the summer of 1919, after Carl had resumed his clinical studies at Prague, he worked in the Pharmacological Institute of Dr. Geza Mansfield in Pozsony, sharing a laboratory with Albert Szent-Györgyi, who later also won a Nobel Prize. Carl's research there resulted in a paper on the physiology and pharmacology of the excitation of the sinus nodes of the heart. The first cooperative work of the Coris, done before their marriage, was on human complement, a substance in the blood that combines with antibodies. After graduation, the collaboration continued with the publication of a paper on the treatment of tuberculosis. Because his father provided him with frogs from the University of Prague, Carl was able to continue his experimental work on the seasonal variation in the action of the vagus nerve of the heart. At the Children's Hospital, Gerty studied the influence of the thyroid on body temperature regulation, research stimulated by patients with congenital myxedema, a disease caused by reduced functioning of the thyroid. She also carried out animal studies after removal of the thyroid and the spleen.

In the autumn of 1921, Carl went to Graz to work in the laboratory of Otto Loewi, a Nobel laureate in 1936, and there developed the idea for a method to study intestinal absorption and the metabolism of sugar in animals. In Buffalo, he learned to use new microanalytical techniques from George Pucher at the Buffalo General Hospital. Together they published several papers in 1922 and 1923 on metabolic disturbances of cats on a milk diet and the biological effect of X rays. Gerty's first paper in English examined the influence of thyroid extract on the rate of multiplication of paramecia. She also studied the effect of X rays on the skin and other organs of mice and, with Carl, their influence on chloride metabolism.

Although Carl published several papers on cancer-related topics while in New York, this period also saw the initiation of the research on sugars and sugar metabolism which earned their Nobel Prize. The discovery of insulin in 1921 had an immediate effect on biomedical as well as clinical research. The fact that this extract from the pancreas could influence the burning of sugar in the body and control diabetes stimulated research throughout the world. The Coris approached their study from a quantitative viewpoint, measuring the amounts of various substances in vivo and determining how insulin affected these amounts. So, in 1924, their papers were concerned with the influence of insulin on phlorizin poisoning, on liver glycogen and free blood sugar in fasting animals, and on the insulin content of the pancreas and other tissues under certain conditions. The Coris' first joint publication on the subject, in 1924, was a comparative study of the sugar content of arterial and venous blood in the presence of insulin. In addition, determinations of changes in inorganic and organic phosphates and of lactic acid when insulin and adrenaline were administered were done, working primarily with the whole animal. Otto Warburg's discovery that tumors used large amounts of glucose at a high rate in vitro led the Coris to experiment on the carbohydrate metabolism of tumors in vivo. They found that a large amount of lactate was produced by growing a Rous chicken sarcoma on one wing of a chicken and analyzing and comparing the content of the venous blood with that of the normal, or control, wing.

During these studies on tumors, it became clear that research on carbohydrate metabolism in normal animals needed to be done. A series of papers on the fate of sugar in the animal body began to appear in 1925, with a study of the rate of absorption of hexoses (six-carbon-atom sugars), such as glucose, fructose, and galactose, and pentoses (five-carbon-atom sugars), such as ribose, from the intestinal tract. A method of analysis was developed for these studies in which the total amount of sugar left in the intestine after absorption was measured after a known quantity had been administered. The Coris also developed other innovative methods for analysis of lactic acid and glycogen; using these techniques, they found that 90 percent of the glucose and fructose absorbed by fasting rats was either oxidized to lactic acid or converted into glycogen, the natural polymer which allows glucose to be stored in the body. They measured the effect of insulin and adrenaline dosage on the amounts of oxidation product and of glycogen in the muscles and in the liver. In 1929, they proposed a "cycle of carbohydrates" (the Cori cycle), in which reactions occur so that blood glucose becomes muscle glycogen, which is changed into blood lactic acid, which can become liver glycogen, which, in turn, forms blood glucose, thus closing the circle. Although the original cycle has been modified, often by later work by the Coris, to make a side reaction of the glycogen portion because glucose and lactic acid can be formed directly from each other, this concept stimulated important research. The Coris also showed that the blood lactate, which is formed by the action of adrenaline, originates in the tissues, and they predicted that it was a contaminant in the insulin, and not the insulin itself, which was responsible for liver glycogen production. This substance, hyperglycemic-glycogenolytic factor, was isolated by the Coris in 1949. The importance of this cycle in understanding glucose metabolism was recognized immediately. The Coris' pioneering quantitative research truly opened up the field of carbohydrate metabolism. During the productive Buffalo period, one hundred papers were published by the couple.

In 1931, the Coris moved to St. Louis, where Gerty was given a laboratory and a position as research associate when Carl became head of the department of pharmacology; they continued a study of hexose monophosphates, compounds (esters) which combine a hexose with one phosphate. They found that, in stimulated muscle tissue, an increase in the monophosphate was accompanied by a decrease in inorganic phosphate, suggesting that this ester was formed directly—without intermediate reactions. One hexose monophosphate, glucose-6-phosphate, had been discovered in which the phosphate is attached to the 6 position. Using water-washed minced muscle and adenylic acid, the Coris were able to isolate glucose-1-phosphate (the Cori ester), which is a precursor to the formation of glucose-6-phosphate from glycogen. The placement of the phosphate in the compound determines whether an enzyme will catalyze a vital specific biochemical reaction. The Coris recognized that the hexose monophosphates were part of the important process of storing glucose as glycogen. The discovery of the role of adenylic acid opened up the study of a new series of reactions.

They now needed to find why the glucose-1-phosphate had been found in the washed muscle: They postulated that by washing they had removed an enzyme which was changing glucose-1-phosphate to glucose-6-phosphate and that another enzyme was responsible for forming the Cori ester from glycogen. This latter enzyme, phosphorylase, was isolated, purified, and crystallized by 1942. Crystallization of an enzyme is necessary to determine its properties. The enzyme which was changing the glucose-1-phosphate to glucose-6-phosphate was also found and was named phosphoglucomutase. Now the mechanism by which the glucose polymer (glycogen), stored in the liver, can be changed to glucose in the blood was clarified. Glycogen becomes glucose-1-phosphate, which becomes glucose-6-phosphate, which is transformed to glucose; the glucose finally becomes lactic acid. All this happens through simple biochemical reactions catalyzed by specific enzymes. The Coris discovered an additional enzyme that is also used in the process whereby glycogen (which has a branched rather than a straight chain structure) forms glucose. As their study of the process continued, it was discovered that glycogen could be formed from glucose-1-phosphate. By using pure enzymes and other necessary compounds, the Coris succeeded in carrying out the first test-tube synthesis of a naturally occurring macromolecule (polymer), glycogen from glucose, thereby confirming the structure of glycogen and showing how branched and straight chain compounds are made in the body.

In 1943, the Coris found that the enzyme phosphorylase existed in two forms, which could change into each other, with hyperglycemic-glycogenolytic factor and adrenaline taking part in the interconversion; one form needed adenosine monophosphate to become active. With this information available, Gerty undertook the study of a group of diseases in which abnormal amounts of glycogen are stored in the tissues. She was the first to show that a hereditary disease could be caused by a specific enzyme deficiency and that because of such a deficiency glycogen could be synthesized in the body with an abnormal structure.

Before Gerty's death in 1957, the Coris continued research on the effect of insulin on carbohydrate metabolism, setting forth a hexokinase theory that was later found to be incorrect. During this period, however, several important enzymes were isolated and/or crystallized, including muscle aldolase, specific hexokinases, and diphosphopyridine nucleotide pyrophosphatase. Enzymatic analysis of polysaccharide structure was carried out, the hormone effects on hexokinase were elucidated, and the role of phosphates in biochemical regulation was clarified. They also showed that diabetes does result from inhibition of hexokinase in certain tissues. The Cori laboratory at Washington University was a major center for biochemical research in the world; among the scientists who studied there were the Nobel laureates, Christian de Duve, Arthur Kornberg, Luis Leloir, Severo Ochoa, and Earl Sutherland. Although Carl did little laboratory work after World War II, he and Gerty continued to supervise and inspire many distinguished students.

After his retirement and move to Boston in 1966, Carl purified the enzyme glucose-6-phosphatase and studied its role in regulation and biosynthesis in diabetics. With Salome Waeland, he showed that chromosome 7 was responsible for the regulation of glucose-6-phosphate in the body but not for its synthesis.

Bibliography

Primary

Joint Publications

BIOCHEMISTRY: "A Method for the Study of Liver Metabolism," *Proceedings of the Society for Experimental Biology and Medicine*, vol. 20, 1923, p. 409; "The Carbohydrate Metabolism of Tumors: II, Changes in the Sugar, Lactic Acid, and CO_2-Combining Power of Blood Passing Through a Tumor," *Journal of Biological Chemistry*, vol. 65, 1925, pp. 397-405; "Glycogen Formation in the Liver from d-and l-Lactic Acid," *Journal of Biological Chemistry*, vol. 81, 1929, pp. 389-403; "The Mechanism of Epinephrine Action: V, Changes in Liver Glycogen and Blood Lactic Acid After Injection of Epinephrine and Insulin," *Journal of Biological Chemistry*, vol. 86, 1930, pp. 375-388 (with K. W. Buchwald); "Mechanism of Formation of Hexosemonophosphatexin Muscle and Isolation of a New Phosphate Ester," *Proceedings of the Society for Experimental Biology and Medicine*, vol. 34, 1936, pp. 702-705; "Resynthesis of Muscle Glycogen from Hexosemonophosphate," *Journal of Biological Chemistry*, vol. 120, 1937, pp. 193-202 (with A. H. Hegnauer); "The Isolation and Synthesis of Glucose-1-Phosphoric Acid," *Journal of Biological Chemistry*, vol. 121, 1937, pp. 465-477 (with S. P. Colowick); "The Enzymatic Conversion of Glucose-1-Phosphoric Ester to 6-Ester in Tissue Extracts," *Journal of Biological Chemistry*, vol. 124, 1938, pp. 543-555 (with S. P. Colowick); "Crystalline Muscle Phosphorylase: III, Kinetics," *Journal of Biological Chemistry*, vol. 151, 1943, pp. 39-55 (with A. A. Green); "The Enzymatic Conversion of Phosphorylase a to b," *Journal of Biological Chemistry*, vol. 158, 1945, pp. 321-332; "The Metabolism of Fructose in the Liver: Isolation of Fructose-1-Phosphate and Inorganic Pyrophosphate," *Biochimica et Biophysica Acta*, vol. 7, 1951, pp. 304-317 (with S. Ochoa and M. W. Slein); "Glucose-6-Phosphatase of the Liver in Glycogen Storage Disease," *Journal of Biological Chemistry*, vol. 199, 1952, pp. 661-667.

Gerty T. Cori

BIOCHEMISTRY: "Glycogen Storage Disease of the Liver: II, Enzymatic Studies," *Pediatrics*, vol. 14, 1954, pp. 646-650 (with J. L. Schulman).

Carl F. Cori

BIOCHEMISTRY: "The Fate of Sugar in the Animal Body: I, The Rate of Absorption of Hexoses and Pentoses from the Intestinal Tract," *Journal of Biological Chemistry*, vol. 66, 1925, pp. 691-715; "Purification of the Hyperglycemic-Glycogenolytic Factor from Insulin and from Gastric Mucosa," *Journal of Biological Chemistry*, vol. 180, 1949, pp. 825-837 (with E. W. Sutherland et al.); "Effect of Hyperglycemic-Glycogenolytic Factor and Epinephrine on Liver Phosphorylase," *Journal of Biological Chemistry*, vol. 188, 1951, pp. 531-543 (with E. W. Sutherland); "Correction of a Genetically Caused Enzyme Defect by Somatic Cell Hybridization," *Proceedings of the National Academy of Sciences, U.S.A.*, vol. 80, 1983, pp. 6611-6614 (with S. Gluecksohn-Waelsch et al.).

AUTOBIOGRAPHY: "The Call of Science," *Annual Reviews of Biochemistry*, vol. 38, 1969, pp. 1-20.

Secondary

Houssay, Bernardo. "Carl F. and Gerty Cori." *Biochimica et Biophysica Acta* 20 (1956): 11-15. An introduction to a volume honoring the Coris on their sixtieth birthdays, this article discusses their research and achievements. Includes a chronology of important work.

Kalckar, H. M. "The Isolation of Cori-ester, 'The Saint Louis Gateway' to a First Approach of a Dynamic Formulation of Macromolecular Biosynthesis." In *Selected Topics in the History of Biochemistry*, vol. 35, edited by G. Semenza. Amsterdam: Elsevier Science Publishers, 1983. A good biography and discussion of the Cori research by a colleague.

Kornberg, Arthur. *For the Love of Enzymes*. Cambridge, Mass.: Harvard University Press, 1989. An excellent autobiography by a Nobel laureate, who describes his time in the Cori laboratory and with them on the faculty at Washington University Medical School. He describes clearly the nature of enzymes and research on their properties.

McCue, George. "Cori + Cori = Nobel Prize." *Science Illustrated* 3 (February, 1948): 19-23. A good popular discussion of the Coris' lives and work, well illustrated.

Ochoa, Severo, and H. M. Kalckar. "Gerty T. Cori, Biochemist." *Science* 128 (1958): 16-17. In this obituary of Gerty Cori, the authors, who worked in her laboratory, pay tribute to her excellent research and influence.

Opfell, Olga S. *The Lady Laureates: Women Who Have Won the Nobel Prize*. Metuchen, N.J.: Scarecrow Press, 1986. Contains a fine overview of the life and work of Gerty Cori.

Yost, Edna. *Women of Modern Science*. New York: Dodd, Mead, 1959. Discusses Gerty's career in a presentation sympathetic to the difficulties encountered by women in science.

Jane A. Miller

1947

Physiology or Medicine

Carl F. Cori, Czechoslovakia and United States
Gerty T. Cori, Czechoslovakia and United States
Bernardo Alberto Houssay, Argentina

Chemistry

Sir Robert Robinson, Great Britain

Physics

Sir Edward Victor Appleton, Great Britain

Literature

André Gide, France

Peace

American Friends Service Committee, United States
Friends Service Council, Great Britain

BERNARDO ALBERTO HOUSSAY
1947

Born: Buenos Aires, Argentina; April 10, 1887
Died: Buenos Aires, Argentina; September 21, 1971
Nationality: Argentine
Area of concentration: Endocrine physiology

Houssay found that the anterior lobe of the hypophysis, or pituitary gland, produces a hormone that blocks the effect of insulin in glucose metabolism. He discovered that diabetes could be induced by administration of anterior pituitary extract and that animals naturally diabetic, or made so by removal of the pancreas, could metabolize glucose normally if the pituitary gland were removed

The Award

Presentation

Professor H. Theorell, the head of the Biochemical Nobel Department of the Royal Caroline Institute, presented the winners of the Nobel Prize in Physiology or Medicine for 1947 to Sweden's King Gustav V on December 10, 1947. Theorell's speech dealt equally with the work of Bernardo Alberto Houssay, who received half of the prize, and Carl Ferdinand Cori and Gerty Theresa Cori-Radnitz, who jointly received the other half for work complementary to Houssay's. After relating the Coris' finding of the enzyme systems that interconvert glucose and its polymer, glycogen, in the liver, and their in vitro synthesis of glycogen, he turned to Houssay's contribution. In his earliest published work, Houssay had noted that acromegaly, a disease of the pituitary, was frequently accompanied by excretion of sugar in the urine, which suggested that carbohydrate metabolism might be connected with that gland. Working both with dogs and with toads, he found that removal of the pituitary made the animals highly sensitive to insulin; some died of glucose and glycogen depletion from amounts of insulin easily tolerated by normal animals.

Implantation of a toad anterior pituitary lobe, even in dogs, relieved the insulin sensitivity. Removal of the insulin-producing pancreas produced diabetes, but removal of the pituitary, followed in a few days by removal of the pancreas, produced no symptoms of diabetes. Growth hormone isolated from the pituitary produced diabetes when injected, and it destroyed insulin-producing cells on prolonged administration. By these and similar experimental observations, Houssay was able to elucidate the interaction of the pancreas and the pituitary in carbohydrate metabolism. Theorell concluded with a tribute to the diligence, patience, and skill of all the winners before presenting them to the king.

Nobel lecture

Houssay's Nobel lecture, delivered in Stockholm on December 12, 1947, was entitled "The Role of the Hypophysis in Carbohydrate Metabolism and in Diabetes." It opened with a brief review of carbohydrate metabolism. Carbohydrates in general are converted into glucose for use in cell metabolism. A constant blood sugar level is maintained by the liver, the removal of which causes hypoglycemia and death. Sugar distribution between the liver and body cells is governed by a dynamic equilibrium among the endocrine glands: The pancreas responds to blood sugar levels by increasing or decreasing insulin production. Pancreatic insulin production increases glucose metabolism and leads to hypoglycemia in a non-equilibrium system. The pituitary (hypophysis), adrenals, and thyroid help raise the blood sugar level, leading to hyperglycemia and, if unchecked, diabetes.

This outline completed, Houssay detailed the laboratory observations, many of them his own or his colleagues', that led to this state of understanding. These included findings already mentioned in Professor Theorell's presentation speech: Animals with the pituitary removed are very sensitive to insulin; this sensitivity is abated when anterior pituitary extract is administered; animals with both pituitary and pancreas removed show little or no diabetes; and these effects cross species lines and apply equally to a number of different laboratory animals. To these observations he added a great many other laboratory findings. The administration of anterior pituitary alone produces diabetes and inhibits the action of separately administered insulin or phlorizin, a drug used to induce hyperglycemia. Removal of the pituitary lowers glycogen, with the decrease lessened if the adrenals are removed as well.

Tabulating all effects of removal of pancreas with or without pituitary (including results of lipid and protein metabolism, which are not seriously affected), Houssay reported that the liver is the target organ for the effect of anterior pituitary, as demonstrated by removal of a number of other major organs, including the brain, with no change in blood glucose level. Examination of pancreas tissue after administration of anterior pituitary extract showed that the insulin-producing islet (the islet of Langerhans) cells were damaged—reversibly after a few days' treatment, but irreversibly after treatment of a few weeks. The chemical entity responsible for all these effects is a protein, and Houssay speculated (correctly) that it is the growth hormone produced by the pituitary. Out of this mass of data, much of it confusing and some appearing to conflict, Houssay surefootedly reached his conclusion: "Carbohydrate metabolism and other metabolic processes are regulated by the balance maintained between the secretion of several endocrine glands. Diabetes and other metabolic diseases are a disturbance in this endocrine equilibrium. . . . [T]he hypophysis is one of the most important organs in the regulation of metabolism and the center of the endocrine constellation." Characteristically, Houssay ended with acknowledgment by name of thirty-nine colleagues in his work.

Critical reception

Reaction to Houssay's Nobel Prize was politely congratulatory in Europe and the United States, but it went to extremes of both adulation and vituperation in Argentina—the former from colleagues and lay people, the latter from the Perón government. The initial announcement of the prize in *La Prensa* on October 24, 1947, noted that this was the first Nobel Prize in Physiology or Medicine to go to an Argentinian and only the second of any Nobel award to do so (Carlos Saavedra Lamas had received the Nobel Peace Prize in 1936). Houssay's work was reviewed very knowledgeably in this long article, and congratulatory opinions were offered in plenty: "[T]he Stockholm Institute recognizes that the tireless work of this investigator during nearly half a century . . . has influenced the advance of human knowledge." Again, "Houssay's school occupies a place in the vanguard" of physiological research, and Houssay himself "was one of the first 'full-time' professors in the country," presenting students with classroom and laboratory research experience rather than the dry theory of earlier instruction. The same article discussed by name the members of Houssay's research "school" and their contributions. It also gave the political background that would lead to government criticism of the prize: In 1943, "he had, together with a nucleus of persons representing various circles in the country, signed a democratically-oriented manifesto, and the 'de facto' government decided to relieve them of their duties, along with many other professors." The "de facto" government was that dominated behind the scenes by Juan Perón. Houssay and his colleagues were restored to their positions in 1945, but a year later, when Perón was fully in charge, Houssay was forced into retirement from the University of Buenos Aires.

As *La Prensa* reported in articles over the next week, letters and telegrams poured in congratulating Houssay on his achievement. Individuals and organizations—lay and professional, Argentinian and foreign—sent best wishes. Many messages from within the country were not without political content. The Argentine Society of Engineers passed a resolution citing Houssay, along with his scientific achievements, for his "position consistent with a democratic citizen." The student organization known as the Atheneum of Democratic Argentine Youth, calling him "un maestro auténtico," added their "regret that this universal homage is not encountered in the teaching chairs and in the Institute of Physiology." The Chamber of Senators of Buenos Aires province telegraphed their unanimous resolution of congratulation. Reaction from government-dominated sources was less temperate. On October 25, Julio V. Otaola, "vice interventor" at the University of Buenos Aires, stated that the university planned no resolution of distinction of any kind. Celebratory meetings or gatherings were officially forbidden. On November 3, *The New York Times* reported that the government organ *Época* had just published an article "plainly libelous by United States standards" that questioned the originality and value of Houssay's work and castigated him for "neglecting" public health problems such as tuberculosis, syphilis, and cancer. "Once again," the article concluded, "the Nobel Prize has been decided on political grounds."

Houssay's response to this attack was merely to repeat an earlier observation that he would not "confuse a big thing [the Nobel Prize] with a little" and to announce plans to lecture at the University of California as he returned from Stockholm. The Perón government in 1947 had not yet developed its later readiness to suppress political opinion, and it dropped the matter without further comment.

Popular and scientific journals elsewhere reported Houssay's receipt of the prize with less passionate advocacy. *The New York Times*, which ran substantially the same news-service story on October 24 as *La Prensa*, followed on October 25 with an editorial that discussed the physiology of Houssay's and the Coris' work and praised it for its implications in the control of diabetes. *Science* noted the award on December 19, 1947, without comment. *Science News Letter*, reporting the physiology prizes on November 1, gave a laudatory discussion of all the work on pituitary, pancreas, and insulin. The British journal *Nature* noted Houssay's prize on November 1, with a short discussion of his work; a year earlier (November 23, 1946) it had reported Houssay's removal from his university post—without overt editorial comment but with evident distaste.

Biography

Bernardo Alberto Houssay was born in Buenos Aires, the fourth of eight children, on April 10, 1887. His parents, Albert (Alberto) and Clara Laffont Houssay, were born in France, and Albert was educated there as well, becoming a doctor in law at Bordeaux before he was invited to return to Argentina to teach. Bernardo was an intellectually precocious child, bilingual in French and Spanish, with a passion for reading history, literature, and natural science and possessing what was later described as a "file card" memory. He received his baccalaureate with highest honors at age thirteen and elected to study pharmacy, graduating in 1904, when he was seventeen. Thereafter he studied medicine, receiving the M.D. in 1910 with a thesis (of his own devising) on pituitary research that also won the science prize of the faculty of medical science. He interned in 1909-1911 and was qualified to practice in the latter year. During his early professional years, Houssay held many concurrent positions, becoming as early as 1907 both a laboratory assistant in physiology and an assistant pharmacist at the Hospital de Clinica. In 1909 he was made acting professor of physiology in the faculty of veterinary science. In 1911, while maintaining a private medical practice, he was named chief of the Unit of Clinical Medicine at the Alvear Hospital. The year after that he was promoted to full professor in the veterinary faculty, and in 1915 he became chief of the Section of Experimental Pathology at the Institute of Bacteriology. It was in this position that he met and worked with Dr. María Angélica Catán, a chemist whom he married in 1920. They had three sons, Alberto, Héctor, and Raúl, all of whom became M.D.'s and two of whom worked for a time in their father's research laboratories.

In 1919, Houssay was named professor of physiology in the faculty of medicine at the University of Buenos Aires, as well as director of the Institute of Physiology, positions to which he devoted his full efforts for the next twenty-four years. In 1943, he and other faculty members were removed from their academic chairs at the university. At this time Houssay founded the privately funded Institute of Biology and Experimental Medicine, which began with an equipment grant from the Rockefeller Foundation; it opened in March, 1944, with Houssay as director. In 1945, the discharged professors were reinstated, but the Perón government established its own rules of governance in the university, installing an "interventor" empowered to make retirement decisions for individual faculty members. Thus, Houssay found himself retired at age fifty-nine. Despite offers from the United States and elsewhere, he elected to stay in Argentina. Many of the researchers who had helped start the Institute of Biology and Experimental Medicine left their restored university posts and joined Houssay at the institute. In 1955, the Perón government fell and Houssay was returned to his position at the university; in 1956 he resigned, however, continuing at the institute as its director until his death on September 21, 1971, at the age of eighty-four.

Scientific Career

Bernardo Houssay was a man uniquely suited to his time and his country. The state of medical and physiological research in Argentina at the beginning of the twentieth century may be compared with that in the United States. In the United States, although many students still looked to Germany for their graduate training, a small number of research schools—Yale University, Harvard University, The Johns Hopkins University—were producing the first generation of native-trained investigators. The Ph.D. was beginning to replace the M.D. as the standard degree for researchers in medically related fields. Between the world wars, the United States would mature and take its place beside England and Europe in medicine, physiology, biochemistry, and microbiology.

Argentina, on the other hand, was perhaps a generation behind this schedule when Houssay's career began. Instruction in physiology was long on theory and woefully short on laboratory practice. No research schools existed; there were few laboratories and little equipment. Pursuing a career in research under such circumstances requires a worker and thinker who is self-motivated and self-fertilizing to an extraordinary degree, since there are no mentors to set research problems and supervise their solution. There are few colleagues with whom to explore ideas on a daily basis. All the ideas, hypotheses, and explanations must come from one's own mind. The person who can flourish under such circumstances will in fact form his own school of research; this is exactly what Houssay did for Argentina, and it is an achievement at least the equal of his research work, with or without the Nobel Prize.

From the start, Houssay showed a capacity for posing and solving his own research problems. His M.D. thesis work, in fact, was undertaken because no one knew much about the pituitary and its secretions and because no one in Argentina was studying it. No one knew much about research methods, either, so Houssay devised his own. Because the thesis won the faculty's science prize, it was published in book form: *Estudios sobre la acción de los extractos hipofisarios* (1911; studies of the action of pituitary extracts). This was the beginning of the lifelong interest in glandular interaction and carbohydrate metabolism that would lead to the Nobel Prize, but it was by no means his only area of research. During the decade after his graduate work, when he held so many professional positions, and for another five or ten years after that, his interests were many and varied. He studied venous pulse rates, hormonal stimulants found in milk, the toxicity of various natural products, the physiological action of curare, strychnine, and veratrine, the material of skin coloration in frogs, and overall rat metabolism. He wrote a series of a dozen papers on the paralytic and hemolytic action of venoms from snakes and spiders.

During these journeyman years, about two-thirds of his output of research papers (published in four languages and in journals all over the world) had to do with pituitary, pancreas, and carbohydrate metabolism. In 1918 he produced an updated examination of the problem, *La acción fisiológica de los extractos hipofisarios* (physiological action of pituitary extracts), and in 1924 he looked at other endocrine effects in *Tiroides e inmunidad: Estudio crítico y experimental* (the thyroid and immunity: a critical and experimental study). In the late 1920's, however, the papers begin to concentrate on the material that led to the Nobel Prize. This was occasioned by the availability of insulin after Frederick Banting and John Macleod's discovery in 1921 and 1922; the hormone became a powerful research tool in Houssay's hands. It was also influenced by the growing success of Houssay's Institute of Physiology within the university and the value of positioning its research work around some central subject. The only major investigation outside the carbohydrate metabolism studies during the years from 1930 to 1947 had to do with the relation of the kidneys and adrenals to blood pressure; even that was an offshoot of the carbohydrate work, because Houssay's original interest was in the effect of adrenal secretions on blood sugar levels. Three more books came out during this time: a collection of lectures originally published in the *New England Journal of Medicine*, entitled *Functions of the Pituitary Gland* (1936); *La acción diabetógena de la hipófisis* (1945; diabetogenic action of the pituitary); and the monumental *Fisiología humana* (1946; *Human Physiology*, 1948), which was translated into a number of languages. It saw two editions in the English version and was considered by some the finest physiology text that had been written.

In the quarter of a century remaining to him after receiving the Nobel Prize, Houssay devoted his efforts to leading the Institute of Biology and Experimental Medicine, but he kept up his output of research papers as well. He still had points to clear up in the pituitary and diabetes work, and he was always prepared to investigate endocrine hormones, particularly as biochemistry elucidated their structure and made them available in pure chemical form. The pace of his production slowed, but his "almost Germanic" determination to explore every aspect of a problem was in evidence up to his final publication, a 1970 study of ketonemia in the pancreatectomized dog. One source gives the number of Houssay's research papers (alone or with coworkers) as more than two thousand.

The worldwide aspects of Houssay's research, however, were only half of his professional career. Within his own country he was a major force in defining, reforming, and improving teaching and research in physiology and, by extension, in all the sciences. His writings in these matters form a series of position papers, published as pamphlets, beginning as early as 1923 with "La investigación es la función primera de la universidad" (investigation is the primary function of the university), continuing in the years just before his suspension with "Concepto de la universidad" (the concept of the university) and "La crisis actual y bases para el adelanto de la universidad" (the real crisis and bases for advancement of the university), and carrying into the 1960's with such papers as "Organization of Scientific Research in Latin America," "My Struggle for Science," and "Role of the Scientist in Modern Society."

The type of science teaching that Houssay found in the state-run universities at the beginning of his career was designed for formal certification, not for real learning—that is, it consisted of much memorization of factual material and frequent examinations to ensure that progress was being made but of little real teaching and no hands-on laboratory experience (a situation that has not been entirely eliminated in Latin American universities to this day). Houssay insisted that there be more real teaching and fewer exams and that students be admitted to the university by competitive examination. By admitting only the best and then truly teaching them, he contended, the university should have few failures, and graduates should be genuinely competent in their subjects. Furthermore, teachers should be "full time," meaning that they should present all aspects of the subject, not only factual lectures. Initially he met with strong resistance from colleagues and students, who suspected him of unacceptable elitism. He quietly persisted in applying his standards at the university, however, and gradually they were proved out by the success of his graduates. Resistance lessened, and his methods were adopted in other departments.

His further concern was that scientific investigation, and the university in general, should be free of outside influences. This is what brought him to the attention of the Perón government, and when he signed the manifesto calling for democracy at all levels of government and for free international cooperation, he placed himself at risk. He accepted that risk because of a quiet, genuine, deep-rooted patriotism. What he wanted, he wanted for Argentina and for other Latin American countries. His reaction to the Nobel Prize expressed this: "I consider this great distinction a recompense and a recognition of the work of scientific investigators carried out by an entire school, and to be a stimulus to men of science of Argentina and the other American nations, who work with a fraternal solidarity for shared ideals." Even more clearly, his refusal to accept posts in other countries underlines his commitment to Argentina. Although it was not clear whether he would be safe from further government interference, he believed that he should remain as a symbol and a center of the research structure that he had worked so hard to establish in his country. A final demonstration of his commitment can be found in his proposal (after the Perón years) of a government agency, the National Council for Scientific and Technical Research. He served as its president in the year of its founding, 1958, and as director until his death.

Distinctions came to Houssay throughout his career. He was a regular or honorary member of dozens of scientific societies and was a recipient of no less than twenty-eight honorary degrees, among them doctorates from many universities: Harvard,

Oxford, Cambridge, and Paris. He was twice honored in ceremonies by colleagues and students: first in 1934, honoring the twenty-fifth year of his career, then in 1967, honoring his eightieth birthday. Both these celebrations were recorded in commemorative volumes. He received these recognitions with an "almost boyish" enjoyment. He remained "unassuming, gentle, and likable," although he also possessed the determination that enabled him to persevere through the most troubled times in his country.

Bibliography

Primary

PHYSIOLOGY: *Estudios sobre la acción de los extractos hipofisarios*, 1911; *La acción fisiológica de los extractos hipofisarios*, 1918; *Tiroides e inmunidad: Estudio crítico y experimental*, 1924 (with A. Sordelli); *Collected Papers on Medical Subjects Including Physiology*, 1924-1934; *Functions of the Pituitary Gland*, 1936; *La acción diabetógena de la hipófisis*, 1945; *Fisiología humana*, 1946 (*Human Physiology*, 1948).

OTHER NONFICTION: *Juan B. Señorans, iniciador de la medicina experimental en la Republica Argentina*, 1937 (with Alfredo Buzzo); *Escritos y discursos*, 1942.

Secondary

"Bernardo Alberto Houssay." In *Current Biography 1948*, edited by Anna Rothe. New York: H. W. Wilson, 1949. A short but well-informed account of Houssay's life and work up to the year of publication, in a biographical series that is widely available in public libraries.

Foglia, Virgilio G. "The History of Bernardo A. Houssay's Research Laboratory, Instituto de Biologia y Medicina Experimental: The First Twenty Years, 1944-1963." *Journal of the History of Medicine* 35 (1980): 380-396. A thorough account of the vicissitudes of the founding of the institute, with descriptions of its organization and operation. With illustrations and a list of the nearly three dozen Foreign Fellows who worked at the institute during the time covered.

"Obituary: Bernardo Alberto Houssay." *The New York Times*, September 22, 1970, p. 50. An obituary of Houssay that presents a brief account of his life, his work, and the political difficulties he encountered.

Sourkes, Theodore L. "1947: Bernardo Alberto Houssay." In *Nobel Prize Winners in Medicine and Physiology, 1901-1965*. London: Abelard-Schuman, 1966. A brief account of the man, the prizewinning work, and its significance, in a volume that is widely available.

Young, Sir Frank, and V. G. Foglia. "Bernardo Alberto Houssay, 1887-1971." *Biographical Memoirs of Fellows of the Royal Society* 20 (1974): 246-270. This is the most complete source available on Houssay, with many personal recollections of longtime colleague Foglia. Includes a two-hundred-item bibliography of Houssay's research papers that actually covers nearly twice that number of publications, as many papers that initially appeared in Spanish were translated into French, German, or English, but all versions of the same paper are included under a single heading.

Robert M. Hawthorne, Jr.

1948

Physiology or Medicine
Paul Hermann Müller, Switzerland

Chemistry
Arne Tiselius, Sweden

Physics
Patrick M. S. Blackett, Great Britain

Literature
T. S. Eliot, Great Britain

Peace
no award

PAUL HERMANN MÜLLER
1948

Born: Olten, Switzerland; January 12, 1899
Died: Basel, Switzerland; October 13, 1965
Nationality: Swiss
Areas of concentration: Synthetic organic chemistry and pest control

By a systematic study of the insecticidal properties of compounds, Müller proved dichlorodiphenyltrichloroethane (DDT) to be an effective insecticide against many disease-carrying insects

The Award

Presentation

G. Fischer, a member of the Staff of Professors of the Royal Caroline Institute, gave the presentation address on December 10, 1948, before Paul Hermann Müller accepted his Nobel Prize. Fischer began his address by connecting the insecticidal properties of dichlorodiphenyltrichloroethane (DDT) with the fight against the disease typhus. Typhus, he noted, has always been a part of war or disaster; it was responsible for destroying Napoleon's Grand Army as it retreated from Russia. French scientist Charles Nicolle had shown that typhus is spread by lice (Nicolle won the 1928 Nobel Prize in Physiology or Medicine for his work), but a means of controlling typhus was still missing. Large numbers of lice could not be destroyed by any practical means. Paul Müller, building on work done by other research groups, systematically synthesized and tested compounds to be used as a contact insecticide to protect plants. The compound DDT proved to be effective against Colorado beetles, flies, and gnats, and was found to maintain insecticidal properties for a long period of time. The next step was to demonstrate its insecticidal properties on blood-sucking and disease-carrying pests such as lice, gnats, and fleas. This miraculous chemical also was not toxic to humans and was cheap, easy to manufacture, and stable.

DDT was able to prove its worth in the winter of 1943, when a typhus epidemic broke out in Naples: Spraying Naples with DDT stopped a winter typhus epidemic. DDT has also been effective in the control of other insects which spread diseases such as malaria, plague, murine typhus, and yellow fever. Thanks to the work of Paul Müller, Fischer said, there is now a way of preventing diseases carried by insects that was unavailable before.

Nobel lecture

Paul Müller delivered his Nobel lecture, "Dichloro-Diphenyl-Trichloroethane and Newer Insecticides," on December 11, 1948. The first part of the lecture explained that it required ninety years of research to develop enough understanding of the field of dyestuffs to be able to make predictions of the behavior of synthetic dyes. The field of pharmaceutical chemistry is more complicated, and although the action of some types of compounds is understood, predictions of physiological activity of synthetic compounds were not yet possible. The field of synthetic insecticides was even more complicated.

In 1935, Paul Müller's work as a commercial chemist brought him to study pesticides to protect plants for his company, based in Basel, Switzerland. There were no points of reference to which he could look. It was too expensive to synthesize natural insecticides, such as pyrethrum, and the known synthetic compounds had less toxic effect than the natural insecticides. The ideal insecticide should be extremely toxic to insects, and its application should achieve results rapidly while not hurting humans, animals, or plants in any way. It should be effective against a broad range of insects and have long-lasting action. In addition to these qualities, it should be cheap and easy to use. Hundreds of compounds were tested before Müller synthesized such a compound, which was chemically based on the results of two research groups. This compound is called dichlorodiphenyltrichloroethane (DDT), and it killed insects more effectively than anything Müller had ever seen. The insecticidal action was so strong on contact that the routine cleaning of a surface was not enough to remove it. Later tests on other insects proved the insecticidal properties to be wide-ranging. DDT met every specification of the ideal insecticide except for immediate action; it sometimes required hours or days for its lethal action. Its long-term action still outweighed the lack of immediate effect. Other, similar compounds have been synthesized and tested, but almost any change in the molecule reduces the insecticidal properties: DDT is apparently unique in its effectiveness against insects.

Since DDT, other compounds, such as chlordane and parathion, have been synthesized. These also exhibit strong insecticidal properties. DDT was evidently the first step in a new era, an era in which compounds would be developed to achieve specific goals of pest control. At the time of this speech, however, the mode of action of DDT was still not understood, nor was the relationship between composition and insecticidal properties. This information and the whole field of pest control were noted as a promising goal for future research.

In his speech, Paul Müller not only laid the foundation of pest control and disease prevention but also challenged science, especially the field of synthetic chemistry, to continue the research.

Critical reception

Time magazine related that DDT's success in the fight against disease in humans was a surprise to Paul Müller. Despite this, DDT continues to be valuable in protecting man from disease. Because of Paul Müller's discovery, the tropics are safer for human life. "DDT has been credited with having saved hundreds of thousands of persons from death and disease," stated the article in *The New York Times* that told of the award of the Nobel Prize to Paul Müller (October 29, 1930). The article also mentioned the Naples epidemic in 1943 and other applications of DDT in Greece and Egypt to prevent disease during World War II. Even more complimentary statements appeared in the next day's issue of *The New York Times.* "Chemists will applaud the award," it said, and "Anyone . . . will recognize the great importance of Dr. Müller's work." The article went on to say that DDT would enable public health officials to control disease-carrying insects. The greatest compliment was in the last paragraph, in which it was proclaimed that DDT did not win the war, but that it did make a difference. Paul Müller deserved the highest award science has to offer because he saved crops at a critical time of need, and also saved the lives of soldiers and civilians. The same article also mentioned that companies such as Geigy, which employed Paul Müller, were having a major impact on problems that had bothered man for centuries.

The *Science News Letter* stressed the internationalism of the Swedish award to Paul Müller, a Swiss, for discovering the properties of DDT, which was first synthesized by a German student, Othmar Zeidler. The insecticidal properties were discovered while trying to fight an American insect pest, the potato beetle. The American Army was the first group to use massive amounts of DDT in attempting to stop an epidemic in Naples, Italy. The article also mentioned the uses of DDT in stopping the transport of insects across national or continental boundaries, and as an aid to entomologists in their fight against insect pests on cultivated plants and domestic animals. The article in *Nature* announcing the award noted that DDT appeared at a critical moment when pyrethrum supplies were falling short because of the war. DDT had proved valuable against typhus and malaria during the war and was now being used to eradicate malaria from the island areas. Other areas in which DDT has shown value were as an aid to agricultural entomology and as a stimulus to continued research in insecticides.

It is not surprising that Paul Müller's award was viewed so favorably. The book *Technology in Western Civilization* (1967) surveyed the impact that DDT had made, and it states the widespread perception about the gifts it would bring to humanity: "It was hailed as a wonder chemical which would revolutionize agriculture and forestry, eliminate insect-borne diseases like malaria, and make cities and recreational areas bug-free." Another history of the time, *DDT*, by Thomas Dunlap, told of an economic entomologist who praised DDT because, before DDT, he had not seen a potato plant without insect damage. Another entomologist proclaimed in 1947 that the time and ability had arrived to wipe out all insects, including the housefly and the horn fly. There was very little DDT had going against it. Articles in *The New York Times* during 1945 did include warnings on misuse, warnings of harm to the environment and people, and reports of DDT's failure to wipe out mosquitos; however, articles also included reports of barnacles being repelled from ships by DDT, the curbing of infantile paralysis (the precipitating virus of which was thought to be spread by insects), and increased yields of crops such as potatoes. For each negative report, people could see positive results.

Books such as *DDT: Killer of Killers* (1946), by O. T. Zimmerman and Irvin Lavine, asserted that DDT would not kill the bee population or destroy the balance of nature; moreover, the book listed seventeen classes of insect pests that could be controlled by DDT. It was attributed to DDT that World War II was the first war in which disease carried by insects did not have a major influence on the outcome. From the viewpoint of the time, Paul Müller was a hero: He had developed DDT. Even in 1965, in Paul Müller's obituary, *Time* magazine called DDT "one of the greatest health saving agents yet developed by man."

Biography

Paul Müller was born January 12, 1899, in Olten, Switzerland, the first of four children, to Gottlieb and Fanny (Leypoldt) Müller. At about the age of five, Paul moved from Lenzburg to Basel with his family. Gottlieb wanted to paint but worked for the Swiss Federal Railroad to support his family. Although not pushing his children into any particular field, he nevertheless supported Müller's interest in chemistry. Müller's mother, however, had little sympathy with the experiments that Müller attempted with chemicals bought from the local pharmacy with his allowance. The Free Evangelical Elementary School and Teachers College in Basel were the sites of Müller's formal schooling. He excelled only in chemistry and physics, to which he devoted outside time. Müller even once corrected a student teacher who wrote a wrong formula on the board. Müller interrupted his schooling in 1916 to work in chemistry laboratories. Convinced that chemistry was the correct field for him, he entered the University of Basel in 1919 and received his doctorate summa cum laude in 1925. A month later, he began work at J. R. Geigy, where he was employed until retirement in 1961. He died of a cardiovascular disease in Basel on October 13, 1965.

On October 6, 1927, Müller married Friedel Rugsegger. He enjoyed his three children, Henry, Nicklaus, and Margaret, spending weekends with them and his wife in the Jura Mountains or the Alps. He loved nature and enjoyed photography and filming as hobbies. Described as slight and dark with a boyish smile, Müller always remained modest, even shy and reserved with strangers, but passionately devoted to research.

Scientific Career

Paul Müller wanted to become a chemist as early as 1916, when he dropped out of school to work in research labs. He first worked as a laboratory assistant in the Cellonite Society. The next year, he worked as an assistant chemist in the Scientific Industrial Laboratory of the Lonza electric works. This practical experience proved useful in his later work, and encouraged him to go back to school.

In 1918 Müller completed his preliminary studies at Obere Realschule and in 1919 at Teachers College. His postgraduate work at Basel University was taken in inorganic chemistry. During the academic year of 1921 to 1922, Müller was assistant lecturer, and in 1922, he began work with Hans Rupe in organic chemistry. Müller's major area was chemistry, but his minors were physics and botany. In 1925, he published his dissertation, receiving his doctorate summa cum laude in April of that year. In May, 1925, he began work at Geigy as the assistant manager of the dyewood department. He worked on both natural vegetable dyes and tanning agents, and is the inventor of the light yellow dye called Legatan. In the field of tanning, Paul developed new synthetic agents that would bleach animals' hides pure white, but these agents were not light-fast (sunlight would cause a change). He also worked on mothproofing agents for textiles. The Swiss farmer benefited from his development of Graminone, a mercury-free seed disinfectant.

In 1935, Müller began to work on a compound to protect plants from insects. Although other insecticides were stomach poisons, he decided that a contact poison would be better for this application. A stomach poison depends upon the consumption of enough plant material that is covered with poison to be lethal to the insect. A contact poison would kill the insect without consumption of plant material and also would kill sucking insects. Sucking insects miss the poison on the surface of the plant and are not affected by it.

Müller decided to use flies instead of moths to test the possible insecticides. Glass boxes that were sprayed with each compound in a nontoxic solvent were the test sites. When the solvent evaporated, it would leave a layer of compound on the glass wall. Then flies were let into the boxes so that the insecticidal activity could be monitored. These experiments led to the nickname "Fly Müller"—an embarrassment to him. He had also made the decision that he needed to test the compounds himself. The testing would encourage him in his work on new compounds, and he might notice something that a technician would miss.

In analyzing other insecticides, both natural and synthetic, Müller had not been able to determine any relationship between composition and toxicity. His experiments did not have good reference points from the start. Testing hundreds of compounds, which he methodically synthesized, he still found few with any insecticidal properties. Müller was persistent, and his attitude was revealed by the statement, "I realized that it is not easy to find a good contact insecticide. In the field of science, one attains something only through obstinacy and steadfast work."

Müller's breakthrough came from putting together separate pieces of information. He knew from earlier work that a chlorine atom bonded to a carbon atom made a group that exhibited toxic characteristics. The research of a group at Geigy had demonstrated oral toxicity to moths of compounds with two parachlorophenyl groups on a central group. Several different central groups could be used and still retain the toxicity. The parachlorophenyl group is a six-carbon ring (phenyl), with one hydrogen atom on each of the carbon atoms numbered two, three, five, and six. Carbon number one was bonded to the central group. The carbon on the opposite side of the ring is carbon number four, in the para position, where the chlorine is bonded.

As Müller studied the literature, he read a paper by F. D. Chattaway and R. J. K. Muir, who described the synthesis of a compound with two phenyl groups bonded to a carbon as a central group. Also bonded to the carbon was another carbon with three chlorine atoms bonded to it. Since one chlorine bonded to a carbon was effective as an insecticide, he was curious about the effect of three chlorines bonded to a carbon. The Chattaway and Muir compound, called diphenyltrichloroethane, did show contact-insecticidal properties. In his methodical, systematic manner, Müller began to make derivatives of diphenyltrichloroethane—that is, compounds in which only one or two atoms have been changed from the original. Remembering the Martin compounds that killed moths, he synthesized dichlorodiphenyltrichloroethane (DDT). When he tested it, it showed a greater toxicity than he had ever seen. It has been calculated that a billionth of a gram will kill a fly. He then began tests against other insects such as bugs, cockroaches, Colorado beetles, mosquitoes, and plant life. It was effective against all of these.

Müller tested DDT against the Colorado beetle in a field test. The plants treated were free of beetles for five to six weeks, while nearby control plots were heavily damaged. Now that Müller had an insecticide, a method of transport was needed to disperse DDT. Müller himself led the way in developing methods such as dusts; 2 to 5 percent DDT in an inert powder such as talc was more effective than pure DDT. Commercial products called Gesarol, Gesapon, and Neocid were 5 percent powder or dust. Neocid was used to stop the Naples typhus epidemic. Another method of dispersal that he developed was an emulsion of DDT. As DDT is insoluble in water, it has to be dissolved in some type of oil, then blended with water. The emulsion can then be sprayed as a liquid. The Swiss and later the English and Americans tested DDT and found it to be effective. Rapidly, large amounts of DDT were being produced to protect people, especially members of the military, from insect-borne diseases.

In searching for a perfect insecticide, Müller found DDT, which satisfied all the criteria. DDT has great insect toxicity, no noticeable mammalian or plant toxicity, a wide range of insect toxicity, good chemical stability, low price, and is not a contact or smell irritant. The only ideal property that DDT does not have is rapid action; the lethal action may require hours or days. Yet the chemical was better than any other insecticide, either natural or synthetic.

One property, however, was a concern to Müller. He voiced his thoughts that DDT was not degradable quickly by sunlight or oxidation, as were the natural insecticides: "Far-reaching ecological changes could result from DDT" was Müller's prophecy in 1946.

Later tests proved the uniqueness of DDT. Almost any change in the molecule reduced the toxicity. Even a slight change, such as moving a chlorine from carbon number four on the benzene ring to another carbon on the ring, changed the action of DDT. Replacing the chlorines with fluorines on each ring did not reduce toxicity, but the new compound was more expensive to make. Müller's discovery was actually a rediscovery. Othmar Zeidler, an Austrian student working on his thesis in 1873, prepared DDT, but he was not looking for insecticidal properties.

Paul Müller's work on DDT brought him many honors, starting with promotion to deputy director of the Department of Scientific Research on Substances for Plant Protection in 1946. The greatest honor was the Nobel Prize in 1948. Müller was made a member of the Reale Academia Internazionale del Parnaso in Naples in 1951. The University of Thessalonika in 1963 awarded him an honorary doctorate.

He was also an honorary member of the Schweizerische Naturforschende Gesellschaft. All the awards and even a promotion did not keep Müller out of the laboratory. He was happiest there. He believed that his work on insecticides must continue. DDT-resistant strains of insects quickly showed that scientists would have to continue to work hard to stay ahead in the war with the insect. Müller's Nobel Prize money was distributed to support research for improved insecticides; other work included studies on the insecticidal mechanism of DDT and other insecticides. Even after retirement in 1961, Müller worked in his private laboratory at home until his death in Basel in 1965.

Paul Müller not only found a weapon against disease carried by insects but also set standards for other scientists by his systematic, methodical approach. His work opened up the field of synthetic chemistry as it applied to insect control. From the foundation laid by Paul Müller, man could now step forward in his quest to understand the composition and mechanism of insecticides.

Bibliography

Primary

CHEMISTRY: "Über Konstitution und toxische Wirkung von natürlichen und neuen synthetischen insektentötenden Stoffen," *Helvetica Chimica Acta*, vol. 27, 1944, pp. 892-928 (with P. Lauger and H. Martin); "Über Zusammenhänge zwischen Konstitution und insektizider Wirkung I," *Helvetica Chimica Acta*, vol. 29, 1946, pp. 1560-1580; "Dichlorodiphenyltrichloroäthan und neuere inzekticide," in *Les Prix Nobel en 1948*, 1949; *DDT: Das Insektizid Dichlorodiphenyltrichloroäthan und seine Bedsutung*, 1955; *DDT: Das Insektizid Dichlorodiphenyltrichloroäthan und seine Bedsutung* (Part 2), 1959.

Secondary

Asimov, Isaac. "Paul Hermann Müller." In *Asimov's Biographical Encyclopedia of Science and Technology*. Garden City, N.Y.: Doubleday, 1982. A well-written if short biography with emphasis on how Müller and his work relate to other outstanding scientists. The organization of scientists is chronological.

Campbell, G. A. "Dr. Paul Müller." *Chemistry and Industry* 52 (December 25, 1965): 2105-2106. This obituary is one of the better biographies of Paul Müller. It tells of his interests in nature and photography, and his life with his family. DDT is covered briefly enough to not interfere with the focus on Paul Müller.

Dunlap, Thomas R. *DDT: Scientists, Citizens, and Public Policy* Princeton, N.J.: Princeton University Press, 1981. This thesis is a well-documented history of DDT. The study is not biologically or chemically based but deals more with the then existing conditions and later with state and federal use of DDT. The controversy over the detrimental effects of DDT is also discussed.

Kransberg, Melvin, and Carroll W. Purcell, Jr., eds. *Technology in Western Civilization*. Vol. 2, *Technology in the Twentieth Century*. London: Oxford University Press, 1967. Provides a good rundown of the technological advances contributing to the vastly enhanced agricultural productivity that has occurred during the twentieth century. DDT figures prominently in this discussion. Written for the general reader.

"Paul Müller Dies; Developer of DDT." *The New York Times,* October 14, 1965, p. 47. This is a long obituary that summarizes Müller's contributions. Its length shows the importance of the control of disease-carrying insects and the respect given to Paul Müller.

Sourkes, Theodore L. *Nobel Prize Winners in Medicine and Physiology, 1901-1965.* New York: Abelard-Schuman, 1966. This is a good biography. It contains several quotes by Paul Müller, and provides a good insight into his humanity and perspectives. The personality of this quiet, dedicated scientist is very evident in this article.

West, T. F., and G. A. Campbell. *DDT and Newer Persistent Insecticides*. New York: Chemical Publishing, 1952. This history of DDT, from men who were there, covers the development, the research at Basel, and the trials and tribulations of the dissemination of DDT throughout the world. Although the chemical research is covered, those chapters are in a language and depth that a layperson can comprehend and appreciate.

Zimmerman, O. T., and Irvin Lavine. *DDT: Killer of Killers*. Dover, N.H.: Industrial Research Service, 1946. A book written during the time that DDT was at its peak use. It outlines the horrors of several diseases spread by insects, the discovery of DDT as an insecticide, its safety, and its formulation. It also provides a good survey of the common insect enemies, how nature will recover from DDT, and a look into the future. Enjoyable reading.

C. Alton Hassell

1949

Physiology or Medicine
Walter Rudolf Hess, Switzerland
António Egas Moniz, Portugal

Chemistry
William Francis Giauque, United States

Physics
Hideki Yukawa, Japan

Literature
William Faulkner, United States

Peace
Lord Boyd-Orr, Great Britain

WALTER RUDOLF HESS
1949

Born: Frauenfeld, Switzerland; March 17, 1881
Died: Locarno, Switzerland; August 12, 1973
Nationality: Swiss
Areas of concentration: Ophthalmology, hematology, and neurophysiology

Walter Rudolf Hess developed methods by which he elucidated the regulatory role of clearly localized sites in the diencephalon and midbrain in the physiology and behavior of higher vertebrates

The Award

Presentation

Professor H. Olivecrona of the Royal Caroline Institute gave the presentation speech on December 10, 1949. Professor Walter Rudolf Hess was honored jointly with Professor António Egas Moniz of the University of Lisbon, Spain, for their brain researches. Professor Olivecrona pointed out that the midbrain had long been known as a higher center of regulation for the autonomic nervous system, but the fine localization of functions within the midbrain had been unknown before Hess's experiments provided a detailed mapping of their distribution.

Professor Olivecrona outlined the procedure that Hess had developed for applying weak electrical stimuli to the subcerebral lower brain areas of conscious cats through fine metal needle electrodes previously implanted under anesthesia. Being insulated except at its very end, such an electrode could apply stimuli to a small, circumscribed area of brain tissue at its tip. Electrodes implanted into different brain centers were found to elicit distinctive changes upon delivery of electrical pulses. From one site, a pronounced defensive behavioral display could be elicited; that cat would act as if it were being attacked by a dog. From another, the behavior of assuming a position typical for sleep and then actually entering a state of sleep could be obtained. Some areas were associated with changes in the characteristics of circulation and respiration; others were associated with the normal eliminative behaviors.

From Hess's findings, it became evident that the brain centers he studied were responsible for coordinating autonomic functions with activation of the skeletal muscles involved in appropriate, corresponding body postures and actions. In summation, Olivecrona said, "Hess has brilliantly answered a number of difficult questions regarding the localization of body functions in the brain."

Nobel lecture

On December 12, 1949, Hess delivered his Nobel lecture, entitled "The Central Control of the Activity of Internal Organs." He began with comments on the interrelationship of a multitude of physiological functions. He alluded to the "advances of specialization" in physiological research being so rapid as to "threaten the ability to grasp, or even to appreciate" the organization of the whole living organism. Thus, he placed his research in the posture of pursuing an understanding of the interrelated functional systems, which would enable it to make practical contributions to the "healing art" of medicine.

The historical background to Hess's research was the anatomical, physiological, and pharmacological elucidation of the peripheral nerves making up the vegetative or autonomic nervous system. This basic research had shown how the autonomic nervous system (ANS) consisted of sympathetic and parasympathetic divisions that generally coinnervate numerous visceral (and other) structures but tend to exert opposing influences on their functions. It had become recognized that the area of the diencephalon known as the hypothalamus served a central controlling function over the activity of the autonomic nerves; however, at the outset of Hess's research there had been little or no localization of the sites for different central regulatory activity. Dr. Hess proceeded to outline the choice and development of his experimental technology that was fundamental to his physiological discoveries. To pry beneath the physical surfaces of the brain for the purpose of exploring the roles of its numerous and complex internal structures required a physical "probe" that could activate nervous tissue physiologically, in a circumscribed manner.

Initial probing with needle electrodes bearing electrical stimuli into the depths of the brain showed Hess that the relationships being explored were more complicated than anyone had anticipated. He realized that a lengthy, painstaking process of high-precision mapping would be required. This involved first a three-dimensional (stereotaxic) aiming of the electrodes based on accurate neuroanatomical information. Second, the confirmation of precisely where the electrodes were delivering stimuli was necessary after completion of a series of experimental observations was completed on each subject. For this objective, Hess applied a higher pulse of electricity that would be sufficient to produce a minute, microscopic lesion at the site of stimulation. This permitted the precise histological localization of sites of the electrode-brain stimulations, which was essential for his observational data to be meaningful. For a permanent record of behavioral manifestations, he introduced cinematography into his laboratory.

Concerning his findings, Hess described his elucidation of a functional dichotomy at the behavioral level paralleling that at the anatomical and physiological levels. He located the hypothalamic centers representing the sympathetic division of the ANS in the posterior and middle parts of the hypothalamus. Moreover, he discovered that stimulation of these areas provoked a behavioral change as well as physiological responses. Cats so stimulated became alerted and even behaved as if they were under attack or being threatened by another animal. Thus, Hess's observations began to bridge the gap between "soma" and "psyche" and to broaden insights into psychosomatic relationships earlier pursued by the renowned Russian physiologist Ivan Pavlov, who received the Nobel Prize in 1904.

Professor Hess coined the terms "ergotropic" and "dynamogenic" to describe the zone of the hypothalamus associated with these sympathetic and behavioral activations. Similarly, he defined another zone composed of portions of the hypothalamus and thalamus that are associated with essentially opposite responses to the ergotropic ones. This included sites subserving not emergency, defensive behaviors, but rather those of relaxation and physiological restoration. These sites and functions he termed a "trophotropic system," which functions via activation of the parasympathetic division of the ANS. It also included those sites that favor the onset of normal sleep. While the ergotropic and trophotropic systems are basically opposite in their roles, they are at the same time complementary relative to the welfare and survival of the organism, as both are essential under different circumstances and at different times.

Critical reception

The announcement of the Nobel award to Walter Rudolf Hess in *Nature* described him as having exceptional ability, farsightedness, and great energy. It expressed an appreciation for the immensity of "these systematic and important researches" on the nervous system "covering almost twenty-five years of tireless work" and concluded that "Hess has richly deserved the present award."

The New York Times of October 29, 1949, carried an Associated Press report of the Nobel awards which indicated that Dr. Hess "has developed important new conceptions on how the nervous system works." It also suggested that Hess's research on cats and dogs had "helped to dispel previous theories concerning the effect of instinct, power of observation and natural intelligence upon their behavior." *The New York Times*' own editorialist, on October 30, described Hess as "one of the bold explorers who discovered some of the brain's correlations with bodily functions and explained why some of the functions are supposedly instinctive."

Biography

Walter Rudolf Hess was born in Frauenfeld, Switzerland, on March 17, 1881, son of a college physics teacher, Clemens, and Gertrud (Fischer Saxon) Hess. In childhood, he became interested in natural history, which may have been instrumental in the biological bent that later led him to study medicine. Hess entered the *Gymnasium* at Frauenfeld when twelve years old. At nineteen he launched a peripatetic journey through the medical curriculum at the University of Lausanne. In completing the ten-semester curriculum, he also attended medical courses at Berne and Zurich in Switzerland and in Germany at Kiel and Berlin. After completing his final two semesters in Zurich, he received his M.D. degree in 1905 from the University of Zurich and was licensed for practice in Switzerland. From 1908 to 1912, Hess carried on a successful practice in ophthalmology. His financial independence enabled Hess to marry (in 1909) Louise Sandmeier, a former doctor's aid in a Zurich eye clinic, who was well prepared to offer help in her husband's practice. She later bore one son and one daughter, Rudolf and Gertrud. Rudolf became chief of the Zurich neurosurgical clinic, and Gertrud became a biology teacher.

Dr. Hess left his practice as an ophthalmologist in 1912 to become an assistant in the Institute of Physiology at the University of Zurich. During the years of World War I, Hess spent some of his time in the military service, but was able also to spend a year on leave of absence for research training at the physiological institute in Bonn, Germany. After one year as acting director, he was appointed professor and director of the institute in 1917. He retired from that position (to professor emeritus) in 1951. Besides his distinguished service as director of Zurich's Institute of Physiology, Hess became head of a committee of the Swiss Society for Scientific Research for the founding of the High Altitude Research Station of the Jungfraujoch, located more than 3,000 meters above sea level. This was accomplished in 1931.

Honors and awards to Walter Hess culminated in 1949 with the Nobel Prize in Physiology or Medicine. Previously, he had been awarded in 1933 the Marcel Benoist Prize (Swiss) and the Ludwig Medal of the German Society for Circulation Research in 1938. Honorary doctoral degrees were awarded by the University of Berne, the University of Geneva, and McGill University, Canada. At the age of ninety, Professor Hess received the Johannes Müller Medal.

During his distinguished research career, Hess was appointed honorary member of various societies of physiology, neurology, and ophthalmology and corresponding member of various academies of science. He was president of the sixteenth International Congress of Physiology in 1938, a responsibility made difficult by the international hostilities that would soon lead to the outbreak of World War II.

Upon notification of the cash award with the Nobel Prize, Dr. Hess said, "It will simplify my work. . . . Now I will be able to hire assistants." The cash award with the 1933 Marcel Benoist prize had enabled him to purchase a simple summer house in the "sun terrace of Switzerland" south of the Alps. There he enjoyed periods of retreat and relaxation, which included successful efforts to grow a harvest of grapes and other garden plants. Hess died at Locarno, Switzerland, on August 12, 1973, at the age of ninety-two.

Scientific Career

During his medical studies, Hess not only satisfied an urge to travel but also displayed the intellectual characteristics of a future research scientist. He wrote a student paper on the structure of the vascular system and even invented a device (viscosimeter) to measure the viscosity of a few drops of blood. Subsequent studies on determinants of blood viscosity that were made possible by his invention became his first research publication. While debating a choice of clinical specialty training, Hess considered which one would both meet his financial needs and permit his further pursuits in medical science research. He decided upon ophthalmology as meeting these two aims. From early 1906 to 1908, he trained as a resident in the department of ophthalmology at the University of Zurich. Seeming again to draw from his paternal inheritance, Hess invented a second device; this one was for making a physical ocular measurement on patients of the department.

In 1908, Dr. Hess established his practice in ophthalmology near Zurich. He set up a laboratory for his continued research activities and kept in touch with research advances by attending scientific meetings. Despite his fairly brief adherence to ophthalmology, he was able to make significant contributions in that area. In 1912, Hess received the offer of a faculty position at the Institute of Physiology in Zurich. His acceptance entailed a significant financial sacrifice. From that time to the end of his life, Hess was fully devoted to teaching and research in the science of physiology. After serving for five years as an assistant in the Institute of Physiology, Hess was elevated to professor and director of the institute in 1917. He continued in that position until his retirement in 1951.

While an assistant at Zurich, Hess took one year on leave of absence, which he spent in further research training at the physiological institute of Bonn University (Germany) under the direction of Max Verworn, whom he acknowledged, in a late-life autobiographical sketch, as having had a great influence on his career. At that time, in 1915 and 1916, and for more than a decade, Hess was still very much involved in research on the circulation. In 1916 and 1917 his work was interrupted, as he was called for active duty in the Swiss army during World War I. From the time of his 1917 promotion, he became responsible for heading and developing the institute's program in both instruction and research. After World War I, to aid his fulfilling this, he visited the lectures and laboratories of distinguished English physiologists of that era.

Initially, the chief subject of Hess's research continued to be the circulatory system, especially concerning the autonomic properties and reactivity of isolated arteries. Arterial rings were removed from various parts of the arterial system, immersed in a physiological salt solution, and stimulated mechanically, electrically, or chemically. The latter stimuli included various biologically active substances, such as adrenaline and acetylcholine. Further studies focused on reflex mechanisms of vascular responses.

Professor Hess's research program in the early 1920's led to the publication of his first book in 1930, *The Regulation of the Circulatory System*. This was followed by a parallel work, *The Regulation of Respiration*, in 1931. By 1925, however, he had begun the exploratory phase of his work on the autonomic regulatory centers of the midbrain and diencephalon (lower forebrain). The first results were presented to a physiology meeting at Frankfurt in 1927. After twenty more years of pursuing the same theme, Hess published two monographs in 1947 and 1948 that served as integrative reviews of his massive accumulation of data. These were well received, especially *Die Organization des vegetative Nervensystems* (1948). They were a foundation for the Nobel Committee's choice of him to receive the 1949 Nobel Prize for discovering "the functional organization of the diencephalon and its role in the coordination of the functions of the inner organs."

Two years after the Nobel award, Professor Hess reached the age of seventy and retired from the institute directorship; however, he continued to publish journal articles and books on his research for another decade and beyond. A 1962 book, *Psychologie in biologischer Sicht* (psychology from the standpoint of a biologist), was republished in English translation in London and Chicago in 1964 as *The Biology of*

Mind. Hess and his delineation of the ergotropic and trophotropic neural systems, with their associated characteristic behavioral/physiological states, had an impact on the emerging era of psychotropic drugs in the latter 1950's and beyond. He gave an address entitled "Psychophysiology and Psychopharmacology" at the 1960 meeting in Basel of the Collegium Neuro-Psychopharmacologium. The congress was organized by, and its published proceedings were edited by, E. Rothlin, one of Hess's early assistants at the institute, who had gone on to become professor of pharmacology at the University of Basel.

A fitting tribute and memorial to the pioneering neuroscience research of Walter Rudolf Hess was the founding of an institute for brain research at the University of Zurich in 1963 and the naming of one of Hess's earlier research collaborators, K. Akert, to be its first director.

Bibliography

Primary

PHYSIOLOGY: *The Regulation of the Circulatory System*, 1930; *The Regulation of Respiration*, 1931; "The Mechanism of Sleep," *American Journal of Physiology*, vol. 90, 1939, pp. 386-387; *Die Organization des vegetative Nervensystems*, 1948; *Diencephalon: Autonomic and Extrapyramidal Functions*, 1954; "The Diencephalic Sleep Center," in *Brain Mechanisms and Consciousness*, edited by E. D. Adrian, F. Bremer, and H. Jasper, 1954; "Experimental Data on the Role of the Hypothalamus in the Mechanisms of Emotional Behavior," *AMA Archives of Neurology and Psychiatry*, vol. 73, 1955, pp. 127-129; *Hypothalamus and Thalamus: Experimental Documentation*, 1956; *The Functional Organization of the Diencephalon Hypothalamus and Thalamus*, 1957; "Psychophysiology and Psychopharmacology," in *Neuro-Psychopharmacology,* vol. 2, edited by E. Rothlin, 1961; *Psychologie in biologischer Sicht*, 1962 (*The Biology of Mind*, 1964); "Causality, Consciousness, and Cerebral Organization," *Science*, vol. 158, 1967, pp. 1279-1283.

Secondary

Breggin, Peter. "The Psychophysiology of Anxiety." *Journal of Nervous and Mental Disease* 139 (1964): 558-568. The author develops several hypotheses, concerning the physiological bases of the emotional state known as anxiety, that are founded significantly upon the work of Hess. Namely, Breggin supposes that anxiety consists of an intitial phase composed of ergotropic activation, followed by a later phase consisting of trophotropic activation.

Brodie, Bernard B., D. J. Prockop, and P. A. Shore. "An Interpretation of the Action of Psychotropic Drugs." *Postgraduate Medicine* 24 (1958): 296-304. The authors present and develop a concept supposing that norepinephrine and serotonin are the respective chemical mediators or neurotransmitters for the two opposing regulatory systems of the hypothalamus that Hess first recognized and named the ergotropic and trophotropic systems. Brodie and his coauthors suggested that hallucinogenic drugs (such as LSD and mescaline) produce ergotropic dominance, whereas tranquilizing drugs (chlorpromazine and reserpine) produce trophotropic dominance. This concept had a major impact on the nascent science of psychopharmacology.

Delgado, Jose M. R. "Free Behavior and Brain Stimulation." *International Review of Neurobiology* 6 (1964): 349-449. Delgado was one of the foremost among several researchers who adopted the approach of stimulating the brains of animals via implanted electrodes and recording by cinematography the behavioral consequences of such artificial activation. These technologies were those primarily pioneered by Hess. Delgado, as this article emphasizes, employed an experimental situation that was more free than Hess's by developing a means to deliver stimuli remotely from a device carried on the bodies of monkeys. Thus, experimental subjects were able to live among other monkeys in a naturalistic, free situation.

Flynn, John P. "The Neural Basis of Aggression in Cats." In *Neurophysiology and Emotion*, edited by D. C. Glass. New York: Rockefeller University Press and Russell Sage Foundation, 1967. The capacity to elicit a display of rage from a cat by electrical stimulation of the hypothalamus was first shown by Hess in 1927, and later by others. Summarized here is an extension and elaboration of Hess's work, in which Flynn studied the ability of electrical stimulation to activate in a controlled manner an attack by a cat toward a rat in its cage.

Gellhorn, Ernest. "The Neurophysiological Basis of Anxiety: A Hypothesis." *Perspectives in Biology and Medicine* 8 (1964-1965): 488-515. Like Breggin above, Gellhorn attempts to formulate a physiological theory of the emotional state of anxiety. Hess's opposing ergotropic and trophotropic systems are the primary foundation of Gellhorn's hypotheses. He sees them as generally operating in a reciprocal relationship, but concludes that chronic anxiety, at least of the excitatory form, arises from the simultaneous activation of both systems at a high level of arousal so that fear coincides with an impulse toward aggression.

____________. "Prolegomena to a Theory of the Emotions." *Perspectives in Biology and Medicine* 4 (1960-1961): 403-436. Gellhorn's elaboration of a "theory of emotion" draws in part upon Hess's findings and terminology. For example, he points out that fright involves activation of Hess's ergotropic system and suggests that a feeling of well-being requires inhibition of that system. He proposes further that the functional concepts of the ergo- and trophotropic systems extend beyond the boundaries of the hypothalamus.

Hess, Walter R. "From Medical Practice to Theoretical Medicine." In *A Dozen Doctors*, edited by Dwight J. Ingle. Chicago: University of Chicago Press, 1963. This article provides an autobiographical sketch that gives insight into childhood and adolescent formative years. It follows highlights of his education and career, from entering medical school to his practice of ophthalmology and through his many years as an academic physiologist.

Koella, Werner P. "Organizational Aspects of Some Subcortical Motor Areas." *International Review of Neurobiology* 4 (1962): 71-116. Dr. Koella initially puts special emphasis on the work of Hess, "since this author's contributions are very extensive and most carefully analyzed." Not merely paying tribute to Hess, Koella also summarizes Hess's works on motor systems and adopts his dichotomous classification of all types of skeletal muscle activity. This work displays the significance of Hess's research not in respect to autonomic and emotional aspects, but rather in regard to integrating mechanisms of motor control.

W. Marvin Davis

1949

Physiology or Medicine

Walter Rudolf Hess, Switzerland
António Egas Moniz, Portugal

Chemistry

William Francis Giauque, United States

Physics

Hideki Yukawa, Japan

Literature

William Faulkner, United States

Peace

Lord Boyd-Orr, Great Britain

ANTÓNIO EGAS MONIZ
1949

Born: Avança, Portugal; November 29, 1874
Died: Lisbon, Portugal; December 13, 1955
Nationality: Portuguese
Areas of concentration: Neurophysiology and psychosurgery

Egas Moniz helped advance the field of psychosurgery by developing prefrontal leucotomy, a surgical procedure used for the recovery and rehabilitation of people with severe psychiatric conditions

The Award

Presentation

Professor H. Olivecrona of the Royal Caroline Institute delivered the presentation address on December 10, 1949. In his address, Olivecrona noted that two important discoveries had been made in the field of neurophysiology; due honor was given to the research of Swiss scientist Walter Rudolf Hess, Egas Moniz's cowinner, in the detailed localization of the primary centers of vital functions.

Olivecrona then discussed the work of António Egas Moniz. Egas Moniz knew that research had long pinpointed the frontal lobes of the brain, directly behind the forehead, as centers for emotional activity. Experiments on animals had proved that the destruction of these lobes led to changes in personality. Once the lobes were removed, certain neuroses experimentally disappeared and were then impossible to reproduce in these animals. Egas Moniz believed that certain psychic states might be alleviated by destroying the frontal lobes or by cutting their connections to other parts of the brain. He developed and named a surgical method, called prefrontal leucotomy because the connections severed run through the white matter of the brain.

Egas Moniz proved that this procedure was helpful for patients suffering from severe psychiatric states, such as schizophrenia and certain forms of persecution mania. Many were able to return to work, and even some of the schizophrenic patients were able to be released from the hospital. The procedure also proved successful in treating serious, bodily conditioned pain. Anguish and anxiety disappeared, making the patient indifferent to pain. Egas Moniz's development of prefrontal leucotomy was important in psychiatric therapy, Olivecrona stated, because it aided in the recovery and social rehabilitation of many seriously ill people.

Nobel lecture

No lecture was given. Egas Moniz, seventy-five years old and in ill health, chose not to travel to Sweden to receive the Nobel Prize personally. It was accepted for him by the chargé d'affaires of the Legation of Portugal.

Critical reception

Since the late nineteenth century, there had been widespread interest in brain surgery as a possible treatment for mental illness. Perhaps Egas Moniz's initial operation was thus an idea whose time had come. By 1934, he had received many honors and much praise for his earlier work in cerebral angiography (visualizing the arteries of the brain). Prefrontal leucotomy—or lobotomy, as it is now called—brought him additional worldwide honors and praise throughout the 1940's.

World War II brought a temporary halt to such work in Europe. During the same period, however, the American popular press stimulated interest in lobotomies with almost uncritical enthusiasm and even some misleading statements. Many variations of the surgery were tried, discussed, and analyzed.

In 1949, Europe was still attempting to recover from the ravages of the war. Only a few nations had again started to encourage research projects. That same year, there had been only a few Nobel Prize nominations—in fact, there were only fifteen for the field of physiology or medicine; the Nobel Committee decided to award the prize to two men.

The New York Times' editorial for October 30, 1949, applauded the selections. Every area of the brain had been explored and investigated since the founding of phrenology, the editorial said. All the information gathered had finally "come together" in 1935 at the International Neurological Conference in London. Following that conference, Egas Moniz had developed a radical surgical procedure that "justified itself . . . [and] taught us to look with less awe on the brain. It is just a big organ, with very difficult and complicated functions to perform and no more sacred than the liver."

Egas Moniz's contribution to cerebral angiography was not mentioned in the award citation issued by the Nobel Committee. That work was considered to be of less importance than the development of lobotomy, according to the editorial in the December 22, 1949, issue of *The New England Journal of Medicine*: "A new psychiatry may be said to have been born in 1935, when Egas Moniz took his first bold step in the field of psychosurgery." Probably because of his important contributions to cerebral angiography and his distinguished career as a politician and diplomat, Egas Moniz was generally treated uncritically and described in only the most complimentary terms. He was Portugal's only Nobel laureate.

Prefrontal leucotomy had received much criticism from its inception, and controversy seemed to grow stronger each year. Yet, despite the increased criticism of the procedure, the 1949 Nobel award created additional interest in psychosurgery. For many in the medical profession, the award seemed to confer approval upon the scientific validity and therapeutic value of the operation.

Biography

António Egas Moniz was born on November 29, 1874, in Avança, Portugal. His early education was carefully supervised by his uncle, Abadelde, a priest. In his senior year at the University of Coimbra, he decided to study medicine. Two years after graduation from medical school, he accepted an appointment as lecturer and married Elvira de Macedo Dias. He periodically studied neurology in France.

He continued to hold his lectureship while pursuing public office; for fifteen years, he served in the Portuguese Parliament. By 1917, he had been named ambassador to Spain; he was president of the Portuguese delegation to the Paris Peace Conference in 1918.

In 1910, Egas Moniz was appointed professor in the newly formed department of neurology at the University of Lisbon and served as director of the Institute of Neurology for Scientific Investigation in that city. Egas Moniz abandoned politics in 1926 to work on cerebral angiography. From 1935 to 1945, he developed the surgical procedure he called leucotomy and concentrated on various modifications of his procedure. In addition to his neurological publications, he wrote about Portuguese heroes and artists. He held memberships in many professional organizations, including the Academy of Science of Lisbon and the Academy of Medicine in Paris, and he was an honorary member of the American Neurological Society. Other awards included honorary degrees from the universities of Bordeaux, Toulouse, and Lyons.

Egas Moniz died in Lisbon in 1955 at the age of eighty-one.

Scientific Career

In the early days of his medical career, Egas Moniz did little of distinction in neurology. He did, however, shock conservative Portugal when he wrote a book on sexual behavior and physiology, *A vida sexual: Fisiologia e patologia* (1901; sexual life: physiology and pathology). During World War I he wrote *A neurologia na querra* (1917; neurology in war). Not a very original work, it had little influence in the neurological field. He also wrote a book entitled *Clinica neurologica* (1925; clinical neurology) and a two-volume work, *Júlio Diniz e a sua obra* (1924; Julio Denis and his works). For almost twenty years he struggled to combine politics and university activities.

By 1926, Egas Moniz had decided to concentrate on neurology. Like many in the profession, he was frustrated by the lack of techniques available for studying the living human brain. Because of its uniform density, its structures could not be distinguished by X rays.

Following up on a suggestion made by Jean Sicard, the neurologist with whom he had studied in Paris, Egas Moniz chose to devote himself to cerebral angiography. Crippled with gout since the age of twenty-four, he needed assistance with his work and thus relied on his colleague Almeida Lima, a young neurology professor who became his lifelong research associate. They began experiments on animals. These led him to perfect the only two substances which proved opaque to X rays without damaging the nervous system. Between 1927 and 1934, Egas Moniz, now a leading neurologist, lectured worldwide and published two books, *Diagnostic des tumeurs cérébrales et épreuve de l'encéphalographie artérielle* (1931; diagnostics of cerebral tumors and application of arterial encephalography) and *L'Angiographie cérébrale, ses applications et résultats en anatomie, physiologie et clinique* (1934; cerebral angiography, its applications and results in anatomy, physiology, and clinic), and 112 articles on the subject.

In 1928, the Nobel Prize Committee received two very brief letters nominating Egas Moniz. The committee declined to award him the prize. Within the next three years, he developed the first X-ray phlebography (pictures of the veins) of the brain. In 1933, he was again nominated, and again the committee declined.

Since 1900, most psychiatrists had regarded mental and emotional disturbances as diseases of the mind and attempted to treat them through various forms of psychoanalysis. Some neurologists in the 1920's and 1930's, however, considered psychological problems as diseases of the brain and searched for new somatic cures for mental illnesses. Earlier somatic treatments for mental disorders were diverse, often extreme, and unsuccessful. Hospital stays were prolonged. Large institutions, operating on limited budgets, were often overcrowded and understaffed. Shock therapy rarely cured hospitalized patients, but it did make them docile and easier to handle.

In 1935, Egas Moniz, then sixty-one, attended the International Neurological Conference in London, where the American neurophysiologists John Fulton and Carlyle Jacobsen presented their study of two monkeys from which they had removed most of the prefrontal lobes of the brain. After the experimental procedure, the monkeys no longer became upset if they made mistakes while carrying out the complex tasks they had learned. Moniz raised questions about the feasibility of using this procedure on humans to relieve anxiety states. Later, in response to critics, he insisted that he had already been thinking of such a procedure for several years prior to the conference.

Egas Moniz moved ahead on an essentially experimental course. Only three months following the conference, he began the operation, which he called leucotomy (from the Greek word for white) because the prefrontal lobes were not severed; only the white matter (neuronal-association fibers) connecting the lobes to the parts of the brain was.

Egas Moniz and Lima selected the prefrontal area where nerve fibers are most concentrated. He believed that abnormal thoughts of mental patients resided in the nerve fiber pathways between the cells and that thus these nerve fibers should be destroyed. Initially, Egas Moniz and Lima used absolute alcohol injections to destroy the fibers. Within a few weeks the technique was modified to cutting nerve fibers with a surgical leucotome, a hollow needle which carried within it a razor-sharp wire as a cutting blade. Four months later, he presented a report, *Tentatives opératoires dans le traitement de certaines psychoses* (1936; tentative methods in the treatment of certain psychoses), on all twenty patients selected: Seven were cured, eight seemed improved, and five were unchanged. The operation also appeared to relieve patients suffering from intractable pain.

The theory behind his procedure was flimsy at best. He seemed unusually willing to take risks, appeared unconcerned about some very troubling side effects, and was much too optimistic in interpreting the clinical results. The report was done too soon postoperatively to be complete or accurate. Yet, Egas Moniz published his results, "Premiers essais de psychochirurgie—Technique et résultats" (1936; first essay on psychosurgery—techniques and results), and presented them before the

Medical Psychological Society in Paris the following year. A few months later, he reported on eighteen additional patients treated and on several modifications to the procedure in *La Leucotomie préfrontale: Traitement chirurgical de certaines psychoses* (1937; prefrontal leucotomy: surgical treatment of certain psychoses). Egas Moniz was eager to report his findings—he was sixty-two years of age, and there might not be another chance to make such a report. He knew also that several other noted European scentists were doing similar research, and he did not wish to share credit with them.

There were no new articles on prefrontal leucotomy after 1937. Egas Moniz remained active in the profession and continued to work on modifications to the procedure, but his publications centered on cerebral angiography. In 1945, he retired and began to write his memoirs, *Confidências de um investigador ciêntífico* (1949; memoirs of a scientific investigator).

At the 1948 International Neurological Congress, held in Lisbon in Egas Moniz's honor, he was publicly thanked for his contributions in advancing the theory of psychosurgery. At that conference, he presented a paper, *Como chequei a realizar a leucotomia pré-frontal* (1948; how I came to perform prefrontal leucotomy). The delegates to the congress, eager to nominate Egas Moniz for the Nobel Prize, accepted by acclamation the Brazilian delegation resolution that all those in attendance use their influence in nominating him.

Yet there was sharp criticism of the procedure itself. Many favored less drastic treatments for mental illness. The papers presented drew conclusions that differed sharply with Egas Moniz's own findings. Some advocated that lobotomy be done only in special cases when all other therapeutic measures had been exhausted and there was no longer any hope of spontaneous improvement. Prefrontal leucotomy had essentially been adopted in the absence of any effective alternative somatic treatment despite all the protests. The number of lobotomies performed worldwide over the years increased, although it never became a common procedure in Portugal. Egas Moniz and his associates performed no more than one hundred such operations.

Between 1949 and 1952, thousands of lobotomies were performed annually. By 1960, however, the use of the procedure was drastically curtailed, as it was becoming apparent that these operations produced brain-damaged people. Within ten years, lobotomies were strictly limited to very specific target areas. Research, discussion, and controversy continued.

Throughout his life, Egas Moniz appeared to need some motivation in the form of an important practical problem to solve. Cerebral angiography and, later, prefrontal lobotomy provided the answer. This was a man who was persistent in his work, had keen observational powers, and had the ability to persuade others to join him in developing and extending basic techniques. Yet he was also able to avoid sharing credit with others. Even Almeida Lima was not acknowledged in any of Egas Moniz's writings until 1936.

In the process of developing prefrontal lobotomy, Egas Moniz did introduce innovations. He invented the leucotome and with it cut only one centimeter of white matter in the lobes. The white matter was not removed but left free in the cavity to undergo autolysis, or self-digestion. In writing about the procedure, Egas Moniz coined the word "psychosurgery"; he is credited with starting a new chapter in the area of brain surgery.

Bibliography

Primary

ANGIOGRAPHY: "L'Encéphalographie artérielle, son importance dans la localisation des tumeurs cérébrales," *Revue neurologique*, vol. 2, 1927, p. 272; *Diagnostic des tumeurs cérébrales et épreuve de l'encéphalographie artérielle*, 1931; "L'Artériophlibographi comme moyen de déterminer la vitesse de la circulation du cerveau, des méninges et des parties molles du crane," *Bulletin de l'Académie de Médecine*, vol. 107, April 12, 1932, pp. 516-518; *Die cerebrale Arteriographic und Phlebographie*, 1940; *Trombosis y otras obstrucciones de las carótidas*, 1941.

NEUROLOGY: *A neurologia na querra*, 1917; *Clinica neurologica*, 1925; L'Angiographie cérébrale, ses applications et résultats en anatomie, physiologie et clinique, 1934; *Tentatives opératoires dans le traitement de certaines psychoses*, 1936; "Premiers essais de psychochirurgie—Technique et résultats," *Lisboa Medica*, vol. 13, 1936, p. 152 (with Almeida Lima); *La Leucotomie préfrontale: Traitement chirurgical de certaines psychoses*, 1937; "Prefrontal Leucotomy in the Treatment of Mental Disorders," *American Journal of Psychiatry*, vol. 93, 1937, pp. 1379-1385; *Como chequei a realizar a leucotomia pré-frontal*, 1948; *Die präfrontale Leukotomie*, 1949.

MEDICINE: *A vida sexual: Fisiologia e patologia*, 1901; *Ao lado da medicina*, 1940; *Confidências de um investigador científico*, 1949.

OTHER NONFICTION: *Um ano de política*, 1920; *Júlio Diniz e a sua obra*, 1924; *O Padre Faria na história do hípnotismo*, 1925; *O Papa Joao, XXI*, 1929; *História das cartas de jogar*, 1942; *Mauríco de Almeida: Escultor, 1897-1923*, 1943.

Secondary

Glaser, Hugo. *The Road to Modern Surgery: The Advances in Medicine and Surgery During the Past Hundred Years*. Translated by Maurice Michael. London: Lutterworth Press, 1960. Each chapter describes the research done in one area of medicine, such as hormones, viruses, and old age. Chapter 6 presents a general history, including a brief description of Egas Moniz's leucotomy procedure.

Koskoff, Yale David, and Richard Goldhurst. *The Dark Side of the House*. New York: Dial Press, 1968. This is the story of Millard Wright, the first patient to be lobotomized without brain damage in 1949. Only three pages in the prologue actually mention Moniz and are confined mainly to his 1936 leucotomy procedure with brief mention of his work in cerebral angiography.

Sackler, Arthur M., et al., eds. *The Great Physiodynamic Therapies in Psychiatry: An Historical Reappraisal*. New York: Hocher-Harper Books, 1956. The articles in this work originally appeared in *The Journal of Clinical and Experimental Psychopathology* and the *Quarterly Review of Psychiatry and Neurology.* Chapter 6 presents Egas Moniz's article "How I Succeeded in Performing Prefrontal Leukotomy." A brief one-page biography with picture is also given at the end of the book.

Stevenson, Lloyd G. *Nobel Prize Winners in Medicine and Physiology, 1901-1950.* New York: Henry Schuman, 1953. This work, for young adults, is part of the Pathfinders in Twentieth Century Science series. It presents brief biographies and explanations of why each of the Nobel laureates became involved in his research. Excerpts are included from Egas Moniz's article "How I Succeeded in Performing Prefrontal Leukotomy."

Valenstein, Elliot S. *Great and Desperate Cures: The Rise and Decline of Psychosurgery and Other Radical Treatments for Mental Illness.* New York: Basic Books, 1986. Intended for scientifically oriented readers, this book contains the most complete information about Egas Moniz. It traces the history of psychosurgery from the late nineteenth century to the 1980's. Three chapters are devoted to Egas Moniz's life and theories, and they present a detailed description of his various procedures.

____________, ed. *The Psychosurgery Debate: Scientific, Legal, and Ethical Practices.* San Francisco: W. H. Freeman, 1980. A lengthy book which requires some knowledge of neurology. Various chapters deal with legal and ethical issues, psychosurgery, and the psychosurgical patient. Seven pages, scattered throughout the book, mention Egas Moniz and deal specifically with his leucotomy procedure.

Walker, A. Earl, ed. *A History of Neurological Surgery.* New York: Hafner Press, 1967. Intended for a scientifically sophisticated readership, the book presents a history of diagnostic procedures and techniques of psychosurgery. Nine pages, scattered throughout the book, give information on Egas Moniz and his leucotomy procedure.

Rita E. Loos

1950

Physiology or Medicine

Edward Calvin Kendall, United States
Tadeus Reichstein, Poland and Switzerland
Philip Showalter Hench, United States

Chemistry

Otto Paul Hermann Diels, West Germany
Kurt Alder, West Germany

Physics

Cecil Frank Powell, Great Britain

Literature

Bertrand Russell, Great Britain

Peace

Ralph Bunche, United States

EDWARD CALVIN KENDALL
1950

Born: South Norwalk, Connecticut; March 8, 1886
Died: Princeton, New Jersey; May 4, 1972
Nationality: American
Areas of concentration: Biochemistry and endocrinology

Kendall distinguished himself as a biochemist by his work on thyroxine, glutathione, and other biologically active substances before turning his attention to the hormones that are produced in the adrenal cortex. One of the hormones he isolated, cortisone, proved effective in ameliorating the symptoms of rheumatoid arthritis. This led to its use in the treatment of many disorders that had been untreatable

The Award

Presentation

Professor Göran Liljestrand, a member of the staff of the Royal Caroline Institute, delivered the presentation address shortly before the Nobel Prize in Physiology or Medicine was awarded jointly to Edward C. Kendall, Tadeus Reichstein, and Philip S. Hench on December 10, 1950. He remarked that for nearly two hundred years following the discovery of the adrenal glands, little was known about their function. In 1855, the English physician Thomas Addison described a life-threatening condition, later known as Addison's disease, that was clearly a result of adrenal insufficiency. Subsequent investigations demonstrated that only the extracts from the adrenal cortex would prolong the life of both adrenalectomized animals and patients afflicted with Addison's disease.

Toward the end of the 1920's, the extracts of the adrenal cortex had been sufficiently purified that the active factor, cortin, could be expected to be isolated and characterized within a short time. In 1934, Kendall and his coworkers at the Mayo Clinic in Rochester, Minnesota, obtained what they thought to be cortin in a crystalline form. Later studies showed that the product was not homogeneous but was a mixture of several substances with closely related structures. In the succeeding years, investigators established the presence of nearly thirty different, yet chemically related, compounds in the adrenal cortex. Six of these compounds were shown to be effective in maintaining the life of adrenalectomized animals. Largely as a result of the work of Reichstein and his associates, the cortical hormones (known also as adrenocortical hormones and corticosteroids), such as the sex hormones, were demonstrated to possess the basic tetracyclic system of the steroids. The best known of the cortical hormones is cortisone, which Kendall initially designated as compound E. It was first isolated simultaneously in four different laboratories, among them Kendall's and Reichstein's.

All the cortical hormones contain twenty-one carbon and three to five oxygen atoms. To varying degrees, they affect carbohydrate and electrolyte metabolism, retention of fluid and nitrogenous waste products, catabolism, and muscular activity. Kendall's group demonstrated that minor variation of structure could produce a significant alteration of biological activities.

In World War II, production of certain cortical hormones was required for military purposes. Among them was cortisone, which was synthesized in minute amounts by a lengthy and arduous process. Only after the end of the war could significant amounts be obtained. The availability of these hormones allowed clinicians at the Mayo Clinic to test the hypothesis that chronic rheumatoid arthritis and the attendant erosion of joints were associated with the dysfunction of the adrenal glands. In April, 1949, Hench, Kendall, Charles H. Slocumb, and Howard F. Polley announced their electrifying results: Bed-ridden arthritic patients given cortisone were able to walk freely, and the pain and tenderness of their joints either had disappeared or were considerably reduced.

Nobel lecture

Kendall delivered his Nobel lecture, entitled "The Development of Cortisone as a Therapeutic Agent," on Monday afternoon, December 11, 1950. He began by acknowledging the contributions made by his colleagues at the Mayo Clinic and by Reichstein and his associates in Zurich, Switzerland. Although approximately thirty compounds were eventually isolated, the group at the Mayo Clinic focused its main effort on four compounds, which they designated as compounds A, B, E, and F. Compounds E and F differ from compounds A and B, respectively, in that the former pair of compounds have an extra oxygen inserted between the hydrogen atom and carbon-17 of the steroid nucleus. Compounds A and B could thus be expected to be synthesized more readily than compounds E and F. Compounds A and E differ from compounds B and F, respectively, in that the former pair of compounds have two fewer hydrogen atoms at the carbon-11 position.

When the National Research Council (NRC) of the United States was requested to furnish the military services with various cortical hormones for possible use by their pilots, it was the consensus of the council that the initial effort should be directed toward the large-scale synthesis of compound A because it possessed the simplest structure of the four hormones then under investigation at Mayo.

Following the method devised by Kendall's group, the pharmaceutical firm Merck and Co. succeeded in synthesizing a large quantity of compound A in 1945. This achievement allowed testing of compound A in humans; however, to the dismay of everyone associated with the project, compound A had little influence on the symptoms of Addison's disease, the condition which was expected to respond most favorably to treatment with the cortical hormones.

Because compounds A, B, E, and F were suspected to possess similar biological activities, many members of the NRC had doubts as to the wisdom of attempting the large-scale synthesis of the other hormones. Kendall and Merck and Co. nevertheless persisted in their combined efforts to convert an intermediary in the synthesis of compound A to compound E, which Kendall and Philip Hench had been looking forward to testing in rheumatoid arthritic patients since 1941. In the summer of 1948, compound E was tested in an Addisonian patient and found to produce a notable improvement in the patient's condition. In September, 1948, the first trial in an arthritic patient was undertaken. Later, substantial improvement was made by Lewis H. Sarett in the synthesis of compound E, which was now renamed cortisone to avoid confusion with vitamin E. This enabled additional patients to be enrolled in the cortisone trial. Included were both patients with rheumatoid arthritis and those with rheumatic fever. Over a period of seven months, convincing evidence was produced to establish the efficacy of cortisone. The process for preparing cortisone was greatly improved from July, 1949, to November, 1950, reducing its cost from two hundred to thirty-five dollars per gram during this period.

The second half of Kendall's lecture was devoted to a discussion of the intricate chemistry involved in the conversion of the bile acid deoxycholic acid into cortisone. Many novel features and improvements of the synthesis were cited. They included contracting the side chain of the bile acid, insertion of an oxygen atom between hydrogen and carbon-17 position, shifting the oxygen function from carbon 12 to carbon 11, and elimination of a pair of hydrogens from carbons 4 and 5.

Critical reception

Public reaction to the awarding of the Nobel Prize to Kendall, Reichstein, and Hench was extremely favorable for several reasons. First, rheumatoid arthritis is a degenerative disease that has plagued humankind since time immemorial. The advent of cortisone gave hope that this disease would soon be conquered. Second, the American recipients of the Nobel Prize were staff members of the Mayo Clinic Foundation, a medical institution recognized worldwide for its preeminence in medical research and care. Third, the development of cortisone illustrated vividly the collaboration of the public and private sectors at its best. Without the support of Merck and Co., investigators at Mayo would not have been able to demonstrate convincingly the utility of cortisone in the treatment of arthritis and a variety of other inflammatory disorders. Fourth, the joint award of the prize to the noted Swiss pharmaceutical chemist Reichstein, as well as to Kendall and Hench, was not only a recognition of the contribution each made to the isolation, structural elucidation, synthesis, and application of the cortical hormones, but also a testimony that scientific research is international in character.

Even before the Nobel Committee announced the winners of the 1950 Nobel Prize, the public was well aware of the importance of cortisone as a therapeutic agent and the vital role that Kendall played in its discovery and development. Following the Mayo Clinic announcement in April, 1949, of the treatment of rheumatoid arthritis with cortisone, a steady stream of reports appeared in both the scientific journals and the lay press announcing the successful application of cortisone to other debilitating disorders and the development of other forms of treatment for arthritis based upon the synthesis of cortisone in the body. The adrenocorticotropic hormone (ACTH), a polypeptide hormone synthesized in the pituitary gland that stimulates the adrenals to synthesize and release the cortical hormones, was tested and found to be effective in the treatment of arthritic patients. The discovery of the effects of cortisone also stimulated the search for still other hormones in the adrenal cortex. In 1953, Sylvia A. Simpson, James F. Tait, Reichstein, and their associates reported the isolation of aldosterone, the most potent agent for the retention of sodium ions in the body.

The therapeutic potential of cortisone and a related hormone, cortisol (Kendall's compound F), appeared so vast that considerable efforts were spent in improving their synthesis. One of the key transformations in the Merck-Kendall synthesis was the multistep introduction of the oxygen function at the carbon-11 position. In numerous laboratories, scientists sought to accomplish this more efficiently by a variety of means.

One biological approach involved perfusing a steroid lacking an oxygen function at carbon 11 (an 11-deoxysteroid) through a mammalian adrenal gland, while another involved incubating the 11-deoxysteroid with different microorganisms. The success achieved in the latter process resulted in the synthesis of a large number of steroids with an oxygen function at carbon 11. Some of these steroids were later found to be even more potent than cortisone as anti-inflammatory agents. The award of the Nobel Prize to Kendall was a foregone conclusion.

In reporting the award to Kendall, *Time* magazine commented, "Kendall kept trying to synthesize compound E, or something like it. At last [he] . . . succeeded, and . . . a colleague, Dr. Philip Hench, directed the first injections of cortisone to human victims of rheumatoid arthritis. The results were dramatic. Suddenly, a vast new field of medical research was opened."

Biography

Edward Calvin Kendall was born on March 8, 1886, to George Stanley and Eva Frances (née Abbott) Kendall of South Norwalk, Connecticut. He was of English and Scottish descent. Both his father and paternal grandfather were dentists and devout members of the Congregational Church of Ridgefield, Connecticut. He was the youngest of three children; his sisters were Florence and Ruth.

As a child, he was intrigued with mechanical devices and natural phenomena. When he was in the eighth grade, he aspired to be a philosopher, thinking that philosophy would enable him to delve into the two areas which intrigued him the most. His first three years of high school were spent at South Norwalk High School. While there, he decided to become a physicist. Because South Norwalk High School was only a three-year school, he transferred to a high school in the neighboring town of Stamford, where he came under the influence of a talented chemistry teacher who had received a doctorate in chemistry from Yale University. As a result, Kendall's interest switched to chemistry.

Following high school, he entered Columbia University as a freshman in September, 1904, after passing the college entrance examination. His choice of Columbia was influenced by his sister Florence's fiancé, Mark W. Norman, who played football at Columbia and whom Kendall admired. At Columbia, he joined a fraternity and was active in intramural wrestling and rowing. He did not consider himself to be a good mixer because of his upbringing. He had no desire to plunge into youthful frivolities; instead, he sought diversion and fascination in the laboratory. His professors made a lasting impression on him. He recalled one of them, saying that in the search for knowledge, there was no substitute for truth. He was graduated with a B.S. degree in 1908 and was immediately appointed laboratory instructor at Columbia for the summer. Living at home in Connecticut, he would commute daily to New York City in the summer. To stay alert for work in the afternoon, he would often take catnaps for fifteen to twenty minutes on one of the laboratory's windowsills before class began.

In the fall of 1908, he commenced graduate work at Columbia University under Professor Henry C. Sherman. He received the M.S. and Ph.D. degrees in 1909 and 1910, respectively. Kendall worked first at Parke Davis and Company in Detroit, Michigan, and then at St. Luke's Hospital in New York City. He went to the Mayo Clinic in 1914 and was appointed to the staff of the clinic the following year. There he remained until 1951, when he reached the mandatory retirement age of sixty-five. The salary he received following his appointment to the staff of Mayo allowed him to think of marriage. On December 30, 1915, he married Rebecca Kennedy of New York. They became parents of three sons and one daughter, Hugh, Roy, Norman, and Elizabeth. Two of his sons, Roy and Norman, preceded him in death. Following his retirement from Mayo, he continued his studies on the adrenal cortex as Visiting Professor of Chemistry at Princeton University. Kendall died at Rahway Hospital in Princeton, New Jersey, on May 4, 1972.

Scientific Career

Throughout his life, Kendall was diligent and purposeful, and he pursued his objectives tenaciously. While a student, he found inspiration and support from the distinguished chemistry faculty at Columbia University. He received the master's and doctorate degrees within two years after receiving the bachelor's degree from the same institution. For his doctoral study, his major professor, Henry C. Sherman, assigned him the problem of studying the enzymatic conversion of starch into maltose and requested him to determine the cause of the erratic results obtained when pancreatic amylose was employed to promote the conversion. In a short time, Kendall found the answer: The enzymatic activity was dependent on the presence of certain salts in the solution. This study formed the basis of his Ph.D. dissertation, which he submitted in 1910.

A committee was convened to examine Kendall on his dissertation. Professor Samuel Tucker was a member of the committee. His role was to examine Kendall's knowledge of electroplating, which was Tucker's area of expertise. At one stage of the examination, Tucker asked Kendall whether he was aware of the recent discovery of the presence of iodine in the thyroid gland. Kendall admitted to not being aware of it. Little did either suspect that this seemingly irrelevant information would later set Kendall on an investigation that would bring him elation, excitement, acclaim, and dejection over the next two decades.

After successfully defending his thesis in 1910 and receiving the Ph.D. the same year, Kendall proceeded to Detroit in September to accept a position in the control laboratory of Parke Davis and Co., America's foremost pharmaceutical firm, at an annual salary of $1,350. His assignment was to isolate the active principles of the thyroid gland. Kendall's stay in Detroit, however, was brief (only four months). He missed the intellectual and professional stimulation of New York City and, particularly, Columbia University. There was no other scientist with a Ph.D. degree in the control laboratory of Parke Davis, so he resigned his position in December and returned to New York City, where he found employment at St. Luke's Hospital, near Columbia. There was no guarantee of salary or tenure, but he would be free to work on projects of his own choosing. No less important, he would be able to attend the opera, which he enjoyed. He began work at St. Luke's in February, 1911, and was given initially an allowance of thirty dollars a month. He resumed working on the isolation of the thyroid hormones. Although he was pleased with his work, he was disenchanted with the attitude of the hospital staff. The administrator and clinicians were indifferent to his work and had no interest in research. To them, the function of a chemist in a hospital was to provide clinicians with analytical services. Once again, Kendall decided to look elsewhere for employment. He considered Rockefeller Institute, whose director was the redoubtable Simon Flexner. Simon and his brother Abraham were fervent advocates of revamping the practice of medicine in the United States. They sought to place it on a sound scientific basis. Despite the interest shown at Rockefeller Institute in the effect of iodine on goiter, Kendall's interview with Simon Flexner was not encouraging, mainly because of Flexner's skepticism of Kendall's ability to isolate the thyroid hormone. Kendall left Flexner's office determined more than ever to isolate the iodine-containing compound in pure crystalline form.

When Kendall learned about the building program at the Mayo Clinic, he applied for a position there. In 1914, he left New York for Rochester, Minnesota. At the Mayo Clinic, he continued his work on the thyroid gland, and on December 23, 1914, he isolated crystalline thyroxine. Less than five years after he had learned of the presence of iodine in the thyroid gland, he had on hand the crystalline iodine-containing hormone. Large-scale isolation was undertaken to produce sufficient quantity of thyroxine for testing in patients. The effects of thyroxine were dramatic. Patients who had been diagnosed as mentally incompetent from myxedema, a deficiency of thyroxine, were restored to a keenness of mind. In 1916, Kendall was invited to present a paper on the isolation of the crystalline hormone from the thyroid gland at a meeting of the Federation of American Societies for Experimental Biology in New York City. He accepted the invitation with pleasure, for the chairman of the meeting was Simon Flexner of Rockefeller Institute.

By the early 1920's, he had become the director of the Section of Biochemistry at the Mayo Clinic and professor of physiologic chemistry in the Mayo Foundation Graduate School of the University of Minnesota. Kendall initiated the oxidation-reduction studies on glutathione, cysteine, and cystine in order to explain the metabolic effects of thyroxine. At the same time, he continued his studies on its structure and synthesis. By 1926, however, he conceded defeat in attempting to deduce the structure. He had misinterpreted the pathway by which several of the degradation products of thyroxine were formed. The successful elucidation of structure, as well as synthesis of thyroxine, was accomplished by Charles R. Harington of University College of London. A few years later, the same man would be the first to synthesize glutathione, the structure of which Kendall and the English biochemist who would receive the Nobel Prize in 1929, Frederick Gowland Hopkins, had independently established as glutamyl-cysteinyl-glycine. Kendall was dejected in not having been the first to synthesize thyroxine, and he believed that he and his staff had caused the Mayo Clinic to suffer a considerable loss of prestige.

Kendall's attention was drawn to the adrenal glands because of the clinical interest at Mayo in Addison's disease, the reported isolation of a hormone from the adrenal cortex, and the visit of Albert Szent-Györgyi to Kendall's laboratories in the autumn of 1929. Szent-Györgyi was the first to isolate vitamin C and had found its highest concentration to be in the adrenal cortex. He stayed at Mayo for eight months in the hope of obtaining adrenal glands from the packing houses in St. Paul, Minnesota. The young and ebullient Hungarian biochemist, who one day would receive the Nobel Prize for his work on vitamin C, was not only a stimulus to Kendall but also a rich source of information on the talent and character of individual European scientists, one of whom had recently beaten Kendall to the structure of thyroxine and another of whom would shortly become his chief rival in the isolation and characterization of the adrenocortical hormones.

Kendall's work on the cortical hormones was facilitated by an agreement with Parke Davis and Co. The pharmaceutical company would supply him bovine adrenal glands at no cost. In return, he would send the adrenaline isolated from the adrenal medulla to Parke Davis, while keeping the cortex extracts for himself. Reichstein, on the other hand, had the collaboration of Organon, Inc., of The Netherlands in the extraction of the adrenal cortex. Both Kendall and Reichstein used letters of the alphabet to denote the molecules.

Until the beginning of World War II, the cortical hormones were of only academic interest. In 1940, however, rumors were circulated that pilots in Germany's Luftwaffe were flying at incredible height with impunity because they had been given adrenal extracts to counteract hypoxemia. Although the rumors were later proved to be false, the National Research Council (NRC) of the National Academy of Sciences appointed a committee on the adrenal cortex to undertake the large-scale preparation of the cortical hormones for military use. Top priority was given to the synthesis of Kendall's compound E (cortisone), which superseded even the priorities for the large-scale production of penicillin and the development of the antimalarials.

Before the synthesis of compound E was undertaken, the committee recommended synthesizing Kendall's compound A first in order both to determine its effect on humans and to acquire the technical skill and knowledge needed for the more difficult synthesis of compound E. World War II, however, came to an end before compound E could be prepared in any sizable amount, which led one critic to comment tartly that the committee on the adrenal cortex of the NRC had failed to produce anything of value during the war. The board of governors of the Mayo Clinic Foundation, however, continued to have faith in the project, as well as in Kendall, and authorized Mayo to continue its collaboration with Merck and Co. on the synthesis of compound E during the postwar period. When the required amount of compound E was synthesized, Harold Mason, at first, and then Kendall personally ground the steroid to a fine powder so that microsuspended samples of compound E in saline could be prepared for administration to the rheumatoid arthritic patients of Philip S. Hench, the head of the department of arthritis at the Mayo Clinic.

Following the announcement of the successful treatment of rheumatoid arthritis with cortisone (compound E) in 1949, Kendall was inundated with honors and awards. For his work on thyroxine previously, he had received the John Scott Prize from the City of Philadelphia in 1921, an honorary doctor of science degree from the University of Cincinnati in 1922, and the Chandler Medal of Columbia University in 1925. In addition, he received the Squibb Award of the Endocrine Society in 1945. Beginning in 1949, he received, among other honors, the Lasker Award of the American Public Health Association, the Nobel Prize in Physiology or Medicine, the Kober Medal of the American Physicians Association, the Passano Foundation Award of the Passano Foundation of San Francisco, the Remsen and Edgar F. Smith awards of the American Chemical Society, the Medal of Honour of the Canadian Pharmaceutical Manufacturers Association, the Scientific Achievement Award of the American Medical Association, the John Phillips Memorial Award of the American College of Physicians, the Cameron Award of the University of Edinburgh, and the Heberden Award of the Heberden Society (London). Honorary degrees were conferred upon him by Yale University, Williams College, Western Reserve University, the National University of Ireland, Columbia University, and Gustavus Adolphus College. Construction of a new laboratory for steroid research at the Mayo Clinic was authorized by the board of governors for Kendall. The esteem which the members of the governing body of the Mayo Clinic Foundation had for him was matched by that of the construction workers who completed the facility in record time.

Kendall was a member of numerous scientific societies, among them the National Academy of Sciences, American Society of Biological Chemists, American Chemical Society, American Physiological Society, American Society of Experimental Biology and Medicine, and the Endocrine Society. He was elected an honorary member of the Royal Society of Medicine of England, the Columbian Society of Endocrinology, and the Swedish Society of Endocrinology.

In addition to providing a new class of drugs for the treatment of a host of inflammatory, allergic, and autoimmune disorders, Kendall's research paved the way for the development of the steroid drug industry. One of his former postdoctoral fellows at the Mayo Clinic involved in the synthesis of compound E, Frank B. Colton, was instrumental in the development of Enovid, the first oral contraceptive.

Bibliography

Primary

BIOCHEMISTRY: *Thyroxine*, American Chemical Society Monograph 47, 1928; "The Influence of the Adrenal Cortex on the Metabolism of Water and Electrolytes," *Vitamins and Hormones*, vol. 6, 1948; "The Hormone of the Adrenal Cortex Designated Compond E," *Proceedings of the Staff Meetings of the Mayo Clinic*, vol. 24, 1949; "Studies Related to the Adrenal Cortex," *Federation Proceedings*, vol. 9, 1950.

MEDICINE: "The Effect of the a Hormone of the Adrenal Cortex (17-Hydroxy-11-Dehydrocorticosterone: Compound E) and of Pituitary Adrenocorticotropic Hormone on Rheumatoid Arthritis," *Proceedings of the Staff Meetings of the Mayo Clinic*, vol. 24, 1949 (with Philip S. Hench, Charles H. Slocumb, and Howard F. Polley); "The Effects of the Adrenal Cortical Hormone 17-Hydroxy-11-Dehydrocorticosterone (Compound E) on the Acute Phase of Rheumatic Fever," *Proceedings of the Staff Meetings of the Mayo Clinic*, vol. 24, 1949 (with Philip S. Hench, Charles H. Slocumb, Arlie R. Barnes, Harry L. Smith, and Howard F. Polley); "Effects of Cortisone Acetate and Pituitary Adrenocorticotropic Hormone on Rheumatoid Arthritis, Rheumatic Fever, and Certain Other Conditions: A Study in Clinical Physiology," *Archives of Internal Medicine*, vol. 85, 1950 (with Philip S. Hench, Charles H. Slocumb, and Howard F. Polley).

AUTOBIOGRAPHY: *Cortisone: Memoirs of a Hormone Hunter*, 1971.

Secondary

Clapesattle, Helen C. *The Mayo Brothers*. Minneapolis: University of Minnesota Press, 1941. A sprightly account is presented of the people associated with the Mayo Clinic, many of whom influenced Kendall's career profoundly. Kendall's success in isolating thyroxine and his early efforts to isolate the adrenocortical hormones are also covered.

Fieser, Louis F., and Mary Fieser. *Steroids*. New York: Reinhold, 1959. In this advanced text on steroids, Fieser and Fieser devote a comprehensive chapter on the chemistry of the adrenocortical hormones.

Kendall, Edward C. "Symposium on Thyroxine." *Mayo Clinic Proceedings* 39 (1964). Commemorating the fiftieth anniversary of the isolation of thyroxine, Kendall recalls his efforts to isolate and synthesize thyroxine. The English biochemist Rosalind Pitt-Russell discusses the successful effort of Sir Charles Harington in synthesizing this hormone. Other noted scientists review its stereochemistry, biochemistry, metabolism, site and action, and physiologic effects.

Sanders, Howard J. "Arthritis and Arthritis Drugs." *Chemical and Engineering News* 46 (August 12, 1968). An excellent account is given of the search for drugs to treat arthritis. The author claims that the discovery of the efficacy of cortisone "touched off the greatest burst of excitement in the entire history of drug therapy."

Shoppee, Charles W. *Chemistry of the Steroids*. 2d ed. Washington, D.C.: Butterworth, 1964. Shoppee was a collaborator of Reichstein in the study of the natural products. His presentation of the cortical hormones is from the vantage point of the Swiss group. This book is also used as an advanced text.

Youcha, Geradine. "The Use and Abuse of Cortisone." *Runner's World*, March, 1984. Use of anabolic steroids among athletes is both illegal and hazardous. Although the use of cortisone is not illegal, it can also be abused and dangerous. Examples are cited in which the chronic use of cortisone for relief of pain and inflammation is a mixed blessing to athletes. The relief produced may mask stress fractures, which when left untreated can result in irreparable damage.

Leland J. Chinn

1950

Physiology or Medicine

Edward Calvin Kendall, United States
Tadeus Reichstein, Poland and Switzerland
Philip Showalter Hench, United States

Chemistry

Otto Paul Hermann Diels, West Germany
Kurt Alder, West Germany

Physics

Cecil Frank Powell, Great Britain

Literature

Bertrand Russell, Great Britain

Peace

Ralph Bunche, United States

TADEUS REICHSTEIN
1950

Born: Włocławek, Poland; July 20, 1897

Nationality: Polish; later, Swiss
Areas of concentration: Organic and pharmaceutical chemistry

Reichstein's work complemented that of Edward Calvin Kendall and Philip S. Hench, and helped in the development of cortisone as a treatment for rheumatoid arthritis. It made possible a more complete understanding of the mechanism of action and means of production of cortisone and other hormones

The Award

Presentation

On December 10, 1950, Professor Göran Liljestrand of the Royal Caroline Institute in Stockholm, Sweden, spoke to an audience that included, among others, His Majesty King Gustav VI of Sweden and the three scientists who were to receive from the king the award of the 1950 Nobel Prize in Physiology or Medicine. Edward Calvin Kendall, Tadeus Reichstein, and Philip S. Hench were to be honored for their discoveries relating to the structure and biological effects of certain hormones found in the outer shell, or cortex, of the adrenal glands of humans as well as animals. The adrenal glands are located in the back, just over the kidneys. Liljestrand began by tracing the history of medical knowledge of the adrenal gland from the anatomists of the Renaissance period up through the English physician Thomas Addison, who first showed the relationship between the symptoms of what is now called Addison's disease and the adrenals. In the search for biologically active chemical constituents of the adrenals, the first discovery was that of the hormone adrenaline, which was isolated from the adrenal medulla and soon synthesized. Adrenaline, although possessing profound physiological effects, failed to relieve the symptoms of Addison's disease. Beginning in about the 1920's, research on adrenal hormones began to concentrate on the cortex of the glands. Crude extracts of the cortex, when injected into animals dying from adrenal insufficiency, relieved the symptoms.

By 1934, Kendall and his coworkers at the Mayo Clinic in Rochester, Minnesota, had achieved the preparation of a crystalline extract from adrenal cortex, but it proved to be a complex mixture of closely related compounds—some inactive, others active in various ways. It was the task of Kendall, Reichstein, and many coworkers to separate this mixture and chemically identify its components. The cortical compounds were eventually found to be twenty-nine in number. To Reichstein went the credit for first isolation of four active hormones from the adrenal cortex, the first synthesis of one of them, and the proof of the chemical structure of the compounds which were shown to be steroids with the same four-ringed structure characteristic of several other biologically important materials, such as sex hormones, cholesterol, and vitamin D.

Nobel lecture

On December 11, 1950, Professor Tadeus Reichstein delivered his Nobel Prize lecture, "Chemistry of the Adrenal Cortex Hormones." The work he described had begun in 1934 and involved the extraction of the hormones from large amounts (1,000 kilograms) of the adrenal glands of cattle. The first stage of concentration produced about 1 kilogram of extract, which proved active when tested on animals. The amounts of material involved initially required the use of industrial-scale equipment, but later stages could be completed on a laboratory scale. Careful use of different liquid solvents (water, benzene, ether, and chloroform) made it possible to reduce the kilogram of extract to 25 grams (about 1 ounce) of material. A special reagent was then applied that had the ability to react selectively with the type of compound known as a ketone. The 25-gram sample was thus divided into two parts: a ketone group, of which about 7 or 8 grams contained most of the biological activity, and a nonketone group, of which 15 or 16 grams were biologically inactive. Final separation of the complex mixture of hormones was accomplished by a sensitive separation technique called chromatography. In this method, the mixture to be separated is mixed with a solvent, and the mixture is allowed to travel downward through a column of dry, finely powdered aluminum oxide held in a vertical glass tube. Each component of the mixture interacts in a slightly different way with the aluminum oxide. As more solvent is added at the top of the column, the components travel down at slightly different rates and may be collected separately. By these methods, Reichstein in Switzerland and Kendall in the United States were able to isolate and purify twenty-nine different pure compounds from the adrenal extracts.

Critical reception

The award of the Nobel Prize was hailed by *The New York Times* as an example of the application of basic scientific research for the betterment of humankind. Naturally, the contributions of Kendall and Hench received more attention, since they were Americans, and also because the chemical work that Reichstein had done was harder for the layperson to appreciate. *The New York Times* reported that, upon hearing of his award, Reichstein had remarked that he would now devote himself to the search for a way to make cortisone cheaper and more abundant.

Newsweek magazine also briefly noted the Nobel Prizes in its November 6, 1950, issue, but gave much greater coverage to the death of King Gustav V of Sweden, who was to have presented the prizes in Stockholm in December, 1950.

The British journal *Nature* devoted a half-page in its November 11, 1950, issue to coverage of the Nobel Prize in Physiology or Medicine. After describing the contributions of the three honorees, the author paid tribute to Reichstein by noting that "[t]he scientific papers coming from Professor Reichstein's laboratory during the past two decades form a remarkable record of technical and theoretical achievement in a field of complex chemistry." Similar sentiments were expressed by the leadership of the Swiss Chemical Society in 1987 in commemorating Reichstein's ninetieth birthday in the August 7 issue (volume 70) of *Helvetica Chimica Acta*. The article praises Reichstein for the fame his work has brought to both Swiss universities with which he was associated, and to Swiss chemistry in general.

Biography

Tadeus Reichstein was born on July 20, 1897, in Włocławek, Poland (located on the Vistula River about eighty miles northwest of Warsaw). He was the eldest son of Isidor and Gustava Reichstein. The family soon moved to Kiev in the Ukraine, where his father was employed as an engineer. In 1914, the Reichsteins took up Swiss citizenship and resided in Zurich, having spent some time in Berlin first.

Reichstein studied first at the Oberrealschule (similar to a junior college) and then at the Eidgenössiche Technische Hochschule (federal technical college) in Zurich, from which he was graduated in 1920 with a degree in chemical engineering. After a short period of work in a factory, Reichstein returned to the technical college, which awarded him a doctorate in organic chemistry in 1922. His doctoral dissertation was published in 1924 and was based on research carried out under the direction of Professor Hermann Staudinger, who won the Nobel Prize in Chemistry in 1953. Reichstein continued to work in Staudinger's laboratory on a project that involved isolating and identifying the flavor and aroma-causing chemicals in roasted coffee. This work is described briefly in Staudinger's memoirs. In 1927, Reichstein married Henriette Louise Quarles van Ufford. The Reichsteins have one daughter, Ruth.

Reichstein continued his research at the Eidgenössiche Technische Hochschule after Staudinger left for Germany, and eventually became a faculty member there. He became interested in sugars and in the recently discovered ascorbic acid (vitamin C). His scientific reputation grew considerably after he published a synthesis of vitamin C in 1933, and he was promoted to assistant professor the next year. The research that led to his Nobel award began in the early 1930's and consisted of the extraction, purification, and identification of some twenty-seven different steroids from the adrenal cortex.

In 1938, Reichstein moved to the University of Basel as director of the Pharmaceutical Institute, and in 1946, he became director of the organic chemistry division there. He continued to direct research on extraction and identification of the chemical constituents of natural products, particularly African plants, and became interested in cardiac glycosides (plant-derived compounds useful in treating heart disease). In 1947, two of Reichstein's assistants actually spent nine months in Africa to obtain botanical specimens. By his retirement in 1967, Reichstein (alone or in collaboration) had contributed more than five hundred research papers to scientific journals. He received many honors besides the Nobel Prize, including honorary doctorates from the Sorbonne (1947) and from the universities of Abidgan, Basel, Geneva, and Leeds. He was also awarded the Marcel Benoist Award (1947) and the Cameron Award (1951), as well as medals from the Royal Society in London (1968) and the Dale Endocrinal Society. His professional affiliations are exceedingly numerous and include memberships in the Royal Society (United Kingdom) and the

National Academy of Sciences (United States). He continued to be active in research until 1987.

Scientific Career

Tadeus Reichstein devoted a long and productive scientific career to graduate-level teaching and chemical research. He is best known for his painstaking studies of the complex mixture of steroid hormones produced by the adrenal cortex. In this work, tiny quantities of the hormones were extracted from one-ton lots of cattle adrenal glands. Chemical and physical methods of separation and purification were developed, so that individual hormone compounds could be isolated and have their molecular structures determined. The biological activity of the compounds was also investigated by animal testing, when amounts were sufficient.

Of the twenty-nine steroid compounds found by Reichstein or others in the adrenal cortex, only six were shown to be biologically active. Animals were surgically deprived of their adrenal glands and began to suffer the symptoms of adrenal insufficiency; in humans this condition is known as Addison's disease. (President John F. Kennedy suffered from this condition.) The active compounds, when administered to the adrenalectomized animals, were able to relieve some of the symptoms of adrenal insufficiency and prolong the lives of the animals. Some of the adrenal hormones became valuable because of other effects. Aldosterone, on the structure and synthesis of which Reichstein published papers in 1953, has powerful effects on water balance and sodium-potassium balance and is now valuable in medicine.

Once the chemical structures of the biologically active compounds had become known, Reichstein was able to pinpoint those aspects of the molecular structure that were essential for activity. In order to improve the availability and lower the cost of the hormones, Reichstein and others tried various schemes for chemical synthesis. A promising synthesis was designed that utilized as starting material a fairly plentiful compound called desoxycholic acid, found in ox bile. Reichstein realized that certain African plants of the genus *Strophanthus* contain compounds called glycosides, which are sugar derivatives of steroidlike compounds that are closely related structurally to the desired hormones. Since the sugar part of these glycoside molecules can easily be split off, the glycosides represented an attractive alternative to ox bile as starting materials for the synthesis of adrenal hormones. Although Reichstein and others were able to determine several syntheses of cortisone starting from plant-derived materials, other routes remain more attractive economically.

Plant glycosides became a major subject of research for Reichstein after he won the Nobel Prize, and his series of numbered publications, *Glycosides and Aglycones*, continued after Reichstein had reached ninety years of age. In the research described in these papers, plant material is made available by a collecting expedition undertaken by Reichstein, his coworkers, or sometimes by others. This material may consist of seeds, flowers, or leaves, and may have been collected in diverse places, such as Africa or closer to home in Ireland. The material is treated with solvents, and the extracts are carefully separated by chromatography. Dozens of components are found, of which some are known compounds, some new. The new compounds are then studied to determine their molecular structures.

Certain glycosides are potent drugs that affect the heart and are invaluable in treating heart disease. Immense effort has gone into the study of so-called cardiac glycosides in the hope that their mode of action can be understood and that a relationship can be found between the chemical structure of the drug and its biological action. Reichstein's work (and the work of many others) contributed the basic chemical information that must precede the work of the physiologists and medical researchers. The medical profession needs a range of heart drugs with different degrees of strength and persistence of action. This need can be met only by continually testing new compounds, many of which come from plants.

Insects feed on plants and fight with predators such as birds. In these activities, glycosides may be involved. Reichstein found compounds in some plants which acted as natural insecticides, tending to protect the plant from marauding insects. Plant-derived insecticides, such as rotenone and pyrethrins, are of considerable importance in agricultural applications. Here again, the structure must be found and an attempt made to study the mode of action. A great potential advantage of "natural" insecticides is their specificity of target and greater safety in the environment.

In one of his publications, Reichstein shows how a certain grasshopper uses cardiac glycosides as part of a defense mechanism. If a bird eats this grasshopper, it gets sick and learns never to eat such an insect again. Also, the grasshopper can spray an irritating liquid from special glands to repel other insects. Chemistry thus contributes to the understanding of insect behavior and predator-prey relationships.

In his work on natural products, Reichstein contributed much knowledge of value in botany. It is often difficult to tell plants apart. Incomplete or anecdotal descriptions of plants often cause confusion when others attempt to find the same plant again. Even the most minute physical descriptions can be subjective or ambiguous. Chemical taxonomy, a field to which Reichstein contributed, is an approach to recognizing and characterizing plants by chemical analysis of their components and by seeking to identify the biosynthetic pathways used by the plant species for production of these components.

In addition to the work already mentioned, Reichstein contributed papers on furan derivatives, sugars, bile acids and derivatives, and toxins from plants and from toads. Some of the toad poisons are used by primitive people; they turn out to be fairly closely related chemically to the cardiac glycosides. Reichstein contributed greatly to the fields in which he worked. His output has been tremendous in quantity and quality and has facilitated many applications of drugs in medicine, particularly the adrenal hormones. By showing the wealth of biologically active compounds that come from plants, his work makes clear how vital the tropical forests of the earth are. Even with the herculean efforts of Reichstein and scientists like him, only a fraction of the estimated 200,000 plant species have been adequately studied, and with deforestation proceeding daily, the potential of many of these species may never be known before they are overtaken by extinction.

Bibliography

Primary

ADRENAL HORMONES: "Die Hormone der Nebennierenrinde," in *Handbuch der biologischen Arbeitsmethoden*, edited by E. Abderhalden, vol. 5, 1938, pp. 1367-1439; "The Hormones of the Adrenal Cortex," in *Vitamins and Hormones*, edited by R. S. Harris and K. V. Thimann, 1943 (with C. W. Shoppee); "Chemistry of the Adrenal Cortex Hormones," in *Nobel Lectures: Physiology or Medicine, 1942-1962*, 1966; "Isolierung eines neuen kristallisierten Hormons aus Nebennieren mit besonders hoher Wirksamkeit auf den Mineralstoffwechsel, *Experientia*, vol. 9, 1953, p. 333 (with R. Neher, S. Simpson, J. Tait, J. von Euw, and A. Wettstein.

CARDIAC GLYCOSIDES: "Cardenolide (herzwirksame Glykoside) als Abwehrstoeffe bei Insekten," *Naturwissenschaftliche Rundschau*, vol. 20, 1967, p. 499; "Cardenolid und Pregnanglykoside," *Naturwissenschaften*, vol. 54, 1967, pp. 53-67.

COFFEE AROMA: "Das Aroma des geroestete Kaffees," *Experientia*, vol. 6, 1950, p. 280 (with H. Staudinger); "Über das Kaffeearoma," *Angewandte Chemie*, vol. 62, 1950, p. 292 (with H. Staudinger); "Das Kaffeearoma," *CIBA-Zeitschrift*, no. 127, 1951, pp. 4692-4694 (with H. Staudinger); "The Aroma of Coffee," *Perfumery and Essential Oil Record*, vol. 46, 1955, pp. 86-88 (with H. Staudinger).

INSECT DEFENSE MECHANISMS: "Cardenolides (Heart-Poisons) in a Grasshopper Feeding on Milkweeds," *Nature*, vol. 214, 1967, pp. 35-39 (with J. von Euw, L. Fischelson, J. A. Parsons, and M. Rothschild); "Aristolochic Acid-I in the Swallowtail Butterfly," *Israel Journal of Chemistry*, vol. 6, 1968, pp. 659-670 (with J. von Euw and M. Rothschild).

VITAMIN C: "Synthesis of *d*- and *l*-Ascorbic Acid (Vitamin-C)," *Nature*, vol. 132, 1933, p. 280 (with A. Gruessner and R. Oppenhauer); "Synopsis of the Chemical and Biological Effect of the Ascorbic Acid Group," *Festschrift Emil C. Barell* (special issue of *Helvetica Chimica Acta*), 1936, pp. 107-138 (with V. Demole).

Secondary

Block, Maxine, ed. *Current Biography Yearbook*. New York: H. W. Wilson, 1951. This reference contains extensive biographical information for the period up to 1951. Also included is material about Hench and Kendall and their contributions to the understanding and use of cortical hormones. It is mentioned that Reichstein and Leopold Ružička (winner of the Nobel Prize in Chemistry for 1939) traveled together to the United States in 1946 on a six-week lecture tour sponsored by the American-Swiss Foundation for Scientific Exchange.

Davis, C. S., and R. P. Halliday. "Cardiac Drugs." In *Medicinal Chemistry*, edited by A. Burger. New York: John Wiley & Sons, 1970. The medical uses of cardiac glycosides are described in this chapter. Some of these compounds were first identified by Reichstein.

Fieser, L. F., and M. Fieser. *Topics in Organic Chemistry*. New York: Reinhold, 1963. Louis Fieser, professor of chemistry at Harvard and an authority on steroids, was in close touch with the cortisone work at the Mayo Clinic. A historical account of the work on adrenocortical hormones is given, together with details on the syntheses worked out by Reichstein, Kendall, and others.

Oesper, Ralph. "Tadeus Reichstein." *Journal of Chemical Education* 26 (October, 1949): 529-530. This short article traces Reichstein's pre-Nobel career (Reichstein once worked in a flashlight factory). Many other biographical works, such as *Current Biographies* and *Who's Who*, cite this article.

Rodig, O. R. "Adrenal Cortex Hormones." In *Medicinal Chemistry*, edited by A. Burger. New York: John Wiley & Sons, 1970. An account of the medical uses of the adrenal cortex hormones.

Schlessinger, Bernard S., and June H. Schlessinger, eds. *Who's Who of Nobel Prizewinners*. Phoenix, Ariz.: Oryx Press, 1986. Contains a short biographical note which mentions some of Reichstein's honors and cites some of his publications.

Sterkowicz, S. "Tadeusz Reichstein: A Polish Winner of the Nobel Prize." *Materia Medica Polona* 20, no. 3 (1988): 201-204. The author has corresponded with Reichstein and obtained some unpublished notes, which are cited here. Also contains several photographs, including one taken in 1987. There is a list classifying Reichstein's 637 published works into ten general subject areas.

Stevenson, Lloyd G. *Nobel Prizewinners in Medicine and Physiology, 1901-1950*. New York: Abelard-Schuman, 1953. Contains a brief account of Reichstein's Nobel Prize work; draws on the review article by Reichstein and Shoppee in *Vitamins and Hormones*. The use of cortisone in treating arthritis is mentioned.

John R. Phillips

1950

Physiology or Medicine

Edward Calvin Kendall, United States
Tadeus Reichstein, Poland and Switzerland
Philip Showalter Hench, United States

Chemistry

Otto Paul Hermann Diels, West Germany
Kurt Alder, West Germany

Physics

Cecil Frank Powell, Great Britain

Literature

Bertrand Russell, Great Britain

Peace

Ralph Bunche, United States

PHILIP SHOWALTER HENCH
1950

Born: Pittsburgh, Pennsylvania; February 28, 1896
Died: Ocho Rios, Jamaica; March 30, 1965
Nationality: American
Areas of concentration: Endocrinology and pathology

Hench envisioned and directed the first administration of cortisone and pituitary adrenocorticotropic hormone (ACTH) to patients with rheumatoid arthritis and other rheumatic diseases

The Award

Presentation

Göran Liljestrand, a professor at the Royal Caroline Medico-Surgical Institute, represented the medical faculty of the Royal Caroline Institute in delivering the presentation address on December 10, 1950, before King Gustav VI Adolf gave the Nobel medals and scrolls to Philip Showalter Hench, Edward Calvin Kendall, and Tadeus Reichstein. Liljestrand began his address by crediting the Italian anatomist Eustachi with first describing the adrenals in 1563. The function of the adrenal glands was unknown at that time and remained unknown as late as 1854, when the German anatomist Ruolf Kölliker reviewed the more detailed structure of the adrenals. In 1855, the English physician Thomas Addison published his observations concerning a rare disease that "made its appearance in persons the greater part of whose adrenals was destroyed."

Liljestrand continued by describing early efforts to obtain extracts from the adrenals, leading to the production from the cortex of "a more or less pure extract" that was called "the cortin." Liljestrand explained the efforts of Kendall, Reichstein, and other investigators, who identified cortin as "a mixture of different substances closely related to one another" and then proceeded to separate these different substances, including "the best known of them all, first named Compound E and now called cortisone or cortone."

After the synthesis of cortisone had been achieved, Liljestrand explained, clinical testing was directed toward chronic rheumatoid arthritis. Hench "had been studying the improvements in chronic troubles in the joints which made their appearance during pregnancy or in cases of jaundice." Liljestrand explained how Hench ultimately associated these effects with the adrenals. In 1949, he said, Hench and his coworkers "published their experiences in respect of the dramatic effects of cortisone in cases of chronic rheumatoid arthritis." Liljestrand further explained that "similar results were obtained with a preparation from the anterior lobe of the pituitary, the so-called ACTH."

Liljestrand characterized the contributions of Hench, Kendall, and Reichstein as an example of close cooperation among representatives of physiology, biochemistry, and clinical medicine, as well as among scientists from different countries. Liljestrand concluded that Hench's "brilliant investigations in respect of the beneficial effects of pregnancy and jaundice on rheumatoid arthritis have been the starting-point for the famous discovery . . . that these diseases and some others are favorably influenced by the hormones from the adrenal cortex."

Nobel lecture

On December 11, 1950, Hench delivered his Nobel lecture, entitled "The Reversibility of Certain Rheumatic and Non-Rheumatic Conditions by the Use of Cortisone or of the Pituitary Adrenocorticotropic Hormone." He discussed "three general aspects of cortisone and pituitary adrenocorticotropic hormone (ACTH)."

In the first part of his lecture, Hench described in detail the "development of the theory which led to the use of cortisone and ACTH in rheumatic diseases." He noted pessimistic earlier opinions on the prognosis of rheumatoid arthritis, then described his observations concerning the ameliorating effect of jaundice on rheumatoid arthritis. Hench noted his early speculations regarding this effect, their therapeutic implications, his attempts to reproduce the phenomenon of relief, and his early speculations concerning "antirheumatic substance X." Hench described a similar ameliorating effect of pregnancy and evaluated the relationship between the antirheumatic agent of jaundice and that of pregnancy. These observations led to speculation that antirheumatic substance X could be a bisexual hormone, and ultimately to speculation that antirheumatic substance X could be an adrenal hormone.

Hench described his decision, with Kendall, in January of 1941, "to administer to rheumatoid patients the adrenal cortical substance, 17-hydroxy-11-dehydrocorticosterone, whenever it might become available." This plan "remained attractive through the several years of waiting" until the adrenal cortical substance, then called compound E and later called cortisone, could be obtained in sufficient quantities. Hench described the first administration of cortisone to a rheumatoid patient on September 21, 1948, followed by the first administration of ACTH to a rheumatoid patient on February 8, 1949.

In the second part of his lecture, Hench characterized "the present status of cortisone and ACTH in general medicine." He explained the clinical effects of these hormones, noted the results of hormonal discontinuance, described their undesirable side effects, and considered their possible potentiation. Hench described gaps in knowledge concerning the administration of cortisone and ACTH and discussed the search for the optimal method of administration, including possible oral administration. He discussed the use of cortisone and ACTH against other conditions, speculated on the mode of action, and noted the search for substitutes.

In the third part of his lecture, Hench briefly described "requirements for the orderly development of cortisone and ACTH as therapeutic agents." He explained the problems in producing cortisone and ACTH, and he emphasized the need to develop a rational method of administration. Hench reviewed the characteristics of antirheumatic substance X and noted that "cortisone appears to possess most of these characteristics." Hench concluded by observing that cortisone and ACTH are like unframed pictures and that the boundaries defining either their full potentialities or their limitations had yet to be established. Hench explained, however, that "whatever the immediate or future destiny of these hormones may be, in the field of practical therapeutics they already have demonstrated clearly the potential reversibility of many disease processes."

Critical reception

The separation, characterization, and synthesis of cortisone proceeded slowly during two decades of research by Kendall, Reichstein, and other investigators. When they were finally available for clinical research, however, the application of cortisone and ACTH to the treatment of rheumatoid arthritis and other rheumatic diseases proceeded with remarkable speed. Public reaction focused on the basic research of Kendall and Reichstein and on the observations of Hench concerning the effects of jaundice and pregnancy on rheumatoid arthritis and other rheumatic diseases.

"Hormone Work Wins Nobel Prize for Two Americans and a Swiss" was the headline of a page-one article in *The New York Times* on October 27, 1950. The article described the independent efforts of Kendall and Reichstein to produce compound E, or cortisone, and explained that "Dr. Hench, a rheumatism specialist at the Mayo Clinic, . . . suggested its use on his rheumatic patients." The article observed that "the treatment was startlingly effective." An article in the November 6, 1950, issue of *Time* magazine described the independent reporting of compound E by Kendall and Reichstein in 1936. "Years passed, during which this hormone had little practical value," the article noted, then explained that Hench "directed the first injections of cortisone to human victims of rheumatoid arthritis" late in 1948. The article concluded that "the results were dramatic. Suddenly, a vast new field of medical research was opened."

Nature magazine reported the award in an article on November 11, 1950: "The award can be regarded as a recognition of the work which has been done leading to the dramatic opening of a new field of scientific medical research—that of rheumatoid arthritis and related diseases." The article explained that "early in 1949, Hench, Kendall, Slocumb and Polley . . . reported on 'the effects of the hormone of the adrenal cortex (17-hydroxy-11-dehydrocorticosterone: compound E) and of pituitary adrenocorticotropic hormone on rheumatoid arthritis.' This was followed soon after by a report of the effects of compound E on rheumatic fever." The article observed that "Dr. Hench has long been a recognized authority on rheumatic diseases" and explained that "the genesis of the discovery of the activity of cortisone is to be found in his belief that an endocrine influence was active in cases of remission of rheumatoid arthritis, for example, in pregnancy."

Biography

Philip Showalter Hench, the son of Jacob Bixler Hench and Clara Showalter Hench, was born in Pittsburgh, Pennsylvania, on February 28, 1896. Hench grew up in the

Pittsburgh area and attended local schools. In 1916, he received his bachelor of arts degree from Lafayette College in Eaton, Pennsylvania. Hench began his medical education at the University of Pittsburgh in 1916. He enlisted in the Medical Corps of the United States Army in 1917, but he was transferred to the reserve corps to complete his medical education. Hench received his doctorate in medicine from the University of Pittsburgh in 1920. (Later, in 1928 and 1929, he studied at Freiburg University in Freiburg, Germany, and at Ludwig-Maximilians-Universität and the von Müller Clinic in Munich, Germany.) He received a master of science degree in internal medicine from the University of Minnesota in 1931.

Hench was an intern at Saint Francis Hospital in Pittsburgh from 1920 to 1921. He participated in advanced training as a fellow of the Mayo Foundation in Rochester, Minnesota, from 1921 to 1923. He served as first assistant in medicine at the Mayo Clinic from 1923 to 1925 and as an associate in the division of medicine from 1925 to 1926. In 1926, he became staff consultant and head of the department of rheumatic diseases at the Mayo Clinic. Hench also served as a consultant at Saint Mary's Hospital in Rochester.

Hench married Mary Genevieve Kahler on July 14, 1927; they had four children, Mary Showalter, Philip Kahler, Susan Kahler, and John Bixler. Hench was appointed an instructor at the University of Minnesota (Mayo Foundation) in 1928. He became an assistant professor in 1932 and an associate professor in 1935. He was promoted to full professor in 1947. During World War II, Hench served as chief of the medical service and director of the Army's Rheumatism Center at the Army and Navy General Hospital in Hot Springs, Arkansas. Hench retired from both the Mayo Clinic and the Mayo Foundation in 1957.

Hench was a vice president in the Kahler Corporation, founded by his father-in-law, John Henry Kahler. Hench was an authority on medical history; his personal interests also included music, photography, and tennis. He was a Republican and a Presbyterian. Hench died while vacationing with his wife in Ocho Rios, Jamaica, on March 30, 1965, one month after his sixty-ninth birthday.

Scientific Career

"Cortisone is the fireman who puts out the fire, it is not the carpenter who rebuilds the damaged house": Hench used this analogy to describe both the power and limitations of cortisone for the treatment of rheumatoid arthritis and other rheumatic diseases. The "fire" of rheumatoid arthritis burned out of control and the prognosis for treatment was pessimistic when Hench first began his work with rheumatic diseases in 1923. Cortisone would ultimately provide dramatic relief from the pain and suffering endured by patients with rheumatoid arthritis and other rheumatic diseases.

On April 1, 1929, Hench evaluated a patient who had suffered from rheumatoid arthritis for the previous four years. The patient explained how he had developed jaundice the previous week; a day later, the pain and swelling in his joints began to diminish. An examination of this patient demonstrated no symptoms of rheumatoid arthritis. The patient's relief from rheumatoid arthritis lasted five months in his feet and eight months in his hands. Between 1929 and 1934, Hench observed sixteen patients with rheumatoid arthritis who obtained similar temporary relief when they developed different types and degrees of jaundice. These observations led to the conclusion that rheumatoid arthritis was potentially a reversible disease. Hench presented these observations in a report that he read before the Second Conference on Rheumatic Diseases of the American Committee for the Control of Rheumatism, in Milwaukee, Wisconsin, on June 12, 1933.

Hench reported on further observations and attempts to reproduce the phenomenon associated with jaundice in a paper that he read before the Fifth Conference on Rheumatic Diseases held by the American Rheumatism Association in Atlantic City, New Jersey, on June 7, 1937 (reported in *The Journal of the American Medical Association* on October 30, 1937). His observations concerning jaundice suggested to Hench that the agent responsible for relieving rheumatoid arthritis was a hepatic or biliary constituent, which he named "antirheumatic substance X." Between 1931 and 1938, Hench studied the beneficial effect of pregnancy on rheumatoid arthritis. Jaundice and pregnancy were also noted sometimes to provide temporary relief from nonrheumatic conditions such as hay fever, asthma, sensitivity to eggs, migraine, and psoriasis. During the 1930's, Hench studied the effect of jaundice on rheumatic diseases, evaluated various types of jaundice associated with the phenomenon, considered the role of the liver in the pathogenesis of rheumatoid arthritis, and reviewed experimental therapy with hepatic, billiary, and related substances.

By the late 1930's, Hench had radically changed his ideas concerning the nature of substance X. Bilirubin and unisexual (female) hormones both had been ruled out as possibilities, and it was concluded that substance X was probably not a disintegration product from damaged liver. Substance X was conjectured to be a biological compound specific in nature and function, and of which the rheumatoid arthritis patient did not have enough. Hench began to suspect that substance X might be a bisexual steroid hormone. Among the substances that he considered in 1938 was whole adrenal cortex extract, then called "cortin."

Harold L. Mason, Charles S. Myers, and Edward C. Kendall, from the division of biochemistry of the Mayo Foundation, isolated compound E, which was later renamed cortisone, in 1935, after five years of attempting to extract hormones from the adrenal cortex. Kendall became Hench's chief collaborator after 1938; they were initially unaware that substance X was actually Kendall's compound E. Hench's perspective on substance X, combined with Kendall's experience with compound E, led to their decision in January of 1941 to administer compound E to patients with rheumatoid arthritis. Unfortunately, only a small amount of natural compound E had been extracted by January, 1941; synthesis of compound E had not yet been attempted, and adequate amounts of compound E would not become available until 1948.

A method to synthesize Kendall's compound E was developed in 1947 by Lewis H. Sarett, from the research laboratories of Merck & Co. Sufficient quantities of compound E were not available for clinical testing in humans until May, 1948. On September 4, 1948, Hench and Kendall sent a letter to Merck & Co. requesting a quantity of compound E sufficient for one patient. A small quantity of compound E was received and was first administered to a patient with rheumatoid arthritis on September 21, 1948. Hench and Kendall, assisted by Charles H. Slocumb and Howard F. Polley, administered daily doses of compound E to this first patient, who was markedly improved within three days and continued to improve until the daily doses were reduced. Similar results were obtained in four more patients with rheumatoid arthritis who received compound E from September, 1948, to January, 1949. In January of 1949, a supply of adrenocorticotropic hormone (ACTH, which stimulates the release of cortisone from the adrenal cortex) was requested from Armour & Co. and was first administered to a patient with rheumatoid arthritis on February 8, 1949. Thereafter, cortisone (compound E), ACTH, or both were administered to a series of patients with severe or moderately severe rheumatoid arthritis.

Hench presented the Heberden oration before the Heberden Society of London on October 15, 1948, in which he presented observations and research leading up to the use of cortisone and ACTH in the treatment of rheumatoid arthritis. In April of 1949, Hench, Kendall, Slocumb, and Polley presented a preliminary report concerning the applications of cortisone and ACTH to the treatment of rheumatoid arthritis, which was first published in the *Proceedings of the Staff Meetings of the Mayo Clinic* on April 13, 1949. Hench described the status of cortisone and ACTH in general medicine in an address to the Royal Society of Medicine on October 10, 1950; the address was published in the *Proceedings of the Royal Society of Medicine* later in 1950. Less than three weeks after this address, while returning to the United States by ship, Hench learned that he had been selected to share the Nobel Prize with Kendall and Reichstein.

From 1949 to 1950, Hench served as chairman of the Arthritis and Rheumatism Study Section of the National Institutes of Health of the United States Public Health Service. From 1950 to 1953, he was a member of the Advisory Council of the National Institute of Arthritis and Metabolic Diseases. He also served as an expert consultant to the surgeon general of the army after 1946. Hench was a member of the Medical and Scientific Committee of the Arthritis and Rheumatism Foundation, a member of the Advisory Committee of the National Research Council, and vice president of the board of managers of the Walter Reed Memorial Association.

The Heberden Medal was awarded to Hench in London in 1942. He shared the Lasker Award from the American Public Health Association with Kendall in 1949. Hench shared a scientific award from the American Pharmaceutical Manufacturers Association with George Thorn from Harvard University in 1950. That same year, he also received the Passano Foundation Award and the Page One Award from the Newspaper Guild of New York for the discovery and development of cortisone. In 1951, Hench received the Criss Award, the Special Citation from the American Rheumatism Association, and the Award of Merit from the Masonic Foundation for Medical Research and Human Welfare. Honorary doctorates were awarded to Hench by Lafayette College, Washington and Jefferson College, the University of Pittsburgh, and other institutions.

Hench was a fellow of the American Medical Association and the American College of Physicians. He was a founding member of the American Rheumatism Association, serving as an executive councillor from 1933 to 1941 and as president from 1940 to 1941. Hench was a member of the American Committee for the Control of Rheumatism, serving as secretary from 1931 through 1938. He was an honorary member of rheumatism societies in Argentina, Brazil, Canada, Denmark, and Spain. He was a member or honorary member of numerous other scientific organizations, among them the American Academy of Arts and Sciences, the Royal Society of Medicine, and the American Society of Clinical Investigation.

Hench observed the beneficial effects of jaundice and pregnancy on rheumatoid arthritis and other rheumatic diseases, and he attributed these beneficial effects to antirheumatic substance X, which he later associated with cortisone from the adrenal cortex. Hench directed the first administration of cortisone and pituitary adrenocorticotropic hormone (ACTH) to patients with rheumatoid arthritis and other rheumatic diseases.

Bibliography

Primary

MEDICINE: "The Analgesic Effect of Hepatitis and Jaundice in Chronic Arthritis, Fibrositis, and Sciatic Pain," *Annals of Internal Medicine*, vol. 7, 1934, pp. 1278-1294; "Effect of Jaundice on Chronic Infectious (Atrophic) Arthritis and on Primary Fibrositis," *Archives of Internal Medicine*, vol. 61, 1938, pp. 451-480; "The Ameliorating Effect of Pregnancy on Chronic Atrophic (Infectious Rheumatoid) Arthritis, Fibrositis, and Intermittent Hydrarthrosis," *Proceedings of the Staff Meetings of the Mayo Clinic*, vol. 13, 1938, pp. 161-167; "The Advantages of Hepatic Injury and Jaundice in Certain Conditions, Notably the Rheumatic Diseases," *The Medical Clinics of North America*, vol. 24, 1940, pp. 1209-1237; "The Potential Reversibility of Rheumatoid Arthritis," *Annals of the Rheumatic Diseases*, vol. 8, 1949, pp. 90-96; "The Effect of a Hormone of the Adrenal Cortex (17-Hydroxy-11-Dehydrocorticosterone: Compound E) and of Pituitary Adrenocorticotrophic Hormone on Rheumatoid Arthritis," *Annals of the Rheumatic Diseases*, vol. 8, 1949, pp. 97-104 (with Edward C. Kendall, Charles H. Slocumb, and Howard F. Polley); "The Effects of the Adrenal Cortical Hormone 17-Hydroxy-11-Dehydrocorticosterone (Compound E) on the Acute Phase of Rheumatic Fever," *Proceedings of the Staff Meetings of the Mayo Clinic*, vol. 24, 1949, pp. 277-297 (with Charles H. Slocumb, Arlie R. Barnes, Harry L. Smith, Howard F. Polley, and Edward C. Kendall); "The Effect of a Hormone of the Adrenal Cortex, Cortisone (17-Hydroxy-11-Dehydrocorticosterone: Compound E), and of Pituitary Adrenocorticotropic Hormone on Rheumatoid Arthritis and Acute Rheumatic Fever," *Transactions of the Association of American Physicians*, vol. 62, 1949, pp. 64-80 (with Edward C. Kendall, Charles H. Slocumb, and Howard F.

Polley); "Effects of Cortisone Acetate and Pituitary ACTH on Rheumatoid Arthritis, Rheumatic Fever, and Certain Other Conditions," *Archives of Internal Medicine*, vol. 85, 1950, pp. 545-666 (with Edward C. Kendall, Charles H. Slocumb, and Howard F. Polley); "The Antirheumatic Effects of Cortisone and Pituitary ACTH," *Transactions and Studies of the College of Physicians of Philadelphia*, vol. 18, 1950, pp. 95-102 (with Edward C. Kendall, Charles H. Slocumb, and Howard F. Polley); "Effect of Cortisone and Pituitary Andrenocorticotropic Hormone (ACTH) on Rheumatic Diseases," *The Journal of the American Medical Association*, vol. 144, 1950, pp. 1327-1335 (with Charles H. Slocumb, Howard F. Polley, and Edward C. Kendall); "The Present Status of Cortisone and ACTH in General Medicine," *Proceedings of the Royal Society of Medicine*, vol. 43, 1950, pp. 769-773.

Secondary

Hench, Philip S. "The Present Status of Cortisone and ACTH in General Medicine." *Proceedings of the Royal Society of Medicine* 43 (1950): 769-773. Based on an address by Hench to the experimental medicine section of the Royal Society of Medicine on October 10, 1950. Explains the differences between cortisone and ACTH and reviews the effects of these hormones on rheumatoid arthritis, rheumatic fever, and other conditions. Speculates on the mode of action of the hormones, identifies side effects, and proposes a plan of administration. As part of this presentation, Hench had projected a film showing the results of the administration of cortisone and/or ACTH to patients with rheumatoid arthritis. The film revealed striking improvement in the posture and movements of patients and the disappearance of joint pain on pressure following only a few administrations of the hormones.

Hench, Philip S., Edward C. Kendall, Charles H. Slocumb, and Howard F. Polley. "Effects of Cortisone Acetate and Pituitary ACTH on Rheumatoid Arthritis, Rheumatic Fever, and Certain Other Conditions." *Archives of Internal Medicine* 85 (1950): 545-666. This is a comprehensive report, presenting further experiences with cortisone and ACTH beyond the preliminary results that had previously been reported. Presents experiences with twenty-three patients with rheumatoid arthritis who were administered cortisone, ACTH, or both. Includes observations and conclusions on a wide variety of other effects associated with cortisone and ACTH. Presented as a study in clinical physiology and not as a report on clinical therapeutics.

Kelley, William N., Edward D. Harris, Jr., Shaun Ruddy, and Clement B. Sledge, eds. *Textbook of Rheumatology.* 3d ed. Philadelphia: W. B. Saunders, 1989. A comprehensive resource on the subject of rheumatology. The first section presents six chapters on the structure and function of connective tissue, muscle, and nerve, and is followed by seven chapters on the immune response and ten chapters on the inflammatory response. There are forty-six chapters on specific disorders and diseases, beginning with five chapters on rheumatoid arthritis. The book concludes with five chapters on medical orthopedics and rehabilitation and eleven chapters on reconstructive surgery in rheumatic diseases.

Kushner, Irving, Ann Forer, and Ann B. McGuire, eds. *Understanding Arthritis*. New York: Charles Scribner's Sons, 1984. Collected from a successful series of pamphlets on rheumatic diseases, edited for lay readers, distributed by the Public Education Committee of the Arthritis Foundation. Part 1 presents nine chapters on the general principles of arthritis, including information on diagnosis, medication, surgery, and living with arthritis. Part 2 presents sixteen chapters on various forms of arthritis, including rheumatoid arthritis. Includes two useful appendices. Provides a variety of information concerning arthritis; easily understandable by the layperson.

McCarty, Daniel J., ed. *Arthritis and Allied Conditions: A Textbook of Rheumatology*. 10th ed. Philadelphia: Lea & Febiger, 1985. The tenth edition of a comprehensive textbook first published in 1940 and generally recognized as the standard textbook on rheumatology. The first section presents seven chapters as an introduction to the study of the rheumatic diseases, while the second section presents twenty chapters on the scientific basis for the study of the rheumatic diseases. There are seven chapters on the clinical pharmacology of the antirheumatic drugs, sixteen chapters on rheumatoid arthritis, and nine chapters on other inflammatory arthritic syndromes.

Steven J. Albrechtsen

1951

Physiology or Medicine
Max Theiler, South Africa

Chemistry
Edwin Mattison McMillan, United States
Glenn Theodore Seaborg, United States

Physics
Sir John Douglas Cockcroft, Great Britain
Ernest Thomas Sinton Walton, Ireland

Literature
Pär Lagerkvist, Sweden

Peace
Léon Jouhaux, France

MAX THEILER
1951

Born: Pretoria, South Africa; January 30, 1899
Died: New Haven, Connecticut; August 11, 1972
Nationality: South African
Areas of concentration: Virology and immunology

Theiler's discoveries that the common mouse is susceptible to yellow fever and that passing the disease from mouse to mouse weakened the yellow fever virus led to the development of a vaccine with which humans could be immunized against the disease

The Award

Presentation

The presentation address was given by Professor H. Bergstrand, Chairman of the Nobel Committee for Physiology or Medicine, on December 10, 1951. In his speech, Bergstrand traced the history of yellow fever research, noting that as early as 1881 a Cuban doctor had linked the spread of the disease to the mosquito. This was confirmed in 1900 by a U.S. Army commission appointed to study yellow fever. The commission proved that the disease is transmitted by the bite of the *Aedes aegypti* mosquito and that yellow fever is caused by a virus.

The next advance in the study of the disease was made in 1927 by researchers at the Rockefeller Foundation, who infected laboratory monkeys with the yellow fever virus. Because monkeys are expensive and difficult to work with as experimental animals, Max Theiler's discovery in 1930 that the common white mouse could also be infected with yellow fever was a major breakthrough. It accelerated the pace of yellow fever research, eventually leading to the development of a variant form of the virus that was harmless to humans (the 17D strain), which was used for large-scale vaccination.

In conclusion, Bergstrand pointed out that the idea of using a variant form of a disease-causing agent to inoculate against a disease was not new. In 1796, Edward Jenner had shown that one could develop immunity to smallpox by being infected with the similar but less serious disease cowpox. A hundred years later, Louis Pasteur had shown that it was possible to transform a severe disease into a mild one by weakening the virus that produced it. Bergstrand noted that the significance of Theiler's work lay not in its originality but in its practical value. Through Theiler's efforts and the efforts of his colleagues at the Rockefeller Foundation, humankind was freed from the scourge of yellow fever and at the same time allowed to hope that other viral diseases might be similarly vanquished.

Nobel lecture

Theiler delivered his Nobel lecture, entitled "The Development of Vaccines Against

Yellow Fever," on December 11, 1951. In it, he divided the study of the disease into two periods. The first was the period in which Walter Reed and his associates had demonstrated that the disease was caused by a virus and was transmitted by the *Aedes aegypti* mosquito. The second period was ushered in by the discovery in 1927 by Adrian Stokes, Johannes Bauer, and N. Paul Hudson of the Rockefeller Foundation that the Indian rhesus monkey was susceptible to yellow fever and could therefore be used in research and experimentation.

Theiler then described his own contribution to the study of the disease: his discovery in 1930 that the mouse, a much less expensive and more readily available experimental animal than the monkey, was also susceptible to yellow fever. Theiler and his coworkers at the Rockefeller Foundation developed a vaccine for yellow fever by passing the disease from mouse to mouse and then later through mouse and chick embryonic tissue to produce a less virulent form of the virus. A marked change in the pathogenicity of the virus, the result of an apparently spontaneous mutation, was noted in what became known as the 17D strain. It was this strain, which produced only mild symptoms of yellow fever in humans and at the same time imparted immunity to the disease, that was adopted for use as a human vaccine.

Critical reception

The announcement that Max Theiler had won the 1951 Nobel Prize in Physiology or Medicine was applauded by the press. *The New York Times* of October 19, 1951, in a front-page story entitled "Nobel Prize Won by New Yorker," hailed Theiler's yellow fever vaccine as "one of the outstanding medical developments in history," comparing it to Edward Jenner's discovery of the smallpox vaccine. In a story that appeared the following day in *The New York Times*, Theiler's work on the development of a yellow fever vaccine was called a "magnificent effort . . . one of the crowning glories of research fostered by the Rockefeller Foundation."

Theiler received the cablegram announcing the decision of the Nobel Committee at his laboratory at the International Health Division of the Rockefeller Foundation in New York City on October 13, 1951. He later told reporters that he was quite surprised. The correspondent for *The New York Times* described Theiler as a shy, introverted man who "spoke modestly about his development of yellow fever vaccine." According to the article, Theiler gave the credit for his achievement to the Rockefeller Foundation and especially to two of his colleagues, Wray Lloyd and Hugh Smith.

The December, 1951, issue of *Scientific American* noted that Theiler had been proposed for a Nobel Prize three times before winning the award. *Newsweek*'s story on Theiler's award, dated October 29, 1951, also mentioned that Theiler had been nominated, though not chosen, in previous years. *Newsweek* stated that each time a more "highly publicized scientist" had won the prize and noted that the unassuming Theiler had "finally received official recognition of the eminence that has long been his professionally."

Most of the stories that appeared in the press made special mention of the extensive use of the vaccine in World War II. During the war, the Rockefeller Foundation organized and oversaw the production and distribution of the vaccine, free of charge, to all Allied troops and personnel assigned to service in the tropics. *Science News Letter* for October 27, 1951, noted that "among vaccinated American servicemen stationed in Africa and South America, not one known case of yellow fever was reported, thanks to Dr. Theiler."

Biography

Max Theiler was born in Pretoria, South Africa, on January 30, 1899. He was the youngest of four children born to Sir Arnold Theiler, a distinguished veterinary scientist, and Emma Jegge Theiler. Theiler's ambition was to become a doctor. He received his early education at Rhodes University College in Grahamstown, South Africa, and the University of Cape Town Medical School. In 1918, he left South Africa for London, where he studied at St. Thomas Hospital and the London School of Tropical Medicine. He received his medical diploma in 1922.

The same year, Theiler decided in favor of a career in medical research. He accepted a research position under Andrew Sellards, an associate professor in the Department of Tropical Medicine, Harvard Medical School, where he studied a number of infectious diseases, including yellow fever. In 1928, while at Harvard, Theiler married Lillian Graham, a laboratory technician. They had a daughter and a son. The boy was killed at the age of eight in an automobile accident.

In 1930, Theiler accepted a position at the International Health Division of the Rockefeller Foundation in New York City, where he continued his research on yellow fever. In 1951, he was named director of the foundation's virus laboratories. That same year he was awarded the Nobel Prize in Physiology or Medicine for his work in developing a vaccine for yellow fever.

Theiler left the Rockefeller Foundation in 1964 to accept a position as professor of epidemiology and microbiology at Yale University. He retired from Yale in 1967. He died of lung cancer on August 11, 1972, at the age of seventy-three.

Scientific Career

For centuries, yellow fever ravaged tropical and subtropical regions of the world, killing millions. The disease was first observed in Central America in the mid-seventeenth century. By the nineteenth century, it had established itself throughout the Caribbean and the rain forests of Africa and South America. Also known as yellow jack, the disease is characterized in its early stages by chills and fever, followed by severe head and back pain and jaundice, from which it gets its name. In humans, yellow fever attacks the liver, spleen, kidneys, and heart. In cases in which the disease proves fatal, the victims often vomit black blood shortly before dying. Those who survive, however, are immune to the disease for life.

In 1881, a Cuban physician named Carlos J. Finlay had written that yellow fever was spread by the bite of the female *Aedes aegypti* (Latin for "unpleasant Egyptian"), a small, silvery mosquito that breeds in stagnant water in or near human dwellings in the tropics. Finlay's discovery, however, was largely ignored. The connection between the insect and the disease was established in 1900 by U.S. Army surgeon Walter Reed. Reed had been appointed to lead a Yellow Fever Commission after more than two hundred U.S. soldiers had died of the disease while stationed in Havana during the Spanish-American War. The commission determined that Finlay had been right. In 1901, Reed's colleague, Dr. William C. Gorgas, chief sanitary officer for the U.S. Army in Havana, launched a rigorous antimosquito campaign. In only eight months' time, he brought the disease under control by killing the mosquito that transmitted it.

Although virtually wiped out in Cuba by 1901, yellow fever continued to plague the coastal towns and cities of Central and South America. Campaigns similar to Gorgas' in Cuba were launched to eradicate the *Aedes aegypti* mosquito, with similar success. Then, in 1911, cases of yellow fever were reported in the jungles of South America and Africa. These outbreaks, far from human habitation, forced the medical world to reexamine its basic ideas about the occurrence and transmission of the disease and the methods used to combat it. Up until this time, yellow fever was considered to be an "urban" disease, and it was believed that the sole carrier of the disease was a single species of mosquito, the *Aedes aegypti*. It was discovered that dozens of different types of mosquitoes could carry the disease and that these mosquitoes could transmit the disease from monkey to monkey and from monkey to man in the jungles. Since it would be impossible to wipe out all the fever-carrying monkeys and mosquitoes in the jungle, another means for controlling the disease had to be found. Medical researchers set about trying to isolate the disease-causing agent in order to develop a vaccine that could be used to immunize whole populations in tropical countries.

The Reed commission had concluded that yellow fever was caused by a virus. Viruses are complete parasites—they depend on the cell they invade to grow and multiply. Unlike bacteria, which can be cultured in artificial media, viruses grow and reproduce only in living tissue. Reed had conducted his yellow fever research using volunteers who had risked their lives. Two members of Reed's commission, Dr. Jesse Lazear and Dr. James Carroll, died as the result of being infected with the virus. To study the virus that causes yellow fever without risking human lives, an experimental animal that could be infected with the disease was needed.

Dr. Adrian Stokes, a British doctor and noted pathologist with the Rockefeller Foundation, tried infecting African monkeys but found that, like much of the native African population, they were immune to yellow fever. Stokes then tried to infect a species of monkey from India. In 1927, he succeeded in inoculating the common Indian rhesus monkey with the blood of a native African named Asibi who was ill with a mild case of yellow fever. The monkey contracted the disease and died. It was an important breakthrough. Scientists could now transplant and grow the virus, passing it from one monkey to another. Tragically, Stokes himself became infected by what came to be known as the Asibi strain of the virus and died of yellow fever while working in Africa.

Max Theiler, already a recognized expert in tropical diseases, was working at Harvard at the time. He had become interested in yellow fever as a result of a controversy then raging over the cause of the disease. Although the Reed commission had reported it was a virus, it had been unable to prove it conclusively. Efforts to see the yellow fever virus, which is only 0.02 micrometer in diameter, had failed because of the limited power of microscopes available at that time. The bacteriologist Hideyo Noguchi, working at the Rockefeller Foundation, announced in 1919 that the disease-causing agent was a bacterium. Noguchi's mistaken ideas about the nature of the yellow fever "germ" would hold back yellow fever research for almost ten years.

Theiler believed that the organism that caused yellow fever was indeed a virus and thus could be cultivated only in living tissue. Stokes's discovery that monkeys could be infected with the disease had been a major advance, but its usefulness was limited, since monkeys are difficult to handle and expensive.

In 1930, Theiler set out to infect white mice with yellow fever. White mice are easy to handle and cheap. He was unsuccessful until he tried injecting ground-up pieces of infected monkey liver directly into the brain of the mouse. Mice so injected sickened and died within a week; however, they showed none of the classic symptoms of yellow fever, namely, the characteristic liver, kidney, and heart damage that occurred in monkeys and man. Autopsies showed that the cause of death in the infected mice was encephalitis, an inflammation of the brain and spinal cord. Instead of giving up, Theiler passed the virus from the infected mice back to monkeys. To his surprise and elation, the monkeys came down with classic yellow fever.

An immediate result of his success was a job offer in New York with the Rockefeller Foundation. The foundation had become involved in the battle against yellow fever in 1915. In 1928, it established a Yellow Fever Laboratory in New York City, with Dr. Wilbur Sawyer as director. At the Rockefeller Foundation, Theiler continued his research using mice. He discovered that as he passed the yellow fever virus from mouse to mouse, it became more virulent for mice but less virulent for monkeys. If the virus was passed through enough mice, Theiler found, it eventually lost its virulence for monkeys. He had successfully attenuated, or weakened, the virus. There were still risks associated with the use of Theiler's mouse-adapted virus as a vaccine, however, most notably, nervous system effects.

Theiler's work had historical antecedents. In the eighteenth century, Edward Jenner had produced immunity to the dreaded disease smallpox by inoculating humans with the organism that caused the related but less serious disease cowpox. Jenner called his method vaccination. Almost a hundred years later, Louis Pasteur showed that humans could be vaccinated against rabies by being inoculated with a form of the virus which had been weakened by serial passage through the brains of laboratory rabbits. The attenuated virus stimulated the production of antibodies in the blood, which provided immunity against the disease.

In 1931, Sawyer and his coworkers developed a vaccine using Theiler's mouse-adapted virus to protect staff members at the Rockefeller Foundation involved in yellow fever research. Both Sawyer and Theiler had contracted mild cases of yellow fever while working with the virus. Both men recovered and were thereafter immune to the disease. Other researchers had not been so lucky. Six scientists at the Rockefeller Foundation, including Stokes and Noguchi, died after being infected with the virus in the course of their research. Sawyer and his associates mixed Theiler's mouse-adapted virus with the blood of persons who had recovered from yellow fever. It proved a successful vaccine but was limited in its usefulness, since the supply of such human immune serum is scarce.

French researchers who read of Theiler's work began using the attenuated virus alone as a vaccine for man. Their results, reported in 1932, showed that when used alone, the mouse-adapted virus produced immunity, but at the risk of serious nervous system complications. Several people vaccinated in this manner died of encephalitis. Theiler opposed the use of his virus by the French in this way. In 1934, he began research to produce a safe vaccine that could be produced in quantity.

With Wray Lloyd, Nelda Ricci, and Hugh Smith of the Rockefeller Foundation, Theiler experimented with tissue-culture methods to produce an attenuated yellow fever virus suitable for human vaccination. They used the Asibi virus, passing it first through minced mouse embryo tissue and then later through chick embryo tissue with the nervous tissue removed. In this way, Theiler and his colleagues kept the virus alive for three years. In 1937, somewhere between the 86th and the 176th passage of the virus through these tissues, the virus underwent a change that rendered it completely harmless to humans. Theiler and his colleagues were unable to repeat the outcome and finally concluded that a spontaneous mutation had occurred for which they could give no explanation. Theiler later told a reporter for *Survey* magazine in December, 1951, "We were lucky. Of course, we worked hard, but more than that, we had a lot of luck."

The mutation became known as the 17D strain. It was tested as a vaccine in Brazil between 1937 and 1940. Once its effectiveness and safety had been demonstrated, the Rockefeller Foundation began producing the vaccine on a mass scale and distributing it free of charge. By 1947, more than 28 million doses had been distributed, much of it for the war effort during World War II. In 1951, Theiler was awarded the Nobel Prize in Physiology or Medicine for his development of a vaccine for yellow fever.

Max Theiler was a pioneer in the science of virology, the study of viruses. Unlike diseases caused by bacterium, viral diseases, such as smallpox, yellow fever, and polio, generally cannot be treated with drugs. Instead, protection against such diseases depends for the most part on the development of safe and effective vaccines. The yellow fever research conducted by the Rockefeller Foundation in general and Theiler's development of a vaccine for the disease in particular have served as models for the study and conquest of other viral diseases.

Bibliography

Primary

VIROLOGY: "Susceptibility of White Mice to Virus of Yellow Fever," *Science*, vol. 71,

1930, p. 367; "Studies on the Action of Yellow Fever Virus in Mice," *Annals of Tropical Medicine and Parasitology*, vol. 24, 1930, pp. 249-272; "Vaccination Against Yellow Fever with Immune Serum and Virus Fixed for Mice," *Journal of Experimental Medicine*, vol. 55, 1932, pp. 945-969 (with S. F. Kitchen and W. D. M. Lloyd); "The Use of Yellow Fever Virus Modified *In Vitro* Cultivation for Human Immunization," *Journal of Experimental Medicine*, vol. 65, 1937, pp. 787-800 (with H. H. Smith); "Yellow Fever," pp. 420-440, in *Viral and Rickettsial Infections of Man* (edited by T. M. Rivers), 1948; *Yellow Fever*, 1951; *The Development of Vaccines Against Yellow Fever*, 1952; *The Arthropod-Borne Viruses of Vertebrates: An Account of the Rockefeller Foundation Virus Program, 1951-1970*, 1973 (with W. G. Downs).

Secondary

De Kruif, Paul. *Microbe Hunters*. New York: Harcourt, Brace, 1926. Considered a classic among popular science books, *Microbe Hunters* profiles the "bold and persistent" scientists who studied and conquered the microbes that cause disease. Chapter 11 recounts as much of the yellow fever story as was then known: the work of Walter Reed and the men who volunteered to participate in Reed's yellow fever research as "human guinea pigs."

Hahon, Nicholas, ed. *Selected Papers in Virology*, Englewood Cliffs, N.J.: Prentice-Hall, 1964. A collection of original papers important in the history of virus research and the development of virology as a science by such pioneers in the field as Edward Jenner and Louis Pasteur. Included is an abridged version of Max Theiler's paper, "Studies on the Action of Yellow Fever Virus in Mice," which describes his breakthrough research at Harvard.

Lapage, Geoffrey. *Man Against Disease*. New York: Abelard-Schuman, 1964. A short history of infectious diseases and the scientists who risked their lives to study them. The emphasis of the book is on the heroism and dedication of the doctors and research scientists involved in the fight against disease. Includes photographs of Carlos Finlay and Walter Reed, a selected bibliography, and an index.

Strode, George K., ed. *Yellow Fever*. New York: McGraw-Hill, 1951. The essays in this book, written by members of the International Health Division (IHD) of the Rockefeller Foundation, describe the work carried out by the IHD in its battle against yellow fever. Included is an essay by Theiler on the yellow fever virus which covers all aspects of his research. The book contains a bibliography of the papers published by the staff of the IHD as well as numerous graphs, maps, and photographs.

Williams, Greer. *The Plague Killers*. New York: Charles Scribner's Sons, 1969. Based on archival materials and interviews with the scientists involved, Williams' book describes the three major campaigns launched by the Rockefeller Foundation against hookworm disease, malaria, and yellow fever. In contrast to the technical essays of the George Strode book, *The Plague Killers* tells the story of the conquest of yellow fever in the form of a dramatic narrative. Includes an annotated bibliography and index.

__________. *Virus Hunters*. New York: Alfred A. Knopf, 1959. Chapter 15, "Theiler: Yellow Fever's Second Exit," presents a shorter account of the yellow fever work carried out by the Rockefeller Foundation than the book *The Plague Killers* by the same author. Here the focus is on the development of a vaccine for the disease. Williams interviewed Max Theiler and, as a result, the book contains a wealth of biographical and anecdotal material. Includes an annotated bibliography.

Nancy Schiller

1952

Physiology or Medicine

Selman Abraham Waksman, United States

Chemistry

Archer John Porter Martin, Great Britain
Richard Laurence Millington Synge, Great Britain

Physics

Felix Bloch, United States
Edward Mills Purcell, United States

Literature

François Mauriac, France

Peace

Albert Schweitzer, France

SELMAN ABRAHAM WAKSMAN
1952

Born: Priluka, Russia; July 22, 1888
Died: Hyannis, Massachusetts; August 16, 1973
Nationality: American
Areas of concentration: Microbiology and pharmacology

Waksman developed methods of screening microorganisms from the soil to determine whether they contained substances that might be effective against pathogens. He thus developed streptomycin—the first chemotherapeutic agent to suppress tuberculosis

The Award

Presentation

A member of the Royal Caroline Institute, A. Wallgren, delivered the presentation speech on December 10, 1952. He began by discussing Robert Koch's isolation of the tubercle bacillus in 1882 and reviewed the attempts to find therapeutic agents against this germ. Several promising agents appeared over the years but proved disappointing. This was the situation when Selman Waksman isolated streptomycin from a soil microorganism in 1943. Streptomycin eventually proved to be the first effective remedy against tuberculosis. This discovery was not a matter of chance, but the result of decades of research by Waksman on soil microbes. The discovery of the first antibiotics in 1939 and 1940 stimulated him to search for such agents in the soil, since he had established during the 1930's the antagonism of soil microbes to other microorganisms. He isolated antibiotics in 1940 and 1942 that were active against many bacteria, but they were too toxic to be of medical value. His research group continued to screen soil microbes and studied some ten thousand cultures before finding one that had antibiotic activity and also low toxicity. This antibiotic, streptomycin, was active against several bacteria, including the tubercle bacillus.

Clinical tests at the Mayo Clinic established its effectiveness in guinea pigs; these were followed by tests on severe cases of different types of tuberculosis in humans that indicated its apparent curative action. Wallgren then noted that streptomycin had had such a long trial throughout the world that it was possible to ascertain its therapeutic value. The most sensational effect was shown in the treatment and reversal of miliary tuberculosis and tubercular meningitis, both fatal diseases with few exceptions. Similarly, streptomycin treatment of early cases of pulmonary tuberculosis reversed its ravages.

Waksman's discovery of streptomycin as an antituberculosis remedy justified his being awarded the Nobel Prize. Yet the antibiotic was effective against many pathogenic bacteria that were not affected by penicillin, which made its therapeutic value even more remarkable.

Nobel lecture

On December 12, 1952, Waksman delivered his Nobel lecture, entitled "Streptomycin: Background, Isolation, Properties, and Utilization." He began with the historical background to antibiotics, which he defined in 1941, at the request of a journal editor, as substances produced by microorganisms that possess the property of inhibiting the growth of and even destroying other microorganisms. From the late nineteenth century, scientists knew that some fungi and bacteria produce chemical substances that inhibit the growth of bacteria, but research in isolating and studying these substances had proven fruitless until recently. He first isolated streptomycin in September, 1943. By the end of 1944, it was undergoing clinical trials, and within two years its possibilities for disease control had been established. The most spectacular clinical application came following the recognition that it was highly effective against the organism responsible for tuberculosis. Within three years of its isolation came the elucidation of its chemical structure, reports on the first one thousand clinical cases, and the beginning of a large manufacturing industry.

Waksman then described his research on soil microorganisms. The isolation of streptomycin was the culmination of decades of study. Since 1915, he had studied the soil microbes known as actinomycetes. Over the years, he established their occurrence, taxonomy, role in soil processes, and associative and antagonistic effects upon bacteria and fungi. His research in the 1920's and 1930's focused on their microbiology and their role in the soil, with no thought of isolating chemical substances of possible therapeutic value. In 1939, he began to investigate this possibility. In 1940, he found the first true antibiotic to be derived from an actinomycetes culture. "Actinomycin" was a highly active antibacterial agent, but it proved extremely toxic in animal tests. This was part of a comprehensive program to screen actinomycetes for their ability to produce antibiotics. The experience gained in this study made possible more effective methods of cultivation of the organisms and the isolation of active substances from them. The organism producing streptomycin was identical to the one he had isolated and identified in 1916 at the beginning of his career.

Waksman then explored the antibacterial properties of streptomycin and its activity against a large number of bacteria found among the gram-negative, gram-positive, and acid-fast groups. Its effectiveness against gram-negative bacteria (in contrast to penicillin, which was effective only against gram-positive ones) and its relatively low toxicity made streptomycin a chemotherapeutic agent of great potential importance. (Gram's stain is a technique used to distinguish among bacteria.) He considered the results of streptomycin therapy on tuberculosis and several other diseases and concluded that medical science and clinical practice had been revolutionized by its introduction.

Critical reception

The response to the announcement of Waksman's Nobel Prize was one of uniform praise. Although there were no extensive notices in newspapers, magazines, or scientific journals, the little publicity that did appear was positive. *The New York Times* responded to the announcement of the prize with an October 24 article by George Axelsson from Sweden. His article was a straightforward sketch of Waksman's life and career and a summary of the reasons for the award. He noted that the decision to award the prize to Waksman was not an easy one. Although the voting is never revealed, apparently there was a deadlock with the nearest competitor until, on the final ballot, Waksman won by a comfortable margin. Another interesting revelation was that, in 1941, Rutgers University, at which Waksman was a faculty member, wanted to release him for economic reasons. A few years later, Rutgers received millions of dollars in royalties from companies manufacturing streptomycin.

The New York Times Magazine issue of November 20, 1941, contained an article about Waksman. The interview for the article was held in Waksman's office at the Rutgers University College of Agriculture. The scientist showed the reporter batches of telegrams that were arriving daily congratulating him on winning the Nobel Prize. Waksman revealed the reasons that he first became interested in microbiology and told why he used microbes from the soil to develop "antibiotics," a term that Waksman was the first to use.

There were brief notices in both *Newsweek* and *Time* magazines (November 3, 1952) and in *Scientific American* (December, 1952) concerning Waksman's research. According to these sources, the majority of the royalties from the discovery of streptomycin went to the university to promote research in microbiology. *The New York Times* covered the award ceremony in an article appearing on December 12, 1952. At the awards ceremony, young Eva Hallström presented Waksman with five red carnations—one for each year she had lived since being diagnosed as having a hopeless case of tuberculosis and receiving streptomycin. This was the most dramatic among many similar incidents. Wherever Waksman traveled to lecture, he would be sure to encounter parents who sought him out to tell him of their gratitude for saving their child's life. The commentary on Waksman's award concerned both Waksman himself and the antibiotics that had revolutionized medicine. Before antibiotics, physicians were not expected to cure disease. Antibiotics revolutionized medicine because physicians could now go beyond diagnosis and prognosis to effect complete cures.

Biography

Selman Waksman was born in Priluka, a small town near Kiev, Russia, on July 22, 1888, to Jacob and Fradia Waksman. He received his early education at a Jewish school and from private tutors. He completed his schooling in Odessa, Russia, receiving a diploma from the *Gymnasium* there in 1910. Shortly afterward, he took the advice of relatives who had emigrated to America and followed them to New Jersey, where he lived on a farm owned by a cousin. He developed an interest in biology and gained acceptance into the College of Physicians and Surgeons at Columbia University on the basis of his *Gymnasium* diploma. He enrolled instead at the Rutgers College of Agriculture on the advice of another Russian immigrant,

Jacob Lipman, head of the bacteriology department there and later dean of the college.

In 1916, Waksman married Bertha Deborah Mitnik, a childhood sweetheart who in 1913 also emigrated from Priluka. They had one child, Byron H. Waksman, who became professor of microbiology at Yale University Medical School. In 1916, Waksman also became a naturalized citizen. At Rutgers, he majored in soil bacteriology. His high aptitude enabled him to begin research in his senior year under Lipman, and he became Lipman's research assistant at the New Jersey Agricultural Experiment Station. Waksman took his Ph.D. in biochemistry from the University of California in 1918.

Lipman invited him to return to Rutgers and take over soil bacteriology. Waksman was lecturer in soil microbiology and microbiologist at the Agricultural Experiment Station. His salary was insufficient to support a family, and he also worked at the nearby Takamine Laboratory until 1921 at three times his salary at Rutgers, where he remained through retirement in 1958. Beginning in 1949, Rutgers used a large portion of the millions of dollars from royalties it received from the patent rights to streptomycin it held to build and support the Rutgers Institute of Microbiology. Waksman was its first director.

Waksman organized a division of marine bacteriology at the Woods Hole Oceanographic Institution in Massachusetts in 1931 and spent his summers there until 1942. He was elected a trustee there and served until his death. He was also the author of more than five hundred articles and twenty-eight books. In addition to his scientific research, he pursued historical studies of microbiology and wrote the biographies of three distinguished microbiologists.

Waksman was the recipient of many honorary degrees and awards from institutions worldwide. He used part of the royalties from streptomycin given to him by Rutgers to establish the Foundation for Microbiology for the support of research, programs, courses, and lectures worldwide. After retirement, he remained active, writing several books and lecturing widely in the United States and abroad. He died in Hyannis, Massachusetts, on August 16, 1973, following a cerebral hemorrhage.

Scientific Career

Prior to the discovery of antibiotics, Waksman was the leading figure in American soil microbiology and was extraordinarily prolific in his research and writing. As an undergraduate at Rutgers, he was inspired in 1915 by Lipman to determine what chemical and biological processes occur in the soil. Lipman asked him to enumerate the different groups of microorganisms in the soil at different levels. He took samples at various depths, sieved and suspended the microbes in water, and cultured them in artificial media. He noted the different kinds of colonies, including the antinomycetes, a little-known type of microbe. After getting his doctorate at the University of California, he returned to Rutgers and decided to focus on the soil actinomycetes and determine their ecology, taxonomy, and activities.

At the request of Lipman, he examined the soil bacteria that oxidize sulfur to form sulfuric acid. He investigated citric and fumaric acid-producing molds, microbes that mineralize nitrogen and corrode iron and steel pipes and that reduce soil erosion and produce enzymes. He devoted many years of study to the decomposition of organic residues in the soil and the origin and nature of humus and peat. His studies of humus and peat revealed these to be the result of the degradation by microbes of their chemical constituents and the animal and plant waste products present. Humus was found to be a newly formed mass of organic matter formed by the activity of microbes on animal and plant wastes that undergoes continuous decomposition with the formation of nutrients essential to soil fertility. His studies of humus became classics. For over two decades, his field was the microbial population of the soil. He wanted to understand how these microbes interact in maintaining the fertility of the soil. He also wrote the fundamental textbooks and monographs on the subject from the 1920's through the 1950's.

During World War II, Waksman investigated the deterioration of war materials by fungi in the tropics and developed antifungal agents to protect such items as batteries, optical equipment, and clothing. His most important endeavor during the war years, however, was his investigation of antibiotics. Almost all of his research from 1939 and afterward was devoted to finding antibacterial drugs in soil microbes. He became a leader in the search for antibiotics as a result of his long experience in soil science and the work of his best-known student, René Dubos.

As early as the late nineteenth century, some biologists thought that microbes might contain substances that inhibit the growth of other microbes. Pathogenic germs introduced into the soil disappeared, apparently destroyed by the microbes in the soil. During the early twentieth century, there were some attempts to obtain chemotherapeutic agents from molds and bacterial cultures, but the field was abandoned until Dubos began to review the previous research and investigated the abandoned ideas.

René Dubos emigrated from France in 1924 and obtained a doctorate under Waksman at Rutgers in 1927. He then entered a research career at the Rockefeller Institute for Medical Research. There, the eminent bacteriologist Oswald Avery told Dubos of his interest in finding a microbe to dissolve the polysaccharide coat of the deadly pneumococcus germ. It was deadly because the coat was not dissolved by the host organism's defenses: The nucleus could not be attacked, and the bacteria remained virulent. Dubos knew that in the soil were organisms capable of digesting polysaccharides. He enriched soil with pneumococcus germs and hoped soil microbes would destroy their coat. In 1931, he discovered that some soil bacteria produce an enzyme that accomplishes this. He refined and extended his soil-enrichment methods. In February, 1939, he announced that he had isolated from *Bacillus brevis* two antibacterial substances, tyrocidine and gramicidin. The latter proved to be the first true antibiotic drug. It was different from any previous chemotherapeutic agent: It was part of a natural process in living bacteria with enough specificity to be toxic to one kind of cell and not at all to others. Unfortunately, this powerful substance was too toxic for human therapy. It found use in the treatment of animals against pneumococcus, staphylococcus, and streptococcus germs. A famous use of gramicidin came at the 1939 World's Fair in New York when sixteen cows at an agricultural pavilion developed an udder infection from streptococci; twelve of them were freed of the bacterium by gramicidin.

Dubos' discovery of antibiotics drew attention to microbial antagonisms in terms of substances produced by microbes themselves. When Howard Florey and Ernst Chain in England, who were then preparing a purely academic survey of antimicrobial mechanisms, learned of Dubos' work, they immediately became aware of the chemotherapeutic potential of penicillin, which was developed in 1928 by Alexander Fleming but not recognized for its therapeutic value until years later. Florey and Chain demonstrated its importance for therapy. Waksman seized on the discovery of gramicidin and converted his research into a search for chemotherapeutic substances among the actinomycetes. These proved to be the most fertile source for antibiotics. He quickly moved to the forefront in the search for antibiotics by developing a screening program by which thousands of soil microbes were cultured and tested for activity. The promising ones were processed chemically to isolate antibiotics. At the time, antibiotics were so novel that when Dubos asked Waksman in 1940 to organize a panel on them for the annual convention of the Society of American Bacteriologists, the two men failed to find enough people to constitute a panel. Within a decade, Waksman had isolated ten antibiotics. The first one was antinomycin in 1940. It proved too toxic for use in medicine, but he and others subsequently isolated several forms of it, known as actinomycin A, B, C, and D. Actinomycin C, discovered by Gerhard Domagk in 1953, proved to be active against cancerous cells of the lymphatic system and became a therapeutic agent for lymphatic tumors and Hodgkin's disease.

Waksman himself isolated actinomycin D in 1954. It was effective against Wilm's tumor, a deadly kidney cancer that is accountable for 20 percent of all malignant growths in children. In 1942, another antibiotic isolated by Waksman, streptothricin, was active against both gram-positive and gram-negative bacteria. Penicillin affected only gram-positive bacteria. Streptothricin was disappointing, however, because it exerted a delayed toxic effect on animals. Waksman therefore searched for a substance that would be active against gram-negative bacteria but with less toxicity. With his students Elizabeth Bugie and Albert Schatz, he developed suitable cultures and isolated from *Streptomyces griseus*, a substance antagonistic to gram-negative microbes. He called it "streptomycin." Two months later, he reported on what was most astonishing about streptomycin: It attacked the tubercle bacillus *Mycobacterium tuberculosis*, the cause of tuberculosis.

Waksman had only a small laboratory at Rutgers, and he was not equipped to perform extensive animal experimentation. He hoped to determine whether streptomycin would be active not only in laboratory cultures but also in live animals. When he began his search for antibiotics, he established an arrangement with the Merck company. According to this arrangement, Merck would have the exclusive right to apply for patents on any processes it developed in the finding and manufacture of antibiotics, Rutgers would receive royalties on their sale, and Waksman personally would receive a much smaller share.

When Waksman found that streptomycin had antitubercular properties, the implications were electrifying. In the early 1940's, tuberculosis was not fully under control. There was no cure—only prolonged bed rest (often in a sanatorium) and a regimen of nutritious food. The tubercle germ could invade any organ of the body, and in its various forms the disease took a horrifying toll. A diagnosis of tuberculosis often entailed lifelong invalidism, and patients died because the available treatment was so limited.

When news about streptomycin reached the Mayo Clinic in Minnesota, William Feldman and H. Corwin Hinshaw, two members of the Mayo Foundation who had been testing drugs for antitubercular effects, requested a sample of the antibiotic from Waksman. They provided the first major clinical trials, the results of which thrilled the medical world. The credit for the revelation that streptomycin is effective against the tubercle bacillus went to them; indeed, some other observers have claimed that they should have shared the Nobel Prize with Waksman. By this time, the award had garnered the degree of prestige it has now.

In December, 1944, the members of the Mayo Foundation had reported the results of experiments with guinea pigs inoculated with the tubercle bacillus. The tests revealed that streptomycin reversed the lethal course of the inoculation, and the reports concluded that it was highly effective in suppressing the growth of the germ.

They were now prepared to initiate tests on human patients. On November 20, 1944, a twenty-one-year-old woman with far-advanced pulmonary tuberculosis (one of her lungs already had undergone surgery; the other was almost eaten away) received streptomycin for the next six months. Discharged with her tuberculosis arrested, she lived to bear three children. This kind of happy ending was to be duplicated thousands of times over the next two years. The Mayo Clinic issued reports during 1945 and 1946 with evaluations of hundreds of cases, demonstrating the effectiveness of streptomycin in treating tuberculosis of the lungs, skin, bones and joints, meninges, and genitourinary organs.

The Mayo Clinic tests were followed by the most extensive study of a single drug ever undertaken. With streptomycin donated by several manufacturers, several thousand patients were tested in a cooperative medical research program involving the Cornell Medical School, the Public Health Service, Veterans Administration hospitals, and the National Tuberculosis Association. These tests determined which patients benefit from streptomycin and how it could be used most efficiently.

Streptomycin was so important that Waksman proposed that any interested company should be able to produce it. Merck agreed to transfer its rights to Rutgers, which, in turn, licensed a number of companies to make it. By 1948, eight companies were producing streptomycin. Rutgers set up a foundation to handle patent and licensing matters. Rutgers would receive 80 percent of the royalties, and Waksman would get 20 percent. Waksman voluntarily reduced his share by one-half in 1949, following a lawsuit initiated by his former student Albert Schatz, who had tested *Streptomyces griseus*. Schatz was a joint applicant on the patent application for streptomycin and thought that he should get both income and credit. Waksman settled out of court. Schatz was legally entitled to credit as codiscoverer of streptomycin. In addition to this outlay, subtracted directly from his share, Waksman distributed a portion of his royalties among twenty-six students and assistants who had helped in the discovery.

Streptomycin was the first effective chemotherapeutic remedy for tuberculosis, including the most hopeless types such as tubercular meningitis and miliary tuberculosis, both hitherto always fatal. The subsequent drop in tuberculosis mortality, especially among children, was remarkable. Manufacture of the drug became an industry that generated some $50 million per year, and by 1950 streptomycin was used against seventy different germs against which penicillin was useless. In addition to tuberculosis, it was effective against gram-negative infections of the abdomen, pelvis, and meninges as well as such diseases as meningitis, tularemia, and urinary tract infections.

After his success with streptomycin, Waksman continued to search for antibiotics among the actinomycetes of the soil. In 1949, he isolated neomycin, a broad-spectrum antibiotic that found a very important niche among the antibiotics as a topical agent. Waksman retired in 1958. He had used his long experience with soil microbes to exploit a new field. He had tested some hundred thousand cultures and discovered eighteen antibiotics. Others found commercially important antibiotics in the soil actinomycetes, and pharmaceutical companies on several continents were mass producing them. Along with his many contributions to the literature on antibiotics, he wrote popular nonfiction. His autobiography, *My Life with the Microbes* (1954), provided an accessible and detailed account of his career. Ten years later appeared his *The Conquest of Tuberculosis*, one of the best books for the general reader on the history, prevalence, treatment, and importance of the disease. Until the widespread use of streptomycin, tuberculosis was the most resistant and irreversible of all major infectious diseases. Streptomycin brought people back from the very edge of death.

Waksman played a major role in the inauguration of the age of antibiotics. His work encouraged others to find antibiotics in the microbial world and to extend his screening methods to make them more effective. Antibiotics brought many infectious diseases within the reach of therapy and greatly diminished both the prevalence and suffering associated with them. Problems, such as that of bacterial resistance to antibiotics, appeared; these have prevented the hoped-for eradication of infectious diseases. Tuberculosis remains a major cause of death in many parts of the world. Antibiotics have established their place in medicine in the treatment of a wide range of infections. The progress in fighting disease germs has been so great as to be fantastic to anyone who had not witnessed the miseries of the preantibiotic era.

Bibliography

Primary
PHYSIOLOGY: *Enzymes*, 1926 (with Wilburt Davidson); *Principles of Soil Microbiol-*

ogy, 1927; *The Soil and the Microbe*, 1931 (with Robert Starkey); *Humus*, 1936; *Microbial Antagonisms and Antibiotic Substances*, 1945; *The Literature on Streptomycin*, 1948-1952; *The Actinomycetes*, 1950-1966; *Actinomycetes and Their Antibiotics*, 1953 (with Hubert Lechevalier); *Soil Microbiology*, 1954.

MEDICINE: *Streptomycin, Its Nature, and Practical Application*, 1949; *Sergei N. Winogradsky*, 1953; *My Life with the Microbes*, 1954; *The Conquest of Tuberculosis*, 1964; *Jacob G. Lipman*, 1966; *Actinomycin*, 1968.

Secondary

Dowling, Harry F. *Fighting Infection: Conquests of the Twentieth Century*. Cambridge, Mass.: Harvard University Press, 1977. Dowling, a physician and medical scientist, covers the antibiotics, sulfa drugs, vaccines, and serums that combat, stop, and prevent infections. The twentieth century is noteworthy for the abundance of these weapons. This is the first large work on the control of infectious diseases over the first seventy-five years of the twentieth century and includes the best description available on the medical applications of streptomycin.

Epstein, Samuel, and Beryl Williams. *Miracles from Microbes: The Road to Streptomycin*. New Brunswick, N.J.: Rutgers University Press, 1946. This is a straightforward record of the research of Waksman that produced the discovery of streptomycin. A chapter on the work of René Dubos on gramicidin is also included.

Lechevalier, Hubert A., and Morris Solotorovsky. *Three Centuries of Microbiology*. New York: McGraw-Hill, 1965. This book reconstructs the main lines of development of microbiology. The largest section is on chemotherapy. It contains an especially good narrative on Waksman and the work of Feldman and Hinshaw at the Mayo Clinic.

Parascandola, John, ed. *The History of Antibiotics: A Symposium*. Madison: University of Wisconsin Press, 1980. A good collection of articles on antibiotic history, including one by a former student of Waksman, Hubert Lechevalier, on the search for antibiotics at Rutgers.

Sokoloff, Boris. *The Miracle Drugs*. New York: Prentice-Hall, 1954. This is a popular book on antibiotics, providing a historical treatment of drug therapy and the work of Louis Pasteur and Paul Ehrlich as well as a discussion of the discovery of penicillin. It is useful for its coverage of the applications, limitations, and toxic effects of streptomycin.

Woodruff, H. Boyd, ed. *Scientific Contributions of Selman A. Waksman*. New Brunswick, N.J.: Rutgers University Press, 1968. This anthology is a commemoration of Waksman's eightieth birthday. In it is contained reprints of many of his most important articles, along with pertinent selections from his books. The anthology also includes a brief biography and listings of honorary degrees, awards, and his graduate students.

Albert B. Costa

1953

Physiology or Medicine

Sir Hans Adolf Krebs, Germany and Great Britain
Fritz Albert Lipmann, Germany and United States

Chemistry

Hermann Staudinger, West Germany

Physics

Frits Zernike, The Netherlands

Literature

Sir Winston Churchill, Great Britain

Peace

George C. Marshall, United States

SIR HANS ADOLF KREBS
1953

Born: Hildesheim, Germany; August 25, 1900
Died: Oxford, England; November 22, 1981
Nationality: German; after 1939, British
Areas of concentration: Biochemistry, metabolism, and enzymology

Krebs discovered the cyclic biochemical process named the Krebs tricarboxylic acid cycle, a major part of the explanation of the cellular mechanisms that allow the body to produce energy and to build and renew itself

The Award

Presentation

On December 10, 1953, Hans Krebs and Fritz Lipmann shared the 1953 Nobel Prize in Physiology or Medicine. Professor Einar Hammarsten, faculty member of the Royal Caroline Institute and representative of the Royal Swedish Academy of Sciences, delivered the allocution. Hammarsten noted that the portion of the Nobel Prize awarded to Krebs, "for the discovery of the citric acid cycle," was for his very significant contribution to research into the functions of the living cell. Hammarsten also pointed out that the complicated participant molecules made it quite difficult to understand the many chemical processes involved. Before Krebs, Hammarsten stated, partial answers and isolated chemical reactions existed; however, "no one could give a uniform picture of a logical over-all mechanism."

Krebs's efforts, Hammarsten said, showed "how individual reactions were linked in a cyclic process" and provided "clear understanding of the essential principle of how released energy is used for the building-up processes which occur in the cell." Hammarsten also reminded the audience that, at the onset, Krebs's idea was "criticized by many." Hammarsten lauded Krebs for explaining both the degradation processes that yield the cell's energy and the building-up processes that use energy, in keeping with the "balance between these two kinds of cell reactions." He also stated that from the chaos of isolated chemical reactions, Krebs had successfully extracted "the basic system for the essential pathway of oxidation within the cell." Krebs's intuition was noted as being so clear that none of his original ideas had to be revised.

Hammarsten ended his commentary on Krebs by stating that the institute was pleased to reward his achievement in seeing the primary pathway of biological combustion and proving the reality of his vision. The prize, Hammersten told Krebs, was being given "in corroboration of the general agreement that you have laid a foundation, which will last for all time," and for the fact that a great development of constructive work founded on his pioneering effort had already been witnessed.

Nobel lecture

Krebs delivered a clear, well-designed Nobel lecture, entitled "The Citric Acid

Cycle," on December 11, 1953. It contained eight portions: early work, crucial experiments, additional evidence, further intermediates, common pathway of foodstuff oxidation, the cycle in different cells and organisms, the role of the cycle in synthetic processes, and common features of different forms of life. The lecture began by crediting the early work of others, "built on the pioneer work of Arthur Harden and Carl Neuberg." Krebs went on to mention his own formative years (from 1926 to 1930) in the laboratory of Otto Warburg. He noted that this experience made attractive the study of the virtually unknown oxidation of biomolecules in higher organisms, and he stated that this endeavor was complicated by the complexity and instability of the test systems studied.

Next, Krebs pointed out that early researchers discovered the rapid biological oxidation of certain important organic acids that contained two to six carbons. These important observations, he said, remained isolated "because they could not be linked to the chief oxidative process, oxidation of sugars." The problem lasted for twenty years, until Albert Szent-Györgyi and coworkers began a study of the process in pigeon muscle preparations (1935) and concluded that several of the organic acids stimulated biological oxidation greatly without being used up themselves (an action that was termed catalytic).

At this point, Krebs's laboratory group entered the picture by showing that six-carbon citric acid was catalytic. Soon, they also showed that citrate could be produced by the chemical combination of four-carbon oxaloacetic acid—one of the other catalytic organic acids already mentioned—and a mysterious two-carbon compound made from sugars. Krebs said that this made it possible to formulate a complete scheme for sugar oxidation. It also linked sugar oxidation with all the organic acids that had been shown to be catalytic and explained both catalytic action and oxidation of those chemicals. He pointed out that the cycle was arbitrarily named the "citric acid cycle" for the sake of convenience and for simplicity.

Krebs stated that the evidence for the importance of the citric acid cycle first came from observations that its individual steps, each mediated by an enzyme (a protein biological catalyst), occurred in animal tissues at rates that supported the view that they were important components of the main respiratory processes, which convert sugars to energy and to cellular building blocks. In addition, Krebs noted that additional proof of this importance came when the use of chemicals that prevent key steps of the cycle—but no other biological processes—stopped the oxidation of sugars both in the test tube and upon their injection into animals.

Next, Krebs acknowledged that the efforts of his colaureate, Fritz Lipmann, and others, showed that the two-carbon chemical, acetyl coenzyme A, was the mysterious two-carbon compound from sugar oxidation that was used to make citric acid. He also noted that the role of acetyl coenzyme A and the conversion of many amino acids to the chemical constituents of the citric acid cycle demonstrated its centrality in the oxidation of fats and proteins, the two other main sources of energy and of cellular building blocks. This cycle, then, is the common metabolic pathway for biological oxidation of foodstuffs and represents a device for simplifying the means by which energy is produced from the many diverse foodstuffs eaten.

Moreover, Krebs pointed out, repetition of the crucial experiments in other species demonstrated that the citric acid cycle occurs in most living organisms, from microorganisms to plants to the highest mammals. He ended the lecture by stating that the remarkable ubiquity of the citric acid cycle allows two important inferences to be made: The mechanism of energy production arose early in the evolutionary process; and life, in its present forms, arose only once.

Critical reception

Scientists around the world applauded Krebs's receipt of the 1953 Nobel Prize because of the great importance of the research he had carried out. Krebs's colaureate, Lipmann, stated that the discovery of the Krebs cycle was attributable to the "remarkable powers in insight, enterprise, and sheer hard work" possessed by Krebs. Krebs had striven to simplify and organize the basic tenets of metabolism. To paraphrase Hammarsten, out of chaos Krebs had successfully extracted the essential pathway of oxidation within the cell. Krebs's intuition, Hammarsten said, was so clear that none of his original ideas needed to be revised.

As noted in *The New York Times* of October 23, 1953, Krebs was cited for what Nobel Committee members called his "brilliant and ingenious description of how energy was generated in living cells." Similarly, the November 2, 1953, *Newsweek* quoted Göran Liljestrand, the secretary of the Nobel Committee, as saying that the work "is of the utmost theoretical significance and likely to have great practical importance in understanding diseases and similar disturbances."

The level of understanding and appreciation of the media for Kreb's research endeavors was exemplified by a group of statements in a much longer, October 23, 1953, article from *The New York Times*: "After much trial and error Krebs found the master key of the cycle, pyruvic acid, he had sought for more than twenty years. The whole process swung around in a circle and rejuvenated its starting materials. The Krebs (citric acid) cycle was a self-perpetuating process in the sense that chemicals were broken to pieces and recreated." The article noted that chemical energy, in the form of sugar, is converted to physical energy—muscle power. Krebs, it stated, believed that the cycle could be applied to other body fuels, such as fatty acids. The Krebs (citric acid) cycle has withstood the tests of time. It can be found, expanded but basically unmodified, in any modern biochemistry textbook. It is often depicted as the central pathway of metabolism.

Biography

Hans Krebs was born at Hildesheim, Germany. He was the son of a Jewish ear, nose, and throat surgeon, Georg Krebs, and of Alma (née Davidson) Krebs. Krebs was educated at Hildesheim's *Gymnasium Andreanum*. He then studied medicine at the universities of Berlin, Freiburg, Göttingen, Hamburg, and Munich. In 1925, Krebs received the M.D. degree from the University of Hamburg.

For the next year, he studied chemistry at the University of Berlin. Then, in 1926, he became a laboratory assistant of Otto Warburg at the Kaiser Wilhelm Institute for Biology, Berlin-Dahlem. Collaboration with Warburg continued until 1930, when Krebs re-entered clinical medical practice, working at Hamburg's Altona Municipal Hospital. He later moved to the medical clinic of the University of Freiburg. At Freiburg, he continued his research efforts and made important discoveries that established his international reputation.

In 1933, Adolf Hitler terminated Krebs's appointment at Freiburg, and Krebs emigrated to England. There, he first worked as a Rockefeller Research Fellow at the University of Cambridge. Krebs next moved to Sheffield University (1935), where he progressed to lecturer-in-charge of the department of biochemistry (1938) and chairman of that department and director of the Medical Research Council Unit for Research in Cell Metabolism (1945). Krebs was married to Margaret Cicely Fieldhouse in 1938; they had two sons (Paul and John) and a daughter (Helen).

In 1953, Krebs won the Nobel Prize; in 1954, he became the Whitley Professor of Biochemistry at the University of Oxford. Krebs remained at Oxford until he retired in 1967. He received many honors and contributed much to the development and understanding of biochemistry. These contributions included discovery of the Krebs (citric acid) cycle; elucidation of the important cyclic mechanism of urea biosynthesis; codiscovery of the glyoxalate cycle (another energy-producing cycle of metabolism); and study of inborn errors of metabolism. Krebs continued with his research efforts after retirement. He died in Oxford, England, on November 22, 1981, at the age of eighty-one.

Scientific Career

The scientific endeavors of Hans Krebs can be summarized as an extensive study of metabolism (the sum of all the chemical reactions carried out by living cells) and the discovery of the existence of cyclic metabolic pathways. Metabolic pathways are groups of enzymes (biological protein catalysts) that convert the chemicals eaten as foods to other biochemicals used for energy production and manufacture all the necessary cellular components. They also carry out many other processes required for life.

Krebs's scientific career began to develop after he received the M.D. degree in 1925 and spent a year in graduate study of chemistry at Berlin University Institute of Pathology. At that time, in 1926, he became a laboratory assistant to Otto Warburg, of Berlin's Kaiser Wilhelm Institute of Biology. Warburg, a famous biochemist, was the winner of the 1931 Nobel Prize in Physiology or Medicine.

During his stay in Warburg's laboratory, Krebs learned Warburg's method for investigating cellular respiration (the biological oxidation of foods that converts them to carbon dioxide, water, and energy). In this method, air and thin slices of living tissue are placed in airtight flasks equipped with gas-pressure gauges. When a tissue slice undergoes respiration, the pressure in the flask decreases. Reading the extent of the gas-pressure decrease allows the exact measurement of the amount of respiration that has occurred.

In 1930, after almost five years of collaboration with Warburg, resulting in the publication of sixteen scientific papers, Krebs returned to clinical practice at hospitals in Hamburg and Freiburg. He practiced medicine and carried out highly sophisticated, self-directed biochemical research for the next four years, from 1930 to 1933. This effort established Krebs's international reputation because of his study of the process that is still called the Krebs urea cycle, which introduced the idea that cyclic processes occur in biochemistry. This research was carried out in collaboration with a medical student, Kurt Henseleit. Amazingly, Krebs managed to carry out this work while in charge of a forty-bed hospital ward.

The Krebs urea cycle depicted the biochemical process by which nitrogen and ammonia are eliminated from the body as urea. This effort, based upon the tissue-slice methodology of Warburg, began with the demonstration that ornithine (an amino acid) acts to catalyze urea biosynthesis. That is, it stimulates urea production without being used up itself. Basically, the urea cycle occurs in three stages. First, ornithine reacts with ammonia to yield citrulline (another amino acid). Next, citrulline is transformed to the amino acid arginine. Then, arginine is broken down to urea—which is excreted—and ornithine, which is able to begin the cycle anew. All the reactions of this cycle, a metabolic pathway, are carried out by enzymes. The enzymology of the pathway was delineated, later, by the research groups of Sarah Ratner and Paul Cohen. This work explains how toxic ammonia, from the respiration of foods that contain nitrogen, is converted to a nontoxic form (urea) for excretion. It also explains the biological function of ornithine and citrulline, which, unlike most amino acids, are not incorporated into body proteins, and explains the biosynthesis of the very important amino acid arginine.

With the advent of the Hitler regime, the violent prejudice against all people of Jewish descent forced Krebs to flee Germany in 1933. Fortunately, a Rockefeller fellowship and an invitation to work at England's University of Cambridge gave Krebs, now an immigrant, a new start. He arrived at Cambridge reputedly with "virtually nothing but a sigh of relief and a few books" and continued biochemical research, under Frederick Gowland Hopkins, at the Institute of Biochemistry. Hopkins, another Nobel laureate (1929) and president of the Royal Society of London, pioneered in vitamin research. During the stay at Cambridge, Krebs published articles on the metabolism of nitrogen-containing chemicals and dicarboxylic acids.

In 1935, Krebs (now possessed of an M.S. in biochemistry) left Cambridge and became a lecturer in pharmacology at the University of Sheffield. By 1938, he was lecturer-in-charge at Sheffield's biochemistry department. There, Krebs contributed to wartime research on diet and nutrition. His efforts to that end were largely responsible for development of the national whole meal loaf: "the economical, healthy standby of a bread-short nation," according to the British Information Service. In 1945, Krebs was appointed professor and chairman of Sheffield's biochemistry department and director of its Medical Research Council Unit for Research in Cell Metabolism. By this time, Krebs was well along in the studies of the citric acid cycle that would earn for him the 1953 Nobel Prize. In this endeavor, Krebs demonstrated that respiration—like urea synthesis—was a cyclic process.

Before their use in the citric acid cycle, the sugars that serve as the main body fuels are first converted enzymatically into two-carbon acetyl coenzyme A. Then, acetyl coenzyme A reacts with four-carbon oxaloacetic acid to produce citric acid. Next, citric acid passes through a series of enzymatic reactions that convert it to energy, carbon dioxide, water, and oxaloacetic acid. The resultant oxaloacetic acid can begin the cycle anew by reacting with another molecule of acetyl coenzyme A. It was later shown that other biological fuels (such as fats and proteins) enter the citric acid cycle, either as acetyl coenzyme A or as one of the several organic acids produced in the enzymatic reactions that compose the cycle. It should be noted that the discovery and identification of acetyl coenzyme A can be attributed mostly to Krebs's colaureate, Fritz Lipmann of Harvard University. The explanation of the Krebs citric acid cycle was exceptionally important. As stated by Einar Hammarsten of the Royal Caroline Institute, it "arranged the many earlier, scattered findings in the area into a unified theory and led to the current understanding of metabolism."

In 1954, Krebs moved to the University of Oxford, accepting an appointment as the Whitley Professor of Biochemistry of its Nuffield Department of Clinical Medicine. He remained there, as head of biochemistry, until his retirement in 1967. Krebs's continued research at Oxford led to further contributions to the understanding of biochemistry and metabolism. For example, in 1957, Krebs and a former student, Hans L. Kornberg, reported the discovery of yet another cyclic metabolic pathway. This was the "glyoxalate cycle," a third Krebs cycle. The glyoxalate cycle is a metabolic pathway which converts acetyl coenzyme A to both the biomolecules that the cell needs for its survival (such as succinic acid and carbohydrates) and the energy it needs to do biological work. The glyoxalate cycle, very important in germinating plant seeds and in microorganisms, is not found in animals. It is composed of several enzymes of the citric acid cycle and others that connect elements of that cycle to the new cycle, which produces succinic acid, carbohydrate, and energy.

After his retirement from Oxford, Krebs continued and extended his research efforts. These additional endeavors included the examination of the control of the rates of metabolic processes and the study of inborn errors of metabolism (genetically heritable diseases caused by the production of defective enzymes). All this work was carried out at the Nuffield Department of Clinical Medicine and at London's Royal Free Hospital School of Medicine. Krebs died in Oxford on November 22, 1981, at the age of eighty-one.

The discovery of the citric acid cycle is viewed as the most important single discovery in metabolic biochemistry, and its importance cannot be overstated. Because of this, as well as his many other important contributions to the understanding of metabolism, Hans Krebs received numerous honors, prizes, memberships in learned societies, and honorary degrees. Among the prizes were the 1953 Nobel Prize; the Lasker Award of the American Public Health Association (1953); the Royal Medal and Copley Medal (in both 1954 and 1961) of the Royal Society of London; the 1958 Gold Medal of the Netherlands Society for Physics, Medical Science, and Surgery; and knighthood, conferred by Britain's Queen Elizabeth II in 1958.

Sir Hans Krebs was also elected to membership in prestigious scientific societies such as the Royal Society of London, America's National Academy of Sciences, the American College of Physicians, and Israel's Weizmann Institute. Many universities around the world awarded him honorary doctorates, among them the University of Chicago, the Sorbonne, Glasgow University, England's universities of London, Sheffield, and Leicester, Berlin University, and Jerusalem University.

Through it all, Krebs remained a quiet, reserved man, who once said of his wide-ranging work, "One cannot have a definite aim in metabolic research. The field is endless." It is reported that when queried about his work credo, Krebs quoted Noël Coward: "Work is fun, and there is no fun like work." He was revered for stimulating his colleagues to productive thought by his example and his own enthusiasm.

Bibliography

Primary

BIOCHEMISTRY: "The Role of Citric Acid in Intermediary Metabolism in Animal Tissues," *Enzymologia*, vol. 4, 1937, pp. 148-156 (with W. A. Johnson); "The Intermediary Stages in the Biological Oxidation of Carbohydrate," *Advances in Enzymology*, vol. 1, 1941, pp. 99-127; "The Tricarboxylic Acid Cycle," *Harvey Lectures*, vol. 44, 1950, pp. 165-177; *Energy Transformations in Living Matter*, 1957 (with H. L. Kornberg); "The Regulation of Release of Ketone Bodies by the Liver," *Advances in Enzyme Regulation*, vol. 4, 1966, pp. 339-354; "The History of the Tricarboxylic Acid Cycle," *Perspectives in Biology and Medicine*, vol. 14, 1970, pp. 154-170; "The Ornithine Cycle of Urea Synthesis," in *The Urea Cycle*, edited by S. Grisolía, R. Baguena, and F. Mayor, 1976.

Secondary

Holmes, F. L. "Hans Krebs and the Discovery of the Ornithine Cycle." *Federation Proceedings* 39 (February, 1980): 216-225. This article provides a detailed description of the events and the thinking involved in discovery of the Krebs-Henseleit cycle. It also traces the development and basis of Krebs's concept of the cyclic pathway. References provided include the original papers in German biochemistry journals.

Kornberg, H. L. "H. A. Krebs: A Pathway in Metabolism." In *The Metabolic Roles of Citrate*. London: Academic Press, 1982. This article, by a former student (another notable scientist), is part of a symposium honoring Krebs. It very succinctly describes Krebs and his career. Krebs is depicted as brilliant, unassuming, and likable. The other eight articles in the book also provide valuable insight into Krebs and into the biochemical roles of citric acid.

Krebs, Hans A., and Anne Martin. *Reminiscence and Recollections*. Oxford, England: Oxford University Press, 1982. This engaging book describes Krebs's life: the development of his career, his most notable discoveries, and the pleasures, trials, and tribulations of employment at Oxford. Krebs emerges as a dynamic scientist, utterly committed to his work yet possessed of a very pleasant personality.

Lehninger, A. L. *Biochemistry.* New York: Worth, 1975. Chapter 17 of this college text provides lucid coverage of the Krebs (citric acid) cycle and the glyoxalate cycle. Lehninger deciphers their history and biochemistry in a very scholarly way. A complete description of the enzymology is given; several direct references to Krebs's work and its importance can be found on pages 444, 447-448, 466, and 579.

____________. *Principles of Biochemistry.* New York: Worth, 1982. Chapter 16 of this text, written at a somewhat lower level than *Biochemistry*, covers the same topics. This text has the advantage of some newer information lacking in the 1975 book. The two texts by Lehninger are complementary.

Williamson, D. H. "Sir Hans Krebs, the First Eighty Years." *Trends in Biochemical Science* 5 (August, 1980): vi-vii. This brief biographical article describes Krebs's life and career. It includes his main research endeavors, placing them in a useful time frame. It also gives some pertinent related references. Throughout the article, Krebs's versatility and ingenuity are made evident.

Sanford S. Singer

1953

Physiology or Medicine

Sir Hans Adolf Krebs, Germany and Great Britain
Fritz Albert Lipmann, Germany and United States

Chemistry

Hermann Staudinger, West Germany

Physics

Frits Zernike, The Netherlands

Literature

Sir Winston Churchill, Great Britain

Peace

George C. Marshall, United States

FRITZ ALBERT LIPMANN
1953

Born: Königsberg, Germany; June 12, 1899
Died: Poughkeepsie, New York; July 24, 1986
Nationality: German; later, American
Areas of concentration: Biochemistry, metabolism, and enzymology

Lipmann was a major participant in deciphering the cellular, catalytic, and energetic mechanisms needed to understand how the body builds and renews itself; he discovered coenzyme A, central to many reactions that yield the cell's energy and to others that use it

The Award

Presentation

Professor Einar Hammarsten, a member of the faculty of the Royal Caroline Institute and the representative of the Swedish Academy of Sciences, delivered the presentation address on December 10, 1953. In his talk, Hammarsten pointed out that the 1953 prize was shared by Hans Krebs and Fritz Lipmann for their important contributions to research into the functions of the living cell. It was pointed out that many extremely complicated molecules are involved there, making it difficult to understand the processes, especially the action of enzymes (the biological catalysts) and the smaller molecules, "coenzymes," required to "awaken enzymes" so that they can work.

Hammarsten went on to note that the efforts for which this Nobel Prize was awarded were important in two complementary ways, generated by Krebs and Lipmann, respectively. Krebs had identified the cyclic process (the Krebs cycle) by which cellular energy is released from foods and which lead to "building-up" processes in cells (anabolism). The cycle, Hammarsten stated, was also called the citric acid cycle after the first compound made from atoms obtained in food.

Understanding the Krebs cycle was not sufficient to understand the process, because it is necessary to introduce "compounds from the outside" if the cycle is to work successfully. Lipmann's discovery of coenzyme A allowed "everything to fit perfectly," as Hammarsten said. That is, reaction between coenzyme A and acetic acid (the metabolic fuel made from food) engenders the ability for formation of citric acid and begins the process. The use of coenzyme A to activate many other important molecules used by cells has been documented; thus, Lipmann's discovery was both ubiquitous and of wide importance.

The value of Lipmann's work became even more clear, Hammarsten said, when it served as a model for other researchers. They theorized that because coenzyme A comes from a B vitamin (pantothenic acid), other vitamins are also active as coenzymes that turn enzymes on. This value was exemplified by citation of later proof (by Swedish biochemist Hugo Theorell) that vitamin B_2 is an important coenzyme. Still other biochemists, unknown to Hammarsten, soon discovered that all the vitamins serve as coenzymes or as the parents of coenzymes made by the body.

Hammarsten ended his commentary on Lipmann by calling him a fighter in the biochemical arena. He noted that Lipmann's fight was to understand the complex biochemical processes related to life and "to make things in this area understandable and distinct." Discovery of coenzyme A was cited as clear demonstration of a reaction of widespread importance and identification of a new way for energy transmission in the cell.

Nobel lecture

Lipmann began his lecture, entitled "Development of the Acetylation Problem: A Personal Account," by modestly stating that receipt of the Nobel Prize encouraged him to view his own research efforts as a serious part of contemporary biochemistry. The remainder of the talk traced, "in Lipmann's segment of interest," the course of development of facts and ideas filling in the understanding of the organism. It was divided into five segments: discovery of acetyl phosphate; identification of coenzyme A; the metabolic functions of coenzyme A; the carboxyl and methyl activation in acetyl coenzyme A; the mechanism of the adenosine triphosphate-coenzyme A-acetate reaction. Throughout the lecture, Lipmann gave credit to all the other research groups involved.

In summary of his own effort, Lipmann noted that his first independent research (study of pyruvate oxidation in bacteria) led to serendipitous observation of dependence upon the presence of inorganic phosphate. This dependence led him to propose and to prove that acetyl phosphate, an acetic acid derivative, was involved and to believe that acetyl phosphate served two purposes in cells: the production of an energy-rich bond that could drive cell processes, and the generation of a building block that was used to make other biomolecules.

Lipmann then generalized that transfer of activated building blocks could be the "fundamental reaction" in biosyntheses. When he tested the function of acetyl phosphate in pigeon liver—a trial system from a higher organism—Lipmann found that this molecule had no effect. He identified a new factor, however—coenzyme A (CoA), a derivative of the vitamin pantothenic acid—which appeared to do the job. Careful chemistry and much work (by Lipmann's group and others) identified the exact structure of coenzyme A and showed that it accounted for all the pantothenic acid in cells of animals, plants, and microorganisms. Coenzyme A, therefore, was the only functional form of the vitamin.

Examination of pantothenic acid deficiency in living organisms made it clear that coenzyme A functioned importantly in many biochemical processes, including the disposition of fats, energy production, and the function of the citric acid cycle. Next, it was shown that coenzyme A activated acetate to form a chemical called acetyl coenzyme A, used both for energy production and for many diverse syntheses in cells. These syntheses included Krebs's citric acid used in energy production, acetylcholine involved in nerve transmission, and other compounds as complex as steroids and terpenes.

Lipmann ended by pointing out that because of the efforts of many researchers, a new picture of biochemistry was developing in his area of interest, synthetic biochemistry and metabolism. He proposed that in the near future the gap between biology and biochemistry would narrow.

Critical reception

The scientific world greeted the announcement that Lipmann had been awarded the 1953 Nobel Prize with enthusiasm, both because of the well-known importance of the research he carried out and because Lipmann was known to be "an intense, dedicated scientist who is always unaffected and very friendly." As the Nobel Committee representative, Hammarsten, had said in the Nobel allocution: "Dr. Lipmann, your opponent, and everybody knows you have only one, is an impersonal opponent, namely the complexity of biochemical processes." Lipmann had endeavored to understand and to clarify metabolism. To quote Hammarsten about Lipmann again: "You have removed an obstructive confusion by the clear demonstration of a very widespread reaction and have discovered simultaneously a new way for the transmission of energy in the cell."

Lipmann had always credited other researchers with the things that they discovered and praised creativity lavishly. Other scientists respected him widely. He was also very learned in his area of research. Consequently, as stated in the October 22, 1953, issue of *The New York Times*, "Dr. Lipmann is regarded by the Nobel committee experts as one of the world's leading experts on the enzymes, substances that promote chemical reactions without themselves being consumed." Similarly, the November 2, 1953, issue of *Newsweek* quoted Dr. Göran Liljestrand, secretary of the Nobel medical committee, as saying that "the work of the two Nobel laureates is of the utmost theoretical significance and very likely to have great practical importance to understanding of diseases and similar disturbances." This statement paralleled commentary made earlier by another famous biochemist, Carl Neuberg, about Lipmann. Neuberg praised Lipmann's contribution to formulation of "the laws of metabolic generation and to the utilization of phosphate bond energy," as well as his research into cancer and cell structure.

The extent of the appreciation of the media for Lipmann's research efforts is best reflected by the following quotation from the November 2, 1953, issue of *Newsweek*: "Dr. Lipmann discovered co-enzyme A, now recognized as the key substance of biological synthesis. Later, he and other Harvard associates demonstrated how this very vital factor contributes to body building. Lipmann's theories are now being widely used in cancer research."

Biography

Fritz Albert Lipmann was born in Königsberg, Germany, the capital of East Prussia. His parents, Leopold Lipmann, a lawyer, and Gertrude (Lachmanski) Lipmann were loving and very supportive. From early childhood, Lipmann loved medicine, a result of the great influence of an uncle who was a pediatrician. Consequently, in

1917, he began studying medicine at the University of Königsberg. Then World War I intervened, and Lipmann joined the Medical Corps.

After the war, Lipmann continued medical studies at Munich and Berlin universities. In 1924, Berlin University awarded him the M.D. degree. Always very interested in the chemistry of life, Lipmann returned to Königsberg to study the science in more depth. This study, under Peter Rona, helped to turn Lipmann toward a career in biochemistry. In 1926, therefore, Lipmann became an assistant in the laboratory of the famous biochemist Otto Meyerhof at Kaiser Wilhelm Institute. There, he completed the Ph.D. degree in 1929. When Meyerhof moved on to Heidelberg, Lipmann went with him.

The next six years of Lipmann's life were peripatetic. He worked in Berlin, Heidelberg, and New York City. During that time, Lipmann worked with biochemists such as Albert Fischer; in 1932, Lipmann moved to the Carlsberg Foundation at Copenhagen to continue working with him. Lipmann remained in Denmark until 1939, studying the mechanisms by which cells make the energy required for life.

By that time, the Nazis were well on the way to controlling Denmark. Lipmann, a Jew, emigrated to America to avoid expected persecution by the Third Reich. At first, he worked for Vincent Du Vigneaud at New York's Cornell University Medical College. Then, in 1944, he became a research fellow in Surgery at Harvard University. At that time, he also became a naturalized American. In 1945, his wife, Elfreda Hall Lipmann, gave birth to their son, Stephen.

By 1949, Lipmann was a full professor of biological chemistry at Harvard because of his research on energy metabolism and his discovery of coenzyme A. In 1953, he received the Nobel Prize in Physiology or Medicine (shared with Hans Krebs), for "discovery of coenzyme A and its importance to intermediary metabolism."

In 1957, Lipmann moved to a biochemistry professorship at Rockefeller University. He remained there, actively engaged in research, until his death on July 24, 1986. Lipmann, an excellent scientist and a decent man, was widely liked and honored. His honors included memberships in prestigious scientific societies, scientific medals, and many honorary degrees from important universities around the world.

Scientific Career

Lipmann's scientific career began in 1922, just after his receipt of the medical degree from the University of Berlin. At that time, Lipmann became "uneasy about charging people for trying to make them healthy" and cast about for another career. Fortuitously, he remained at the university for a very intensive course in biochemistry taught by Peter Rona. This course made him decide to become a life science researcher. He began with a pharmacology research fellowship, under Ernst Laquer in Amsterdam. There, becoming acquainted with biochemistry, Lipmann decided to focus on that area of endeavor.

Ever practical, Lipmann decided that he needed a better grasp of chemistry to function well as a biochemist. To obtain the needed expertise, he returned to the University of Königsberg and spent three years in the superb chemistry department chaired by Hans Meerwein. Then, he passed the *Staatsexamen* and carried out doctoral research on the biochemistry of muscle cells in the Berlin University laboratory of Otto Meyerhof (cowinner of the 1922 Nobel Prize in Physiology or Medicine, for research in the area). In 1929, Lipmann was awarded his Ph.D.

Much of Lipmann's work at this time was based on the fact that by the 1920's Meyerhof and other scientists had identified the general schema for carbohydrate metabolism, working mostly with glucose. It was known, for example, that this very plentiful sugar was chemically degraded by a fermentation process (glycolysis) and also by oxygen-utilizing (aerobic) respiration. In the aerobic process, glucose is first made into pyruvic acid. Then it is oxidized to carbon dioxide and water. Glycolysis also produces pyruvate; however, in the fermentation, the puruvate is converted to lactic acid.

Lipmann continued with Meyerhof for two years after obtaining his Ph.D. During this time, he was employed as a graduate research associate. When Meyerhof moved to Heidelberg, Lipmann went with him. During his collaboration with Meyerhof, Lipmann studied the effect of toxic fluoride ion on muscle and showed that it was caused by the diminished oxidation of lactic acid.

Then, in 1930, Lipmann returned to Berlin to pursue additional postgraduate research with Albert Fischer. In Fischer's laboratory, he learned to culture fibroblast cells, a new technique essential to any high-powered contemporary biochemical research. In 1931, however, Lipmann won a Rockefeller fellowship and spent the year at New York's Rockefeller University, where he learned about the metabolism of phosphorus, an area in which he later worked very extensively. One example of a paper he published from this work was "Serine Phosphoric Acid Obtained on Hydrolysis of Vitellinic Acid," published in 1932 in *The Journal of Biological Chemistry.* After the fellowship ended, Lipmann rejoined Fischer and followed him to a new laboratory at the Carlsberg Foundation, in Copenhagen.

Lipmann spent the next seven years in Copenhagen. During this time, he began to examine the mechanisms by which cells produce the energy they require to survive. He began with the study, in bacteria, of a phenomenon called the Pasteur effect. The term "Pasteur effect" indicates the ability of oxygen to stop glycolysis in many cells that can grow in its presence or absence. Lipmann's research tool here was examination of the oxidation of pyruvate to acetate, the main metabolic fuel. Early in his research effort, Lipmann discovered that the process was completely dependent upon inorganic phosphate. This phosphate dependence, he found, was intimately related to the production of the metabolite acetyl phosphate. Consequently, Lipmann postulated that phosphate might be the universal basis for biological energy production; however, he later learned that although the acetyl phosphate was very important in bacteria, it was more of a side issue in the higher organisms.

By 1939, Lipmann was forced to flee from Nazi persecution as the German war machine began to occupy Denmark; he emigrated to the United States. Penniless, Lipmann began anew in his adopted country. Initially a research associate again, Lipmann soon rose to a professorship at Harvard Medical School.

Among Lipmann's contributions to biochemistry between 1940 and 1945 was the proposal (now universally accepted) that the main source of energy in all living cells was adenosine triphosphate (ATP). He hypothesized that the phosphate groups of this chemical are used to drive most energy-requiring reactions in living organisms. Later, when his research group identified coenzyme A, Lipmann and coworkers showed many of the ways in which the coenzyme participates in conversion of phosphate-bond energy from ATP into other useful forms of cellular energy. They also discovered that coenzyme A was ubiquitous in living cells. One excellent review of the area that Lipmann wrote was "The Metabolic Function of Pantothenic Acid" (1954).

Lipmann's findings on coenzyme A clarified many biochemical issues of the time, including solidification of understanding of the metabolic cycle proposed by Hans Krebs for conversion of foods to cellular energy. The importance and the close interrelationship of Lipmann's efforts with coenzyme A and the work of Hans Krebs on the citric acid (Krebs) cycle, led to their joint receipt of the 1953 Nobel Prize in Physiology or Medicine. This highly interrelated work, done independently by Lipmann and Krebs, was acknowledged by the Nobel Committee as "vast and significant contributions to research into the function of living cells."

During the next thirty-five years, Lipmann continued to delve into the secrets of biochemistry. Much of his intense effort was carried out at Rockefeller University, where he became a full professor of biochemistry in 1957. The endeavors Lipmann carried out related to many aspects of the use of phosphate-bond energy to power biochemical reactions, to protein synthesis, to hormone action, and to cancer.

For example, Lipmann and coworkers did much to describe and identify the formation of chemicals called organic sulfates. Organic sulfates are produced by interaction between adenosine triphosphate and a wide variety of important body chemicals. Lipmann and coworkers isolated "active sulphate" (3′-phosphoadenosine-5′-phosphosulfate), the chemical utilized to make the organic sulfates of biochemicals including carbohydrates, lipids, proteins, and many hormones. They also began the efforts at studying the enzymes (protein biochemical catalysts) that produced these organic sulfates and the application of examination of sulfation of biomolecules to study of cancer and other disease processes.

Lipmann's research group also participated in delineation of the mechanism of protein synthesis. Here again, Lipmann was interested in the role of adenosine triphosphate in powering the process. To this end, he and his group examined the catalysis of amino acid activation, a primary issue in protein synthesis. They participated in identification and study of the three proteins, called chain elongation factors, involved in growth of protein molecules during their biosynthesis. A review of this effort can be found in an article called "Polypeptide Chain Elongation in Protein Biosynthesis" (1969). An interesting offshoot of Lipmann's interest in protein synthesis was the observation that some bacteria are capable of producing small, proteinlike antibiotics by a method that utilizes a chemical cousin of coenzyme A called phosphopantetheine.

Fritz Lipmann was recognized as a superb scientist, filled with love for research. He was possessed of skill, insight, and determination. Consequently, Lipmann made exceptional contributions to scientists' current understanding of cellular metabolism and the mechanisms whereby cells produce their energy. Working in this area, he made it clear, whereas before it had been mostly speculative. As Hammarsten had said in his 1953 Nobel Prize presentation speech, Lipmann was a "fighter in the biochemical arena" who had labored "to understand complex biochemical processes related to life and make things in this area understandable and distinct." His research efforts greatly enriched the reputation of Harvard University and of Rockefeller University, helping to keep those universities at the cutting edge of the research in biochemistry during the periods when he was associated with them.

Lipmann was also known as a pleasant, well-liked person. He was an idealist full of respect for others, honesty, and decency. These characteristics were recognized by the people who knew Lipmann and worked with him. He was also a role model because of his willingness to strive and his determination.

Lipmann was honored for his scientific endeavors with membership in prestigious scientific societies, numerous scientific prizes, and many honorary degrees from universities around the world. His society memberships included the American National Academy of Sciences, the American Society of Biological Chemists, the Harvey Society, the Faraday Society, the Danish Royal Academy of Sciences, and the British Royal Society of London. Lipmann's major prizes, in addition to the 1953 Nobel Prize, were the Carl Neuberg Medal (1948), the Mead-Johnson Award (1948), and the National Medal of the U.S. National Science Foundation (1966). His honorary doctoral degrees in science included those from the Sorbonne, the University of Marseille, the University of Chicago, the University of Copenhagen, Harvard University, Rockefeller University, and the Albert Einstein College of Medicine. Lipmann was also awarded a doctorate of humane letters by Brandeis University.

Bibliography

Primary

BIOCHEMISTRY: "Serine Phosphoric Acid Obtained on Hydrolysis of Vitellinic Acid," *Journal of Biological Chemistry*, vol. 98, 1932, pp. 109-117 (with P. A. Levene); "Metabolic Generation and Utilization of Phosphate Bond Energy," *Advances in Enzymology*, vol. 1, 1941, pp. 99-162; "Biosynthetic Mechanisms," *Harvey Lectures*, vol. 44, 1950, pp. 99-123; "The Metabolic Function of Pantothenic Acid," *The Vitamins*, vol. 2, 1954, pp. 598-618; "Polypeptide Chain Elongation in Protein Synthesis," *Science*, vol. 164, 1969, pp. 924-1031; "Protein Biosynthesis," *Annual Review of Biochemistry*, vol. 40, 1971, pp. 409-448 (with J. Lucas-Leonard); "Sulfate Activation," *The Wanderings of a Biochemist*, 1971, pp. 63-79; "The Roots of Bioenergetics," *Energy Transformation in Biological Systems*, 1975, pp. 3-22; "A Long Life in Times of Great Upheaval," *Annual Review of Biochemistry*, vol. 53, 1984, pp. 1-33.

Secondary

Huxley, A. F. *Energy Transformations in Biological Systems.* Amsterdam: Elsevier, 1975. This CIBA Symposium was in honor of Lipmann's seventy-fifth birthday. Articles cover areas including mitochondrial energy generation, phosphate transfer, vision, bioluminescence, transport across cell membranes, and muscle contraction. The centrality of ATP is clear throughout. The symposium was dedicated to Lipmann because he initiated the proposition that ATP is the primary energy carrier in cells.

Lehninger, A. L. *Biochemistry.* New York: Worth, 1975. Chapter 17 of this college text provides lucid coverage of the Krebs cycle. Lehninger deciphers its history and biochemistry in a scholarly way. Complete description of the enzymology and the coenzymes is given. The importance of coenzyme A is also made clear. Several direct references to Lipmann's work and its importance are found on pages 342, 388, 519, and 715.

____________. *Principles of Biochemistry.* New York: Worth, 1982. Chapter 16 of this text, written at a somewhat lower level than *Biochemistry*, covers the same topics. This text has the advantage of providing some newer information lacking in the 1975 book. References to the importance of Lipmann's endeavors is made on pages 256, 372, and 443. The two texts by Lehninger complement each other.

Metzler, David. *Biochemistry: Chemical Reactions of Living Cells.* New York: Academic Press, 1977. Chapter 28 of this excellent text deals with coenzymes. It contains a solid description of coenzyme A, including reasons Lipmann expected its existence; aspects of its isolation; and brief descriptions of both its structure and functions. References to the overall importance of coenzyme A are listed in chapter 8 and described throughout the book.

Scott, Thomas, and Mary Brewer. *Concise Encyclopedia of Biochemistry.* New York: Walter de Gruyter, 1983. The brief but useful entry on coenzyme A in this biochemistry encyclopedia gives its structure, the chemical basis for its action in metabolism, and some of its biochemical functions. This is a good starting point for those who wish to look into coenzyme A action in more depth.

Sanford S. Singer

1954

Physiology or Medicine

John Franklin Enders, United States
Thomas Weller, United States
Frederick Robbins, United States

Chemistry

Linus Pauling, United States

Physics

Max Born, Great Britain
Walther Bothe, West Germany

Literature

Ernest Hemingway, United States

Peace

Office of the U. N. High Commissioner for Refugees

JOHN FRANKLIN ENDERS

THOMAS WELLER

FREDERICK ROBBINS

JOHN FRANKLIN ENDERS, THOMAS WELLER, and FREDERICK ROBBINS 1954

John Franklin Enders

Born: West Hartford, Connecticut; February 10, 1897
Died: Brookline, Massachusetts; September 8, 1985
Nationality: American
Areas of concentration: Virology and immunology

Thomas Weller

Born: Ann Arbor, Michigan; June 15, 1915

Nationality: American
Areas of concentration: Virology and immunology

Frederick Robbins

Born: Auburn, Alabama; August 25, 1916

Nationality: American
Areas of concentration: Virology and immunology

Enders, Weller, and Robbins developed techniques for propagating poliomyelitis virus in tissue culture, an essential step in the development of a polio vaccine and a major breakthrough in the study of viruses in general in the laboratory

The Award

Presentation

Professor Sven Gard, a member of the Staff of Professors of the Royal Caroline Institute, gave the presentation speech on December 10, 1954, on behalf of the Swedish Academy of Sciences. John Enders, Thomas Weller, and Frederick Robbins received their medals and Nobel diplomas the next day from King Gustav VI Adolf of Sweden. Gard began by contrasting the progress that had been made in isolating, cultivating, and developing prophylactic methods against bacterial diseases in the preceding seventy-five years with the difficulties encountered in attempting to isolate and cultivate viruses. Because bacterial diseases had lost some of their prominence as human pathogens, viral diseases had come to assume a more critical role as a public health problem. Poliomyelitis, scarcely mentioned in medical texts published before 1900, accounted for nearly one-fifth of all deaths from infectious disease in

Sweden in the early 1950's. Progress in virology was hampered by the fact that viruses could be propagated only in a living host—a costly, time-consuming process that produced uncertain results.

The report in 1949 by Enders, Weller, and Robbins concerning the successful cultivation of poliomyelitis virus in human tissue culture was a scientific milestone for several reasons. First, it gave virologists a practical, standardized method for isolating and propagating a variety of different viruses in the laboratory; it also gave vaccine researchers a reliable source of viral material from which to produce vaccines. Second, it provided a system in which the activities and properties of the virus could be studied directly. Third, it shed light on the nature of the poliomyelitis virus itself and demonstrated conclusively that it was not dependent on nerve tissue. It also represented a significant refinement in tissue culture techniques overall. Professor Gard expressed optimism that the groundwork laid by Enders and his colleagues would lead rapidly to new discoveries of immediate practical benefit. He praised them for their "biological common sense" and their practical approach to medical research in an era increasingly characterized by concern with technology and gadgetry.

Nobel lecture

The Nobel lecture, entitled "The Cultivation of Poliomyetlitis Virus in Tissue Culture," was presented by Enders, Weller, and Robbins on December 11, 1954. It displays a masterful command of the English language because of John Enders, who was nearly as well qualified as an English scholar as he was as a virologist. It recounts how the three collaborators came to study the polio virus, the details of their experimental work, and probable applications of their work to other areas of virology.

In 1937, when Enders first began working with viruses at Harvard Medical School, the science of virology was in its infancy in the sense that neither the underlying principles nor experimental techniques of the research were well established. Theory was inadequate to suggest more than the vague outlines of experimental design, and to some extent researchers were "fishing in troubled waters" in the hope that some of their manipulations would at least suggest future avenues for profitable experimentation. The discovery for which the three men won the Nobel Prize in 1954 was the direct result of a series of experiments conducted between 1937 and 1949, none of which was specifically aimed at poliomyelitis. The final result could not have been predicted at any but the latest step in the series.

In 1937, Enders, a bacteriologist at Harvard Medical School, turned his attention to growth of the herpes simplex and measles viruses. He became convinced that tissue culture techniques were an ideal means of investigating viruses, and the expertise he acquired in tissue culture led Thomas Weller, who was pursuing a specialty in tropical medicine and parasitic nematodes (elongated cylindrical worms), to collaborate with him. After World War II, operations moved to Boston Children's Hospital, where Frederick Robbins joined the team. Their first joint project was the cultivation of the mumps virus, a choice that proved fortunate because the slow-growing mumps virus could be propagated in culture only in tissue cultures maintained over long periods of time.

In 1948, following the successful completion of the mumps virus experiments, Robbins was preparing to study the viral agent of infantile diarrhea in tissue culture. At the time, a debate was raging about whether the polio virus would grow only in nerve tissue. It had been speculated that it could grow in the human intestinal tract as well. Enders and his colleagues suspected that the cultures of fetal intestinal tissue established for Robbins' experiments could provide the answer. They therefore inoculated some of the cultures with the Lansing strain of polio viruses. The results were far more successful than they had anticipated. The virus clearly multiplied in a variety of human tissues, including fetal intestine, brain, kidney, and skin tissue. Changes in the cells and in the growth medium were correlated with virus growth. Before this discovery, the only method of propagating or determining the presence of polio virus had been to inoculate a suitable host. Since two of the strains attacked only humans and primates, the process was laborious, costly, difficult to quantify, and morally difficult to justify.

The development of the tissue culture technique permitted screening and selection for strains with altered pathogenicity, a prerequisite for development of an effective polio vaccine. Passage of a strain of virus through many successive generations in tissue culture, using the highest possible dilution of the material used for inoculating, produced viral strains that were capable of infecting monkeys and producing an immune response. The tissue culture technique also made it possible to produce antibodies for epidemiological studies and to culture the virus as a diagnostic procedure. This enabled polio researchers to form a better picture of the distribution of the disease and the proportion of nonparalytic cases. Tissue cultures were already proving a useful tool in identifying and characterizing previously unknown viruses, such as cocksackie and human respiratory viruses, and in experimental manipulation of known viruses, notably that of measles.

Of the many discoveries by other researchers that contributed to this research, the three laureates singled out the discovery of antibiotics, which made it possible to maintain tissue cultures over long periods of time and to isolate viruses from bacterially contaminated substrates (such as feces), to be particularly significant.

Critical reception

Public response to the announcement that Enders, Weller, and Robbins had been awarded the Nobel Prize was immediate and uniformly laudatory. It could scarcely have been otherwise in an era when poliomyelitis was the most feared public health menace in the industrialized world. The first extensive field trials involving immunizing half a million American schoolchildren with Salk vaccine had just been completed in the spring and summer of 1954.

With the possible exception of the acquired immune deficiency syndrome (AIDS) epidemic of the 1980's, no single infectious disease has loomed so large in the modern public imagination as polio did in the 1940's and 1950's. Aside from its obvious virulence, it is a singularly frightening disease, striking apparently healthy children and young adults without warning and leaving many of them permanently paralyzed. Until it was demonstrated that the majority of cases were nonparalytic and were never diagnosed as polio, the epidemiology of the disease was mysterious, and quarantine methods were ineffective in halting its spread.

Although records of what was presumably poliomyelitis exist from ancient Egypt to the present, the disease was not formally recognized as such until the nineteenth century. It had assumed the status of an important epidemic disease in the mid-twentieth century. It is, in essence, a disease exacerbated by modern sanitation. In preindustrial times (and under typical conditions in the Third World), children were exposed to the polio virus in infancy and contracted a mild nonparalytic intestinal form of the disease which conferred permanent immunity. In the twentieth century United States, however, the virus was usually absent from the environment, and periodic epidemics swept through susceptible populations of older children and young adults, among whom a certain proportion became paralyzed. Moreover, the severity of epidemics was increasing with time. Franklin Delano Roosevelt fell victim during the epidemic of 1921 and was partially paralyzed for the remainder of his life.

Through the "March of Dimes" campaign, the National Foundation for Infantile Paralysis made people acutely aware of the devastating effects of the disease while raising impressive amounts of money both for direct aid to victims and for basic research. Enders, Weller, and Robbins were supported in part by the National Foundation for Infantile Paralysis, a circumstance that was gratifying to the foundation and its myriad supporters and was a coup for popularly based philanthropic efforts in general, as noted in an editorial in *The New York Times* on October 23, 1954. The Nobel Committee had initially been inclined to award the prize to Enders alone, but Enders, with characteristic modesty and generosity, insisted that it be shared equally with his two younger colleagues.

In recounting interviews with colleagues several years after the award, Greer Williams presents the personal views of some members of the scientific community, who believed that Enders and his colleagues were excessively modest about the unique contribution of their research. Enders, according to one fellow faculty member, "had a green thumb for growing viruses," a phrase that sums up a quality of persistence and attention to detail without which it is impossible to manipulate difficult biological systems successfully. What the prizewinners themselves viewed as something of a chance discovery, the scientific community was more ready to recognize as being the product of many years of uniquely competent and inspired research.

Biographies

John Franklin Enders was born on February 10, 1897, in West Hartford, Connecticut, into a family that possessed a substantial private fortune and was firmly entrenched in the commercial, social, and intellectual elite of New England. He was the son of John O. Enders and Harriet (née Whitmore) Enders. His father was president of the Hartford National Bank, and his grandfather was president of Aetna Life Insurance Company. After completing his secondary education at St. Paul's school in Concord, New Hampshire, in 1915, Enders enrolled at Yale University, but he left in 1917 to become an aviator and flying instructor in the United States Marine Corps.

At the end of World War I, he returned to Yale, from which he was graduated in 1920. After a brief, unrewarding period as a real estate agent, he enrolled in the school of arts and sciences of Harvard University, intending to get a graduate degree and teach English. In four years, he completed a master's degree in English and was close to finishing a Ph.D. (with a specialization in Celtic and Teutonic languages) when a student with whom he shared lodgings introduced him to Dr. Hans Zinsser, a charismatic professor of bacteriology who was to become his mentor in a newfound métier. With Zinsser, Enders completed the Ph.D. in microbiology and immunology in 1930 with a thesis on serology of pneumococcus. His association with virology began with an investigation of feline distemper. In 1930, he was appointed to the teaching staff of Harvard Medical School.

It is tempting to characterize (or caricature) Enders as a stereotypical product of an upper-class New England family, and such a portrait would have at least an element of truth. His biographers describe him as crusty, undemonstrative, modest, and cultured. Financial security afforded him the leisure to pursue an academic career according to his own schedule and to explore many avenues. Because he was wealthy, he was immune—as English scholar, as brilliant biologist, and as a member of the boards of directors of numerous corporations—to any pressures to obtain quick results or pursue the latest trends.

Enders married Sarah Francis Bennet of Brookline, Massachusetts, in 1927. After her death in 1943, he married Carolyn Keane of Newton Center, Massachusetts. He had one son and one daughter by his first marriage. He died on September 8, 1985, in Brookline.

Thomas Weller was born in Ann Arbor, Michigan, on June 15, 1915, the son of Carl Vernon Weller, a member of the faculty of the pathology department of the University of Michigan Medical School. He received his A.B. from the University of Michigan in 1936 and went on to pursue graduate work at the University of Michigan Biological Station, obtaining the M.S. degree in 1937 for work on parasites of fish. In the meantime, he had entered Harvard Medical School and had begun work with two distinguished parasitologists, E. E. Tyzzer and Donald Augustine, from whom he acquired a lifelong interest in protozoology and helminthology. In 1939, he began work with Enders on viruses in tissue culture. He obtained his M.D. in 1940 and was in clinical training at the Children's Hospital in Boston until joining the Army Medical Corps in 1942. He became head of the departments of bacteriology, virology, and parasitology of the Antilles Medical Laboratory in Puerto Rico, and he attained the rank of major. After the war he returned to the Children's Hospital, and after completion of residential training became assistant director of the research division of infectious diseases of the Children's Medical Center. He also joined the faculty of Harvard Medical School, first as an instructor in pathology and tropical medicine, then as an associate professor of public health. In 1954, he was given an endowed chair as Strong Professor of Tropical Public Health and head of the department of public health of Harvard Medical School.

Frederick Chapman Robbins was born in Auburn, Alabama, on August 25, 1916. He was the son of William J. Robbins, a well-known botanist who later became director of the New York Botanical Gardens, and Christine (née Chapman) Robbins. He received the A.B. degree from the University of Missouri in 1936 and his B.S. there in 1938. In 1940, he was graduated with an M.D. from Harvard Medical School and was appointed resident physician at the Children's Hospital Medical Center in Boston, where he worked until joining the United States Army in 1942. He was appointed chief of the virus and rickettsial disease section of the Fifteenth Medical General Laboratory, and he served in the United States, North Africa, and Italy, conducting significant research on viral hepatitis, typhus, and Q fever.

Upon discharge, he returned to the Children's Hospital, retaining an appointment to its staff as well as to that of Harvard Medical School in 1948. In May, 1952, he moved to Cleveland, Ohio, to accept a position at Western Reserve University School of Medicine. In 1948, he married Alice Northrop, daughter of John Northrop, who shared the 1946 Nobel Prize in Chemistry. The couple have two daughters.

Scientific Careers

Many observers have commented upon the large element of chance involved in the bringing together of three men with such diverse backgrounds and research interests as Enders, Weller, and Robbins. Their scientific careers as collaborators coincide only during the period 1946 to 1952; subsequently, they all worked in different laboratories with different areas of concentration in the general field of epidemiology and parasitology. Enders was, above all, a virologist; Robbins was a specialist in contagious diseases of children; and Weller was a scholar and practitioner in the specialty of tropical medicine. A contrast can be drawn between the careers of the two medical doctors, Weller and Robbins, who became heavily involved in administration, and that of Enders, with his academic Ph.D., for whom, first, teaching, and later, research, were paramount.

The team that thus coalesced at the Infectious Disease Laboratory of the Boston's Children's Hospital in 1946 and that was to win the Nobel Prize in Physiology or Medicine eight years later drew upon experiences that were intimately associated with the members' various services for the United States during World War II. Enders, who was anxious to focus his research on medical problems of military significance, happened serendipitously to have chosen to work with Joseph Stokes at the University of Pennsylvania developing a vaccine against the mumps virus years before. Stokes and Enders relied on monkey hosts as a source of the virus. Enders was convinced that the virus could be successfully cultivated in tissue culture.

Thomas Weller came to the laboratory following a three-year stint in the Army Medical Corps. While a student at Harvard Medical School before the war, he had been introduced to virus research and tissue culture techniques by Enders. His primary speciality was parasitology—the study of protozoa and parasitic worms and the source of health problems that are most prominent in the tropics. These problems are the result of obligate parasites, which cannot reproduce independent of the host. Robbins, the third member of the team, wished to specialize in infectious diseases of children. After a three-year term in the United States Army, he accepted a fellowship from the National Foundation for Infantile Paralysis to work with John Enders on viral disease.

It is impossible to appreciate the revolutionary nature of this work without understanding something of the nature of viruses and previous attempts to cultivate them. Viruses are the most obligate of obligate parasites, able to reproduce themselves only within living cells. Most viruses, including important viral diseases of man, are quite host-specific, attacking only one host species or a few closely related species. In contrast, it is possible to grow a wide range of bacteria pathogenic to humans in nonliving media. Finally, the minute size of viruses made it impossible to see individual virus particles directly with methods available in 1948.

The scientists working on mumps, polio, and other host-specific human viral diseases could do very little without recourse to primate (monkey) hosts: They could not demonstrate unequivocally that the virus was present; they could not produce antiserums for immunological work, and they could not produce additional virus particles for research or for commercial production of a killed or attenuated virus vaccine. Vaccines prepared from infected monkey tissues were not only prohibitively expensive, they also produced such violent allergic reactions in humans that their use could only be justified in genuinely life-threatening situations.

In tissue culture, isolated animal (or plant) cells are maintained in a nutrient medium in which they live and metabolize; in early experiments, there was typically little reproduction of cells in tissue culture, but with subsequent refinements it has become possible to propagate lines of cells nearly indefinitely. Various workers had proposed and experimented with tissue culturing methods in the 1920's and 1930's, and the approach which proved most appropriate for polio virus research was described by Hugh and Mary Maitland in 1928. The importance of the Maitlands' technique, which was not widely used because of its complexity, lay in the length of time that a culture could be maintained. In order to demonstrate the growth of a slow-growing virus, it was necessary that the same cells be kept alive for a period of weeks. This task was considerably easier after the discovery of antibiotics, which were effective in preventing bacterial contamination of cultures.

In early 1948, Enders and Weller, supported by a grant from the National Foundation for Infantile Paralysis to Harvard University for research on unspecified viruses, set out to grow mumps and chicken pox viruses in cultures of suspended chick embryo cells. They were able to show that, given a sufficient amount of time, the mumps virus multiplied, and the culture fluid produced the positive hemagglutination reaction characteristic of mumps. These results did not capture public attention directly, but they were important in setting the stage for later work.

Having established a successful routine for cultivating slow-growing viruses in tissue culture, each member of the team proceeded to establish a series of cultures to investigate a particular viral problem. Weller established cultures of human embryonic brain, skin, and intestinal tissue in order to cultivate chicken pox, and Robbins was attempting to cultivate the agent of viral diarrhea in infants using mouse intestine. None of the members of the team specifically intended to work with polio, but it occurred to Enders that it would be worth testing to see whether the Lansing strain of poliomyelitis, which had been sent to him by a colleague, would grow in established cultures of intestinal tissue. Epidemiologists had determined that polio virus was present in large quantities in the intestines of patients, which suggested that it was not restricted to nervous tissue as had been supposed by earlier researchers. The virus failed to grow in mouse intestine, but after eight to twenty-eight days, an increase in virus concentration could be demonstrated in human embryonic skin.

At first, virus multiplication could only be demonstrated by inoculating mice with culture fluid. It was soon noticed, however, that changes in the color and acidity of the medium were correlated with viral activity and that the cells themselves showed pathological changes when observed microscopically. Refinements in the tissue culture technique itself improved the sensitivity and reliability of such direct methods for determining virus presence without recourse to infecting live animals. These results were published in *Science* in January, 1949, and immediately became the foundation for a new generation of poliomyelitis research. Enders, Weller, and Robbins continued to work together on a variety of problems in virology for which the tissue culture methodology was appropriate (Enders worked on measles, Robbins on mumps, herpes simplex, and vaccinia, and Weller on varicella, herpes zoster, and cocksackie viruses).

In 1952, Robbins moved to Cleveland, Ohio, to take a position as professor of pediatrics at Western Reserve School of Medicine and director of the department of pediatrics and contagious diseases at Cleveland Metropolitan Hospital. In 1961, he was elected president of the Society for Pediatric Research and in 1962 became a member of the American Academy of Arts and Sciences. He has served as a consultant on the boards of numerous governmental and private health agencies and has published widely on a variety of public health problems.

As a professor at Harvard Medical School, Weller continued active research in both parasitology and virology, making important contributions to the literature on trichinosis and schistosomiasis. The latter is one of the most serious, debilitating, and intractable of tropical parasitic diseases. He was able to cultivate this parasite in vitro and to develop improved diagnostic tests for it. His analyses stressed the importance of ecological and social factors in the spread of schistosomiasis as well as purely parasitological considerations. Weller cultivated and demonstrated that the viruses responsible for varicella (chicken pox) and herpes zoster (shingles) were identical and that this ubiquitous pathogen, relatively benign for normal individuals, constitutes a serious threat to immune-deficient patients. He also isolated and characterized the viral agent of cytomegalic inclusion disease in infants.

John Enders continued to investigate viral agents of disease in culture, and he was instrumental in the development of a measles vaccine, first used clinically in 1961.

He was also active in researching connections between viruses and cancer. He retired from active scientific work in 1977 and occupied himself in his remaining years to his first scholarly love, literature, until his death on September 8, 1985.

Bibliography

Primary

MEDICINE: "Virus Disease of Cats, Principally Characterized by Aleucytosis, Enteric Lesions, and Presence of Intranuclear Inclusion Bodies," *Journal of Experimental Medicine*, vol. 69, 1939, pp. 327-352 (Enders, with W. D. Hammon); *Immunity: Principles and Application in Public Health*, 1939 (Enders, with Hans Zinsser and L. Fothergill); "Evaluation of Test for Antihemagglutinin in Diagnosis of Infections by Mumps Virus," *Journal of Immunology*, vol. 61, 1949, pp. 235-242 (Enders and Robbins, with L. Kilham and J. H. Levens); "Cultivation of Lansing Strain of Poliomyelitis Virus in Cultures of Various Human Embryonic Tissues," *Science*, vol. 109, 1949, pp. 85-87 (Enders, Weller, and Robbins); "Studies on Cultivation of Poliomyelitis Viruses in Tissue Culture: Direct Isolation and Serologic Identification of Virus Strains in Tissue Culture from Patients with Nonparalytic and Paralytic Poliomyelitis," *American Journal of Hygiene*," vol. 54, 1951, pp. 286-293 (Enders, Robbins, and Weller, with G. L. Florentino); *Poliomyelitis: Second International Poliomyelitis Conference*, 1952 (Enders); "Application of Tissue Culture Methods to Study Viral Infections," *Pediatrics*, vol. 13, 1954, pp. 283-292 (Robbins and Weller); "The Etiologic Agents of Varicella and Herpes Zoster: Isolation, Propagation, and Cultural Characteristics in Vitro," *Journal of Experimental Medicine*, vol. 108, 1958, pp. 843-868 (Weller, with H. M. Witton and E. J. Bell); "Remarks on Oncogenic Virus-Cell Relationships," *Proceedings of the National Cancer Society*, vol. 5, 1968, pp. 725-733 (Enders); "The Long-Term Effects of Infection in Early Life," *Pediatric Research*, vol. 8, 1974, pp. 972-976 (Robbins); "Schistosomiasis: Its Significance in a Changing World," *Journal of Toxicology and Environmental Health*, vol. 1, 1975, pp. 185-190 (Weller); "Varicella and Herpes Zoster: Changing Concepts of the Natural History, Control, and Importance of a Not-So-Benign Virus," *New England Journal of Medicine*, vol. 309, 1983, pp. 1362-1368, 1434-1440 (Weller); "Isolation of the Human Cytomegaloviruses," *Birth Defects*, vol. 20, 1984, pp. 15-19 (Weller).

Secondary

Calder, Richie. "Man's Struggle Against Poliomyelitis." *World Health* 14 (1961): 29-35. A brief illustrated history of polio in a journal published by the World Health Organization, covering the same material treated by Paul (1971) but with considerably less technical detail.

Paul, John R. *A History of Poliomyelitis*. New Haven, Conn.: Yale University Press, 1971. Paul traces the history of polio from Egyptian times through its emergence as an epidemic disease in the 1800's to the development of a successful vaccine in the 1950's. The book is aimed at nonspecialists but assumes a college-level background in the biological sciences. Chapter 35 is devoted to the work of Enders and colleagues and includes biographical information as well as a thorough account of the work.

Riedman, Sarah R., and Elton T. Gustafson. *Portraits of Nobel Laureates in Medicine and Physiology.* New York: Abelard-Schuman, 1963. This readable, nontechnical account is organized according to subdiscipline; each chapter treats a number of laureates who worked on related topics. The section devoted to polio research provides a personal portrait of Enders, Weller, and Robbins and a lucid description of their joint work.

Sourkes, Theodore L. *Nobel Prizewinners in Medicine and Physiology.* New York: Abelard-Schuman, 1966. The article on Enders, Weller, and Robbins contains a brief biographical sketch, a two-page description of the prizewinning work aimed at the nonspecialist, and a brief assessment of the consequences of the work for medicine. Contains a minimum of bibliographic information.

Waterson, A. P., and Lise Wilkinson. *An Introduction to the History of Virology.* New York: Cambridge University Press, 1978. Chapter 6, "Development of Cell and Tissue Cultures," gives a nontechnical but thorough account of the history of attempts to culture viruses. It also provides a clear explanation of the contrast between bacterial and viral cultures. There is a short biography of Enders.

Williams, Greer. *Virus Hunters.* New York: Alfred A. Knopf, 1959. A lively journalistic account of research on viruses, somewhat outdated from a scientific point of view but full of fascinating historical detail. Chapters 21 to 26 deal with polio research. Chapter 22, "Enders: Polio Research's Debt to Mumps," presents a personal portrait of Enders and his colleagues and a lucid account of their research.

Martha Sherwood-Pike

1955

Physiology or Medicine
Axel Hugo Theodor Theorell, Sweden

Chemistry
Vincent du Vigneaud, United States

Physics
Willis Eugene Lamb, Jr., United States
Polykarp Kusch, United States

Literature
Halldór Laxness, Iceland

Peace
no award

Uggla

AXEL HUGO THEODOR THEORELL 1955

Born: Linköping, Sweden; July 6, 1903
Died: Stockholm, Sweden; August 15, 1982
Nationality: Swedish
Areas of concentration: Biochemistry and enzymology

Theorell's research on the structure and activities of those enzymes that facilitate oxidation and reduction reactions in certain cells advanced scientific understanding not only of how cells use oxygen but also of how enzymes themselves function in all their interactions

The Award

Presentation

Professor Einar Hammarsten, a member of the Royal Caroline Institute and a former teacher of Theorell, gave the formal presentation address on December 10, 1955, before Theorell received his Nobel Prize from the hands of King Gustav VI Adolf. Hammarsten chose a historical approach, tracing Theorell's principal research area, oxidative enzymes, back to Jöns Jakob Berzelius, who, early in the nineteenth century, developed the notion of catalysts (substances that speed chemical changes without suffering change themselves). Berzelius used the term to include inorganic as well as organic (or biological) catalysts, but it was not until the late nineteenth century that scientists were able to separate enzymes from cells whose many reactions these biological catalysts carefully mediate. In the twentieth century, biochemists showed that enzymes are proteins which, in minuscule amounts, can accelerate, in an extremely specific way, certain cell reactions a billionfold or more.

Theorell's work dealt largely with the enzymes of cell respiration—that is, with substances that promote the reactions through which organisms transform nutrients, with the participation of oxygen, into usable energy. He discovered the basic components of important enzymes as well as how these parts fit together to enable enzymes to encourage certain chemical reactions. Because enzymes are extremely reactive, their isolation and purification proved difficult, but Theorell's great experimental expertise permitted him to obtain and study uncontaminated samples of such iron-containing enzymes as the peroxidases and the cytochromes. Hammarsten concluded by praising both the "fertile imagination" and the technical skill of his former student. In these attributes he found Theorell an exemplary intellectual descendant of Berzelius, their fellow Swede.

Nobel lecture

Theorell delivered his lecture, "The Nature and Mode of Action of Oxidation Enzymes," on December 12, 1955. He began by pointing out that enzymes direct all chemical reactions in living things. As Hammarsten had done, Theorell mentioned

Berzelius, who, more than a century before, had gone to the same secondary school as he had.

Otto Warburg, who had won the 1931 Nobel Prize for his discovery of the nature and mode of action of the respiratory enzyme, became Theorell's guide to the large and important group of oxidative enzymes. In 1932, Warburg and an associate had isolated from yeast an impure sample of a yellow substance that was instrumental in the oxidation of cell sugars. The yellow color fascinated Theorell, since it faded on reduction (combination with hydrogen) and returned on oxidation (combination with oxygen). Theorell capitalized on Warburg's work by constructing an electrical instrument of his own design to obtain extremely pure yellow enzyme. He then showed that this enzyme had two components: a protein part, or apoenzyme, which is biologically inactive unless joined to a second part, a coenzyme—a small non-protein molecule, also inactive alone. Theorell investigated why this coenzyme, with its yellow color and its structure related to riboflavin (vitamin B_2), is inactive when isolated but active when anchored to its large, colorless protein carrier (the apoenzyme). He was able to show how the colored part of the yellow enzyme (eventually called FMN, for flavin mononucleotide) brings about the oxidation of the sugar glucose by binding this substrate with certain atoms to a specific site on the flavin moiety.

Theorell then discussed his work on another enzyme system, alcohol dehydrogenase; like the yellow enzyme, it consists of an apoenzyme (a large protein) in reversible combination with a coenzyme—in this case, diphosphopyridine nucleotide (DPN). These alcohol-burning enzymes occur in the livers of animals and in yeast. They may either oxidize alcohol to aldehyde (a process which occurs principally in the liver) or reduce aldehyde to alcohol (which occurs in yeast).

In the 1930's, Theorell became interested in yet another enzyme, cytochrome *c*, a red substance that had been recognized in muscle as early as 1886. It was not until 1925, however, that David Keilin, a professor of biology at the University of Cambridge, rediscovered the substance. Keilin named it "cytochrome" (meaning colored cell) and showed that it was widely distributed in aerobic organisms. He discovered three different cytochromes and called them *a*, *b*, and *c*. Theorell's research focused on cytochrome *c*, and he determined the exact nature of the chemical linkage between its apoenzyme and its iron-containing prosthetic group (the nonprotein unit necessary for a protein's biological activity). Specifically, in 1938, he and his colleagues showed that cytochrome *c*'s prosthetic group is bonded to its apoenzyme by means of bridges of sulfur atoms. After Linus Pauling had discovered that proteins have a helical structure, Theorell confirmed, by chemical methods, that Pauling's alpha helix was present in cytochrome *c*.

Theorell concluded by discussing some other important oxidative enzymes, catalase and the peroxidases. Catalase breaks down hydrogen peroxide into oxygen and water; the peroxidases activate hydrogen peroxide so that it oxidizes various compounds. Despite the great amount of information biochemists have garnered about these and other enzymes, they actually know, Theorell felt, only about the most accessible parts of the smallest enzymes. Since the ultimate goal of enzyme research is "the filling of the yawning gulf between biochemistry and morphology"—that is, the detailed determination of the spatial arrangement of all atoms in every enzyme—biochemists have herculean labors ahead of them.

Critical reception

Theorell, who worked at the Royal Caroline Institute, and who had helped found the Nobel Medical Institute, did not confront the difficulties encountered by many foreign scientists in familiarizing the relevant Nobel Committees with his work. His successes in biochemistry were well known in Sweden, and most scientists believed that it was only a matter of time before he would be awarded a Nobel Prize. Indeed, some scientists, both in Sweden and abroad, believed that a Nobel Prize for Theorell was long overdue. Despite this strong support for Theorell's candidacy, it initially seemed that he would have to wait another year for his prize: Premature newspaper reports indicated that, according to ranking members of the Caroline Institute, Vincent du Vigneaud of Cornell University might receive the 1955 award for his work on hormones (as, in fact, he did—in chemistry, however, rather than in physiology or medicine).

In announcing that Theorell had won the medical prize, Göran Liljestrand, the secretary of the Nobel Committee on Medicine, called Theorell "the indisputable leader in his field," and the Swedish press followed Liljestrand's tone and analysis in their accounts. Stories were accompanied by a picture of Theorell celebrating his honor by sharing champagne in laboratory beakers with his associates. Theorell was the first Swede to win the award in medicine since 1911, when Allvar Gullstrand won it for his work on the dioptrics of the eye, and national pride was obvious in both professional and popular accounts. Considerable human interest surrounded Theorell's Nobel Prize, since he had been a victim of polio in his youth; as several reporters pointed out, he had risen above his handicap to become an outstanding scientist as well as an adept amateur musician.

In England and the United States, the award to Theorell also met with a favorable response. *The Times* of London praised his work on oxidative enzymes as "an outstanding contribution to our understanding of the complicated mechanism of cell division and cell growth." In assessing Theorell's work on enzymes, several American newspapers mentioned the seminal work of the American James B. Sumner, who had won the 1946 Nobel Prize in Chemistry for having isolated and crystallized enzymes and demonstrated their protein nature. *The New York Times* for October 21, 1955, mentioned Theorell's indebtedness to two other Americans: Linus Pauling, for his work on protein structure, and Britton Chance, for his work on the mechanisms of enzyme reactions. An article in *The New York Times* for October 23, 1955, explained how Theorell advanced Sumner's work by showing precisely how an enzyme's activity depends on the relationship between the apoenzyme and coenzyme. Like the Swedish newspapers, *The New York Times* wondered why it had taken the Nobel Committees "so long to honor a scientist whose technical methods and explorations of a dozen different fields command the admiration of his peers."

As had become traditional, American newsmagazines also commented on the Nobel Prize winners. For example, *Time* for October 31, 1955, reported on the false leak that preceded the revelation of Theorell's Nobel Prize. In fact, until a few minutes before the actual announcement, the Associated Press was distributing extensive background information about the "winner," du Vigneaud. Despite this distraction, *Time* and other newsmagazines viewed the award to Theorell as richly deserved. *Newsweek*'s account was in the same vein, though it added the information that Theorell planned to split his $36,720 prize money between an expansion of his research facilities and a larger apartment for himself, his wife, and his three sons.

Biography

Axel Hugo Theodor Theorell, the second of three children, was born in Linköping, Sweden, a small town about 190 kilometers southwest of Stockholm, on July 6, 1903. His father, Thure Theorell, was the town's general medical practitioner and was a medical officer for a regiment located a few kilometers away. His mother, the former Armida Bill, was descended from a Peruvian Indian who had settled in Sweden in the eighteenth century. She was a talented pianist and singer, and she instilled in Hugo a lasting love of music. When he was three years old, a severe attack of poliomyelitis crippled him (a later muscle transplant helped him to walk unaided, but he was never able to run, skate, or ski).

After attending the junior school and state secondary school in Linköping, Theorell followed in his father's footsteps by deciding to study medicine. In 1921, he began his association with the Royal Caroline Institute in Stockholm, from which he received his bachelor of medicine degree in 1924, his M.D. degree in 1930, and in which he became lecturer in physiological chemistry as a doctor. He married Elin Margit Elizabeth Alenius on June 5, 1931. They had met through playing music together, and their marriage produced three sons (their only daughter died of tuberculosis when very young).

In 1932, Theorell was appointed associate professor of biochemistry at Uppsala, and in 1933, in what became the turning point in his career, he received a Rockefeller Fellowship to work with Otto Warburg in Berlin, where his productive research continued until 1935. In 1936, the Caroline Institute established a Nobel Institute with a biochemistry department, where Theorell had the opportunity to expand his research. Under his direction, this institute became a significant international center of biochemical research. Even during World War II, when the influx of foreign scientists was cut off, Theorell was able to carry on important work in the institute.

Although he never abandoned research, Theorell found more of his time taken up with scientific administration in the postwar period. In 1947, his new Nobel Medical Institute at Solnavägen was opened. He also helped get the Wenner-Gren Center in Stockholm constructed (a facility where visiting scientists could live and work). He suffered a stroke in 1974, and this caused him to relinquish many of his burdensome administrative duties. In the summer of 1982, while visiting the island of Ljusterö, off the Swedish coast near Stockholm, he died at the age of seventy-nine.

Scientific Career

Enzymes were the focus of most of Theorell's scientific research. His earliest work on the chemical nature of the yellow enzyme led him into the field of oxidative enzymes, which provided vast opportunities for him to exercise his great experimental and theoretical talents. He was especially fascinated by the chemical interactions between the protein apoenzymes and their nonprotein cofactors. So significant were his contributions to this field that he is considered one of the founders of enzymology.

Upon graduating from secondary school in 1921, he focused on a career in medicine, fully intending, despite his handicap, to practice as a doctor. At the Caroline Institute he became increasingly attracted to biochemistry, largely through the influence of teacher Einar Hammarsten. After receiving his bachelor of medicine degree in 1924, Theorell spent the first three months of 1925 studying bacteriology at the Pasteur Institute in Paris. Upon his return to Sweden, he continued his biochemical studies under the direction of Hammarsten, who suggested the topic for Theorell's M.D. thesis. Hammarsten thought that lipids (fats) in the blood might influence the erythrocyte (red blood cell) sedimentation rate (the erythrocyte sedimentation rate, or ESR, was a new clinical test for blood). Theorell showed that lipids tend to reduce the ESR.

In the early 1930's, Theorell worked on myoglobin, an iron-containing protein found in muscle cells. First discovered at the end of the nineteenth century and called "myohaematin," this red substance was initially confused with hemoglobin, since, like hemoglobin (the oxygen-carrying molecule in erythrocytes), myoglobin has a strong affinity for oxygen. Theorell proved that myoglobin is a distinct protein by purifying it and then studying its physical and chemical properties. He purified myoglobin's protein portion by spinning samples at very high speeds in a centrifuge (a process called ultracentrifugation) and by electrophoresis. He then measured myoglobin's sedimentation rate, affinity for oxygen, and magnetic properties. He demonstrated conclusively that myoglobin and hemoglobin are not the same.

Myoglobin proved to be an iron-containing protein associated with cellular respiration, and to pursue his interest in oxidative enzymes, he went to Otto Warburg's Institute for Cell Physiology in Berlin-Dahlem. By the time that Theorell began his research on oxidative enzymes, a biochemical model of biological oxidation was emerging. It had become clear that each of the complicated reactions by which such food molecules as carbohydrates are converted into carbon dioxide and water are orchestrated by enzymes. At Berlin-Dahlem, therefore, Theorell decided to study the oxidative yellow enzyme that investigators had discovered in yeast, heart muscle, and milk.

He had two electrophoresis apparatuses built, and he used them to purify the yellow enzyme and to separate it into two fragments. One fragment was a colorless protein of high molecular weight; the other fragment was a yellow derivative of vitamin B_2 with a low molecular weight. Neither fragment was biologically active by itself, but when Theorell recombined them, he obtained the yellow enzyme with its oxidative ability fully restored. He had clearly demonstrated that this enzyme was a compound of protein and cofactor, an observation that he would later generalize to other enzymes. Warburg was deeply impressed with Theorell's work.

When he returned to Stockholm in 1935, Theorell concentrated his efforts on another enzyme, cytochrome *c*. He was able to separate this enzyme into an apoenzyme (which was pure protein) and a prosthetic group (an iron-containing heme unit). He was able to purify this cytochrome and determine how its heme group is joined to its large protein part. In 1937, his work on cytochrome *c* continued at the new Nobel Medical Institute, a research facility with close ties to the Caroline Institute. Here, in the late 1930's, Theorell showed how other forms of the cytochromes could be analyzed in a way similar to his earlier studies.

To help him in this work, he spent three months in 1939 with Linus Pauling at the California Institute of Technology in Pasadena. Working with Charles D. Coryell, one of Pauling's associates, he measured the magnetic properties of ferric cytochrome *c* over a wide range of acidity using a very accurate balance that Pauling had used in his magnetic studies of hemoglobin derivatives (the term "ferric" indicates that the iron is in a more oxidized form than in the "ferrous" state). Theorell was able to elucidate how the iron-containing heme group is bonded into a crevice of the protein portion of the cytochrome. More specifically, he showed how the heme group was surrounded and protected by amino acid chains.

During World War II, Sweden's neutrality enabled Theorell to continue his research on iron-containing enzymes, in particular, the peroxidases and catalase. The peroxidases catalyze the oxidation of various substances by hydrogen peroxide and are found in many plants. Catalase is also widely distributed in living things. Hydrogen peroxide, a by-product of certain cell reactions, is a corrosive substance that oxidizes various amino acids. To counter its potential damage to vital proteins, cell organelles contain ample amounts of catalase. Theorell prepared catalase in a very pure form and investigated its properties. He was also able, in 1942, to obtain pure peroxidase from horseradish and establish the nature of its iron-containing prosthetic group. In all his studies of these iron-containing enzymes—myoglobin, cytochrome *c*, catalase, and the peroxidases—his overriding objective was to delineate the variety of ways in which the iron atoms are bonded to the protein portion of the enzyme, since he felt that this region of the enzyme's structure was largely responsible for its properties.

After the war, Theorell was able to expand his research on oxidative enzymes by returning to myoglobin and its connection with myoglobinuria (a paralytic disease, one of whose symptoms is excessive myoglobin in the urine). In his investigations of this and other enzymes, he and his colleagues were able to develop new techniques, particularly methods that required only very small samples. In the late 1940's, he used these techniques to study alcohol dehydrogenase (ADH), a liver enzyme that catalyzes the oxidation of alcohol. Two of his collaborators crystallized ADH from horse liver in 1948; during the years following this crystallization, the reactions of the enzyme, its coenzyme (nicotinic acid adenine dinucleotide, or NAD), and its substrate or inhibitors were probably more thoroughly studied than any other enzymatic system. The changes in fluorescence and other optical properties that occurred made these reactions particularly attractive to experimenters. In a classic series of researches in the late 1940's and early 1950's, Theorell, in collaboration with Britton Chance, studied the details of how ADH catalyzes the oxidation of ethyl alcohol to acetaldehyde in liver cells. Theorell and his associates were able to show that the oxidations of alcohol through ADH proceeds via a highly ordered mechanism (now known as the Theorell-Chance mechanism). These studies had a great influence on later work on the chemical kinetics of enzymatic systems.

Throughout the 1950's, Theorell continued to work on ADH; for example, he investigated precisely how ADH's coenzyme (NAD) is bonded to the apoenzyme. More concretely, he revealed how one of the two zinc atoms in liver ADH is situated at the active center of the enzyme. He accomplished this by using inhibitors, substances that compete with the coenzyme. Although this work on ADH seems highly abstract, it did have practical consequences, for the knowledge that Theorell obtained was used to develop a specific analytical method for measuring the alcohol content of bodily fluids (Swedish law courts eventually accepted these methods). His work also led to the development of sensitive blood tests that have been extensively applied in determining legal standards of drunkenness.

During the 1960's and 1970's, Theorell's Nobel Institute became "a Mecca of biochemistry" that attracted scientists from all over the world. He found that more and more of his time was taken up with scientific administration. He served as administrator of the Wenner-Gren Society and the Wenner-Gren Center, and he was president of the International Union of Biochemistry. After he became professor emeritus in 1970, he continued to work in the Laboratory for Enzyme Research on alcohol dehydrogenase, collaborating in constructing a three-dimensional structure of this enzyme. He also worked with a clinical group involved in studying animals and humans with the aim of preventing the ill effects of alcoholism through the use of highly specific inhibitors of ADH. His failing health interfered with these projects, but his work on his beloved enzymes ended only with his death.

Throughout his career, Theorell manifested the ability to choose significant problems and to invent the best methods for solving them. He was the first scientist to produce a pure form of myoglobin. Fellow scientists have stated that his work on yellow enzyme was fundamentally important in the understanding of oxidation enzymes. He was the first scientist to isolate a coenzyme, and he was the first to divide an enzyme into its constituent parts (apoenzyme and coenzyme). His studies of alcohol dehydrogenase became a model for other enzymologists to emulate. Theorell's sure mastery of traditional and modern biochemical techniques allowed him to obtain important structural information about a whole series of enzymes crucial in cell respiration, and his discoveries made the work of other scientists on other enzymes much easier. His enthusiasms were contagious, and his collaborators carried his ideas throughout the world. His discoveries were so basic and so beautiful that they will continue to influence enzymologists far into the future.

Bibliography

Primary

BIOCHEMISTRY: "Studies of Cytochrome *c*: I, Electrophoretic Purification of Cytochrome *c* and Its Amino Acid Composition, II, The Optical Properties of Pure Cytochrome *c* and Some of Its Derivatives, III, Titration Curves" (with Åke Åkeson), and IV, the Magnetic Properties of Ferric and Ferrous Cytochrome *c*," *Journal of the American Chemical Society*, vol. 63, 1941, pp. 1804-1827; "Heme-Linked Groups and Mode of Action of Some Hemoproteins," *Advances in Enzymology*, vol. 7, 1947, pp. 265-303; "Liver Alcohol Dehydrogenase: I, Equilibria and Initial Reaction Velocities," *Acta Chemica Scandinavica*, vol. 5, 1951, pp. 1105-1126 (with Roger Bonnichsen); "Liver Alcohol Dehydrogenase: II, Kinetics of the Compound of Horse-Liver Alcohol Dehydrogenase and Reduced Diphospho Pyridine Nucleotide," *Acta Chemica Scandinavica*, vol. 5, 1951, pp. 1127-1144 (with Britton Chance); "Flavin-Containing Enzymes," in *The Enzymes*, vol. 2, edited by J. B. Sumner and K. Myrbäck, 1951; "The Iron-Containing Enzymes—Catalases and Peroxidases—Hydroperoxidase," in *The Enzymes*, vol. 2, edited by J. B. Sumner and K. Myrbäck, 1951; "On the Interaction Between Coenzymes and Enzymes," *Discussions of the Faraday Society*, no. 20, 1955; "Function and Structure of Liver Alcohol Dehydrogenase," *Harvey Lectures*, ser. 61, 1965-1966; *The Physical Chemistry of Enzymes*, 1966; "Historical Aspects of Physiological Alcohol Combustion," in *Alcohol and Aldehyde Metabolising Systems*, edited by R. G. Thurman, T. Yonetani, J. R. Williamson, and B. Chance, 1974; "Enzymes Revisited: From Berzelius to Sumner," in *Reflections on Biochemistry*, edited by A. Kornberg, B. L. Horecker, L. Cornudelia, and J. Oro, 1975; "My Life with Proteins and Prosthetic Groups," in *Proteolysis and Physiological Regulation*, 1975.

Secondary

Boyer, Paul D., ed. *The Enzymes*. 3d ed. Vol. 1, *Structure and Control*. New York: Academic Press, 1970. This work, in its many volumes and in its previous two editions, is the classic reference source for anyone seeking detailed information on enzymes. Theorell wrote for and had his work discussed in previous editions; in this third edition, his work is extensively analyzed in volume 2, *Kinetics and Mechanism* (1970); volume 11, *Oxidation-Reduction: Part A, Dehydrogenases (I), Electron Transfer (I)* (1975); and volume 13, *Oxidation-Reduction: Part C, Dehydrogenases (II), Oxidases (II), Hydrogen Peroxide Cleavage* (1976). These and the other volumes are intended as a reference tool for biochemists, biophysicists, and molecular biologists, and a background in biochemistry is necessary to use them with full understanding.

Dalziel, D. "Axel Hugo Theodor Theorell, 6 July 1903–15 August 1982," *Bio-*

graphical Memoirs of Fellows of the Royal Society 29 (1983): 585-621. This biographical article provides a good account of Theorell's family background and early life as well as of his later career as a biochemist. The author makes some use of chemical formulas in explaining Theorell's accomplishments in biochemistry, but his emphasis is on his subject's overall development as a scientist. Dalziel includes sections on Theorell's awards, his activities as a scientific administrator, his avocations as a musician and sailor, and his personal qualities. Appended to the article is a bibliography of 258 of Theorell's publications.

Dixon, Malcolm, and Edwin C. Webb. *Enzymes*. 2d ed. New York: Academic Press, 1964. In this book, the authors strive to present in an organized and understandable way the general principles of enzymology. This book treats enzymes in a less detailed way than the multivolume work by Boyer given above. Nevertheless, Theorell's work is adequately analyzed. At the book's end is an extensive list of more than a hundred pages of most of the enzymes known by the middle of 1962. Also includes a compilation of 2,972 references and a detailed index.

Keilin, David. *The History of Cell Respiration and Cytochrome*. Prepared for publication by Joan Keilin. Cambridge, England: Cambridge University Press, 1966. Keilin, a pioneer researcher in enzymology, worked on this book for several decades of his life, and it was left uncompleted at his death. His daughter prepared the work for publication in truncated form. Although he intended at the start to write a history of respiration, Keilin soon realized that this subject was too broad, and he restricted his treatment to material in which he was personally interested, especially the hemoprotein oxygen carriers. Keilin makes some use of chemical formulas, but his approach is basically historical, so the work is accessible to students and others without a biochemical background. A bibliography of text references and a comprehensive index concludes the book.

Schwert, George W., and Alfred D. Winer, eds. *The Mechanism of Action of Dehydrogenases: A Symposium in Honor of Hugo Theorell*. Lexington: University Press of Kentucky, 1969. This book, the result of a symposium held at the University of Kentucky in 1965 on the mode of action of a certain class of dehydrogenases, consists mainly of papers presented at the meetings and the discussions that ensued. Hugo Theorell wrote the foreword, in which he presents his interesting reminiscences about his early research at Warburg's institute in Berlin-Dahlem. The book has a list of contributors but no index.

Robert J. Paradowski

1956

Physiology or Medicine

André Frédéric Cournand, France and United States
Werner Forssmann, Germany
Dickinson W. Richards, Jr., United States

Chemistry

Sir Cyril Norman Hinshelwood, Great Britain
Nikolai Semenov, Soviet Union

Physics

William Shockley, United States
John Bardeen, United States
Walter H. Brattain, United States

Literature

Juan Ramón Jiménez, Spain

Peace

no award

ANDRÉ FRÉDÉRIC COURNAND
1956

Born: Paris, France; September 24, 1895
Died: Great Barrington, Massachusetts; February 19, 1988
Nationality: French; after 1941, American
Areas of concentration: Cardiovascular and pulmonary physiology and pathology

Cournand developed the technique of cardiac catheterization for clinical applications to study the physiology and pathology of the heart, lungs, and circulation in healthy and diseased humans

The Award

Presentation

Göran Liljestrand, a professor at the Royal Caroline Institute, gave the presentation address for the awarding of the 1956 Nobel Prize in Physiology or Medicine. Representing the Royal Caroline Institute, he paid homage to the work of the three winners, Werner Forssmann, André Frédéric Cournand, and Dickinson W. Richards, Jr., before King Gustav VI Adolf presented them with the Nobel medals and scrolls. Liljestrand began by stating that the two decisive factors in the functioning of the heart are pressure and flow and by describing the limitations inherent in early attempts to study those factors. Although direct methods of observation were possible in animal studies, indirect methods had to suffice in human studies.

This situation changed in 1929, when Forssmann performed heart catheterization experiments on himself demonstrating how "the methods well known from animal experiments could also be adapted for studies in man." Cournand and Richards saw the potential of Forssmann's discovery; eventually, they developed the technique for clinical applications in man. As a result of these efforts, cardiac catheterization became an accepted and valuable technique in the world of clinical medicine.

Liljestrand discussed the clinical applications of cardiac catheterization, including investigations of secondary wound shock, acquired heart disease, congenital heart disease, and pulmonary diseases. These investigations by Cournand and Richards had "been instrumental in promoting the remarkable advances in heart surgery made in recent time." Liljestrand stated that the extensive investigations he had briefly mentioned involved "the cooperation of a large number of highly skilled research workers," but that Cournand and Richards had "consistently been the pioneers and the leaders." Summarizing the contributions of Forssmann, Cournand, and Richards, Liljestrand stated that "the practical value of cardiac catheterization has been definitely proved" by Cournand and Richards. In their hands, the technique led to many diagnostic and therapeutic advances.

Nobel lecture

On December 11, 1956, Cournand delivered his Nobel lecture, entitled "Control of the Pulmonary Circulation in Man with Some Remarks on Methodology." Cournand began with an extended preamble on methodology in which he characterized the cardiac catheter as "the key in the lock" and discussed the development and limitations of the methodology. He explained the Fick principle for measuring flow and expressed caution in applying physical principles to biological measurements; he indicated, however, that extensive investigations had shown that the Fick principle could be applied in most situations.

Cournand then moved to the main theme of his lecture, concerning the control of the pulmonary circulation in normal man. He explained how "the relationship between pressure and flow in the pulmonary circulation was quite different from that in the systemic circuit." He described these differences in the pulmonary circulation based on pressure and resistance, anatomic observations, mechanical factors, and distensibility. He emphasized the importance of distensibility in creating a nonlinear relationship between pressure and flow in the pulmonary circulation. Explaining how hypoxia and acetylcholine "appear to affect the resistance to flow in the pulmonary circulation by modifying the muscular tone of its vessels," he discussed how hypoxia causes pulmonary vasoconstriction, which results in an increase in pulmonary arterial pressure. He suggested various unresolved questions concerning where and how pulmonary vasoconstriction occurs in response to hypoxia, then proposed the possibility of a local effect of hypoxia and described experiments to examine this hypothesis.

Cournand then turned to the effects of acetylcholine, which was known "to have a strong vasodilating influence throughout the systemic arterial tree." He explained that "as far as the pulmonary circulation is concerned, however, reports on the effects of this preparation in animals have been contradictory." Cournand described experiments involving the administration of acetylcholine while breathing room air and during the administration of hypoxia.

Summarizing present knowledge, Cournand noted that "it can be said that we have acquired some understanding of the relations between pressure and flow in the pulmonary vessels of normal man." He contrasted what was known with mechanisms of action that were poorly understood and presented several doubts that confronted fitting what was known "into an integrated concept of the control of the pulmonary circulation." Looking ahead to the future, he stated, "The only incontestable prophecy that can be made is that advances in methodology and advances in understanding will go hand in hand."

Critical reception

At the time that Cournand and his fellow laureates won the 1956 Nobel Prize, the tremendous importance of cardiac catheterization had been realized by the medical profession as well as by much of the general public. Reaction to announcement of the award, therefore, was enthusiastically favorable. Much attention was given to the experiments that Forssmann had performed on himself. The work of Cournand and Richards was considered an archetypal example of the benefits that basic medical research can offer to clinical medicine and the treatment of disease.

An article on the award in *The Times* (London) stated that "the award of the Nobel Prize for Medicine to Professors Forssmann, Cournand, and Richards is a well deserved tribute to three of the pioneers in a method of investigation without which it would have been almost impossible for surgeons to achieve the striking successes which they are now obtaining in the treatment of certain forms of heart disease." *Time* magazine ran an article noting that Forssmann's discovery was "ignored" in Germany, where researchers "scoffed at Forssmann's catheterization of the heart as a circus stunt." The article continued that Cournand and Richards "read of Forssmann's experiment and developed a way to use it both for research and diagnosis. They showed that it could be used in studies of shock, in revealing defects inside the heart or abnormal connections between arteries."

An article in *The New York Times* on October 19 explained that Forssmann, Cournand, and Richards "were cited for their work in exploring with a thin tube the interior of the functioning human heart." The article explained how Cournand and Richards "eventually showed how every known means for measuring pressures and blood compositions inside the heart could be safely applied by the method first tried by Dr. Forssmann on himself." In an editorial, *The New York Times* stated that "it is not unusual nowadays for a surgeon to run a catheter or hollow plastic tube through a vein in the arm into the heart." The editorial regarded the work of Cournand and Richards as "a brilliant example of what can be accomplished by fundamental research on the heart."

Biography

André Frédéric Cournand, the second of the four children of Jules Cournand and Marguerite Weber, was born in Paris, France, on September 24, 1895. His father was a dentist who also was awarded some twenty-five patents as an inventor. He received his early education at the Lycée Condorcet, working with a private tutor in philosophy and gaining experience in a private laboratory. He obtained his baccalaureate degree at the Faculté des Lettres of the Sorbonne in 1913 and took the diploma of physics, chemistry, and biology at the Faculté des Sciences in 1914.

After his first year of medical studies, Cournand volunteered, in 1915, for service in the French Army during World War I. He initially served as a "private medical student," a special rank created to provide help for surgeons at the front. Because of the high fatality rate among battalion surgeons, he received four months of training in 1916 and became an auxiliary battalion surgeon. Gassed and wounded near the end of the war, he was awarded the Croix de Guerre with three bronze stars.

Cournand resumed his medical studies after the war, passing the competitive examinations required for an appointment in the public hospitals and serving first as an extern and then as an intern from 1925 through 1930. (In France, the internship included the equivalent of a residency and preceded completion of the medical degree.) He completed his thesis and was awarded the medical degree of the Faculté de Médecine of the University of Paris in 1930. Cournand moved to the United

States in 1930 and began his affiliation with Bellevue Hospital and Columbia University in New York City. He ultimately became a visiting physician at Bellevue Hospital, a professor in the College of Physicians and Surgeons at Columbia University, and director of the Cardio-Pulmonary Laboratory of the Columbia University Division of Bellevue Hospital. Cournand became a naturalized citizen of the United States in 1941.

In 1924, Cournand married Sibylle Blumer, who was the widow of Birel Rosset. Cournand adopted their son, Pierre Birel Rosset-Cournand, who was killed in France in 1944 while serving as a parachutist with the Free French Army. Cournand and his wife had three daughters—Muriel, Marie-Ève, and Marie-Claire. Cournand's first wife died in 1959, and in 1963 he married Ruth Fabian, who had been the administrative assistant in his laboratory. His second wife died in 1973. In 1975 he married Beatrice Bishop Berle, who was the widow of Adolph Berle. After a long illness, Cournand died of pneumonia at his home in Great Barrington, Massachusetts, on February 19, 1988, at the age of ninety-two.

Scientific Career

When asked how he became interested in heart work, Cournand once responded, "I'm what you call a versatile Frenchman. I'm interested in a lot of things. Lungs were among them. It was through the lung work that we came to use the heart tubes." Commenting on the medical profession in an interview after the announcement that he would share the Nobel Prize in 1956, Cournand noted that "for the practice of medicine, one needs to be dedicated to the desire to serve."

Cournand's medical residency and early research experiences took place during the decade of the 1930's. He traveled to the United States in 1930 to spend a single year of residency in the chest service (then known as the tuberculosis service) of the Columbia University Division of Bellevue Hospital. He served as an assistant resident and resident physician in the chest service, which was directed by James Alexander Miller and J. Burns Amberson. He decided to remain in the United States after 1931 when he was offered the opportunity to become chief resident and to participate in research with Dickinson Richards on the physiology and pathology of respiration.

Cournand and Richards began their collaborative research efforts in 1932, using available early techniques to study the physiology and pathology of respiration. Their research was based on the application of a concept propounded by Lawrence J. Henderson of Harvard University, who postulated that the heart, lungs, and circulation form a single physiological system for the exchange of respiratory gases between the atmosphere and the tissues of the organism. Cournand and Richards developed a battery of tests to evaluate lung function and determined standard values of the various parameters in normal subjects. These lung function tests were then used to investigate pulmonary function in patients with various types of pulmonary disease, including tuberculous lesions, chronic emphysema, and various forms of fibrosis.

In 1936, the need to obtain mixed venous blood from the right atrium of the heart led them to consider the technique of cardiac catheterization first demonstrated on humans by Werner Forssmann in 1929. After four years of preliminary experiments on dogs and a chimpanzee, Cournand and Richards began cardiac catheterization in human subjects in 1940. The initial importance of cardiac catheterization was that it established a safe method for obtaining mixed venous blood to determine blood flow by application of the Fick principle. This application of the Fick principle was used to measure cardiac output in evaluating a new model of the ballistocardiograph. The results of this investigation were presented at the annual meeting of the American Physiological Society in 1941 and were published in 1942.

New catheters and improved recording equipment were developed, including a mobile multiple recording apparatus. Cardiac catheters were advanced beyond the right atrium into the right ventricle in 1942, then advanced into the pulmonary artery in 1944. A double-lumen catheter allowed the simultaneous measurement of pressures in two different places. These developments were presented in 1944 and 1945. The applications of cardiac catheterization opened a whole new range of studies to investigate functions of the heart, lungs, and circulation in various diseases. Cournand and Richards used cardiac catheterization to investigate various types of shock, leading to treatment for shock based on physiological measurements. Their studies of hemorrhagic shock identified the importance of replacing lost blood both quantitatively and qualitatively through the administration of other fluids or through the use of drugs.

Cournand and Richards investigated systemic hypertension and acquired heart disease and continued their investigations of various types of pulmonary disease. These studies eventually included the effects of pulmonary diseases upon the pulmonary circulation and right ventricular function. They investigated the consequences for the heart and lungs of various obstructive diseases of the lungs, studied the relationship between the electrical and mechanical events of the cardiac cycle, and evaluated the effects of drugs upon the hemodynamic aberrations associated with various cardiac diseases.

Cournand worked with Janet S. Baldwin and Aaron Himmelstein to apply the technique of cardiac catheterization to the investigation of congenital heart disease. The technique demonstrated unusual communications between the heart chambers, among the large blood vessels, or between these vessels and the heart chambers. During World War II, Cournand was an investigator with the Office of Scientific Research and Development and was a consultant with the Chemical Warfare Service. He was later a member of the Cardiovascular Study Section of the National Heart Institute, serving as its chairman from 1956 through 1959. He was a member of the subcommittee on circulation of the National Research Council and a consultant to the Manhattan Veterans Administration Hospital. He also served as adviser to the Délégué Général de la Recherche Scientifique et Technique of the French government after 1958.

Cournand had scientific interests that extended beyond physiology and pathology. He was a science historian and biographer and a student of the sociology of science.

After his retirement, he became interested in the philosophy of prospective developed by Gaston Berger and his followers. Prospective is a composite intellectual and social movement dedicated to discovering how to analyze in depth the consequences of accomplished or proposed actions. Cournand contributed articles on the philosophy of prospective and applied the prospective philosophy and method to medical education and science. In 1973, Cournand and Maurice Lévy edited *Shaping the Future: Gaston Berger and the Concept of Prospective*.

Cournand delivered the Harvey Society Lecture in 1950 and served as president of the Harvey Society in 1960 and 1961. He gave the John Phillips Memorial Lecture before the American College of Physicians in 1952; he delivered the Einthoven Memorial Lecture at the University of Leiden in The Netherlands in 1958 and presented the Dr. Albert Wanderer Gedenkvorlesung at the University of Berne in Switzerland in 1962.

Cournand won numerous awards other than the Nobel Prize, and he was granted membership or honorary membership in many scientific societies throughout the world. He won the Lasker Award, given by the American Public Health Association, for example, in 1949, and medals from the French and Belgian academies of medicine in 1956. He became an officer in France's Legion of Honor in 1957 and was made a commander in 1970. He also received honorary degrees from many universities, including the University of Strasbourg and Columbia University. Cournand was a member of the American Physiological Society and an honorary member of the British Cardiac Society and the Swedish Cardiac Society, among many organizations.

Cournand developed the technique of cardiac catheterization in order to study the heart, lungs, and circulation as a single physiological system, and he subsequently used cardiac catheterization to study the physiology and pathology of the heart, lungs, and circulation in both healthy and diseased humans. His clinical applications of cardiac catheterization included pulmonary diseases, shock, systemic hypertension, acquired heart disease, and congenital heart disease. His work was a brilliant example of the benefits that basic medical research can provide to the practice of clinical medicine and the treatment of disease.

Bibliography

Primary

MEDICINE: *Cardiac Catheterization in Congenital Heart Disease: A Clinical and Physiological Study in Infants and Children*, 1949 (with Janet S. Baldwin and Aaron Himmelstein); *L'Insuffisance cardiaque chronique: Études physiopathologiques*, 1952 (with Jean Lequime and Paul Regniers); *Du concept de la conjonction de l'air et du sang dans le poumon: Développement historique contribution récent*, 1966; "Cardiac Catheterization: Development of the Technique, its Contributions to Experimental Medicine, and its Initial Applications in Man," *Acta Medica Scandinavica*, supplement 579, 1975; *From Roots to Late Budding: The Intellectual Adventures of a Medical Scientist*, 1986 (with Michael Meyer).

EDITED TEXTS: *Shaping the Future: Gaston Berger and the Concept of Prospective*, 1973 (with Maurice Lévy).

Secondary

Cournand, André, Janet S. Baldwin, and Aaron Himmelstein. *Cardiac Catheterization in Congenital Heart Disease: A Clinical and Physiological Study in Infants and Children*. New York: Commonwealth Fund, 1949. Discusses applications of cardiac catheterization to the diagnosis and treatment of congenital heart disease. Part 1 describes the physiological methods; part 2 presents case studies in which the technique was applied. Well-illustrated and generally easy to understand.

Cournand, André, and Michael Meyer. *From Roots to Late Budding: The Intellectual Adventures of a Medical Scientist*. New York: Gardner Press, 1986. Cournand wrote this autobiography near the end of his life. He first presents an overview of his life, emphasizing his education, his experiences in World War I, his return to medical education, and his research in the United States with Richards. Part 2 includes an introduction to the concept and method of prospective and presents historical perspectives on cardiopulmonary physiology. Includes many photographs.

Fishman, Alfred P., and Dickinson W. Richards, Jr., eds. *Circulation of the Blood: Men and Ideas*. New York: Oxford University Press, 1964. Contains chapters concerning the history of cardiovascular physiology written by prominent researchers. Divided into three parts: the heart, the blood vessels, and special circulations. The first chapter, by Cournand, is entitled "Air and Blood" and considers the historical development of understanding the relationship between the heart and the lungs.

Forssmann, Werner. *Experiments on Myself: Memoirs of a Surgeon in Germany.* Translated by Hilary Davies. New York: St. Martin's Press, 1974. This is the translation of the autobiography of Cournand's cowinner Forssmann. It is a lively account of his life and work, much of which is directly relevant to Cournand's own work; Forssmann discusses influences on his generation of researchers. Includes a preface written by Cournand.

Green, David E., and W. Eugene Knox, eds. *Research in Medical Science*. New York: Macmillan, 1950. Aimed at "inspiring" the nonspecialist reader, this book presents essays on more than twenty topics concerning medical research. One chapter is by Cournand's cowinner Richards; it is entitled "Pulmonary Physiology" and emphasizes various types of pulmonary function and malfunction.

Grossman, William, ed. *Cardiac Catheterization and Angiography.* 3d ed. Philadelphia: Lea & Febiger, 1986. Written by prominent researchers and clinicians and aimed at the instruction of physicians training to become cardiologists. Includes general principles of cardiac catheterization and angiography, the historical development of cardiac catheterization, and its relationship to present practice. There are also chapters on techniques of cardiac catheterization and hemodynamic principles. Intended for a medical audience, this book is a comprehensive resource.

Yang, Sing San, Lamberto G. Bentivoglio, Vladir Maranhao, and Harry Goldberg. *From Cardiac Catheterization Data to Hemodynamic Parameters*. 3d ed. Philadelphia: F. A. Davis, 1988. This book's first chapter provides a historical perspective on cardiac catheterization, beginning with the research of Forssmann, Cournand, and Richards. Chapters 2 through 6 explain various measurements associated with cardiac catheterization. Most of the writing is technical and explains specific applications of cardiac catheterization to obtain and utilize data about the heart, lungs, and circulation.

Steven J. Albrechtsen

1956

Physiology or Medicine

André Frédéric Cournand, France and United States
Werner Forssmann, Germany
Dickinson W. Richards, Jr., United States

Chemistry

Sir Cyril Norman Hinshelwood, Great Britain
Nikolai Semenov, Soviet Union

Physics

William Shockley, United States
John Bardeen, United States
Walter H. Brattain, United States

Literature

Juan Ramón Jiménez, Spain

Peace

no award

WERNER FORSSMANN
1956

Born: Berlin, Germany; August 29, 1904
Died: Schopfheim, West Germany; June 1, 1979
Nationality: German
Areas of concentration: Cardiovascular experimentation, surgery, and urology

Forssmann demonstrated the safety of and potential for cardiac catheterization and contrast radiography in human beings through courageous experiments on himself

The Award

Presentation

Göran Liljestrand, a professor at the Royal Caroline Institute and secretary of the Nobel Committee for Physiology or Medicine, represented the medical faculty of the Royal Caroline Institute in delivering the presentation address on December 10, 1956, before King Gustav VI Adolf offered Nobel medals and scrolls to Werner Forssmann, André Frédéric Cournand, and Dickinson W. Richards, Jr. Liljestrand began his address by borrowing a statement from William Harvey to describe the heart as "the sun of the microcosm formed by the human body." He explained the two factors that are crucial in the work of the heart, pressure and flow, and discussed the limitations of early techniques for studying these factors. While direct methods were possible in animal experiments, the study of humans "was naturally confined to the use of the indirect methods."

Liljestrand explained how this situation changed in 1929, when Forssmann demonstrated—"by making, with the intrepidity of youth, by no means harmless experiments on himself—that a narrow catheter could be advanced from a cubital vein into the right atrium itself, a distance of almost two-thirds of a metre." Forssmann thereby demonstrated how the methods developed in animal experiments could be adapted for studies on human beings.

Forssmann conducted further experiments on himself to further "röntgenologic" examination of the right side of the heart and the pulmonary vessels, through direct injection of contrast medium. Liljestrand observed that "it must have required firm conviction of the value of the method to induce self-experimentation of the kind carried out by Forssmann. His later disappointment must have been all the more bitter." Liljestrand explained that Forssmann was not given adequate support; on the contrary, he was criticized so severely that he lost interest in pursuing his experiments. Liljestrand explained how Cournand and Richards recognized the potential of Forssmann's discovery and after several years of research developed the technique for clinical applications in man.

Liljestrand praised Forssmann for his courage in submitting himself to heart catheterization. In conclusion, Liljestrand called the work of Forssmann, Cournand, and Richards "an outstanding example of the great possibilities implied by the application of physiological methods to clinical problems."

Nobel lecture

On December 11, 1956, Forssmann delivered his Nobel lecture, entitled "The Role of Heart Catheterization and Angiocardiography in the Development of Modern Medicine." Forssmann's lecture described three periods in the historical development of modern cardiology. The first period, the sixteenth and seventeenth centuries, involved the characterization of the circulation. Forssmann explained the discovery of the lesser circulation by Miguel Serveto and noted that Caesalpinus traced the path of the greater circulation. Jacobus Sylvius, Canani, and Fabricius of Aquapendente concurred in recognizing the direction of blood flow in the venous circulation. The first period reached a climax when William Harvey "combined all these individual findings with the results of his own research to form the general picture of what we today call the circulation of the blood." Forssmann also noted the explanation and description of capillaries by Marcello Malpighi.

The second period did not develop immediately, but had to wait "until, at the end of the eighteenth and the beginning of the nineteenth centuries, scientific methods of examination made their appearance in medicine." The beginning of this period was marked, said Forssmann, by William Withering's introduction of digitalis for the treatment of edema. Percussion was introduced by Leopold Auenbrygger von Auenbrugg, auscultation by René-Théophile-Hyacinthe Laënnec, and the electrocardiogram by Willem Einthoven.

The modern period of research, according to Forssmann, was launched by "classic French experimental physiology." Noting the trials on animals of Claude Bernard and the manometer procedure developed by others, Forssmann credited the Reverend Stephen Hales, an Englishman, with the first catheterization of the heart of a living animal for a clear experimental purpose. He noted research concerning "intra-arterial therapy" and explained how one investigator probed the right heart in animals and human cadavers. In 1929, Forssmann himself began experiments in probing the right heart. He also undertook experiments in angiography, in which "for the first time the living heart of a dog was successfully visualized radiologically with the aid of a contrast medium."

The year 1941, according to Forssmann, was a turning point, for it was in this year that Cournand and his colleagues began publishing the results of their experiments with the heart catheter as a method of clinical investigation. Forssmann also noted the research of John McMichael, who used cardiac catheterization "to solve pharmacological problems," the selective angiography of the lung vessels by another physician, and extensions of cardiac catheterization to access the liver and kidneys.

"One may compare the art of healing," concluded Forssmann, "with a work of art, which from different standpoints and under different lighting reveals ever new and surprising beauty." He warned against "the mistake which runs all through the history of medicine: that of concentrating dogmatically upon first one, then another facet of research, instead of standing back to view the whole as a growing entity."

Critical reception

Cardiac catheterization was well recognized as an important clinical technique by both medical professionals and the general public by the time Forssmann, Cournand, and Richards received the Nobel Prize in 1956. Public reaction focused on the courageous experiments of Forssmann on himself and on the subsequent development and applications of the technique by Cournand and Richards. Forssmann's experiments, in particular, captured the public's imagination.

In an article in *The Times* of London on October 19, 1956, an anonymous medical correspondent wrote:

> [T]he award of the Nobel Prize for Medicine to Professors Forssmann, Cournand, and Richards is a well deserved tribute to three of the pioneers in a method of investigation without which it would have been almost impossible for surgeons to achieve the striking successes which they are now obtaining in the treatment of certain forms of heart disease.

An article in the October 29, 1956, issue of *Time* magazine described Forssmann's experiments on himself, noting that he had been "young (25) and eager to prove the worth of a revolutionary idea: that it should be possible to learn more about the inside of a diseased human heart by inserting a thin rubber tube (catheter) into it." Yet "older men, who should have been wiser, scoffed at Forssmann's catheterization of the heart as a circus stunt." The article continued by explaining that Cournand and Richards "read of Forssmann's experiment and developed a way to use it both for research and diagnosis." A page-one article in *The New York Times* on October 19, 1956, reviewed the fascinating history of Forssmann's work and then explained how Cournand and Richards "eventually showed how every known means for measuring pressures and blood compositions inside the heart could be safely applied by the method first tried by Dr. Forssmann on himself."

An editorial in the same issue of *The New York Times* commended Forssmann for his courageous self-experimentation. The editorial noted the risk associated with the experiment but explained that Forssmann "emerged from the ordeal with no ill consequences" and thus promoted subsequent investigation of the condition of the heart in "cases of rheumatic fever, congestive heart disease and other heart 'troubles.'" The editoral concluded that "if more is known about the normal and abnormal heart and physicians know better than ever before how to deal with it, we have reason to be thankful to the winners of this year's Nobel Prize in Medicine."

Biography

Werner Theodor Otto Forssmann, the son of Julius Forssmann and Emmy Hindenberg, was born in Berlin, Germany, on August 29, 1904. His father was trained as an attorney and worked for the Victoria Life Insurance Company. He served as a captain in the German army during World War I and was killed in Galicia in 1916.

From 1910 through 1922, Forssmann was a student at the Askanisches Gymnasium in Berlin. It was consistent with family tradition that his parents chose for him a conventional humanistic school that would provide a broad liberal education. Forssmann received his medical education at the Friedrich Wilhelm University in Berlin, from 1922 through 1929. He took the state examinations on February 1, 1928, and spent his probationary year in the University Medical Department at Moabit Hospital, during which time he also completed his doctoral thesis. Forssmann received his license to practice medicine and his doctoral diploma on February 1, 1929.

Forssmann married Elsbet Engel on December 7, 1933. His wife was also a physician and surgeon who ultimately specialized in urology. Six children were born to the couple between 1934 and 1943.

Forssmann continued his medical training by serving as an assistant to prominent surgeons and urologists at hospitals in Eberswalde, Berlin, Mainz, and Dresden. During World War II he served as a surgeon with the German army and was interned for a time in an Allied prisoner-of-war camp. Following the war, he gradually resumed the practice of medicine and eventually established a practice in surgery and urology with his wife in the Black Forest town of Bad Kreuznach.

Following the awarding of the Nobel Prize, Forssmann was appointed honorary professor of surgery and urology at the Johannes Gutenberg University in Mainz. He eventually became director of the surgical department at the Evangelical Hospital in Düsseldorf, from which he retired in 1970. His leisure activities included gardening, walking, and watercolor painting. Forssmann died in Schopfheim, West Germany, on June 1, 1979, at the age of seventy-four.

Scientific Career

Forssmann received his medical education at the Friedrich Wilhelm University in Berlin, from 1922 through 1929. Among his professors was Rudolf Fick, the son of Adolph Fick, whose "Fick Principle" would ultimately be applied to measure blood flow based on samples obtained through cardiac catheterization. Forssmann received his clinical training in the new teaching department at Moabit Hospital under Georg Klemperer in internal medicine and Moritz Borchardt in surgery. During the winter semester of 1925-1926 he received training in obstetrics at the gynecology clinic in the Women's Hospital in Artillerie-strasse.

Forssmann took the state examinations on February 1, 1928, and spent his probationary year in the University Medical Department at Moabit Hospital under William Beck. It was during this probationary year that Forssmann conducted his first experiments on himself while working on the research for his doctoral thesis. This research involved the effects on the blood of feeding liver, and the subjects were himself and a small group of students. During the winter of this year, he assisted Fick in teaching anatomy at the university. Forssmann received his license to practice medicine and his doctoral diploma on February 1, 1929.

Forssmann initially practiced medicine at a private women's hospital in Spandau. He then moved on to work under Richard Schneider in Eberswalde, a small Prussian town northeast of Berlin. Schneider was head of the second surgical department in the Auguste Viktoria Home, a regional headquarters of the Red Cross. It was in Eberswalde that Forssmann conducted the most famous of his experiments on himself.

Forssmann had been fascinated by old diagrams illustrating the work of Bernard, Chauveau, and Marey. Hoping to be able to carry out on a man what they had done on animals, he discussed his ideas with Schneider, who acknowledged that his ideas were sound. Yet Schneider declined to allow Forssmann to carry out such an experiment on a patient, and further forbade Forssmann to experiment on himself.

Now on his own, Forssmann decided to override Schneider's prohibition and proceed with the experiment on his own heart, secretly and quickly. He obtained the necessary instruments, anesthetized his left elbow, made an incision in his skin, inserted a needle under the vein, opened it, and pushed the catheter about a foot inside. He walked downstairs to the X-ray room, where he was placed in front of the fluoroscope screen. Bursting into the room, a young colleague tried to stop him and pull out the catheter. Fighting the attempted interference, Forssmann used a mirror and saw through the fluoroscope that the catheter had reached the head of the humerus. Again his young colleague urged him to stop, but Forssmann pushed the catheter in further, almost to the two-foot mark. Now the mirror showed the catheter inside the heart, with its tip in the right ventricle, just as he had envisioned it. He had some X rays taken as documentary evidence.

At first Schneider accused Forssmann of betraying his trust, but he quickly congratulated him on making a great discovery, offered his complete support, and urged Forssmann to publish a paper immediately. "Probing the Right Ventricle of the Heart" was published in *Klinische Wochenschrift* on November 5, 1929. In recognition of Forssmann's potential and to facilitate further research, Schneider, Wilhelm His, and August Bier assisted him in obtaining a position under Ferdinand Sauerbruch at the Charité in Berlin.

Forssmann arrived at the "Mecca of German Surgery" on October 1, 1929. The publication of his article the following month made him a celebrity, and he was quickly besieged by hordes of reporters. Controversy quickly developed, and his work was challenged for priority by Ernst Unger, based on the latter's work with Bleichroder and Loeb concerning intra-arterial therapy. Although Unger's claim was not valid, the controversy combined with professional jealousy, and young Forssmann found himself dismissed by Sauerbruch after less than three months at the Charité.

Forssmann returned to Auguste Viktoria Home on January 1, 1930, where Schneider took special care that he gained experience steadily and systematically. Forssmann also continued his work on heart catheterization, experimenting with contrast radiography of the heart. He arranged with Willi Felix of the Neukolln Municipal Hospital in Berlin to use that institution's more up-to-date X-ray facilities. He initially tried experiments with rabbits but then switched to dogs, which were kept in his mother's apartment. His experiments on animals proved that the central portion of the circulatory system can tolerate the introduction of a flow of highly concentrated contrast medium.

Forssmann decided to carry out two further experiments on himself at Eberswalde. Altogether, he catheterized his own heart nine times without any side effects. Although the X-ray equipment at Eberswalde was not powerful enough to take short-exposure photographs efficiently, he was able to prove that it was possible to inject contrast medium into the human heart. Forssmann submitted an article to the *Münchner medizinische Wochenschrift* and presented his contrast medium results to the Eberswalde Region Society of Physicians on November 29, 1930. He was also allowed to present a short report to the 1931 Conference of Surgeons. At the next meeting of the Berlin Society of Surgeons, Sauerbruch suddenly asked Forssmann to return to the Charité.

Back at the Charité, Forssmann was assigned regular duties as an anesthetist, even after a time as "anesthetist to the chief." He also became "traffic director," with responsibility for supervising the operating schedule. During this time he applied for research support to the German Scientific Aid Council, but he never received a response. The criticism and opposition to his experiments and ideas continued. In the face of this venomous opposition, and without support, he could not continue his research. In the early summer of 1932, Sauerbruch advised him to move away from research to a career as a practicing surgeon at another hospital.

Forssmann traveled to the hospital in Mainz on July 31, 1932. He met his future wife in the hospital dining room immediately after his arrival. The department of surgery was headed by Willi Jehn, who was assisted by two senior physicians, Alfred Duhrssen and Axel Lezius. Forssmann was given a privileged position in the surgical department and immediately took over the women's ward. He worked at the hospital in Mainz through August of 1933.

In the fall of that year, Karl Heusch opened the first urology department in a Berlin municipal hospital, at the Rudolf Virchow Hospital. Heusch invited Forssmann to become his senior physician and offered to teach him urology. Together with Heusch, Forssmann performed his last experiment on himself. This experiment involved aortography: Contrast medium was injected into the aorta to provide X-ray pictures of the blood vessels in the kidneys. They attempted to inject the contrast medium into the aorta at the tip of the shoulder blade under a local anesthetic. Forssmann experienced excruciating pain when the tip of the needle reached the wall of the aorta. After three unsuccessful attempts, they abandoned the experiment, and the exhausted Forssmann went to bed. Following this failure, Forssmann's wife forbade him to conduct further experiments on himself, citing his responsibilities to his family.

Forssmann had made it clear to Heusch that he did not intend to remain in urology permanently. He was interested in developing experience in urology to support his interest in surgery. In the summer of 1936, Albert Fromme chose Forssmann for the post of senior surgeon in his large and famous department in Dresden. Forssmann regarded his two years with Fromme as the consummation of his surgical training. In Dresden, Forssmann came of age as a surgeon.

In 1938, Forssmann was transferred to the third surgical department at Robert Koch Hospital (formerly Moabit Hospital) as senior surgeon. He remained there for less than a year and was then called to duty as a surgeon with the German army during World War II. During the war Forssmann served with various medical units and was frequently responsible for the care of the most severely wounded. Near the end of the war, he escaped from the Russians to the American lines, where he was captured. He was transferred to various prisoner-of-war camps and eventually released.

Forssmann returned from World War II to find his house in ruins, with his family having fled to the south. He joined his family in the tiny hamlet of Wambach, high in the mountains in the Black Forest. His wife had established a medical practice in the community, and Forssmann became her partner. In 1948, they moved down into the valley, to Wies, where Forssmann continued his limited general practice. He returned to surgery and urology in 1950, when he and his wife moved to a specialized urology practice in Bad Kreuznach, a small town southwest of Mainz. He remained in Bad Kreuznach through 1957.

The experiments that Forssmann had conducted on himself had long been forgotten in his own country. More than a decade after Forssmann demonstrated the safety and potential for cardiac catheterization, Cournand and Richards began to develop his technique for clinical applications. Priority for Forssmann was firmly established in a statement that Cournand included in his first journal article concerning cardiac catheterization. Yet the realities of World War II kept Forssmann from having any part in the work of his fellow researchers in the United States.

Following the war, the continuing development and application of cardiac catheterization expanded beyond Cournand and Richards to other investigators. There was increasing interest in Forssmann and his contributions. In 1951, Forssmann discussed his experiments in a documentary film about cardiac catheterization that was produced in Great Britain. Beginning in the early 1950's, he was increasingly invited to lecture on his experiments and on the broader historical development of cardiac catheterization.

The Nobel Prize changed Forssmann's way of life dramatically. It quickly became clear that he could not remain in Bad Kreuznach after winning the Nobel Prize, but that he must find a wider sphere of activity. Immediately after the announcement of the Nobel award, Forssmann was named an honorary professor at the Johannes Gutenberg University in Mainz. At the start of 1958, Forssmann became director of the surgical department at the Evangelical Hospital in Düsseldorf. After overcoming early political difficulties with the chairman of the hospital's board of directors, Forssmann went on to modernize surgery at the Evangelical Hospital. He remained at this hospital until his retirement in 1970.

Forssmann was elected a member of the American College of Chest Physicians in

1954 and became a member of the Executive Board of the German Surgical Society in 1962. In 1966 he became a foreign corresponding member of the British Medical Society and in 1967 an honorary fellow of the Indian Academy of Sciences. He was also an honorary member of the Royal Swedish Society for Cardiology and a member of the German Society for Urology, the German Child Welfare Association, and the German Society for Emergency Medicine. Forssmann received the Liebnitz Medal of the German Academy of Sciences in East Germany in 1954. He was the guest of honor at the National University of Córdoba in Argentina in 1954 and was named an honorary professor at this university in 1961. Numerous other international honors followed upon the Nobel Prize.

Through his creative self-experimentation, Forssmann was the first to show that cardiac catheterization could be performed safely on human beings. He went on to conduct animal experiments and further experiments on himself involving contrast radiography. Rejected and ignored in his own country, he was forced to abandon further research for a more practical career as a surgeon and urologist; yet his experiments ultimately provided the foundation for modern cardiology.

Bibliography

Primary

MEDICINE: *Experiments on Myself: Memoirs of a Surgeon in Germany*, 1974.

Secondary

Cournand, André. "Cardiac Catheterization: Development of the Technique, Its Contributions to Experimental Medicine, and Its Initial Applications in Man." *Acta Medica Scandinavica*, 579 (1975). An edited and expanded version of the Jiménez Díaz Memorial Lecture presented by Cournand in Madrid, Spain, on May 19, 1970. Presents a comprehensive historical review of the development of cardiac catheterization and its early clinical applications. Part 1 considers the initial period, 1844 through 1900, including the development of cardiac catheterization by Claude Bernard. Part 2 considers the period from 1929 through 1936, emphasizing the experiments of Forssmann on himself; part 3 considers the third period, 1936 through 1945, describing the work of Cournand and Richards. Well illustrated; includes extensive footnotes and references.

Fishman, Alfred P., and Dickinson W. Richards, Jr., eds. *Circulation of the Blood: Men and Ideas*. New York: Oxford University Press, 1964. Twelve chapters concerning the history of cardiovascular physiology written by prominent researchers. Divided into three parts with five chapters on the heart, three on the blood vessels, and four on special circulations. The first chapter, by Cournand, is entitled "Air and Blood" and considers the historical development of understanding the relationship between the heart and lungs. Richards also wrote a chapter with William F. Hamilton entitled "The Output of the Heart," surveying the history of investigations of cardiac output.

Forssmann, Werner. *Experiments on Myself: Memoirs of a Surgeon in Germany.*

Translated by Hilary Davies. New York: St. Martin's Press, 1974. Forssmann always enjoyed telling stories; his family and friends encouraged him to tape-record his stories and have them transcribed. Forssmann organized these transcribed stories to render an account of both his life and the times in which he lived, including discussion of his personal philosophy of research and medicine. Includes a preface by Cournand.

Grossman, William, ed. *Cardiac Catheterization and Angiography.* 3d ed. Philadelphia: Lea & Febiger, 1986. Written by prominent researchers and clinicians and aimed at the instruction of physicians training to become cardiologists. Begins with three chapters on general principles of cardiac catheterization and angiography, including a chapter on the historical development of cardiac catheterization and its relationship to modern practice. Intended for a medical audience, this book is a comprehensive resource.

Yang, Sing San, Lamberto G. Bentivoglio, Vladir Maranhao, and Harry Goldberg. *From Cardiac Catheterization Data to Hemodynamic Parameters.* 3d ed. Philadelphia: F. A. Davis, 1988. This work aims "to transform raw data into meaningful hemodynamic parameters to be used, with the clinical data, in cardiovascular diagnosis." The first chapter provides a historical perspective on cardiac catheterization, beginning with the research of Forssmann, Cournand, and Richards. A technical publication that explains specific applications of cardiac catheterization to obtain and utilize data about the heart, lungs, and circulation.

Steven J. Albrechtsen

1956

Physiology or Medicine

André Frédéric Cournand, France and United States
Werner Forssmann, Germany
Dickinson W. Richards, Jr., United States

Chemistry

Sir Cyril Norman Hinshelwood, Great Britain
Nikolai Semenov, Soviet Union

Physics

William Shockley, United States
John Bardeen, United States
Walter H. Brattain, United States

Literature

Juan Ramón Jiménez, Spain

Peace

no award

DICKINSON W. RICHARDS, JR.
1956

Born: Orange, New Jersey; October 30, 1895
Died: Lakeville, Connecticut; February 23, 1973
Nationality: American
Areas of concentration: Cardiovascular and pulmonary physiology and pathology

Richards developed the technique of cardiac catheterization for clinical applications to study the physiology and pathology of the heart, lungs, and circulation in healthy and diseased humans

The Award

Presentation

Göran Liljestrand, a professor at the Royal Caroline Institute and secretary of the Nobel Committee for Physiology or Medicine, represented the medical faculty of the Royal Caroline Institute in delivering the presentation address on December 10, 1956, before King Gustav VI Adolf gave the Nobel medals and scrolls to Werner Theodor Otto Forssmann, André Frédéric Cournand, and Dickinson W. Richards, Jr. Liljestrand began his address by borrowing a statement from William Harvey to describe the heart as "the sun of the microcosm formed by the human body." He explained the two decisive factors for the work of the heart—pressure and flow—and discussed the limitations of early techniques in studying those factors. While direct methods were possible in animal experiments, the study of humans "was naturally confined to the use of the indirect methods."

This situation changed in 1929, when Forssmann demonstrated through heart catheterization experiments on himself how "the methods well known from animal experiments could also be adapted for studies in man." Cournand and Richards recognized the potential of Forssmann's discovery and developed the technique for clinical applications in man. As a result of these efforts, cardiac catheterization "made its triumphant entry into the world of clinical medicine."

Liljestrand continued by discussing the clinical applications of cardiac catheterization developed by Cournand and Richards, including investigations of secondary wound shock, acquired heart disease, congenital heart disease, and pulmonary diseases. He explained how these investigations had "been instrumental in promoting the remarkable advances in heart surgery made in recent time." Liljestrand stated that the extensive investigations he had briefly mentioned involved "the cooperation of a large number of highly skilled research workers," but that Cournand and Richards had "consistently been the pioneers and the leaders."

Liljestrand said that "the practical value of cardiac catheterization has been definitely proved" by Cournand and Richards. He further stated that this method "led to many important new observations, to diagnostic as well as therapeutic advances." Liljestrand concluded by stating that the work of the three laureates was "an outstanding example of the great possibilities implied by the application of physiological methods to clinical problems."

Nobel lecture

On December 11, 1956, Richards delivered his Nobel lecture, entitled "The Contributions of Right Heart Catheterization to Physiology and Medicine, with Some Observations on the Physiopathology of Pulmonary Heart Disease." Richards began by stating that measurements made in the right side of the heart in man "have provided a key to almost all the syntheses, all the integrations that we have attempted, in elucidating the nature of cardiopulmonary function." Early research concerning the integration of the heart, lungs, and circulation was noted to lack important measurements concerning "the state of the blood as it enters the right heart, its respiratory gas contents, its pressure relationships, and its rate of flow."

"We were aware of the earlier experiment of Forssmann," explained Richards, "and had followed closely its isolated uses in Germany, Portugal, South America, and France." Richards explained how Cournand and Hilmert A. Ranges utilized the technique of cardiac catheterization in man to obtain "consistent values for blood gases" that allowed them to determine cardiac output. Not long after, additional techniques were developed for pressure measurements, while techniques to measure blood volumes were also applied: "The stage was now set for study of cardiac and pulmonary functions in many forms of clinical disease."

"First to be undertaken was an investigation of traumatic shock in man," explained Richards. Cardiac catheterization was applied to the diagnosis of congenital heart disease; it also contributed to the surgery of congenital heart disease. The physiology of heart failure was studied; many forms and degrees of heart failure were defined, and their responses to treatment were measured. The action of digitalis glucosides was evaluated, and the original Starling principle was critically reviewed; acquired heart disease was studied. Richards explained that "excursions into cardiac physiology . . . have indeed been a major feature of our work" but that they somewhat obscured the fact that Cournand and he had consistently thought of themselves as primarily pulmonary rather than cardiac physiologists.

"The heart in chronic pulmonary disease is at a crossroads," stated Richards, "itself a consequence of both pulmonary and cardiocirculatory disturbances." He characterized pulmonary heart disease as "cardiac hypertrophy and dilation secondary to disease of the lungs." Using chronic diffuse pulmonary emphysema as a prototype, he described pulmonary heart disease. He divided pulmonary emphysema into four physiological groups and then discussed the characteristics of each of these four groups, "concentrating on the features concerned with the flow of blood through the lungs and the action of the right heart."

Richards concluded by mentioning "a few of the areas in which we believe that further basic research might well be concentrated." He noted the importance of further basic research concerning "the pharmacodynamics of the lung, and especially of the pulmonary circulation," and he emphasized the need to bring together function and structure. In conclusion, he summarized his lecture as an endeavor to present "a brief account of the development of cardiac catheterization in our hands, and some of the adventures that we have had with it."

Critical reception

The importance of cardiac catheterization as a clinical technique was well recognized both by medical professionals and by the general public when Forssmann, Cournand, and Richards received the Nobel Prize in 1956. Public reaction focused on Forssmann's experiments on himself and on the subsequent development and applications of the technique by Cournand and Richards. The work of Cournand and Richards was considered a brilliant example of the benefits of basic medical research to the practice of clinical medicine and the treatment of disease.

On October 19, 1956, the medical correspondent of *The Times* of London wrote that "the award of the Nobel Prize for Medicine to Professors Forssmann, Cournand and Richards is a well deserved tribute to three of the pioneers in a method of investigation without which it would have been almost impossible for surgeons to achieve the striking successes which they are now obtaining in the treatment of certain forms of heart disease."

An article in the October 29, 1956, issue of *Time* magazine explained Forssmann's experiments on himself, noting that "his discovery was ignored in Germany" where "older men, who should have been wiser, scoffed at Forssmann's catheterization of the heart as a circus stunt." The article continued by explaining that Cournand and Richards "read of Forssmann's experiment and developed a way to use it both for research and diagnosis. . . . Conditions that formerly were invariably fatal could be detected and corrected by surgery."

A page-one article in *The New York Times* on October 19, 1956, explained that Forssmann, Cournand, and Richards "were cited for their work in exploring with a thin tube the interior of the functioning human heart." The article went on to credit them with "providing a new technique for cardiology, including the diagnosis and treatment of heart disease." The article explained how Cournand and Richards "eventually showed how every known means for measuring pressures and blood compositions inside the heart could be safely applied." Forssmann was quoted in the article expressing his appreciation to Cournand and Richards. "No one in West Germany has paid any attention to me," he said. "The Americans were the ones who recognized my work."

An editorial in *The New York Times* on October 19, 1956, began by stating that "it is not unusual nowadays for a surgeon to run a catheter or hollow plastic tube through a vein in the arm into the heart." The editorial regarded the work of Cournand and Richards as "a brilliant example of what can be accomplished by fundamental research on the heart" and concluded that "if more is known about the normal and abnormal heart and physicians know better than ever before how to deal with it, we have reason to be thankful to the winners of this year's Nobel Prize in Medicine."

Biography

Dickinson Woodruff Richards, Jr., the son of Dickinson Woodruff Richards and Sally Lambert Richards, was born in Orange, New Jersey, on October 30, 1895. His maternal grandfather was a physician who had received his medical training at Bellevue Hospital; three maternal uncles were also physicians associated with either Bellevue Hospital or the College of Physicians and Surgeons at Columbia University.

Richards followed family tradition and received his early education at the Hotchkiss School in Lakeville, Connecticut. At the Hotchkiss School he received a classical education in the humanities, emphasizing English, Greek, and history. Family tradition continued with his undergraduate education at Yale University, from which he was graduated in 1917. At Yale, he continued his studies in the humanities, but he also developed a background in mathematics and the natural sciences. During World War I, Richards served as a lieutenant with an artillery unit. He traveled to Europe with the American Expeditionary Force in 1918.

Family tradition resumed after the war, when Richards entered the College of Physicians and Surgeons at Columbia University in 1919. He received his master's degree in physiology in 1922 and completed his medical degree in 1923. He was an intern from 1923 to 1925 and a resident in medicine from 1925 to 1927 at Presbyterian Hospital in New York City. This was followed by a research fellowship at the National Institute for Medical Research in London, England, from 1927 to 1928.

Richards returned to the United States in 1928 and resumed his affiliation with Presbyterian Hospital and the College of Physicians and Surgeons at Columbia University. He later became affiliated with Bellevue Hospital, also in New York City. He ultimately became an attending physician at Presbyterian Hospital, a visiting physician at Bellevue Hospital, director of the Columbia University Division of Bellevue Hospital, and Lambert Professor of Medicine in the College of Physicians and Surgeons at Columbia University.

Richards married Constance Burrell Riley on September 19, 1931. Their four children were Ida, Gertrude, Ann, and Constance. Richards was a Presbyterian and a member of the Century Association in New York City. He died in Lakeville, Connecticut, on February 23, 1973, at the age of seventy-seven.

Scientific Career

"Modesty and greatness seldom harmonize in one individual," stated André Cournand in a biographical sketch of Richards that he included in his autobiography. Cournand cited Richards as "one of those few in whom these apparently opposite qualities balanced one another. Although modest to the point of shyness, he implemented his natural intellectual gifts through strong character and hard work, reaching the heights in whatever he undertook."

Late in his life, Richards himself characterized his investigative work as belonging to three sequences. He termed the first sequence "blood and circulation," to describe his early research from 1922 to 1932. He called the second sequence "blood to lung," to describe his development of various tests of pulmonary function from

1932 to 1942. He termed the third sequence "lungs, blood and circulation," to describe his research involving the development of cardiac catheterization for clinical applications from 1940 to 1961.

Richards began his affiliation with Columbia University and its associated hospitals as a medical student from 1919 to 1923. The relationship continued from 1923 to 1927, when he was an intern and a resident in medicine at Presbyterian Hospital. During this time he developed a relationship with Lawrence J. Henderson of Harvard University, who became his mentor in physiology and his ideal as a scientist. With the encouragement of Henderson, Richards published three papers during his residency concerning his research on the circulatory adjustments to anemia, his research on blood flow through the lung and systemic circulations in a patient with tetralogy of Fallot, and his research on the influence of posture upon the mechanics of blood flow.

Richards followed his residency with a research fellowship at the National Institute for Medical Research in London, England, from 1927 to 1928. During this fellowship he received training in experimental physiology under his other mentor, Henry Hallet Dale. Richards published two papers during his research fellowship concerning his research with Walter Bauer on the vasodilator effect of acetates and his research with Bauer and Dale on the control of the circulation in the liver. Looking back on his early influences, Richards said, "A man's mind and his actions are chiefly molded by a very few. For me, in the early years, these were Lawrence J. Henderson and Henry Hallet Dale."

Richards returned to the United States in 1928 and joined the department of medicine at Presbyterian Hospital. He served as an assistant attending physician and associate attending physician at Presbyterian Hospital (becoming an attending physician in 1945). He also joined the faculty of the College of Physicians and Surgeons at Columbia University. Richards continued his early research efforts after his return to Presbyterian Hospital in 1928. His research involved the problem of how to equilibrate oxygen and carbon dioxide in a lung-bag system in order to estimate their concentration in mixed venous blood. This technique (called the indirect Fick method) was used to study the effect of therapeutic pneumothorax on the pulmonary blood flow.

Richards began his collaborative research efforts with Cournand in 1932. Their research was based on the application of the concept propounded by Henderson, who postulated that the heart, lungs, and circulation form a single physiological system for the exchange of respiratory gases between the atmosphere and the tissues of the organism. Cournand and Richards developed a battery of tests to evaluate lung function and determined standard values of the various parameters in normal subjects. These lung-function tests were then used to investigate pulmonary function in patients with various types of pulmonary diseases, including tuberculous lesions, chronic emphysema, and various forms of fibrosis.

In 1936, the need to obtain mixed venous blood from the right atrium of the heart led them to consider the technique of cardiac catheterization first demonstrated on humans by Forssmann in 1929. After four years of preliminary experiments with dogs and a chimpanzee, Cournand and Richards began cardiac catheterization in human subjects in 1940; these efforts were presented in an article published in the *Proceedings of the Society for Experimental Biology and Medicine* in 1941.

The initial importance of cardiac catheterization was that it established a safe method for obtaining mixed venous blood to determine blood flow by application of the Fick principle. This application of the Fick principle was used to measure cardiac output in evaluating a new model of the ballistocardiograph. The results of this investigation were presented at the annual meeting of the American Physiological Society in 1941 and were published in 1942.

Cardiac catheterization also allowed the measurement of blood pressures in the right side of the heart, once the catheter was connected to a recording manometric system. The initial pressure measurements in man were presented in an article in 1941. An exhaustive report that included experience in animals as well as in man was presented the following year. Improved catheters were soon developed, along with improved recording equipment, including a mobile multiple recording apparatus. Cardiac catheters were advanced beyond the right atrium into the right ventricle in 1942 and advanced into the pulmonary artery in 1944. A double-lumen catheter was developed to allow the simultaneous measurement of pressures in two different places.

Cardiac catheterization opened a whole new range of studies to investigate functions of the heart, lungs, and circulation in various diseases. Cournand and Richards used cardiac catheterization to investigate various types of shock, leading to treatment for shock based on physiological measurements. Their studies of hemorrhagic shock identified the importance of replacing lost blood both quantitatively and qualitatively through the administration of whole blood, rather than treating shock through the administration of other fluids or through the use of drugs.

Cournand and Richards investigated systemic hypertension, acquired heart disease, and congenital heart disease, and they continued their investigations of pulmonary disease. These studies eventually included the effects of pulmonary diseases upon the pulmonary circulation and right ventricular function. They investigated the consequences for the heart and lungs of various obstructive diseases of the lungs, studied the relationship between the electrical and mechanical events of the cardiac cycle, and evaluated the effects of drugs on the hemodynamic aberrations associated with various cardiac diseases.

During World War II, Richards was a member of the subcommittee on shock of the National Research Council (from 1941 to 1945) and deputy chief of the division of physiology of the committee on medical research of the Office of Scientific Research and Development from 1944 to 1946. Richards served as medical adviser to the research organizations of Merck and Company after 1935 and was a senior consultant to the New York Veterans Administration after 1954. In 1947 he was named Lambert Professor of Medicine in the College of Physicians and Surgeons at Columbia University. He became Lambert Professor of Medicine Emeritus and continued as a special lecturer in the College of Physicians and Surgeons at Columbia University following his retirement in 1961.

Richards delivered the Harvey Society lecture in 1943 and served as president of the Harvey Society in 1962. He received the citation of the American Heart Association in 1957. The John Phillips Memorial Award of the American College of Physicians was presented to Richards in 1960, and he received the Chevalier of the Legion of Honor from France in 1963. Richards received the Trudeau Medal of the National Tuberculosis Association in 1968 and the Kober Medal of the Association of American Physicians in 1970.

Richards accepted only two of the numerous honorary doctoral degrees that were offered to him. In 1957, he accepted a degree from Yale University, his alma mater; in 1966, he accepted a degree from Columbia University, where he had received his medical training and served his medical and academic career. Richards became a member of the National Academy of Sciences in the United States in 1957 and a member of the American Academy of Arts and Sciences in 1968. He was a fellow of the American College of Physicians and a diplomate of the American Board of Internal Medicine. Richards was a member of the Association of American Physicians, serving as its president in 1962; he was also a member of the American Society for Clinical Investigation, the American Trudeau Society, the American Medical Association, and the American Clinical and Climatological Association.

Richards developed the technique of cardiac catheterization for clinical applications to study the heart, lungs, and circulation as a single physiological system. He subsequently utilized cardiac catheterization to study the physiology and pathology of the heart, lungs, and circulation in healthy and diseased humans. His clinical applications of cardiac catheterization included pulmonary diseases, shock, systemic hypertension, acquired heart disease, and congenital heart disease. His work was a brilliant example of the benefits of basic medical research to the practice of clinical medicine and the treatment of disease.

Bibliography

Primary

MEDICINE: *Medical Priesthoods and Other Essays*, 1970.

EDITED TEXT: *Circulation of the Blood: Men and Ideas*, 1964 (with Alfred P. Fishman).

Secondary

Cournand, André. "Cardiac Catheterization: Development of the Technique, Its Contributions to Experimental Medicine, and Its Initial Applications in Man." *Acta Medica Scandinavica*, supp. 579 (1975). An expanded version of a lecture presented by Cournand in 1970, this presents a comprehensive historical review of the development of cardiac catheterization and its early clinical applications. Part 1 considers the initial period from 1844 through 1900; part 2 considers the period from 1929 through 1936, emphasizing the experiments of Forssmann on himself; part 3 considers the period from 1936 through 1945, describing the work of Cournand and Richards in the clinical development of cardiac catheterization. Well-illustrated; includes extensive footnotes and references.

Cournand, André F., and Michael Meyer. *From Roots to Late Budding: The Intellectual Adventures of a Medical Scientist*. New York: Gardner Press, 1986. This is the autobiography that Cournand wrote near the end of his life; part 2 includes historical perspectives on cardiopulmonary physiology, with a biographical sketch of Richards. Cournand clearly communicates his respect and appreciation for Richards as his longtime collaborator. Intended for a general audience; includes an extensive collection of photographs.

Fishman, Alfred P., and Dickinson W. Richards, Jr., eds. *Circulation of the Blood: Men and Ideas*. New York: Oxford University Press, 1964. Twelve chapters concerning the history of cardiovascular physiology written by prominent researchers. Divided into three parts: five chapters on the heart, three chapters on the blood vessels, and four chapters on special circulations. Coedited by Richards, who also wrote a chapter with William F. Hamilton entitled "The Output of the Heart." This chapter begins with the discovery of the circulation and early research concerning hemodynamics. Discusses the Fick methods and indicator dilution methods for measuring cardiac output and concludes by discussing the regulation of stroke volume.

Green, David E., and W. Eugene Knox, eds. *Research in Medical Science*. New York: Macmillan, 1950. This is a collection of essays on twenty-six different aspects of medical research; it is aimed at "enlightening and inspiring" the nonspecialist reader. Includes a chapter by Richards entitled "Pulmonary Physiology" that emphasizes the classification of pulmonary function and forms of pulmonary insufficiency; Richards also considers oxygen and nitrogen poisoning and respiratory gas exchange in the blood.

Grossman, William, ed. *Cardiac Catheterization and Angiography.* 3d ed. Philadelphia: Lea & Febiger, 1986. Written by prominent researchers and clinicians and aimed at the instruction of physicians training to become cardiologists. Includes three chapters on general principles of cardiac catheterization and angiography, including a chapter on the historical development of cardiac catheterization. There are chapters on techniques of cardiac catheterization, hemodynamic principles, angiographic techniques, and other related topics. Intended for a medical audience, this is a comprehensive resource.

Richards, Dickinson W., Jr. *Medical Priesthoods and Other Essays*. Hartford: Connecticut Printers, 1970. A collection of six essays on medicine and four essays on physiology; most were edited from formal lectures presented by Richards between 1952 and 1966. The essays on medicine begin with the title essay, "Medical Priesthoods, Past and Present," which was originally delivered as the Presidential Address to the Association of American Physicians in 1962. The book includes Richards' Nobel lecture.

Yang, Sing San, Lamberto G. Bentivoglio, Vladir Maranhao, and Harry Goldberg.

From Cardiac Catheterization Data to Hemodynamic Parameters. 3d ed. Philadelphia: F. A. Davis, 1988. Written with the main objective of transforming raw data "into meaningful hemodynamic parameters to be used, with the clinical data, in cardiovascular diagnosis." The first chapter provides a historical perspective on cardiac catheterization, beginning with the research of Forssmann, Cournand, and Richards. Other chapters explain various measurements associated with cardiac catheterization and discuss the assessment of various pathological conditions through cardiac catheterization. A technical publication that explains specific applications of cardiac catheterization to obtain and utilize data about the heart, lungs, and circulation.

Steven J. Albrechtsen

1957

Physiology or Medicine
Daniel Bovet, Switzerland and Italy

Chemistry
Sir Alexander Robertus Todd, Great Britain

Physics
Chen Ning Yang, China and United States
Tsung-Dao Lee, China and United States

Literature
Albert Camus, France

Peace
Lester B. Pearson, Canada

DANIEL BOVET
1957

Born: Neuchâtel, Switzerland; March 23, 1907

Nationality: Swiss; after 1947, Italian
Areas of concentration: Chemotherapy and pharmacology

Daniel Bovet pursued studies of molecular competitive phenomena involving synthetic organic compounds designed as potential antagonists of endogenous chemical transmitters, and he discovered important medicinal agents

The Award

Presentation

The presentation speech was delivered on December 10, 1957, by Professor B. Uvnäs, representing the faculty of the Royal Caroline Institute. Dr. Uvnäs began by reviewing the background for Daniel Bovet's researches, which was laid by discoveries in the 1920's concerning the importance of neurotransmitter molecules—acetylcholine and adrenaline—released by the peripheral autonomic and motor nerves, and of histamine as a mediator of allergic responses of various organs. Collectively, these biogenic amines provided a great opportunity for developing synthetic molecules that could serve important therapeutic purposes by imitating or antagonizing their functions. Bovet focused his efforts on finding molecules that could antagonize or block the actions of such biogenic amines. The discovery of the first such blocker for histamine, termed an "antihistamine," was made in 1937 by Bovet and A. M. Staub. This breakthrough led to the synthesis of numerous other new compounds to be tested in many pharmacology laboratories for antihistaminic activity.

For many years, Bovet studied the relationships of chemical structure to biological activity among compounds synthesized as substitutes for the naturally occurring alkaloids of curare and ergot. The most notable success was in discovering chemically simpler molecules capable of medical use as muscle paralyzants in surgery. These act as blockers of the neurotransmitter acetylcholine in the muscles. Use of such agents permits a lesser degree of general anesthesia while still attaining full muscle relaxation. Less anesthetic means a greater margin of safety for the patient; for this, Uvnäs noted, Bovet deserves credit. His similar studies for improving on ergot alkaloids as blockers of adrenaline have importance, although they have not directly yielded new medicinal agents. Professor Bovet's more recent transition to research in the important new field of psychopharmacology was recognized at the close of Professor Uvnäs' presentation speech.

Nobel lecture

The imposing title of Daniel Bovet's lecture, delivered on December 11, 1957, was "The Relationships Between Isosterism and Competition Phenomena in the Field of Drug Therapy of the Autonomic Nervous System and that of Neuromuscular Transmission." An "isostere" is defined as a substance that stands in place of another compound, as in the situation of "competitive inhibition." This in turn is defined as the prevention of a normal action of an effector substance by another agent (an isostere) that also enters into a combination with the element ("receptor") that is essential to the effector substance. Thus, "isosterism and competitive phenomena" describes Bovet's searches for competitive blockers of the endogenous amines—histamine, acetylcholine, adrenaline (epinephrine), and serotonin. Such searches, Bovet emphasized, have sometimes been facilitated by the prior identification of plant alkaloids that act in the desired manner—with cocaine as a model for synthetic local anesthetics, atropine and curare as natural antagonists of acetylcholine, and ergot alkaloids as prototypes for anti-adrenaline agents. No naturally occurring antihistamines, however, have ever been found. Neither was there known, in 1957, an antiserotonin agent from nature.

By the early 1930's, Dr. Bovet had begun to publish on research concerning compounds that showed inhibition of adrenaline's actions. Initially drawing on the structure of adrenaline itself as a pattern from which to begin, Bovet later pursued studies on fragments of the ergot alkaloid basic structure as antiadrenaline agents. Unfortunately, neither Bovet and his colleagues, nor many others similarly pursuing this subject, were rewarded with a new, useful therapeutic agent.

In 1946, Bovet, his wife, and other coworkers began a search for synthetic curare substitutes: agents that would act by blocking the excitatory action of acetylcholine on the skeletal muscles. Earlier, the structure of curare's active constituent, d-tubocurarine, had been elucidated, and it had been introduced into medical use in 1946. Working with chemists of the French pharmaceutical company Rhone-Poulenc, Bovet found already by 1946 one compound that was the first synthetic curarizing agent having comparable selectivity of action to that of the natural alkaloid. In 1947, Bovet reported one of the simplest compounds possessing a true tubocurare-like action; it later entered medical use under the name gallamine (Flaxedil). In addition, Bovet's group first recognized the muscle paralyzant activity of another compound, succinylcholine, which soon entered medical use and continues to be important because of its short duration of action and the innocuous nature of its quickly produced metabolites. Professor Bovet elaborated on the details of two modes of action that are correlated with chemical features that divide all curarizing drugs into classes for which he coined the term "pachycurares" and "leptocurares."

At this point, Professor Bovet discussed his third area of work exemplifying the pursuit of isosteric inhibitors, that involving the "local hormone" histamine. In Ernest Fourneau's laboratory at the Pasteur Institute, Bovet began to search for antihistamine activity. The first success, with the compound thymoxyethyldiethylamine (designated 929-F, the initial standing for Fourneau), was achieved by 1937. It was able to protect guinea pigs fully against a lethal intravenous injection of a histamine solution. In 1944, the work of Bovet led to the first clinically effective and nontoxic histamine blocker, pyrilamine (Neo-Antergan), which continues in use today despite the advent of scores of newer compounds. Bovet stated that in less than ten years about five hundred chemists had performed about five thousand syntheses of potential antihistamines. He described three major chemical subgroupings into which the many active compounds could be divided.

For the latter part of his lecture, Dr. Bovet turned to the subject of the central nervous system (CNS) and its neurotransmitters as a target for intrepid pharmacologists, who he termed the "enfants terribles" of the science of physiology—this perhaps for their lack of awe at such a task. He cited W. Feldberg's analysis, which caused him to conclude that acetylcholine must also be a CNS neurotransmitter. Bovet himself was among those becoming psychopharmacologists as he turned his attentions to the CNS. Early evidence of this was provided by his studies of the electroencephalogram of rabbits as an index of changes in brain activity induced by drugs that modify CNS acetylcholine mechanisms—physostigmine (eserine), atropine, and nicotine. He also showed the ability of a new group of therapeutic agents for Parkinson disease to block effects of nicotine on the CNS. This supported the characterization of the anti-Parkinson agents as centrally acting acetylcholine blockers.

In closing, Dr. Bovet gave a fleeting view of the topic of drug-receptor interactions, a field only beginning its rise at that time. The note he sounded at that point was to be sounded again from the same platform at greater intensity and length by another pharmacologist and developer of new drugs thirty-one years later: James W. Black. So it was that Bovet paid homage to his mentors and colleagues for their contributions to his success; there would be others to come who would build their success on the foundation that Bovet had laid.

Critical reception

Popular news media found Daniel Bovet somewhat anomalous as a Nobel laureate because of his prior obscurity. *Time* magazine headed its story, "Unknown Giant," making much of Bovet's never having been listed by the "Who's Who" of his country and never even having been interviewed before by newsmen. He was, however, referred to as one of the "research stars" at the Istituto Superiore di Sanita of Rome "who has spent a lifetime in quiet laboratories." *Time* also highlighted his not having taken a patent on his inventions in his own name and thus his not having received any income from commercial exploitation of his discoveries. The story also gave Dr. Bovet the major credit for discovering the active antibacterial agent sulfanilamide, which "took the lead in chemotherapy away from Germany in helping to create the succession of sulfa drugs that have saved millions of lives."

The editorialist for *Nature* (London, November 9, 1957) remarked that Bovet's Nobel Prize would "give pleasure to all chemists and pharmacologists who are concerned with the discovery of new drugs" and that "he has made a long series of discoveries in chemical pharmacology, many of which have led to important advances in medicine." After summarizing Bovet's work in developing the first antihistamines and the first synthetic curare-like drug, the writer added that "he also seems to have an instinctive genius for deciding what chemical compounds would be most likely to have the desired pharmacological properties."

Biography

Daniel Bovet was born on March 23, 1907, at Neuchâtel, Switzerland, to Pierre and Amy (Babut) Bovet. His father was a professor of education at the University of Geneva, for whom his children served as "guinea pigs for testing father's educational theories. . . . It was wonderful," according to Bovet. He took his secondary education and his initial university studies at Geneva, graduating in 1927. After serving as an assistant in physiology, he obtained his doctor of science degree in 1929, based on his thesis in zoology and comparative anatomy. He joined the staff of the Pasteur Institute in Paris in 1929 as assistant in the Laboratory of Therapeutic Chemistry, of which Professor Ernest Fourneau was director. Fourneau's influence on Bovet's future researches was great. Bovet became director in 1939 and served until 1947, when he moved to Italy to organize and become the director of a new Laboratory of Therapeutic Chemistry at the Istituto Superiore di Sanita (an Italian institute of health) of Rome. He continued in that position until 1964, when he became professor of pharmacology at the University of Sassari. In 1971 he left Sassari to become professor of psychobiology at the University of Rome until his retirement in 1982. From 1969 to 1975, Bovet served also as director of the Laboratory of Psychobiology and Psychopharmacology of the Consiglio Naziona delle Recerche in Rome.

Daniel Bovet became a citizen of Italy in 1947. Since 1938 he had been married to a native of Italy, the former Filomena Nitti, whose father Francesco Nitti had served as prime minister before he went into exile in France during the Fascist regime. It was in Paris, at the Pasteur Institute, that Bovet met his future wife as another researcher. Except for time out to bear their three children, Filomena Bovet-Nitti worked as a collaborator in her husband's researches after their marriage.

Professor Bovet was honored a number of times prior to his receiving the Nobel Prize in 1957: In 1934, he was awarded the Plantamour Prize of the faculty of science of the University of Geneva; in 1936, the Martin Damourette Prize of the Academy of Sciences of the Institute of France; in 1941, the General Muteau Prize of the Italian Academy of Science; in 1949, the Cameron Prize of the University of Edinburgh, the Burgi Prize of the Faculty of Medicine of Berne, and, jointly with his wife, the E. Paterno Prize; in 1952, the Addingham Gold Medal of the University of Leeds. Bovet received honorary doctorates from the universities of Palermo, Rio de Janeiro, Geneva, Montpelier, Paris, Nancy, Prague, and Strasbourg. In 1946 he was elected to the Legion of Honor of France, and in 1959 he was elected a Grand Official of the Order of Merit of the Italian Republic.

Scientific Career

Upon receiving his D.Sc. degree from the University of Geneva, Daniel Bovet left Switzerland; he was to divide his subsequent research career between France and Italy. He remained from 1929 to 1947 at the Pasteur Institute in Paris. He considered himself most fortunate to join the research group directed by Ernest Fourneau in the Laboratory of Therapeutic Chemistry. In comparison to contemporary academic research institutions of the United States, that laboratory would be equivalent to the combination of a department of medicinal chemistry and a department of pharmacology. Bovet's activities were such as to be aptly described as those of a "chemical pharmacologist," although that phrase (and that sort of researcher) is seldom encountered now.

In his early years, Bovet became part of a team that began to investigate the basis for the antibacterial action of a new chemotherapeutic agent from Germany, Prontosil, discovered by Domagk in 1935. Fourneau, Bovet, and coworkers deduced from the fact that Prontosil was inactive in vitro, although protective when given to streptococcal-infected mice, that it must be metabolically transformed to the active molecule. Pursuing this hypothesis, they discovered the antibacterial substance sulfanilamide, which became a most important anti-infective drug on its own, as well as becoming a prototype from which were developed many other agents of the "sulfa drug" family. These were the first and only truly effective therapy for many sorts of infections before the antibiotic era dawned. Another important benefit to Dr. Bovet's research career that was imparted at the Pasteur Institute was his research collaborator who became his wife, Filomena Bovet-Nitti. She continued to work with him throughout his career, coauthoring books and many of his research papers, as well as presenting some on her own.

Before and during the period of his work on Prontosil and sulfanilamide, Daniel Bovet was launching the main thrust of his career: the pursuit of competitive inhibitors, or blocking agents, toward endogenous amines serving important transmitter/mediator roles. This led him to another major discovery, more nearly his alone, in respect to the mediator of allergic responses, histamine. In 1937, Bovet and A. M. Staub published on the first known histamine blockers, one of which (929-F) gave 100 percent protection of guinea pigs against an otherwise lethal intravenous dose of histamine. In 1939, Bovet became head of the laboratory upon the retirement of Fourneau. Further studies were directed toward finding antihistamine compounds suitable, after human testing, to be marketed for medicinal use. Bovet and his colleagues accomplished this with the 1944 introduction of pyrilamine (Neo-Antergan).

Bovet's early papers on antihistamines clearly indicated that his agents of that new group were incapable of blocking some physiological responses to histamine; they could not oppose histamine-induced gastric secretion. Thus, it remained for others to delineate the concept of two histamine receptors and for James W. Black and his colleagues in 1972 to define the second receptor and supply a blocker for it. For this and earlier discoveries, Black would receive the Nobel Prize in 1988. The new family of antihistamine drugs which Bovet fathered came to consist of at least three subgroups, grouped by chemical patterns. One of these, exemplified by promethazine (Phenergan), later became the source of the "phenothiazine tranquilizers" or antipsychotic agents, mainly because the prominent sedative properties of promethazine provoked further exploration of exploitable new depressant properties. Chlorpromazine (Thorazine) was the initial success of this group (coming from another French drug development program). Another subgroup became the source of antinausea-antiemetic agents for treating motion sickness and vertigo.

In 1947, Bovet left Paris for Rome and the challenge of founding and directing a new laboratory of therapeutic chemistry at the Istituto Superiore de Sanita. This move to his wife's native country was quickly followed by Bovet's becoming a citizen of Italy. During his years at the institute, much of Dr. Bovet's attention focused on another area of major success, the study of structure-activity relationships among synthetic agents having curare-like activity. A culmination of his earlier researches at the Pasteur Institute on autonomic agents came in the form of a 1948 book, coauthored by Mrs. Bovet-Nitti, entitled *Structure et activité pharmacodynamique des médicaments du système nerveux végétatif*.

Whereas most, if not all, of his previous journal papers had been published in French, after 1947 many began to appear in Italian; by 1950, some were in English. American journal publications on antihistaminic agents in 1950 and on curare-like agents in 1954 brought greater accessibility of Bovet's researches in those areas to English-speaking scientists. French-language journals, however, were never totally deserted by Bovet. Between 1934 and 1952, Bovet received seven prizes or medals for his research from Swiss, Italian, French, and British sources. It is evident that his work had gained considerable notice prior to his receiving the ultimate recognition of the Nobel Prize in 1957.

During his years at the institute in Rome, Bovet became increasingly oriented toward psychopharmacology; this was especially evident at first in his joint papers with Victor Longo concerning nicotine and other drugs affecting acetylcholine functions of the brain. In 1969, Bovet became director of the Laboratory of Psychobiology and Psychopharmacology of the national research council in Rome, continuing through 1975. In 1964, he left the institute to become professor of pharmacology at the University of Sassari, a position he held until 1971. Then he became professor of psychobiology at the University of Rome from 1971 until his retirement in 1982. The period from 1967 to the early 1970's was one of active publication, centering on contrasts among several inbred strains of mice in their behavioral responses to psychopharmacologic drugs. What may have been the last such experimental research publication was one appearing in 1980, coauthored by Bovet, that dealt with a genetic analysis of behavior of mice in a three-path maze apparatus.

Two 1990 reviews of the three classes of histamine receptors and their antagonists each found occasion to cite papers by the discoverer of blocking drugs for the original histamine receptor (now the H_1-receptor). Greater continuing recognition is seen in the fact that a 1990 book on nerve-muscle function recalls clearly Bovet's contributions to that area of drug development.

Bibliography

Primary

PHYSIOLOGY: *Structure et activité pharmacodynamique des médicaments du système nerveux végétatif*, 1948; "Curare," *Experientia*, vol. 4, 1949, pp. 325-348 (with F. Bovet-Nitti); "Introduction to Antihistaminic Agents and Antergan Derivatives,"

Annals of the New York Academy of Sciences, vol. 50, 1950, pp. 1089-1126; "Some Aspects of the Relationship Between Chemical Constitution and Curare-Like Activity," *Annals of the New York Academy of Sciences*, vol. 54, 1951, pp. 407-432; "The Action on Nicotine-Induced Tremors of Substances Effective in Parkinsonism," *Journal of Pharmacology and Experimental Therapeutics*, vol. 102, 1951, pp. 22-30 (with V. G. Longo); *Curare and Curare-Like Agents*, 1959 (with F. Bovet-Nitti and G. B. Marini-Bettolo); "Isosterism and Competitive Phenomena in Drugs," *Science*, vol. 129, 1959, pp. 1255-1264; "Effects of Nicotine on Avoidance Conditioning of Inbred Strains of Mice," *Psychopharmacologia*, vol. 10, 1966, pp. 1-5 (with F. Bovet-Nitti and A. Oliverio); "Genetic Aspects of Learning and Memory in Mice," *Science*, vol. 163, 1969, pp. 139-149 (with F. Bovet-Nitti and A. Oliverio); "Synthetic Inhibitors of Neuromuscular Transmission, Chemical Structures, and Structure Activity Relationships," in *Neuromuscular Blocking and Stimulating Agents*, vol. 1, pp. 243-294, 1972.

Secondary

"Antihistamines (Systemic)." In *United States Pharmacopeia Drug Information for the Consumer*. Mt. Vernon, N.Y.: Consumers Union, 1988. An authoritative, thorough source on this class of drugs with respect to the information needs of consumers. Includes seventeen prescription and nonprescription chemical entities in the class with a multitude of trade names for such products. Covers matters to be considered before using, proper manner of use and storage, precautions while using, and an array of possible side effects. Does not pertain to the history of antihistamines.

Bowman, William C. *Pharmacology of Neuromuscular Function*. 2d ed. London: John Wright & Sons, 1990. A book on skeletal muscle and its innervation that describes Bovet's discoveries in the area concerning gallamine triethiodide, which became the first widely used synthetic neuromuscular blocking drug, and the neuromuscular blocking action of succinyldicholine, which became and continues to be a significant drug in the practice of anesthesiology.

Feinberg, Samuel M. "Antihistamine Drugs." *Journal of the American Pharmaceutical Association, Practical Pharmacy Edition* 8, no. 9 (1947): 546-549. An early review by an allergist on antihistamines when only two were available in the United States. The author credits "Fourneau and his collaborators" in France for opening this new class of drugs. He describes the therapeutic benefits and the unwanted side effects for Pyribenzamine and Benadryl and indicates that chemists and pharmacologists of the pharmaceutical industry "are feverishly at work attempting to find a drug which will come closer to perfection."

Flieger, Ken. "It's Spring Again and Allergies Are in Bloom." *FDA Consumer* 23 (May, 1989): 16-19. In the only historical note, the author indicates that before the 1940's there was essentially no drug to benefit "hayfever" sufferers. Antihistamines currently are the most widely used treatments for this allergy, known as seasonal allergic rhinitis. A list of twenty-three available antihistamines (by generic name only) is provided. The use of oral and topical decongestants is also covered.

Friend, Dale G. "The Antihistamines." *Clinical Pharmacology and Therapeutics* 1 (September/October, 1960): 5-10. A review of six major antihistamines of varied chemical nature and side-effect profiles. Being considerably farther removed than Feinberg's review from their introduction, no reference is made to the discovery of this group of drugs. Both generic and trade names are given; toxicity and therapeutic uses are discussed.

Melville, K. I. "Antihistamine Drugs." In *International Encyclopedia of Pharmacology and Therapeutics*. Vol. 1, *Histamine and Antihistamines*. Oxford, England: Pergamon Press, 1973. The author begins his broad review with a summary of the search for a specific histamine antagonist by Bovet at the Pasteur Institute and the development of the first clinically useful one, mepyramine or NeoAntergan.

Talley, James R., and A. G. Danti. "Antihistamines: Their Actions and Interactions." *U.S. Pharmacist* 2 (May, 1977): 51-55. Tissue-level actions and therapeutic uses are described, but the main emphasis is on potential adverse reactions and on reported interactions with drugs from other diverse classes. No historical references.

W. Marvin Davis

1958

Physiology or Medicine

George Wells Beadle, United States
Edward Lawrie Tatum, United States
Joshua Lederberg, United States

Chemistry

Frederick Sanger, Great Britain

Physics

Pavel Alekseyevich Cherenkov, Soviet Union
Ilya Mikhailovich Frank, Soviet Union
Igor Yevgenyevich Tamm, Soviet Union

Literature

Boris Pasternak, Soviet Union

Peace

Dominique Georges Pire, Belgium

GEORGE WELLS BEADLE
1958

Born: Wahoo, Nebraska; October 22, 1903

Nationality: American
Areas of concentration: Genetics and biochemistry

Beadle helped to define one of the basic tenets of biology: the one gene, one enzyme hypothesis. With Edward L. Tatum and Boris Ephrussi, he studied eye color mutants of the fruit fly Drosophila melanogaster *and nutritional mutants of the pink bread mold* Neurospora crassa *to demonstrate that each gene in an organism encodes a unique protein enzyme for controlling various metabolic reactions*

The Award

Presentation

Professor T. Caspersson of the Royal Caroline Institute presented the Nobel Prize in Physiology or Medicine to George Beadle, Edward Tatum, and Joshua Lederberg on Wednesday, December 10, 1958. In his short presentation, Caspersson discussed the various aspects of heredity, the transmission of basic organismal characteristics from parents to offspring. He also described the uses of radiation in studying genetics, the science dealing with genes and their mechanisms of expression and inheritance, plus the dangers of atomic energy, recently harnessed, to living organisms.

Beadle and Tatum studied nutritional mutants of the pink bread mold *Neurospora crassa*, a filamentous fungus that easily can be cultured in test tubes. These nutritional mutants could grow only on special media (food) supplemented with a variety of nutrients; they would not grow on a medium containing only the most basic nutrients needed for growth and reproduction. Beadle and Tatum determined that each mutant was deficient for a single nutrient, usually a vitamin or amino acid. From these studies, they deduced that each nutritional mutant lacked an enzyme that helped to synthesize that particular nutrient. The enzyme was missing because the gene encoding it was mutated (damaged). This evidence supported their hypothesis that one gene encodes one enzyme.

In living organisms, genes encode protein enzymes that act in series to synthesize various needed nutrients for the cell. These series of enzymes are called biochemical, or metabolic, pathways: One enzyme modifies substance A to create substance B, which is modified by a second enzyme to create substance C, which is modified by a third enzyme to create substance D, and so on. Each enzyme of a pathway is encoded by a single unique gene. A mutation of that gene prevents proper enzyme functioning, thereby disrupting the entire biochemical pathway. The only solution to the problem is to supply the organism with a nutrient synthesized by another enzyme in the pathway located after the site of action of the damaged inactivated enzyme.

Nobel lecture

George Beadle delivered his Nobel lecture, entitled "Genes and Chemical Reactions in *Neurospora*," on Thursday, December 11, 1958. While not addressing the entire history of biochemical genetics, Beadle did provide a concise, informative survey of the breakthrough experiments that he, Tatum, and Lederberg conducted en route to discovering the one gene, one enzyme concept. His lecture was divided into four principal sections: inborn errors of metabolism, eye pigment mutants of *Drosophila melanogaster*, nutritional mutants (called auxotrophs) of *Neurospora crassa*, and the implications of the one gene, one enzyme concept to genetics and biology.

In 1865, the Austrian monk Gregor Mendel developed the science of genetics by discovering the inheritance of traits (genes) in a predictable fashion for garden peas. Mendel's work was mostly ignored for the next forty years, whereupon several investigators rediscovered his work and began speculating upon the nature, structure, and function of genes. The English biochemist Sir Archibald E. Garrod observed that humans suffering from the disorder called alcaptonuria released urine that turned black upon exposure to air. Garrod determined that the causative substance for this malady is homogentisic acid. He observed that the incidence of the disorder was inherited and surmised that the affected individuals lacked an enzyme that normally modified homogentisic acid. He correctly theorized, furthermore, that such individuals lacked the normal gene (by mutation) that encoded this particular enzyme. For alcaptonuria and other, similar disorders, Garrod coined the phrase "inborn errors of metabolism."

In the 1930's, Beadle and Boris Ephrussi began studying the biochemistry and genetics of the eye pigments (eye color molecules) in the fruit fly *Drosophila melanogaster*, working along the same pathway as Garrod. Normal, or wild-type, fruit flies have reddish-brown eyes. Two radiation-induced mutations, vermilion (v) and cinnabar (cn), lack brown pigment; affected flies have bright red eyes. Beadle and Ephrussi transplanted eye buds between fruit fly larvae, which subsequently developed into adult flies having three, not two, eyes. Vermilion or cinnabar buds transplanted into wild-type larvae resulted in wild-type eyes. A vermilion bud transplanted into cinnabar larvae becomes wild-type. A cinnabar bud transplanted into vermilion larvae becomes cinnabar. From these seemingly bizarre results, they surmised that the biochemical reaction pathway for *Drosophila* brown eye pigment is precursor to vermilion substance to cinnabar substance to brown pigment. Adolf Butenandt and coworkers determined the vermilion substance to be kynurenine and the cinnabar substance to be 3-hydroxykynurenine. Ephrussi, Beadle, and Tatum correctly theorized that a mutation in the gene encoding the enzyme which converts *n*-formylkynurenine to kynurenine produces vermilion eyes. A mutation in the gene encoding an enzyme that converts kynurenine to 3-hydroxykynurenine produces cinnabar eyes.

Looking for a simpler organism with which to verify the one gene, one enzyme hypothesis, Beadle and Tatum turned to the pink bread mold *Neurospora crassa*. They irradiated *Neurospora* spores, followed by growth on fully supplemented growth media. Mutants were found that could not grow on minimally supplemented media, food that contained the minimum nutrients needed for wild-type *Neurospora* to grow and reproduce. Further testing showed that each mutant was deficient for a single nutrient, usually an essential vitamin or amino acid. These mutants lacked the enzymes needed for synthesizing these nutrients from chemical precursors. Detailed genetic studies showed that each mutant was affected at a specific chromosomal location, at a specific gene. They verified the one gene, one enzyme hypothesis. Each *Neurospora* auxotroph was mutated for a specific gene encoding a specific protein for synthesizing an essential vitamin or amino acid.

Critical reception

The awarding of the 1958 Nobel Prize in Physiology or Medicine to Beadle, Tatum, and Lederberg reflected a shift in medical and biological research toward genetics and biochemistry to the very basis of life itself. They were the beginning of a wave of great biologists who would unravel the nature of the gene, the code of life. Beadle and Tatum performed their breakthrough work before the 1950's, when such Nobel laureates as Alfred Hershey, Martha Chase, Francis Crick, and James Watson determined that deoxyribonucleic acid (DNA) is the genetic material. Nobel laureates Linus Pauling and Frederick Sanger unraveled the structures and enzymatic actions of proteins. The current dogma of molecular biology, DNA encodes ribonucleic acid (RNA), which encodes protein, hinges upon Beadle and Tatum's one gene, one enzyme concept. They discovered the nature of the gene and its role within the cell before its structure and exact mechanisms of action were discovered.

The November 10, 1958, issue of *Time* magazine cited the three Americans for their genetic research. Beadle and Tatum shared half the prize, and Lederberg received the remaining half. *Time* briefly described their research, discussing *Neurospora*, X-irradiation to produce mutations, and the first isolated mutant for vitamin B_6. Heredity and the linkage of genetics to biochemistry were the emphasized topics.

The November 10, 1958, issue of *Newsweek* cited Beadle and Tatum for their work in improving knowledge of biochemical genetics. The applications of their work to the treatment of cancer and other diseases were stressed. Much emphasis was placed upon Lederberg's discovery of a sexual cycle in bacteria. Most magazines and newspapers placed the spotlight on the plight of the Russian poet and 1958 Nobel laureate in Literature, Boris Pasternak, whose novel *Doctor Zhivago* (1958) was banned in the Soviet Union and who was forced by the Soviet government to refuse the Nobel Prize. The December 22, 1958, issue of *Newsweek* again highlighted the Nobel Prize recipients following the presentations in Stockholm.

The Nobel Prize opened up new avenues for Beadle, including the presidency of the University of Chicago and involvement in several important causes, such as the mutational effects of radiation and radioactive fallout from nuclear explosions. Both the United States and the Soviet Union were conducting above-ground nuclear tests at the time. Beadle served as chairman of the Committee on the Genetic Effects of

Atomic Radiation for the National Academy of Sciences.

From the 1960's, onward, virtually all undergraduate and graduate genetics textbooks included a summary of *Neurospora crassa* and the famous experiments of Beadle and Tatum. Their experiments, while simple in scope, have emerged as among the most important in the history of genetics. Their work serves as an example of selecting the proper organisms for experimentation and for clear interpretation of data. Most important, the one gene, one enzyme hypothesis, its connection to Garrod's inborn errors of metabolism, and its direct applications to the treatment of genetic disease make Beadle and Tatum's work immensely important.

Biography

George Wells Beadle was born in Wahoo, Nebraska, on October 22, 1903. His parents were Chauncey Elmer Beadle and Hattie Albro Beadle. He received his B.S. and M.S. degrees in 1926 and 1927, respectively, from the University of Nebraska, Lincoln. In 1931, he received the Ph.D. from Cornell University.

With a National Research Council fellowship, he studied at the California Institute of Technology from 1931 to 1936, where he collaborated with the eminent geneticists Theodosius Dobzhansky, Alfred H. Sturtevant, and S. Emerson. In 1935, he studied at the Institut de Biologie Physico-Chimique in Paris. He became assistant professor of genetics at Harvard University in 1936. From 1937 to 1946, he was professor of biology and genetics at Stanford University. He became professor and chairman of the Division of Biology at the California Institute of Technology in 1946. In 1961, he became chancellor, then president, of the University of Chicago. After retirement in 1968, he worked from 1968 to 1970 with the American Medical Association Institute for Biomedical Research.

Beadle holds honorary doctorates from several universities, including Nebraska, Yale, Northwestern, Rutgers, and Oxford. He has received awards from the American Public Health Association, the American Cancer Society, and the National Academy of Sciences, as well as the Albert Einstein Commemorative Award in Science. He is a member of the National Academy of Sciences, the Genetics Society of America, the American Association for the Advancement of Science, the American Cancer Society, and the Royal Society of London. He has been married twice. He and his second wife, author Muriel McClure Beadle, gave birth to a son, David Beadle.

Scientific Career

George Beadle was interested in genetics as far back as his undergraduate days at the University of Nebraska. As a geneticist, he has studied a variety of species from the animal, plant, and fungal kingdoms. His devotion to the subject can be traced to his upbringing in a farming family and to his excellence in science during high school.

He studied hybrid wheat at the University of Nebraska en route to an M.S. degree in 1927. From 1927 to 1931, he pursued and earned a doctorate at Cornell University. He studied Mendelian asynapsis in corn (*Zea mays*). Asynapsis is a situation in which two homologous (identical) chromosomes fail to pair during meiosis, the process by which chromosomes are evenly distributed between gametes (pollen and egg) in reproductive organs (flowers). The result can be an abnormal distribution of chromosomes in the corresponding gametes and future offspring. Beadle continued to study the genetics of *Zea mays* from 1931 to 1936 at the California Institute of Technology.

In 1935, Beadle began collaborating with the eminent *Drosophila* geneticist Boris Ephrussi at the Institut de Biologie Physico-Chimique in Paris. They studied the genetics and biochemistry of eye pigment hormones in the fruit fly *Drosophila melanogaster.* Eye pigments are the substances that confer the reddish-brown eye color for the wild-type flies. Over two dozen radiation-induced eye color mutations had been generated in the fruit fly. The vermilion mutation had been genetically mapped to the X chromosome. Female flies have two X chromosomes; males have only one. The geneticist Alfred H. Sturtevant constructed gynandromorphs, flies that had started development as females (XX) but that had lost one X chromosome in some cells, thereby making those cells "male" (X__). Sturtevant observed that in heterozygous gynandromorphs, where one eye color gene is wild-type and the other is vermilion, eye color is always wild-type, indicating that a chemical messenger (a hormone) is diffusing from wild-type eye tissue to vermilion eye tissue, thus making the vermilion eye wild-type.

Vermilion and cinnabar eye color mutants have bright red eyes; they lack brown eye pigment. Ephrussi and Beadle continued Sturtevant's work to try to determine the genetic basis of these two eye-color mutations, which apparently affected the biochemical pathway for the synthesis of brown eye pigment in *Drosophila*. They based their work upon the transplantation of eye buds, also called eye imaginal disks, from larva to larva. An imaginal disk is a clump of undifferentiated cells in the larval stage of the fruit fly's life cycle. There are, for example, two eye imaginal disks, six leg imaginal disks, and two wing imaginal disks (one imaginal disk for every corresponding structure) located in the respective regions of the larval body. During metamorphosis (pupariation), these imaginal disks differentiate into the appropriate adult structures under the influence of the hormone 20-hydroxyecdysone, with the mature adult emerging from the pupal case after several days. Ephrussi and Beadle developed a technique for transplanting these disks between larvae using tiny micropipets.

They transferred eye imaginal disks from larvae of cinnabar flies into wild-type larvae; the cinnabar eye disks became wild-type eyes. In like manner, vermilion eye disks transplanted into wild-type larvae also yielded wild-type eyes. Wild-type eye disks transplanted into cinnabar or vermilion larvae remained wild-type. Obviously, there was some diffusible substance moving from the wild-type tissue to the mutant tissue, thereby converting the mutant eye tissue to wild-type. Transplants between vermilion and cinnabar larvae yielded more interesting results. Vermilion eye disks transplanted into cinnabar larvae became wild-type, whereas cinnabar eye disks transplanted into vermilion larvae remained cinnabar. From these data, Beadle and Ephrussi determined the biochemical pathway for brown eye color pigment production in *Drosophila melanogaster.* Transfusions of larval lymph from larva to larva corroborated their conclusions.

In 1937, Beadle became professor of biology at Stanford University, where he teamed with Edward L. Tatum and several others to attempt to identify the vermilion and cinnabar substances. Ephrussi and Tatum had discovered that the brown pigment precursor was the amino acid tryptophan. The German scientist Adolf Butenandt determined that the vermilion substance is kynurenine and that the cinnabar substance is 3-hydroxykynurenine. Eventually, the brown eye pigment biochemical pathway was roughly established. The vermilion mutation is in a gene encoding the enzyme that converts *n*-formylkynurenine to kynurenine. The cinnabar mutation is in another gene encoding an enzyme which converts kynurenine to 3-hydroxykynurenine.

The problem with working with *Drosophila* eye pigment was that the mutations preceded the understanding of the biochemistry behind the mutation. With the one gene, one enzyme concept in mind, they decided to switch to an organism whose biochemistry was already well understood, which was easy to grow and manipulate in the laboratory, and which was haploid, having one copy of every chromosome and, therefore, one copy of every gene, so that any induced mutations would be visible immediately. The ideal organism that met these requirements turned out to be the pink bread mold *Neurospora crassa*.

Beadle obtained wild-type strains of *Neurospora* from two former colleagues from Cornell, B. O. Dodge and Carl C. Lindegren. They exposed wild-type *Neurospora* asexual spores to X rays, mated them to wild-type *Neurospora*, collected the sexual spore offspring, and grew these spores on media containing all possible nutrient types that might be needed. At this point, they did not know which spores had been mutated and which had not; however, they did have isolated individuals growing on fully supplemented media.

The next step was to attempt to grow each of the irradiated *Neurospora* on minimal media, food containing just enough nutrients to allow growth and reproduction for wild-type *Neurospora*, with nothing extra included. Any *Neurospora* whose biochemical genes were not mutated would grow on minimal media; however, any *Neurospora* whose biochemical reaction genes were mutated would not grow on minimal media. This difference helped Beadle and Tatum to identify biochemical mutants of *Neurospora crassa*. Unaffected *Neurospora* were disregarded. Mutants not growing on minimal media could be retrieved from their original fully supplemented media cultures. The next step was to determine for which nutrient each mutant was deficient. This involved taking each *Neurospora* mutant and attempting to grow it on a series of media each supplemented with a different single additional nutrient, usually an amino acid or vitamin. The one medium supplemented with a single extra nutrient upon which a particular *Neurospora* mutant grew identified the exact nutrient for which that particular *Neurospora* strain was deficient. For example, a *Neurospora* strain deficient for the amino acid arginine (an arginine mutant) will grow on fully supplemented media, will not grow on minimal media, but will grow on minimal media supplemented only with arginine.

Beadle and Tatum isolated many nutritional mutants of *Neurospora crassa*; these mutants are termed auxotrophs because of their nutritional requirements. Their 299th isolated spore turned out to be deficient for vitamin B_6, the 1,085th isolated spore was deficient for vitamin B_1, and so on. Special genetic crosses of these mutants to themselves, to wild-type strains, and to other mutant strains of *Neurospora* demonstrated that these mutations were located at specific locations on the chromosomes of *Neurospora*. In other words, specific genes that encoded specific enzymes for synthesizing specific amino acids and vitamins were mutated. Beadle and Tatum had demonstrated that one gene encodes one enzyme.

In their famous 1941 paper, entitled "Genetic Control of Biochemical Reactions in *Neurospora*," Beadle and Tatum described the generation, growth, and genetics of three mutants—one of which could not synthesize vitamin B_6, one of which could not modify vitamin B_1, and one of which could not synthesize para-aminobenzoic acid. In a subsequent paper, published in 1946 and entitled "Genes and the Chemistry of the Organism," Beadle outlined the various known biochemical pathways of *Neurospora*, mutations that disrupt these biochemical pathways, and the nature of the one gene, one enzyme concept. A biochemical pathway involves a long series of chemical reactions in which one substance is converted to another, then another, and so on. Each chemical reaction is catalyzed, or assisted, by an enzyme. Each enzyme type is encoded by a specific gene. Mutating a gene results in a poorly functional or nonfunctional enzyme, resulting in the disruption of a specific chemical reaction in a particular biochemical pathway. Something is not broken down that should be broken down, or something is not made that should be made. In some cases, the mutation can have fatal effects (as in the human genetic diseases cystic fibrosis, Tay-Sachs disease, and sickle-cell anemia). This is the nature and importance of the one gene, one enzyme concept that Beadle and Tatum extended from Garrod's earlier work.

Before sharing the Nobel Prize with his close colleagues Tatum and Lederberg in 1958, Beadle pursued further research elucidating the genetics and biochemistry of *Neurospora crassa*. This work involved the radiation-induced generation of more mutants and genetic mapping of these mutants to specific regions on the chromosomes of *Neurospora*. After receiving the Nobel Prize, he became chancellor and president of the University of Chicago in 1961, a position he held until retirement in 1968.

Bibliography

Primary

GENETICS: "Development of Eye Colours in *Drosophila*: Pupal Transplants and the Influence of Body Fluid on Vermilion," *Proceedings of the Royal Society of London*, series B, vol. 122, 1937, pp. 98-105 (with C. W. Clancy and Boris Ephrussi); "Development of Eye Colors in *Drosophila*: Extraction of the Diffusible Substances Concerned," *Proceedings of the National Academy of Sciences*, vol. 23, 1937, pp. 143-152 (with Kenneth V. Thimann); "A Comparison of the Diffusible Substances Concerned with Eye Color Development in *Drosophila*, *Ephestia*, and *Habrobracon*," *Proceedings of the National Academy of Sciences*, vol. 24, 1938, pp. 80-85 (with R. L. Anderson and Jane Maxwell); "Development of Eye Colors in *Drosophila*: Some Properties of the Hormones Concerned," *Journal of General Physiology*, vol. 22, 1939, pp. 239-253 (with Edward L. Tatum); "Genetic Control of Biochemical Reactions in *Neurospora*," *Proceedings of the National Academy of Sciences*, vol. 27, 1941, pp. 499-506 (with Edward L. Tatum): "Heterocaryosis in *Neurospora crassa*," *Genetics*, vol. 29, 1944, pp. 291-308 (with Verna L. Coonradt); "Genes and the Chemistry of the Organism," *American Scientist*, vol. 34, 1946, pp. 30-53, 76; "Linkage Studies with Biochemical Mutants of *Neurospora crassa*," *Genetics*, vol. 34, 1949, pp. 493-507 (with Mary B. Houlahan and Hermione Grant Calhoun); "Genes and Chemical Reactions in *Neurospora*" (Nobel lecture), *Les Prix Nobel en 1958*, 1959.

Secondary

Beadle, George Wells. *Genetics and Modern Biology.* Philadelphia: American Philosophical Society, 1963. This short work, reprinted from the American Philosophical Society's "Jayne Lectures for 1962," is Beadle's account of the development of genetics from Mendel up through Watson and Crick. He discusses important advances in genetics, including his own work with Ephrussi and Tatum.

Beadle, Muriel. *Where Has All the Ivy Gone? A Memoir of University Life*. Garden City, N.Y.: Doubleday, 1972. This entertaining work is a description of life with George Beadle during his presidency of the University of Chicago in the turbulent 1960's, as seen by his second wife. The book offers a close view of Beadle and his views on science and education in the United States.

Gardner, Eldon J., and D. Peter Snustad. *Principles of Genetics*. 7th ed. New York: John Wiley & Sons, 1984. This undergraduate-level genetics textbook provides a comprehensive survey of genetics, including all relevant phenomena, important experiments, and major figures in the history of genetics, such as Beadle and Tatum. The book is clearly written, well illustrated, and well referenced.

Goodenough, Ursula. *Genetics*. 2d ed. New York: Holt, Rinehart and Winston, 1978. This undergraduate genetics textbook is an excellent survey of the subject. The book provides exceptionally good coverage of the great classical genetics experiments and of the history of genetics. *Neurospora crassa* and the work of Beadle and Tatum are described in detail.

Judson, Horace Freeland. *The Eighth Day of Creation: The Makers of the Revolution in Biology.* New York: Simon & Schuster, 1979. Judson's work is a wonderful in-depth study of the development of genetics and molecular biology in the twentieth century. The book describes the research and personal lives of many Nobel Prize winners, including Beadle and Tatum. Judson concentrates on the major themes in biology, including the one gene, one enzyme concept, as well as the politics and methods of science.

Perkins, David D., and Edward G. Barry. "The Cytogenetics of Neurospora." *Advances in Genetics* 19 (1977): 133-285. This exhaustive work by two top *Neurospora* geneticists is probably the most complete reference source for the genetics of the pink bread mold *Neurospora crassa*. The work of Beadle and Tatum is discussed, along with the works of other researchers in the field. An extensive reference list is provided.

David Wason Hollar, Jr.

1958

Physiology or Medicine

George Wells Beadle, United States
Edward Lawrie Tatum, United States
Joshua Lederberg, United States

Chemistry

Frederick Sanger, Great Britain

Physics

Pavel Alekseyevich Cherenkov, Soviet Union
Ilya Mikhailovich Frank, Soviet Union
Igor Yevgenyevich Tamm, Soviet Union

Literature

Boris Pasternak, Soviet Union

Peace

Dominique Georges Pire, Belgium

Fabian Bachra

EDWARD LAWRIE TATUM
1958

Born: Boulder, Colorado; December 14, 1909
Died: New York, New York; November 5, 1975
Nationality: American
Areas of concentration: Genetics and biochemistry

Tatum's work helped popularize the idea that each gene on a chromosome contains the information necessary for the production of an enzyme, which in turn catalyzes one step in the synthesis of growth factors such as amino acids, nucleosides, and vitamins. The idea became known as the one gene, one enzyme hypothesis

The Award

Presentation

On December 10, 1958, Professor T. Caspersson, a member of the Staff of Professors of the Royal Caroline Institute, introduced to the Royal Swedish Academy of Sciences Edward Lawrie Tatum, George W. Beadle, and Joshua Lederberg by describing the importance of their research.

Caspersson explained how Tatum and Beadle's work contributed to an understanding of what genes are and how they function. At Stanford University, Tatum and Beadle irradiated a bread mold, *Neurospora crassa*, with X rays to change its hereditary information. They obtained a number of mutant molds that could no longer make amino acids and would not grow unless supplied the amino acids or precursor molecules that could be used by the mutant mold to synthesize the required amino acid. By determining the amino acid or precursor molecule required for growth by the different mutant molds, Tatum and Beadle were able to show that amino acids were synthesized step by step in a chain of chemical reactions. Each gene controlled the activity of a single enzyme involved in one of the steps in the synthesis of an amino acid. They reasoned that irradiation of chromosomes with X rays damaged or destroyed a gene, which in turn resulted in the loss of an enzyme activity. Tatum and Beadle's research demonstrated that there was a relationship between genes, the enzymes they coded for, and the steps in a biochemical pathway. Their research also led to procedures for determining biochemical pathways.

Caspersson further related that Joshua Lederberg used nutritional mutants of bacteria to prove that these tiny, single-cell organisms lacking nuclei and visible chromosomes had genes like those in higher organisms. In addition, Lederberg and Tatum showed that bacteria could be crossed to produce offspring with new genetic characteristics. Tatum, Beadle, and Lederberg were then awarded the 1958 Nobel Prize in Physiology or Medicine by the Royal Caroline Institute.

Nobel lecture

On December 11, 1958, Tatum delivered his Nobel lecture, entitled "A Case

History in Biological Research." Tatum explained how each new study undertaken had led to an advancement in his basic understanding of the relationship between genetics and biochemistry. His graduate study at the University of Wisconsin resulted in vitamin B_1 (thiamine) being identified as a growth factor in propionic acid bacteria. His postdoctoral research at the University of Utrecht in Holland introduced him to the nutritional requirements of the mold *Neurospora* and its need for a growth factor, biotin. Tatum's study of the fruit fly *Drosophilia* at Stanford University in California introduced him to another growth factor, tryptophan, which was necessary for the production of eye color. His genetic studies with the fly impressed upon him the need to use an experimental organism in which mutations could be easily isolated. The choice and use of *Neurospora* depended upon its characterization by many other scientists and the identification and synthesis of a number of growth factors, including biotin needed for the growth of *Neurospora*. From his studies in Europe, Tatum had learned how to grow, mate, and manipulate the mold's spores. He knew that *Neurospora* had a single set of chromosomes. This latter characteristic made it a useful organism for obtaining mutations that affected each step in a biosynthetic pathway. Some of the first mutants studied help elucidate the biochemical steps in the synthesis of tryptophan.

Tatum and Beadle also obtained mutant bacteria (*Escherichia coli* K-12) that were unable to catabolize tryptophan to indole. A large collection of bacteria requiring various growth factors was developed. In 1945, Tatum's move to Yale University in New Haven, Connecticut, led to a collaboration with a medical student, Joshua Lederberg, who used some of the bacterial mutants isolated at Stanford to demonstrate that bacteria were capable of conjugating. It was luck that the bacterial mutants had been isolated in a strain of *Escherichia coli* that was able to transmit chromosomes to recipient bacteria, since most strains of bacteria do not have this ability.

Tatum predicted how the one gene, one enzyme concept would be basic to understanding such diverse areas as microbial resistance to antibiotics and drugs, the development of cancer, and the improvement of plants and animals through genetic engineering. He emphasized that studies on mutant *Neurospora* and *Escherichia* were of great importance in detecting and understanding not only conjugation but also how chromosomes and genes recombined with each other. These mutants were also used to determine the steps involved in the biosynthesis and biodegradation of cellular constituents.

Tatum's 1958 Nobel lecture was prophetic. He predicted that the DNA code would be determined and that this would "permit the improvement of all living organisms by processes which we might call biological engineering." In fact, scientists worked out the genetic code in the 1960's, and by the 1980's were producing all sorts of useful genes, proteins, and organisms by genetic engineering.

Critical reception

The importance of Tatum and Beadle's work was summarized by the science writer for the journal *Science* in the November 14, 1958, issue when he wrote, "They proposed to prove the tenet that all biochemical and enzymatic reactions are controlled by genes." Biochemical genetics had been extremely difficult to study in higher organisms mainly because it is hard to obtain biochemically deficient mutants; however, the use of fungi and bacteria made it relatively easy to obtain all sorts of biochemically deficient mutants. One of the first mutants they found was a fungus that failed to produce an enzyme necessary for synthesizing vitamin B_6. This fungus would not grow unless it was supplied vitamin B_6. They proceeded to prove that the mutations were inherited.

The science writer for *Time* magazine of November 10, 1958, explained how important the isolation of mutants was: "This provided a means of studying genetic changes by corresponding changes in the organism's ability or failure to produce specific chemicals, thus giving genetics a new exactness and turning it into a predominantly chemical science." There were now two types of genetics: classical and molecular. The bacterial mutants that Tatum's laboratory had isolated were also important because they allowed his graduate student, Joshua Lederberg, to discover sex in bacteria. The writer for *Time* also indicated what he felt might be an important practical consequence of the Nobel recipients' work when he wrote, "The most baffling problem of medicine, cancer, is caused by a genetic change in human cells that make them multiply irresponsibly. Increased knowledge of genetics may eventually cure or prevent cancer."

It was, however, the science writer for the journal *Nature* of November 15, 1958, who really understood the significance of Tatum and Beadle's work. Genetic crosses between the growth factor requiring mutants and normal fungi always showed that the mutant differs from the normal strain by a single altered gene. "Thus, single genes appeared to control biochemical reactions and, by inference, the formation of single enzymes. This first successful attempt to relate genetic and biochemical function experimentally gave birth to the stimulating 'one-gene-one-enzyme' hypothesis and initiated the expanding field of biochemical genetics." Also of importance was their discovery that some of the mutants, which appeared to have the same growth factor deficiency, were not identical, but had defects at different steps in the biochemical pathway that led to the synthesis of the growth factor. These mutants made it possible to determine the biochemical pathways involved in the synthesis of a number of growth factors. Without these mutants, knowledge of intermediary metabolism would be rudimentary.

Lederberg's use of the bacterial mutants isolated by Tatum's research allowed Lederberg to demonstrate sexuality in bacteria and the fact that some of the genes were linked, "thus showing, for the first time, that bacteria are fundamentally similar to other types of cells in their genetic and biochemical constitution."

Biography

Edward Lawrie Tatum was born in Boulder, Colorado, on December 14, 1909. He received a B.A. in chemistry in 1931, an M.S. in microbiology in 1932, and a Ph.D.

in biochemistry in 1934. After a year of postdoctoral work in biochemistry, he obtained a fellowship to study bacteriological chemistry at the University of Utrecht, in Holland. In 1937, Tatum accepted a position as a research associate at Stanford University, where under the direction of Beadle, he attempted to study the fruit fly *Drosophila* and its nutritional needs. Realizing the practical difficulty of doing this, Tatum and Beadle turned to a simpler organism, the mold *Neurospora*. Tatum worked at Stanford University from 1937 to 1945. His collaboration with Beadle led to a classic paper published in 1941 and to the Nobel Prize in 1958.

Tatum moved to Yale University in 1945, where he continued his work in genetics and biochemistry. In the summer of 1946, a young medical student, Joshua Lederberg, who was in his second year at Columbia College of Physicians and Surgeons, began a research fellowship under Tatum's direction. Lederberg discovered that the common intestinal bacterium *Escherichia coli* could conjugate, and shared in the Nobel Prize.

In 1948, Tatum returned to Stanford University, where he continued to work on the genetics and biochemistry of *Neurospora*. Tatum moved to New York in 1957 to work at Rockefeller Institute (now known as Rockefeller University), where he specialized in the genetics and biochemistry controlling the morphological development of *Neurospora*. His genetic and biochemical studies also included research on cytoplasmic inheritance in *Neurospora*. In 1965, Tatum's research group demonstrated that one type of cytoplasmic inheritance in *Neurospora* was apparently attributable to genes associated with the mitochondria. They extracted mitochondria from an abnormal mutant mold that grew slowly, demonstrated maternal inheritance, and had abnormal numbers of cytochromes. They then injected whole mutated mitochondria into normal *Neurospora*. After growing the mold for a few days (during which it moved normally), the slow-growing characteristic appeared. This change in activity rate could only have resulted from a gene-mediated change in the mitochondrial enzymes responsible for the movement. The observation provided evidence for the one gene, one enzyme concept, and for the hypothesis that mutations alter enzyme characteristics.

According to fellow Nobel Prize winner Joshua Lederberg, "The last years of [Tatum's] life were marred by increasingly poor health, substantially self-inflicted by a notorious smoking habit. His mental outlook was further scarred by the agonizing death of his second wife." Edward Tatum died in New York on November 5, 1975. In a eulogy at Rockefeller University, at which he remained on the faculty until his death, speakers stressed how Tatum had generously helped and inspired researchers, noting that he had been elected a member of the National Academy of Sciences in 1957 and that he was a founding member of the editorial committee for the *Annual Review of Genetics*, on which he served from 1961 to 1967.

Scientific Career

Edward Tatum's father, an M.D. and a Ph.D., was professor of pharmacology at the University of Wisconsin. This and the fact that a number of other family members were also college professors influenced Edward to enter the University of Wisconsin and major in chemistry. After graduating from the University of Wisconsin with a bachelor's degree in chemistry, Tatum continued his education there, becoming a graduate student in microbiology and biochemistry. The identity of growth factors, sometimes called nutritional requirements, was one of the many unsolved microbiological problems that Tatum began to study. Tatum and a visiting researcher were able to identify thiamine (vitamin B_1) as one of the growth factors required for the growth of propionic acid bacteria. In the 1930's, most scientists did not realize that the various nutritional requirements of organisms had a genetic basis. Today, thanks to Tatum and Beadle's research, it is known that mutated genes result in missing or defective enzymes that block steps in the synthesis of amino acids and vitamins. Unless these necessary growth factors are supplied, the mutant organism will not be able to maintain itself and will die. Continuing his postdoctoral study of growth factors, Tatum traveled to Europe in 1935 to study at the University of Utrecht with the discoverer of another growth factor called biotin.

In 1937, Tatum joined Beadle at Stanford University in California to study the genetics and biochemistry of the fruit fly *Drosophila*. This was an important move for Tatum because his studies made him think about the relationship between genes, enzymes, and metabolic conversions. Tatum and Beadle wanted to demonstate that X-ray induced mutations altered genes and, in turn, inactive enzymes. In addition, they wanted to show that a missing or defective enzyme blocks one of the steps in a metabolic pathway. The problem was, how to do this.

To investigate the relationship between genes, enzymes, and metabolic pathways, many different types of mutants needed to be isolated. Detection of mutants is very difficult and time-consuming in higher organisms that have paired genes on homologous chromosomes. A mutation in one of the paired genes would generally be compensated by the normal gene and no change would be detected. Tatum and Beadle realized that they needed to use an organism other than *Drosophila*. They needed an organism that had only a single copy of each gene to make the discovery of mutants feasible. They chose to study the pink bread mold *Neurospora crassa* because it was one of the best characterized and most easily grown microorganisms, and it had only one set of chromosomes. The normal and mutant fungi could be propagated indefinitely without genetic changes or they could be mated to one another to produce new gene combinations. This made it possible to show that the changes were actually genetic. *Neurospora* grew rapidly on an agar medium supplemented with a sugar, a few salts, and the B vitamin biotin. Unlike *Drosophila*, *Neurospora* could make all the molecules it needed for growth from the nutrients in a defined minimal medium. The sexual cycle, from sexual spores of one generation to sexual spores of the next, requires only ten days.

Neurospora produces two types of spores: the microscopic, single-celled conidia that arise during asexual propagation of the fungus, and the larger, single-celled ascosopores that arise from matings between different sexes of the fungus. When conidia are placed on a nutrient that supports growth, they begin to elongate and divide. Because the dividing cells remain attached to one another and branching occurs, a growth that resembles a thick bush develops. The fungal bush is called a mycelium, while a branch is referred to as a hypha. The ends of some hyphae develop into the string of cells called conidia. No mating or genetic recombination precedes the formation of conidia; this is why they are often referred to as asexual spores. If cells from two different sexes fuse, a fruiting body forms that bears asci containing ascospores. Ascospores are sometimes called sexual spores because their formation is dependent upon sex: a mating, genetic recombination, and meiosis. Ascospores are able to form mycelia that are genetically different from either parent because recombination preceded their formation.

To test the hypothesis that genes control enzymes, which in turn control metabolism, Tatum and Beadle treated conidia with X rays or ultraviolet light to induce mutations. These mutations would sometimes damage a gene and this in turn would inactivate the enzyme controlled by the gene. Theoretically, a mutant conidium could be detected if it did not grow on the simple medium that promoted growth of the wild type; however, this would not show that the mutations had anything to do with genes. Consequently, Tatum and Beadle mixed the irradiated conidia with the wild mycelium of the opposite mating type. A mating would produce ascospores that could be separated using a dissecting microscope and a dissecting knife. The descendants of the mutated genes would be discovered in those ascospores that did not grow on a defined minimal medium. In addition, if they found a one-to-one ratio of mutant ascospores to normal ascospores and the appropriate order of mutant and normal ascospores in the fungal asci, this would conclusively demonstrate that the defect was the result of a single abnormal gene or very closely linked genes if more than one was involved in controlling the activity of an enzyme. Heavy ultraviolet irradiation of conidia would yield about two mutant ascospores out of every hundred tested.

The individual wild and mutant ascospores were transferred to a rich medium so that the mutants would grow. After the mutants grew, sample conidia and hyphae could be transferred to defined minimal media to determine which organisms would not grow. The particular defect was detected by testing each mutant on a defined minimal medium supplemented with a particular necessary substance that might not be naturally manufactured by the mutated spores. The mutant fungus might be placed on different defined minimal media supplemented with one of the following growth factors: thiamine, riboflavin, pyridoxine, pantothenic acid, niacin, para-aminobenzoic acid, inositol, choline, or folic acid. If the spores grew only on the agar supplemented with pantothenic acid, for example, this indicated that the mutation affected the biosynthesis of pantothenic acid.

Tatum and Beadle were able to prove that the mutations were the result of the effect of the X rays upon the genes rather than upon other conceivable parts of the spores or upon the processes of cell metabolism directly. (At first, some scientists speculated that the X rays were, for example, affecting protein synthesis or interfering with the action of the enzymes, which many thought controlled their own replication.) Tatum and Beadle showed that the inability to make a growth factor acted like a unit of inheritance after a mating. The inability to make a growth factor was thus linked only to a gene.

Some of the fungal mutants were defective not only in their ability to synthesize the amino acid tryptophan, but also in their ability to synthesize niacin (vitamin B_1). How did Tatum and Beadle demonstrate that only one gene was mutated and, by inference, only one enzyme? Tatum and Beadle found that both the tryptophan and niacin requirements could be satisfied in some of their mutants by the addition of anthranilic acid or indole. They postulated that these were precursors of tryptophan, and that tryptophan was the precursor of niacin. In other mutants defective in tryptophan and niacin synthesis, the growth factor requirements could only be synthesized by indole or tryptophan. Some mutants that could synthesize tryptophan but not niacin accumulated kynuremine. Other niacin-requiring mutants accumulated 3-hydroxy-anthranilic acid. The foregoing information and other data indicated the biosynthetic pathway:

anthranilic acid → ? → indole → tryptophan → kynurenine →
? → 3-hydroxy-anthranilic acid → ? → niacin.

This pathway explained how a single mutation affecting a single enzyme could make an organism unable to synthesize two different growth factors.

From 1944 to 1946, Tatum isolated mutant bacteria that had defects similar to those found in *Neurospora*. The growth-factor-requiring bacterial mutants were used by Tatum and Lederberg to demonstrate conjugation and recombination in bacteria. In their 1946 paper, "Gene Recombination in *Escherichia coli*," Tatum and Lederberg describe an experiment in which a triple mutant requiring threonine, leucine, and thiamine for growth was crossed with another triple mutant needing phenylalanine, cysteine, and biotin for growth. They obtained wild strains with no growth factor requirements. These wild strains were never found in pure cultures of the triple mutants, indicating that the wild strains that appeared in the mixed cultures were not the result of reversions of the three mutations.

In the 1940's and 1950's, Tatum demonstrated that the chemical composition of the growth medium could significantly influence the morphology of *Neurospora*. When he limited the building blocks necessary for cell membrane synthesis, the normal bushlike growth of the fungus was inhibited and a small colonial morphology resulted. Eventually, Tatum and other researchers found that lysosomes are damaged by limiting necessary membrane building blocks. Enzymes escaping from the damaged lysosomes cause the breakdown of the wall, which inhibits growth and branching. Tatum's research indicated that *Neurospora*'s morphology is determined directly by the structure and chemical composition of its cell wall, not the cell membrane. In the early 1960's, it became clear that morphological changes are always accompanied by changes in chemical composition of the cell wall. From the mid-1960's to the mid-1970's, the chemical structure of the wall was analyzed. It was discovered, using the electron microscope, that the cell wall consists of two distinct layers. The outer layer is composed of a polysaccharide-protein complex and a beta-1,3-glucan (another type of polysaccharide), while the inner layer was composed of chitin. Protein is found in both layers and accounts for 10-14 percent of the wall's weight. Chemically or genetically altering the peptides found in the wall significantly affects fungal morphology, while altering the chitin component has little effect on fungal morphology. Tatum's research indicated that the wall proteins are covalently linked to the polysaccharides. In the 1960's and 1970's, hundreds of mutants that produced unusual patterns of growth were found and classified into six groups according to their type of growth. Some fungi formed small, tight colonies like bacteria, while others formed spreading colonies. Still other mutants spread extensively, forming distinctive patterns. All the morphological mutants analyzed showed decreased amounts of cell-wall protein. Tatum was unable to affect morphology by interfering with chitin synthesis and concluded that chitin has no role in determining morphology; however, some other researchers have found that chitin levels also play a role in determining the morphology of *Neurospora*.

Tatum, Beadle, and Lederberg's studies showed the scientific world that microorganisms such as fungi, bacteria, and viruses have a genetic system much like that of higher organisms and that these simpler organisms could be used to answer genetic questions on a molecular level. Using microorganisms, scientists in the 1950's and 1960's worked out the multitude of biosynthetic and biodegradative pathways that biochemists called intermediary metabolism—the bread and butter of most biochemistry courses. In the 1960's, bacteria were used to determine how the hereditary information of deoxyribonucleic acid (DNA) replicated, how DNA was transcribed into messenger ribonucleic acid (mRNA), and how the mRNA was then translated into protein. Bacterial mutants were used to work out each step of protein synthesis and to demonstrate how many antibiotics and drugs interfered with protein synthesis. Most significantly, the genetic code was uncovered. In the 1970's and 1980's, genetic engineering blossomed with the discovery of numerous bacterial restriction endonucleases for specifically cutting DNA and the development of techniques for cloning specific pieces of DNA. The understanding of viral genetics and how viruses replicate has continued to expand since Lederberg's discoveries. Tatum, Beadle, and Lederberg must certainly be considered the fathers of the genetic revolution that occurred during the last half of the twentieth century.

Bibliography

Primary

GENETICS: "Vitamin B Requirements of *Drosophila melanogaster*," *Proceedings of the National Academy of Sciences*, vol. 27, 1941, pp. 193-197; "Genetic Control of Biochemical Reactions in *Neurospora*," *Proceedings of the National Academy of Sciences*, vol. 27, 1941, pp. 499-506 (with G. W. Beadle); "Gene Recombination in *Escherichia coli*," *Nature*, vol. 158, 1946, p. 558 (with J. Lederberg); "Biochemical Mutant Strains of *Neurospora* Produced by Physical and Chemical

Treatment," *American Journal of Botany*, vol. 37, 1950, pp. 38-46 (with Barratt, Fries, and Bonner); "Synthesis of Aromatic Compounds by *Neurospora*," *Proceedings of the National Academy of Sciences*, vol. 40, 1954, pp. 271-276 (with Gross, Ehrensvard, and Garnjobst); "Heterocaryon Incompatibility in *Neurospora crassa*—Micro-Injection Studies," *American Journal of Botany*, vol. 48, 1961, pp. 299-305 (with Wilson and Garnjobst); "Thiamine Metabolism in *Neurospora crassa*," *American Journal of Botany*, vol. 48, 1961, pp. 702-711 (with Eberhart); "The Relationship of M-Inositol to Morphology in *Neurospora crassa*," *American Journal of Botany*, vol. 48, 1961, pp. 760-771 (with Shatkin); "A Relationship Between Cell Wall Structure and Colonial Growth in *Neurospora crassa*," *American Journal of Botany*, vol. 50, 1963, pp. 669-677 (with de Terra); "Relationship of the Major Constituents of the *Neurospora crassa* Cell Wall to Wild-Type and Colonial Morphology," *Journal of Bacteriology*, vol. 90, 1965, pp. 1073–1081 (with Mahadevan); "A Survey of New Morphological Mutants in *Neurospora crassa,*" *Genetics*, vol. 57, 1967, pp. 579-604 (with Garnjobst); "Effect of L-Sorbose on Polysaccharide Synthetase of *Neurospora crassa*," *Proceedings of the National Academy of Sciences*, vol. 69, 1972, pp. 313-317 (with Mishra); "Differential Inhibition of Branching Enzyme in a Morphological Mutant and in Wild Type *Neurospora*: Influence of Carbon Source in the Growth Medium," *Biochimica et Biophysica Acta*, vol. 421, 1976, pp. 106-114 (with Abramsky).

Secondary

Beadle, George Wells. "The Genes of Men and Molds." In *Facets of Genetics: Readings from Scientific American*, edited by Adrian Morris Srb. San Francisco: W. H. Freeman, 1970. This paper, written in 1947, explains how Tatum and Beadle manipulated *Neurospora* to obtain mutants and how they used these mutants to deduce the steps in biochemical pathways. The article is ten pages long and contains numerous figures that help the reader understand *Neurospora*'s genetics and the experiments that led to Tatum and Beadle sharing the 1958 Nobel Prize.

Judson, Horace F. *The Eighth Day of Creation*. New York: Simon & Schuster, 1979. This book is a comprehensive history of molecular biology with detailed information on the isolation of fungal and bacterial mutants and their importance in learning what genes are and what they do. There are numerous interviews with scientists familiar with these Nobel laureates that help to explain how they developed the idea that genes coded for proteins.

Lederberg, Joshua. "Edward Lawrie Tatum." *Annual Review of Genetics* 13 (1979): 1-5. This paper summarized Tatum's contribution to the field of biochemical genetics, now known as molecular biology; it was written by Tatum's most famous graduate student, who shared the 1958 Nobel Prize. There is some information about Tatum's administrative duties and his personal life.

____________. "Forty Years of Genetic Recombination in Bacteria: A Fortieth Anniversary Reminiscence." *Nature* 327 (1986): 627-628. Lederberg describes the history and circumstances that led to the discovery that bacteria have genes and can conjugate. Lederberg makes it clear that luck was important in his being able to discover conjugation in bacteria. Tatum had by chance chosen a bacterium that was able to conjugate, and he isolated mutants of this bacterium.

____________. "Genetic Recombination in Bacteria: A Discovery Account." *Annual Review of Genetics* 21 (1987): 23-46. This paper is a brief autobiography of Lederberg's early studies and the research that led to the Nobel Prize in 1958. Lederberg's account of what was known in molecular biology in the 1940's and 1950's introduces the discussion of his work in Tatum's laboratory at Yale University. A brief insight into Tatum's character is provided when Lederberg describes how Tatum helped him obtain his Ph.D. and a position at the University of Wisconsin.

Riedman, Sarah R., and Elton T. Gustafson. *Portraits of Nobel Laureates in Medicine and Physiology.* New York: Abelard-Schuman, 1963. This book contains a history of Alfred Nobel and most of the Nobel Prize recipients in medicine or physiology from 1901 to 1963. This is a short history of Tatum, Beadle, and Lederberg and a discussion of their involvement in the isolation of fungal and bacterial mutants. The importance of the mutants in determining what genes are and what they do is discussed.

Zuckerman, Harriet, and Joshua Lederberg. "Postmature Scientific Discovery?" *Nature* 327 (1980): 629-631. Zuckerman considers why recombination in bacteria was not discovered in bacteria before 1946. Before this time, scientists had many erroneous ideas about bacteria, most important of all that they lacked genes. The biochemical analysis of fungi and bacteria by Tatum and Beadle made it clear that bacteria had genes. This led to Tatum and Lederberg's investigation into whether they were also capable of conjugation and recombination.

Jaime S. Colomé

1958

Physiology or Medicine

George Wells Beadle, United States
Edward Lawrie Tatum, United States
Joshua Lederberg, United States

Chemistry

Frederick Sanger, Great Britain

Physics

Pavel Alekseyevich Cherenkov, Soviet Union
Ilya Mikhailovich Frank, Soviet Union
Igor Yevgenyevich Tamm, Soviet Union

Literature

Boris Pasternak, Soviet Union

Peace

Dominique Georges Pire, Belgium

JOSHUA LEDERBERG
1958

Born: Montclair, New Jersey; May 23, 1925

Nationality: American
Areas of concentration: Genetics, biochemistry, and molecular biology

Lederberg made essential contributions to the development of bacterial genetics and to proving the similarity of the genetic mechanisms in bacteria and higher organisms via discoveries about organization of bacterial genetic material and its genetic recombination

The Award

Presentation

Professor T. Caspersson, a member of the faculty of the Royal Caroline Institute and the representative of the Swedish Academy of Sciences, delivered the Nobel presentation address on December 10, 1958. He first pointed out that one of the most striking features in the development of science in the 1940's and the 1950's had been a very rapid advance in biology and that often "the step from basic biological research to important advances in medical treatment and diagnosis is short."

Caspersson also indicated that progress has been "especially rapid in experimental genetics and that its methods and point of view have been indispensable in many fields of our modern medicine." He pointed out that the work of the 1958 Nobel laureates is "on this plane, being concerned with the basis of heredity and the manner in which genes function."

Lederberg and coworkers, Caspersson said, were "primarily responsible for the development of bacterial genetics into an extensive research field" and for the proof that genetic mechanisms of bacteria and higher organisms correspond. He also noted that one of Lederberg's particularly important contributions was the discovery that sexual fertilization is not the only process leading to the recombination of genetic material, because "bits of genetic material introduced into a bacterium" can become parts of its genome and change its constitution via transduction.

Caspersson also noted that the processes of transduction and related phenomena have greatly improved the means of "penetrating experimentally into the processes of cell growth and cell function." He predicted that both cancer and growth problems "will be much better understood and very strongly influenced by the discoveries of the 1958 Nobel Prize winners." The talk ended with congratulations to the laureates and the statement that Lederberg, "in collaboration with his cowinners . . . made possible the advance of research" of the structure of the genetic material.

Nobel lecture

On May 29, 1959, Lederberg began his Nobel lecture, entitled "A View of Genetics," by stating that in lieu of simply reviewing genetic recombination and the organization of bacterial genetic material, he would examine the context of contemporary science and scrutinize future prospects of experimental genetics. Genetics, he noted, was reaching its height "in coalescence" with biochemistry and the principle that the genetic characteristics eventually will be denoted as an exact sequence of amino acids derived from a corresponding DNA sequence.

Lederberg also noted that the utility of bacteria and of their genetics to biology is attributable to the simplicity and to the synthetic power of these tiny organisms. The idea that genetic information is encoded in a linear sequence of the subunits of deoxyribonucleic acid (DNA), the nucleotides, he pointed out, is strongly supported by the work of the scientific community over the past decade.

Next, Lederberg outlined what the scientific community had discovered about DNA as a substance and how the DNA-directed synthesis of proteins might occur. First, he stated, as a linear polymer of thousands of units, DNA can carry a very large amount of genetic information. Lederberg also noted that a probable model for its synthesis was derived as a corollary to the work of James Watson and Francis Crick, who identified DNA's double helix structure.

Then, he predicted that the genetic code for amino acid incorporation would involve "code words" consisting of three or four nucleotides. The mode of information transfer from DNA to proteins was envisioned as occurring in two main steps: information transfer from DNA to ribonucleic acid (RNA) by a mechanism analogous to synthesis of DNA, and protein synthesis by aminoacylation of RNA, assembly of aminoacylated RNA molecules on a larger RNA that directs the synthesis of proteins, and the condensation of amino acids to the desired protein.

Lederberg also noted that the understanding of the relationship between DNA and bacterial mutation arose from the use of natural analogues of the "bases" that make up the code words in DNA, pointing out the importance of genetic recombination to this understanding, and described the value of the work of François Jacob and coworkers with viruses. He continued by philosophizing about the importance and the suitability of the mutualism of DNA, RNA, and proteins to the creation of life.

Lederberg's concluding statement pointed out that the experimental control of cellular genotypes is one of the measures of the scope of genetic science and predicted that methods of stepwise analysis and assembly of nucleotides would be perfected in the near future. He also predicted that both biological and chemical approaches would be used here.

Critical reception

The world greeted the announcement that Lederberg had been awarded the 1958 Nobel Prize with enthusiasm because of the great importance of the research he conducted. For example, *The New York Times* stated on October 31, 1958, that "Lederberg was recognized for use of bacteria through which more extensive studies of genetic mechanisms might be conducted. He was cited specifically for discoveries concerning genetic recombination and organization of the genetic material of bacteria. . . . He is also credited with having discovered a method of artificially giving organisms such as bacteria a new look by introducing genes into them, thereby providing valuable means of investigating heredity."

Other media sources that commented on Lederberg's work were also laudatory. For example, *Time* magazine (November 10, 1958) indicated that Lederberg had shown that after a bacterium is infected by a virus, the virus "breaks up into hundreds of new virus particles. If these particles in turn infect another bacterium and it survives, they sometimes turn it into a new strain. Apparently, the viruses, acting somewhat like submicroscopic spermatozoa, take hereditary material from the first bacterium and transfer it to the second." The article also suggested that increased knowledge of genetics may eventually cure or prevent cancer.

The feelings of the scientific community about Lederberg's work are well summarized by highlights of the allocution speech by T. Caspersson, representative of the Nobel Committee. For example, Caspersson noted that "one of Lederberg's particularly important contributions was the discovery that sexual fertilization was not the only process leading to the recombination of genetic material" but that "bits of genetic material introduced into a bacterium" can become part of its genome and "change its constitution" via transduction. Caspersson also stated that "transduction and related phenomena" have greatly improved means of "penetrating experimentally into the processes of cell growth and cell function." He then predicted that the understanding of cancer and growth problems "will be much better understood and strongly influenced" by the discoveries of Lederberg and his cowinners. More than thirty years later, the 1990 *Encyclopædia Britannica* made very similar comments about Lederberg's efforts.

Biography

Joshua Lederberg, the son of Rabbi Zwi Lederberg and Esther (Goldenbaum) Lederberg, was born in Montclair, New Jersey. He grew up in the Washington Heights area of New York City. Young Lederberg received his primary and secondary education at New York's Public School Number 46, Junior High School Number 164, and Stuyvesant High School, from which he was graduated in 1941. Next, he studied at Columbia University from 1941 to 1944, obtaining a B.A. with honors in zoology at the age of nineteen. Then he began medical school at the Columbia University College of Physicians and Surgeons. During medical school, he undertook part-time research in zoology with Francis Ryan. After two years of medical school, Lederberg spent the summer of 1946 as a research assistant at Yale University's department of botany and microbiology.

Lederberg never resumed his medical training. He instead became a graduate student of Yale's Edward Tatum, a biochemist and microbiologist who had done pioneering work in biochemical genetics. In 1946, he married Esther (Zimmer) Lederberg. Lederberg's work was considered to be so good that he left Yale in 1947 to become an assistant professor of genetics at the University of Wisconsin even before obtaining his Ph.D., which he received in 1948 from Yale. By 1954, Lederberg was a full professor at the University of Wisconsin. In 1957, he organized the university's

Department of Medical Genetics and became its first chairman. In 1954, he was also elected to membership in the National Academy of Science. In 1958, Lederberg shared the Nobel Prize in Physiology or Medicine with Beadle and Tatum. In 1959, Lederberg moved to Stanford University, organized a department of genetics, and became its executive head. In 1962, he was appointed director of Stanford's Kennedy laboratories for Molecular Medicine. Lederberg remained at Stanford until 1978, when he became president of New York's Rockefeller University.

During his career, Lederberg has served as a consultant to the National Aeronautics and Space Administration because of his scientific eminence and his interest in the medical consequences of the exploration of space. He has also been a scientific adviser to the World Health Organization on matters concerning biological weapons and biological warfare.

Scientific Career

Joshua Lederberg's scientific career has always been aimed at "understanding human origin and purpose and seeking to forestall hunger, disease, and death." He began his efforts as a Columbia University undergraduate, working with Francis Ryan, in the zoology department. This endeavor continued when Lederberg entered medical school at Columbia University. At the end of Lederberg's second year as a medical student, Professor Edward Tatum invited him to undertake a three-month summer study course in biochemical genetics at Yale University. Lederberg accepted and did so well that he was offered a graduate research fellowship at Yale. He accepted the fellowship, began graduate study, and his great ability led to a meteoric rise to fame.

In order to consider Lederberg's scientific contributions intelligently, it is valuable to trace the development of the science of genetics up to the start of his collaboration with Tatum. Scientific genetics formally began in 1865 with Dominican monk Gregor Mendel, who then published his studies of the laws of inheritance in pea plants. Mendel proposed that "characters" (now called genes) govern the heritability of physical traits. (Heritability is the ability of organisms to transmit the qualities of their physical substance to their offspring.)

By the early 1900's, Mendel's laws (ignored during his lifetime) became the basis for genetic research. Other scientists applied Mendel's methods to examination of primroses, fruit flies, rodents, and many other creatures. All these efforts agreed on the two principles called Mendel's laws. The first law, called the law of segregation, is that each hereditary characteristic (each gene) is controlled by two "factors" (called, technically, alleles) that segregate (separate) into distinct germ cells; furthermore, these distinct units remain distinct and extant even when they seem to be lost in the offspring. The second law, called the law of independent assortment, states that pairs of factors separate independently in germ cells, which recombine randomly when hybrids interbreed. The randomness and independence of the separation allows for the appearance of the gene-encoded characteristics according to predictable proportions. Soon it was shown that genes were pieces of the chromosomes of living cells. By 1940, it was known that genes were composed of DNA. At that time, George Beadle and Edward Tatum (with Lederberg, cowinners of the 1958 Nobel Prize in Physiology or Medicine) carried out pioneering research that proved that DNA directs the cellular production of enzymes, the protein catalysts that mediate all chemical reactions that occur in living cells. DNA therefore controls the biochemical processes of living cells; collectively, these are referred to as metabolism.

Bacteria, however, were believed to be limited to asexual reproduction via cell division to two daughter cells. It was unclear how new genetic information or evolution could occur in those tiny organisms. Lederberg's early studies in Tatum's laboratory dealt mostly with a search for sexual reproduction in bacteria. He soon found that some strains of the colon bacteria *Escherichia coli* were capable of sexual reproduction. Observed sexual reproduction in these bacteria was achieved by the process named conjugation. In conjugation, the two bacteria involved become joined together by a conjugation tube; the "male" bacterium injects its chromosomal information into the "female" bacterium. Then, the daughter cell produced by this conjugation divides asexually.

These observations led Lederberg and Tatum to carry out experiments in bacterial genetic recombination by examining the consequences of crossing (mating) two different bacterial strains. The resultant bacterial offspring they isolated were found to be a third strain, possessing characteristics of both parent strains used in the cross. Lederberg and Tatum named the process sexual genetic recombination and laid down the foundation for the modern science of bacterial genetics.

In the course of his research efforts, Lederberg developed a number of important techniques for the isolation and study of recombinant bacteria. The best known of these is called replica plating. To conduct replica plating, researchers first grow recombinant bacteria in culture dishes (plates). After growth is complete, they are transferred onto a sterile velveteen pad. The pad is then used to inoculate a large number of other plates that contain different types of growth media. The bacterial inoculum on each of the plates becomes an exact replica of the original plate. Consequently, comparison of bacterial growth on each different kind of medium can be done exactly. This allows the exact determination of the genetic nature of the recombinants and of the frequency with which recombination occurs. Replica plating allows sophisticated examination of the nature of chromosomal sequence and of the location of specific genes.

Lederberg continued his studies at the University of Wisconsin, collaborating with his wife and other research associates. Then, he and graduate student Norton Zinder showed that new genetic information could enter a bacterium by another process, called transduction. Unlike the sexual recombination process, which can transfer an entire chromosome into a female bacterium, transduction transfers only small fragments of the hereditary material. Soon, Zinder and Lederberg demonstrated that transduction was mediated by bacterial viruses. Among the gene transfers that Lederberg carried out were the immunity to antibiotics and the resistance to these therapeutic drugs. These studies demonstrated that disease production and the resistance to disease by microorganisms were mediated by genetic processes. The identification of conjugation and transduction as means of introducing desired new genes into bacteria enlarged the methodology for investigation of the chemistry of heredity.

Lederberg's other scientific interests include the basis for antibody production, computer applications to both biology and chemistry, and exobiology, the search for extraterrestrial life. The last area is particularly interesting. Lederberg's effort here began during the early years of the United States' space program, when he speculated on the biological and medical consequences of space exploration. This interest led to his participation, as a consultant, in the Viking program's exploration of Mars.

Some of Lederberg's ideas on exobiology are expressed in an article entitled "Moondust," which appeared in 1958 in *Science*. This article points out that many important clues about the origin of life may be derived from study of the layer of dust of great antiquity that has been trapped by the Moon's gravitational field. Lederberg and Cowie warned that these clues might be destroyed by nonsterile rockets reaching the earth's satellite. They suggest that this might occur because such rockets could carry terrestrial organisms, which would then grow and cause misconceptions about extraterrestrial microbiology and answers to the question of whether or not all life in the universe has a similar genetic basis. In later years, Lederberg's involvement in exobiology led to important statements about the utilization of the biological, chemical, and engineering technology that could help science to decipher the mysteries of the cosmos.

Joshua Lederberg has been a preeminent shaper of the modern science of genetics, and he is primarily responsible for proof that the genetic mechanisms of bacteria and those of the higher organisms correspond. His endeavors are viewed as important to the future of research to combat cancer, to understand immunology, and to advance medicine. Lederberg, therefore, has become a symbol of the achievement that can be possible for persons of great scientific ability who work at the frontiers of scientific knowledge. His efforts as a scientific adviser to the World Health Organization and to the National Space Agency point out, by example, that scientists can become deeply involved in social and moral issues.

Lederberg has earned many honors for his scientific works. Preeminent among these are the 1958 Nobel Prize and the presidency of Rockefeller University, one of the world's finest scientific institutions. He has also been a member of the Presidential Scientific Advisory Council and has written nationally syndicated columns in the public press. He has also received honorary degrees from many major universities (Yale, New York University, and Columbia in the United States, and the University of Turin, in Italy). Lederberg's many scientific society memberships include the National Academy of Science, the Royal Society of London, Sigma Xi, and Phi Beta Kappa.

Bibliography

Primary

GENETICS: "Gene Recombination in *Escherichia Coli*," *Nature*, vol. 158, 1946, p.

558 (with E. L. Tatum); "Replica Plating and Indirect Selection of Bacterial Mutants," *Journal of Bacteriology*, vol. 63, 1952, pp. 399-406 (with E. M. Lederberg); "Genetic Exchange in Salmonella," *Journal of Bacteriology*, vol. 64, 1952, pp. 679-699; "Sex in Bacteria: Genetic Studies, 1945-1952," *Science*, vol. 118, 1954, pp. 169-175; "Prospects for the Genetics of Somatic and Tumor Cells," *Annals of the New York Academy of Science*, vol. 63, 1956, 662-665; "Genetic Transduction," *American Scientist*, vol. 44, 1956, pp. 264-280; "Viruses, Genes and Cells," *Bacteriological Reviews*, vol. 21, 1957, pp. 133-139; "A View of Genetics," *Les Prix Nobel*, 1958, pp. 170-189; "Forty Years of Genetic Recombination in Bacteria: A Fortieth Anniversary Reminiscence," *Nature*, vol. 327, 1986, pp. 627-628; "Perspectives: Gene Recombination and Linked Segregations in *Escherichia coli*," *Genetics*, vol. 117, 1987, pp. 1-4; "Genetic Recombination in Bacteria: A Discovery Account," *Annual Review of Genetics*, vol. 27, 1987.

BIOLOGY: "Moondust," *Science*, vol. 127, 1958, pp. 1473-1475; "Reflections on Darwin and Ehrlich: The Ontogeny of the Clonal Selection Theory of Antibody Formation," *Annals of the New York Academy of Science*, vol. 546, 1988, pp. 175-182.

Secondary

Hayes, William. *The Genetics of Bacteria and Their Viruses*. New York: John Wiley & Sons, 1964. This book, though dated, describes research techniques in bacterial and viral genetics. Chapters 21 ("Transduction") and 22 ("Conjugation") describe the work of Lederberg's group and comment on its great value. The bibliography contains many of the most relevant papers by Lederberg and coworkers.

Jacob, François, and Élie Wollman. *Sexuality and the Genetics of Bacteria*. New York: Academic Press, 1961. This book describes bacterial genetics and sexual conjugation. It is divided into three portions: origin and development of bacterial genetics; detailed analysis of sexual conjugation; use of bacterial conjugation to attack genetic problems. Lederberg's work is cited throughout the text and thirty of his relevant papers are in the bibliography.

Lehninger, Albert. *Principles of Biochemistry*. New York: Worth, 1982. This college biochemistry text covers well the issues involved in modern molecular genetics and DNA chemistry. Portions of chapter 30 cover the concepts of transduction and bacterial conjugation. The book contains clear diagrams of the processes.

Stent, Gunther. *Molecular Biology of Bacterial Viruses*. San Francisco: W. H. Freeman, 1963. The book compiles many historical and technical issues in the development of the molecular biology of bacteriophages. It includes sections on infection of bacteria, growth and reproduction of viruses, genetic recombination, lysogeny, transduction, and expression of hereditary information. Reference to Lederberg's work is most extensive in chapter 13, on transduction.

Sanford S. Singer

1959

Physiology or Medicine

Severo Ochoa, Spain and United States
Arthur Kornberg, United States

Chemistry

Jaroslav Heyrovský, Czechoslovakia

Physics

Emilio Gino Segrè, United States
Owen Chamberlain, United States

Literature

Salvatore Quasimodo, Italy

Peace

Philip Noel-Baker, Great Britain

SEVERO OCHOA
1959

Born: Luarca, Spain; September 24, 1905

Nationality: Spanish; after 1956, American
Area of concentration: Enzymology

Ochoa prepared a pure enzyme from acetic acid bacteria, with the aid of which enzyme he was able to synthesize large molecules analogous to natural nucleic acids, one of the two basic principles of living matter, proteins and nucleic acids

The Award

Presentation

Professor Axel Hugo Teodor Theorell, member of the Staff of Professors of the Royal Caroline Institute and recipient of the Nobel Prize in Physiology or Medicine himself in 1955, made the presentation address on Thursday, December 10, 1959, to King Gustav VI Adolf and other assembled guests, introducing Arthur Kornberg and Severo Ochoa, the joint recipients of the Nobel Prize in Physiology or Medicine for 1959.

Theorell opened with a phrase from an old Danish song, "There must be two if life shall succeed," to introduce the idea that from a biological standpoint two principles are necessary for life: proteins and nucleic acids. The two scientists being honored had succeeded, in different ways, in synthesizing nucleic acids. The ribonucleic acids that Ochoa synthesized also assist in the further synthesis of proteins, Theorell said. He stated that uric acid, the first representative of the purines (a class of nitrogen-bearing compounds that make up part of the nucleic acids), had been discovered in Sweden two centuries earlier, independently, by Torbern Bergman and Carl Wilhelm Scheele, in a curious parallel to the work of the two currently honored scientists, Ochoa and Kornberg—a reminder of Sweden's great era in chemistry in the eighteenth century.

Ochoa isolated an enzyme that causes ribonucleotides to unite to form molecules indistinguishable from natural nucleic acids. In order to start the reaction, a small amount of the desired nucleic acid must be added, as a sort of template, after which the enzymes then permit this model molecule to replicate itself to produce more of the same nucleic acid. Ochoa's work has helped researchers to advance markedly in their understanding of the mechanisms involved in living matter, Theorell concluded.

Nobel lecture

On December 11, 1959, Severo Ochoa began his Nobel lecture, entitled "Enzymatic Synthesis of Ribonucleic Acid," by reviewing the recent work on the synthesis of ribonucleic acid. The growth of living cells is one of nature's most important mechanisms, and the nucleic acids play a role in such growth by transmitting hereditary traits. Ribonucleic acid (RNA) helps in the synthesis of proteins, whereas deoxyribonucleic acid (DNA) acts as the principal component of nuclear chromosomes, the threadlike bodies within the cell (so called because of their affinity for certain dyes). In certain viruses, Ochoa noted, RNA is the carrier of genetic information.

Ochoa isolated an enzyme that acts as a catalyst (that is, it speeds the reaction) in the synthesis of RNA from molecules containing phosphate, called nucleosides, by releasing some of the phosphate and combining the rest of the molecules into still larger molecules, synthetic RNA. This synthetic RNA proved to be identical with natural RNA. He suggested that specific forms of RNA require the presence of some of the desired form of RNA as a template at the beginning of the reaction, in order that the particularly desired form of RNA could be replicated. In other words, a small added amount of the desired form of RNA must act as a nucleus on which more molecules can condense, in much the same way that sublimation nuclei act in cloud precipitation. The added RNA nucleus becomes a template for the growth of new RNA molecules of the same kind. The enzyme itself, completely free of this template RNA, would probably prove inactive, Ochoa suggested.

He named his enzyme polynucleotide phosphorylase and added that its occurrence in nature appeared to be widespread enough to be involved in the natural biosynthesis of RNA. Other investigators had described enzymes which catalyzed the addition of a few nucleotide units to an already existing RNA molecule, but none had previously succeeded in synthesizing a complete RNA molecule.

Ochoa concluded his address with a reference to the work of Arthur Kornberg, cowinner of the 1959 Nobel Prize in Physiology or Medicine, who had succeeded in synthesizing the other nucleic acid, DNA. Such syntheses, he concluded, may lead to general methods for making genetic material in a test tube.

Critical reception

Two United States biochemists, Severo Ochoa of New York University and Arthur Kornberg of Stanford University, would share the 1959 Nobel Prize in Physiology or Medicine, *The New York Times* announced on October 16, 1959. The two scientists were being honored for their contribution to the "understanding of the life process," the reporter said. The account continued, "Professor Hugo Theorell, a Nobel laureate himself in 1955, said the [Caroline] Institute was honoring two of the best biochemists of the present time during their most active age. Dr. Ochoa is 54 years old and Dr. Kornberg is 41." Ochoa was described as dedicated to his work but wholly aware of the world around him—exacting, but not lacking in a sense of humor.

Two of the substances that represent the distinction between life and nonlife are ribonucleic acid (RNA) and deoxyribonucleic acid (DNA), said *Time* magazine, and two U.S. scientists have succeeded in synthesizing RNA and DNA. *Time* described how Ochoa's life had been sharply disrupted in his native country, Spain, by Francisco Franco's revolution in the 1930's. He left for Germany, then England, and finally the United States in 1940. In 1946 at New York University he had a brilliant postdoctoral student, Arthur Kornberg, with whom (and others) Ochoa was able to make an enzyme with which to build RNA and DNA molecules.

Science magazine told a similar story, adding that DNA is the chemical that is the carrier of hereditary traits in living things. *Science* said that DNA provides the master pattern of each cell, allowing that cell to reproduce itself in its own image. Furthermore, DNA plays a role in the production of RNA, which in turn is essential to the production of proteins.

Newsweek headlined "A Mighty Step" in describing Ochoa's work and pictured him toasting his colleagues with champagne in paper cups. "What is the value of synthesizing RNA and DNA?" *Newsweek* asked, then answered its own question: "Conceivably, scientists might be able one day to transplant into animals or man synthetic DNA capable of adding desirable traits, and thus improve their offspring genetically."

Science News Letter noted that the award to Ochoa and Kornberg was presented for their "joint work in discovering the mechanisms in the biological synthesis of DNA and RNA, and thus contributing to our understanding of the life process." Such molecules as the two men have produced in a test tube, the article stated, appear to be identical to natural RNA and DNA. Their work may also contribute to cancer research, since this disease is characterized by abnormal growth of cells, and the work of Ochoa and Kornberg contributes greatly to solving the problems of cellular reproduction, the article concluded.

None of the reviewers made note of what might be an item of considerable interest, the fact that Ochoa was one of only three Nobel laureates in science originally from the Iberian peninsula, the other two being Santiago Ramón y Cajal (Spain, 1906) and António Egas Moniz (Portugal, 1949).

Biography

Severo Ochoa, son of Severo Ochoa, a lawyer, and Carmen (de Albornoz) Ochoa, was born on September 24, 1905, in Luarca, on the Bay of Biscay, province of Asturias, in the Basque region of northern Spain. For his education, Ochoa traveled across Spain to the Costa del Sol on the Sea of Alboran and the ancient city of Malaga. There he took his bachelor of arts degree at the university, at the unusually early age of sixteen. He was then attracted to the medical school of the University of Madrid, where Santiago Ramón y Cajal was professor of histology and pathological anatomy. (Ramón y Cajal won the Nobel Prize in Physiology or Medicine in 1906 for his work on the nervous system.) Ochoa obtained his doctor of medicine degree at Madrid in 1929, where he was assistant to Professor Juan Negrin. During this period, in 1927, he also spent a summer at the University of Glasgow, Scotland, where he worked with Diarmid Noel Paton.

Ochoa next proceeded to the Kaiser Wilhelm Institute for Physiology in Heidelberg, Germany, where he worked from 1929 to 1931 on the physiology of muscle with Otto Meyerhof, cowinner of the 1922 Nobel Prize in Physiology or Medicine for his work in the biochemistry of muscle. On July 8, 1931, Ochoa was married to Carmen Garcia Cobian.

He was then appointed to the faculty at the University of Madrid in physiology, where he stayed from 1931 until 1935. He did his first work on enzymes when he worked briefly in 1932 with Harold Ward Dudley, biochemist for the laboratories of the Medical Research Council in London, England.

The Spanish revolution forced Ochoa to leave his native country permanently in 1936. He first returned to Meyerhof's laboratory in Heidelberg, then proceeded to various posts in England—at Plymouth Marine Biological Laboratory, then at the University of Oxford medical school, where he worked with Rudolf Albert Peters from 1938 to 1941.

In 1941, Ochoa went to the United States to Washington University school of medicine in St. Louis, Missouri, where he was a research assistant in pharmacology with Carl and Gerty Cori (who received the Nobel Prize in Physiology or Medicine jointly in 1947). In 1942, Ochoa moved to New York University, where he was to remain for the rest of his professional career. In 1942 he was appointed an assistant professor of biochemistry, and a year later he became professor of pharmacology. In 1954 he became professor of biochemistry and chairman of the department of biochemistry. Ochoa and his wife became United States citizens in 1956.

Ochoa was elected to membership in the National Academy of Sciences (U.S.), the American Academy of Arts and Sciences, and the Deutsche Akademie der Naturforscher; he holds honorary degrees from many universities throughout the world. He was elected to honorary membership in organizations including the Royal Society (London), 1965; the Academy of Science, U.S.S.R., 1966; the Royal Academy of Medicine, Sevilla (Spain), 1971; and the Academy of Science, D.D.R., 1977. He was awarded the Gold Medal of Madrid University in 1969 and the Albert Gallatin Medal of New York University in 1970.

Scientific Career

Ochoa worked and studied with many well-known physiologists and biochemists, several of whom were Nobel laureates themselves. Some of his work with Meyerhof at Heidelberg, for example, was reported in 1937, when he described the action of glucolytic enzyme on heart muscle to form lactic acid. He gave a summary of this work on the biochemistry of muscle tissue in an address in 1938, reported in the journal *Chemistry and Industry.*

In 1938, Ochoa moved to England, where he worked on the biological function of vitamin B with Peters at the University of Oxford. In this period, 1938 to 1941, he also began to work on enzymatic mechanisms in various brain tissues, using pigeon and rat brains, and reporting on the necessity of having certain metal ions (dissolved metal atoms), such as magnesium or manganese, present in solution in order for oxygen to be taken up by the tissue.

In 1941, he moved to the United States and began to work with the Coris at Washington University in St. Louis, where he studied enzymology further. He reported on the use of extracts from the heart tissue of cats as a source of the enzyme alpha-ketoglutaric dehydrogenase in the *Journal of Biological Chemistry* in 1943.

In 1942, Ochoa found his professional home at New York University in Manhattan, where he remained until his retirement in 1974. There he continued his research on enzymes, including enzymes from pig heart tissue that catalyze carbon dioxide coupling, and enzymatic linkage with cytochrome-C. By 1948 he was able to publish his series of three articles on the biosynthesis of tricarboxylic acids by carbon dioxide fixation. In the first of these three articles, he described the synthesis of oxalosuccinic acid (OSA), a relatively unstable compound that he isolated by precipitation in the form of its insoluble barium salt. The preparation of OSA, Ochoa said, "made possible a better understanding of the mechanism of biological reactions involving tricarboxylic acids." This was a critical step in his journey toward the eventual synthesis of RNA. He also studied the effect of metallic cations (positively charged metal atoms in solution) on decarboxylation of OSA (that is, removal of carbon dioxide from the molecule) and found magnesium and manganese ions to be the most effective in preventing the decomposition of OSA.

In the second of these three landmark articles, Ochoa described how decarboxylation of OSA was promoted by the presence of an enzyme—he called it OSA-carboxylase—extracted from the tissue of pig hearts, but only in the presence of manganese ions in the solution. OSA-carboxylase itself, free of manganese ions, did not act on OSA.

In the third and longest article of the three papers, Ochoa described the conditions necessary for enzymatic carboxylation and decarboxylation of various tricarboxylic acids, such as citric acid and isocitric acid. With these results he was ready for the next phase of his research—the polymerization of nucleotides, the process which led to his synthesis of RNA.

Notable advances had been made prior to Ochoa's work in the synthesis of smaller related molecules, the so-called nucleotides, the building-block molecules for the nucleic acids, but Ochoa (and Kornberg) were the first to bring these nucleotides together in the laboratory to form the giant molecules of the nucleic acids, RNA and DNA. Their discovery, which made this synthesis possible, was an enzyme, polynucleotide phosphatase (PNP), which Ochoa isolated and prepared in very pure form from certain bacteria, *Azotobacter vinelandii*. Ochoa first reported the isolation of this enzyme in 1955. The nucleotide that he used as the building material for RNA was called a nucleoside diphosphate, which in the presence of magnesium ions in solution was able to unite with itself (polymerize) to form polymeric molecules, long-chain molecules made up of repeated units of the smaller building-block molecules, with the simultaneous liberation of phosphate. The polymeric molecular product had a molecule of high molecular weight, a polyribonucleotide.

Specifically, among the nucleotide building blocks that Ochoa used were the organic bases—adenine, guanine, uracil, and cytosine—which had been identified earlier by others as being constituent parts of RNA and DNA. The corresponding nucleoside diphosphates were called adenosine, guanosine, uridine, and cytidine diphosphates. When these nucleosides were reacted individually or in varying combinations, synthetic polyribonucleotides were formed; the nature of the product depended on the particular combination of nucleoside diphosphate used in the synthesis. Ochoa reported in 1957 that the structures of these polymeric products were found to conform in all respects to the structural pattern of natural RNA. The polymeric products could be decomposed by the use of alkalis, enzymes such as snake venom, or extracts of the spleen or pancreas, and the original nucleotides could be recovered. In this work Ochoa used the radioactive element phosphorus 32 as a tracer in order to follow the course of the reaction.

If the monomeric substance, the nucleoside diphosphate, used as starting material was adenosine diphosphate (ADP) and it was polymerized in the presence of the catalytic enzyme PNP, the polyribonucleotide product was called Poly A. If the starting material was guanosine diphosphate (GDP), the product obtained was called Poly G. Uridine diphosphate (UDP) similarly yielded Poly U, and cytidine diphosphate (CDP) Poly C. All these products were obtained using only a single nucleoside diphosphate as the starting material. Ochoa then tried various binary combinations as starting materials. ADP and UDP yielded the polynucleotide that he called Poly AU; GDP and CDP yielded Poly GC. In each case he showed by degradation with alkali that these polyribonucleotides consisted of linear chains in which the component nucleoside units were linked to one another by phosphate diester bridges. Similar degradation of natural RNA had revealed the natural bases, adenine, guanine, uracil, and cytosine, whose diphosphates were then used in the final synthesis of RNA. The final step in the synthesis of RNA was to combine all four nucleoside diphosphates, ADP, GDP, CDP, and UDP, together with the enzyme catalyst to obtain Poly AGCU, which proved to be identical to natural RNA.

Ochoa's work did not end with the synthesis of RNA. He still had to demonstrate convincingly that his synthetic RNA was identical to natural RNA. Thus he showed that the size of the synthetic RNA molecules was similar to that of natural RNA molecules, with molecular weights varying between thirty thousand and several million. This was shown, for example, when sedimentation constants for samples of his synthetic RNA were found to be similar to constants determined for RNA isolated from *Azotobacter vinelandii* bacterial cells.

Ochoa also studied the mechanism by which the synthetic reaction took place, but first he had to purify the enzyme he used. This was done by ion exchange through a long column of the mineral hydroxy apatite in a method developed by Arne Tiselius, Nobel laureate in chemistry in 1948. Ochoa estimated that the enzyme was separated from contaminants and that purification of "some six hundred fold over the initial extract from the Azotobacter cells" was thus obtained. Even so, the highly purified enzyme contained about 3.5 percent of a firmly bound oligonucleotide contaminant that could not be removed without destroying the enzyme itself. He reported that it was therefore still undecided what the role of this contaminant, if any, might be in the synthesis.

Another of Ochoa's discoveries, essential to his synthesis of RNA, was that it was necessary to have a small amount of the desired product nucleotide present in the reaction mixture as a primer to get the reaction started. Thus, if highly purified enzyme preparations were used, equilibrium was not reached "even after many hours of incubation." The reaction rate was markedly stimulated, however, by the addition of small amounts of the desired product; they seemed to act as a primer, or template, for further reaction, Ochoa hypothesized. This priming effect was not entirely specific, however: The polynucleotide from adenine could prime the synthesis of a polynucleotide from uracil, as well as that of RNA. RNA, whether natural or synthetic, primed the synthesis of RNA as well as that of other polynucleotides from single bases. Thus Ochoa did not claim to understand the complete mechanism of the synthetic process. He did suggest that the primer molecules serve as nuclei for growth of polynucleotide chains in a manner similar to the action of sublimation nuclei in bringing about precipitation in clouds. The primer nuclei may serve as templates for their own replication, Ochoa suggested, even though this had not yet been established experimentally. It appeared justified to conclude that the enzyme catalyst by itself might not be able to start the synthesis of a polynucleotide chain from nucleoside diphosphates as the only reactants. The presence of a small amount of the desired product to serve as a nucleus for growth is "probably indispensable," Ochoa suggested.

James D. Watson and Francis Crick had already proposed their double-stranded helical structure for DNA, although they were not to receive their Nobel Prizes for this work until three years later, in 1962. Ochoa stated that he assumed the same double-stranded helical structure for RNA as Watson and Crick had proposed for DNA. He cited the work of Alexander Rich, professor of biology at Massachusetts Institute of Technology, and coworkers for showing that triple-stranded helical polynucleotide structures can also be formed. Rich had used X-ray diffraction and optical density studies to elucidate the molecular structure of nucleic acids. One such study demonstrated that a complex molecule consisting of one Poly A and two Poly U molecules was formed in the presence of magnesium ions, and the only possible structure for such a complex was a triple-stranded helix, Ochoa stated.

In his Nobel address, Ochoa referred to the work of Arthur Kornberg, his colaureate, as providing deep insight into the mechanism of the replication of DNA. Such insights, Ochoa implied, might lead to the general ability to synthesize genetic material in a test tube. Since RNA is the genetic material of some viruses, Ochoa's work might "pave the way for the artificial synthesis of biologically active viral RNA" and thus for the synthesis of viruses themselves, Ochoa stated. These particles are at the very threshold of life and may be the first steps in synthesizing living matter.

Bibliography

Primary

PHYSIOLOGY: "Biosynthesis of Tricarboxylic Acids by Carbon Dioxide Fixation: I, Preparation and Properties of Oxalosuccinic Acid," *Journal of Biological Chemistry*, vol. 174, 1948, pp. 115-122; "II, Oxalosuccinic Carboxylase," *Journal of Biological Chemistry*, vol. 174, 1948, pp. 123-132 (with Erna Weisz-Tabori); "III, Enzymatic Mechanisms," *Journal of Biological Chemistry*, vol. 174, 1948, pp.

133-172; "Enzymatic Synthesis of Nucleic Acidlike Polynucleotides," *Science*, vol. 122, 1955, pp. 907-910 (with Marianne Grunberg-Manago and Priscilla J. Ortiz); "Enzymatic Synthesis and Breakdown of Polynucleotides: Polynucleotide Phosphorylase," *Journal of the American Chemical Society*, vol. 77, 1955, pp. 3165-3166 (with M. Grunberg-Manago); "Small Polyribonucleotides with 5′-Phosphomonoester End-Groups," *Science*, vol. 123, 1956, pp. 415-417 (with L. A. Heppel and P. J. Ortiz); "Studies on Polynucleotides Synthesized by Polynucleotide Phosphorylase: I, Structure of Polynucleotides with One Type of Nucleotide Unit," *Journal of Biological Chemistry*, vol. 229, 1957, pp. 679-694 (with L. A. Heppel and P. J. Ortiz); "II, Structure of Polymers Containing a Mixture of Bases," *Journal of Biological Chemistry*, vol. 229, 1957, pp. 695-711 (with L. A. Heppel and P. J. Ortiz); "IV, P-32 Labeled Ribonucleic Acid," *Journal of Biological Chemistry*, vol. 234, 1959, pp. 1208-1212 (with P. J. Ortiz).

Secondary

Cohen, Seymour S. *Introduction to the Polyamines*. Englewood Cliffs, N.J.: Prentice-Hall, 1971. The polyamines are low-molecular-weight nitrogenous bases. Putrescine and cadaverine are examples of simple diamines. Structures for polyamines and ribosomes are compared. Mechanisms of synthesis of polyamines, ribosomes, proteins, and RNA are discussed.

Fraenkel-Conrat, Heinz. "Ribonucleic Acid: The Simplest Information Transmitting Molecule." *Journal of Chemical Education* 40 (1963): 216-222. In this article, Fraenkel-Conrat discusses the chemical nature of the nucleic acids, both RNA and DNA, which he says are the carriers of genetic and possibly also other types of information in all organisms. Methods by which this information can be changed through chemical modification, and how this process may result in mutation are also included.

Gait, M. J., ed. *Oligonucleotide Synthesis: A Practical Approach*. Washington, D.C.: I.R.L. Press, 1984. Sixteen contributors. Chapter 8, "Enzymatic Synthesis of Oligoribonucleotides," by Dorothy Beckett and Olka C. Uhlenbeck, discusses much work done since the earlier work of Ochoa. The availability of synthetic RNA, since Ochoa's pioneering work, and especially RNA of defined sequence of amino units, has greatly aided the investigation of the structure and functions of RNA, these authors state.

Gale, E. F. *Synthesis and Organization in the Bacterial Cell*. New York: John Wiley & Sons, 1959. RNA and DNA differ in the nature of the pentose units in the bases making up the polynucleotide, with RNA containing adenine, guanine, uracil, and cytosine, and DNA containing adenine, guanine, cytosine, and thymine. RNA synthesis in vivo takes place only in the presence of the complete mixture of amino acids required for protein synthesis. This book gives a picture of the state of the art at the time of Ochoa's work.

Lesk, Arthur M. "Progress in Our Understanding of the Optical Properties of Nucleic Acids." *Journal of Chemical Education* 46 (1969): 821-826. The dependence of the optical properties on conformation can be predicted; conversely, the conformation of a (nucleic acid) molecule may be inferred from its optical properties. Conformation of RNA in ribosomes from *Escherichia coli* and tobacco mosaic virus RNA have been so deduced.

Ochoa, Severo. "Biosynthesis of Ribonucleic Acid." In *Cellular Biology*. Vol. 5, *Nucleic Acids and Viruses*. New York: Academy of Sciences, 1957. Ochoa gives here much of the same material that he was to present in his Nobel Prize address. He discusses the synthesis of RNA and includes the procedure for purification of the enzyme polynucleotide phosphorylase from *Azotobacter vinelandii*. He shows how he synthesized polynucleotides containing adenylic acid, uridylic acid, cytidylic acid, or inosinic acid, using the enzyme to form Poly A, Poly U, Poly C, Poly I, Poly AU, and Poly AGUC.

Joseph Albert Schufle

1959

Physiology or Medicine

Severo Ochoa, Spain and United States
Arthur Kornberg, United States

Chemistry

Jaroslav Heyrovský, Czechoslovakia

Physics

Emilio Gino Segrè, United States
Owen Chamberlain, United States

Literature

Salvatore Quasimodo, Italy

Peace

Philip Noel-Baker, Great Britain

ARTHUR KORNBERG
1959

Born: Brooklyn, New York; March 3, 1918

Nationality: American
Areas of concentration: Enzymology and synthetic biochemistry

The discovery of DNA polymerase by Kornberg led to the elucidation of an enzymatic mechanism for DNA replication and ultimately to the biological synthesis of DNA

The Award

Presentation

On December 10, 1959, Professor Hugo Theorell, a member of the Staff of Professors of the Royal Caroline Institute, delivered the presentation address prior to the awarding of the Nobel Prize in Physiology or Medicine to Arthur Kornberg. Theorell began his address by making an analogy between proteins and nucleic acids and men and women, in terms of their necessity for the continuation of life. He also compared the nucleic acids and proteins based on size, structure, elementary composition, and the regulated order of the building blocks of each. Previous research relating to protein and nucleic acid synthesis was noted, beginning with Carl Wilhelm Scheele and Torbern Bergman, who discovered the first of the purines, uric acid, in 1776. Albrecht Kossel, in 1910, elucidated the chemistry of the nitrogenous bases of nucleic acids, and, in 1957, Alexander Todd detailed the chemical properties of nucleic acids. It was Kornberg's own earlier research using *Escherichia coli* to produce highly purified enzymes, however, that aided him most in the successful synthesis of deoxyribonucleic acid (DNA) polymerase.

Theorell predicted that great discoveries would result from the research done by Kornberg. He reminded his listeners that Friedrich Wöhler bridged the first gap between living and dead material in the nineteenth century when he synthesized urea and stated that the artificial synthesis of DNA marked the second major step along this pathway. Dr. Kornberg was congratulated by King Gustav VI Adolf, from whom he accepted the 1959 Nobel Prize in Physiology or Medicine.

Nobel lecture

Arthur Kornberg gave his Nobel lecture, entitled "The Biologic Synthesis of Deoxyribonucleic Acid," on December 11, 1959. Appropriately, he explained the structure of the DNA molecule in terms of the basic components and their specific chemical linking patterns. The components, known as nucleotides, are made of nitrogen-containing organic bases called purines and pyrimidines, a five-carbon sugar, and a phosphate group. The purines (adenine and guanine) of one nucleotide are always paired with the pyrimidines (thymine and cytosine) of another nucleotide, and they are attached to one another by hydrogen bonds. These molecules form the "rungs" of the ladder-shaped DNA molecule. The sides of the ladder are formed by the five-carbon sugars, which are themselves linked together by the phosphates.

This entire assemblage results in a double cylindrical spiral shape known as a helix. The DNA helix is stabilized by the relatively weak hydrogen bonds, which essentially provide the mechanism by which DNA can be replicated. To accomplish this, two strands of the DNA molecule can separate, and new strands complementary to each of the single strands can be made. Two new and identical DNA molecules would thereby be produced. Kornberg detailed the process of DNA replication at the enzymatic level and presented experimental proof that a DNA-synthesizing enzyme (DNA polymerase) catalyzes the reactions that result in the production of new strands of DNA. It was thoroughly explained how a single strand of DNA acts as a pattern for the formation of a new strand of nucleotides. The new strand is complementary to the original DNA strand, so new double-stranded DNA results. The length of the new DNA is determined by the length of the pattern DNA.

Kornberg referred to several researchers whose work was pertinent to his studies. Among these were Ervin Chargaff, who demonstrated that there are two consistencies in DNA composition and that an equivalency exists between purines and pyrimidines, regardless of the source. James Watson and Francis Crick constructed a model of the DNA molecule based on the crystallography studies of Maurice Wilkins and Rosalind Franklin; Howard K. Schachman's research gave evidence that enzymatically synthesized DNA is not distinguishable from DNA isolated from nature.

The conclusion that the synthesizing enzyme purified from *Escherichia coli* is responsible for the production of new double-stranded DNA from a DNA template and that hydrogen bonding of the nitrogenous bases is the guiding mechanism of action is based on experimental results involving five major findings: the physical properties of enzymatically synthesized DNA; the equal control of the DNA polymerase reaction on natural DNA and analogues by hydrogen-bonding restrictions; the process of base-composition replication during enzymatic synthesis; the replication of nucleotide sequences, showing the pattern of sequence frequency and antiparallel orientation; and the necessity for the presence of template DNA and the triphosphates of all four nitrogenous bases (adenine, guanine, cytosine, and thymine) for DNA synthesis.

Critical reception

When the Nobel Prize was awarded to Arthur Kornberg, he was already a highly respected research investigator in the scientific community. His enzyme discoveries involving diphosphopyridine nucleotide (DPN) and flavin adenine dinucleotide (FAD) had been duly noted. This discovery of an enzyme capable of copying a DNA template and producing an exact replica focused attention on the question of the origin of life in the community at large. Yet, Nobel Prize recipient Hugo Theorell stated in *The New York Times*, December 10, 1959, that this research "clarified many of the problems of regeneration and the continuity of life" but had no real impact on questions concerning the origin of life.

The response to the synthesis of DNA polymerase was duly noted in the scientific community, but according to various newspaper accounts, such as those in *The Times* (of London), *The New York Times*, and *The Washington Post*, the general public seemed only slightly aware of the implications of this achievement. This was perhaps because the genetic replica produced as a result of the action of deoxyribonucleic acid polymerase was inactive. Additionally, it was rapidly attached by extraneous enzymes that damaged the molecules. Therefore, this DNA was unable to simulate the activity of DNA in living cells.

In congratulatory remarks to Kornberg, President Dwight Eisenhower stated that a new pathway had now been opened for studying causes and cures for life-threatening diseases. In particular, he stressed the relationship of this discovery to cancer treatment and possible cure. *The Times* (of London) immediately noted that the key to how DNA might produce exact copies of itself was predicated upon the X-ray diffraction studies of Maurice F. H. Wilkins, a British scientist, and his collaborators. When Kornberg accepted the Nobel Prize, he had already begun the research that would lead to still greater accomplishments.

Biography

Arthur Kornberg was born in Brooklyn, New York, on March 3, 1918, the son of Joseph and Lena (née Katz) Kornberg. He attended local public schools, achieving a brilliant scholastic record, and was graduated from Abraham Lincoln High School in June, 1933, at the age of fifteen. On a New York State scholarship, he attended City College of New York, where he majored in premedicine and received his B.S. degree with honors in 1937. He was a recipient of a Buswell scholarship to the University of Rochester School of Medicine, from which he received the M.D. degree in 1941. He interned at Strong Memorial Hospital in Rochester, New York, from 1941 to 1942.

In 1942, Kornberg served briefly in the United States Coast Guard as a medical officer with the rank of lieutenant, junior grade. In this same year he was commissioned an officer in the United States Public Health Service and was assigned to the National Institutes of Health (NIH) in Bethesda, Maryland. On November 21, 1943, Arthur Kornberg and Sylvy Ruth Levy were married. Sylvy was a biochemist and his collaborator. They would have three sons, Roger David, Thomas Bill, and Kenneth Andrew. From 1942 to 1945, he worked in the nutrition section of the Division of Physiology. He was chief of the enzyme and metabolism section at NIH from 1947 to 1953. On leaves of absence from the NIH, Kornberg worked with Severo Ochoa at the New York University College of Medicine in 1946, with Carl and Gerty Cori at Washington University School of Medicine in St. Louis, and with H. A. Barker at the University of California at Berkeley in 1951.

In 1953, Kornberg left the National Institutes of Health to become head of the department of microbiology at Washington University School of Medicine, where he remained until 1959. From 1959 to 1969, he was professor and executive head of the department of biochemistry at Stanford University School of Medicine. He has remained as professor at Stanford University. Keenly interested in enzymology and synthesis biology, he has performed his investigative research in those areas.

Included among Kornberg's honors are the Nobel Prize in 1959; honorary degrees from City College of New York, the University of Rochester, Yeshiva University, Washington University (St. Louis), and Notre Dame; the Paul-Lewis Laboratories Award of the American Chemical Society in 1951; and the Scientific Achievement Award of the American Medical Association in 1968. He was made a foreign member of the Royal Society of London in 1970.

Scientific Career

From the beginning of his educational career, Kornberg exhibited academic excellence. He was the "smart kid" on the block in his hometown, attending the public schools of Brooklyn, New York. At the age of fifteen, he was graduated from Abraham Lincoln High School. His interest in life processes and their regulators was apparently initiated as a result of taking a premedical course at City College of New York. He received his B.S. in 1937 from CCNY with a double major in biology and chemistry and, in 1941, received his M.D. from the University of Rochester School of Medicine. While attending the University of Rochester, Kornberg became interested in enzymes and decided to dedicate himself to enzyme research instead of medical practice. He published his first scientific paper while at the University of Rochester, then interned for one year at Strong Memorial Hospital in Rochester, New York.

He served briefly as a medical officer in the Coast Guard in 1942. The following year he was assigned to the National Institutes of Health (NIH) in Bethesda, Maryland, as a commissioned officer in the United States Public Health Service. Kornberg remained at NIH from 1943 through 1952, except for the period from 1945 to 1947. During this period he took leaves of absence from NIH to work with Carl and Gerty Cori at Washington University in St. Louis, with H. A. Barber at the University of California at Berkeley, and with Severo Ochoa, with whom he later shared the Nobel Prize. While carrying on research in these laboratories, he greatly increased his expertise in isolating and purifying enzymes. In 1947, he returned to NIH and served as chief of the enzymes and metabolism division until 1952. It was at NIH that he first designed research procedures that led to the synthetic production of the coenzymes diphosphopyridine nucleotide (DPN) and flavin adenine dinucleotide (FAD). The mechanism he used to produce the coenzymes was a condensation reaction involving activation of nucleoside precursors. Kornberg would apply this knowledge in his DNA experiments at a later time.

In 1953, he joined the faculty at Washington University and was professor and chairman of the department of microbiology. It was at Washington University that he discovered the enzyme that catalyzes the reaction for bacterial high-molecular-weight phosphates. It was also there that Kornberg began the study that would culminate in the discovery that won for him the Nobel Prize in 1959. The research pathway to the discovery of DNA polymerase was an arduous yet exciting one for Kornberg. He firmly believed that enzyme purification was the key to the solution of the complex reactions involved in DNA replication. This belief proved to be correct. As purification of the enzyme continued, more information on the possible synthetic replication of DNA was revealed. In 1956, Kornberg and his associates isolated and purified DNA polymerase from the intestinal bacterium *Escherichia coli*. The following year, 1957, they used DNA polymerase to produce a giant molecule of artificial DNA. This DNA molecule was biologically inert, but it possessed the genetic properties of natural DNA.

As executive head of the department of biochemistry at Stanford University in 1959, Kornberg (and his research associates) set about the task of synthesizing a biologically active DNA. This synthesis had eluded Kornberg earlier because of impurity of the DNA polymerase, complexity of the DNA template, and damage to DNA polymerase by extraneous enzymes. The solution to the problem was initiated, however, when Robert L. Sensheimer of California Institute of Technology provided Kornberg with a simpler template. Kornberg and associate Mehran Goulian continued their purification procedures for DNA polymerase. In 1966, they discovered an enzyme with joining properties sufficient to close the DNA ring. This enzyme, called ligase, was discovered simultaneously by Kornberg and researchers in other laboratories. By using the natural virus DNA as a template and adding the DNA nucleotides—plus DNA polymerase and ligase—in a test tube, Kornberg could produce a biologically active DNA molecule. In a statement to Harold Schmeck of *The New York Times* on December 15, 1967, Dr. Kornberg commented that this research opened the way for more in-depth study of genetics and the nature of viruses and cancer and, maybe most important, might help in disclosing intimate processes of life itself. He further stated that this achievement represented eleven years of research, both by his laboratory and by other researchers around the country. When asked if they had created life in a test tube, Kornberg replied that he might be able to answer that "if you'd first care to define life."

Kornberg's scientific career has been punctuated with numerous awards and honors. In 1951, he received the Paul-Lewis Laboratories Award in enzyme chemistry from the American Chemical Society; in 1952, he received a silver medal from the Federal Security Agency for superior service. He has received honorary degrees from the City College of New York, the University of Rochester, Yeshiva University, Washington University in St. Louis, and Notre Dame. He was elected to the National Academy of Sciences in 1957 and the American Academy of Art and Sciences in 1961. In 1968, he received the Scientific Achievement Award of the American Medical Association, the Lucy Wortham James Award of the Society of Medical Oncology, and the Borden Award of the American Association of Medical Colleges. In 1970, he was made a foreign member of the Royal Society of London. He was president of the American Society of Biological Chemists in 1965 and 1966. He is a member of the National Academy of Sciences, Phi Beta Kappa, Sigma Xi, American Society for Clinical Investigation, the American Chemical Society, and the Harvey Society.

Bibliography

Primary

BIOCHEMISTRY: *Enzymatic Synthesis of DNA*, 1962; *Biosynthesis of DNA*, 1964; *DNA Synthesis*, 1974; *DNA Replication*, 1980.

Secondary

American Men and Women of Science: Physical and Biological Sciences. 8 vols. 17th ed. New York: R.R. Bowker, 1989. Presents a biographical sketch of Kornberg's life, emphasizing both the research for which he received the Nobel Prize and more recent work on the synthesis of an active form of DNA.

Johnson, Leland G. *Biology*. 2d ed. Dubuque, Iowa: Wm. C. Brown, 1987. A brief, clear explanation of the methods used to show how DNA is replicated is included in this standard biology textbook.

Modern Scientists and Engineers. Vol. 2. New York: McGraw-Hill, 1980. A discussion of the procedure used to extract DNA polymerase from *Escherichia coli* bacteria and how these procedures elucidated the mechanism by which DNA replicates. References.

Moritz, Charles, ed. *Current Biography Yearbook, 1968*. New York: H. W. Wilson, 1968. This article relates detailed information on Kornberg's professional career in education and research as well as his education and training that led to the M.D. and Ph.D. degrees. It includes a press conference interview with Kornberg on his synthesis of active DNA molecules in 1967. A brief reference to his family is given. References appended.

Stent, Gunther S. *Molecular Genetics: An Introductory Narrative*. San Francisco: W. H. Freeman, 1971. An explanation of how the DNA of the infected bacterium participates in the production of proteins and enzymes necessary for virus DNA replication. The complete process of the formation of virus DNA is explained with diagrams.

Bennye S. Henderson

1960

Physiology or Medicine

Sir Macfarlane Burnet, Australia
Peter Brian Medawar, Great Britain

Chemistry

Willard Frank Libby, United States

Physics

Donald A. Glaser, United States

Literature

Saint-John Perse, France

Peace

Albert Lutuli, South Africa

SIR MACFARLANE BURNET
1960

Born: Traralgon, Victoria, Australia; September 3, 1899
Died: Melbourne, Victoria, Australia; August 31, 1985
Nationality: Australian
Areas of concentration: Virology and immunology

Burnet's work played a pivotal role in revolutionizing modern immunology through his discoveries concerning the nature of viruses and antibodies as well as through his highly influential clonal selection theory of the immune response

The Award

Presentation

On December 10, 1960, shortly before Frank Macfarlane Burnet and Peter Brian Medawar received their Nobel Prizes in Physiology or Medicine from the hands of King Gustav IV, Sven Gard, a member of the Royal Caroline Institute, gave a presentation address that centered on biochemical individuality, a theme pervasive in the prizewinning work of both laureates. Most people are aware of the individuality of their fellow human beings, and some may know that this individuality is involved in such traits as fingerprints. Not so well known, however, is the individuality of many of the complex organic substances that constitute the molecular underpinnings of this individuality. Doctors have successfully grafted tissue from one section of a person's body to another, but grafts between different individuals have often failed. Burnet, who studied the mechanism by which an organism distinguishes between "self substances" and "foreign substances," showed both how this valuable property allows the body to identify an immense variety of material as potentially harmful and how this capacity could be overcome by inducing in animals, during their embryonic period, an immunological tolerance. This could be done because Burnet recognized that the ability to produce immunity is not inherited (it is lacking in the fetus) but develops gradually (animals attain full immunological maturity only after birth). By constantly interacting with self substances during the embryonic stage, the maturing immune system develops a mechanism to recognize and remember those substances making up the body's individuality. Burnet predicted that the introduction of foreign tissue into an embryo should cause no immune response; instead, the body's immune system would always interpret this tissue as self, and so tolerate it if it were reintroduced (a prediction verified experimentally by Medawar). Because of the work of Burnet and Medawar, doctors now have a deeper understanding of immunity, which should lead to new treatments for various immune disorders and to techniques for transplanting tissues between different individuals.

Nobel lecture

In his lecture, "Immunological Recognition of Self," given on December 12,

1960, Burnet emphasized the issue of an animal's identification of self substances and its rejection of foreign substances. The largely theoretical lecture had three main sections and a brief conclusion. The first section dealt with the nature of antigens and antibodies. Early in the history of immunology, scientists believed that all types of immunity were produced by antibodies (protein molecules discharged into the blood because of stimulus by such antigens as toxins, foreign proteins, and bacteria). Burnet considered that the basic problem of immunological theory was to determine both the nature of antibody and the conditions under which it will be produced. The difference between immunologically active and inactive molecules is limited to very small, specialized sites by means of which the antibody reacts specifically with antigen.

Burnet spoke about immunological information in the second part of his lecture. A living thing recognizes the difference between self and nonself substances through various chemical structures. Burnet compared this recognition system in organisms to a dictionary—that is, a collection of structures with which a potentially harmful chemical configuration can be compared to decide whether it fits or fails to fit into a particular living thing. "Immunologically competent cells" carry out this function, said Burnet, through being specifically stimulated by contact with a particular antigen. According to his "selective theory," any given antigen has a corresponding set of preformed immunocytes (the short term for the immunologically competent cell), which are then selected to form the antibody for a particular antigen.

In the third section of his lecture, Burnet discussed the evolution of the immune process. Immunity against harmful substances and organisms clearly provides a living thing with an advantage in the struggle to survive, and the question naturally arises of how certain animals developed this powerful mechanism, allowing them to sense the presence of alien materials and to eliminate them. According to Burnet, the mechanism evolved through chance mutations, for when the various elements of this mechanism happened to develop, the living thing could then maintain a surveillance over the "orthodoxy" of its chemical structures by stamping out structural "heresies" before they could spread. For him, this ability of immunological recognition and control is an inevitable consequence of a complex living thing's need for a feedback system to preserve its healthy functioning.

Burnet concluded by noting that immunological tolerance, the loss of the ability by an individual to respond specifically to an antigen, occurs naturally and may be actuated experimentally, as his cowinner Peter Medawar showed by administering an antigen to the fetus of an experimental animal. Although Burnet considered his own part in this discovery "a very minor one," he did formulate the hypothesis that prompted these experiments. At that time immunologists were only beginning their studies of the body's mechanism of self-recognition, but Burnet's hope was that these mechanisms by which structural and functional integrity are maintained might also act like "Ariadne's thread" to guide scientists through the "biological labyrinth" of differentiation—that is, the process by which a single fertilized egg becomes an extremely complex living thing.

Critical reception

Shortly before he won the Nobel Prize, Macfarlane Burnet had received a series of honors that led several scientists to believe that he was ripe for medical science's highest honor. In 1957, he had become a foreign member of the Royal Swedish Academy of Sciences, which increased his visibility to members of the Royal Caroline Institute, the awarders of the medical Nobel Prize. In 1958 he also received the Order of Merit and in 1959 the Copley Medal of the Royal Society, the two highest awards available to a British scientist. In the late 1950's, Burnet's clonal selection theory of antibody formation was being widely discussed and becoming increasingly influential. Despite these indicators of a possible Nobel Prize, Burnet was completely surprised when he was informed that he was the 1960 recipient of "the conventional peak" of the scientific hierarchy of recognition, as he later described it. The reason for his surprise was twofold: First, he had interpreted his election to the Swedish Academy of Sciences as a consolation prize for having lost to others for the Nobel Prize; second, he was a theoretician, and it was experimental discoveries that Alfred Nobel had intended to be rewarded. Nevertheless, Burnet also realized, as the prizes evolved, the trend had been away from experimental and toward theoretical achievements in medical research.

His Nobel Prize was announced in Australia on October 20, 1960, and Burnet learned of it through a telephone call from a Melbourne newspaper. Then came a call from Stockholm, but the poor connection resulted in confusion on Burnet's end, and he did not clearly understand that he had shared the prize with Medawar until he heard it on a British Broadcasting Corporation broadcast. Since he was the first resident Australian to win the Nobel Prize in Physiology or Medicine, the press and journals of the island continent were overwhelmingly favorable toward and proud of Burnet in their reporting and analysis of his award. The Melbourne *Herald* even sent a reporter to accompany Burnet and his family to Stockholm, so that people in Australia would be able to read about the details of their new hero's European adventures.

Because both awardees had been previously honored by the Queen of England and the Royal Society, *The Times* of London for October 21, 1960, noted with approval the further honor for this "Briton and Australian." They quoted Swedish authorities who said that the discovery by Burnet and Medawar of acquired immunological tolerance was "one of the greatest events in the history of immunology and the starting point of a new era in experimental biology." *The Times* also ran a second article, "Step to Grafting Human Tissues," which explained how the laureates' work dealt with one of the most fundamental questions of medicine: how the implantation of foreign cells in an animal embryo allowed the adult animal to develop a tolerance of these alien cells.

The Nobel Prize to Burnet and Medawar was extensively discussed in American newspapers and journals. For example, *The New York Times* for October 21, 1960, quoted with approval the Royal Caroline Institute's acclaim of the researchers for having discovered a solution to a vexing problem that had blocked the replacement of defective organs in animals and humans. Like the London papers, *The New York Times* reported that some cautious attempts to apply the laureates' discoveries to human transplants had already been made. Burnet, in particular, was praised for his idea that a body does not inherit the capacity to recognize tissues as its own, but that it gradually develops this ability during the embryonic period. The article emphasized that the two laureates formed a closely complementary pair, since Burnet's theoretical prediction that immunological tolerance could be acquired if foreign tissues were introduced during the embryonic period was indeed experimentally confirmed by Medawar.

No controversy developed over the award to Burnet and Medawar. Burnet traveled back to Australia from Sweden via India, where he commented: "All the world loves a lover and (apparently) a newly chosen Nobel laureate, or at least so it seemed in Asia." Upon his return to Australia, he was selected as "Australian of the Year" for an important social and political function. Other honors from appreciative Australians followed, and it was some time before he was able to come "down to earth" and return to his scientific work.

Biography

Frank Macfarlane Burnet was born on September 3, 1899, in Traralgon, a small town in the province of Victoria in southeastern Australia. He was the second of six children of Frank Burnet, a bank manager, and of the former Hadassah Pollock MacKay. He was brought up on the Shorter Catechism of the Presbyterian church, and the Calvinist influence of his religious training led him, as he has stated, to concentrate on the genetic influences on human behavior. He was educated at various Victoria schools and at Geelong College (1913-1916), and he completed his medical course at Ormond College of the University of Melbourne, from which he was graduated, second in his class, with a B.S. in 1922 and an M.D. in 1924. In his first professional assignment, he was resident pathologist at the Royal Melbourne Hospital.

In the middle 1920's, he was Beit Fellow in medical research at the Lister Institute of Preventive Medicine in London, where he received his Ph.D. in 1928. Returning to Australia, he became assistant director of the Walter and Eliza Hall Institute for Medical Research in Melbourne (he later became its director from 1944 to 1965). He married Edith Linda Druce, a schoolteacher, on July 10, 1928, a union that produced two daughters and a son. His work at the Hall Institute moved from phages and viruses into immunology and finally into cancer and gerontology. With the exception of several visits to various foreign countries, where he studied and lectured, he did most of his medical research at the Hall Institute.

World War II did not change the basic pattern of his life, though the tempo of his work accelerated. His principal war job was helping develop influenza vaccines. Throughout his professional life, but particularly in the postwar period, he received many offers of distinguished academic positions from English and American institutions, but he preferred to remain at the Hall Institute, from which he retired in 1965. During his retirement years, he continued to do some medical research, but most of his time was dedicated to writing several books on interdisciplinary issues in biology, medicine, ethics, and the humanities. Three years after the death of his first wife, he married Hazel Jenkin. His death from cancer occurred in Melbourne on August 31, 1985.

Scientific Career

Almost all Burnet's scientific career centered on medical research, not from a clinical or chemical perspective but from his distinctive biological viewpoint. The most important theme running through his work in virology, immunology, and gerontology was his application of Darwinian ideas to cellular processes. For him, survival was not only the business of the evolution of species but also intimately involved in viral mechanisms and antibody production. More specifically, his selection theory's basic idea is that differences between antibodies result from the genetic differences among cells producing the antibodies, which was a far different approach from the detailed chemical explanations of such scientists as Linus Pauling. Burnet was, like Pauling, primarily a theoretician, and the conception and development of his theories benefited from his isolation in Australia, where he, a "social misfit" with an extremely "cerebrotonic temperament," could develop his ideas largely protected from the pressures of competition and conformity.

After receiving his M.D. degree in 1924, he became immersed in clinical work, but he also read Felix d'Hérelle's classic work on bacteriophages, the viruses that invade, multiply, and destroy bacteria. This deepened his interest in the biological underpinnings of medicine. Burnet became particularly interested in the genetic relationship between these microorganisms and their hosts. He began to write theoretical papers about them (he once said that he had an uncontrollable urge all of his life to generalize from his particular observations). His time spent working with disease-causing organisms at the Melbourne Hospital revealed to him how little doctors knew about the body and its illnesses. Bacteria were then beyond the control of drugs, and doctors could do little to treat a bacterial disease such as pneumonia. Essentially, they could only wait for the disease to run its course either to recovery or to death.

At the end of his residency, Burnet was firmly convinced that he wanted to go into clinical neurology. Some of his advisers believed, however, that he was much better suited to laboratory work than to a clinical career, and they steered him away from the wards and into the laboratory, which he found suited him perfectly. To further his career as a medical researcher, he went to England for two years to work at the Lister Institute. While a Beit Fellow at this institute, he received a solid education in bacteriophages and a doctorate, which gained for him a senior post at the Hall Institute when he returned to Australia.

In his new position he quickly encountered an opportunity to do research of genuine significance. Twelve children had died after receiving diphtheria vaccinations. In investigating this tragedy, Burnet discovered that the deaths had been caused by contamination of the vaccine sample by staphylococcus, a common bacterium responsible for wound and skin infections. This discovery stimulated him to begin probing the way the body defends itself against such invasions—that is, to discover how antibodies are produced.

During the early 1930's, both as a Rockefeller Fellow at the National Institute for Medical Research in London and at the Hall Institute in Melbourne, Burnet developed a technique for growing viruses in live chick embryos. When certain parts of the membrane of these embryos are spotted with a very weak solution of material suspected of containing a virus (he first used canary-pox virus), these points become round areas of proliferating cells after incubation, if indeed a virus is present. With the use of various dilutions, this technique could also measure the number of virus particles in the sample. Burnet's method became the standard way to study viruses for more than two decades, because egg membrane is very inexpensive and requires little attention (tissue-culture methods supplanted Burnet's procedure in the late 1940's).

From the mid-1930's onward, Burnet and his colleagues investigated outbreaks of influenza, poliomyelitis, and other diseases. Having seen periodic waves of influenza spread around the world every few years, Burnet used his new method of cultivating viruses to discover how each wave of the influenza virus was caused by a mutant of the previous virus. He published papers on variations in the virulence of the influenza virus and on its mutation rates. He also discovered that influenza viruses are able to merge with virus particles of other types, giving rise to new offspring. With the outbreak of a polio epidemic in 1937, he isolated a virus and studied it, showing that it was different from the standard Rockefeller-Institute virus. This was the start of differentiating the polio virus into various types, an important step toward modern methods of vaccination against the disease.

Burnet's work on influenza and polio continued into the war years, since government and military officials were concerned about controlling epidemics during the conflict. He also traveled to the United States to work with an American army research unit at Fort Bragg. While in the United States, he met Linus Pauling, a theoretical physical chemist who had proposed, in 1940, an increasingly influential explanation of how antibodies are produced. Building on earlier theories, Pauling proposed that gamma globulin, a class of plasma proteins that have sites of antibody activity, initially has no immunological properties, but when this long polypeptide chain is brought into contact with an antigen molecule, it folds into a more detailed configuration, and a structure complementary to the antigen is molded. This instructive or template theory, as it came to be called, explained how a highly specific protein (the antibody) could be formed. Burnet, however, with his interest in biology, could not fully understand what Pauling, a structural chemist, was saying. He criticized the Pauling theory not on the basis of the chemical specificity of the antibody but on the basis of the biological production of the entire antibody molecule. Burnet would come to believe that antibody production is a function not only of the cells originally stimulated but also of their descendants—that is, the function of the antigen is to instigate a preexistent (or old) configuration into activity. In Pauling's theory, the antigen impresses a new configuration onto a nascent polypeptide chain.

World War II energized basic research in a number of medical areas of interest to Burnet, including viral diseases and the rejection of skin grafts on burn and wound victims. This work continued after the war. For example, he investigated the disease called Q fever—named, not as many think, for Queensland, where it was first recognized, but for "query," because its causal agent was unknown. Burnet was able to isolate the organism that causes Q fever, now called *Rickettsia burneti* in his honor (*Rickettsia* is a genus of bacteria containing small rod-shaped organisms that, in Q fever, are propagated in sheep and other animals, including humans).

Burnet had long speculated about how a living organism distinguishes self from nonself, and from his work on chick embryos, he began to think that an organism's ability to distinguish its own substances from foreign substances had not yet developed at the embryonic stage. It seemed to him, therefore, that the ability of a chick embryo to form antibodies against foreign proteins might not be inborn. In humans, antibodies against disease develop only after exposure to the microorganism causing the disease. When in the course of life, he wondered, did this ability to resist foreign material develop? If it occurred at the embryonic stage, the immunological tolerance to certain substances might be induced artificially at this stage. After developing these ideas, Burnet published in 1949 the monograph that would later win for him the Nobel Prize. In it he predicted that if an antigen were injected into an animal embryo, then the animal would not form antibodies against the antigen but would instead become tolerant of it. Peter Medawar demonstrated this conclusively in 1953, when he and his coworkers showed that the inoculation of the fetus of an inbred strain of mice with living cells from a different breed (and a future donor) made them tolerant of grafts from these alien donors in later life, a phenomenon Medawar named "acquired immunological tolerance."

During the middle and late 1950's, Burnet developed what many consider his greatest contribution to immunological theory. He himself stated on several occasions that this clonal selection theory of antibody formation was his most important contribution to science. He developed this theory from the work of others. Niels K. Jerne, who, like Burnet, had been a pathologist and an immunologist, proposed in 1955 a selection theory that had considerable influence on Burnet. Jerne's theory, called the natural selection theory, suggested that organisms initially possess very small numbers of a great variety of antibodies against every possible antigen, and when an antigen enters the body, the antibodies capable of binding to it are naturally selected and increase in number. Burnet gave Jerne's theory a cellular foundation: He replaced Jerne's natural antibodies with the cells that produced them and applied Darwinian selection to the antibody-producing cells. What was new in Burnet's theory was the idea that the cell (or, more precisely, a clone of identical cells) is the structure selected to form the antibody for a particular antigen. Each immunocyte is therefore subject to an evolutionary process of selective survival within the internal world of the living thing (just as its species is subject to this process in the external world). At the time of Burnet's proposal in 1957, the cells responsible for reacting with antigens were unknown, although many immunologists were fairly certain that the white blood cells produced large amounts of antibodies. Not until the early 1960's were lymphocytes shown to be reactive with antigen, and not until years later was it proved that each antigen does indeed select a particular clone of lymphocytes, as Burnet had envisioned.

In the years following his proposal, Burnet spread his clonal selection theory through papers, lectures, and conferences in Europe and America. Initially, the clonal selection theory was unpopular, because many scientists found it unreasonable that so many different immunocytes should be produced, even in small quantities, with the capacity to bind to such widely different antigens. Furthermore, chemically trained scientists wanted a structural antibody theory, but Burnet was biologically oriented and paid little attention to chemical specificity. His strategy met with success when such phenomena as booster immunization seemed to confirm his ideas. More specifically, when scientists administered antigens to test animals, not only did the quantity of antibodies increase but their quality increased as well—that is, their affinity for antigen. With the acceptance of Burnet's theory, immunology shifted away from a primarily chemical to a sophisticated biological approach. In 1967, Burnet announced at a scientific meeting that his theory was the new paradigm now directing the theoretical development of immunology. In his later career, Burnet found his main intellectual interest in the nature of aging, especially after he retired from the Hall Institute in 1965. He tried to develop a genetic theory of human aging and wrote some papers and books on the subject. He also became more interested in social, political, and ethical questions. His work in medical research had convinced him that the solutions to most social and political questions must be based on genetics, for several millions of years of evolution had provided living things with much natural wisdom. Diseases and wars were now the causes of much of the world's sufferings, and he wanted to use scientific knowledge in whatever ways he could to minimize these sufferings. His death in 1985 interrupted his thinking about these problems, but some of his writings were published posthumously.

Burnet was an important part of the great discoveries in virology before World War II and of the immunological revolution after it. His peers regarded him as the world's expert on viruses and viral diseases, and he fundamentally changed the knowledge of these diseases and their propagation. Although he did excellent and extensive laboratory work, he was essentially a theoretician, and his theories were, for the most part, couched in biological, Darwinian, and genetic terms, rather than the chemical terms of many of his precursors and contemporaries. Because of some controversies surrounding several of his theories, he himself experienced doubts about his own career and about the world of medicine within which he worked. Many of his critics were strict experimentalists who held that Burnet often went beyond what he could establish in the laboratory, but he believed that science needed both detailed experimental work and highly imaginative speculations. His biological approach to the problem of antibody production met with success. His many discoveries played an important part in the changes in diagnosis and treatment of various human diseases. Influenced by his Presbyterian background, he was sometimes uneasy about his position as a researcher, wondering whether he might have done more good in a clinic. Despite his doubts, his discoveries have been recognized as leading to basic changes in medical practice and to vaccines that have greatly benefited humanity. Ultimately, he saw medicine as primarily concerned with human suffering, and he deeply believed that however involved he might become in his research, he must always return to his responsibility toward his fellow human beings.

Bibliography

Primary

VIROLOGY: *Biological Aspects of Infectious Disease*, 1940 (also as *Natural History of Infectious Disease*, 1953); *The Production of Antibodies: A Review and a Theoretical Discussion*, 1941 (with M. Freeman, A. V. Jackson, and D. Lush), 1949 (with F. Fenner); *Virus as Organism*, 1945; *Viruses and Man*, 1953; *Principles of Animal Virology*, 1955; *Enzyme, Antigen, and Virus*, 1956; *The Viruses*, 1959 (edited, with W. M. Stanley).

IMMUNOLOGY: *The Clonal Selection Theory of Acquired Immunity*, 1959; *Autoimmune Diseases*, 1963 (with I. R. Mackay); *The Integrity of the Body: A Discussion of Modern Immunological Ideas*, 1966; Cellular Immunology, 1969; *Self and Not-Self*, 1969; *Immunological Surveillance*, 1969; *Auto-immunity and Auto-immune Disease*, 1972; *Immunology*, 1976; *Immunology, Aging, and Cancer: Medical Aspects of Mutation and Selection*, 1976.

GENETICS: *Intrinsic Mutagenesis: A Genetic Approach to Ageing*, 1974; *Endurance of Life: The Implications of Genetics for Human Life*, 1978.

BIOLOGY: *Biology and the Appreciation of Life*, 1966; *Genes, Dreams, and Realities*, 1971; *Biological Foundations and Human Nature*, 1983.

HUMANITIES: *Dominant Mammal*, 1970; *Credo and Comment: A Scientist Reflects*, 1979.

AUTOBIOGRAPHY: *Changing Patterns: An Atypical Autobiography*, 1968.

Secondary

Bibel, Debra Jan, ed. *Milestones in Immunology: A Historical Exploration*. Madison, Wis.: Science Tech, 1988. This book, intended for historians of medical science, presents a general account of the history of immunology. Bibel is director of the Metchnikoff Memorial Library in Oakland, California, which possesses a collection of materials on the history of immunology. Her book consists of a series of important immunological papers covering the field from 1880 to the present, each accompanied by an introduction. Though far from being a systematic or comprehensive history of immunology, this book does provide much information about the development of this discipline not previously easily available.

Burnet, Frank Macfarlane. *Changing Patterns: An Atypical Autobiography*. Reprint. New York: Elsevier, 1969. Burnet's autobiography is atypical because it avoids a chronological treatment of his life and work (thus it is not comprehensive) and because it deals with much more than his own experiences (he wanted to show how medicine has changed in the twentieth century). He has thematic chapters dealing with his work on viruses, poliomyelitis, immunological tolerance, clonal selection, and autoimmune disease. Intended for a general audience. There is a curriculum vitae in an appendix as well as a bibliography and an index.

Mazumdar, Pauline M. H., ed. *Immunology, 1930-1980: Essays on the History of Immunology.* Toronto: Wall & Thompson, 1989. Some of the essays in this collection are useful to students of Burnet's thought—for example, G. L. Ada's "The Conception and Birth of Burnet's Clonal Selection Theory" and G. J. V. Nossal's "The Coming of Age of the Clonal Selection Theory." Because of Burnet's far-reaching involvement in immunology, his work is discussed in several of the other articles. The book is distributed by the University of Toronto Press.

Silverstein, Arthur M. *A History of Immunology.* San Diego: Academic Press, 1989. Silverstein, of The Johns Hopkins School of Medicine, has written the only complete history of immunology. It covers the development of the field from 1720 to 1970. Though the book is aimed at young immunologists, its general historical approach makes it readable by those with a modicum of knowledge in the biological sciences. It has three appendices: a calendar of immunological progress, a list of Nobel Prize highlights in immunology, and a biographical dictionary of scientists who contributed significantly to immunology. Also included: a glossary, and a name and subject index.

Stent, Gunther S. *Molecular Genetics: An Introductory Narrative*. 2d ed. San Francisco: W. H. Freeman, 1978. Stent provides an excellent historical introduction to modern molecular genetics, and he discusses Burnet's work in this disciplinary context. The book is intended for readers with two years of undergraduate science training. The book contains extensive references to the scientific literature. Indexed.

Wintrobe, Maxwell M. *Blood, Pure and Eloquent: A Story of Discovery, People, and Ideas*. New York: McGraw-Hill, 1980. This book, containing twenty-one sections written by twenty authors, is designed to tell the story of how the study of blood began, how the understanding of it evolved, and how well it is understood today. Intended both for the layperson and the scientist, it successfully communicates the work of many scientists whose discoveries are in some way related to blood. Burnet's work is discussed by various authors of the sections, all of whom have participated in and contributed to the advances about which they write.

Robert J. Paradowski

1960

Physiology or Medicine
Sir Macfarlane Burnet, Australia
Peter Brian Medawar, Great Britain

Chemistry
Willard Frank Libby, United States

Physics
Donald A. Glaser, United States

Literature
Saint-John Perse, France

Peace
Albert Lutuli, South Africa

PETER BRIAN MEDAWAR
1960

Born: Rio de Janeiro, Brazil; February 28, 1915
Died: London, England; October 2, 1987
Nationality: British
Areas of concentration: Experimental zoology and immunology

Medawar presented the first experimental evidence to sustain the prediction that an animal could be prepared in an experimental manner to make it later able to accept certain foreign substances within its body which it would otherwise reject, a result which Medawar called "immunological tolerance"

The Award

Presentation

Professor S. Gard, member of the faculty of the Royal Caroline Institute, made the presentation speech on Saturday, December 10, 1960, introducing to King Gustav VI Adolf and other eminent guests the corecipients of the Nobel Prize in Physiology or Medicine, Sir Frank Macfarlane Burnet and Peter Brian Medawar. In his introduction, Gard reviewed the history of biological individuality, referring to characteristics such as facial features, manner of motion, fingerprints, and other attributes that distinguish an individual animal from others of its kind. The differences between patterns of biological cells are usually too subtle to be detected by chemical tests, yet they seem to be recognized immediately by some mechanism in the individual organism which acts to neutralize or otherwise counteract invading foreign materials. Hence, when grafting of tissue in an animal is attempted, the operation often results in rejection, depending on the origin of the tissue being grafted.

It was Burnet's insight to predict that an individual might be experimentally transformed or adapted to make him later amenable to foreign substances that he might otherwise reject. Medawar and his coworkers were the first to provide experimental evidence to sustain Burnet's prediction, so the recognition by the Nobel Committee of Burnet and Medawar together was particularly appropriate.

Medawar performed grafting experiments on twin calves to support Burnet's theory and to indicate that grafting of tissue was a system of testing well suited to corroborate the theory. Experiments were carried out on mice, for which a large number of genetically homogeneous lines are available. Mouse embryos in the womb were inoculated with foreign tissues to develop in them an immunological tolerance to the substances introduced. Grafting of tissue was then performed on the mice after they had matured, and it was shown that the transformed mice accepted not only their own tissue as grafts but also foreign tissue of the same immunological variety as that which was introduced into the fetus.

The result, Gard stated, has been the opening of a new chapter in the history of experimental biology and the nature of zoological immunity: "Immunological tolerance," as Medawar called it, meant an enlargement of the content of the "self" components of the animal body by experimental methods to include foreign components that previously would have been rejected.

Nobel lecture

Medawar's lecture, delivered on Monday, December 12, 1960, was entitled "Immunological Tolerance," which he said might be described as a state of nonreactivity toward a substance that would normally be expected to excite an immunological response. This latter term, "immunological response," he illustrated by an example. If living cells from a mouse of a certain strain, designated as strain A, are injected into a mouse of a different strain (call this strain B), the cells of strain A will be destroyed by an immunological response within the body of the mouse of strain B. If the strain A cells are injected into an unborn fetus of strain B, however, they are for some reason accepted. In addition, Medawar found that when the strain B mouse matured from the injected fetus, it would accept any later graft of tissue from a strain A donor as if it were its own strain B tissue. The strain B mouse is then said to have acquired an immunological tolerance for strain A cells or tissue.

Medawar explained fetal acceptance in the following way. The blood systems of fetal twins—twin cattle for example—are homogenous to the extent that fetal twins can have a prolonged exchange of blood before birth. It follows that the fetal twins must exchange red-cell precursors, not only red blood cells, in their mutual transfusion before birth. They thus develop an immunological tolerance to each other's red cells, a fact discovered in 1945 by Ray David Owen. A few years after this, Medawar and coworkers showed that such fetal twins would accept skin grafts from each other as well. They then began to reproduce in the laboratory the very same state of affairs that had occurred in nature in the fetal twins, a phenomenon called chimerism. In 1953, chimerism was shown to occur naturally in human twins. It followed that human chimeric twins could accept skin grafts from each other.

Medawar then found that the state of immunological tolerance prevailed throughout the body: If any one part of the body tolerated foreign grafts, so would any other part. He also found that the state of tolerance was specific in the sense that tolerance for grafts from one individual did not imply tolerance for grafts from a second individual unrelated to the first. Further work showed that injection of white cells or lymphoid cells could confer tolerance of skin grafts and thyroid tissue grafts as well as of grafts of ovaries, kidneys, and adrenal glands.

The immunological defenses of the body are directed against foreign materials, called antigens. Burnet (the corecipient of the prize with Medawar) predicted that antigens inoculated into an animal sufficiently early in its life (in the fetal state, for example) should come to be accepted as if they were its own. The literature indicates that a mammalian infant may be especially tolerant of antigens originating in its mother.

Medawar said that Burnet and he had agreed upon a "division of labor," which absolved Medawar from speculating on the causes of this tolerance. Burnet, in his

Nobel address, delivered immediately preceding Medawar's, discussed such theoretical aspects of immunological tolerance.

Critical reception

The award of the 1960 Nobel Prize in Physiology or Medicine, made jointly to Sir Frank Macfarlane Burnet of the University of Melbourne, Australia, and Peter Brian Medawar of University College, London, England, was in recognition of their discovery of a fundamental revision in the theory of immunity, said the *Scientific American* in its account of the awards in its December, 1960, issue. The article went on to say that Burnet in 1949 proposed that immunity is not inherited but is acquired during the embryonic period. Medawar confirmed Burnet's proposal in 1953 in a series of skin graft experiments with mice. They found that mice of strain A, when inoculated in the embryo with cells from mice of strain B, acquired a tolerance for the foreign cells and would accept skin grafts from strain B after birth.

The New York Times for October 21, 1960, observed that Burnet was regarded as one of the world's great experts on viruses and virus diseases and that his predictions of immunological patterns of tolerance had been confirmed experimentally by Medawar. Medawar showed that immunity developed in the embryo and that full tolerance was reached only some time after birth. The problem with grafts from other animals had been that such grafts often appeared to take hold satisfactorily for several days but almost invariably began to decay and slough off eventually. Prior inoculation in the embryonic state, however, could make such grafts be accepted permanently. The article cautioned that this was still work in the pioneering stage and that much research was still needed. If such work were to be finally successful, however, a defective human body could perhaps be rebuilt by transplanting tissue and organs from another body.

Time magazine for October 31, 1960, said that Burnet shared the Nobel Prize "with towering (6 ft., 4-1/2 in.) British zoologist Peter Brian Medawar who has been working on tissue transplants for the past 17 years." *Time* said that Medawar was the first to solve the puzzle of the rejection reaction. *Time* observed further that the Burnet-Medawar discovery had no direct medical use but that it represents "a long step closer to the day dreamed of by many doctors when surgeons will be able to shift hearts, lungs, kidneys, and even limbs, from one body to another."

Science for November 4, 1960, noted that Medawar gave particular credit to coworkers Rupert Billingham and Leslie Brent, who were first his students and later his colleagues. *Science* further reported that since the confirmation of Burnet's theory by Medawar it had been found that X rays and cortisone can cause similar tolerance to foreign tissue in an adult animal that has not received prenatal treatment.

Biography

Peter Brian Medawar was born in Rio de Janeiro, Brazil, on February 28, 1915. His father, Nicholas Medawar, a native of Lebanon, was a naturalized British citizen temporarily residing in Brazil. Medawar had his schooling at Marlborough College, Marlborough, Wiltshire, England, in the pleasant valley of the river Kennet.

In 1932, he went to Magdalen College of the University of Oxford, where he studied zoology with J. Z. Young. He received his bachelor's degree at Oxford, and he stayed on to work in Lord Howard Walter Florey's school of pathology. The great Australian pathologist aroused an interest in medicine in Medawar. He was a Christopher Welch Scholar at Magdalen College, and in 1938 he became a Fellow of Magdalen. Medawar married Jean Shinglewood Taylor, the daughter of a Cambridge physician, in 1937; they had two sons, Charles and Alexander, and two daughters, Caroline and Louise. In 1942 he won the Rolleston Prize; in 1944 he became a senior research fellow and University Demonstrator in Zoology and Comparative Anatomy at St. John's College, Oxford. From 1947 to 1951, he was Mason Professor of Zoology at the University of Birmingham, England. He then became Jodrell Professor of Zoology at the University College, London University, where he served from 1951 to 1962, when he was appointed director of the National Institute for Medical Research in London. He served in this position from 1962 to 1971 and became Director Emeritus in 1975.

The Royal Society of London, where he was the Croonian Lecturer in 1958, elected him a Fellow in 1949 and gave him its Royal Medal in 1959. Also in 1959 he was Reith Lecturer for the British Broadcasting Corporation. He was elected a foreign member of the New York Academy of Sciences, the American Academy of Arts and Sciences, and the U.S. National Academy of Science. Other honors he has received include the Copley Medal (1969) and honorary degrees from the universities of Cambridge, Liège, Aston, Birmingham, Hull, Glasgow, Alberta, Dundee, Dalhousie, British Columbia, Chicago, Exeter, Southampton, and London. Medawar died in London on October 2, 1987.

Scientific Career

Medawar's original research at the University of Oxford was done on tissue culture, regeneration of peripheral nerves, and the mathematical analysis of the changes of shape of organisms that occur during this development.

During World War II, at Oxford, Medawar studied ways of uniting the ends of severed nerves, and he achieved fame by devising a biological cement to accomplish this purpose. Also during World War II, he was asked by the British Medical Research Council to investigate the healing of wounds and to find out why skin taken from one human donor would seldom graft permanently onto another human body. In this work, Medawar proposed theorems of transplantation immunity that led him to further experimental work in this area. He moved to Birmingham in 1947, where he continued the same work. In collaboration with Rupert Everett Billingham, the lecturer in the department of zoology there (later professor of zoology at the University of Pennsylvania, Philadelphia), he studied pigmentation and skin grafting in cattle and the use of skin grafting in distinguishing types of twins.

Medawar has said that the first example of what he called immunological tolerance was the remarkable discovery in 1945 by Ray David Owen that twin cattle are born with a stable mixture of each other's red blood cells. As a consequence, he said, "the twin cattle must have exchanged red-cell precursors and not merely red cells in their mutual transfusion before birth." It also followed that defensive mechanisms such as macrophages (tissue cells originating in the bone marrow that function as the body's response to invading foreign matter) may also be exchanged and perhaps neutralized.

In 1951, in collaboration with Billingham (then research fellow in zoology at University College, London) and other coworkers, Medawar published various papers on skin grafting and its use in distinguishing different types of twins in cattle. In one report they said that thirty-six out of forty-two cattle twins were completely tolerant to skin grafts from their respective twins, whereas grafts from mother to offspring were not tolerated. They had not begun with the idea of studying immunological tolerance, but rather hoping to find a method of distinguishing various types of cattle twins. They found that only monozygotic twins—twins from the same egg—are completely tolerant to grafts of each other's skin.

The connection between Owen's discovery and their own was obvious, Medawar said. In addition, Frank Macfarlane Burnet had read a general significance into Owen's discovery and come up with a general theory of the tolerance. Tolerance must be a consequence of an alteration in the host. This alteration was found to occur most effectively in the fetal animal, and, once established, the state of tolerance existed throughout the animal's system. If one part of the body would tolerate a foreign graft, any other part of the same body would as well. Medawar also found that the state of tolerance is specific to one individual: An animal tolerant to grafts from one individual donor would not accept grafts from a different individual donor. He found that the injection of blood cells into the fetus can also confer tolerance of skin grafts after birth.

Medawar recognized that Burnet was the first to attempt to explain this tolerance by his idea that foreign tissue, such as antigens, injected into an animal early in its life (as in the fetal state) could be accepted by the host as if they were its own tissue. This would be expected to be especially true in cases where the gestation period is relatively long, as is the case with cattle and with humans.

Medawar cautioned that tolerance was becoming a testing ground for other theories of immune response and that far too much was still uncertain about it. Dangers exist in such studies—for example, in the fact that the permeation of the fetus by foreign substances that gain access through the mother might weaken the resistance of the fetus to infectious diseases later. Thus he recommended that traffic between maternal and fetal blood circulatory systems should be closely observed and controlled.

Modern molecular biology and the biochemistry of immunity have made great progress since Medawar's work, but he was among the pioneers who made scientists realize that there is indeed such a field open to investigation. Antibodies, or immunoglobulins, are now being studied with regard to their specificity of binding with a wide variety of molecules, and they are seen to constitute a critical element in the immune system. If the immune system functions properly, no antibodies are produced against the individual's own cells or proteins; Medawar's work showed how to suppress antibody production against foreign tissue in the fetal state.

Medawar also had a great interest in the philosophy of science. He published a number of books that dealt with the subject later in his career, among them *The Art of the Soluble* (1967) and *Pluto's Republic* (1982). Medawar's own philosophy was greatly (and admittedly) influenced by twentieth century British philosopher Sir Karl Raimund Popper. Popperian influences can be seen in Medawar's disparagement of the so-called scientific method and his denigration of induction, or inductivism—a method of logical reasoning from the particular to the universal. (Popper once stated that in his view "there is no such thing as induction.") Medawar wrote that the idea of science being completely accountable to reason "is no longer believed in by most people who have thought deeply about the nature of the scientific process." He believed that science begins in speculation rather than observation. Advances in scientific understanding, he stated, "begin with a speculative adventure, an imaginative preconception of what might be true."

Bibliography

Primary

BIOLOGY: "The Use of Skin Grafting to Distinguish Between Monozygotic and Dizygotic Twins in Cattle," *Heredity*, vol. 5, 1951, pp. 379-397 (with D. Anderson, R. E. Billingham, and G. H. Lampkin); "Tolerance to Homografts, Twin Diagnosis, and the Freemartin Condition in Cattle," *Heredity*, vol. 6, 1952, pp. 201-212 (with Billingham, Lampkin, and H. L. Williams); "Actively Acquired Tolerance of Foreign Cells," *Nature*, vol. 172, 1953, pp. 603-606 (with Billingham and L. Brent); *The Uniqueness of the Individual*, 1957; *Recent Advances in the Immunology of Transplantation: Genetics and the Future of Man*, 1968.

EDITED TEXT: *Essays on Growth and Form*, 1945 (with Clark).

PHILOSOPHY OF SCIENCE: *The Art of the Soluble*, 1967; *Pluto's Republic*, 1982; *Aristotle to Zoos: A Philosophical Dictionary of Biology*, 1983.

Secondary

Bibel, Debra Jan. *Milestones in Immunology: A Historical Exploration*. Madison, Wis.: Science Tech, 1988. Part 7, "Immunogenetics," discusses Medawar's work in 1944 on the behavior and fate of skin grafts in rabbits and his 1953 work on actively acquired tolerance of foreign cells. The papers and a summary are included. Medawar's paper, with R. E. Billingham and L. Brent, was published in *Nature* (vol. 172, 1953, pp. 603-606), and it discusses actively acquired tolerance of foreign cells and includes the results of skin-grafting experiments.

Cunningham, Alastair J. *Understanding Immunology*. New York: Academic Press, 1978. A table of ideas in immunology includes Medawar's work on self-tolerance by grafting cells. The mechanism of transplantation tolerance is illustrated with a figure. Other possible mechanisms of tolerance are also illustrated with figures.

Hood, L. E., I. L. Weissman, W. B. Wood, and J. H. Wilson. *Immunology.* Menlo Park, Calif.: Benjamin/Cummings, 1984. Clonal selection underlies tolerance. Organisms typically do not mount immune responses against their own macromolecules and are thus said to be tolerant of their own antigenic determinants. Subject matter is organized into thirteen chapters, such as "Immune System" and "Antibodies." Chapter 8, "Immune Response," surveys the cellular biology of vertebrate immunological response. Chapter 10, "Tolerance," analyzes the regulation of immunity and considers in detail the development of immunological tolerance.

Klein, Jan. *Immunology: The Science of Self-Nonself Discrimination.* New York: John Wiley & Sons, 1982. Chapter 2, "The History of Immunology," includes an "immunological hall of fame." Medawar's work on artificial induction of immunological tolerance is included; a figure illustrates the principles he discovered.

Nossal, G. J. V. *Antibodies and Immunity.* New York: Basic Books, 1978. Chapter 12, "Immunological Tolerance," discusses the Nobel Prizes awarded to immunologists: E. A. von Behring (1901); Élie Metchnikoff and Paul Ehrlich (1908); Karl Landsteiner (1930); F. M. Burnet and Peter Medawar (1960); and G. M. Edelman and R. R. Porter (1972). Medawar's work in World War II on skin grafts for burn patients is included in the discussion.

Joseph Albert Schufle

1961

Physiology or Medicine

Georg von Békésy, Hungary and United States

Chemistry

Melvin Calvin, United States

Physics

Robert Hofstadter, United States
Rudolf Ludwig Mössbauer, West Germany

Literature

Ivo Andrić, Yugoslavia

Peace

Dag Hammarskjöld, Sweden

GEORG VON BÉKÉSY
1961

Born: Budapest, Austro-Hungarian Empire; June 3, 1899
Died: Honolulu, Hawaii; June 13, 1972
Nationality: Hungarian; later, American
Area of concentration: Aural physiology

Georg von Békésy studied the detection and analysis of sound by the human ear. He discovered how the inner ear transforms the mechanical vibrations of sound into electrical impulses by which the brain can distinguish pitch; he was also instrumental in the discovery of treatments for various forms of deafness

The Award

Presentation

Professor Carl Gustaf Bernhard, member of the Staff of Professors of the Royal Caroline Institute, represented the Royal Swedish Academy of Sciences in delivering the presentation address for the Nobel Prize in Physiology or Medicine awarded to Georg von Békésy on December 10, 1961. The address began with Bernhard commenting on von Békésy's initial interest in how a ship's foghorn could be heard for many miles at sea while being inaudible in the cabin of the ship. This effect is similar to the human ear's high sensitivity to sounds coming from outside and low sensitivity to the sound produced from a nearby source within the body. He pointed out the extremely large range of the human hearing ability, which can almost record the bouncing of an air molecule against the eardrum while being able to withstand the pounding of strong sound waves that can set the body to vibrating. At the same time, the ear can selectively analyze words as well as instrumental and vocal expressions.

Bernhard proceeded to explain the mechanism of hearing, emphasizing the different parts that are essential in hearing, such as the ossicle chain (the subtle system of levers), the cochlea (a long, coiled tube in the fluid-filled inner ear), and the receptors (the sense cells). He also stressed the contributions of the scientists before von Békésy who set the foundations of acoustics, such as Hermann von Helmholtz. At that point he praised von Békésy's unique work, which combined physics and anatomy and justified the earlier scientists' assumptions that the "frequency of the sound waves determines the location along the basilar membrane at which stimulation occurs." Those findings were determined via model experiments that gave a clear insight of the overall mechanism.

He finally pointed out the effect that von Békésy's work had in audiology and its clinical application in treating the diseases of the ear. Bernhard closed his address by expressing his satisfaction that this award was being given according to Alfred Nobel's wish that "the prize [should be awarded] for outstanding discoveries which are entirely the result of one single scientist's work."

Nobel lecture

On December 11, 1961, Georg von Békésy opened his address, entitled "Concerning the Pleasures of Observing, and the Mechanics of the Inner Ear," by giving credit to Helmholtz's book *Die Lehre von den Tonempfindungen*, published in 1863. That work became the main source in the area of acoustics, since the field went through a period of stagnation that lasted almost one hundred years. The whole field made very little progress during that period in comparison with other fields of physics. Strangely enough, the concepts of waves and acoustics served new theories in the meantime: for example, the wave postulated by Ernst Mach was the model for the light radiation discoveries that earned for Pavel A. Cherenkov, Ilya M. Frank, and Igor Tamm the Nobel Prize in Physics in 1958.

He then proceeded to explain his own observations. First he demonstrated the extremely small vibration amplitudes that are detected by the human ear. He pointed out the role of the amplifier invention that provided a way to measure these small amplitudes. Von Békésy surprised his audiences by showing illustrations of several ancient statues and artifacts to prove his point that nature cannot be outdone by human fantasy but that instead, man should learn from nature. That, he said, would lead to the production of "something of enduring interest." He described his initial scientific experience with the malfunctioning of the telephone lines in Hungary and his efforts to localize the disturbance, comparing this to the musician who tests his violin by plucking a string and tuning it at the same time.

His next endeavor was to improve the sound quality of telephone communication. He started by comparing the human eardrum and the telephone earphone and showed, by means of a graph, the unquestionable superiority of the ear. He pointed out that at the time of his initial research, there was a general belief that the mechanical properties of the tissues of the ear changed rapidly after death and that there was therefore no chance of determining the mechanical properties of the inner ear of man. As a result, he started working with the eardrum first. He considered it the most sensitive part of the inner ear. He noticed that the amplitude of oscillations, their resonant frequencies, and the change in their decay could be precisely measured and that those same vibrations showed no change when applied to a metallic membrane for days.

The next problem he confronted was the analysis of the traveling wave. He observed that when a tuning fork was struck by an object of internal elasticity, waves could be detected traveling from the vibrator to the edge of the object and were then reflected back. A sensitive experiment using the inner ear of a guinea pig (as large as a drop of water at the end of an eye dropper) provided evidence that over the lower frequency range the ordinary bending of the basilar membrane produced vibrations that stimulated the nerve endings. Moreover, the vibration pattern seemed to be quite stable irrespective of whether the wall of the spiral canal of the inner ear, known as the cochlea, was open. He then proceeded building an enlarged model of the cochlea and attempted to apply his theory to it. The model consisted of a plastic tube filled with water and a membrane 30 centimeters in length. When stimulated with a vibration, traveling waves similar to those seen with the normal human ear were detected. As a nerve supply, he used his arm against the model and showed that the ear has a frequency analyzer that produces a subsequent sharpening of the sensation area.

He concluded his address by suggesting that every local stimulus in contact with the skin provides strong inhibition around the place of stimulation, not only for the ear and the skin but also for the retina. As a result, von Békésy expressed the hope that one day physiology would realize that there are some chapters in common between eye, ear, and skin and that this would lead to "a simplification of the descriptions of the sense organs."

Critical reception

Von Békésy received the Nobel Prize in a decade that also saw the prize given to another scientist who worked on the human organs that provide senses: Haldan Keffer Hartline, for his work on visual receptors and retinal interaction in 1967. *The New York Times* (October 20, 1961) announced von Békésy's selection by the Royal Caroline Institute on the first page, with the indication that a prize of $48,300 accompanied the award. It also pointed out that Helmholtz's theory (stating that the basilar membrane in the inner ear contained fibers which were activated much like strings of a piano) was actually replaced by von Békésy's theory. The article quoted a spokesman from the Royal Caroline Institute stating that the selection was a result of von Békésy's "discoveries concerning the physical mechanisms of stimulation within the cochlea" and his numerous other contributions, such as the audiometer—a device that tests the hearing function. It also added that there is hardly any problem concerning the physical mechanics of acoustic stimulation to which von Békésy has not added clarity. A separate article in that same issue announced his winning an honor from the Deafness Research Foundation in New York. At a luncheon at the Waldorf-Astoria Hotel, he was cited for his "pioneering investigations into the nature of hearing and auditory problems" by Dr. Gordon D. Hoople, medical adviser of the foundation. A third article, entitled "Scientist in Sound: Georg von Békésy," in the same issue described his life. A citation awarded him by the Acoustical Society of America in May, 1961, described him as "physicist, anatomist, physiologist and experimenter." It declared that the modern ear seems almost "as much a matter of Békésy's contrivance as it is of nature's patient evolution."

A correspondent from *The Times* of London (October 20, 1961) announced the selection with an article entitled "Helper of Deaf Wins Nobel Prize." Together with a biographic abstract came the acknowledgment that he "is regarded as probably the greatest living expert on the mechanism of the inner ear." Another article in *The Times* (on October 23, 1961) ended by noting von Békésy's belief that the difference between successful and unsuccessful research is basically a problem of asking the right question.

As a Nobel Prize recipient, Georg von Békésy was unique. He was the only one until the mid-1970's to have been working in a university until his retirement without being a professor. Only ten out of ninety-two laureates (including von Békésy) permanently based in the United States at the time they received their awards changed their affiliations in the five years following the prize. Only he and Joshua Lederberg chose not to list their Nobel Prizes in *American Men and Women of Science*. Finally, the *Medical Tribune* (January 17, 1973), six months after his death, announced that von Békésy had named the Nobel Foundation heir to his estate of $400,000 in art objects—about ten times the amount he had received from his prize. The Nobel Foundation in turn placed his art collection on public exhibition for the first time on December 9, 1974.

Biography

Georg von Békésy, the son of Alexander von Békésy, a member of the diplomatic service, and Paula Mazaly von Békésy, was born in Budapest, Hungary, then part of the Austro-Hungarian Empire, on June 3, 1899. He had a brother and a sister who lived all of their lives in Hungary. He received his early education in Munich, Constantinople, Budapest and in a private school in Zurich. After completing his high school education in Budapest, he enrolled at the University of Bern in Switzerland (1916-1920) and later at the University of Budapest, where he earned a Ph.D. in physics in 1923. He then proceeded to work as a communications engineer at the Hungarian telephone system for twenty-three years. He worked for one year at the central laboratory of Siemens and Halske A.G. in Berlin, which at the time was one of the centers of development of telecommunications. In 1946 he emigrated to Sweden, where he worked at the Royal Caroline Institute in Stockholm and at the Royal Institute of Technology. A year later he went to Harvard University as a research lecturer; he was later promoted to the rank of senior research fellow in psychophysics, and he remained there until 1966.

Georg von Békésy was never married and had no offspring. Extremely dedicated to his work, he was known to stay at the laboratory from nine in the morning to ten o'clock at night. He used to eat lunch at work and dinner at a restaurant before he walked home. According to a report in *The Times* of London, his verbal command of the English language upon his arrival in the United States in 1947 was negligible, although he could read the language well. In a very short time, however, he managed to speak it fluently ("with a Hungarian accent supplemented by expressive gestures") and published practically all of his subsequent publications in English. His main hobby was the collection of primitive art pieces. According to a reporter of the *Sunday News* (October 29, 1961), he looked "like the little, pale, stoop-shouldered, anonymous man you often see hunched over a foreign-language newspaper . . . in the Automat or on the Lexington Avenue IRT." He was an unassuming man with gray hair, light blue eyes, and a small mustache. He claimed to like the lonely life, maintaining that "concentration on one field is possible only if you are lonely to a certain degree."

In 1966, von Békésy left Harvard University for the University of Hawaii, where he worked as a professor of sensory sciences until the time of his death on June 13, 1972, at the age of seventy-three.

Scientific Career

Georg von Békésy was fortunate to have been born into a well-to-do family. He obtained his baccalaureate degree in chemistry at the University of Bern, after having passed the Swiss *Maturitätsprüfung*. He remained in science despite the brief military service he had to go through upon his return to Budapest. His interest in sound and the ear first developed when he heard high-pitched gypsy music as a boy in his native Hungary. He later decided to devote his life in this field, after earning his Ph.D. at the University of Budapest in 1923. His doctoral research in physics at Budapest was in a branch of optics known as interference microscopy, and he first tried to find a position in optics. Such jobs were scarce at the time, however, so he elected to work as a communications engineer in the research laboratory of the Hungarian telephone system (at the time, this was a division of the postal service). This was the only laboratory that was still equipped after World War I. It had financial support because the government was forced by postwar treaties to maintain the telephone and telegraph lines that crisscrossed the country. Although the laboratory did not have an open position for a physicist at the time, he was still hired, but at a small salary.

Von Békésy's question at the time was, "How much better is the ear than the telephone system?" To determine how much of a sound range a new cable should be capable of relaying, he decided to investigate how the human ear receives sound. The newly installed Hungarian telephone system was directly connected to many European countries, and any failures in the national system created international complaints. His first major project was to determine which of the three basic components was primarily responsible for the malfunctions—the sending microphones, the transmitting line, or the receiving earphones. After some preliminary work, von Békésy realized that the fault lay in the earphones, whose membranes produced much greater distortions of vibration than those of the eardrum. As a result, he became directly involved with the investigation of the hearing phenomenon.

Hearing occurs when sound waves enter the ear and strike the eardrum, creating vibrations that pass the leverlike bones of the middle ear and are transmitted to the cochlea. The cochlea is divided lengthwise into two sections by the basilar membrane, which carries specialized hair cells that transmit the vibrations to the nerve fibers of the auditory nerve. By the mid-1920's, the anatomy of the ear was fairly well documented; the problem concerned the way the basilar membrane responds to sound pressure. Helmholtz's theory stated that each fiber has its natural period of vibration and responds to a sound that vibrates in that natural period. Since any sound is a combination of pure vibrations, it would vibrate a combination of fibers that would send the message to the brain.

Research on the ear was very difficult at the time, since it was generally believed that the ear tissues deteriorated rapidly upon death. Von Békésy discovered that this was true only if the tissues were dehydrated and that the properties remained pretty much intact as long as the ears from cadavers were kept in an environment that provided 100 percent humidity. He used a special underwater microscope to observe the progress of his work closely. Most of the work was done on the acoustic organs of guinea pigs that were smaller than those of the human being, and von Békésy was forced to develop microsurgical tools that would not irreversibly destroy the various components of the middle and inner ear. He earned a reputation of being a nuisance to the autopsy rooms and local hospitals, as well as at the mechanical workshops of the post office. Workers were often confronted with a drill-press full of human bone dust upon their arrival at work in the morning. He managed, however, to be on friendly terms with most everyone through his warm personality.

The first paper he published in 1928 proved to be the turning point of his scientific career. In it, he discussed the pattern of vibration in the membranes of the cochlea of the ear; this became the platform on which he based all of his studies on the mechanics of the ear.

The second task he had to accomplish was to establish the way the basilar membrane moves upon sound wave impact. At the time, there were four theories: A tone would make part of the membrane vibrate; it would make the whole membrane vibrate; it would send a traveling wave down the length of the membrane; or it would be reflected back to create a standing wave. Von Békésy devised a model membrane out of rubber and showed that the vibrations in the basilar membrane are traveling waves. He also demonstrated that the fact that the basilar membrane is not uniform (it is stretched at its base and wider and floppier at the apex of the cochlea) is responsible for the differentiation of high- and low-pitched sounds, since the brain receives information about the location from nerve fibers in the cochlea.

Georg von Békésy continued his work with the Hungarian post office until the end of World War II, except for a year of work at the central laboratory of Siemens and Halske A.G. in Berlin (1926-1927), at the time a center in the development of communication technology. In 1939, he was named professor of experimental physics at the University of Budapest while still working for the post office.

In 1946, he went to Sweden and worked on his research at the Royal Caroline Institute under Y. Zotterman. It was at that time that he developed a new type of audiometer, a hearing device that could be operated by the patient and that has applications outside the field of hearing. One year later, he emigrated to the United States and started working at Harvard University's psychoacoustic laboratory. There he developed an enlarged model of the cochlea and attempted to show how sound travels in the ear. The model consisted of a water-filled plastic tube with a piston in one end that produced traveling waves through the fluid and along the membrane. He simulated the spiral membrane in the body canal of the cochlea (known also as the organ of Corti) by placing his arm on the tube. He decided that, although the traveling waves ran along the whole length of the membrane with almost the same amplitude, only a one-inch section was vibrating. He concluded, therefore, that nervous inhibition must play an important role in the way it is perceived.

Von Békésy continued his research on the biomechanics of the cochlea, and his work led to significant advances in the diagnosis and development of methods for the treatment of hearing disorders. As a result, microsurgeons have been able to develop ways of constructing new eardrums of skin or vein tissue and are able to replace small bones of the ear with plastic parts.

Von Békésy retired from Harvard in 1966 and became a professor of sensory sciences at the University of Hawaii—an endowed chair provided by the Hawaiian telephone company. He continued his research in trying to establish the similarities between hearing and the other senses in a new laboratory that was built for him. He remained there almost until the day of his death in 1972. The obituary column in *The Washington Post* of June 6, 1972, described his achievements as "a scientific basis for advances in the treatment of deafness and a tremendous contribution to the knowledge of acoustics." One day later, *The Times* of London announced his death with the indication that his work had made it possible to differentiate among certain forms of deafness and to select the proper treatment more accurately.

The first recognition of von Békésy's work came in the early 1930's, with honors including the Denker Prize (1931), the Leibnitz Medal of the Berlin Akademie der Wissenschaften (1937), the Guyot Prize for Speech and Otology (1939), the Academy Award of the Hungarian Academy of Science in Budapest (1946), the Shambaugh Prize in Otology (1950), the Warren Medal of the Society of Experimental Physiologists (1955), the gold medals of the American Otological Society (1957) and the Acoustical Society of America (1961), as well as the Achievement Award of the Deafness Research Foundation (1961). He was awarded honorary M.D. degrees from Wilhelm University, Münster (1955), the University of Bern (1959), the University of Padua (1962), and the University of Budapest (1969). Honorary doctorate degrees were awarded by Gustavus Adolphus College (1963) and the universities of Pennsylvania (1965), Buenos Aires (1968), Córdoba (1968), and Hawaii (1968). He was a member of the American Academy of Arts and Sciences and the U.S. National Academy of Sciences.

Georg von Békésy's numerous publications included three books: *Hearing: Its Psychology and Physiology* (1938), *Experiments in Hearing* (1960), and *Sensory Inhibition* (1967). The second book is a compilation of his papers from a period of thirty years (from 1928 to 1958), considered models of technical skill and clarity. His third book gives a detailed picture of the inhibitory interactions of hearing, vision, taste, and skin senses.

Georg von Békésy was an ardent lover of art. Music and sculpture were an important part of his life to the extent that he integrated them into his Nobel Prize lecture. One of his last papers dealt with the study of contour and contrast effects present in Oriental art. His comment upon his first view of the organ of Corti is reported in his *Biographical Memoirs*: "I found the inner ear so beautiful under a stereoscopic microscope that I decided I would just stay with that problem. It was the beauty and the pleasure of beauty that made me stick to the ear."

Bibliography

Primary

PHYSIOLOGY: "Über den Einfluss der nichtlinearen Eisenverzerrungen auf die

Güte und Verständlichkeit eines Telephonie-Übertragungssystemes," *Elektrische Nachrichten-Technik*, vol. 5, 1928, pp. 231-246; *Hearing: Its Psychology and Physiology*, 1938; *Experiments in Hearing*, 1960 (edited by E. G. Wever); *Sensory Inhibition*, 1967. A complete list of von Békésy's publications is given in *Biographical Memoirs*, vol. 48, published by the National Academy of Sciences (1976).

Secondary

Asimov, Isaac. *Asimov's Biographic Encyclopedia of Science and Technology*. 2d rev. ed. Garden City, N.Y.: Doubleday, 1982. This book contains the biographies of thousands of scientists whose pioneer work helped establish today's advancements in technology. Von Békésy's entry is a short biography that gives a concise but clear outline of his career and his contributions in science.

"Georg von Békésy." In *Current Biography Yearbook, 1962*, edited by Charles Moritz. New York: H. W. Wilson, 1962. An excellent article that presents a good description of Georg von Békésy's life, outlines his discovery, and justifies his earning the Nobel Prize. It also gives several references, mostly newspaper articles with rare interviews. The 1972 *Cumulative Index* issue includes a short paragraph announcing his death.

National Academy of Sciences (U.S.). *Biographical Memoirs*. Vol. 48. Washington, D.C.: Author, 1976. This book contains an excellent biography of von Békésy, written by Floyd Ratliff, that includes a description of his passion for the mechanism of hearing and his primitive art collection, a list of his honors, and a complete listing of his publications.

Nobelstiftelsen. *Nobel: The Man and His Prizes*. New York: Elsevier, 1972. Discusses in general the contributions of each of the Nobel laureates and the politics behind their election. In a short paragraph (pp. 267-268), the justification for the Nobel Prize award to von Békésy is presented by outlining his discovery and its importance in people's lives.

____________. *Physiology or Medicine, 1942-1962*. Amsterdam: Elsevier, 1964. This series of volumes contains the presentation speeches during the award ceremonies for the Nobel Prize recipients. The section on von Békésy (pp. 719-748) contains the presentation speech by C. G. Bernhard, member of the Staff of Professors of the Royal Caroline Institute and the acceptance speech of von Békésy, which includes several figures and a two-page biography.

Schlessinger, Bernard S., and June H. Schlessinger. *Who's Who in Nobel Prize Winners*. Phoenix: Oryx Press, 1986. This is a concise biography of all Nobel Prize recipients that includes selected publications, main jobs, and awards, as well as some details on their private life. It concludes with a "commentary" that justifies awarding the scientist.

Tyler, Wasson, ed. *Nobel Prize Winners*. New York: H. W. Wilson, 1987. This book contains biographies of all Nobel Prize recipients up to 1987. Von Békésy's biography describes his methods of study of the hearing mechanism and includes selected works and other references about his biography.

Zuckerman, Harriet. *Scientific Elite: Nobel Laureates in the United States*. New York: Free Press, 1977. Discusses general details of American Nobel laureates, such as their ages at full professorship, their affiliations at the time of their winning the award, and the final position they held. Discusses Békésy's decision to appoint the Nobel Foundation heir to his estate.

Paris Svoronos

1962

Physiology or Medicine

Francis Crick, Great Britain
James D. Watson, United States
Maurice H. F. Wilkins, Great Britain

Chemistry

Max Ferdinand Perutz, Great Britain
John Cowdery Kendrew, Great Britain

Physics

Lev Davidovich Landau, Soviet Union

Literature

John Steinbeck, United States

Peace

Linus Pauling, United States

FRANCIS CRICK
1962

Born: Northampton, England; June 8, 1916

Nationality: British
Areas of concentration: Molecular biology, biophysics, biochemistry, and genetics

Crick and James Watson made one of the most important biological discoveries of the twentieth century: the three-dimensional structure of deoxyribonucleic acid (DNA), the molecule that encodes every inherited characteristic of every living organism on earth

The Award

Presentation

Professor A. Engström of the Royal Caroline Institute presented the Nobel Prize in Physiology or Medicine to Francis Crick, James Watson, and Maurice Wilkins on Monday, December 10, 1962. In his presentation speech, Engström discussed the structure of deoxyribonucleic acid (DNA), the means by which DNA encodes proteins, and the profound effect that the discovery of its structure had upon all areas of biology. He highlighted the artistic nature of the molecule and the creative thinking of its three discoverers.

DNA consists of two very long antiparallel polynucleotide chains. The molecule is termed antiparallel because the two polynucleotide chains run in opposite directions beside each other. Each polynucleotide consists of many nucleotides. Each nucleotide is composed of the sugar deoxyribose, a phosphate, and one of four possible nitrogen-containing bases: adenine, guanine, cytosine, or thymine. Nitrogenous bases on opposite polynucleotide chains pair with each other by sharing hydrogen atoms, thereby forming hydrogen bonds which hold the two antiparallel chains together. An adenine on one polynucleotide chain always pairs with a thymine on the opposite complementary polynucleotide chain, and vice-versa. A cytosine on one chain always pairs with a guanine on the complementary chain, and vice versa. Furthermore, the two chains twist into a helical structure resembling a spiral staircase.

The order of nitrogenous bases on a given DNA polynucleotide chain serves as the genetic code for a living organism having that particular sequence. Every few thousand nitrogenous bases constitute a gene, which is copied to produce the polynucleotide ribonucleic acid (RNA), some of which (messenger RNA) is used to encode protein. Therefore, DNA encodes RNA which encodes protein—the major theme of molecular biology that was established by Crick, Watson, Wilkins, and many other molecular biologists.

Nobel lecture

Francis Crick delivered his Nobel lecture, entitled "On the Genetic Code," on

Tuesday, December 11, 1962. In his lecture, Crick focused not on his discovery of the structure of DNA but on a major problem facing molecular biology: the nature of the genetic code. His talk summarized the current knowledge and experiments describing how DNA encodes protein.

At the time, experimental evidence indicated (correctly) that the nitrogenous base sequence of a DNA polynucleotide chain is copied to produce a complementary messenger RNA (mRNA) polynucleotide chain. Subsequently, the messenger RNA is translated to generate a long series of amino acids called a protein. The information content of DNA and RNA lies in their respective nucleotide nitrogenous base sequences, but how this actually happened was not known.

Numerous possible genetic codes had been considered, such as two consecutive RNA nucleotides encoding an amino acid, three consecutive RNA nucleotides, four, five, six, and so on. Some scientists suggested overlapping coding units, or codons, where overlapping series of nucleotides encoded amino acids. There are twenty types of amino acids in the proteins of all living organisms, and these twenty amino acids are encoded by some combination of four types of nucleotide nitrogenous bases (adenine, guanine, cytosine, and thymine).

If the twenty amino acid types were encoded by two-nucleotide codons, and the two nucleotides of a codon each could be any combination of the four nitrogenous base types, then there would be $4 \times 4 = 16$ codon types, which would not be enough to encode twenty amino acids. If the codons had three random nucleotides, then there would be $4 \times 4 \times 4 = 64$ codon types. If the codons had four random nucleotides, then there would be $4 \times 4 \times 4 \times 4 = 256$ codon types, and so on. While two-nucleotide codons are insufficient for coding amino acids, four-, five-, and six-nucleotide codons are simply too many. Numerically speaking, a three-nucleotide codon is most plausible, even though it requires the existence of sixty-four total codons to encode twenty amino acids.

Experimental evidence supported the three-nucleotide codon. Frameshift mutations, where a nitrogenous base is added or deleted from the DNA nucleotide sequence of a gene, were produced in bacteria and viruses. Single frameshift mutations completely inactivated the proteins encoded by the mutated genes. If two nucleotides were added within a single gene (a double frameshift), the protein was still inactivated, thus disproving the two-nucleotide codon. If three nucleotides were added, the protein was functional. Four or five added nucleotides resulted in inactive proteins. Six added nucleotides within a single gene resulted in an active protein. Therefore, the gene protein was active only when the added nucleotide mutations occurred in multiples of three. This was compelling evidence in favor of the three-nucleotide codon. Additionally, Crick cited the recent research of eventual Nobel laureates Marshall Nirenberg, Robert Holley, and Har Gobind Khorana, who were deciphering which three-nucleotide codons encoded which amino acids.

Crick listed eleven important properties of the genetic code, including the facts that the codons are triplet (they have three consecutive nucleotides), that the codons do not overlap, that the encoded amino acid sequence comes directly from the linear RNA codon sequence, and that the codons are redundant (more than one codon encodes each amino acid). Furthermore, Crick noted the fact that the genetic code is universal, being virtually the same in every known living organism from viruses to humans.

Critical reception

The awarding of the 1962 Nobel Prize to Crick, Watson, and Wilkins was applauded worldwide because of their penetration into the secrets of the cell. In fact, their awards were practically inevitable, given the magnitude of their discovery. Since their unraveling of the structure of DNA in 1953, the science of molecular biology had virtually exploded, the three men had delved deeper into the secrets of DNA, and their discovery had been corroborated by several prominent investigators, including Rosalind Franklin, Raymond Gosling, Frank Stahl, and Matthew Meselson.

Their joint Nobel Prize was announced in newspapers, magazines, and professional journals worldwide. The importance of their work and their subsequent Nobel Prize elevated Crick, Watson, and Wilkins to celebrity status. Announcements of their Nobel Prize appeared in the October 26, 1962, issue of *Science*, the October 26, 1962, issue of *Time*, the October 29, 1962, issue of *Newsweek*, and the November 2, 1962, issue of *Life*.

Time magazine cited the three scientists for their discovery of the structure of DNA, the basis for all life on earth. *Time* described the structure of DNA, the methods by which the structure was determined, and the academic atmosphere at England's University of Cambridge in the early 1950's during their discovery. *Newsweek* also described DNA's structure and the importance of its understanding. Both magazines emphasized the applications of Crick, Watson, and Wilkins' work to the improved scientific understanding of heredity, reproduction, genetic disease, and cancer. *Life* included photographs and brief biographies of the three men as well as a photograph of two unique DNA models on display in Seattle, Washington.

The impact of their discovery and subsequent Nobel Prize made the names Watson and Crick household words; their names are synonymous with molecular biology. Since winning the Nobel Prize, Crick has emerged as one of the great biological theoreticians, a scientist whose insight, ideas, and critical, objective thinking have driven the directions of many biological disciplines.

Crick, Watson, and Wilkins split the $49,650 Nobel Prize. Had not another scientist, Rosalind Franklin, died of cancer in 1958, the 1962 Nobel Prize in Physiology or Medicine might conceivably have been awarded to a foursome. The atmosphere surrounding their discovery from 1950 to 1953 has been the subject of much writing, some controversial, including Watson's autobiographical *The Double Helix* (1968) and Horace Freeland Judson's 1979 compendium, *The Eighth Day of Creation*.

In 1983, the thirtieth anniversary of their discovery, Crick and Watson were honored in Boston. The event included both reminiscences and discussions on new breakthroughs in DNA research. The anniversary meeting was cited in the October 3, 1983, issue of *Time* and in the October 7, 1983, issue of *Science*. In the *Time* article, entitled "Commemorating a Revolution," authors Frederic Golden and Jamie Murphy compared Crick and Watson's discovery to Charles Darwin's publication of *On the Origin of Species* in 1859.

Biography

Francis Harry Compton Crick was born in Northampton, England, on June 8, 1916; he is the son of Harry Crick and Annie Elizabeth Wilkins. He received his early education at Northampton Grammar School and Mill Hill School. In 1937, he received his B.S. degree in physics from University College, London. He subsequently pursued a doctorate in physics. Unfortunately, this work ended with the destruction of the physics laboratory during the German bombing of London in World War II. During the war, he was a research scientist studying magnetic and acoustic mines for the British Admirality.

In 1949, Crick entered a biology doctoral program at the Medical Research Council's Cavendish Laboratory of Cambridge University. He worked with X-ray diffraction studies of biological molecules, specifically proteins, under the supervision of Nobel laureate Sir Lawrence Bragg and future laureate Max Perutz. At Cambridge, he met and collaborated with James D. Watson in determining the structure of DNA. After receiving his Ph.D. in 1954, he remained with the Medical Research Council's Laboratory of Molecular Biology through 1976. In 1961, he became a fellow of the Salk Institute for Biological Studies in La Jolla, California, where he took a permanent position in 1976.

Crick is a member of numerous scientific societies and has received many honors, including the Prix Charles Leopold Meyer of the French Academy of Sciences, the Lasker Foundation Award, and honorary membership in the American Academy of Arts and Sciences. He has been married twice, first to Ruth Doreen Dodd (1940-1947) and then to Odile Speed in 1949. He has a son, Michael F. C. Crick, by his first marriage and two daughters, Gabrielle A. Crick and Jacqueline M. T. Crick, by his second marriage.

Scientific Career

Like many of his colleagues involved in the molecular biological revolution of the 1950's and 1960's, Francis Crick is a physicist turned biologist. Originally he was devoted purely to physics. After receiving his B.S. degree in physics from University College, London, he pursued a Ph.D. in physics, which abruptly ended with a German bomb destroying his laboratory during World War II. After leaving the British Admiralty in 1947, he shifted his scientific interests to biology, specifically with the goals of describing the physical aspects of biological problems and of discrediting vitalistic views of biology. (With respect to the latter goal, Crick is an atheist.) From 1947 to 1949, he studied cell biology at the Strangeways Research Laboratory in Cambridge, England. During this period, he earned a reputation for his critical analytical abilities and his voracious reading of the biological literature.

In 1949, Crick became a research staff member at the Medical Research Council's

Cavendish Laboratory at the University of Cambridge. He entered the Ph.D. program and began studying protein structure under the direction of Sir Lawrence Bragg, Max Perutz, and John Kendrew. These three eminent biochemists were working on the structure of the blood plasma protein hemoglobin at the time Crick began his doctoral research. Crick studied protein structure using two basic techniques practiced at the Cavendish Laboratory: crystallography and X-ray diffraction.

Protein crystallography involves the concentration of pure protein and its subsequent crystallization; the protein molecules will orient in a specific pattern during the crystallization process. The crystallized protein can be photographed by beaming X rays through the crystals; the diffraction, or scattering, of the X rays as they strike particular protein atoms generates a pattern of dots on a photographic plate. The pattern of dots and the precise distances between the dots on the X-ray diffraction photograph give the scientist an idea of the three-dimensional structure of the protein molecule. Based upon the X-ray diffraction data and biochemical tests of the protein's atomic components, the investigator can then attempt to construct a physical model of the protein. The techniques of crystallization and X-ray diffraction are difficult; interpretation of the data that is obtained is even more difficult.

During Crick's first two years at the Cavendish Laboratory, from 1949 to 1951, he developed expertise in these experimental methods but did not generate any relevant results. He was very skilled at pinpointing flaws in his colleagues' experiments and at solving problems which baffled them, but his own research was relatively stagnant. He was, however, entranced with the structure of genes and how they encoded proteins.

In early October, 1951, Crick met twenty-three-year-old Dr. James D. Watson, an American biologist who had recently arrived at the Cavendish Laboratory to research genetics and biochemistry. They quickly became close scientific colleagues and began to speculate upon the structure of DNA. At the time, DNA had not been firmly established as being the genetic material. Oswald Avery had provided, in 1944, strong evidence that the genetic material of bacteria is DNA. Not everyone was convinced, however, until Alfred Hershey and Martha Chase performed their famous "Waring blender" experiment in 1953.

Based upon Avery's conclusions, Crick and Watson considered DNA to be the genetic material. They studied X-ray diffraction photographs of DNA produced by many investigators, including their Cambridge colleagues Maurice Wilkins, Rosalind Franklin, and Raymond Gosling. They already knew the chemical composition of DNA: the sugar deoxyribose, phosphate, and the nitrogen-containing bases adenine, guanine, cytosine, and thymine. From these data and from Linus Pauling's discovery of the alpha helix in protein structure, Crick and Watson proposed a single-chain helical DNA model in late 1951. The model contained some very serious flaws, and it was rejected.

After this episode, Crick and Watson were ordered not to work on DNA because they were junior staff members who were competing against the Wilkins-Franklin-Gosling group. Crick returned to his doctoral dissertation, studying the alpha-helical models of protein structure. Watson studied the genetics of viruses. Their hiatus from DNA structure research lasted for about one year. During this period, other scientific groups actively pursuing DNA structure were slowed by scientific, personal, and political problems. The Wilkins-Franklin group was plagued by personality conflicts and incorrect data interpretation. The American government, in an era suspicious of any political dissent, prohibited Linus Pauling from traveling abroad to foreign laboratories because of his antinuclear views.

Nevertheless, Pauling proposed a structure for DNA in a paper submitted to the *Proceedings of the National Academy of Sciences (USA)* in late January, 1953. The news of Pauling's proposed DNA structure was unnerving to the Cambridge scientists; however, analysis of Pauling's structure revealed several errors. The structure was incorrect. Consequently, Crick and Watson were freed to tackle DNA again. In their second attempt, they were equipped with better knowledge of the molecule. They had seen some of Rosalind Franklin's excellent DNA X-ray diffraction photographs, which clearly showed that there were two helically arranged DNA polynucleotide chains having a diameter of 20 angstroms (0.000000002 meter), with 3.4 angstroms (0.00000000034 meter) separating each nucleotide of the chain. Furthermore, each turn of the helix was 34 angstroms long, indicating that ten nucleotide pairs existed per turn. Additionally, they had met Erwin Chargaff of Columbia University during the previous summer. Chargaff had demonstrated that the amount of adenine (A) in DNA equals the amount of thymine (T) and that the amount of guanine (G) equals the amount of cytosine (C).

Equipped with these data, Crick and Watson started building cardboard and metal models of DNA. By late February, 1953, they had brainstormed to the correct structure. A complete model was assembled by March 7. Their colleagues could not find any flaws in their proposed structure, so Crick and Watson began writing a short paper laying claim to the discovery. Even Pauling endorsed the structure.

The Crick and Watson DNA structure is two "antiparallel" polynucleotide chains—antiparallel because the two chains are running beside each other in opposite directions, polynucleotide because each chain consists of millions of sequential nucleotides. Each nucleotide consists of the sugar deoxyribose, a phosphate, and one of four nitrogenous bases (adenine, guanine, cytosine, or thymine). An adenine nucleotide on one polynucleotide chain always pairs with a thymine nucleotide on the opposite complementary polynucleotide chain, and vice-versa, by sharing two hydrogen atoms (that is, forming two hydrogen bonds). A cytosine nucleotide on one polynucleotide chain always pairs with a guanine nucleotide on the opposite complementary chain, and vice-versa, by sharing three hydrogen atoms (three hydrogen bonds). This pairing explained the Chargaff A = T, G = C ratios. The pairing also suggested a possible means of replication (duplication) for DNA, in which the two polynucleotide chains separate and a new complementary antiparallel chain is made for each original chain prior to cell division.

Crick and Watson described their DNA structure and this possible replication mechanism in their famous April 25, 1953, *Nature* paper, entitled "Molecular

Structure of Nucleic Acids: A Structure for Deoxyribose Nucleic Acid," and again in a later *Nature* paper on May 30, 1953. Soon thereafter, their DNA structure was corroborated by Rosalind Franklin and Raymond Gosling. Matthew Meselson and Frank Stahl verified Crick and Watson's "semi-conservative" replication model in the late 1950's.

The impact of Crick and Watson's discovery quickly seized the biological science community. In 1953 and 1954 they presented the DNA structure at numerous scientific conferences, including Cold Spring Harbor and the Royal Society of London. After receiving his Ph.D. in 1954, Crick stayed with the Cavendish Laboratory, where he began studying—and became a major figure in solving—the genetic code. Experiments had showed that DNA encoded messenger RNA which, in turn, encoded the amino acid sequence of proteins. The mechanism behind this process remained to be determined.

The astrophysicist George Gamow was the first to suggest that a unit of nucleotides encoded each amino acid. The genetic code lay in the order of messenger RNA nucleotide nitrogenous bases: the order of the adenines, guanines, cytosines, and thymines on a single messenger RNA polynucleotide chain. How many nucleotides constituted a coding unit, or codon? Two nucleotides per codon would not be enough, because the proteins of all living organisms use twenty amino acid types. Some scientists considered four-, five-, and six-nucleotide codons. Crick and colleagues correctly theorized and experimentally demonstrated a three-nucleotide codon, where every three successive nucleotides on a messenger RNA polynucleotide chain encodes successive amino acids on the corresponding protein.

After receiving the Nobel Prize in 1962, Crick began to venture into other areas of biological research. He collaborated with colleagues from numerous fields, including astrophysics, cosmology, and psychology. He became affiliated with the Salk Institute in La Jolla, California, while remaining at Cambridge. With biochemist and researcher into the origin of life Leslie Orgel, Crick reinvigorated the directed panspermia hypothesis (first advanced by the famous Swedish chemist Svante Arrhenius) that life on earth was seeded from outer space. While their proposal has been ridiculed by many, directed panspermia is an active area of research in several countries. Crick also participated in the first Soviet-American International Conference on Communication with Extraterrestrial Intelligence (CETI), held in 1971.

In 1975, Crick and P. A. Lawrence performed developmental genetics experiments, verifying the results of Antonio Garcia-Bellido that cellular development and differentiation in insects occurs by tissue compartmentalization. Working with the fruit fly *Drosophila melanogaster*, they demonstrated that groups of cells which eventually become a wing, for example, do so by multiplying into the thousands, followed by compartment-by-compartment differentiation. Different groups of cells change into different portions of the wing based upon their compartment positions.

In 1976, Crick resigned from the Medical Research Council in order to take a full-time research position at the Salk Institute. In the early 1980's, he and Graeme Mitchison of Cambridge proposed some major new ideas concerning how the brain functions and why higher mammals dream. They have proposed that REM (rapid eye movement) sleep, which is when dreaming occurs in most mammals having a cerebral neocortex, functions to erase irrelevant and meaningless memories. Their hypotheses on dreaming have evoked much controversy.

Bibliography

Primary

BIOLOGY: "Molecular Structure of Nucleic Acids: A Structure for Deoxyribose Nucleic Acid," *Nature*, vol. 171, 1953, pp. 737-738 (with James D. Watson); "Genetical Implications of the Structure of Deoxyribonucleic Acid," *Nature*, vol. 171, 1953, pp. 964-967 (with Watson); "The Structure of DNA," *Cold Spring Harbor Symposia on Quantitative Biology*, vol. 18, 1953, pp. 123-131 (with Watson); "The Complementary Structure of Deoxyribonucleic Acid," *Proceedings of the Royal Society of London*, series A, vol. 223, 1954, pp. 80-96 (with Watson); "The Structure of the Hereditary Material," *Scientific American*, vol. 191, 1954, pp. 54-61; "Nucleic Acids," *Scientific American*, vol. 197, 1957, pp. 188-200; "The Genetic Code," *Scientific American*, vol. 207, 1962, pp. 66-74; "On the Genetic Code," *Les Prix Nobel en 1962*; "On the Genetic Code," *Science*, vol. 139, 1963, pp. 461-464; "The Genetic Code: III," *Scientific American*, vol. 215, 1966, pp. 55-62; "Compartments and Polyclones in Insect Development," *Science*, vol. 189, 1975, pp. 340-347 (with P. A. Lawrence); "Thinking About the Brain," *Scientific American*, vol. 241, 1979, pp. 219-230; *Life Itself*, 1981.

Secondary

Crick, Francis H. C. "Lessons from Biology." *Natural History* 97 (November, 1988): 32-39. This article, adapted from the author's 1988 book *What Mad Pursuit: A Personal View of Scientific Discovery* (Basic Books, New York), is a summary of scientific methodology and its potential flaws. Crick uses numerous examples, including his own work with the genetic code.

Felsenfeld, Gary. "DNA." *Scientific American* 253 (October, 1985): 58-67. This article clearly describes the structure of DNA, how it is organized into genes, and how DNA folds up to form a chromosome. The article includes excellent diagrams, relevant experiments, and a summary of gene regulation mechanisms.

Gardner, Eldon J., and D. Peter Snustad. *Principles of Genetics*. 7th ed. New York: John Wiley & Sons, 1984. This very clearly written, wonderfully illustrated undergraduate genetics textbook provides a comprehensive survey of the field. Chapter 5, "Genetic Material: Properties and Replication," provides a brief history of Crick and Watson's work and a thorough discussion of DNA as the genetic material.

Judson, Horace Freeland. *The Eighth Day of Creation: The Makers of the Revolution in Biology*. New York: Simon & Schuster, 1979. Judson's wonderful book is an extensive history of the development of biology in the twentieth century, especially genetics and molecular biology. Special emphasis is placed upon the events leading up to and following Crick and Watson's discovery of DNA structure. Judson's work is a major contribution to this history.

Lewin, Benjamin. *Genes II*. New York: John Wiley & Sons, 1985. Lewin's work is one of the most complete, detailed surveys of current knowledge in molecular biology and biochemical genetics. This textbook, which is suitable for advanced undergraduates and graduate students, provides many chapters on DNA structure and function.

Melnechuk, Theodore. "The Dream Machine." *Psychology Today* 17 (November, 1983): 22-34. This article is a summary of Crick and Graeme Mitchison's work on dream research. The article describes REM sleep and Crick's proposal that such sleep is the mammalian brain's way of removing useless information.

Sagan, Carl, ed. *Communication with Extraterrestrial Intelligence (CETI)*. Cambridge, Mass.: MIT Press, 1973. This exciting book is a transcript of the first international conference dealing with contacting intelligent life elsewhere in the universe, held in Soviet Armenia in 1971. The list of conference participants is a who's who of world-famous scientists. Francis Crick is a prominent figure in many of the lively discussions.

Watson, James D. *The Double Helix*. New York: Atheneum, 1968. This controversial book is Watson's own account of his collaboration with Crick and Wilkins on discovering DNA's structure. A number of scientists, including Crick, strongly protested the publication of this book for various reasons.

David Wason Hollar, Jr.

1962

Physiology or Medicine

Francis Crick, Great Britain
James D. Watson, United States
Maurice H. F. Wilkins, Great Britain

Chemistry

Max Ferdinand Perutz, Great Britain
John Cowdery Kendrew, Great Britain

Physics

Lev Davidovich Landau, Soviet Union

Literature

John Steinbeck, United States

Peace

Linus Pauling, United States

JAMES D. WATSON
1962

Born: Chicago, Illinois; April 6, 1928

Nationality: American
Areas of concentration: Genetics, biochemistry, and molecular biology

Watson and Crick's model for the structure of DNA inspired the "central dogma," the idea that DNA dictates not only its own replication but also the synthesis of RNA and that RNA determines the type of protein synthesized

The Award

Presentation

On December 10, 1962, Professor A. Engström, a member of the Staff of Professors of the Royal Caroline Institute, introduced to the Royal Swedish Academy of Sciences Francis Harry Compton Crick, James Dewey Watson, and Maurice Hugh Frederick Wilkins by describing the importance of their research.

Professor Engström explained that Crick, Watson, and Wilkin's work was of great importance because it indicated how deoxyribonucleic acid (DNA) could control the general and individual properties of an organism. DNA is a huge molecule that is constructed from small subunits called deoxyribonucleotides; these consist of a nitrogen-containing ringed molecule (the base), a deoxyribose sugar, and a phosphate. In Watson and Crick's model for DNA, deoxyribonucleotides are chemically connected to form long, unbranching strands. The four bases (adenine, thymine, cytosine, and guanine) of the deoxyribonucleotides could be in any order in the DNA strand. In addition, two helical strands are held together by hydrogen bonds between complementary bases in the two strands, forming a double helix. Watson and Crick proposed that adenine in one strand is complementary to thymine in the second strand, while guanine is complementary to cytosine. Because the two strands of the DNA chromosome are complementary, each strand can dictate the synthesis of a complementary strand. During replication, the double helix would unwind, and each strand would function as a template for the synthesis of a complementary strand.

Professor Engström also mentioned that the nucleotide sequence in one of the DNA strands would determine the order of nucleotides in another type of nucleic acid, called ribonucleic acid (RNA). The sugar in RNA is a ribose (rather than the deoxyribose in DNA) and the base uracil replaces thymine. RNA dictates the order of amino acids in proteins. In other words, DNA determines the order of bases in RNA, and the sequence of bases in RNA then dictates the order of amino acids in protein. The multitude of proteins coded for by the DNA determines the characteristics of the organism. Watson, Crick, and Wilkins were awarded the 1962 Nobel Prize in Physiology or Medicine by the Royal Caroline Institute for their insight into genetics and physiology. His Majesty the King of Sweden presented the awards.

Nobel lecture

On December 11, 1962, Watson delivered his Nobel lecture, entitled "The Involvement of RNA in the Synthesis of Proteins." Much of Watson's presentation was concerned with how scientists discovered that there were three categories of RNA: messenger RNA (mRNA), ribosomal RNA (rRNA), and transfer RNA (tRNA). Only one of these types of RNA acted as the genetic code for protein synthesis.

Watson explained that studies in the 1940's and early 1950's had shown that protein synthesis was associated with ribosomes in the cytoplasm, not with DNA in the nucleus of cells. The facts that cells actively synthesizing protein have high levels of RNA and that ribosomes are composed of RNA suggested that RNA is an intermediate between DNA and the protein that it encoded. Even before Watson and Crick had published their structure for DNA in 1953, Watson had expressed the idea that the information in the DNA molecule was passed to an RNA molecule and that this information was then somehow translated into protein. This was the beginning of what became known as the "central dogma": DNA makes RNA that makes protein. After many experiments in the 1950's, scientists proved that the stable RNA found in ribosomes is not the RNA that coded for proteins. Experiments with bacterial viruses and bacteria indicated that protein synthesis depends upon an unstable RNA with a half-life of only a few minutes, which François Jacob and Jacques Monod named messenger RNA (mRNA).

Since amino acids do not directly bind to RNA, they cannot simply line up on an RNA template and be hooked together by some enzyme. As a working hypothesis, Crick proposed, in the mid-1950's, that there might be twenty different adaptor molecules that could both hydrogen-bond to the linear code of bases in the mRNA and attach to one of the twenty amino acids. Possibly a third type of RNA, transfer RNA (tRNA), discovered in 1956, was the adaptor molecule. By 1958, scientists had demonstrated that the small tRNA molecules were indeed the adaptors predicted by Crick.

In the mid-1950's, it was discovered that bacterial ribosomes consist of two unequal subunits that are constructed from numerous proteins and three different rRNA molecules. Experiments hinted at the fact that the stable rRNA in ribosomes was not the messenger RNA: The addition of an abnormal nucleotide, which alters the RNA code, to growing cells resulted in the synthesis of abnormal proteins within a few minutes. Clearly, the stable rRNA was not directing protein synthesis. If it had been, not all the new proteins would have been defective. Other experiments indicated that viral protein synthesis was using a rapidly synthesized RNA distinct from the bacterial rRNA found in the bacterial ribosomes. Experiments in which protein synthesis was carried out in a test tube convinced everyone that mRNA was distinct from rRNA. It was possible to add an artifical mRNA such as polyU, which consists entirely of uracil, to a protein-synthesizing complex in a test tube and produce a distinct polypeptide consisting of a single amino acid. This was direct proof that a single-stranded RNA other than rRNA or tRNA is the template for protein synthesis.

In the early 1960's, various researchers demonstrated that the mRNA base sequence determines which of the twenty different amino acid-tRNA complexes will bind to the mRNA-ribosome complex. It also became clear that the tRNA molecules are responsible for reading the genetic code contained within the linear sequence of bases in the mRNA.

Watson concluded his discussion of RNA by pointing out that the process of protein synthesis is much more complex than indicated by the central dogma (DNA makes RNA, which makes protein). Instead of the one RNA, scientists found three different classes of RNA involved in protein synthesis.

Critical reception

The scientific community throughout the world enthusiastically supported the award of the 1962 Nobel Prize in Physiology or Medicine to James Watson, Francis Crick, and Maurice Wilkins for determining the molecular structure of DNA. The Royal Caroline Institute of Sweden, which presented the Nobel Prize, wrote that the discovery of the DNA structure had "no immediate practical application, but determining the molecular structure of the substance that is responsible for the forms that life takes is a discovery of tremendous importance." The DNA model stimulated research on exactly how DNA could act as a template for its own duplication and how the sequence of bases in a strand functions as the genetic code. In addition, scientists wanted to know exactly what enzymes and proteins were involved in winding and unwinding the DNA strands and synthesizing DNA. Furthermore, the DNA model and the central dogma stimulated research into how the RNA code was read and how protein synthesis was regulated. By 1962, many of these questions were being answered in detail. John T. Edsall of the biological laboratories at Harvard University wrote in *Science* (October 26, 1962) that the Watson-Crick discovery "has been hailed as perhaps the most significant single advance made in biology during the 20th century."

In addition to stimulating research into the replication and expression of DNA, the Watson-Crick model explained how mutations affect the structure and activity of DNA. In the October 26, 1962, issue of *Time* magazine, the science editor wrote that the "determination of DNA's structure was as important to studies of the secrets of life as was the splitting of the atom to physics." He reasoned that when chromosomes in a cell were "altered by radiation, chemicals, or in any other way, the result may be the aberrant growth that is called cancer." On the other hand, altered chromosomes might cause genetic defects or diseases that could perhaps be reversed some day "by supplying tailor-made, corrective DNA."

Almost all scientists realized that the model for DNA proposed by the 1962 Nobel Prize recipients had exerted a profound influence on biochemical and biological research. There was at least one scientist, however, Barry Commoner at Washington University in Saint Louis, Missouri, who was unable to believe in the simplicity of the central dogma: DNA → RNA → protein → the organism's characteristics. According to Commoner, DNA was not the sole hereditary information, since various forms of DNA polymerase could alter the hereditary information during DNA replication. Also, mutated tRNAs and ribosomal proteins could result in the synthesis of abnormal proteins. He concluded that "biochemical specificity within the cell is fundamentally circular rather than linear and the total system rather than any single constituent is responsible for the biochemical specificity which gives rise to biological specificity." According to the central dogma, the DNA sequence of nucleotides in new DNA should be determined only by the template sequence, not by DNA polymerases. Furthermore, the sequence of amino acids should be determined only by the DNA and complementary mRNAs, not by the structure of tRNAs or ribosomal proteins. This kind of argument, however, is essentially nothing more than rhetoric. The machinery involved in DNA duplication and protein synthesis does not provide precise information in the same sense that DNA itself does. Machinery needed for DNA duplication and for the expression of the code, if defective, may produce a mixture of many different defective DNA molecules and proteins. There is no information being transmitted in this random and abnormal process. Commoner also conveniently overlooked the fact that even the altered machinery is coded for by the DNA.

Biography

James Dewey Watson was born in Chicago, Illinois, on April 6, 1928. He was educated at Chicago schools and was a brilliant student. At age fifteen, Watson received a scholarship to the University of Chicago. He received a B.S. degree in zoology in 1947. A fellowship for graduate study at Indiana University in Bloomington led to a Ph.D. in zoology in 1950.

From 1950 to 1951, Watson studied in Copenhagen, Denmark, where he worked with bacterial viruses. Because of his lack of interest in the research he was doing in Copenhagen and his interest in the structure of DNA, Watson moved to the University of Cambridge in England, where he met Francis Crick. Using their knowledge of the chemistry of nucleotides and of DNA as well as the new X-ray diffraction data provided by Rosalind Franklin and Maurice Wilkins, Watson and Crick proposed a structure for the DNA molecule in 1953. This led to the publication of three papers that are considered classics and that revolutionized genetics and molecular biology.

In 1953, Watson became a senior research fellow in biology at the California Institute of Technology, where he attempted to learn something about RNA from X-ray diffraction studies. Returning to England in 1955, he worked with Crick on the structure of viruses. Another move, in 1956, took him to Harvard University, where he became professor of biology. While at Harvard University, Watson published his classic *Molecular Biology of the Gene* (1965). Watson became director of the Cold Spring Harbor Laboratory in 1968; that same year, he published another classic book, *The Double Helix*. Watson has also coauthored *Molecular Biology of the Cell*, which was first published in 1983. In 1988, he became associate director of the National Center for Human Genome Research at the National Institutes of Health (NIH).

Watson was elected to the National Academy of Sciences in 1962, the year he was awarded the Nobel Prize in Physiology or Medicine. In 1971, he was awarded the National Academy of Sciences' J. J. Carty Medal, and in 1977 the president of the United States awarded him the Presidential Medal of Freedom, the highest civilian award, for his outstanding scientific achievements.

Scientific Career

After being graduated from the University of Chicago, James D. Watson began his graduate work at Indiana University. His Ph.D. thesis was a study of bacteriophage proliferation and the effect of X rays on this process. Salvador Edward Luria, a microbiologist and a Nobel Prize recipient in 1969, was Watson's thesis adviser. Luria and geneticist Hermann Joseph Muller, a Nobel Prize recipient in 1946, greatly influenced Watson's interest in genetics and prepared him for a brilliant career in microbiology and genetics. After obtaining his Ph.D. in zoology in 1950, Watson moved to Copenhagen, Denmark, where he worked with bacterial viruses, trying to discover what happens to viral DNA when it infects a bacterium.

At a meeting in Italy, Watson met Maurice Wilkins, who was presenting a paper on X-ray diffraction through crystalline DNA. The X-ray diffraction data indicated that DNA might be helical in shape. Because of his lack of interest in the research he was doing in Copenhagen and his increasing interest in the structure of DNA, Watson moved to the Cavendish Laboratory at the University of Cambridge in England in 1952. At the Cavendish Laboratory, Watson met Francis Crick, a physicist studying protein structure who also was interested in the structure of DNA. Using their knowledge of the chemistry of nucleotides and of DNA, as well as the X-ray diffraction data provided by Rosalind Franklin and Maurice Wilkins, researchers at King's College in the University of London, Watson and Crick proposed a structure for the DNA molecule in 1953 that turned out to be correct. At the ages of twenty-five and thirty-five, respectively, Watson and Crick published three papers that were to change genetic research drastically and lead to the Nobel Prize.

Watson and Crick's first 1953 *Nature* paper proposed that DNA consists of two nucleic acid strands that are coiled around a common axis, forming a double right-handed helix. The number of strands was determined from the density of DNA, as found from X-ray diffraction studies. The bases (adenine, thymine, guanine, cytosine) are on the inside of each of the helices, holding them together, and the phosphates are on the outside. A base pair was found every 0.34 nanometers along the length of the DNA molecule, and there was a complete twist every 3.4 nanometers. The diameter of the DNA molecule was reported as 2 nanometers. The bases in each pair were proposed to be held together by hydrogen bonds. Most important, adenine paired with thymine, and guanine paired with cytosine: No other pairings were possible. This restricted pairing of the bases was explained by the chemistry of the bases, which would cause the bases to attract or repel each other. Watson and Crick hinted that their model would explain how DNA might replicate itself with the often-quoted words, "It has not escaped our notice that the specific pairing we have postulated immediately suggests a possible copying mechanism for the genetic material." In their subsequent 1953 *Nature* and *Cold Spring Harbor Symposia on Quantitative Biology* papers, they showed how the two nucleic acid strands were held together by hydrogen bonds between the bases and showed that the only hydrogen bonding possible was between adenine and thymine and between guanine and cytosine. Any order of the four bases could occur in one strand of the DNA, but the order of the four bases on the complementary strand would be determined by the hydrogen-bonding restriction. The pairing restriction was supported by the fact that the amount of adenine equaled thymine and the amount of guanine equaled cytosine in all nucleic acids tested. These equalities held even when the ratio of adenine to guanine in DNA from different organisms varied considerably. X-ray studies of DNA with different amounts of water showed that water changed DNA's shape. The wet (more than 30 percent water) B structure had paired bases every 0.34 nanometer along the length of the double helix, while the drier (less than 30 percent water) A structure was about 30 percent shorter and had paired bases every 0.28 nanometer.

Watson and Crick observed that the complementary nature of the two DNA strands could explain how DNA might duplicate itself. They suggested that DNA duplication would require the breaking of hydrogen bonds and the unwinding of the two DNA strands. Then each DNA strand would act as a template for the formation of a complementary strand. This would result in two complete and identical DNA molecules. A major problem for DNA duplication was the unwinding of the two helical strands: The two strands of a chromosome would have to be turned many millions of times to untwist it and separate the strands. Moreover, in addition to the double helical structure of the strands, the entire molecule was supercoiled.

Watson and Crick explained the appearance of spontaneous DNA mutations by assuming that bases would undergo temporary chemical changes that altered their hydrogen bonding specificity. Thus, adenine could hydrogen-bond abnormally with cytosine, and guanine could hydrogen-bond abnormally with thymine. During DNA duplication, this would introduce the incorrect nucleotide into a growing DNA strand.

Watson became a senior research fellow in biology at the California Institute of Technology in 1953; there, he investigated RNA using X-ray studies. Watson returned to the Cavendish Laboratory in 1955, where he worked with Crick on the structure of viruses. In 1956 he moved to Harvard University, where he eventually became professor of biology. At Harvard, Watson's main focus was on RNA and its role in protein synthesis.

On December 11, 1962, Watson delivered his Nobel lecture, in which he discussed some of the experiments that he and other scientists had performed to determine how DNA controlled the synthesis of proteins. In the early 1950's, Watson had expressed the idea that the information in the DNA molecule was passed to an RNA molecule and that this information was somehow translated into protein. Mutated DNA would lead directly to an altered protein, according to the central dogma (DNA makes RNA, which makes protein). No one at this time had any indisputable evidence that this was how things worked. In fact, many scientists believed that mutated proteins were normal when they were made and that they were changed afterward by a mutated enzyme. According to the central dogma, a mutated gene makes an altered RNA, and this in turn codes for a defective protein. Scientists eventually discovered that there are three categories of RNA: A multitude of short-lived messenger RNA (mRNA) molecules function as the templates for protein syntheses, sixty-one different transfer RNA (tRNA) molecules with covalently bound amino acids read the mRNA, and three different ribosomal RNA (rRNA) molecules function as structural components of the ribosomes.

While at Harvard University, Watson published three editions of his classic *Molecular Biology of the Gene* (1965, 1970, 1976), which a generation of students has appreciated. *The Double Helix* (1968) was an account of the scientists and the politics involved in Watson and Crick's discovery of the structure of DNA. Concern about the dangers of constructing recombinant DNA and the developing recombinant DNA technology stimulated Watson to publish *The DNA Story* in 1981 and *Recombinant DNA: A Short Course* in 1983. The 1987 fourth edition of *Molecular Biology of the Gene* was coauthored with four other researchers, and it blossomed into a 1,163-page book. Watson also coauthored *Molecular Biology of the Cell* (1983).

In 1968, while still at Harvard University, Watson began an association with the Cold Spring Harbor Laboratory, where he became director. Watson made tumor virology a major research area at Cold Spring Harbor. Much of the present understanding of oncogenes (cancer-causing genes) and the molecular biology of cancer has come from work carried out at this laboratory. He eventually left Harvard in 1976 so that he could devote more time to his directorship at Cold Spring Harbor. Cold Spring Harbor Laboratory is located in Cold Spring Harbor on Long Island in New York and has been a major research center for biologists since its inception in 1933. Each year about four thousand visiting scientists from around the world take part in fifty or more professional meetings and advanced courses in molecular biology. Since 1933, the laboratory has sponsored an annual scientific symposium in a specific area of biology. The papers presented are then published in a volume entitled *Cold Spring Harbor Symposia on Quantitative Biology.* One of the classic 1953 Watson and Crick papers on the structure of DNA appeared in the volume that was devoted to viruses. Watson, as director of the Cold Spring Harbor Laboratory, was involved in planning and organizing each year's symposium. Since 1968, when he became director, the majority of the symposia have been concerned with DNA and its expression.

In the mid-1980's, scientists and government agencies began to consider the best approach to sequencing the twenty-four different chromosomes (twenty-two autosomes, an X chromosome, and a Y chromosome) found in humans. The DNA sequencing project became known as the Human Genome Project. The physicists and biologists at the Department of Energy (DOE), having a mandate to monitor the inherited effects of low-level exposure to radiation and other environmental hazards, were interested in sequencing the human genome and developing cheap and quick sequencing techniques so that they might monitor mutations caused by radiation and chemical exposures. Charles R. Cantor became director of the Human Genome Center at the Lawrence Berkeley Laboratory in Berkeley, California.

In response to the DOE's preparations to sequence the 3 billion base pairs of the human genome, molecular biologists became organized in 1986 after a meeting at Cold Spring Harbor Laboratory. Lobbying by the molecular biologists stimulated the National Institutes of Health (NIH) to become involved in the Human Genome Project. James D. Watson, director at Cold Spring Harbor Laboratory, became associate director of the National Center for Human Genome Research at the National Institutes of Health in Bethesda, Maryland, in 1988. The molecular biologists were interested in sequencing the human genome for a number of reasons. For example, sequencing data on defective genes and controlling sites would indicate exactly what the mutations were doing, and this information would suggest useful therapies for cancers and other genetic diseases such as cystic fibrosis, sickle-cell anemia, thalassemia, familial hypercholesterolemia (premature heart disease), diabetes, Alzheimer's disease, and schizophrenia. The knowledge derived from the Human Genome Project might lead to the development of drugs that would help people afflicted by genetic illnesses. In addition, comparison of known genes in other organisms with those in the human genome would indicate the function of the gene in humans. This would add to the understanding of how humans and other animals develop from a single cell into a multicellular organism and how this development is sometimes disrupted. Knowledge of the human genome would make genetic counseling more effective and would give prospective parents more choices in cases where defective genes were discovered in the family or in a developing fetus.

Watson's numerous meetings with committees and the press made it clear that he was concerned with "the ethical and social implications raised by an ever-increasing knowledge of human genes and the genetic diseases that result from variations in our genetic messages." At least 3 percent of the funds for sequencing human DNA were to go to study of the ethical and social implications of the Human Genome Project. Watson proposed that everyone must "work to ensure that society learns to use the information only in beneficial ways and, if necessary, pass laws at both the federal and state levels to prevent invasions of privacy of an individual's genetic background by either employers, insurers, or government agencies and to prevent discrimination on genetic grounds." He concluded, "If we fail to act now, we might witness unwanted and unnecessary abuses that eventually will create a strong popular backlash against the human genetics community."

The Department of Energy and the National Center for Human Genome Research under the National Institutes of Health signed a memorandum of understanding in 1988 that established formal coordination between the two agencies by way of a joint advisory committee. This helped Watson and Cantor work together to ensure that their research groups would complement one another. In 1990, the National Center for Human Genome Research received just under $60 million, while the Department of Energy program was funded at $28 million. The first five years of the Human Genome Project were devoted to developing new techniques for cheaply and rapidly sequencing DNA as well as developing computer programs for storing the data. In addition, various groups were to test techniques and strategies for mapping the human genome. Watson predicted in 1990 that the Human Genome Project would be completed within fifteen years and would cost about $3 billion.

Watson and Crick's model for the structure of DNA was the spark that ignited the field of molecular genetics during the last half of the twentieth century. Watson was also a major force in promoting government involvement in the Human Genome Project. Without government support and coordination, the project might have taken more than a hundred years to complete and been very wasteful of resources. Watson not only played a part in discovering the structure of DNA but was also fortunate to have been involved in the many discoveries that have been and will be made by sequencing the human genome.

Bibliography

Primary

GENETICS: "The Transfer of Radioactive Phosphorus from Parental to Progeny Phage," *Proceedings of the National Academy of Sciences*, vol. 37, 1951, p. 507 (with O. Maaloe); "Molecular Structure of Nucleic Acids: A Structure for Deoxyribose Nucleic Acid," *Nature*, vol. 171, 1953, pp. 737-738 (with F. H. C. Crick); "Genetical Implications of the Structure of Deoxyribonucleic Acid," *Nature*, vol. 171, 1953, pp. 964-967 (with F. H. C. Crick); "The Structure of DNA," *Cold Spring Harbor Symposia on Quantitative Biology*, vol. 18, 1953, pp. 123-131 (with F. H. C. Crick); "The Complementary Structure of Deoxyribonucleic Acid," *Proceedings of the Royal Society*, series A, vol. 223, 1954, pp. 80-96 (with F. H. C. Crick); "Physical Studies on Ribonucleic Acid," *Nature*, vol. 173, 1954, p. 955; "Unstable Ribonucleic Acid Revealed by Pulse Labelling of *Escherichia coli*," *Nature*, vol. 190, 1961, p. 581 (with F. Gros, W. Gilbert, H. Hiatt, G. Attardi, and P. F. Spahr); *Molecular Biology of the Gene*, 1965; *The Double Helix*, 1968; *The DNA Story*, 1981 (with John Tooze); *Recombinant DNA: A Short Course*, 1983 (with John Tooze and David Kurtz); *Molecular Biology of the Gene*, rev. ed., 1987 (with Nancy H. Hopkins, Jeffrey W. Roberts, Joan Argetsinger Steitz, and Alan M. Weiner); *The Human Genome Project: Past, Present, and Future*, 1990.

BIOLOGY: *Molecular Biology of the Cell*, 1983 (with Bruce Alberts, Dennis Bray, Julian Lewis, Martin Raff, and Keith Roberts).

Secondary

Cantor, Charles R. "Orchestrating the Human Genome Project." *Science* 248 (April, 1990) 49-51. This is Cantor's account of how the Department of Energy became involved in the Human Genome Project and how he became director of the Human Genome Center at Lawrence Berkeley Laboratory in Berkeley, California. Cantor explains how his and Watson's agencies will complement each other in the project.

Commoner, Barry. "Failure of the Watson-Crick Theory as a Chemical Explanation of Inheritance." *Nature* 220 (October, 1968): 334-340. Commoner uses rhetoric to try to show that DNA is not the sole determinant of heredity. Mutations that affect enzymes involved in DNA replication, RNA synthesis, and protein synthesis are known to alter the DNA, RNA, and protein, respectively. Commoner equates mutant enzymes with information such as that found in the genetic code.

Crick, Francis. *What Mad Pursuit: A Personal View of Scientific Discovery.* New York: Basic Books, 1988. Crick describes how speculation played an important role in the discoveries that he and Watson made in the early 1950's. He explains how he was led to propose the adaptor hypothesis several years before tRNA's were discovered and how he and Brenner deduced that messenger RNA must exist and that the code was comma-less, non-overlapping and consisted of three nucleotides.

Judson, Horace Freeland. *The Eighth Day of Creation: The Makers of the Revolution in Biology.* New York: Simon & Schuster, 1979. A comprehensive history of molecular biology with detailed information on the discovery of the structure of DNA by Watson and Crick. There are numerous interviews with Watson and Crick as well as with scientists familiar with these Nobel laureates; provides an in-depth understanding of how they developed their ideas on the structure of DNA.

Riedman, Sarah R., and Elton T. Gustafson. *Portraits of Nobel Laureates in Medicine and Physiology.* New York: Abelard-Schuman, 1963. This book contains a history of Alfred Nobel and most of the Nobel Prize recipients in medicine or physiology from 1901 to 1963. There is a short history of Wilkins, Crick, and Watson's involvement in the discovery of the structure of DNA. The development of the central dogma is also discussed.

Jaime S. Colomé

1962

Physiology or Medicine

Francis Crick, Great Britain
James D. Watson, United States
Maurice H. F. Wilkins, Great Britain

Chemistry

Max Ferdinand Perutz, Great Britain
John Cowdery Kendrew, Great Britain

Physics

Lev Davidovich Landau, Soviet Union

Literature

John Steinbeck, United States

Peace

Linus Pauling, United States

MAURICE H. F. WILKINS
1962

Born: Pongaroa, New Zealand; December 15, 1916

Nationality: British
Areas of concentration: Biophysics and chemistry

Wilkins performed X-ray diffraction studies on the DNA molecule, revealing evidence of the molecule's basic structure

The Award

Presentation

In presenting the laureates in science on December 10, 1962, Professor Arne Engström, member of the Staff of Professors of the Royal Caroline Institute, likened the discovery of the structure of deoxyribonucleic acid (DNA) and its significance to a caricature. The success of a portrayal in a caricature depends upon the genuineness of the fusion of generalities and individualities. Comparatively, the discovery of the overall helical structure of DNA by Maurice Wilkins and the demonstration of the specificity of base pairing within the helices by James D. Watson and Francis Crick revealed the vehicle by which the commonalities and individualities of living things could be derived. Engström further endeavored to explain briefly the composition of DNA and the mechanism of the genetic code. DNA is the hereditary material that makes up the gene; it is composed of chemical units called nucleotides that are in turn made up of three types of building blocks: sugar, phosphate, and a nitrogen-containing chemical base.

The X-ray diffraction photographs of DNA made by X-ray crystallography techniques show a cross-pattern of dark spots in the center of the picture, which indicated that DNA is helical. This information was used by Wilkins to determine the double spiral staircase formation of DNA. In a like manner, the black areas of the top and bottom of the photograph indicated to Watson and Crick that the nitrogen bases are stacked inside the helices like rungs on a ladder. These "rungs," made up of four types of bases, are always paired in a specific order that constitutes the genetic code. Each three of these bases denotes a code that, along with ribonucleic acid (RNA), determines which amino acids will compose the proteins synthesized. This code is transferred in cell divison in normal body cells and sex cells so that DNA can both start and control the development of the individual. Thus, Engström stated, the discovery of the structure of deoxyribonucleic acid opens the door to various avenues of study that will lead to more knowledge of the control and transfer of genetic information. The Nobel Prize was then received by Maurice Wilkins from the hands of His Majesty King Gustav VI.

Nobel lecture

The Nobel lecture, entitled "The Molecular Configuration of Nucleic Acids," was given by Dr. Maurice H. F. Wilkins on December 11, 1962. Before explaining the details of the research which earned for him this honor, Wilkins described background research which eventually led to the nucleic acid studies. After receiving his degree in physics from the University of Cambridge in 1938, Wilkins studied luminescence and the motion of electrons in crystals. He also participated in the making of the atomic bomb during World War II. Later, however, he became interested in the complex molecular structures of the macromolecules that apparently control life processes.

About this time he was invited by J. T. Randall of St. Andrews in Scotland to join a biophysics project that utilized X radiation in studying genetic material. From this time on, Wilkins became increasingly more fascinated with the structures of macromolecules and with the bonding relationships among these molecules. Quite by accident, he isolated single strands of DNA fibers while manipulating a DNA gel. Because of the uniformity of structure, Wilkins thought that these fibers would make excellent X-ray diffraction studies that might possibly yield much information about function as well as structure of these macromolecules. This marked the beginning of his DNA X-ray diffraction studies.

Many scientists were carrying out research designed to determine the genetic substance. Among these were Alfred Hershey and Martha Chase, who studied bacteriophages by using radioactive isotopes and concluded that the genetic substance is DNA. Erwin Chargaff showed that the proportions of the nitrogen-containing bases are the same in all cells of the same species; J. M. Gulland and D. O. Jordan showed that the bases are hydrogen-bonded together, both for stabilization and for ease of chain separation. Other scientific experiments showed DNA to be a pure chemical substance with outstanding possibilities for self-replication and reproduction. The question then became: If DNA is truly the genetic material, how is the genetic information contained in DNA? The answer would come when the concise structure of DNA was determined. This was accomplished by X-ray diffraction studies, coupled with molecular model building.

From X-ray diffraction photographs, the helical nature of DNA was shown. These helices are made up of five-carbon sugars and phosphate groups that appear to form the vertical sides of a ladder. The vertical sides are held together by nitrogenous bases known as purines and pyrimidines. The five-carbon sugars, phosphates, and nitrogenous bases make up nucleotides, which are the building blocks of DNA. The purines are named adenine and guanine, and the pyrimidines are cytosine and thymine. All the bases are stacked at equal distances from one another, with adenine and thymine always pairing and cytosine and guanine pairing, so that the ladder's vertical sides are uniformly equidistant from end to end. The bases are held together by hydrogen bonds. From the crystallography studies of Wilkins and associates, Watson and Crick theorized what the structure should be and constructed models to prove their theory. They noted that it was the exactness of the base pairing that formed the foundation for DNA replication and information transfer. Wilkins noted that there are several configurations of the DNA molecule and that each is determined by the water and salt content of the DNA fibers and cations used in neutralizing the phosphate groups. The three configurations of the DNA molecule are denoted A, B, and C. The A configuration is a crystalline formation, the B configuration is a higher-moisture molecule, and the C configuration is an artifact resulting from drying of the fibers.

Continuing his explanation of the DNA configuration, Wilkins noted that another nucleic acid was needed to transfer genetic information. This nucleic acid is RNA, which acts as a middleman between the raw genetic information and actual life processes such as protein synthesis. Wilkins concluded his lecture on an optimistic note, pointing out that X-ray diffraction could in the future be used for direct analysis of both DNA and RNA molecules. He finished by thanking the many scientists who contributed to his work.

Critical reception

The announcement that Maurice H. F. Wilkins was one of the recipients of the Nobel Prize in Physiology or Medicine in 1962 was met with optimistic enthusiasm by laymen and scientists alike. Dr. Alfred E. Mirsky, a geneticist from the Rockefeller Institute, stated in *Newsweek* that their "work is a step toward biology's Rosetta Stone." *The New York Times* recorded the event as the first physical description of the chemical that makes up the genes; further, it said, this achievement was probably the greatest genetic advance since Gregor Mendel illustrated the fundamentals of inheritance.

At the time of the presentation of the award, Wilkins was an internationally recognized expert on the molecular structure of nucleic acids. He had participated in research teams in England and the United States. He was known by his colleagues as a man of few words but great ideas. He was so consumed with finding the structure of DNA and determining its role in inheritance, however, that he once said to Watson and Crick that "DNA, you know, is Midas' gold. Everyone who touches it goes mad."

Their great accomplishment has started scientists on one of the most exciting chases since the splitting of the atom, one which may ultimately unravel the last secrets of the living cell. The significance of such findings may only be realized when this information is used to deter disease and prevent inheritable abnormalities. A sad note concerning the presentation of this award to Wilkins is that his research associate, Rosalind Franklin, who made the X-ray diffraction photograph that pinpointed this information, did not live to see the fruition of her work. Wilkins' research provided the first stimulus for the DNA structure determination and supplied the proof that the structure proposed by Watson and Crick was essentially correct.

Biography

Maurice Hugh Frederick Wilkins was born on December 15, 1916, in Pongaroa, New Zealand, to Edgar Henry and Eveline Constance Jane (née Whittaker) Wilkins, both of Dublin, Ireland. His father was interested in research, but because of his duties as a school doctor in New Zealand, he had little opportunity to pursue research.

At the age of six, Maurice was sent to England, where he attended King Edward's School in Birmingham. He obtained the B.A. degree from St. John's College, University of Cambridge, in 1938. His studies on the luminescence of solids and the electron trap theory of phosphorescence earned for him the Ph.D. degree in 1940.

When England entered World War II, Wilkins changed his studies to weaponry research and joined other physicists studying the separation of uranium isotopes for making an atom bomb. He participated in Britain's military nuclear research as a member of the Manhattan Project team in Berkeley, California. There he involved himself in mass spectrograph studies of the separation of uranium isotopes. After the war, in 1945, he took a position at St. Andrew's University in Scotland in biophysics. In 1946, he moved to King's College in London and became a member of the staff of the Medical Research Council's biophysics research unit until 1950, when he became assistant director. In 1955 he was named deputy director. From 1946 to 1955, he investigated the genetic effects of ultrasonics, studied microscopy, and performed spectrophotometric studies of nucleic acids and tobacco mosaic viruses. At this time, he began his X-ray diffraction studies of DNA, which led to the delineation of its molecular structure. He has many publications on X-ray diffraction and nucleic acids.

In 1959, he was elected a fellow of the Royal Society; in 1960, he received the Albert Lasker Award, which he shared with Watson and Crick; and in 1962, he was made a Companion of the British Empire. Also in 1959, he married Patricia Ann Chidgey. They would have two children, Sarah and George.

Scientific Career

It seemed a bit incredible to Wilkins that he should receive the Nobel Prize for his studies in macromolecular structure. Many scientists were involved in these types of studies as a result of the "coming of age" of two scientific fields—molecular biology and biophysics—in the mid-1940's. These fields seemed to offer the means of solving the problems of the mechanisms of life processes and a means, possibly, of controlling them to improve the health conditions of man. During the middle to late 1940's, Wilkins considered changing his research field from physics to molecular biology or biophysics as a result of his disenchantment with the field after he became involved with the making of the atom bomb during World War II. Notwithstanding his years of training and work in the field of physics (beginning in 1938 with his taking the B.A. degree in physics from St. John's College, Cambridge, and in 1940 earning the Ph.D. degree in physics from Birmingham University for his studies on the luminescence of solids and the electron trap theory of phosphorescence), Wilkins decided that after the war in 1945 he should apply his knowledge of physics to biological systems. He believed that much biological data could thus be accumulated that could be used to solve the fundamental problems of life, especially those concerned with heredity and disease control.

In 1945, he became a lecturer in physics at St. Andrew's University in Scotland, and in 1946, with much apprehension, he joined the biophysics unit of the Medical

Research Council at King's College, University of London. It was at this time that scientists at the Rockefeller Institute announced that the genes, the carriers of hereditary traits, were made up of DNA, an extremely complicated chemical substance. This may well be considered the turning point in Wilkins' career. He was so fascinated with DNA that he immediately began his dichroism pattern analysis of microscopy studies. Specifically, he placed the DNA molecules under the microscope, then illuminated the molecules with one color of transmitted light and another color of reflected light. For proper orientation of the DNA molecules under the microscope, he placed them in a gel and adjusted the DNA fiber positions with a glass rod. In the course of observation—and somewhat by accident—Wilkins noticed that very thin fibers stretched between the gel and the tip of the glass rod each time he picked up the glass rod. These fibers, according to the literature on structure studies of crystalline proteins, would be especially amenable for analysis by X-ray diffraction techniques. With great zeal and curiosity, Wilkins began his X-ray diffraction studies that would earn for him in later years the Nobel Prize.

The first results of the crystallography studies were excellent. They indicated that DNA was a spiral; it seemed much like a rope ladder that was fixed at one end and twisted upon itself. This pattern was observed to be the same irrespective of the source of the DNA. Wilkins, along with his colleague, Rosalind Franklin, discerned from the sharpness of the diffraction patterns that DNA molecules were highly regular and were probably helical. Further analysis showed the diameter of the helix to be 2 nanometers, with its purine and pyrimidine bases stacked 0.34 nanometer apart. The width of the helix suggested that it was composed of two strands, which accounts for the now-familiar term "double helix." It was evident that DNA was a long polymer chain of alternating sugar and phosphate groups with the nitrogen-containing bases attached as side chains to each of the sugars. It was also clear that the phosphate groups were on the outside of the unit and, as density measurements indicated, that there were probably two coaxial molecules in the helix. To prove that the DNA structure was true (and not an artifact of isolation), Wilkins took X-ray diffraction photographs of intact biological systems. They very closely matched the isolated molecules.

Wilkins shared his information with a British biochemist, Francis Crick, who, with American biologist James Watson, constructed an acceptable model of DNA. With more research results, Wilkins refined his X-ray techniques and added experimental confirmation to the Watson-Crick DNA model. After several years of X-ray diffraction studies on ribonucleic acid (RNA), in 1962, Wilkins obtained the first really clear X-ray diffraction patterns of RNA and noted that it, like DNA, had a helical structure. He continued his studies of DNA and RNA, but increasingly placed more emphasis on RNA.

Bibliography

Primary

BIOPHYSICS: "Molecular Structure of Deoxypentose Nucleic Acids," *Nature*, vol.

171, 1953, p. 737 (with A. R. Stokes and H. R. Wilson); "A New Configuration of Deoxyribonucleic Acid," *Nature*, vol. 182, 1958, pp. 387-388 (with D. A. Marvin and M. Spencer); "Molecular Configuration of Nucleic Acids," *Science*, vol. 140, 1963, pp. 941-950; "X-Ray Diffraction Study of the Structure of Nucleohistone and Nucleoprotamines," *Journal of Molecular Biology*, vol. 7, no. 6, 1963, pp. 756-757 (with Geoffrey Zubay); "X-Ray Diffraction Studies of the Molecular Configuration of Nucleic Acids," in *Aspects of Protein Structure*, edited by G. N. Ramachandran, 1963; "A Note on Reversible Dissociation of Deoxyribonucleohistone," *Journal of Molecular Biology*, vol. 9, no. 1, 1964, pp. 246-249 (with Geoffrey Zubay).

Secondary

Crick, Francis. *What Mad Pursuit: A Personal View of Scientific Discovery*. New York: Basic Books, 1988. Wilkins' fellow Nobel laureate Crick presents his own view of the DNA research in which he was involved. Focuses on the work of Watson and Crick in the 1950's; Wilkins' work is included.

Curtis, Helena, and Sue Barnes. *Biology*. New York: Worth, 1989. This text includes a discussion of the critical X-ray diffraction photographs of DNA fibers; reflections of crossings in the middle indicate the helical nature of the molecule. Makes note of the importance of Rosalind Franklin's contribution to Wilkins' work.

Darnell, James, Harvey Lodish, and David Baltimore. *Molecular Cell Biology*. 2d ed. New York: W. H. Freeman, 1990. Contains a good general discussion of how images formed by the refractions of an X-ray beam can reveal extensive detail of molecules. Special emphasis is placed on the DNA molecule.

Judson, Horace Freeland. *The Eighth Day of Creation: The Makers of the Revolution in Biology*. New York: Simon & Schuster, 1979. This history of molecular biology devotes considerable attention to DNA discoveries. Contains interviews with many of the scientists involved and gives a clear idea of how DNA research proceeded.

Modern Scientists and Engineers. Vol 3. New York: McGraw-Hill, 1980. A brief biographical reference, in which emphasis is placed on the work that earned the Nobel Prize for Wilkins. Details of experimental protocol are given, as is a discussion of related work.

Watson, James D. *The Double Helix*. New York: Atheneum, 1968. Watson presents his version of the discovery of the structure of DNA and details his collaboration with both Wilkins and Crick. This book generated some controversy because of its subjective (some would say gossipy) "behind-the-scenes" portrayals of scientists and their work.

Watson, James D., and F. H. Crick. "Molecular Structure of Nucleic Acids: A Structure for Deoxyribose Nucleic Acid." *Nature* 171 (1953): 737. This article was for the scientific community a final confirmation that the genetic material is DNA, which is a double helix consisting of two complementary strands of nucleotides.

Bennye S. Henderson

1963

Physiology or Medicine

Sir John Carew Eccles, Australia
Alan Lloyd Hodgkin, Great Britain
Andrew F. Huxley, Great Britain

Chemistry

Karl Ziegler, West Germany
Giulio Natta, Italy

Physics

Eugene Paul Wigner, Hungary and United States
Maria Goeppert Mayer, Germany and United States
J. Hans D. Jensen, West Germany

Literature

George Seferis, Greece

Peace

International Red Cross Committee
League of Red Cross Societies

SIR JOHN CAREW ECCLES
1963

Born: Melbourne, Australia; January 27, 1903

Nationality: Australian
Area of concentration: Neurophysiology

Eccles investigated the electrical changes by which nerve cells communicate with one another. He concluded that an ionic mechanism involving sodium and potassium ions carries the nerve impulse across the synapse

The Award

Presentation

Professor Ragnar Arthur Granit, a member of the faculty of the medical school of the Royal Caroline Institute in Stockholm, delivered the presentation address for the 1963 Nobel Prize in Physiology or Medicine on Tuesday, December 10, 1963, before King Gustav VI Adolf, assembled members of the royal family, and guests. The award was presented jointly to John Eccles, Alan Lloyd Hodgkin, and Andrew Fielding Huxley. Granit's address began with a summary of the basic processes involved in nerve impulses and their transmission through the body by nerve fibers. The results obtained by this year's Nobel laureates, Granit said, concerned the electrical changes in the nerve cells caused by the impulse. The processes were measured by means of minute electrodes and then amplified a million times so they could be displayed on the screen of a cathode-ray tube.

These experiments, begun in 1939 by Hodgkin and Huxley, were performed using the giant nerve fiber from a squid. They found that a nerve impulse delivered a potential change that exceeded by one-third the potential measured inside the fiber membrane. Their experiments following World War II were designed to test a theory advanced by Ernest Overton in 1904 which suggested that the nerve impulse involved transfer of sodium and potassium ions across the fiber membrane.

Eccles' work, Granit said, used microelectrodes—with tips of the order of one one-thousandth of a millimeter in diameter—which were placed inside the motoneurons, the nerve cells, in the spinal cord. Eccles showed how excitation of the nerve cell caused changes in the membrane potentials. The excitation caused a potential decrease until a value was reached sufficient to "fire off" an impulse. Eccles suggested that this impulse was carried along the nerve fiber by sodium ions. The nerve impulse, then, corresponds to an ionic current, Granit concluded.

Nobel lecture

On December 11, 1963, Eccles gave his Nobel lecture, entitled "The Ionic Mechanism of Postsynaptic Inhibition." (The synapse is the junction between nerve cells.) In an illustrative diagram accompanying his lecture, Eccles showed a drawing of a nerve cell, which consisted of a central nucleus surrounded by branching nerve fibers that end in knobs. These branching fibers may contact similar fibers from adjacent nerve cells at synapses, the points of contact. Transmission of nerve impulses across these synapses is brought about by secretion of chemical substances, or ions, which act across the synaptic gap between the nerve cells. Eccles used an electron microscope to obtain images of motoneurons and microelectrodes to penetrate the cell and make the potential measurements.

The technique that Eccles and his coworkers devised consisted of the introduction of a fine glass pipette having a tip diameter of about 0.5 micron (1 micron = 0.001 millimeter) and filled with a conductive salt solution such as concentrated potassium chloride. Potential measurements were then made and recorded; they showed the variation of electromotive force across the membrane making up the wall of the nerve cell. Two kinds of synaptic potentials were noted, excitatory and inhibitory, which were "virtually mirror images of each other," according to Eccles.

Experiments were made involving altering the concentration gradient across the membrane for various cations and anions and measuring the resulting potential produced and its decay with time. Changes in relative ionic concentrations across the membrane were affected by altering the concentration of the external solution. Conversely, ions could be injected into the interior of the nerve cell and measured by passing a given amount of electrical current through the microelectrode. In accompanying diagrams, Eccles illustrated how an inhibitory potential could be changed to a depolarizing potential by the addition of chloride ions into the nerve cell.

Eccles tested the depolarizing ability of thirty-three different anions, including bromide, nitrate, sulfate, and phosphate. In general, the smaller the ionic size, the greater the depolarizing effect. He attributed this effect of size to the ability of the anion to penetrate the membrane and thus counteract the membrane potential established by the cation. The smaller the size of the anion, the greater its ability to penetrate the membrane. He estimated that the membrane was permeable to all anions of a diameter less than 1.14 times the diameter of the potassium ion, or not more than 2.85 angstrom units (1 angstrom unit = 0.0000000001 meter). This is in accordance with the theory that the membrane potential may be attributable to differences in potassium concentration across the membrane.

In conclusion, Eccles presented a picture of the synaptic reaction as he believed it to be. In effect, he said that chloride and potassium ions move across the membrane and produce the current that makes up the nerve impulse.

Critical reception

The Nobel Prize in Physiology or Medicine for 1963 was awarded to two Britons, Alan Lloyd Hodgkin, forty-nine, and Andrew Fielding Huxley, forty-five, and an Australian, Sir John Carew Eccles, sixty, reported *Facts on File: World News Digest*. The three men were honored for their research on nerve cells and shared a $51,158 cash award.

The New York Times for October 18, 1963, carried the headline "3 Win Nobel Prize for Nerve Studies" and said that the award was made "for their work in analyzing the functions of nerve cells in transmitting impulses along a nerve fiber." Hodgkin and Huxley were the fourteenth and fifteenth Britons to be chosen for the award, and Eccles the second Australian, since the first Nobel Prizes were distributed in 1901. The United States, with twenty-seven winners, has dominated the field, the article said.

Eccles was a brilliant scholar from childhood, *The New York Times* reported, and attended Magdalen College, University of Oxford, as a Rhodes Scholar. He had "completed 35 years of studying communication between nerve cells but had never worked with colleagues. . . . 'My work grows out of theirs,' " he explained.

In an accompanying feature article, *The New York Times* said that the laureates had clarified nerve-impulse transmission and that data from axons of squid were the basis for research on the phenomenon of the synapse. The *Times* carried an additional article following the actual prize awards on December 11, 1963.

"Nobels for Nerves" was the alliterative headline in *Newsweek* for October 28, 1963; *Newsweek* reported that "squidows was the word that the wives of Cambridge physiologists Alan Hodgkin and Andrew Huxley used in referring to themselves." Hodgkin and Huxley (a half-brother of novelist Aldous Huxley and grandson of the famous nineteenth century biologist Sir Thomas Huxley) "discovered how electrochemical activity within the nerve cell fiber transmits the impulses that carry information along nerves, like a telephone carries conversations." While the British researchers concerned themselves with the flow of impulses, *Newsweek* continued, Eccles uncovered new information about how these same impulses "jump from one nerve cell to another." He inserted ultrathin glass electrodes into the spinal cords of cats to map the electrical changes involved in the inhibition and excitation of nerve cells at synaptic junctions.

Science for October 25, 1963, carried a two-page article by M. G. F. Fuortes of the National Institutes of Health on the Nobel Prizes in Physiology or Medicine for 1963. Walther Nernst, Fuortes wrote, had first suggested that the "electrical properties of nerves should be ascribed to accumulations of ions and movement of ions across a barrier permeable to some ions only." Hodgkin and coworkers "measured the amounts of various electrolytes entering and leaving the nerve fibers at rest, and during activity. The results proved to be in agreement with the view that the membrane is permeable mostly to potassium when it is at rest, and mostly to sodium during activity," *Science* reported. Eccles' results "showed that the synaptic transmission is analogous to transmission from motor nerves to muscles."

Biography

John Carew Eccles was born in Melbourne, Victoria, Australia, on January 27, 1903. His father, William James Eccles, was a teacher, as was his mother, Mary (Carew) Eccles. He was graduated in medicine with first-class honors by Melbourne University in 1925 and entered Magdalen College of the University of Oxford in England on a Rhodes Scholarship in the same year. Eccles was married to Irene Frances Miller on July 3, 1928. They would have nine children, Rosamond Margaret

(Mrs. Richard Mason), Peter James, Alice Catherine, William, Mary Rose (Mrs. Brian Mennis), John Mark, Judith Clare, Frances Joan, and Richard Aquinas Eccles.

He continued to win honors at Oxford—first-class honors in natural sciences, the Christopher Welch Scholarship, and a Junior Research Fellowship at Exeter College, Oxford, where he began to do research on nerve reflexes with Sir Charles Scott Sherrington, Waynflete Professor of Physiology, until 1934. From 1934 to 1937, Eccles served as a tutorial fellow at Magdalen College.

In 1937, Eccles returned to Australia, where he was director of the Kanematsu Memorial Institute of Pathology in Sydney until 1943. He then moved to New Zealand as professor of physiology at the University of Otago in Dunedin, where he served until 1951. In 1952 he returned to Australia as professor of physiology at the National University in Canberra, and he remained there for the next fifteen years. In 1966 he moved to the United States to become a member of the American Medical Society's Institute for Biomedical Research in Chicago.

Eccles was knighted by the queen in 1958. Other honors include Fellow (1941) and Medalist (1962) of the Royal Society of London; the Cothenius Medal of the Deutsche Akademie der Naturforscher Leopoldina (1963); honorary member of the American Philosophical Society; and honorary foreign member of the American Academy of Arts and Sciences.

Scientific Career

Synaptic transmission—the movement of nerve impulses between nerve cells—was Eccles' area of research in his early days at Oxford in the early 1930's. This research was carried out on the central nervous system and peripherally in affected sympathetic ganglia and heart muscles using newly developed electrical techniques. In this early period, there were at least two rival theories of synaptic transmission—one chemical, the other electrical. At first Eccles resisted the idea of chemical transmission of nerve impulses, but he later came to accept chemical transmission as the moving force in the great majority of both central nervous system and peripheral synapses.

In 1937, Eccles moved to Australia to become director of a medical research group in Sydney. There he had Bernard Katz and Stephen William Kuffler as collaborators in research on the microphysiology of neuromuscular junctions using cats and frogs. Then, as professor of physiology at the University of Otago in New Zealand, Eccles continued his studies on the central nervous system. In 1951, with L. G. Brock and J. S. Coombs, he succeeded in inserting a microelectrode into the heart of nerve cells of the central nervous system and was able to measure the electrical responses produced by excitatory and inhibitory synapses. Also in New Zealand, Eccles met philosopher Karl Raimund Popper, with whom he later collaborated on a book, *The Self and Its Brain*. Popper's revolutionary ideas in the philosophy of science impressed Eccles very much, and from Popper he learned the transitory nature of scientific theories, the necessity of testing such theories as rigorously as possible, and how theories are either falsified or corroborated but never truly verified.

In 1952, Eccles returned to Australia, to the Australian National University in Canberra. In the earlier years, from 1953 to 1955, he concentrated on the biophysical properties of synaptic transmission, the research for which he was given the Nobel Prize. He reported on some of this work in the *Annals of the New York Academy of Science* in 1959, when he said that the electron microscope had fully confirmed the neuron theory of Santiago Ramón y Cajal (winner of the Nobel Prize in 1906)—that each nerve cell was structurally an independent unit. Further, there was a gap, the synaptic cleft, of 150 to 400 angstroms between the nerve cells, across which the nerve impulses must be transmitted. This transmisson, or synaptic action, was of two types, Eccles wrote, excitatory and inhibitory: Excitatory synaptic action evoked the discharge of nerve impulses, whereas inhibitory synaptic action tended to prevent this discharge or impulse. A nerve impulse is discharged when a specific chemical transmitter is released from one nerve cell (the presynaptic terminal), traverses the synaptic cleft, and acts on the second (or postsynaptic) cell. Because of the relatively high concentration of potassium, sodium, and chloride ions in the nerve cells, he believed that these ions were the ones principally involved. Under the influence of the excitatory synaptic transmitter, receptive areas of the membrane making up the body of the receiving cell become permeable to all diffusible ions, both inside and outside the membrane; consequently, ions move from higher to lower concentration through the membrane and create a membrane potential. Eccles stated that the current moving inward across the activated patches would be carried largely by sodium ions that would be "moving down a steep electrochemical gradient of over 100 millivolts, across a membrane of about 50 angstroms thickness." In general, he said, the activated membrane behaves like a sieve that allows the passage of ions of diameter below a certain value.

Eccles and coworkers measured both excitatory postsynaptic potentials (EPSP) and inhibitory postsynaptic potentials (IPSP) across membranes permeable to various relatively small ions under the influence of changes in concentration artificially produced inside the cell by injection. Muscle fibers were also found to influence the potentials. Thus, using crustacean nerve cells, the IPSP was found to act in a certain direction only when the nerve cell was depolarized by the stretching of its associated muscle fiber.

In a further corroboration of the theory of chemically transmitting synapses, Eccles reported that anesthetics, such as Nembutal, in moderate dosages prolonged and increased the inhibition of nerve reflexes. He pointed out that this was probably attributable to depression of the transmitter action at synapses responsible for presynaptic inhibition. In 1964, Eccles reported on the correlation between the size of the ions in the aqueous solutions inside and outside the nerve cells and the effects of their injection into the cell on the IPSP. The inhibitory membrane is permeable, he found, to all ions smaller than the potassium ion. He concluded that potassium and chloride ions, "moving across the membrane thousands of times more readily than normally," produce an ionic flux that causes the IPSP.

In a ten-page article in *Scientific American* (January, 1965), Eccles summarized many of these studies to show how one nerve cell transmits the nerve impulse to another nerve cell by delivering a "squirt of transmitter substance." He said that he and his colleagues studied large nerve cells called motoneurons that lie in the spinal cord and whose function is to activate various muscles in the body. The spinal cord connects at one end to the brain, and, in "trying to understand the workings of his own brain man meets his highest challenge." Eccles reported that their studies of nerve-cell potentials indicated a concentration of potassium ions inside the nerve cell that is about thirty times greater than that outside the cell. He and his coworkers determined that to maintain the large difference in concentration, the inside of the membrane would have to be charged 90 millivolts negative with respect to the exterior. The effects of some drugs, he concluded, could be demonstrated by the effects of certain toxic substances (strychnine and tetanus toxin) in the spinal cord: "They specifically prevent inhibitory synaptic action and leave excitatory action unaltered." The result is convulsions, because the synaptic excitation of nerve cells is uncontrolled.

The philosophical problem of the relation between the mind and the body was the difficult subject that Eccles and philosopher Karl Popper tackled together in the 1970's. During the month of September, 1974, the two men and their wives were guests of the Rockefeller Foundation at its Villa Serbelloni on Lake Como. Eccles and Popper held daily discussions, which were recorded and were eventually published in 1977 as *The Self and Its Brain*. Thus, they continued the close relationship begun a quarter of a century earlier in New Zealand.

Popper, in part 1 of the book, stated that humankind's consciousness of self and knowledge of death were among its great "achievements." He also divided experience into three "worlds": World 1 is the world of physical objects, world two that of states of consciousness, world three that of objective knowledge (this is the world that includes man-made culture). In part 2, Eccles discussed the neuronal machinery involved in the various manifestations of the self-conscious mind and its implications for Popper's three worlds. He also commented on "misleading" ideas about how the brain works. People are told, he said, that "the brain 'sees' lines" and other forms, yet "all that is known to happen in the brain is that neurons of the visual cortex are caused to fire trains of impulses in response to some specific visual input." Eccles had earlier summarized the difficulties inherent in trying to understand the workings of the brain in his 1965 *Scientific American* article: "The task of understanding in a comprehensive way how the human brain operates staggers its own imagination."

Bibliography

Primary

PHYSIOLOGY: *The Neurophysiological Basis of Mind: The Principles of Neurophysiology*, 1953; "Excitatory and Inhibitory Synaptic Action, *Annals of the New York Academy of Sciences*, vol. 81, 1959, pp. 247-264; "Pharmacological Studies on Presynaptic Inhibition," *Journal of Physiology*, vol. 168, 1963, pp. 500-530 (with

R. Schmidt and W. D. Willis); "Ionic Mechanism of Postsynaptic Inhibition," *Science*, vol. 145, 1964, pp. 1140-1147; "The Synapse," *Scientific American*, vol. 212, pp. 56-66; "The Ionic Mechanisms of Excitatory and Inhibitory Synaptic Action," *Annals of the New York Academy of Sciences*, vol. 88, 1966, pp. 473-494; *The Physiology of Nerve Cells*, 1968; *The Understanding of the Brain*, 1973.

PHILOSOPHY: *Facing Reality: Philosophical Adventures of a Brain Scientist*, 1970; *The Self and Its Brain*, 1977 (with Karl Popper).

Secondary

Brodal, Alf. *Neurological Anatomy: In Relation to Clinical Medicine*. New York: Oxford University Press, 1969. This book was first published in Norwegian in 1943; the English translation was first issued in 1946. It is of interest in that it presents the view of neurological anatomy that prevailed at the time Eccles was first performing his work on neurons.

Galbraith, G. C., M. L. Kietzman, and E. Donchin, eds. *Neurophysiology and Psychophysiology.* Hillsdale, N.J.: Erlbaum, 1988. Sixty-one contributors cover topics such as neural control, visual discrimination, attention, motor performance, development, and higher cognitive processes. Both excitatory and inhibitory synaptic actions are discussed by F. B. Krasne of UCLA; he used crayfish tailflip locomotion in connection with his neural studies.

LeDoux, Joseph E., and William Hirst, eds. *Mind and Brain: Dialogues in Cognitive Neuroscience*. New York: Cambridge University Press, 1986. The purpose of this book is to encourage neuroscientists and cognitive scientists to consider whether mutual interdependence is their most prudent course. In eighteen chapters by different authors, the subjects taken up include perception, attention, memory, and emotion. Eccles' book *The Brain and the Unity of Conscious Experience* is considered under problems of consciousness.

Newman, P. P. *Neurophysiology.* Jamaica, N.Y.: Spectrum, 1980. A course of lectures at the University of Leeds, England, provides a comprehensive account of the nervous system and its functions. In chapter 3, "Synaptic Transmission," both excitatory and inhibitory postsynaptic potentials are explained. Newman agrees with Eccles that in mammals the action potentials at presynaptic endings cause liberation of chemical transmitter substances that produce a change in ionic permeability of postsynaptic membranes.

Ryle, Gilbert. *The Concept of Mind.* New York: Barnes & Noble Books, 1949. This book, about which Eccles has written, offers a theory of the mind. The key arguments are intended to show why certain sorts of operation with the concepts of mental powers and processes are breaches of logical rules. The official doctrine is that every human being is both a body and a mind; however, minds are not in space, nor are their operations subject to mechanical laws.

Joseph Albert Schufle

1963

Physiology or Medicine

Sir John Carew Eccles, Australia
Alan Lloyd Hodgkin, Great Britain
Andrew F. Huxley, Great Britain

Chemistry

Karl Ziegler, West Germany
Giulio Natta, Italy

Physics

Eugene Paul Wigner, Hungary and United States
Maria Goeppert Mayer, Germany and United States
J. Hans D. Jensen, West Germany

Literature

George Seferis, Greece

Peace

International Red Cross Committee
League of Red Cross Societies

ALAN LLOYD HODGKIN
1963

Born: Banbury, Oxfordshire, England; February 5, 1914

Nationality: British
Area of concentration: Neurophysiology

Hodgkin clarified the source of the "action potential" that carries messages along a nerve in terms of the voltage that arises from different concentrations of potassium and sodium ions inside and outside the nerve and the flow of these ions across the nerve membrane

The Award

Presentation

Professor Ragnar Granit of the Royal Caroline Institute presented Alan Lloyd Hodgkin and his cowinners Andrew Huxley and John Carew Eccles to Sweden's King Gustav VI Adolf, in a speech delivered in Stockholm on December 10, 1963. Granit's presentation dealt with all three men's work. He sketched in the background of nerve impulses as voltage peaks of about 1 millisecond duration that move along the nerve axon (the long fiber that reaches away from the central nerve cell and its nucleus) and indicated that Hodgkin and Huxley's research was thus electronic as much as physiological.

The "resting potential" of a nerve is a voltage difference across the nerve membrane equal to that of a "concentration cell"—a type of battery in which the electromotive force is developed solely by differences in anode and cathode concentration of a single ion—in this case, potassium. If a stimulus causes potassium ions to flow freely across the cell membrane, reducing potential difference to zero, the action potential should have a force the same as that of the resting potential. Hodgkin's earliest work, in 1939, showed that the action potential was in fact greater than the resting potential. Clearly another ion was contributing to the action potential: sodium.

Working with giant axons (about 1 millimeter in diameter) from squid, Hodgkin and Huxley devised a series of experiments in which they altered the resting potential with an internal electrode, then altered the concentration of sodium and potassium in the external solution. These variations allowed them to determine at what levels of force and at what concentrations sodium and potassium ions flowed through the nerve membrane and to elicit the mechanism of the action potential: Sodium permeability of the membrane increases, sodium flows into the nerve, and the first half of the voltage peak of the action potential results from the electromotive force change of the sodium concentration cell. In the second half of the peak, sodium flow closes down rapidly and potassium flow out of the nerve takes place, which falls off much more slowly than sodium flow. The overall voltage falls below the resting potential after the action potential has passed a region of the nerve. This makes that region unresponsive for about a millisecond and ensures that no nerve impulse can go backward. Granit closed this section of his talk with mention of clinical applications then being investigated. He then discussed Eccles' work and presented the three men to the King to receive the 1963 Nobel Prize in Physiology or Medicine.

Nobel lecture

Hodgkin's lecture, delivered on December 11, 1963, was entitled "The Ionic Basis of Nervous Conduction." He began by recalling that Trinity College, University of Cambridge, where he was a fellow, had a distinguished history of neurophysiological research. He cited the men upon whose work he had built, then moved on to his own first major finding—that the action potential exceeds the resting potential by a factor of up to two. (Nerve impulses take the form of an action potential; this is a transient voltage peak propagated down the nerve fiber, with a constant potential dictated by the sodium and potassium concentration cells.) This finding was made in 1939, and work had to be put away during World War II.

In 1945, work began in earnest on both sides of the Atlantic, and in less than a decade, most of the findings that led to the Nobel Prize had been published. The first piece of information was made possible by use of the giant axon of the squid, which provided enough material to determine solution concentrations of ions. The resting potential was found to correspond to the electromotive force (emf) of the potassium concentration cell, with potassium ion concentrations being measured inside and outside the axon. To explain the remainder of the action potential, Hodgkin and his coworkers adopted the "sodium hypothesis," which stated simply that the remainder of the potential arose from a sodium concentration cell if the axon membrane could be shown to be permeable to sodium ion. (All electrochemical cells require a controlled exchange of the materials that cause the emf difference across a solution interface, an intermediate conducting solution, or, in this case, a biological membrane.) By manipulating sodium concentrations in the fluid external to the axon, they showed that sodium was indeed responsible for the extra voltage of the action potential: Reducing sodium concentration lowered the action potential (and slowed it as well), reducing it to the resting potential alone when external sodium concentration was zero. When the concentration was increased, the action potential was increased.

Experiments with radioactive sodium showed that sodium did indeed flow across the membrane—about twenty thousand sodium ions into the axon per square micrometer of surface for each nerve impulse, and an equal number of potassium ions out. Hodgkin and Huxley then devised a method for both measuring and controlling the potential across the membrane, which they dubbed the "voltage clamp." Two fine electrodes were inserted into the axon's interior, one to sense voltage and the other to control internal potential by electronic feedback methods. By controlling both potential (in stepwise increments) and external ionic concentrations, Hodgkin and his colleagues were able to determine exactly which ionic influx and efflux carried each part of the current that produced the action potential and eventually could give the description of that potential found above in Professor Granit's introduction.

Hodgkin concluded his Nobel address with a brief discussion of current work. Each nerve impulse, he noted, exchanges about one millionth of the axon's concentration of sodium and potassium. How are these restored? A "sodium pump" was proposed, using energy-rich phosphate compounds such as adenosine triphosphate (ATP) to drive the ions against their concentration gradient; the idea was only a hypothesis under investigation at the time of the address. To test whether biological solutions were necessary in the axon, Hodgkin replaced the gel in the axon with simple potassium chloride solution and found that the nerve continued to fire thousands of times before it ran down from lack of ATP to operate the ion pump. Hodgkin concluded by turning the podium over to cowinner Huxley, who would, he said, show some of the quantitative aspects of the nerve work, in particular the laboratory confirmation of a number of predictions that arose from the mathematical equations they had developed to describe the ionic-electronic action of the nerve impulse.

Critical reception

The 1963 Nobel Prize in Physiology or Medicine was noted with comment by such widely scattered medical jounals as *Nordisk Medicin* (Stockholm), the *Medical Services Journal, Canada, Deutsche medizinische Wochenschrift*, and *Orvosi Hetilap* (Budapest). Of the accounts in semipopular science publications in English, perhaps the most surprising was that in *Science News Letter*, which discussed the unconfirmed sodium pump theory and failed to mention the potassium-sodium nerve transmission work at all. The British journal *Nature* merely announced the award, noting in conclusion that the three laureates "are well known for their work in neurophysiology." As all were fellows of the Royal Society, the laconic treatment was perhaps justified.

Science gave a more complete response. At the time of the prize announcement in late October, the journal printed a brief but thorough discussion of the state of knowledge of nerve transmission by M. G. F. Fuortes, chief of the section of neurophysiology at the National Institute of Neurological Diseases and Blindness, and sometime colleague of Hodgkin and Huxley. The views of the three prizewinners, he concluded, "have been subjected to rigorous tests in many laboratories all over the world and have stimulated fruitful research which promises to continue for some time to come." He continued, "The recent advances in our understanding of the function of nerves and synapses are largely due to the work" of the three laureates. An equally knowledgeable and laudatory assessment appeared in *The New York Times* at the time of the announcement (October 18, 1963), in a signed article by Harold M. Schmeck, Jr. Reviewing the work of all three men, he concluded that their contribution was "extremely fundamental" and could have valuable clinical consequences. In the same issue, in addition to the announcement of the awards, biographical sketches of the winners appeared. The one for Hodgkin included a description by his sixteen-year-old daughter, who mentioned his "deep blue eyes" and "tiny feet": "If you said he was distinguished looking, we'd all be delighted."

The Times of London, on the same date, amplified the award announcement with a brief but well-informed description of the squid axon work, focusing on the experimental technique but adding that scientific "ability of this kind had to be combined with a clear grasp of basic electrical theory and the imaginative insight to arrive at a model of how a nerve might work." The writer concluded that, except for a molecular description of mechanism, "Hodgkin and Huxley have solved the problem of nerve action." Overall, the responses to the Nobel award to Hodgkin and his cowinners can be summed up in the phrase "well-deserved."

Biography

Alan Lloyd Hodgkin was born February 5, 1914, the eldest son (of three) of George L. and Mary F. (Wilson) Hodgkin. George Hodgkin died during World War I, when Alan was four years old. The boy showed an early interest in ornithology and natural history. He was sent to a preparatory school at age nine, and to Gresham's School, Holt, at thirteen. In 1932, he was admitted on scholarship to Trinity College, University of Cambridge, where he did his undergraduate work and earned the M.A. and Sc.D. degrees. In 1936, he became a fellow of Trinity College, a research position he has held (except between 1978 and 1984) since that time. In 1937 and 1938, he worked with Herbert Gasser at the Rockefeller Institute in New York, as well as at the marine biology laboratory at Woods Hole, Massachusetts. Returning in 1938 to Cambridge and the marine biology laboratory at Plymouth, Hodgkin began the work on nerve conduction that would occupy the rest of his career; it was interrupted, however, by England's declaration of war against Adolf Hitler's Germany in September, 1939.

Hodgkin worked during the war at the Royal Air Force Establishment in Farnborough, initially in aviation medicine. He helped develop an oxygen system for high-altitude flyers, then investigated the problem of high-altitude bends. After a year, he was assigned to do research on radar for the remainder of the war. During that time he married Marion Rous, daughter of the American tumor researcher Peyton Rous; they would later have one son and three daughters.

Back at Cambridge and Plymouth in 1945, Hodgkin became lecturer, then assistant director of research. In 1948, he was elected a fellow of the Royal Society; in 1952, he was named Foulerton Research Professor of the Royal Society, in which position he worked until 1969. From 1970 to 1981 he was Humphrey Plummer Professor of Biophysics at Cambridge, and served as president of the Royal Society from 1970 to 1975. From 1966 to 1976 he was president of the Marine Biological Association, and from 1971 to 1984 the chancellor of the University of Leicester. Hodgkin was knighted (KBE) in 1972 and presented with the Order of Merit the following year. He has received many medals, awards, and honorary degrees in addition to the Nobel Prize.

Scientific Career

To an unusual degree, Hodgkin's scientific work has revolved around a single topic: the mechanism of nerve transmission. His very first experimental investigation, as a twenty-year-old undergraduate at Cambridge, was an unsuccessful effort to demonstrate increased membrane (electrical) conductivity in a frog nerve blocked by freezing a portion of the nerve at the center of its length. In the following year, with improved electronic equipment, he demonstrated electrical conduction past the block, but the membrane permeability still eluded him. These results were published in two papers in 1937 in the *Journal of Physiology* (London), where nearly all of his laboratory results would appear over the years.

In 1936, as he moved into graduate work, Hodgkin was named a fellow of Trinity College, Cambridge, signaling the research direction that his career was to take. On the suggestion of neurophysiologist E. D. Adrian (later master of Trinity), Hodgkin began to work on nerve fibers from shore crabs (Carcinus), because they are unmyelinated (not surrounded by a fatty sheath, which alters conduction patterns) and because a single axon could be dissected out of a nerve bundle fairly easily. He got interesting results with subthreshold excitation voltages but was held back by the limitations of his measuring devices. Fortunately, he received a fellowship to work at the Rockefeller Institute in New York in 1937. This placed him among people who were doing the kind of nerve work in which he was interested, at the Rockefeller as well as at Columbia University and Woods Hole. At least equally important, it showed him the kind of electronic design that he needed for the delicate tasks he set for himself in the laboratory. As Hodgkin himself put it, "to work in a big well-organized laboratory . . . helped to turn me from an amateur into a professional scientist." With the equipment available in New York, he was able quickly to demonstrate alteration of conduction velocity with alteration of the external resistance of a nerve fiber (in oil versus sea water as an external medium). At Woods Hole, he was introduced to the giant axon of the squid (of the genus *Loligo*), with which he would obtain the results leading to the Nobel Prize.

Back in England in 1938 and 1939, Hodgkin was able to obtain the initial results on the discrepancy between resting potential and action potential that would eventually lead to the potassium-sodium mechanism, with Huxley collaborating in some of the work. He also began a mathematical description of conductance, using measurements from crab and lobster nerve as well as squid nerve, but the data proved refractory and the analysis had to wait for completion until after the war. World War II uprooted Hodgkin and Huxley, as it did so many other scientists, causing them to suspend their investigations completely and engage in altogether different activities. Hodgkin spent a year in aviation medicine, then nearly six years in radar, on the electronic design side. Asked later whether this experience affected his scientific life, Hodgkin responded, "I would like to be able to say that it made a profound difference, and I expect it did, indirectly. But the fact remains that when I returned to Cambridge in August 1945 I continued working on crustacean nerve using almost exactly the same equipment as before the war." This was principally because electronic components were not readily available. When the technologies developed during the war were brought into the laboratory, radioactive tracers rather than electronic circuitry brought the first success in the research at Cambridge, allowing measurement of sodium flow across the nerve membrane. Moreover, war surplus equipment soon allowed construction of the measuring and feedback devices necessary for the voltage-clamp experiments.

The unique feature of the Hodgkin-Huxley voltage clamp was the use of two microelectrodes inserted into the interior of the squid axon. One electrode sensed voltage across the nerve membrane; the second provided an electric current, which, in conjunction with the resistance of the membrane, established a definite voltage across the membrane. In this way the problem of polarization (buildup of a layer of charged particles at the current-carrying electrode, which affects both current and voltage characteristics) was circumvented: The sensing electrode carried no current and did not polarize, while the polarization at the current-carrying electrode was simply corrected by external feedback circuitry.

A second feature of this work was the mathematical formulation of the potassium-sodium flow and its effect on potential across the nerve membrane, which has been described as "a four-dimensional system of ordinary nonlinear differential equations." When phenomena have been expressed mathematically, the stage is set for experimentally holding certain variables (such as voltage, concentrations, and temperature) in the equations at set levels so that values of the equations' constants can be determined. This in turn allows prediction of the effect of the variables under conditions not yet measured, or perhaps not even attainable. This is what Hodgkin's group did, and they were successful in predicting the shape and velocity of the action potential, the time changes of potassium and sodium permeability of the membrane, and a number of other features.

Hodgkin and his colleagues also proposed the "sodium pump" to restore the concentration of sodium ions in the axon after the nerve impulse, and they demonstrated that energy-rich phosphate compounds were required to operate the pump. This they did by inhibiting sodium flow with cyanide ion, then injecting arginine phosphate or adenosine triphosphate (ATP) into the nerve. Either phosphate compound restored sodium flow for a time that depended upon the amount injected. It was left for others to quantify flow with energy (three sodium ions out and two potassium ions in per ATP molecule) and to suggest molecular mechanisms for ion transport (configurational changes in the protein molecules of the nerve membrane). The necessity for the sodium pump, however, with its ATP energy source, was clearly understood by Hodgkin and his coworkers.

In the years following the Nobel award, Hodgkin's professional life became increasingly concerned with external professional activities and administration. As noted above, he was president of the Marine Biology Association for ten years and of the Royal Society for five. In addition, he accepted the chancellorship of the University of Leicester for a thirteen-year period, from 1971 to 1984. His investigations continued, however, with papers appearing in the *Journal of Physiology* at irregular intervals into the 1980's. His interests continue to be mechanisms of nerve action, but they have focused more specifically on vision in reptiles and amphibians. His lifetime output numbers fewer than one hundred research papers, but many of these are so thorough and complete that a worker more dedicated to the publications game might have made half a dozen papers out of each one. Hodgkin is a foreign member or an honorary member of a number of scientific societies and has received several awards in addition to the Nobel Prize. Sixteen universities have given him honorary doctorates, including the University of Oxford and the Rockefeller University in New York.

The importance of Hodgkin's work in physiology is twofold. First, because of his unique combination of biological, electronic, chemical, and mathematical understanding, he settled the complex question of nerve transmission almost completely. Second, and equally important, the set of ideas and mechanisms developed in his description of nerve action is so rich that it has been useful in other aspects of nerve activity and even in more general physiology. Transmission in the Purkinje nerve fibers of the heart, for example, conforms to the same mathematical expressions of sodium flow as those developed for squid axons. Transmission across the nerve synapse is seen as a chemically generated electrical signal. Transmission in myelinated (sheathed) mammalian nerves proceeds by the same mechanism as in the unmyelinated squid axon, but it leaps from node to node where the myelin coating is interrupted; this accounts for the speed of transmission in myelinated nerves. Ion transport across cell membranes in general follows the same pattern as that postulated in the sodium pump, triggered by concentration differentials and powered by ATP. Hodgkin's work has had many reflections in unexpected areas of physiology.

Bibliography

Primary

NEUROPHYSIOLOGY: "The Ionic Basis of Nervous Conduction," *Science*, vol. 145 (Septemer 11, 1964), pp. 1148-1154; *The Conduction of the Nervous Impulse*, 1964; "Chance and Design in Electrophysiology: An Informal Account of Certain Experiments on Nerve Carried Out Between 1934 and 1952," *Journal of Physiology*, vol. 263, 1976, pp. 1-21 (also in *The Pursuit of Nature*, Hodgkin et al., 1977).

OTHER NONFICTION: "Beginning: Some Reminiscences of My Early Life (1914-1947)," *Annual Reviews in Physiology*, vol. 45, 1983, pp. 1-16.

Secondary

Bullock, T. H., R. Orkland, and A. Grinnell. *Introduction to Nervous Systems*. San Francisco: W. H. Freeman, 1977. Chapter 4 of this good college-level book on nervous systems explains the work of Hodgkin and Huxley. Bibliographies at the end of each chapter provide selected further readings. Illustrations.

Cronin, Jane. *Mathematical Aspects of Hodgkin-Huxley Neural Theory.* Cambridge, England: Cambridge University Press, 1987. A thorough treatment of the original mathematical work of Hodgkin and Huxley, together with other models and theories up to the publication date. Highly technical.

Fuortes, M. G. F. "Nobel Prize: 1963 Award Honors Three for Research on Nerve Functioning." *Science* 142 (October 25, 1963): 468-471. Brief but very well-informed review of the state of the art in nerve transmission research, and where the work of Hodgkin, Huxley, and Eccles fits.

Hodgkin, Alan Lloyd. *The Conduction of the Nervous Impulse*. Liverpool, England: Liverpool University Press, 1964. This is a short book (only 108 pages), but it provides a fine summary of the work of Hodgkin and Huxley. Its focus is on the processes occurring within a single nerve cell as the nerve impulse is being conducted. Illustrated with many helpful graphs; includes an extensive bibliography of works on single-neuron physiology.

Sourkes, Theodore L. *Nobel Prize Winners in Medicine and Physiology, 1901-1965*. New York: Abelard-Schuman, 1966. Provides brief biographies of the winners, with an account of their work and its wider significance, in a volume that is widely available.

Robert M. Hawthorne, Jr.

1963

Physiology or Medicine

Sir John Carew Eccles, Australia
Alan Lloyd Hodgkin, Great Britain
Andrew F. Huxley, Great Britain

Chemistry

Karl Ziegler, West Germany
Giulio Natta, Italy

Physics

Eugene Paul Wigner, Hungary and United States
Maria Goeppert Mayer, Germany and United States
J. Hans D. Jensen, West Germany

Literature

George Seferis, Greece

Peace

International Red Cross Committee
League of Red Cross Societies

ANDREW F. HUXLEY
1963

Born: London, England; November 22, 1917

Nationality: British
Areas of concentration: Neurophysiology and muscular physiology

Together with Alan L. Hodgkin, Huxley studied the electrical properties of giant axons during nerve transmission and discovered the true nature of the nerve impulse; he also independently studied muscle contraction and helped perfect the ultramicrotome

The Award

Presentation

The presentation speech was made by Professor Ragnar Granit, a member of the Staff of Professors of the Royal Caroline Institute, on December 10, 1963. Dr. Granit outlined the collaborative work of Hodgkin and Huxley in studying the fibers (axons) of nerve cells, especially the large nerve cells of the squid. Their studies used microelectrodes to record electrical impulses, which were then amplified about one million times and displayed on an oscilloscope. In 1939, Hodgkin and Huxley attempted to check an earlier theory concerning the nature of the nerve impulse, "an electrical pulse which lasts 1/1,000 second." Nerve cells that are not conducting impulses have a higher concentration of potassium ions than their surroundings. It had been theorized that the nerve impulse caused a temporary increase in the permeability of the membrane, allowing the potassium ion concentrations to become equal. Hodgkin and Huxley tried to confirm that the difference in electrical potential (voltage) across the membrane disappeared when an impulse passed, but they obtained a surprising result: The electrical potential did not simply disappear, it reversed by about one-third of its original strength.

World War II interrupted this work, but after the war Hodgkin and Huxley returned to the study of nerve impulses using squid axons. They were able to measure the electrical resistance of the membrane, from which they could calculate its conductance or permeability. By carrying out their measurements in solutions of various ionic concentrations, they found that two different changes in membrane permeability were occurring. First, the permeability of the membrane to sodium ions increased, allowing sodium ions outside the cell to leak inside rapidly, producing the observed voltage reversal; second, the permeability of the membrane to potassium increased about half a millisecond later, allowing the potassium concentrations to equalize on opposite sides of the membrane. These ion movements were described in terms of equations by which Hodgkin and Huxley were able to predict with great accuracy the shape of the nerve impulse that they observed on the oscilloscope.

Nobel lecture

Huxley's Nobel lecture, entitled "The Quantitative Analysis of Excitation and Conduction in Nerve," delivered on December 11, 1963, was really a continuation of the previous address by his collaborator, Alan L. Hodgkin, outlining the nature of the nerve fiber and the nerve impulse. After mentioning his debt to Hodgkin, who was his professor at Trinity College of the University of Cambridge, Huxley explained the apparatus that the pair had used. In particular, they were able to measure the flow of charged ions across the membrane at various times during the passage of a nerve impulse.

By repeating their measurements in sodium-free seawater, Hodgkin and Huxley were able to show that the initial ion movements were those of sodium ions passing inward across the membrane. The subsequent movement of potassium ions in the opposite direction was confirmed by measurements using radioactive potassium. Huxley was able to develop equations to predict both the rate at which sodium and potassium ions would flow across the cell membrane and the nature of the electrical impulses that would result. Huxley first made these calculations in the 1940's on desktop calculators, but improved calculations were later made far more rapidly by computer. Huxley found that these calculated results agreed very closely with the measured voltages and the oscilloscope tracings, many of which he used to illustrate the lecture. Most of the observed properties of nerve impulses could therefore be explained in terms of the movements of sodium and potassium ions across the nerve cell membrane.

Critical reception

Since the explanation of the nerve impulse had been considered an important goal of physiology throughout the early decades of the twentieth century, the awarding of the Nobel Prize to Hodgkin and Huxley was hardly surprising. In fact, since the prize was awarded twenty-four years after Hodgkin and Huxley made their initial discovery, it was regarded by many as a recognition long due. *Science*, for example, remarked that "there is no doubt that the recent advances in our understanding of the function of nerves . . . are largely due to the work of the three scientists [Hodgkin, Huxley, and John C. Eccles] who were honored this year by the award of the Nobel Prize."

An article in *The New York Times* stated that the three prizewinners had done much to make nerve-impulse transmission clear and noted that data from axons of squid formed the basis for research being performed on the synapse. The article noted that Hodgkin and Huxley were the fourteenth and fifteenth British winners of the physiology or medicine prize. In an article entitled "3 Win Nobel Prize for Nerve Studies," it was stated that they were being recognized for their work in "analyzing the functions of nerve cells" in the transmittal of impulses along the nerve fiber.

Newsweek reported that Huxley and Hodgkin discovered the electrochemical activity within the nerve cell fiber that allows information to be carried along nerve cells "like a telephone carries conversations." The *Newsweek* article, entitled "Nobels for Nerves," noted that the wives of Huxley and Hodgkin (in a commentary on their husbands' long hours in the laboratory) sometimes referred to themselves as "squidows." Writing in *Science*, M. G. F. Fuortes noted that German scientist Julius Bernstein had previously described the nerve impulse as being attributable to membranes permeable to potassium ions. Huxley, Hodgkin, and coworkers had "measured the amounts of various electrolytes entering and leaving the nerve fibers."

Biography

Andrew Fielding Huxley came from a distinguished family: His grandfather, Thomas Henry Huxley, had been an anatomist and a prominent early supporter of the evolution theories of Charles Darwin. Other prominent family members included biologist Julian Huxley and novelist Aldous Huxley, both half-brothers to Andrew. Andrew attended University College School and Westminster School for five years each. In 1935, he entered Trinity College, University of Cambridge, where his interest in physiology was first stimulated. He received his B.A. from Cambridge in 1938 and his M.A. in 1941. In the summer of 1939, he began doing research with Hodgkin at the Marine Biological Laboratory at Plymouth, England, but this study was interrupted by World War II.

In 1946, Huxley returned to Cambridge, where he held both teaching and research positions until 1960. In 1947, he married Richenda Pease, the daughter of a geneticist, with whom he had six children. He also served as an editor of the *Journal of Physiology* from 1950 to 1957 and was elected to the Royal Society in 1955. From 1960 to 1983, Huxley was head of the department of physiology at University College, London. In 1983, he returned to Cambridge as a professor and administrator. Huxley was awarded the Nobel Prize in 1963, together with Hodgkin and John Carew Eccles. He was awarded the Royal Society's Copley medal in 1973 and was knighted in 1974.

Scientific Career

In his early education, Andrew Huxley was inclined first toward classics (his father's specialty) and then toward physics. At Cambridge's Trinity College, he took courses in physics and chemistry, both of which served him well in his later work. A third science course, however, was also required; on the advice of a friend, he took a course in physiology, which immediately sparked his interest in that subject. He soon fell under the influence of four eminent teachers, of whom Alan L. Hodgkin proved to be the most influential.

In the summer of 1939, Huxley began doing research with Hodgkin at the Marine Biological Laboratory at Plymouth, England. The British physiologist J. Z. Young had recently called attention to the existence in squids (*Loligo*) and cuttlefish (*Sepia*) of a pair of giant axons, associated with their manner of escaping predators by "jet propulsion." These axons were unusually long, and, more important, their exceedingly large diameter of about a millimeter permitted the insertion of various recording devices. Once removed from the animals, the giant nerve cells would continue to function for several hours if they were maintained in fresh seawater. Neither the nerve cells nor the intact animals could be maintained away from the coast, however, so Hodgkin and Huxley joined the many other physiologists who spent their summers at the Marine Biological Laboratory studying the squids.

At the time when Hodgkin and Huxley began their work on the squids' giant axons, the nature of the nerve impulse was only partly known. Recordings made from electrodes placed outside nerve cells showed that the outer surface was positively charged; when a nerve impulse passed by, however, this positive charge momentarily disappeared. At the beginning of the twentieth century, a German physiologist named Bernstein had hypothesized that the nerve impulse was propagated by a sudden increase in the permeability of the cell membrane, allowing all charged ions, particularly those of potassium, to reach an equilibrium quite rapidly. Hodgkin and Huxley began by attempting to test Bernstein's hypothesis in the giant axons of the squid, using microelectrodes placed inside the cell as well as outside. Hodgkin and Huxley also displayed their fleeting results on an oscilloscope screen so that events of 0.001-second duration could accurately be recorded. Their initial results were surprising and unexpected: During the passage of a nerve impulse, the electrical polarity of the membrane not only disappeared, it momentarily reversed. This initial result, reported in 1939, meant that Bernstein's interpretation was inadequate and that further study would have to be undertaken. The study, however, was interrupted by World War II.

In 1946, following the war's end, Hodgkin and Huxley resumed their research on squid axons. Taking advantage of the unusually large diameter of the axons, Hodgkin and Huxley withdrew enough fluid to measure the concentration of various ions. They found that the internal concentration of potassium ions was high but that the concentration of sodium ions inside the axon was low compared to that of the surroundings. They proposed that the positive charge on the outside of the cell membrane was caused by the excess of sodium ions and that it was the inward movement of these sodium ions that caused the momentary reversal in electrical polarity that they had recorded. They tested this "sodium hypothesis" by bathing a squid axon in sodium-free seawater and measuring the resulting voltage changes when a nerve impulse passed. They also used the technique, relatively new at the time, of "voltage clamping," in which an electronic feedback circuit maintains a constant voltage difference across the membrane while the tendency of charged particles (such as ions) to move and cause voltage changes is measured. When the normal polarity, or "resting potential," of the membrane failed to reverse as the impulse passed, the expectations of Hodgkin and Huxley were confirmed. They concluded that the normally observed voltage reversal was caused by a sudden increase in the permeability of the membrane to sodium ions, allowing sodium ions outside the cell to leak inside rapidly. This change was determined to be highly specific to sodium ions, for no other ionic movements occurred at the beginning of the nerve impulse.

The reversal of polarity was very brief, lasting about 0.001 second; afterwards, the polarity reversal disappeared. Hodgkin and Huxley attributed the disappearance of reversed polarity to the outward movement of potassium ions. They tested this hypothesis using radioactive potassium ions, whose movement they could easily follow by measuring the radioactivity. Again, their results were confirmed.

Hodgkin and Huxley now thought that they could explain nerve impulse conduction as a two-step process. In the first step, sodium ions rushed inward, causing a brief reversal of polarity. In the second step, potassium ions rushed outward, causing the reversed polarity to disappear. Equations for the movement of sodium, potassium, and other types of ions were devised, and Huxley tested these equations by comparing the predicted movement of charged ions with the electrical changes recorded on the oscilloscope tracings. The initial computations were tediously performed on desk calculators, but the computations were repeated under vastly improved conditions on electronic computers some ten years later. The agreement between the mathematical model and the observed results was extremely close. The equations describing the ion movements had enabled Hodgkin and Huxley to predict with great accuracy the shape of the nerve impulse that they had observed on the oscilloscope. Huxley and Hodgkin concluded that they had correctly accounted for nerve conduction by a series of changes in membrane permeability and the ensuing movement of ions.

From 1946 to 1951, Huxley and Hodgkin continued to study nerve impulses in the giant axons of squids. Most of the experimental work had to be done during the summer and early fall months when the squids were available at the marine laboratory in Plymouth. The major results of these studies were published in 1952 and have served as the basis for all subsequent studies.

While he was working on squid axons with Hodgkin, Huxley also collaborated with R. Stämpfli, studying the myelinated nerve fibers of vertebrates during those months in which fresh squids were unavailable for study. Huxley found that many of the electrical changes in vertebrate axons followed the same course that they did in squid axons, implying a similar mechanism in vertebrate nervous systems. The presence of a myelin sheath around the nerve fibers, however, had a complicating effect: Squid axons (and unmyelinated vertebrate axons) conducted their impulses smoothly along their membrane surfaces, but the fatty myelin sheath interfered with this process. Huxley found that electrical charges kept building up between segments of myelin (at the nodes of Ranvier) until they were large enough to "jump" across the myelinated segment to the next node of Ranvier. This type of "saltatory conduction" was first reported in 1949.

Beginning in 1952, Huxley turned his attention to the physiology of muscle contraction, developing an interference microscope for studying the alternating striations. His studies on muscle fibers led to the characterization of the bands now known as A and I (originally "anisotropic" and "isotropic" under Huxley's interference microscope) and later to the development of the sliding filament theory of muscle contraction. According to this theory, now widely accepted, the alternating A and I bands are caused by the alignment of fibers of the proteins actin and myosin, arranged at right angles to the bands.

As a nerve impulse is received, the initiation of muscle contraction begins with a change in membrane permeability comparable to that associated with the nerve impulse, but resulting in an inward movement of calcium ions. After calcium ions enter the cell, contraction is brought about by the sliding of actin and myosin filaments past one another. A third protein, troponin, inhibits contractions from taking place by binding with myosin most of the time. The influx of calcium ions causes the troponin to bind to the calcium ions, releasing the myosin at the onset of contraction. Once the myosin becomes free to bind to the actin, contraction ensues.

Huxley developed a micromanipulator and an ultramicrotome for cutting very thin sections for viewing under the electron microscope in connection with his studies on muscles. With these materials, he sectioned and examined muscle that was fixed in the relaxed state, muscle that was fixed under conditions of strong contraction (tetany induced by large concentrations of acetylcholine), and muscle that was stretched and then fixed. In each case, Huxley was able to correlate the observed changes in the width of the A and I bands and in their component sub-bands with postulated changes in the sliding of actin and myosin filaments past one another.

Because of his direct involvement in research with both nerve conduction and muscle contraction, Andrew Huxley may truly be said to have participated in two of the most important physiological discoveries of the twentieth century.

Bibliography

Primary

PHYSIOLOGY: "Action Potentials Recorded from Inside a Nerve Fibre," *Nature*, vol. 144, 1939, p. 710 (with A. L. Hodgkin); "Resting and Action Potentials in Single Nerve Fibres," *Journal of Physiology*, vol. 104, 1945, p. 176 (with A. L. Hodgkin); "Evidence for Saltatory Conduction in Peripheral Myelinated Nerve Fibres," *Journal of Physiology*, vol. 108, 1949, pp. 315-339 (with R. Stämpfli); "Effect of Potassium and Sodium on Resting and Action Potential in Single Myelinated Nerve Fibres," *Journal of Physiology*, vol. 112, 1951, p. 476 (with R. Stämpfli); "Measurement of Current-Voltage Relations in the Membrane of the Giant Axon of *Loligo*," *Journal of Physiology*, vol. 116, 1952, pp. 424-448 (with A. L. Hodgkin and B. Katz); "The Dual Effect of Membrane Potential on Sodium Conductance in the Giant Axon of *Loligo*," *Journal of Physiology*, vol. 116, 1952, pp. 497-506 (with A. L. Hodgkin); "Properties of Nerve Axons: I, Movement of Sodium and Potassium Ions During Nervous Activity," *Cold Spring Harbor Symposia on Quantitative Biology*, vol. 17, 1952, pp. 43-52 (with A. L. Hodgkin); "Movement of Radioactive Potassium and Membrane Current in a Giant Axon," *Journal of Physiology*, vol. 121, 1953 (with A. L. Hodgkin); "Local Activation of Striated Muscle Fibres," *Journal of Physiology*, vol. 144, 1958, pp. 426-441 (with R. E. Taylor); *Reflections on Muscle*, 1980.

Secondary

Bullock, T. H., R. Orkland, and A. Grinnell. *Introduction to Nervous Systems*. San

Francisco: W. H. Freeman, 1977. A good college-level introduction to the anatomy, physiology, and psychology of nervous systems. The explanations are clear, and the book is very well illustrated throughout. The bibliography at the end of each chapter is confined to a few well-chosen works, most of which will guide the reader to further references in the primary research literature. Huxley's work on nerve impulses is explained in chapter 4. The essential equations are given, but the nonmathematical reader can easily ignore them.

Eccles, J. C. *The Physiology of Nerve Cells*. Baltimore: The Johns Hopkins University Press, 1957. A good, somewhat technical, but well-written summary of the physiology of individual nerve cells and the connections between them. Written by a Nobel laureate (he shared the prize with Huxley and Hodgkin), this book summarizes the principal findings of Huxley, Hodgkin, and their fellow workers on nerve conduction and ion movements across membranes in single nerve cells. A greater portion of the book, however, is devoted to Eccles' own research specialty, the connections or synapses between adjacent nerve cells. The book is adequately illustrated with graphs and diagrams, and it contains a good bibliography.

Handbook of Physiology. Section 1, *The Nervous System*. Bethesda, Md.: American Physiological Society, 1977. This standard reference has convenient summaries, each by a different author, of various topics related to the physiology of nerve cells. In particular, chapters 3 through 7 all deal with the work of Huxley and his coworkers. Each chapter is well written, though somewhat technical, and is amply illustrated. A lengthy bibliography occurs at the end of each chapter, making the book a gold mine of information about important research findings and an essential tool for any serious researcher.

Hodgkin, A. L. *The Conduction of the Nervous Impulse*. Liverpool, England: Liverpool University Press, 1964. This book of 108 pages is probably the best summary of the work of Hodgkin, Huxley, and their coworkers at Cambridge. The book focuses very clearly on processes that take place within a single nerve cell, especially along its membrane, during the conduction of a nerve impulse. The book is very well illustrated, mostly with graphs, and very well explained. An appendix contains the differential equations used by Hodgkin and Huxley to describe the movements of sodium and potassium ions across the nerve cell membrane. The bibliography is more exhaustive than any other on the subject of single-neuron physiology.

Jack, J. J. B., D. Noble, and R. W. Tsien. *Electric Current Flow in Excitable Cells*. Oxford, England: Clarendon Press, 1975. A highly detailed account of the physics of ion flow and electrical activity in nerve cells. Equations are numerous throughout the book, but a lengthy bibliography makes the book useful even for those who have no patience with the mathematical models.

Eli C. Minkoff

1964

Physiology or Medicine

Konrad E. Bloch, United States
Feodor Lynen, Germany

Chemistry

Dorothy Crowfoot Hodgkin, Great Britain

Physics

Charles Hard Townes, United States
Nikolay Gennadiyevich Basov, Soviet Union
Aleksandr Mikhailovich Prokhorov, Soviet Union

Literature

Jean-Paul Sartre, France

Peace

Martin Luther King, Jr., United States

KONRAD E. BLOCH
1964

Born: Neisse, Upper Silesia, Germany; January 21, 1912

Nationality: American
Areas of concentration: Biochemistry and lipid metabolism

Bloch helped develop the modern understanding of the mechanism and regulation of the synthesis and degradation of cholesterol and fatty acids

The Award

Presentation

Sune Bergström, a biochemist and member of the staff of the Royal Caroline Institute, delivered the presentation address on December 10, 1964, before the Nobel Prize was awarded to Konrad Bloch by His Majesty the King. In his address, Bergström surveyed the early history of research on the chemistry of cholesterol and analyzed how Bloch's work was of fundamental importance in understanding the diseases that had become the most common causes of death in the developed countries. He explained that cholesterol, which actually means "gallstone," has long been associated with human disease; cholesterol was first isolated from human gallstones. Although many aspects of the chemical nature of cholesterol were identified during the first two decades of the twentieth century, the long series of steps by which the body builds this complex molecule could not be solved until Bloch and his associates successfully exploited the technical advantages of using radioactive isotopes of hydrogen and carbon to track the fate of the building blocks of cholesterol and fatty acids.

In addition to refining the technique of using radioactive isotopes to work out the steps by which small building blocks are linked together to form cholesterol, Bloch proved that cholesterol is the precursor of bile acids and steroid hormones. By providing a complete map of the steps involved in the metabolism of cholesterol, Bloch's work gave biomedical scientists a means of understanding the development of major cardiovascular diseases and the possibility of treating such diseases in a rational manner.

Nobel lecture

On December 11, 1964, Konrad Bloch delivered his Nobel lecture, entitled "The Biological Synthesis of Cholesterol." It provided a detailed historical and experimental review of one of the most challenging biosynthetic puzzles confronting organic chemists in the 1930's. When the structure of cholesterol was finally completely elucidated in the early 1930's, Bloch explained, one of the most brilliant chapters in the history of organic chemistry came to a close. At that point, chemists and biochemists had confronted a molecule whose architecture seemed entirely "enigmatic."

The complex structure of cholesterol did not seem to offer any clues as to how cells could construct such a molecule from simpler constituents. In a very general way, some of the early speculations were nevertheless remarkably close to the truth. Chemists suggested that the tetracyclic steroidal ring system (a large complex molecule made up of four smaller rings) might arise from an appropriately folded long-chain precursor molecule. The chemical substances that make up the steroid family include many hormones, vitamins, cell constituents, and drugs. Further research on this problem was influenced by the suggestions that the terpenes and steroids might arise from a common precursor and that cholesterol might be formed by the cyclization of the hydrocarbon squalene. By 1926, investigators had demonstrated that the cholesterol content of tissues could be increased by feeding squalene (a polyisoprenoid hydrocarbon) to experimental animals.

The first phase of experimental studies of cholesterol biosynthesis began in 1937, when scientists using stable isotopes suggested that cholesterol was formed by the linkage of certain small molecules that served as intermediates in fat and carbohydrate metabolism. At the very beginning of his scientific career, Bloch was able to exploit the exciting new tool of isotopic tracers as a means of solving the riddles of biosynthesis. In the early 1940's, Bloch initiated his systematic studies of the biosynthesis of cholesterol. Utilizing labeled acetic acid, he was able to show that acetate was a major contributor to the synthesis of sterol molecules. His goal was to establish the origin of all the carbon atoms in the cholesterol skeleton. As expected, cholesterol, like other related natural substances, seemed to be derived from a polyisoprenoid intermediate. Bloch's general hypothesis was that the major stages in the biosynthesis of cholesterol involved the formation of squalene from acetate and cyclization to form cholesterol. Labeled squalene was soon shown to be a precursor of cholesterol, but a formidable amount of rigorous chemical work was needed to provide an unequivocal demonstration of the origin of each carbon in the cholesterol skeleton.

In attempting to put his work into perspective, Bloch noted that the direction of further investigations of sterol biosynthesis seemed clearly indicated. Research would have to progress from the level of intact animals or whole cells to in vitro experimentation with highly purified enzymes. Only by working with such isolated enzymes could researchers elucidate the nature of the individual reaction mechanisms for the many steps involved in cholesterol biosynthesis. In 1964 this elucidation was still a distant goal for many of the later steps in the biosynthetic pathway that involved hydrophobic (insoluble in water) molecules and enzymes that were tightly bound to particulate constituents of the cell. Progress in finding methods of studying the enzymes that acted on lipophilic (soluble in lipids) substrates was essential for establishing a "rational approach to the problem of metabolic regulation." Although it was clear that many environmental, dietary, and hormonal factors influence the rate of cholesterol synthesis, the mechanism of metabolic control was obscure. The role of sterols as cell constituents and the conversion of cholesterol to steroid hormones and bile acids were also important areas for further research.

Critical reception

When the Nobel Prize in Physiology or Medicine for 1964 was announced, E. P. Kennedy and F. H. Westheimer wrote in the journal *Science* that, because of the work of Konrad Bloch and others, the outlines of the chemistry of life were "now plainly visible." During the course of a quarter century, biochemists had discovered many of the chemical reactions that occur in living cells. Despite the remaining gaps in the knowledge of cellular metabolism, the establishment of the outlines of the chemistry of life was certainly among the greatest accomplishments of twentieth century science. Konrad Bloch's work on the biosynthesis of steroid molecules was hailed as "one of the most far-reaching developments in the field of intermediary metabolism."

Science writers explained that Konrad Bloch and his colaureate Feodor Lynen had independently studied the way in which animal cells produce cholesterol, the necessary precursor of the sex hormones and the hormones of the adrenal cortex. On the other hand, cholesterol was also associated with atherosclerosis and coronary disease. According to *Time* magazine of October 23, 1964, Bloch and Lynen had revealed the "secrets" of a "mysterious substance called cholesterol" that was a "root cause of much artery disease and many heart attacks." Bloch was credited with discovering that most of the cholesterol in the body came not from dietary cholesterol but from "built-in cholesterol factories."

The scientific community joined the Swedish Academy of Sciences in recognizing the contributions that Bloch had made to elucidating the complex pattern of reactions involved in the biosynthesis of cholesterol. Although the work of Lynen and Bloch was closely interwoven, Bloch had specialized in the study of cholesterol, while Lynen had focused his attention on fatty acid biosynthesis. It seemed obvious that the knowledge gained from Bloch's work on the biosynthesis of cholesterol would have widespread applications to other biologically significant substances; moreover, basic research on the metabolism of cholesterol had profound implications for progress in medicine. In the 1960's, it was already known that certain cardiovascular diseases involved some derangement of lipid metabolism associated with high levels of cholesterol in the blood. Although the exact role of cholesterol in the development of atherosclerosis was not understood, physicians and scientists were sure that information about the biosynthesis of the steroids would contribute to progress in understanding the mechanisms that normally regulate the level of cholesterol in the body and to rational means of preventing and treating cardiovascular disease.

Scientists noted that, in addition to the work on cholesterol, Bloch had made outstanding contributions to other areas of biochemistry, such as the biosynthesis of glutathione and the metabolism of fatty acids. His studies of glutathione had provided a valuable model for investigations of the mechanisms by which amino acids are activated to form peptide bonds. Another area in which Bloch had made significant contributions was the analysis of the pathways leading to the biosynthesis of unsaturated fatty acids. These investigations led him into new areas of comparative evolutionary biochemistry. Bloch found that the biosynthetic pathway found in aerobic organisms is different from that utilized by anaerobes. While the details of these metabolic pathways might be of interest only to specialists in lipid metabolism, Bloch's findings and hypotheses are of general scientific interest in mapping out the complex chemistry of life. Many journalists would probably agree with a report in *The Nation* of November 9, 1964, however, that their readers would be more interested in the Nobel Prize in Literature and the Nobel Peace Prize, because "laymen frequently cannot appreciate the worth of creative scientists and physicians."

Biography

Konrad Emil Bloch, the second child of Fritz Bloch and Hedwig (née Striemer) Bloch, was born on January 21, 1912, in Neisse, Upper Silesia, then Germany. Bloch attended the elementary school and the *Realgymnasium* in Neisse. In 1930, he went to Munich to study chemical engineering at the *Technische Hochschule*. Under the influence of Hans Fischer, he became attracted to organic chemistry, especially the structure of natural products. Lectures at the Münchner Chemische Gesellschaft by some of the great organic chemists, such as Adolf Windaus and Heinrich Wieland, sparked his interest in the steroids, porphyrins, and enzymes. Because of the Nazi racial laws being instituted in German schools, however, Bloch's studies in Munich ended in 1934 when he received the degree of *Diplom-Ingenieur* in chemistry. Fortunately, he was able to obtain a temporary position at the Schweizerische Forschungsinstitut in Davos, Switzerland, where he carried out research on the phospholipids of tubercle bacilli.

Bloch's first published researches revealed that previous claims that tubercle bacteria contained cholesterol were false. His first encounter with cholesterol confirmed experiments by Erwin Chargaff, Rudolph J. Anderson, and Rudolf Schönheimer, scientists he would later meet at Columbia University. With his nonrenewable residential permit in Switzerland about to expire, Bloch was delighted to receive a letter of appointment as assistant in biological chemistry, School of Medicine, Yale University; however, there were actually no funds available for this position.

In December, 1936, Bloch arrived in the United States, with "great hopes" but no money. Rudolph Anderson suggested that he pursue graduate studies with Hans T. Clarke at Columbia University rather than Yale. With help from Max Bergmann and support from the Wallerstein Foundation, he entered the department of biochemistry in the College of Physicians and Surgeons at Columbia University as Clarke's student. After Bloch obtained his Ph.D. in 1938, Rudolf Schönheimer asked him to join his research group at Columbia's College of Physicians and Surgeons. Later Bloch referred to these years with Schönheimer and David Rittenberg as the most influential of his *Lehrjahre*. Bloch married Lore Teutsch, a native of Munich, on February 15, 1941; they had first met many years before in Munich. The Blochs had two children, Peter and Susan.

After Schönheimer's premature death in 1941, members of his research group were encouraged by Clarke to continue to develop their own special interests. During this period, Bloch's interest in intermediary metabolism and the problems of biosynthesis was keenly developed. In 1942, in collaboration with Rittenberg, Bloch began work on the biological synthesis of cholesterol, which was to remain a fertile field of research for some twenty years. In 1946, he moved to the University of Chicago as assistant professor of biochemistry. He was promoted to associate professor in 1948 and professor in 1950. He found the intellectual atmosphere in the biochemistry department, then headed by E. A. Evans, Jr., stimulating and productive. During this period he continued his studies of cholesterol biosynthesis and the enzymatic synthesis of the tripeptide glutathione. A Guggenheim Fellowship in 1953 provided a productive year at the Organisch-Chemisches Institut, Eidgenössische Technische Hochschule in Zurich with renowned chemists Leopold Ružička and Vladimir Prelog. In 1954, Bloch became Higgins Professor of Biochemistry, department of chemistry, Harvard University. In 1968 he was appointed chairman of the department. He remained at Harvard until 1978.

Scientific Career

Although cholesterol had been isolated from gallstones in the 1820's and its structure had been elucidated in the 1930's, little was known about its biosynthesis when Bloch took up the problem in the 1940's. Cholesterol is the most common steroid in animal tissues, especially abundant in bile and gallstones. In classical experiments at Columbia University in 1937, Rudolf Schönheimer and David Rittenberg used deuterium as a tracer to show that cholesterol is built up in animal tissues from small molecules. Bloch was introduced to the powerful new methodology of isotopic tracers and its potential in the investigation of previously intractable problems of intermediary metabolism as a graduate student. Five years later, Bloch and Rittenberg, using acetic acid labeled with deuterium, proved that this compound is a major precursor of cholesterol in rats. With this work Bloch began the pursuit of a goal—the complete elucidation of the biosynthesis of sterols.

Bloch's research objective became the establishment of the origin of all the carbon atoms in the cholesterol skeleton. Analysis of the pattern of distribution would presumably provide clues to the biosynthetic pathway that led to cholesterol. Early evidence suggested that a two-carbon metabolite of acetate was the principal building block of cholesterol. Studies were concerned with explaining the steps in the biosynthesis of sterols, which involved the conversion of acetic acid to squalene, the cyclization of squalene, and the metabolism of a series of intermediates to form cholesterol. Working out the details of this pathway involved truly prodigious labors, because it was subsequently discovered that the transformation of acetic acid to cholesterol involves about thirty-six steps.

As a working hypothesis for the biosynthesis of cholesterol, Bloch suggested the general outline:

acetate →isoprenoid intermediate →squalene →cyclization produce →cholesterol.

To verify this hypothesis, Bloch tried to demonstrate the formation of squalene from labeled acetate in the shark. This seemingly peculiar choice of experimental animal was based on the fact that sharks accumulate very large amounts of the hydrocarbon squalene in their livers; indeed, the name squalene comes from that of the dogfish *Squalus*. The hydrocarbon squalene deserves special attention for its role in unraveling the biosynthetic pathway of the steroids. It thus seemed logical to inject radioactive acetic acid into sharks, isolate squalene from their livers, and then determine whether the labeled squalene served as an intermediate in the synthesis of cholesterol.

Bloch set out for Bermuda, where marine biologists could supply him with dogfish. Unfortunately, captured sharks proved refractory to experimental manipulation and invariably died before properly metabolizing the labeled acetic acid. After a few days on the beaches of Bermuda, Bloch returned to the University of Chicago and the more mundane rat liver system. Bloch and R. G. Langdon were successful in isolating labeled squalene from the livers of rats injected with radioactive acetate. Labeled squalene was then used to show that this hydrocarbon served as a precursor of cholesterol in intact animals. Further experimental evidence was obtained by exploiting mutants of *Neurospora crassa* (isolated by fellow Nobel Prize winner Edward L. Tatum); these were deficient in pyruvate metabolism, which meant that acetate had to be supplied to them in their growth medium. When the mutant mold was grown on labeled acetate, the labeling pattern of ergosterol provided strong evidence for Bloch's hypothesis.

In 1953, Robert B. Woodward and Bloch proposed a mechanism for the cyclization of squalene to form lanosterol. Their hypothesis received strong support from the experiments of John W. Cornforth and others, whose chemical degradation of the sterol nucleus revealed the pattern of labeling from radioactive acetate which was predicted by the Woodward-Bloch formulation. Not all the steps between lanosterol and cholesterol had been established in 1964, but Bloch and his associates had isolated many of the intermediates, purified many of the enzymes involved in specific biosynthetic steps, and provided a well-documented outline of this complex biosynthetic pathway.

Putting his many years of research into perspective in 1964, Bloch predicted that future research on terpene and sterol biosynthesis, like all biosynthetic studies, would progress from the level of intact animals or whole cells to in vitro experimentation. Biochemists had learned that it was only possible to understand reaction mechanisms by the use of isolated, purified enzymes. Understanding the enzymology of the cholesterol pathway would provide a rational approach to broader questions of metabolic regulation. Such questions transcended narrow academic curiosity because basic research was essential to an understanding of the complex environmental, dietary, and hormonal factors that influence the rate of cholesterol synthesis and the diseases associated with lipid metabolism; moreover, comparative biochemistry would shed light on the role sterols play as structural elements of the cell. Because the sterols had not been found in bacteria or the blue-green algae, it seemed that the development of the sterol biosynthetic pathway indicated an evolutionary division between primitively organized cells lacking various membrane-bound intracellular organelles and more complex, differentiated cells.

More than twenty years after winning the Nobel Prize, Bloch still found the question of anaerobic versus aerobic life-styles in relation to evolution an intriguing area for research and speculation. "Fitness for biological function," he wrote, "not chance, appears to be the driving force for structural modifications of a biomolecule." He was intrigued by the concept that Darwinian evolution might be "manifest at the level of small molecules as well as at the organismic and genomic level." In the case of cholesterol, it is possible that the molecule originally served as a hormonelike signal calling for the assembly of certain cell membranes. This was a question that Bloch planned to pursue in further researches. In 1987, when reflecting on the rewards and privileges of a career in science, Konrad Bloch still saw the scientific enterprise as a "glorious entertainment."

Bibliography

Primary

BIOCHEMISTRY: "Biological Conversion of Cholesterol to Cholic Acid," *Journal of Biological Chemistry*, vol. 149, 1943, pp. 511-517 (with B. Berg and D. Rittenberg); "The Utilization of AcOH for Fatty Acid Synthesis," *Journal of Biological Chemistry*, vol. 154, 1944, pp. 311-312 (with D. Rittenberg); "Biosynthesis of Squalene," *Journal of Biological Chemistry*, vol. 200, 1953, pp. 129-134 (with R. G. Langdon); *Lipid Metabolism*, 1960; "Enzymatic Synthesis of Monosaturated Fatty Acids," *Accounts of Chemical Research*, vol. 2, 1962, pp. 193-202; "The Biological Synthesis of Cholesterol," *Science*, vol. 150, 1965, pp. 19-28; *Biological and Chemical Aspects of Oxygenases: Proceedings of the United States-Japan Symposium on Oxygenases*, edited by Bloch and Osamu Hayaishi, 1966; "Enzymatic Desaturation of Stearyl-ACP," in *Biological and Chemical Aspects of Oxygenases*, 1966, pp. 3-11 (with J. Nagai); "On the Evolution of a Biosynthetic Pathway," in *Reflections in Biochemistry*, edited by A. Kornberg, B. Horecker, L. Cornudella, and J. Oro, 1976; "Summing Up," *Annual Reviews of Biochemistry*, vol. 56, 1987, pp. 1-19.

Secondary

Dawson, R. M. C., and D. N. Rhodes, eds. *Metabolism and Physiological Significance of Lipids*. New York: John Wiley & Sons, 1964. Although written for a scientifically sophisticated audience, this text provides valuable insight into the biochemistry of the lipids during the period in which Bloch was conducting the research for which he was awarded the Nobel Prize. This monograph provides an authoritative and comprehensive account of the field in the early 1960's.

Florkin, Marcel, and E. H. Stotz. *Comprehensive Biochemistry*. Vol. 31, *A History of Biochemistry*. Amsterdam: Elsevier, 1975. Part 3, entitled "History of the Identification of the Sources of Free Energy in Organisms," presents relevant information. Although written for a scientifically sophisticated audience, much of the material on the history of research on the lipids should be accessible to general readers. The text provides extensive explanations and references.

Fruton, Joseph S. *Molecules and Life: Historical Essays on the Interplay of Chemistry and Biology.* New York: Wiley-Interscience, 1972. This well-written, lucid text is historical and general in approach, even though it is intended for the scientifically knowledgeable reader. The section "Pathways of Biochemical Change" provides valuable accounts of the use of radioactive tracers in metabolic research and the metabolism of fatty acids.

Greenberg, D. M., ed. *Metabolic Pathways*. Vol. 2. New York: Academic Press, 1968. This text contains valuable review articles concerning fatty acid and lipid synthesis; written for a knowledgeable audience.

Haslewood, G. A. D. *Bile Salts*. London: Methuen, 1967. This is a brief, readable book about a rather narrow topic; however, the study of cholesterol biosynthesis is closely related to the history of studies of bile salts and bile stones.

Kennedy, E. P., and F. H. Westheimer. "Nobel Laureates: Bloch and Lynen Win Prize in Medicine and Physiology." *Science* 146 (1964): 504-506. This analysis of the work for which Bloch won the Nobel Prize was written for the "News and Comment" feature of the journal *Science*. It provides valuable information about the life and work of Bloch and the history of research on the biosynthesis of cholesterol and fatty acids.

Kornberg, A., B. L. Horecker, L. Cornudella, and J. Oro, eds. *Reflections on Biochemistry: In Honour of Severo Ochoa*. Oxford, England: Pergamon Press, 1976. A collection of essays by some of Severo Ochoa's students and colleagues celebrating progress in biochemistry over the course of almost fifty years. Several essays concerning lipid research describe work done by Bloch. The essays provide some biographical material and reflect the development of fields, concepts, and techniques in biochemistry in a manner accessible to the general reader.

Masoro, E. J. *Physiological Chemistry of Lipids in Mammals*. Philadelphia: W. B. Saunders, 1968. This short textbook provides a good review of the state of knowledge about lipids in the 1960's.

Richards, J. H., and J. B. Hendrickson. *Biosynthesis of Steroids, Terpenes, and Acetogenins*. New York: W. A. Benjamin, 1964. Written for chemists, this book provides a useful review of the state of knowledge of the organic chemistry of these important classes of chemicals at the time Bloch was awarded the Nobel Prize.

Lois N. Magner

1964

Physiology or Medicine

Konrad E. Bloch, United States
Feodor Lynen, Germany

Chemistry

Dorothy Crowfoot Hodgkin, Great Britain

Physics

Charles Hard Townes, United States
Nikolay Gennadiyevich Basov, Soviet Union
Aleksandr Mikhailovich Prokhorov, Soviet Union

Literature

Jean-Paul Sartre, France

Peace

Martin Luther King, Jr., United States

FEODOR LYNEN
1964

Born: Munich, Germany; April 6, 1911
Died: Starnberg, West Germany; August 9, 1979
Nationality: German
Area of concentration: Biochemistry

Lynen was the first biochemist to explain the functions of the vitamin biotin and to determine the process by which cells produce cholesterol

The Award

Presentation

Professor Sune Bergström, member of the staff of professors of the Royal Caroline Institute, presented the 1964 Nobel Prize in Physiology or Medicine to Feodor Lynen and Konrad Bloch on December 10, 1964. In the presence of the Royal Swedish Academy of Science and the Swedish royal family, Bergström lauded the joint recipients "for their discoveries concerning the mechanism and regulation of the cholesterol and fatty acid metabolism."

Bergström began his citation by reminding his audience that cholesterol had been demonstrated to be associated with gallstones more than two hundred years ago. He also pointed out that more recently, scientists had discovered a correlation between the amount of fats and cholesterol in the human diet and atherosclerosis. This association of cholesterol and disease, he continued, prevented the realization until very recently that cholesterol is "a necessary constituent of all our cells and that it fulfills important functions." Bergström then recalled that two German chemists, Adolf Windaus and Heinrich Wieland, had won Nobel Prizes in Chemistry for their research into the structure of cholesterol, which demonstrated that cholesterol was an active ingredient in vitamin D, in male and female sex hormones, and in the hormones produced by the adrenal cortex. Despite this pioneering work into the nature of cholesterol, however, it fell to Lynen and Bloch to discover the method by which cholesterol and related fatty acids form and to establish the relationship between them.

Bergström credited a research group at Columbia University, of which Bloch was a member, with discovering the important tool of radioactive isotopes, which made possible the close study of the structure of living cells. Using that tool, Bloch and Lynen made the discoveries which won for them the 1964 Nobel Prize in Physiology or Medicine. Bergström related how Lynen, using the radioactive isotope technology discovered at Columbia, managed to isolate activated acetic acid, a substance which Bergström characterized as "the precursor of all lipids in our body and the common denominator of a number of metabolic processes." Shortly after Lynen's discovery, Bloch and his colleagues established the ways in which the two carbon atoms of acetic acid result in the synthesis of squalene, which in turn becomes a steroid called lanosterol. The body then transforms lanosterol into cholesterol. Bergström also acknowledged the contributions of biochemists in several countries in clarifying the complicated process of cholesterol formation, but he noted that the three discoveries of greatest importance in understanding the mechanisms of cellular metabolism were made by Lynen and Bloch. Lynen, he said, established the nature and explained the actions of the vitamin biotin and was also able to determine the structure of cytohemin. Bloch proved experimentally that cholesterol is an ingredient of bile acids and of one female sex hormone. Taken together, the discoveries of Lynen and Bloch allowed other researchers to show that cholesterol is the basic ingredient of all steroid substances in the human body.

Bergström concluded his presentation by crediting Lynen and Bloch with performing the biochemical research that led to present knowledge of how cholesterol and fatty acids are formed in the body and how they function. The discoveries of the 1964 prize winners, he said, should help future researchers understand the origins of many lethal diseases of the human cardiovascular system and help devise cures or preventions for those diseases, which are the most common cause of death in the industrialized nations of the world.

Nobel lecture

Lynen delivered his Nobel lecture in German on December 11, 1964. He entitled it "Der Weg von der 'Aktivierten Eissigsäure' zu den Terpenen und den Fettsäuren" (the passage of "activated acetate" through terpenes and fatty acids) and augmented it with numerous illustrations, chemical formulas, charts, and graphs. Lynen first gave a brief account of his earliest research efforts in what he called "dynamic biochemistry," initiated in 1937. He mentioned biochemists whose discoveries inspired and influenced him, in particular Otto Warburg, the recipient of the 1931 Nobel Prize in Physiology or Medicine. He then recalled his first independent research project, in 1939, which concerned the metabolism of cells and the fermentation of alcohol. These first experiments, he explained, led to his lifelong interest in cell metabolism and to the research that resulted in his Nobel Prize.

Lynen then recounted his isolation of "activated acetate" from yeast in 1951. He demonstrated through illustrations and complex chemical formulas that it is chemically indistinguishable from acetyl coenzyme A, a substance similar to vinegar which is essential in the formation of cholesterol. Lynen paid tribute to his mentor/father-in-law as being the inspiration for his early work. In addition, he mentioned all the other scientists with whom he worked during the research which led to his discovery. Lynen discussed his discovery of the so-called fatty-acid cycle with the aid of numerous illustrations and chemical formulas. Again, he mentioned the many coworkers who aided in his research, especially his colaureate, Konrad Bloch, with whom he corresponded regularly after World War II. Lynen and Bloch discovered a sequence of thirty-six steps by which animal cells produce cholesterol.

Lynen explained one of his most important discoveries—the nature and function of the little-known vitamin biotin. First isolated in 1935, biotin occurs in minute quantities in yeast. Lynen also explained the biosynthesis of terpene. He concluded his lecture by characterizing himself as only one of many researchers who were slowly progressing toward solving the mysteries of human metabolism and expressing the conviction that someday all those mysteries would be revealed.

Critical reception

Perhaps because he shared the prize with an American, or perhaps because the political climate was right, Lynen's reception of the Nobel Prize received much more notice in the United States than was usual for European laureates. Although he was German, Lynen's past was not tainted by Nazi affiliations, and the general spirit of reconciliation between the United States and Germany which followed the Berlin crisis of 1961 established a climate in which his selection was popular.

According to the newspaper press in the United States and the Federal Republic of Germany, the selection of Lynen and Konrad Bloch as cowinners of the 1964 Nobel Prize in Physiology or Medicine generated enthusiasm and applause from both the chemistry and medical communities worldwide. Articles in *The New York Times* and the German newspaper *Der Spiegel* on October 16, 1964, identified both men as pioneers in their field who have made fundamental contributions to scientific knowledge concerning cholesterol and fatty acids in cell metabolism, which may lead to cures for a variety of circulatory diseases.

In addition to a short biography of each recipient and an account of the research for which they received their prizes, *The New York Times* included a lengthy assessment of the significance of the work of the two laureates. In a long article beginning on page 1 and continued on page 3, the unnamed reporter for *The New York Times* concluded that although the discoveries of Lynen and Bloch were important, much research remained to be done before their findings would yield practical results. In a follow-up article on October 30, 1964, another reporter for *The New York Times* was much more generous in his assessment of Lynen's and Bloch's work. He praised the Nobel Committee's selection of the two men, saying that "their work provides an excellent sample of what scientists mean when they speak of basic research as distinct from applied research." He went on to speculate that the laureates' research would eventually lead to the prevention or treatment of circulatory diseases.

Biography

Ida Frieda Lynen (née Prym) gave birth to Feodor Felix Konrad Lynen in Munich, Germany, on April 6, 1911. Feodor's father, Dr. Wilhelm Lynen, was professor of mechanical engineering at the Technical Institute of Munich. His mother was the daughter of the noted manufacturer Gustav Prym.

After successfully completing his elementary education despite the confusion and dislocations in Germany which accompanied World War I and the subsequent abortive attempts at revolution by political groups from the extreme left and the extreme right, Lynen entered the exclusive Luitpold Oberrealschule in Munich in 1921. The Munich in which Lynen grew to adulthood was a hotbed of political activity. The birthplace of Adolf Hitler's National Socialist movement, Munich witnessed frequent armed clashes between rival political groups throughout the 1920's. Unlike many of his peers, Lynen was able to resist the lure of high adventure seemingly offered to the youth of Germany by political activity. Instead, he concentrated on his studies and his favorite hobbies, skiing and hiking.

In 1930, Lynen entered the University of Munich to study chemistry under Professor Heinrich Wieland, who had received the Nobel Prize in Chemistry for 1927. Lynen completed the requirements for the doctor of philosophy degree in February, 1937. Three months later he married Eva Wieland, the daughter of his mentor, who eventually bore him five children. Through the influence of his father-in-law, Lynen was awarded a stipend from the national research foundation for postdoctoral study at the University of Munich, where he undertook a career in research. The German government deemed his studies important enough to exempt him from military service when World War II erupted in 1939. Lynen's research earned for him a *Habilitation* (a certificate which qualified him as a university lecturer) in 1941, and his father-in-law arranged a position for him at the university as lecturer the next year. The university administration promoted him to associate professor of biochemistry in 1947 and to full professor in 1952. Sponsored by Nobel laureate Otto Warburg, Lynen became director of the Max Planck Institute for Cellular Chemistry in 1954. The Planck Institute already enjoyed the reputation as the world's leading research facility in biochemistry and served as a training center for aspiring biochemists from Europe and America.

During a long and productive scientific career, Lynen lectured at most major universities in Europe and the United States. In addition to the Nobel Prize, he won many awards and prizes. These included the Neuberg Medal of the American Society of European Chemists and Pharmacists (1954), the Liebig Medal of the Association of German Chemists (1955), the Carus Medal of the German Academy of Natural Science (1961), and the Otto Warburg Medal of the Association for Physiological Chemistry (1963). He also received a number of honorary doctorates from major universities in Europe and the Americas. Lynen spent his last seven years as director of the Max Planck Institute for Biochemistry. He died in his home in Starnberg, a small town outside Munich, West Germany, on August 9, 1979.

Scientific Career

Lynen's scientific career began during his postdoctoral studies in his father-in-law's laboratory at the University of Munich in 1937. His first published scientific paper concerned the reduction of amber acid and citric acid by means of yeast, and it showed the role of phosphoric acid in the respiratory process of yeast. In 1938 and 1939, he became interested in viruses and published three papers on the subject before the outbreak of World War II. During the war, he moved his family to the small town of Starnberg outside Munich to escape the escalating American and British bombing raids. During that period, he became friends with Berthold von Bohlen und Halbach, director of the vast firm of Krupp. Most of his attention in research during the war years was directed toward further investigations of phosphoric acid and toward the studies of cholesterol that eventually won international fame.

After the war, Lynen continued his investigations into the nature of cholesterol. Through reading American biochemical journals, he discovered that Konrad Bloch at Columbia University in the United States was pursuing research along the same lines. The two men began a correspondence that eventually led to the discovery of the thirty-six steps by which animal cells produce cholesterol, a major achievement in unraveling the mysteries of cell metabolism. Cholesterol is a fatlike crystalline alcohol belonging to a group of related substances called sterols. The liver produces these substances, which occur in blood, bile, brain and nerve tissues, adrenal glands, the liver, and the kidneys. Cholesterol itself is a major component of gallstones.

In 1947, Lynen received promotion to associate professor of biochemistry at the University of Munich. By 1951, his research led him to the isolation of "activated acetate" from yeast. He showed that activated acetate is chemically identical with acetyl coenzyme A, which plays a vital role in the formation of cholesterol. His discovery was an essential step toward understanding the ways in which sterols and fatty acids form in animal cells. Bloch's previous isolation of a hydrocarbon called squalene was a necessary prerequisite to Lynen's discovery of activated acetate. The correspondence and cooperation between the two men greatly accelerated the success of their research. Lynen also cooperated closely with Bloch in finding a way to convert mevalonic acid to squalene by means of isopentenyl prophosphate—another important step in defining cell metabolism.

In 1952, officials at the University of Munich promoted Lynen to full professor of biochemistry and, in 1954, appointed him director of the renowned Max Planck Institute for Cellular Chemistry. This latter position, obtained with the help of former Nobel laureate Otto Warburg, allowed Lynen to devote all of his time to research. In the late 1950's, the medical community in Europe and the United States began to show increasing interest in the work of Lynen and Bloch concerning cholesterol because of increasing evidence of a link between that substance and heart disease. Several studies published in the United States showed that victims of arteriosclerosis, heart attacks, and strokes had abnormally high levels of cholesterol in their bloodstreams. Some studies suggested that excessive cholesterol in the diet is a major cause of cardiovascular disease. These studies led the National Heart Association of the United States to issue a report in 1964 which concluded that people with high cholesterol levels develop more coronary disease than those with lower levels. The growing concern of the international medical community with cholesterol as a cause of circulatory diseases, in fact, was a major factor in the decision of the Nobel Committee to name Lynen and Bloch the corecipients of the 1964 prize.

Lynen's research also led to a number of important discoveries in areas other than cholesterol metabolism. During World War II he had undertaken a study of fatty acids related to cholesterol. In the 1950's, this research led him to the isolation of a multi-enzyme complex from yeast which acts as a catalyst in the synthesis of long-chain fatty acids from acetyl coenzyme A and malonyl coenzyme A. Lynen found a number of the intermediate steps of this process through enzymological techniques and the use of analogues of coenzyme A. This research defined the series of chemical reactions through which energy is produced when fatty acids in foods are combusted to form carbon dioxide and water in the cell. Lynen's friend, Berthold von Bohlen und Halbach, director of the Krupp firm, had convinced the German government of the importance of this work for the war effort, so the government continued to subsidize Lynen's research throughout the war.

Another important discovery of Lynen's during the 1950's and 1960's concerned the vitamin biotin. Although scientists had known of biotin since 1935, its nature and function were not well understood until Lynen began to study it during the 1950's. In a famous paper in 1959, Lynen showed that biotin is an essential element in fat metabolism. His study also showed that biotin and protein working together inject carbon dioxide into molecules that are essential in producing fat and other bodily substances. Lynen continued to elucidate the importance of the role of biotin throughout his career and was preparing a paper on the subject at the time of his final illness. During the years before his Nobel Prize, Lynen's laboratory also produced important findings in other areas of biochemistry. These included studies of the biosynthesis of terpenes and of carotinoids, the mechanism producing the action of water-soluble vitamins, and the relationship between fatty acids and diabetes. During that period, his laboratory was host to a steady flow of postgraduate students of biochemistry from around the world who came to Munich to study with Lynen. Their work greatly enhanced his own research. Lynen inspired in them a love of research as well as a fierce loyalty to him. Many of them went on to make important contributions to biochemistry in their own right, and several of them were recipients of Nobel Prizes in later years.

Lynen's research activities did not diminish after he won the Nobel Prize in 1964: He continued to publish important papers in the areas of research for which he won the prize, and he turned his attention to other subjects as well. With the help of an ever-increasing number of aspiring biochemists who competed for the scarce postdoctoral slots in his laboratory, Lynen investigated such subjects as the bacterial oxidation of Vitamin B_6, cytohemin, and even the biochemical problems associated with the making of synthetic rubber. In later years he became increasingly interested in practical applications of his research, particularly in the relationship between cholesterol and arteriosclerosis. He published an important paper on that topic in 1972. Lynen received an appointment as director of the Max Planck Institute for Biochemistry in 1972. In that capacity he continued to be active in research and to publish numerous papers in scientific journals in Europe and the United States until his final illness and his death in 1979.

Bibliography

Primary

BIOCHEMISTRY: "Biosynthesis of Fatty Acids," *Proceedings of the Symposium on Drugs Affecting Lipid Metabolism*, 1961; "The Function of Biotin and Vitamin B_{12}-Coenzyme in the Oxidation of Fatty Acids with an Uneven Number of Carbon Atoms," *Proceedings of the Symposium on Drugs Affecting Lipid Metabolism*, 1961 (with E. R. Stadtman, P. Overath, and H. Eggerer); "Regulatory Mechanism in Aerobic Carbohydrate Metabolism of Yeast," in *Control Mechanisms in Respiration and Fermentation*, edited by B. Wright, 1963; "The Biochemical Function of Biotin: VI, Chemical Structure of the Carboxylated Active Site of Propionyl Carboxylase," *Proceedings of the National Academy of Sciences (USA)*, vol. 49, 1963, pp. 379-385 (with M. D. Lane); "The Cellular Control of Fatty Acid Synthesis at the Enzymatic Level," in *Molecular Basis of Enzyme Action and Inhibition*, edited by P. A. E. Desnuelle, 1963 (with M. Matsuhashi, S. Numa, and E. Schweizer); "Crystallization of a Multienzyme Complex: Fatty Acid Synthetase from Yeast," *Proceedings of the National Academy of Sciences (USA)*, vol. 63, 1969, pp. 1377-1382; "The Role of Phosphopantetheine in the Yeast Fatty Acid Synthetase Complex," *Vitamins and Hormones*, vol. 28, 1970, pp. 329-343 (with E. Schweizer, K. Willecke, and W. Winnewisser); "Patulin Biosynthesis: The Role of Mixed Function Oxidases in the Hydroxylation of m-Cresol," *European Journal of Biochemistry*, vol. 49, 1974, pp. 443-455.

Secondary

Bloch, Konrad, ed. *Lipide Metabolism*. New York: John Wiley & Sons, 1960. Edited by Lynen's corecipient of the 1964 Nobel Prize. The articles in Bloch's book contain many references to Lynen's work, including the research that led to his Nobel Prize. Lynen's central place in research into fatty acids and cholesterol is evident from the large number of times his work is cited. Contains much technical terminology and assumes knowledge about biochemistry on the part of the reader.

Greenberg, David M., ed. *Metabolic Pathways*. Vol. 2, *Lipids, Steroids, and Carotenoids*. New York: Academic Press, 1968. The six articles in Greenberg's book contain more than one hundred references to scientific literature published by Lynen in various biochemical journals; the numerous references to his work demonstrate the centrality of Lynen's research. Written as a textbook for college-level biochemistry classes.

Hartmann, Guido R., ed. *Die aktivierte Essigsäure und ihre Folgen: Autobiographische Beiträge von Schülern und Freunden Feodor Lynens*. Berlin: Walter de Gruyter, 1976. More than one-third of the eighty-seven articles by Lynen's former students and colleagues contained in this book are in English. The English-language articles will give the reader an idea of the warm personal relationships formed by Lynen with many of those who worked with him and the intense loyalties he inspired. Also contains a complete listing of all of his scientific publications.

McGilvery, R. W. *Biochemistry: A Functional Approach*. Philadelphia: W. B. Saunders, 1979. McGilvery's book does not discuss Lynen's work directly, but it can provide a relatively simple explanation of the problems with which Lynen dealt and the areas of biochemistry in which he worked. Provides definitions for the various technical terms necessary for an understanding of Lynen's research and explanations of chemical symbols and tables which permeate his published work.

Sabine, J. R. *Cholesterol*. New York: Marcel Dekker, 1977. Contains the best explanation in English of the nature and significance of Lynen's work. Although the book does contain technical jargon and chemical formulas, the interested reader without formal training in biochemistry can follow most of the arguments without much difficulty.

Paul Madden

1965

Physiology or Medicine

François Jacob, France
André Lwoff, France
Jacques Lucien Monod, France

Chemistry

Robert Burns Woodward, United States

Physics

Shin'ichirō Tomonaga, Japan
Julian Seymour Schwinger, United States
Richard P. Feynman, United States

Literature

Mikhail Sholokhov, Soviet Union

Peace

United Nations Children's Fund

FRANÇOIS JACOB
1965

Born: Nancy, France; June 17, 1920

Nationality: French
Areas of concentration: Molecular biology, biochemistry, and genetics

Jacob was a major contributor to seminal discoveries concerning genetic control of enzyme and virus synthesis, which were a landmark in producing molecular biology; they spanned virology, biochemistry, and microbiology

The Award

Presentation

Professor Sven Gard, a member of the faculty of the Royal Caroline Institute and representative of the Swedish Academy of Sciences, delivered the allocution address on December 10, 1965, before the King of Sweden awarded the Nobel medal and scroll. In his talk, Gard pointed out that the 1965 prize was given for discoveries on genetic regulation of enzyme and virus synthesis. He noted that this research area was quite difficult to deal with and that the research had represented a long, hard effort.

He continued by pointing out that earlier Nobel laureates, who included Francis Crick, James D. Watson, Arthur Kornberg, and Severo Ochoa, had helped to set the stage for this effort by describing the hereditary material, deoxyribonucleic acid (DNA); identifying its composition; showing it to be composed of double-stranded molecules; demonstrating that it contains the information (in the genes) required for the production of all the cellular proteins; and denoting the tremendous number of possible structures for individual genes.

Gard then reminded his audience that the cellular hereditary material provides two levels of information: first, the ability of each half of the double-stranded DNA molecule to become an exact copy of the initial hereditary material when the cell reproduces, and second, a series of code words that determine what component is incorporated into each position of every protein for which it codes. With all this, however, the main question of how the hereditary information can become chemical processes was unanswered before the efforts being honored by the 1965 Nobel Prize.

Gard then described how François Jacob, Jacques Monod, and André Lwoff had done this by identifying messenger ribonucleic acid (mRNA) and by developing the concept of the operon, with its inherent adaptability, necessary for survival. He pointed out that the great endeavors of this Nobel group had opened up a new field of research that deserved to be named "molecular biology."

Gard ended by pointing out that in their joint endeavor, Lwoff, Monod, and Jacob represented the necessary expertise in microbiology, biochemistry, and cellular genetics, respectively. The great strength of the team was their special qualities of intellect, collaborative ability, imagination, and scientific intuition, without which the discoveries could not have been made. He also predicted that their research would greatly stimulate discoveries in all areas of life science and spread out like ripples in a pond, leading to phenomenal things.

Nobel lecture

On December 11, 1965, François Jacob delivered his Nobel lecture, entitled "The Genetics of the Bacterial Cell." He began by modestly crediting much of the basis for his receipt of the prize to the fact that he had been in the right place at the right time. Jacob also indicated that the Pasteur Institute had been an excellent place for such work because of its rare atmosphere of enthusiasm, very lucid constructive criticism, nonconformity, and amicable interaction between scientists.

After this, Jacob divided the lecture into five concise parts, in which he discussed the essence of the joint efforts of the French group. The first four portions of the lecture dealt with lysogeny and bacterial conjugation, expression of the genetic material via messenger ribonucleic acid (mRNA), the regulation of the genetic activity of bacterial cells by the operons, and the organization of bacterial genetic material. The last portion of the talk delineated the conclusions derived from the effort.

Throughout his lecture, Jacob stressed the great importance of understanding the chemistry of the hereditary material (DNA) to deciphering all aspects of genetics and molecular biology. His concluding statements began with the description of the main biochemical activities of the DNA—the transcription, or copying, of one chain to produce the messenger RNA, and the replication of both DNA chains when a cell reproduces. He then related that these are subject to numerous specific molecular regulatory interactions determined by the genes. Jacob pointed out that the messages inscribed in the DNA contain the plans for all cellular components and programs that coordinate necessary syntheses, assuring their appropriate execution.

Jacob also noted the major importance of microbial genetics in giving a definitive answer to the problem of how the genes interact with the cytoplasm, coordinating the environment and heredity. He mentioned that regulatory effectors of microbial genetics do not simply have a stimulatory role; rather, they act as signals that allow synthesis of products whose nature depends solely on the nucleic acid sequence utilized.

Jacob likened the action of the gene regulators to signals determining which pages of a book, the hereditary information, were read at any given moment. Finally, he pointed out that the exact chemical basis for the various control processes was not yet known. He correctly intimated that eventually they would become known. Time has allowed their identification, and the Pasteur group played a very important part in the research necessary to attain this goal.

Critical reception

The scientific world greeted the announcement that Jacob, Monod, and Lwoff had received the Noel Prize with as much enthusiasm as had been communicated by

Dr. Gard. There was very little discord here. The efforts of Jacob and his coworkers had contributed so significantly and so definitively to the understanding of genetics, biochemistry, and microbiology that it was clear that they deserved the prize. Many other famous scientists commented favorably on their efforts. For example, Dr. Gunther Stent (himself a famous molecular biologist at the University of California, Berkeley) pointed out in the October 22, 1965, issue of *Science* that "the influence of the endeavors of Jacob, Monod, and Lwoff transcends the boundaries of molecular biology" and that "it will alter the face of developmental biology and embryology." Stent also stated that "it would be difficult to imagine anyone more deserving of the Nobel prize" than the three Pasteur Institute scientists.

The public was not entirely clear about the exact nature of the work carried out by the Pasteur group. Even *The New York Times* limited its response to thumbnail sketches of the lives of the three great scientists, noting their academic positions, their scientific awards, and the fact that all three scientists had been war heroes, winning medals for bravery, including the Medal of the Resistance (Lwoff), the French War Cross (both Jacob and Monod), the American Bronze Star (Monod), and the Companion of the Liberation (Jacob).

The world responded to Jacob very positively as a great writer and speaker in biology. Even ten years later, Jeremy Bernstein, in the course of a review of Jacob's book, *The Logic of Life: A History of Heredity* (in the October 13, 1975, issue of *The New Yorker*), complimented Jacob's Nobel Prize effort, saying that "it is not possible to easily sketch the depth and richness of Dr. Jacob's contribution" to the understanding of molecular biology and molecular genetics. In addition, Bernstein complimented *The Logic of Life* for its brilliance. He pointed out that after reading Jacob's work, "one feels better, more serene, and in possession of enlarged perspective of who one is and what one's place is in the natural order of things."

Biography

François Jacob, only child of Simon Jacob, a merchant, and Thérèse (Franck) Jacob, was reared in the Jewish religion. His prosperous parents sent young Jacob to excellent schools, including Paris' Lycée Carnot. Jacob was an excellent student, who wished earnestly to become a surgeon, after falling in love with the race against death and the precision he perceived upon viewing an operation. His goal was encouraged by a physician uncle, Henri Jacob, and by his parents. On graduation from the *lycée*, Jacob enrolled at the Sorbonne, with medicine his major. He did well and also developed an interest in research. Yet Jacob's first love remained surgery.

Jacob's studies ended abruptly when Germany invaded France and he fled to London. There, Jacob joined the Free French Army Medical Corps. Throughout World War II, he saw action in North Africa, with General Jacques Philippe Leclerc. During the Normandy invasion, Jacob was attached to the American Second Armored Division. In 1944, at Le Mans, he was wounded severely while trying to help an injured soldier. Injuries to his hand and arm ended his hopes of becoming a surgeon. Jacob's valorous war record won for him the French War Cross and the Companion of the Liberation, two of the highest French war medals.

Returning to Paris after the war, Jacob passed the rigorous second-year medical exams at the Sorbonne and changed to medicine after unsuccessful attempts to continue surgical training. He did well but felt trapped and flirted briefly with careers in journalism, politics, and civil service. None of these professions held Jacob's interest. At this time, he met and married Lise (née Bloch) Jacob.

Interaction with Lise's cousin, Henri Marcovich, a physician turned biological researcher, led Jacob to realize that he had the ability and the desire to go in that direction too. He decided that genetics was the area for him because it dealt with "quantitative biology" and sat at the "core of things." This decision led Jacob to his life's work, to the 1965 Nobel Prize, and to his long, successful career at Paris' Pasteur Institute.

Jacob and his wife, Lise, had four well-loved children, Henri, Laurent, Odile, and Pierre. Professionally, his honors include membership in the French Academy of Science, the Royal Society of London, and the American Academy of Arts and Sciences.

Scientific Career

François Jacob's life's work may be described as being the investigation and the definition of the cellular genetics of bacteria. His contributions to the area are many and varied. He began his career by seeking a research fellowship at the National Research Center and the National Hygiene Institute, where he was rejected by Émile Terroine and Louis Bugnard, the directors of the two agencies. Finally, Jacques Trefouel, the director of the Pasteur Institute, offered Jacob a fellowship. There, he did his doctoral work with the well-known geneticist André Lwoff, whose great scientific virtuosity Jacob attempted to emulate.

Jacob completed his doctoral work under Lwoff in 1954. His efforts stemmed from Lwoff's study of lysogenic bacteria. Unlike most bacteria, lysogenic bacteria are not destroyed by viral offspring soon after infection with bacterial viruses (the bacteriophages). When lysogenic bacteria are subjected to various external stimuli such as ultraviolet light, they are destroyed by the multiplication of the viruses in the cell and the release of the viral offspring produced. The overall process is called lysogeny.

Lwoff had shown that the bacteriophages in lysogenic cells first existed as noninfectious forms of the viruses, called prophages, carried inside the bacteria. Jacob's doctoral research extended the understanding of lysogenic bacteria and prophages, carrying Lwoff's efforts forward. It included the concept that prophages were carried hooked into the bacterial chromosome as one of its genetic elements. Jacob later proved this to be correct, but at the time of his thesis defense it was not entirely acceptable to the scientific community.

Immediately after the completion of his doctoral work, Jacob began collaborating with Elie Wollman in the study of the genetics of bacterial chromosomes. This work was made possible by their discovery that bacteria were differentiated sexually into male and female cells, which mated by attaching themselves together with a conjugation tube. As Jacob and Wollman explained, beginning in the July, 1956, issue of *Science*, this tube forms between mating cells and the male cell passes its genetic material through the tube into the female.

The data that Jacob and Wollman collected on mating bacteria showed that bacterial chromosomes are circular deoxyribonucleic acid (DNA) molecules that contain numerous genes arranged in an ordered array. They found that this ordered gene array could be mapped by an experimental technique that used a food blender to break the conjugating pairs at desired time intervals. Via this technique, Jacob and Wollman demonstrated that chromosomes, attached to the cell membrane, always contain genes arranged in the same consecutive order from their point of attachment. Genes, then, were subunits (pieces) of the DNA in the bacterial chromosome. All bacterial variants which exhibited lost genetic attributes were found to have portions of their chromosomes missing or inactive. Any variant bacteria observed that exhibited new genetic characteristics were found to contain additional chromosomal material.

Next, Jacob collaborated with Jacques Monod in the discovery (in bacteria) of a special type of ribonucleic acid (RNA) called messenger RNA. Today, because of these efforts, the three main types of cellular RNA molecules have been identified: ribosomal RNA, messenger RNA, and transfer RNA. These three kinds of RNA cooperate in the synthesis of proteins, the means by which the hereditary information in the cellular chromosomes is actualized. Ribosomal RNAs are structural RNA components of the ribosomes on which cellular proteins are manufactured. Messenger RNA is responsible for carrying the genetic code transcribed from DNA to specialized sites within the cell; each contains the "blueprint" for the synthesis of a protein. Transfer RNA is responsible for the assembly of the amino acids that make up a protein chain, which is synthesized at a ribosome.

In their examination of the genetics of protein synthesis, Jacob and Monod also discovered that chromosomal DNA contains structural and regulatory genes. Structural genes are copied to produce messenger RNA blueprints for production of proteins that cause observed genetic characteristics. Messenger RNAs produced from regulatory genes are blueprints for repressor proteins. Repressor proteins combine with chromosome operator sites (special pieces of DNA, into which they fit) and turn off messenger RNA production from structural genes. Operator-repressor combination can be viewed as an "off" signal for protein synthesis. These efforts of Jacob and Monod were first described in 1961 in a *Journal of Molecular Biology* paper entitled "Genetic Regulatory Mechanisms in the Synthesis of Proteins."

Jacob and Monod hypothesized that all cellular chromosomes were divided into units called operons. They defined an operon as a portion of a chromosome composed of a regulatory gene, an operator site, and several structural genes. The operon hypothesis indicates how cells adapt to environmental changes. Such adaptation is necessary if cells are to survive the constant changes in their surroundings.

Among the phenomena explained by the operon hypothesis is enzyme induction—rapid production of enzymes (the biological catalysts) needed to respond to a sudden change in the supply of a food (for example, the sugar lactose) given to bacteria. Jacob and Monod hypothesized that this occurred because the food combines with the repressor protein to inactivate it, acting as an "inducer." Repressor inactivation by inducers was proposed to allow the operon to function, producing its enzymes via the action of its structural genes. The operon hypothesis stated that when the food (inducer) was used up, the repressor again became functional. Consequently, it then turned off the operon. Numerous repressor proteins have been isolated, and their properties validate the operon hypothesis.

In the course of this effort, Jacob, Monod, and coworkers also demonstrated that lysogeny, which had occupied Jacob's doctoral work, was the result of the addition of the viral genome to the chromosome of the host bacteria. This was accomplished by a process that prevented viral reproduction—the result of the action of a repressor protein. The reproduction of a bacteriophage in lysogenic bacteria therefore behaved like the expression of an operon in protein synthesis. Ultraviolet light and other "lysogenic factors" were viewed as the inducers that led to this reproduction and to the destruction of the host cell that followed it, via repressor inactivation.

Great things began to happen to Jacob in 1960, when he became the chief of the Department of Cellular Genetics at the Pasteur Institute. In 1964, the Collège de France established a chair in cellular genetics for him. In 1965, he shared the Nobel Prize with Lwoff and Monod for great "discoveries concerning the genetic control of enzyme and virus synthesis," including the operon hypothesis. This research is viewed by most scientists as the wedge that opened the field of molecular biology by explaining how genetic information is converted into chemical processes. Some other honors bestowed upon Jacob include the Essec Prize of the Anticancer League (1958), the Mayer Prize of the French Academy of Science (1962), appointment as a commander in the French Legion of Honor (1965), and an honorary doctorate from the University of Chicago (1965).

Jacob has continued to contribute to molecular biology by filling in, developing, and editing important concepts about molecular genetics. Among his major interests has been proof of the viral theory of human cancer production. This theory proposes that cancer-causing viruses such as the prophage in a lysogenic bacterium lie dormant within human cells until they are activated by environmental factors. Once activated, Jacob envisions these viruses as taking over human cells and converting them to wildly growing cancer cells. It is significant that the research of Howard Temin and others has implicated viruses in certain types of cancer production, supporting Jacob's hypothesis and leading to the concept of cancer genes (oncogenes).

François Jacob has always been known as a man of probity, an idealist imbued with respect for the law, honesty, decency, strong character, and respect for other people. He is also recognized as a superb scientist, filled with a transcendent love for research. He has made exceptional contributions to molecular biology. Working in a defined area, he made it quantitative, whereas before it was mostly speculative. His efforts have greatly enriched the reputation of the Pasteur Institute, helping to keep it in the forefront of research in the area. Before the research to which Jacob contributed so greatly, it was not understood how the biological expression of the cell's genetic information was accomplished. Without that research, there might be no molecular biology. In addition, the high technology of recombinant DNA research and of genetic engineering might never have been developed.

Bibliography

Primary

BIOLOGY: "Transduction of Lysogeny in *E. coli*," *Virology*, vol. 1, 1955, pp. 207-220; "Genetic Aspects of Lysogeny," in *The Chemical Basis of Heredity*, edited by W. D. McElroy and B. Glass, 1957; "Genetic Control of Viral Functions," *Harvey Lectures*, vol. 554, 1960, pp. 1-39; "Genetic Regulatory Mechanisms in the Synthesis of Proteins," *Journal of Molecular Biology*, vol. 3, 1961, pp. 318-356 (with Jacques Monod); *Sexuality and the Genetics of Bacteria*, 1961 (with Elie Wollman); *The Logic of Life: A History of Heredity*, 1975; *The Actual and the Possible*, 1982.

Secondary

Hayes, William. *The Genetics of Bacteria and Their Viruses*. New York: John Wiley & Sons, 1964. This book describes early modern methods of research in bacterial and viral genetics. It also deals with lysogeny and Jacob's contributions. Its bibliography contains thirty-five of Jacob's publications.

Jacob, François. *The Statue Within*. Translated by Philip Franklin. New York: Basic Books, 1988. This intriguing autobiography was funded by the Sloan Foundation. It gives important insights into François Jacob, his contemporaries, and the development of molecular biology. It contains many interesting anecdotes about the environment and the scientists of the Pasteur Institute, as viewed by Jacob.

Jacob, François, and Jacques Monod. "Genetic Regulatory Mechanisms in the Synthesis of Proteins." *Journal of Molecular Biology* 3 (1961): 318-356. This important, insightful article describes the messenger RNA concept and explains the operon concept as to function of repressors, operators, and structural genes. It is a must for those who wish to gain in-depth insight into the concepts and basic chemistry of the processes involved.

Jacob, François, and Elie Wollman. *Sexuality and the Genetics of Bacteria*. New York: Academic Press, 1961. This valuable book describes bacterial genetics and sexual conjugation in bacteria. As the authors explain in their preface, the book is divided into three portions: the origin and the early development of bacterial genetics, the detailed analysis of sexual conjugation in bacteria, and the use of bacterial conjugation to attack relevant genetic problems of the time.

Lehninger, A. L. *Biochemistry*. New York: Worth, 1975. Chapter 35 of this college text provides lucid coverage of regulation of gene expression. Lehninger deciphers the history and the biochemistry of the area in masterful, scholarly fashion. Much is said about the work of Jacob and Monod in induction of enzymes and related topics. Repressors, operons, and enzyme inducers are described completely.

———. *Principles of Biochemistry*. New York: Worth, 1982. Portions of chapter 29 of this text, written at a somewhat lower level than *Biochemistry*, cover the work of Jacob and Monod.

Stent, Gunther S. *Molecular Biology of Bacterial Viruses*. San Francisco: W. H. Freeman, 1963. The book compiles many historical issues in the development of the molecular biology of bacteriophages. It includes sections on infection of bacteria, growth/reproduction of viruses, genetic recombination, lysogeny, transduction, and expression of hereditary information. Its bibliography/citation index contains thirty of Jacob's most relevant publications with Wollman and others.

Sanford S. Singer

1965

Physiology or Medicine
François Jacob, France
André Lwoff, France
Jacques Lucien Monod, France

Chemistry
Robert Burns Woodward, United States

Physics
Shin'ichirō Tomonaga, Japan
Julian Seymour Schwinger, United States
Richard P. Feynman, United States

Literature
Mikhail Sholokhov, Soviet Union

Peace
United Nations Children's Fund

ANDRÉ LWOFF
1965

Born: Ainay-le-Château, France; May 8, 1902

Nationality: French
Areas of concentration: Molecular genetics and virology

Lwoff helped discover the regulatory-processes in body cells that contribute to genetic control of enzymes and the synthesis of viruses. He showed that a virus can become part of a cell's genetic material and can be passed to following generations of cells

The Award

Presentation

Sven Gard, member of the Royal Caroline Institute and a member of the Nobel Committee for Physiology or Medicine, represented the Royal Swedish Academy of Sciences in delivering the presentation address on Friday, December 10, 1965, before King Gustav VI gave the Nobel medals and scrolls to André Lwoff, François Jacob, and Jacques Monod. In his presentation, Gard announced that the Nobel Prize in Physiology or Medicine (1965) was shared for "discoveries on genetic regulation in the synthesis of enzymes and viruses."

Gard pointed out that this topic is hardly an easy subject for research, noting that he once heard Professor Jacob warn an audience of specialists that if one had to describe genetic mechanisms, one had to choose between being inaccurate or being incomprehensible. As Gard presented the three scientists, he pointed out that he was going to be as inexact as his conscious would allow. Gard noted that many former Nobel laureates worked in this area of research, providing the foundation upon which the French scientists have built. He presented an overview of the significance of the double helical structure of deoxyribonucleic acid (DNA) as well as of the significance and mechanism of base pairing in protein synthesis. He continued with the fact that one of the principal functions of genes must be to determine the nature and number of enzymes in a cell; genes must also determine the chemical means by which the reactions take place that form cellular substances and release the energy that is required for all life functions. Each enzyme must correspond to one specific gene. The gene, therefore, contains the information concerning the number, nature, and order of each specific part in the construction of a certain enzyme or protein. The question remained: How was the information used and transformed chemically?

A group of French scientists managed to show how the structural information of genes is used chemically. An exact copy of the genetic code is produced; it is called a structural messenger. The structural messenger is then locked in a chemical warehouse in the cell and bound up in magnetic band around a cylinder. Every time a new "word" comes into the cylinder, a portion of the band is attached. It is a complement to the word, adapting to it like a piece of a puzzle. Each piece of the construction is formed this way, and they are lined up one after the other to create a correctly conjugated albumin.

Since the structural messenger has a limited "life span," there is only time for the creation of a few "copies." Therefore, for the cell to keep functioning, there must be a continuous production of structural messengers that corresponds to uninterrupted gene activity. There are two kinds of regulatory genes: An emitter sends chemical signals that are capped by a receptor, which then controls one or more structural genes. As long as the signals are capped, the receptor is blocked and the structural genes are inactive.

These French scientists have opened up a field of research that is aptly named molecular biology, Gard stated. Lwoff handles the microbiology, Monod has the biochemistry, and Jacob deals with the cellular genetics. Their crucial discovery would not have been possible without their mastery of all technical phases of these fields and their perfect cooperation. Although there are no practical uses yet for these scientific results, they have strongly stimulated scientific research in all areas of biology and in other fields as well.

Nobel lecture

André Lwoff delivered his lecture, "Interactions Between Virus, Cell, and Organism," on December 11, 1965. In it, he said that an organism is an independently functioning system of integrated structures composed of cells, which are composed of molecules that work together in harmony—each one knowing what the others do. Each must be able to receive messages and must be able to obey them. For many years, Lwoff noted, countless scientists have devoted themselves to the virus—Lwoff's own work has been an extension of a long series of ideals and discoveries. Lwoff considered certain aspects of the relation between the cell and the virus: cellular metabolic interactions. He subsequently set out to follow their development and evolution.

When one examines the mechanics of the production of different proteins, one sees that it is done in a specific order, as if a sequence of repression and depression were present. As far as is known, it is the phage that regulates itself. The host infected by a phage becomes a phage factory that stops only when the host is destroyed. Bacteria have no control over the development of a virulent phage in the most extreme case; however, there are less severe cases, and there are phages that do not kill every infected bacteria. Certain bacteria survive in order to penetrate the phages indefinitely. These are lysogenic bacteria, the study of which has profoundly changed our ideas on cell-virus relations.

It is known, Lwoff continued, that viruses and chromosomes from their host cells have numerous nucleotide sequences in common. This can hardly be a coincidence. Many virologists think that the virus is created by mutation from normal cellular elements—that the virus is a disorder created from cellular order. These ideas were hotly contested for years. In a bacterium, DNA-RNA polymerase synthesizes ribonucleic acid (RNA) on a DNA matrix, not on an RNA matrix. In vitro, however, the same enzyme can use RNA polymerase. In a bacterium, then, DNA-RNA polymerase can be said to be "on the job," rather than being elsewhere getting into trouble. In a normal cell, each molecule is in its place; that is why each part of the molecule does its own work. That phenomenon led Lwoff to wonder whether certain cellular diseases are not caused by the unwanted presence of some foreign visitor at some particular place.

Why is it, he wondered, that lysogenic bacteria do not reproduce bacteriophage? It is known that one gene of the prophage is expressed, producing a repressor that attaches to an operator gene and blocks expressions of the structural gene that determines the formation of the enzymes necessary for autonomous phage reproduction. If the lysogenic bacteria are depressed, they will produce virions.

The repressor is produced by a regulating gene, and it acts on an operator gene. Both are subject to mutations. A mutated regulator gene produces a repressor that can no longer block the operator, and a mutated operator no longer responds to the repressor. In the last analysis, then, it is the environment that governs the bacterial metabolism, which in turn governs the genetic constitution of the bacteria, in turn governing the gene or portions of the phage. This renders the bacteria capable of producing phage—or even of producing diphtherial toxin or synthesizing a new antigen that can modify the structure of the bacterial cell wall.

Critical reception

Thirty years had elapsed between the reception of the Nobel Prize in Chemistry by Frédéric and Irène Joliot-Curie (1935) and the presentation of the award in Physiology or Medicine to Lwoff, Monod, and Jacob (1965). This apparent lack of recognition of leading French scientists had become a matter of public concern in France. While Lwoff, Monod, and Jacob had long been recognized abroad as among the world's leading modern biologists, they remained virtually unknown and without influence on scientific affairs in their own country.

As reported in *Science*, "News and Comments" (1965), the practical use of Lwoff's conclusions in "typing" strains of organisms recovered in epidemics appeared in developments such as those obtained by Shapiro and coworkers, who isolated a complex of genes controlling a single function representing the lactose operon. It appears, the article stated, that complex problems of bacterial variation may eventually explain the origin of hereditary diseases.

To investigate these hypotheses, *Time* magazine reported, Lwoff chose to work with single-celled organisms, such as bacteria, because they have a single chromosome (man has forty-six). As "stand-ins" for genes, he chose viruses that infect bacteria (bacteriophages), because their cores consist of nucleic acid. Lwoff found that what actually happens is not as simple as had been thought. The viral nucleic acid, the *Time* article stated, masquerading as a gene, might do one of two things after invading a bacterium. It might stimulate the bacterium to produce hundreds of copies of the various particles and destroy itself in the process, or it might attach itself to the host cell's genetic material and then lie dormant, only to reappear in successive generations. After this dormant phase, chemicals or radiation can still trigger the intruder gene into becoming infective and destructive.

The article in *Science* observed that the influence of the work for which Lwoff, Monod, and Jacob were honored "far transcends the bounds of molecular biology." Probably the most important impact has been on developmental biology, a field concerned with the understanding of regulation of gene activity, or ontogeny.

Biography

André Lwoff, born May 8, 1902, at Ainay-le-Château, was the son of Russian parents who settled in France. He studied science and medicine at the University of Paris and was attached to the Pasteur Institute from 1921, becoming head of the department of microbic physiology. He performed services for which he was awarded the Medaille de la Resistance in 1964 and became commandeur of the Légion d'Honneur in 1966. He shared the Nobel Prize in Physiology or Medicine in 1965 for his research on episomes.

His research interests have been multifaceted and have included parasitic cilia (their evolutionary cycle and morphogenesis); hematin, a growth factor in flagella, and protohematin and its qualitative action on growth; factor V, which influences *Hemophilus influenza*, and its specific role in bacterial metabolism; poliovirus and the relation between viral sensitivity and temperature; and the mechanism of specific inhibitors to viral development. The Rockefeller Foundation awarded several grants to Lwoff so that he could execute his research programs. Much of his research was performed in collaboration with Edward Chatton.

Scientific Career

Although André Lwoff is certainly best known for the work that was to win the 1965 Nobel Prize, that research on lysogenic bacteria and "prophage" was actually the third area that Lwoff had investigated in his career. In the 1920's, he studied the morphogenesis of protozoa (morphogenesis is the process by which tissues are formed and then differentiate). In the 1930's, he became interested in the nutrition of protozoa.

Lwoff's work on protozoan morphogenesis in the 1920's culminated in the discovery of extranuclear inheritance in those organisms. Because of this work, Lwoff, at a young age, gained a reputation as a leading protozoologist of the time. In order to study ciliated protozoa (cilia are microscopic hairlike structures), Lwoff and Edward Chatton developed a process that became known as the Chatton-Lwoff silver-impregnation technique.

Silver-impregnation techniques permit protozoologists to study not only the static pattern on the bases of the somatic and oral ciliature in their material but also the dynamic aspects of these structures during the morphogenetic phenomena of binary fission and stomatogenesis. Data from such investigations were of considerable value in taxonomic considerations. They also provided a more precise understanding of the cortical anatomy in the trophont (vegetative), or nondividing, ciliate, which contributed to a determination of its most appropriate position in the scheme of ciliate classification.

The Chatton-Lwoff silver-impregnation technique was used for studies of ciliated protozoa at the University of Illinois and Howard University. Utilization of the silver-line system in systematics of the ciliate protozoa became very popular during the decade of the 1950's, primarily through the outstanding monographic works of French protozoologists.

When Lwoff turned to the study of protozoan nutrition in the 1930's, his work led him to initiate the use of chemically defined media for the growth of protozoa. He came to identify vitamins as important factors in microbial growth. In 1936, he published a famous paper with his wife Marguerite; it showed that vitamins function as coenzymes. Because of this discovery, Lwoff was soon viewed not only as a protozoologist but also as a figure in the development of nutrition as a science in its own right.

In 1941, Lwoff published his classic and influential treatise *l'Évolution physiologique* (physiological evolution), in which he theorized that biochemical evolution is brought about by progressive losses of biosynthetic capacity. Lwoff is given credit for formulation of "the unitary concept," a model to which all the properties of lysogenic bacteria are ascribed. This unitary concept is accounted for by the presence and position of a specific structure representing the genetic material of the phage—the properties of a lysogenic bacterium being the consequences of the right particle being at the right place.

Lwoff's work in the 1930's was performed at the Pasteur Institute in Paris, and it was his friendship with another researcher there, Emanuel Wollman, that was to lead him to the study of lysogenic bacteria. Wollman was an early student of these bacteria; he was killed in a Nazi concentration camp in World War II. After the war, Lwoff decided to continue the work that Wollman had begun. At that time, the field of lysogeny was not a well-respected area of research; it was out of favor with the new school of bacteriologists, many of them American scientists.

In 1950, however, Lwoff showed that lysogenic bacteria can indeed pass on the ability to produce viruses, in the non-infective form of the prophage. With his co-workers, he also discovered that ultraviolet light can be used to induce prophage to produce infective virus. With this proof that lysogenic bacteria do perpetuate viruses, lysogeny suddenly became a respectable field of study. Views on the relationship between virus and host cell began to change; it began to be viewed as a sort of "peaceful coexistence." The process of prophase induction, however, remained somewhat mysterious for nearly ten years after its initial discovery by Lwoff.

In the 1950's, Boggs undertook the study of the mechanisms of specific inhibitors of viral development. These inhibitors probably act by modifying the tertiary or quaternary structure of a protein. The phenomenon of virus interference may have important implications for the clinician; in general, it is manifested when a virus that is capable of causing illness or death fails to do so when inoculated along with (or following) a second virus that by itself fails to produce symptoms.

The growth of influenza viruses in the allantoic cavity of the chick embryo provides an excellent situation for the study of interference. If a large dose of undiluted virus is inactivated by ultraviolet irradiation and injected into the allantoic cavity, subsequent inoculation of a small dose of active virus of any type will produce no demonstrable evidence of infection. Killed virus, heated to 56 degrees Celsius for thirty minutes, is equally effective as an interfering agent. The implications for the physician are complex, and although double infection in an animal is recognized, clinically it is rare to see a patient who is suffering from one viral disease become acutely infected by another. This would seem like a logical or opportune time to attack, but the phenomenon of virus interference may be a very significant mechanism of nature to minimize or prevent double, triple, or other multiple infections.

In 1957, Lwoff tackled poliovirus and the relation of viral sensitivity to temperature and retrovirulence; this led him to the question of viral infection. It seemed to him that nonspecific factors played a key role in the evolution of primary infection. (Paralytic polio is a viral disease of the central nervous system that causes inflammation and damage to nerve cells and tissue in the lower brain and spinal cord.) The poliovirus enters the body through the nose or throat, then passes into the bloodstream.

Lwoff identified macromolecules in *Escherichia coli*, a bacterium that is normal in the intestinal tract of man and other vertebrates. He also provided some insight into the nuclear cycle of *Stephanopogon mesnili*. These are very small marine benthic organisms with two or more nuclei. The cytostome is apical and slitlike; cilia are confined mostly to several rows on the central surface. The cytopharynx is supported by bundles of microtubules. Mitosis in this organism involves an intranuclear spindle, with no dissolution of the nuclear envelope; division is by palintomy within a cyst.

Lwoff received an honorary doctor of science degree from the University of Chicago in 1959. He was influential in the creation of the European Organization of Molecular Biology in 1963. André Lwoff is a member of several organizations, including the Royal Society of London, the National Academy of Sciences (USA), and the Society of General Biochemistry (USA). Lwoff was a recipient of the Medal of Resistance (France) and, in 1961, was presented with the Leeuwenhoek Medal by the Royal Dutch Academy; he is president of the Microbiological Society of France.

Bibliography

Primary

VIROLOGY AND BIOCHEMISTRY: "The Saline-Gelatin Method (Wet Method) for Staining Protozoa," *Comptes rendus des séances de la société de biologie*, vol. 118, 1930, pp. 1068-1072 (with E. Chatton); "The Nuclear Cycle of *Stephanopogon mesnili*," *Archive of General Experimental Zoology*, vol. 78, 1936, pp. 117-132; *Problems of Morphogenesis in Ciliates*, 1950; "Identification of Macromolecules in *Escherichia coli*," in *Biological Order*, 1962; "Introduction to Biochemistry of

Protozoa," *Biochemistry and Physiology of Protozoa*, vol. 1, 1964, pp. 1-7 (with Seymour Hunter); "Concept of Kinetid in Locomotor Apparatus," in *General Protozoology*, 1965 (with E. Chatton).

Secondary

Adams, John M. "Diseases Caused by Enteroviruses: Coxsackie Viruses (A & B), The Polioviruses, ECHO Viruses." In *Newer Virus Diseases*. New York: Macmillan, 1960. This discusses the discovery of the adenoviruses in tonsils and adenoids removed at operation, new tissue culture methods, and the production of successful adenovirus vaccines. The ECHO viruses (enteric cytopathogenic human orphan) are considered as major etiologic agents in the production of diarrhea and various other human diseases.

Browing, Carl H., ed. *Encyclopedia of World Biography*. Vol. 7. New York: McGraw-Hill, 1965. This book gives a view of André Lwoff that includes his major works (genetics, morphogenesis, polio research, silverline system, and biochemistry). Lwoff's association with Edward Chatton as well as his early experiences at the Pasteur Institute are included.

Smithies, Oliver. "Antibody Variability." *Science* 157 (1967): 227-230. This article discusses peptide and amino acid sequences in Bence Jones Proteins (abnormal plasma or urine proteins) and the analysis of amino acid sequence data from thirty myelomatosis-derived proteins. A modified multiple gene hypothesis is proposed by W. J. Dreyer and W. J. Bennet.

Stent, Gunther S. "Nobel Laureates in Medicine or Physiology." *Science* 150 (October 22, 1965): 462-464. This article discusses the salient research areas of André Lwoff: nutrition morphogenesis, the poliovirus, protozoology. It presents an explanation for two concepts by Jacob and Monod, messenger RNA and the operon. The former represents a "copy" of a region of a cell's DNA (genome) used as a template for protein synthesis, and the latter is a regulatory unit of DNA that determines what sequence of base pairs will be used as a template for mRNA synthesis.

Wada, Akyoshi, and Suyama Akira. "Local Stability of DNA and RNA Secondary Structure and Its Relation to Biological Functions." *Proceedings in Biophysics and Molecular Biology* 47 (1986): 113-157. This article treats chemical and geometrical pictures (base-pairing modes in DNA and RNA secondary structure) and discusses the correlation between the double-helix stability distribution and genetic structure in DNA. Topics indicating experimental evidence for DNA are discussed: electron microscopy, electrophoresis, and endonuclease digestion and kinetics.

Nathaniel Boggs

1965

Physiology or Medicine

François Jacob, France
André Lwoff, France
Jacques Lucien Monod, France

Chemistry

Robert Burns Woodward, United States

Physics

Shin'ichirō Tomonaga, Japan
Julian Seymour Schwinger, United States
Richard P. Feynman, United States

Literature

Mikhail Sholokhov, Soviet Union

Peace

United Nations Children's Fund

JACQUES LUCIEN MONOD
1965

Born: Paris, France; February 9, 1910
Died: Cannes, France; May 31, 1976
Nationality: French
Areas of concentration: Cellular biochemistry, molecular biology, and bioethics

Monod, in collaboration with André Lwoff and François Jacob, discovered the process through which genes regulate vital biochemical processes, thereby setting the direction for a revolution in genetics while widening the fields of microbiology and medicine

The Award

Presentation

Sven Gard, Sweden's leading virologist and a member of Stockholm's Royal Caroline Institute of Medicine and Chemistry, represented the Royal Swedish Academy of Sciences in delivering the presentation address on December 10, 1965. Before the laureates received their awards from King Gustav VI, Gard began his address by pointing out that their work was in an area of science that is not easily understood and quoted François Jacob's admonition that to describe the operation of a genetic mechanism, it is necessary to be somewhat "inexact," even "incomprehensible." He promised to try to follow this principle of uncertainty within the confines of his own conscience in explaining the nature of the work of the three men honored by the committee.

In summarizing the previous history of research in this area (which he romantically designated as the secrets of life itself), Gard pointed out that such other Nobel laureates as Francis (Charles) Crick and James Watson had built a basis for the research of Monod and his colleagues, and described it as a series of stages and angles of approach that had determined that one of the principal functions of the gene is to determine the nature and number of enzymes in a particular cell. Previous researchers in the field had discovered that the cell's structure could be described as the result of the cell's deoxyribonucleic acid (DNA)—a long, double chain composed of four separate chemical units designated by the letters A, C, G, and T, designating the bases adenine, cytosine, guanine, and thymine. Gard explained how the relationship between the units led to the nearly infinite possibilities for combinations and characteristics in cell formation. This model could be seen as a communication code that determines the hereditary changes that occur through cellular division. Each gene contains information concerning the number, the character, and the structural order of the amino acids that constitute a basic protein molecule, the building blocks of all living substances. What remained a mystery was the manner in which the genetic information contributed to the chemical reactions involved in cell division.

Gard then described how the group of researchers led by Monod discovered what could be considered a "messenger" that carries a crucial "word" that is assimilated by another cell, similar to the action of a magnetic band on a recording surface of a tape. Each "messenger" contributes to the full message, like a part of a puzzle, until the entire process of transmission has occurred. Gard called this aspect of Monod's research remarkable in that it revealed chemical processes previously unknown or misunderstood. Gard went on to explain that the identification of the activating agent in the process was crucial to the understanding of cellular growth and reproduction. Cells tend to be inactive without it. Gard speculated that the activity of viruses might be controlled in the same manner, and that tumors studied in terms of their similar patterns of growth not only might provide information about "normal" cell processes but also could contribute to the understanding of disease mechanisms.

In concluding, Gard remarked that scientists have an inflated opinion of their abilities because of recent advances in many fields, and that little had really been known about essential cellular structure. Within the confines of a single cell spanning relatively large distances of millionths of a millimeter, scientists would be able to study activity of extraordinary complexity because of Monod's research. Gard suggested that Monod and his colleagues had originated a new field, which he labeled "molecular biology," citing André Lwoff as the specialist in microbiology, Jacob as a geneticist, and Monod as a biochemist. Calling their discovery "decisive," he stated that it would not have been possible without the total cooperation of the three men and observed that technical competence was not sufficient to penetrate the secrets of life: The capacity for fantasy, intuition, determination, logical thinking, and intellectual synthesis is also vital for a discovery of this magnitude. Gard closed his remarks by pointing out that this work did not have practical applications yet but would stimulate much more research, and that it held great promise for further advances in the field of medical science.

Nobel lecture

On December 11, 1965, Jacques Monod delivered his Nobel lecture, entitled "From Enzymatic Adaptation to Allosteric Transitions." It contained his personal philosophy concerning the methods of scientific inquiry and a detailed explanation of the work that led to his groundbreaking discoveries. Recalling the lack of support he received from the French government before the implications of his work became clear, Monod described a primitive laboratory in the old Sorbonne, where he worked surrounded by stuffed monkeys. His enthusiasm for returning to his research after World War II carried him past any limitations in his facilities. He resumed his work on a doctoral dissertation on chemical changes occurring during the growth of various bacteria, discovering that there were two distinct stages of growth under certain conditions. From his senior colleague, André Lwoff, he found that this discovery had important implications for learning about the manner in which enzymes are produced and how they changed. Convinced from his previous research in genetics in the United States that these enzyme changes were connected to the genetic code of the protein under examination, he examined all the studies in this area that he could find, attended symposia in several countries, and determined that the central problem concerned the role of the inducing agent leading to the enzymatic change. As he stated the question, "Does the change in the enzyme develop from a total process of synthesis, or is it an aspect of remodeling, conversion, or just the activation of material already present?" Monod believed that some additive was responsible for inducing the change, and through further experimentation and his consultation with other scientists, he began to realize that there was a repressing agent that prevented any change until a particular element removed its capability.

Utilizing a "double negative" approach proposed by Leo Szilard, Monod concluded that the eventual change in an enzyme was the result of what he called, initially, an antirepressor, but he still did not know what the repressing agent was. (The term antirepressor was eventually changed to operon, which essentially means gene cluster.) To solve this problem, he likened himself to a police inspector who has to find a criminal (or "assassin," as he called the repressor) based on a composite portrait drawn from several clues. The work of Crick and Watson in 1954 had led to the proposal of what was called the genetic code theory: The structure of proteins is determined and defined by the linear sequence of the nucleotides (sugar in a nitrogen base) in DNA. For Monod, this meant that some kind of "messenger" was involved in transmitting the signal that led to enzymatic change and that this messenger was intricately involved in the function of the repressor he sought. To determine how the relationship worked and to identify the messenger and the repressor, Monod hypothesized that there was only one repressing agent and began a series of experiments to determine its chemical nature. Working with what are called regulatory enzymes, Monod determined how they were activated and noted the primary properties exhibited in transforming a protein molecule through interaction. He called this an "allosteric effect," since there was a change in the structure caused by the attachment of a separate substance—an indirect effect. The allosteric reaction was not dependent on chemical reactivity between the various substances. From this, Monod concluded that a metabolic change had taken place and that it was coordinated by a network of specific interactions dependent on the structure of the protein itself, or its genetic code.

This concept, Monod observed, was dangerous, because it seemed to explain so much but it led to the interpretation of the essential structure of the RNA polynucleotide that turned out to be the messenger he sought, and to the beginning of an understanding of how the operon regulating the function of the repressor worked. As he had hoped, it also opened the gateway to an analysis of even more complex biological phenomena.

Critical reception

The awarding of the Nobel Prize in Physiology or Medicine to Jacques Monod and his colleagues André Lwoff and François Jacob of the Pasteur Institute in Paris was received with great enthusiasm in both Europe and the United States. The three men had been near-winners in previous years, and there was considerable expectation that they would be honored for their groundbreaking work "concerning genetic control of enzymes and virus synthesis." Their names were among eighty that had been considered by a fifteen-man Nobel committee from the Royal Caroline Institute, Sweden's leading medical college and research organization. The top faculty of the institute approved the decision unanimously. One of the reasons for jubilation was the fact that no French scientist had been awarded a Nobel Prize since Frédéric and Irène Joliot-Curie had received the chemistry prize in 1935, an apparent lack of recognition that had wounded French national pride and was becoming a matter of some public concern. While the award delighted the French press, some observers noted the irony involved in the fact that the scientists themselves had not received very much recognition during the course of their careers from the French scientific establishment. They remained comparatively unknown and "without much influence" in the scientific affairs of their own country. Knowledgeable people in the field were aware of their work, however, although none of the three had been elected to the French Academy of Sciences at the time of the award. Lwoff already held memberships in the Royal Society of London and the United States National Academy of Sciences, however, and Monod had received awards from the French Academy in 1955 and 1962.

Another reason for enthusiasm among commentators in France was the distinguished war record of Monod and Jacob. Monod had joined the French Resistance movement when France fell and had eventually risen to the post of commander of one of its underground military units before joining the French army after liberation. He had been awarded a Croix de Guerre and was made a Chevalier of the Legion of Honor, two of France's highest military awards, and had also been given a Bronze Star by the United States Army. The idea that an intellectual was also a man of action was very appealing to the French, while Monod's American colleagues who knew him from his work at the California Institute of Technology in the mid-1930's and from his heroic service in World War II were also very pleased to see Monod honored.

The public response to Monod's prize was exceeded by that within the scientific community. No one disputed the verdict that the research was "brilliantly imaginative," and the consensus was that the three not only had provided answers to one of the most important questions in microbiology but also had opened a field of immense possibility for future discovery. As Gunther S. Stent wrote in the October, 1965, issue of *Science*, "[T]he influence of the work for which Lwoff, Monod and Jacob are being honored by this prize now far transcends the bounds of molecular biology." Sven Gard, who made the prize presentation, pointed out that their discoveries had already led to a considerable amount of work in research laboratories throughout the world and that it would likely provide the initial basis for genetic alteration that would benefit humankind. While noting that their work had "no present practical application," *Time* magazine, in its October 22, 1965, issue, forecast the possibility that it might be possible to extrapolate "all the way from microbe to man" to determine how "long-dormant viruses may belatedly trigger cancerous changes in human cells." Stent maintained that the face of embryology had been altered and pointed out that "the three laureates" had also made "one further enormous scientific contribution: in their laboratories they trained a phalanx of young workers whose work was to transform the landscape of modern biology." He concluded his essay by remarking that it would be "hard to imagine anyone more deserving of this prize." In a general summary of the decision by the Swedish Academy members, the *Time* article stated, "the Nobel Prize committee, which has sometimes been as much as 30 years late in recognizing achievement, has now reached toward the future in making its 1965 award."

Biography

Jacques Lucien Monod was born on February 9, 1910, in Paris, France, the son of Lucien Monod, a painter, and Charlotte Todd MacGregor, an American who was originally from Milwaukee. Monod's father was considered an anomaly in a family of Huguenot descent whose members for centuries had become physicians, clergymen, teachers, and civil servants. Monod claims that he was heavily influenced by his father's combination of artistic sensitivity and intellectual erudition. The family moved to the south of France when he was seven, and Monod always saw himself less a product of Parisian culture than country life.

He returned in 1928 to study for a bachelor's degree in natural sciences at the University of Paris, and earned a *licencié ès sciences* degree in 1931, the year he published his first scientific paper. He joined the Faculté des Sciences at the university in 1934 and continued to work there through the decade except for a year spent at the California Institute of Technology (1936-1937) on a Rockefeller Foundation Fellowship. He married Odette Bruhl, a conservator at the Musée Guimet, in 1938, and was at work on his doctorate when war broke out. When France surrendered, he joined the Resistance, eventually becoming a commander of an underground unit, and was awarded the Croix de Guerre, the Legion of Honor decoration, and the American Bronze Star. In 1946, he joined André Lwoff's Department of Microbial Physiology at the world-famous Pasteur Institute. For the next fifteen years, he, Lwoff, and François Jacob worked on the research that would eventually lead to his Nobel Prize. He accepted a professorship at the Sorbonne in 1959 and became the director of the Pasteur Institute in 1971.

In addition to his renown as a Nobel Prize winner, Monod also gained fame as a best-selling author when a translation of his book, *Le Hasard et la nécessité* (*Chance and Necessity*) was published in 1970. More than 150,000 copies of the book were sold during the first three months of the year, and Monod spent the early 1970's as a participant in several international conferences which debated the place of the scientist in the political affairs of the world and considered the ethical questions raised by such philosophers as Pierre Teihard de Chardin, with whose teleological evolutionary theory Monod disagreed in his book. From 1968 until his death in 1976, Monod was a nonresident fellow of the Salk Institute, and in 1973 he visited the United

States as a part of a fund-raising trip to save the Pasteur Institute from bankruptcy. At the time of his death, he was an honored member of the international scientific community, belonging to the Washington Academy of Science, the Royal Society of London, and the Czechoslovak Academy of Science.

Scientific Career

Jacques Monod always regarded science as much more than a series of experiments in the laboratory. He maintained throughout his career that a scientist has a responsibility not only to the intellectual traditions of unbiased exploration but to the moral obligations and social and political consequences of his work as well. He cited as an early influence his father's "passionate love of the works of the mind" and acknowledged his debt to his father's "positivist faith in the joint progress of science and society." Like his father, who broke an old family tradition of professional service by following his instincts to become an artist, Monod remained something of a maverick throughout his life, never hesitating to put aside the work he clearly loved when another problem demanded his attention and never sacrificing his principles even when cooperation with those in positions of power would have made it easier for him to accomplish his scientific goals. When Monod was a graduate student at the University of Paris in the early 1930's, he found the faculty "twenty years or more behind contemporary biology," and his teachers tried to discourage his interest in the relatively new field of genetics by telling him that his work fell somewhere between the boundaries of what was then known as microbiology and chemistry, and that if he continued he would have no future in the university. At this time in his life, Monod entertained thoughts of leaving the sciences altogether and attempting to pursue a career as a classical musician, since he played the cello with professional competence.

In a display of determination that marked his entire career, Monod found a way to continue his work, accepting an assistantship in zoology at the University of Paris in 1932 and then securing a Rockefeller Foundation fellowship to work with the renowned geneticist Thomas Hunt Morgan at the California Institute of Technology in 1937. Monod seems to have instinctively realized that since his teachers in France were relatively ignorant of the genetic implications of the work he was doing on the chemical processes involved in the development of bacterial cultures, he would have to find other instructors in foreign countries. In doing this, he began to develop the cross-cultural framework that enabled him to pull together the prior work of scientists in many different locations. Returning to France, he continued to pursue his interests in bacterial growth rates, publishing his first noteworthy papers in the mid-1930's, but he was unable to complete the dissertation he had proposed for his doctoral degree by the time World War II broke out. In a typical gesture of complete commitment to his convictions, Monod did not travel abroad to continue with his research during the war but joined the Resistance movement, eventually becoming a commander of an underground military unit and then joining the French regular army; he ultimately completed his service as a member of the military government that occupied Germany. When the war ended, Monod returned to Paris to join the department of microbial physiology at the Pasteur Institute under the supervision of André Lwoff, whose work he already knew and admired. In his Nobel lecture, Monod recalls that he resumed his scientific work with "desperate eagerness" during the somber winter of 1940 after France fell, and that when Lwoff told him that his ideas might have something to do with "enzymatic adaptation," Monod replied, "Never heard of it." Lwoff explained what was involved, and Monod recalls that "the die was cast." When he was finally able to begin again in 1946, he concentrated all of his attention on the phenomena of enzyme adaptation, pulling together the ideas he had pondered during the war and some of the experiments he had performed clandestinely at Lwoff's laboratory during the Occupation.

Monod felt that the people he had met in Morgan's laboratory in California were a "revelation of what a group of scientists could be like when engaged in creative activity and sharing in a constant exchange of ideas, bold speculations, and strong criticisms." He hoped to gather a similar group in Paris, and he felt confident that the concepts of genetics he had learned in the United States might eventually be applied to bacteria. Working with Lwoff and François Jacob, a former member of the Free French who joined the Pasteur Institute in 1950, Monod began to study the synthesis of the bacterial enzyme beta galactosidase, attempting to solve the problem of how specific protein enzymes were formed. The enzymes with which he chose to work were ideal for a study of how a cell makes its enzymes, because that formation only began when a substratelike inducer (that is, the material upon which the enzyme acts) was added. During the first ten years of his work, Monod was able to demonstrate that induced formation of beta galactosidase was actually part of a new synthesis, rather than the conversion of any previously existing protein. Although it was already understood that genes arranged in the chromosomes of the nucleus of every cell were responsible for the manner in which a cell reproduces, almost nothing was known about the complex chemical interactions by which hereditary information was actuated. Monod and Lwoff were able to show by 1950 that viruses infesting sewer bacteria sometimes invaded and destroyed a cell, while at other times they changed the cell's structure, so that it reproduced in altered form. The work that Monod and his colleagues had accomplished pointed to the need for determining how the production of enzymes was triggered and halted, and through the monumental experiments of James Watson and Charles Crick, who proposed the model for deoxyribonucleic acid (DNA), Monod realized that the blueprint for cellular reproduction was available for analysis and that he could combine his own work with the genetic advances that had taken place during the early 1950's.

From this point, the divergent strands of the work of many scientists began to coalesce. Monod was never concerned about sharing his insights, never fearful that his theories might be proved wrong, since his goal was to learn everything about his subject, regardless of who was given the credit for his work. He was also confident enough in his own ability to know that it would be acknowledged and respected by his colleagues. Monod had been appointed the head of the department of cellular biochemistry in 1954 and was then in a position to hire other scientists to join him in his work. He suggested to Georges Cohen and Howard Rickenberg that they try to isolate the specific protein (galactoside permease) that supported the theory that each enzyme in a cell has its own production-regulating gene. Working with Arthur Pardee and François Jacob in 1958, Monod established for the first time that the role of the inducer in enzyme adaptation is to neutralize the repressor—the "assassin" that interrupted protein formation. From there, Monod and his colleagues were to formulate the concepts that led to the awarding of the Nobel Prize in 1965. In essence, they discovered that the basic arrangement of the DNA gene is transcribed to an RNA molecule, which they called messenger RNA. This combines with other RNAs to form protein. They also proposed the concept of the operon, which explained why the instructions carried by RNA were not carried out constantly, to the point of chemical chaos, but intermittently. Their work demonstrated that the repressor instructions were also encoded in DNA and transmitted constantly by RNA, but that the operon (or gene cluster) was like a circuit with a negative feedback safeguard. Whenever there is a threat to the cell, the operon cuts into the repressor message so that a positive message is conveyed and the cell continues with enzyme adaptation. Monod, who had become a professor on the faculty of sciences at the University of Paris in 1959, wrote an essay with Jacob called "Genetic Regulatory Mechanisms in the Synthesis of Proteins," which was published in the *Journal of Molecular Biology* in 1961. It has been called "one of the monuments in the literature of molecular biology." The essay was immediately recognized as a landmark statement, and Monod was awarded the Léopold Mayer Prize of the French Academy in 1962. He became a member of the true scientific elite in 1965 when he shared the Nobel Prize in Physiology or Medicine.

In accepting the responsibilities of his international reputation, Monod began to spend less time in actual laboratory work (although he continued to publish important papers through the 1960's, including a genetic mapping of part of the universally used *Escherichia coli* bacterium in 1965 and an essay for a Nobel symposium entitled "Symmetry and Function in Biological Systems" in 1968, but believed that he could begin to address some of the problems he had recognized in the French government's system of support for the sciences. In an interview in *Le Nouveau Observateur*, he expressed gratitude for grants from the United States government and from private agencies that made his work possible, praising the American attitude of spontaneous and natural scientific research. He complained that the French Ministry of Education had always favored those projects with immediate applicability to medicine or industry, thus neglecting the pure research that made such practical projects possible. He mentioned that the French government had recently approached the Pasteur Institute with offers to assist if the experiments were directed to specific applications, and defiantly proclaimed, "We refused. These people don't know what research is. We don't have to justify research." Monod was direct in his criticism, but always open to opportunity, especially if he could work toward his goal of establishing a laboratory. In 1967, he accepted an appointment as professor of biology at the Collège de France. On the other hand, it was not surprising that he joined student protesters in the streets of Paris during the political upheaval of 1968, recalling the limits placed on his own studies by conventional authority and reactionary thinking.

His involvement with governmental agencies led him to spend much of his time in reflection on the role of the scientist in an ideal society. In 1969, he delivered before a symposium in Stockholm an address entitled "The Place of Value in a World of Facts." Although he had once considered himself a Communist, he broke with the party when Joseph Stalin promoted the fraudulent genetic theories of Trofim Lysenko, and in his address in Stockholm, he expressed his view that all the value systems of the past, including religion, Marxism, and rationalism, had been invalidated by modern scientific discoveries. Instead of blindly following dogmatic ideologies, humans must find a new moral standard in a manner similar to science's method of finding truth through "logic confronted by experience." His reflections on these and other matters concerning what he believed to be the high "risk of the race committing suicide" led him to the highlight of what might be considered the second (although complementary) part of his career, the publication of his book *Le Hasard et la nécessité* in 1970.

Drawing on the existentialist thinking of his friend Albert Camus, and using Camus's great vision of the mythic Sisyphus "happy" in his struggle, Monod tried to frame for a nonscientific audience the philosophical implications of "the revolutionary discoveries made about basic life processes by scientists." Refusing to accept any explanation of existence in terms of what "ought" to be, Monod began with the fundamental postulate that "there is no plan, there is no intention in the universe." What must be recognized, he insisted, is that "chance alone is at the source of all novelty." Monod believed that human evolution is a product of unpredictable mutations and the necessity of natural selection in a Darwinian sense. The book was not only a best-seller in France but also the source of an ongoing debate in the realm of the philosophy of biology, typified by a conference sponsored by the Rockefeller Foundation, "Problems of Reduction in Biology," held in Bellagio, Italy, in September, 1972. The last session included an introductory address by Monod, followed by a discussion session including Monod and some of the most prominent scientists of the day, among them the Nobel laureate Peter Medawar and the noted philosopher Karl Popper.

In 1971, Monod became the director of the Pasteur Institute, forcing him to discontinue his own research work; but he did publish a number of papers with younger colleagues during the early 1970's, including further work with the *E. coli* bacteria, and a study of the beta galactosidase bacterial enzyme to examine how immunological systems operate. He visited the United States in 1973 in an effort to save the Pasteur Institute from bankruptcy, supporting his appeal by pointing out that he had trimmed the staff, patented a new influenza vaccine, and was continuing the work begun by Louis Pasteur in 1888 which had resulted in eight men who had studied or worked there winning Nobel Prizes in Physiology or Medicine. Although he felt the necessity of making a public appeal, he was speaking from the heart, since his own work—removed from the mainstream of French science, with its rigid, government-controlled administrative structure—had found a "home" at the privately supported institute.

Monod died on May 31, 1976, in Cannes, located in the southern French countryside that he considered to be his home, in spite of his many years in Paris. An accurate assessment of his career was made by his old friend and collaborator, André Lwoff, who wrote in a preface to his *Selected Papers in Molecular Biology* in 1978, that sometimes a career of a scientist is marked by a great discovery, but that "it is most unusual that it be illuminated by an uninterrupted series of great discoveries, and still more unusual when each discovery gives rise to new concepts and opens new vistas." Lwoff noted that Monod established a "school" that exhibited his dominance in his field, that he had the insight to set a direction for research, the ability to judge the potential of a young scientist, and the personality to inspire and encourage others to work in harmony. Monod's contribution to the development of molecular biology and the philosophy of science was impressive during his lifetime, and remains significant toward the close of the twentieth century.

Bibliography

Primary

BIOLOGY: *Selected Papers in Molecular Biology*, edited by André Lwoff and Agnes Ullmann, 1978.

PHILOSOPHY OF SCIENCE: *Le Hasard et la nécessité*, 1970 (*Chance and Necessity: An Essay on the Natural Philosophy of Modern Biology*, 1971).

Secondary

Ayala, Francisco José, and Theodosius Dobzhansky, eds. *Studies in the Philosophy of Biology: Reduction and Related Problems.* London: Macmillan, 1974. A collection of essays concerning the implications of biological discoveries in the second half of the twentieth century. The source for the book was a conference held in Bellagio, Italy, in September, 1972, where Jacques Monod was one of the featured speakers. His work is discussed in many of the selections, and he was the leader of a session which considered many of the issues raised in his book *Chance and Necessity.*

Fuller, Watson, ed. *The Biological Revolution: Social Good or Social Evil?* Garden City, N.Y.: Anchor/Doubleday, 1972. The text of the book is composed of papers and discussions presented at an international conference held in London in November, 1970. The issues covered included genetic engineering and other applications of new techniques in the sciences. Monod presented a paper entitled "On the Logical Relationship Between Knowledge and Values" and participated in many panels on the ethics of scientific exploration.

Judson, Horace Freeland. *The Eighth Day of Creation: The Makers of the Revolution in Biology.* New York: Simon & Schuster, 1979. While Monod is referred to only tangentially, this book provides a clear, informative, and engaging account of the origins and development of molecular biology. Extensively quoting many of the primary participants in the field, it offers a solid background for the context of Monod's work and provides information about the leading scientists to whose work he often refers.

Lewis, John, ed. *Beyond Chance and Necessity: A Critical Inquiry into Professor Jacques Monod's "Chance and Necessity."* Atlantic Highlands, N.J.: Humanities Press, 1974. A thorough examination of Monod's basic philosophical position, combining explanatory analysis of Monod's thinking with considerable critical disagreement.

Mayr, Ernst. *Toward a New Philosophy of Biology: Observations of an Evolutionist.* Cambridge, Mass.: Belknap Press of Harvard University Press, 1988. Nearly two decades after Monod's statement of his philosophical position, this book considers the implications of his original position, the critical commentary it engendered, and its relevance and validity in the last decade of the twentieth century. The book also covers many issues related to Monod's work, concentrating on advances in biology since Monod's Nobel award experiments.

Monod, Jacques. *Selected Papers in Molecular Biology.* Edited by André Lwoff and Agnes Ullmann. New York: Academic Press, 1978. In addition to collecting many of the important papers Monod and his colleagues presented during Monod's career, this book includes a complete bibliography of his scientific publications, as well as a list of other books Monod wrote. In addition, it lists interviews in periodicals and radio and television interviews with Monod. Many of Monod's articles are in English, including his Nobel lecture, and there are extensive diagrams and charts for the more advanced student of molecular biology.

Leon Lewis

1966

Physiology or Medicine

Peyton Rous, United States
Charles Brenton Huggins, Canada and United States

Chemistry

Robert S. Mulliken, United States

Physics

Alfred Kastler, France

Literature

Shmuel Yosef Agnon, Israel
Nelly Sachs, Sweden

Peace

no award

PEYTON ROUS
1966

Born: Baltimore, Maryland; October 5, 1879
Died: New York, New York; February 16, 1970
Nationality: American
Areas of concentration: Virology and oncology

Rous and his associates discovered that viruses were able to cause cancer. He demonstrated that the development of a cancer was a stepwise process induced by mutagens such as radiation, ultraviolet light, chemicals, and viruses

The Award

Presentation

On December 10, 1966, Professor Georg Klein of the Royal Caroline Medico-Surgical Institute, introduced Peyton Rous to the Royal Swedish Academy of Sciences by briefly explaining the significance of his research and its place in history. In 1911, Rous reported that cell-free filtered material from chicken tumors would cause new tumors when injected into healthy chickens. The fact that the tumor-inducing material was filtered, so that it was free of cancer cells and bacteria, indicated that a virus might be involved in causing the cancer. The agent that caused the chicken sarcomas eventually became known as the Rous sarcoma virus (RSV). In the years that followed the discovery of RSV, Rous's research group found two other viruses that caused bone, cartilage, and blood vessel tumors. The three cancers could each be transmitted by cell-free filtrates from the cancers. Each filtrate produced tumors identical to those from which it had originated.

In 1932, one of Rous's colleagues discovered that warts (papillomas) in wild cottontail rabbits could be transmitted by cell-free extracts. Warts are considered benign tumors because they do not spread to other parts of the body. Rous discovered that some wart cells, however, would mutate and become malignant cancers. The change from benign to malignant wart cells would occur more rapidly than usual if the warts were exposed to chemicals that caused cancer. Rous found that cancers develop in a stepwise fashion from normal cells.

By the mid-1960's, much had been learned about how bacterial viruses modified the physiology of their host cells. Some bacterial viruses were able to insert their hereditary information into their host's chromosomes. It was suggested that some animal viruses might also insert their hereditary information into their host cell's chromosomes. This might be enough to convert a normal cell into a malignant one. These speculations were resolved a few years after Rous's death by studying RSV and RNA tumor viruses similar to RSV.

Nobel lecture

On December 13, 1966, Peyton Rous delivered his Nobel lecture, entitled "The

Challenge to Man of the Neoplastic Cell." He began with his ideas on what cancer was and what caused it. Tumors and cancers, according to Rous, develop from abnormally regulated reproducing cells. A mass of abnormal cells forms a neoplasm ("new tissue") or tumor. When a neoplasm or tumor remains intact and does not spread to other tissues, it is said to be benign. On the other hand, a neoplasm that fragments, that spreads into other tissues, and that proliferates where it should not, is said to be malignant. Thus, cancer is a malignant neoplasm. Benign neoplasms can become cancers by suffering additional mutations, by losing chromosomes, and by increasing the chromosome number. These alterations affect many different aspects of a cell's regulation and metabolism. Thus, a malignant neoplasm generally consists of cells from different stages of the developing cancer. The cells that dominate are those that reproduce most rapidly and avoid the host's immune system most successfully.

Rous demonstrated that normal cells could be converted into neoplasms by subjecting the cells to certain chemicals, radiation, ultraviolet light, and viruses. He distinguished between the event that initiates a transformation and the events that promote the subsequent development of a cancer. The agents that induce the first mutations, converting normal cells into neoplastic cells, are called initiators. Chemicals, radiation, ultraviolet light, and viruses are all common inducers. A tumor or cancer may never develop after the induction step unless further mutations and rearrangements of the hereditary information occur. Subsequent changes require the long-term presence of, or repeated exposure to, promoters. Promoters induce new mutations or damage nearby tissue so that hormones are released that stimulate the growth of neoplastic cells. The more neoplastic cells grow, the more likely that one of them will undergo a further alteration and start on a pathway toward cancer. This idea that there must be an initiating event and then promotional events over a long period of time explains why naturally occurring cancers take years to develop.

In 1909, Rous showed that cells from a malignant chicken sarcoma could be transplanted to other chickens, where they would reproduce and form new sarcomas. The following year, he discovered a virus infecting the chicken sarcoma cells, which could be used to induce sarcomas in other birds of an inbred flock. Because scientists were unable to find viruses that caused neoplastic growths in mammals and because no cancers known were infectious, Rous's discovery of a virus that could cause cancer was discounted as being an oddity associated only with chickens. Rous himself was unable to find any viruses associated with mammalian cancer, and he consequently turned to other research until the 1930's.

In 1933, Richard Shope of the Rockefeller Institute discovered a virus associated with warts (papillomas) on wild cottontail rabbits. Because this virus was able to cause warts in wild and domestic rabbits, Shope suggested that this might be an example of a mammalian cancer induced by a virus. Since Rous was an expert on neoplasms and cancers, Shope gave him the virus to study. Rous's studies indicated that the virus-infected warts were not cancers but benign skin tumors. Nevertheless, malignant growths often appeared on warts induced by viruses but almost never on virus-free warts induced by chemicals. Rous concluded that the papilloma virus could act both as an initiator and as a promoter to cause cancer.

An important discovery made by Rous and his assistants was that cancerous tumors were not composed of a single type of cell but of cells at all stages of the neoplastic development. He discovered this by separating the cells of a mouse mammary carcinoma and scattering these cells subcutaneously in mice. Some of the cells gave rise to tumors and stimulated the growth of blood vessels and supporting mouse tissue, while others simply survived without significant growth. At the time Rous received the Nobel Prize, only herpes viruses that cause fever blisters and shingles were known to cause human cancers. Rous noted in his Nobel lecture that cancer sometimes arose after repeated herpes outbreaks had disturbed the same regions of skin. Since 1966, however, a number of viruses have been discovered that initiate and/or promote human cancers.

Critical reception

Rous had demonstrated that a chicken cancer was caused by a virus in 1911; the fact that his work was not recognized by a Nobel Prize until 1966 showed how long it had taken cancer research to place Rous's work into the overall picture of how cancer develops. Initially, scientists had speculated that the cause of cancer had been discovered, but this idea was soon proved incorrect. Rous's work was then seen to have no relevance to cancer in mammals. It was not until the 1930's that Rous's faith that viruses would be important in understanding cancer would be vindicated. Discoveries that viruses could indeed cause mammalian cancers convinced scientists that the study of tumor viruses might shed light on the causes of cancer.

W. Ray Bayan of the National Institutes of Health, writing for *Science* magazine in 1966, nicely summarized Peyton Rous's scientific achievements. In 1910, Rous had been able to propagate chicken tumors in closely related chickens but not in other flocks of the same breed. This showed that genetic factors of the host animals were important in controlling the growth of cancers. According to Bayan, transplanting cancers "represented a notable achievement for its time since only a few cancer investigators throughout the world had succeeded in transplanting tumors of any animal species."

During the years when the viral etiology of cancer had fallen into disrepute, Rous and his associates had developed new procedures and techniques for the study of animal viruses. The most notable of these were the propagation of viruses on chorioallantoic membranes of fertilized eggs and the dispersion of tissue cells by trypsinization. The procedure for quantifying and growing viruses in eggs and for establishing cell cultures has allowed scientists to learn about viruses and make numerous vaccines against viruses. Rous and his colleagues showed that benign rabbit warts could progress to malignant cancers and that carcinogenic chemicals and viruses would increase the rate of transition from benign to malignant neoplasm.

Strangely, the significance of Rous's research was not made clear by a number of reviewers announcing the 1966 Nobel Prize. The science editor for *Nature* commented that Rous's work half a century earlier was prophetic; this is actually an odd interpretation of Rous's work, since very few cancers are caused by viruses. In fact, his research was more stimulatory than prophetic. The procedures that he developed and the knowledge he passed on encouraged scientists to study RSV and other tumor viruses. Study of these viruses in the 1980's led to an understanding of how oncogenes and tumor suppressor genes are involved in cancer.

The science editor for *Scientific American* commented that Rous's Nobel Prize was for "work that was done many years ago and has already become part of the tradition of science." The editor, however, left unexplained his comment that "the significance of Rous' initial discovery has been enhanced with every passing year." Although Rous's experimentation with RSV and his many discoveries in molecular biology during the 1960's provided a hypothetical explanation for how RSV might cause cancer, it was not until the 1980's that experiments demonstrated exactly how RSV and other RNA tumor viruses cause cancer.

Biography

Francis Peyton Rous was born in Baltimore, Maryland, in 1879. He attended local schools and began college in 1896 at The Johns Hopkins University in Baltimore, then newly established. After receiving a bachelor's degree in 1900, Rous trained at The Johns Hopkins Medical School, graduating in medicine in 1905. He completed a year of residency at The Johns Hopkins Hospital.

In 1906, Rous joined the staff at the University of Michigan, where he became an instructor and began his research in pathology. He spent a year in Dresden, Germany, studying pathology. Rous left the University of Michigan in 1909 for The Rockefeller Institute, where he was to work on the etiology and pathology of cancer. Two years after Rous was hired at The Rockefeller Institute, he reported that chicken sarcomas were caused by a virus. By 1914, Rous's laboratory had discovered a total of three distinct avian cancers caused by three distinct viruses. Research on tumor-causing viruses gave way to studies on blood preservation, the fate of erythrocytes, transfusions with preserved blood, production of antiserums to protect against infections, function of the liver and gall bladder, measurement of tissue pH, and permeability of blood and lymph capillaries.

In 1921, Rous became coeditor (and later editor) of the *Journal for Experimental Medicine*, published by The Rockefeller Institute (now Rockefeller University); he was an editor until just before his death in 1970. In 1927, Rous was elected to the National Academy of Sciences for his many discoveries in pathology and medicine. Beginning in 1934, Rous and his associates published a series of reports on the papilloma virus that induced warts on cottontail rabbits. His research group studied the effects of chemical carcinogens and reported their results in numerous papers from 1935 to 1964.

Rous officially retired from The Rockefeller Institute in 1945. He remained at the institute for an additional twenty-five years, however, where he continued to stimulate new research on chemical carcinogens. Rous received the Nobel Prize in Physiology or Medicine in 1966 at the age of eighty-seven, in recognition of his discovery that viruses and chemicals were able to cause cancer. He continued to do research at the Rockefeller University until his death from cancer; he died in 1970 at the age of ninety.

Scientific Career

At the beginning of the twentieth century, nothing was known about the cause of cancer; however, this situation soon began to change. In 1908, researchers reported on a virus that caused leukemia in chickens; they carried out six passages of the virus from fowl to fowl and induced leukemia at each transfer. In the years that followed, they discovered a second distinct chicken leukemia virus. Unfortunately, the significance of these viruses was not appreciated because leukemia was not thought of as a cancer.

In 1909, Peyton Rous began a study on tumors that grew on Plymouth Rock hens. Microscopic investigation indicated that the tumors consisted of connective tissue cells that were often highly malignant. Small portions of the tumor inoculated into other chickens of the same inbred flock grew into tumors. At first, the tumor could only be grown in chickens of one flock; later, it grew more malignant and could be grown in unrelated chickens. Injected tumors seeded themselves throughout the body, eventually killing the chicken. These observations demonstrated that the tumors were malignant cancers of the connective tissue called sarcomas. Rous discovered that cell-free material from the chicken sarcomas would cause sarcomas to develop when injected into chickens. This suggested that the sarcomas were caused by viruses, the extremely small entities that were known to cause rabies, poliomyelitis, and foot-and-mouth disease. No one knew at the time what viruses were.

In 1912, Rous and James B. Murphy found that they were able to induce tumors by inoculating developing chick embryos with dried viruses. This represented the first use of embryos for maintaining tumors and for growing viruses. The cultivation of viruses in fertilized eggs was an extremely important achievement because it meant that viruses could be purified and grown to produce vaccines. (Today, vaccines for use in humans are no longer made by growing viruses in eggs but by growing them in human cell cultures.) By 1914, three different viruses that caused distinct chicken cancers had been isolated by Rous and his assistants. The viruses could be differentiated not only by the cancer they produced but also by the different antibodies the chickens made against the viruses. Unfortunately, not much progress was made in discovering the cause of mammalian cancers after Rous's important discoveries. Scientists were not convinced that Rous had discovered anything of importance, and Rous saw no future in continuing cancer research. Consequently, he turned to a number of studies that kept him busy until the 1930's, when he returned to cancer research and made more breakthrough discoveries.

During the early years of World War I, many soldiers died from loss of blood because they did not receive transfusions at the front. This predicament stimulated Rous and his colleagues to look for some way of storing red blood cells (RBCs) so that blood could be transfused on the battlefield. Direct transfusion from donor to patient was not feasible, and many wounded soldiers were dying before they could receive blood at hospitals behind the front lines. Rous determined the normal life span of RBCs and then looked for a fluid that would preserve them. Rous and Joseph R. Turner soon discovered that a standard physiological salt solution with added sodium citrate and glucose would protect RBCs for nearly a month. This solution became known as the Rous-Turner solution. The sodium citrate prevented clotting, while the salt and glucose protected the cell membranes. Rous and Turner reported their findings in a number of papers published in 1915 and 1916. In 1917, Oswald Robertson, one of Rous's colleagues, was able to test blood stored in Rous-Turner solution under battlefield conditions in Belgium. The lives of many badly wounded soldiers were saved because of the battlefield transfusions. The blood that Robertson used for transfusions was cooled in a makeshift icebox, and it represented the world's first blood bank. A report of Robertson's success is found in the *British Medical Journal* of 1918. In recognition of the many lives that were saved, Robertson received the medal and ribbon of the British Distinguished Service Order in 1919.

The discovery of blood preservation by Rous and his colleagues at The Rockefeller Institute was not appreciated again until World War II began. The Rous-Turner solution, which had been forgotten since the end of World War I, was reinstated. Once more, countless lives were saved throughout the world by transfusions. After the war, blood banks that preserved blood with the Rous-Turner solution became common. In recognition of Rous's part in the discovery of the Rous-Turner solution, Rous was awarded the Kober Medal by the Association of American Physicians in 1953.

From 1915 to 1916, Rous and Frederick S. Jones attempted to separate cells from tissues so that individual cells could be grown and studied. Mechanical separation always led to cell death. Rous and Jones found that they could separate cells by first growing tissue fragments in clotted plasma and then by treating the tissue with the pancreatic enzyme trypsin. This treatment did not damage the cells. Many years later, Rous and his associates used trypsin-separated cells to study how cells protected viruses from serum antibodies. Tissues are still treated with trypsin to separate them so that they can be grown in cell cultures. Studies on the fate of circulating RBCs stimulated Rous and his colleagues to determine what happened when RBCs degenerated and how the hemoglobulin was metabolized. They found that a colored product of hemoglobulin metabolism was excreted by the liver into the bile. If the liver was not functioning correctly because of viral infections or cancer, the pigment was stored in the body, turning the tissues yellow. Studies concerned with the fate of red blood cells were published in 1917.

In the 1920's, Rous and his assistants studied the secretory function of the liver. They confirmed that bile was produced by the liver and was altered in the gall bladder. They found that the lining of the gall bladder removed water from the bile and concentrated it. Storage in the gall bladder made the bile thicker and much richer in bile pigments; in addition, the gall bladder produced mucus that facilitated the movement of the viscous bile through the bile duct into the intestines. Rous's colleagues showed that the gall bladder was not simply a sac for storing bile but was an important organ of digestion. The gall bladder and bile studies were published from 1920 to 1925.

Rous and his associates used a number of dyes to learn about anatomy and physiology. To understand why certain antiseptics were not effective against some infections, tissue acidity or alkalinity was measured. The degree of acidity or alkalinity was determined using pH indicator dyes that changed color in response to the hydrogen ion concentration. They showed that tissues metabolizing slowly tended to be alkaline while very active tissues were acidic. Nontoxic dyes were used to discover that blood capillaries leak the most fluid into surrounding tissue where they are the narrowest. Dyes were also used to visualize the lymphatic capillaries of the body. Rous's studies demonstrated that the lymphatic system is extensive and extremely fine. Injections into the skin would disrupt lymphatic capillaries and allow bacteria, dyes, and other material to enter the lymph. In 1932, Rous's associates published a study in which they used dyes to visualize the drainage of tissue fluid into the lymphatic system.

In 1934, Rous's interest in tumor viruses was rekindled when Richard E. Shope gave him a papilloma virus that caused warts in wild cottontail and domestic rabbits. Rous and his associates demonstrated that the rabbit warts were benign tumors. They noticed that malignant cancers arose very infrequently from the benign neoplastic cells. Rous also discovered that the virus not only caused normal cells to develop into neoplastic cells but also caused more neoplastic cells to become malignant than normal. Rous confirmed Shope's observations that viruses could not be extracted from virally induced warts on domestic rabbits. Yet, the viruses were still present in some hidden form, since tumor and malignant cells transplanted into rabbits induced the synthesis of antibodies against the virus. Rous extrapolated these results and hypothesized that all malignant tumors are induced by viruses. He believed that radiation or chemical carcinogens (such as tar and polycyclic hydrocarbons) induce hidden viruses that are the actual cause of transformations. This generalization turned out to be untrue: Most cancers are not associated in any way with viral infections.

One particularly malignant tumor that arose from a virally induced rabbit papilloma was serially transplanted from rabbit to rabbit for twenty-eight years. The cancer never yielded a virus of any sort, but blood tests of the first few successive hosts showed that the viral antigen-inducing antibodies gradually disappeared. This meant that the virus initiated and promoted the development of malignant skin cancers but was not required for the maintenance of the cancerous state. Rous and his colleagues found that malignant tumors would eventually shut off the host animal's immune system, which initially fought the tumor. This loss of the immune system could be demonstrated by tissue grafts from other animals. Even grafts from animals of alien species would not be rejected from animals with dispersed cancer.

In 1941, Peyton Rous, John Kidd, and Ian Mackenzie showed that many neoplastic cells would develop on rabbits after painting the skin with tar. Only a few of the neoplastic cells ever developed into visible tumors. Subsequent stimulation of the changed cells by viral infections or chemicals caused some of the neoplastic cells to form tumors and some of the tumor cells to become malignant cancers. The substances that stimulated neoplastic cells to proliferate and become cancerous became known as promoting agents, or promoters. Promoters were distinguished from initiating agents or initiators: Initiators change normal cells into neoplastic cells. Rous concluded that normal cells become cancerous by a stepwise progression: Normal cells become neoplastic cells, which become benign tumor cells; benign tumor cells become malignant cells (cancer), which become extremely malignant cells.

In 1943, Peyton Rous and William Smith transplanted epithelial tissue from mouse embryos into adult mice and subjected the transplanted material to the carcinogen methylcholanthrene. This induced a large number of very different malignant carcinomas. From 1948 to 1949, Rous, Smith, and E. Stanfield Rogers produced lung tumors in newborn mice by injecting their mothers during pregnancy with urethane. In 1949, Rous and Rogers discovered that simultaneous use of the Shope papilloma virus and chemical carcinogens would speed the development of malignant epithelial cells. These experiments showed that undifferentiated and rapidly growing cells subjected to chemical carcinogens or viruses would give rise to cancerous cells more rapidly than differentiated older cells.

Peyton Rous's many studies on the relationship between cancer and carcinogens helped to explain what caused malignant neoplasms. His research made it clear that malignant cells develop from normal cells in a stepwise manner. Rous's pioneering work stimulated researchers to discover exactly how tumor viruses and other carcinogens cause cancer. Because of Rous's influence and his characterization of RSV, this virus became a research tool in many laboratories throughout the world. The study of RSV and other RNA tumor viruses has proved to be extremely informative and has helped scientists discover exactly how viruses cause cancer. The year Rous died, David Baltimore and Howard Temin reported that the Rous sarcoma virus, as well as other related retroviruses, contained a special enzyme. This enzyme, reverse transcriptase, catalyzes the synthesis of DNA copies of the viral RNA. The discovery of reverse transcriptase provided the first solid evidence that RNA tumor viruses converted their hereditary information into DNA and then integrated into the host cell's chromosomes. It was hypothesized that the integrated viral DNA could disrupt controlling genes and/or stimulate genes that should not be activated. Baltimore and Temin received the 1975 Nobel Prize in Physiology or Medicine for their discovery of reverse transcriptase.

In the late 1970's and the 1980's, Harold Varmus and Michael Bishop, among others, showed that retroviral DNA did, in fact, insert itself into the host cell's chromosomes. This required the activity of another viral-encoded enzyme called an integrase. They found that viruses only proliferated if they were able to insert their DNA into the host's chromosome. Most important of all, Varmus and Bishop finally provided a mechanism by which retroviruses could cause cancer. They discovered that many retroviruses carried oncogenes that promoted the rapid transformation of cells. These special genes were called oncogenes because they caused cells to become cancerous. Retroviral DNA lacking oncogenes could also cause cancer by inserting next to important regulatory genes and activating them. Varmus and Bishop discovered that the oncogenes carried by retroviruses were slightly altered forms of a number of cellular genes. These observations suggested how the Rous sarcoma virus caused tumors. It was found that RSV carries an oncogene (*src*) that is an altered form of the cellular enzyme protein kinase. Varmus and Bishop shared the 1989 Nobel Prize in Physiology or Medicine because of two important discoveries: They proved that viral oncogenes carried by some RNA tumor viruses are derived from cellular genes, and they demonstrated how retroviruses could induce and promote cancers. The study of the Rous sarcoma virus has led to Nobel Prizes for a number of scientists and to a better understanding of the cause of cancer.

Bibliography

Primary

MEDICINE: "Transmission of a Malignant New Growth by Means of a Cell-Free Filtrate," *Journal of the American Medical Association*, vol. 56, 1911, p. 198; "On the Causation by Filterable Agents of Three Distinct Chicken Tumors," *Journal of Experimental Medicine*, vol. 18 (1914), pp. 52-69 (with J. B. Murphy); "The Normal Fate of Erythrocytes: I, The Findings of Healthy Animals," *Journal of Experimental Medicine*, vol. 25, 1917, pp. 651-653 (with O. H. Robertson); "Experiments on the Production of Specific Antisera for Infections of Unknown Cause: I, Type Experiments with Known Antigens—A Bacterial Hemotoxin (Megatheriolysin), the Pneumococcus, and Poliomyelitis Virus," *Journal of Experimental Medicine*, vol. 29, 1919, pp. 283-304 (with O. H. Robertson and Jean Oliver); "Experiments on the Production of Specific Antisera for Infections of Unknown Cause: III, The Effects of a Serum Precipitin on Animals of the Species Furnishing the Precipitinogen," *Journal of Experimental Medicine*, vol. 31, 1920, pp. 253-265 (with G. W. Wilson and Jean Oliver); "The Concentrating Activity of the Gall Bladder," *Journal of Experimental Medicine*, vol. 34, 1921, pp. 47-73; "Suppression of Bile as a Result of Impairment of Liver Function," *Journal of Experimental Medicine*, vol. 41, 1925, pp. 611-622 (with D. R. Drury); "Selection with the Magnet and Cultivation of Reticuloendothelial Cells (Kupffer Cells)," *Journal of Experimental Medicine*, vol. 59, 1934, pp. 577-591 (with J. W. Beard); "The Neoplastic Traits of a Mammalian Growth Due to a Filterable Virus: the Shope Rabbit Papilloma," *Science*, vol. 79, 1934, pp. 437-438 (with J. W. Beard); "The Fixation and Protection of Viruses by the Cells of Susceptible Animals," *Journal of Experimental Medicine*, vol. 61, 1935, pp. 657-688 (with P. D. McMaster and S. S. Hudack); "The Progression to Carcinoma of Virus-Induced Rabbit Papillomas (Shope)," *Journal of Experimental Medicine*, vol. 62, 1935, pp. 523-548 (with J. W. Beard); "The Virus Tumors and the Tumor Problem," *The Harvey Lectures*, vol. 31, 1936, pp. 74-115; "The Carcinogenic Effect of a Papilloma Virus on the Tarred Skin of Rabbits: II, Major Factors Determining the

Phenomenon—the Manifold Effects of Tarring," *Journal of Experimental Medicine*, vol. 68, 1938, pp. 529-561 (with J. G. Kidd); "The Initiating and Promoting Elements in Tumor Production: An Analysis of the Effects of Tar, Benzpyrene, and Methylcholanthrene on Rabbit Skin," *Journal of Experimental Medicine*, vol. 80, 1944, pp. 101-125 (with W. F. Friedewald); "Viruses and Tumour Causation: An Appraisal of Present Knowledge," *Nature*, vol. 207, 1965, pp. 457-463; "The Challenge to Man of the Neoplastic Cell," *Science*, vol. 157, 1967, pp. 24-28.

Secondary

Baltimore, David. "Viral RNA-Dependent DNA Polymerase." *Nature* 226 (1970): 1209-1211. A classic paper in which Baltimore shows that Rauscher mouse leukemia virus and Rous sarcoma virus contain the enzyme reverse transcriptase. This enzyme converts viral RNA into DNA. The discovery of this enzyme provided evidence for the idea that insertion of viral DNA into the chromosomes of animal cells was responsible for transforming normal cells into cancer cells.

Bishop, J. Michael. "The Molecular Genetics of Cancer." *Science* 235 (1987): 305-311. This article describes a number of oncogenes that have been discovered in retroviruses and how these oncogenes resemble normal cellular genes called protooncogenes. Bishop explains how oncogenes, introduced by retroviruses, can transform cells and convert them into cancerous cells. How retroviruses that lack oncogenes can cause cancer is also considered. A model for how the various different classes of oncogenes might be involved in the stepwise progression leading to cancerous cells is presented.

Bryan, W. Ray. "Peyton Rous." *Science* 154 (1966): 364-365. An easy-to-read and informative summary of Rous's important discoveries.

Dulbecco, Renato. "Francis Peyton Rous." *Biographical Memoirs* 48 (1976): 275-306. An informative and easy-to-read biography of Peyton Rous written by a Nobel prize recipient who worked with RSV as well as the transforming DNA viruses polyoma and SV40.

Temin, Howard M., and Satoshi Mizutani. "RNA-Dependent DNA Polymerase in Virions of Rous Sarcoma Virus." *Nature* 226 (1970): 1211-1213. A second classic paper in which the authors demonstrate that RSV has the enzyme reverse transcriptase.

Varmus, Harold. "Lessons from the Life Cycle of Retroviruses." *The Harvey Lectures, 1987-1988* 83 (1989): 35-56. This manuscript presented a simple discussion of what was known about retroviruses in the late 1980's. It clearly explains how retroviruses were believed to cause cancer.

Jaime S. Colomé

1966

Physiology or Medicine

Peyton Rous, United States

Charles Brenton Huggins, Canada and United States

Chemistry

Robert S. Mulliken, United States

Physics

Alfred Kastler, France

Literature

Shmuel Yosef Agnon, Israel

Nelly Sachs, Sweden

Peace

no award

CHARLES BRENTON HUGGINS
1966

Born: Halifax, Nova Scotia, Canada; September 22, 1901

Nationality: Canadian; after 1933, American
Areas of concentration: Hormonal physiology and oncology

Huggins applied the results of his basic research on sex hormones to the development of a new form of cancer therapy in which hormones were used to retard and reduce the growth of cancers of the prostate gland and breast

The Award

Presentation

Professor Georg Klein of the Royal Caroline Medico-Surgical Institute delivered the presentation address, citing the achievements of Charles Huggins and Peyton Rous, at the Nobel awards ceremony on December 10, 1966. He noted that Huggins' work on cancer of the prostate had been published in a number of journals in the late 1930's and early 1940's. Finally, after more than twenty-five years, Huggins was to receive the Nobel medal and diploma for his work.

In his address, Klein first discussed the history of research on viral causes of cancer and Peyton Rous's contributions to that research. Klein began the second part of his address by commenting on the relatively quick applicability of Huggins' research, compared with the fifty or more years which passed before Rous's work was fully recognized. Despite their very different approaches, Klein stated that the work of both winners addressed the same question: "Is the cancer cell a completely self-sufficient normal cell?" Huggins' work showed that some tumor cells were affected by, and even dependent on, natural hormones of the body. Huggins took this basic research and used it to develop a treatment for prostatic cancer in which male sex hormones that encouraged tumor growth were eliminated through surgery or antagonized by the addition of female sex hormones. This therapy was later applied, though with less dramatic results, to breast cancer.

Klein praised this "completely new type of cancer therapy" that "has already given many valuable and relatively symptom-free years to gravely ill cancer patients throughout the civilized world." He also included in his address a quotation by Rous recognizing the importance of Huggins' work. Professor Klein concluded his address by praising both Huggins and Rous for clarifying the behavior of cancer cells.

Nobel lecture

Huggins' lecture, delivered on December 13, 1966, was entitled "Endocrine-Induced Regression of Cancers." In a rather technical lecture, he reviewed his own work of the past three decades and paid tributes to other researchers, both students and colleagues, who worked in endocrinology (the study of hormones) and related fields.

In the first part of his lecture, Huggins described the steps which led him from investigating chemical secretions of accessory sex glands in dogs to developing human cancer therapies. As Huggins commented, "A program was not prepared in advance for this basic physiologic study. . . . There were blind alleys but eventually . . . we were somewhat amazed to find ourselves studying the effects of hormonal status on advanced cancers of people."

In 1940, Huggins and his students observed that following orchiectomy (surgical removal of the testes) or treatment with the female hormone estrogen, prostate tumors in male dogs shrank rapidly. They also found that the response of prostate cancer to hormone treatment could be monitored by measuring the relative amounts of acid or alkaline phosphatases (a class of enzyme) in the blood. Similar results were found when both surgical and hormonal treatments were applied to humans. Although only four of the first twenty-one cancer patients treated by orchiectomy survived for more than twelve years, Huggins pointed out that lives had been prolonged and pain lessened for many.

In the second part of his lecture, Huggins discussed his interest in the treatment of breast cancer. It did not seem to present as clear a picture as prostate cancer treatment, because breast cancer can be found in both men and women, and in women who have had their ovaries removed. Huggins identified a hormone secreted by the adrenal gland that seemed to encourage the growth of cancer of the breast. He then applied this idea clinically by treating cancer patients by adrenalectomy (surgical removal of the adrenal glands). Huggins noted that research in breast cancer was being hampered by the lack of a suitable animal model. Mice were used at first, but few of their tumors were found to respond to hormones in any way. Rats, however, proved more useful, and Huggins developed a reliable technique for selectively inducing breast cancers in rats within a month using a chemical.

Studies of mammary cancer in rats led to a surprising discovery: Cancer could also be inhibited by excessive amounts of steroid hormones. Huggins referred to this as "cancer control by hormone-interference." Application of this observation also led to clinical treatments for breast cancer in men and women and for certain lymphomas and leukemias. Huggins concluded his talk by asserting that the hormone-dependence of some cancers proves that cancer is not "autonomous," nor are all cancers the same.

Critical reception

An article published in *The Atlantic Monthly* shortly before the announcement of the 1966 Nobel Prizes examined the record of the Academy in selecting appropriate winners for its physiology or medicine prize. In "Nobel's Hits and Errors," Donald Fleming criticized the Nobel Committee for its lack of consistency and foresight. Prophetically, he specifically mentioned Peyton Rous, the 1966 cowinner, as a "shocking" omission. While Fleming did not similarly single out Charles Huggins, many others believed that his award was an appropriate highlight to a lifetime of achievement.

In "Belated Recognition," *Time* magazine praised the choice of Huggins and Rous, pointing out that Huggins' award came more than twenty-five years after his initial work and praised the Academy for correcting its "glaring" omission. An editorial in *The New York Times* called Huggins "an outstanding cancer fighter" and labeled his work on hormones and cancers of the prostate and breast "of historic importance both for therapy and basic understanding." While more subdued in tone, similar articles appeared in *Science*, *Nature*, the *Journal of the American Medical Association*, *Newsweek*, and *Science News*.

Huggins' award was announced only two days after the close of an international symposium on host-tumor interactions held in his honor, on the occasion of his sixty-fifth birthday and his nearly forty-year association with the University of Chicago. At this time, Huggins received much praise from those whose opinions he respected most: his colleagues and coworkers. After the award was announced, Huggins said that the Nobel Prize was "not a great event like a birth or marriage. The greatest thing is to have favorable recognition from colleagues in the same field who suffer as I do from the seven-day week."

Paul Talalay, one of Huggins' many students, was called upon to write several tributes at the time of Huggins' award; he praised Huggins' skills as a teacher as well as a scientist. In an article for the journal *Science*, cowritten with Guy Williams-Smith, he showed the admiration he felt for his mentor:

> The extraordinary breadth of his scientific interests and achievements, his great courage in the clinic and at the laboratory bench, and his utter dedication to the cancer problem have excited world-wide admiration. The award of a Nobel Prize to one who has done so much for human cancer patients is richly deserved.

Biography

Charles Brenton Huggins was born on September 22, 1901, in Halifax, Nova Scotia, Canada. He was the first of two boys born to Charles Edward Huggins, a pharmacist, and Bessie Marie (née Spencer) Huggins. Huggins grew up in Halifax, where he attended the local public schools. Huggins received his B.A. from Acadia University, a small college in Wolfville, Nova Scotia, where he was one of a graduating class of only twenty-five. At the age of nineteen, he began medical school at Harvard University, and four years later he received both his M.A. and M.D. degrees. Following graduation, Huggins did an internship at the University of Michigan Hospital in Ann Arbor, studying surgery under Dr. Frederick A. Coller; he then spent a year as instructor in surgery at the University of Michigan Medical School.

On July 29, 1927, Huggins married Margaret Wellman, whom he had met in Ann Arbor; they later had two children: a son, Charles Edward, who became a professor of surgery at Harvard, and a daughter, Emily Wellman Huggins Fine. Also in 1927, Huggins began his long association with the University of Chicago, starting as an instructor in surgery. Huggins was promoted to assistant professor in 1929, and the following year he traveled abroad to train further in the field of clinical urology. He first visited the laboratory of Dr. Robert Robison of the Lister Institute in London, then worked for a time in Germany with Otto Warburg, who won the Nobel Prize in Physiology or Medicine in 1931. In 1933, Huggins became a naturalized citizen of the United States, and in the same year he was promoted to associate professor at the University of Chicago.

He was promoted to professor of surgery at the University of Chicago in 1936 and served as director of the Ben May Laboratory for Cancer Research from 1951 until his retirement in 1969. Huggins continued his research at his laboratory at the University of Chicago until 1972, when he became chancellor of his alma mater, Acadia University. He retired from that position in 1979 and returned to Chicago.

Huggins once described himself as "addicted" to his work, but he maintained other interests, including a love of music, especially the works of J. S. Bach and Wolfgang Mozart. Like many scientists, he was also interested in current affairs. In 1967, he was one of sixteen Nobel scientists who signed a petition urging the United States to work for direct peace talks between the Arab nations and Israel.

Scientific Career

At the time that Charles Huggins' Nobel Prize was announced, he tried to convey his feelings to a group of reporters at a press conference. "This is terribly exciting," he said, "like the time your house burned down. However, if you gentlemen will permit me, I will be back in my lab this afternoon." He went on to explain, "I started an experiment Monday, and it comes out today." Hard work and dedication were the foundations of Huggins' success. Upon completing medical school at Harvard, Huggins continued his training under Frederick A. Coller at the University of Michigan, specializing in surgery. After joining the faculty of the University of Chicago, he concentrated on the field of urology, the study of the urinary system. In this, he was encouraged by the university's chief of surgery, Dr. Dallas B. Phemister, who sent him to Europe for further training; there, he met Otto Warburg. Warburg had recently discovered some interesting details in the energy mechanism of tumor cells. He found that tumor cells, unlike most normal cells, can break down carbohydrates without oxygen. Huggins maintained a long friendship with Warburg, with their interest in cancer being one common denominator.

After returning to Chicago in the early 1930's, Huggins used his training to develop ways to transform normal connective tissue into specialized bone tissue; he used the cells lining the urinary tract, especially the bladder. His interest in urology, however, gradually led him to concentrate more and more on the physiology and diseases of the male urogenital system. In particular, he worked on the prostate gland, a small gland located around the neck of the bladder in males, whose secretions form a major part of the ejaculatory fluid.

Initially, Huggins was interested in looking for organic phosphates in prostate fluid. In order to isolate secretions of the prostate, Huggins developed a surgical procedure to collect prostatic secretions of dogs over a period of years. It was luck that dogs were used, since these were the only laboratory animals known to develop prostate tumors. At first, Huggins was vexed by the appearance of tumors in his subjects, but he later began to search for such animals as his interest in cancer grew. Huggins measured prostate secretions in cancerous animals and found that increased testosterone levels increased cancer growth. Moreover, he found that by inhibiting the concentrations of male hormones in the bloodstream, either by removing the source of the hormones through surgery or by adding antagonistic female hormones, growth of prostate cancer could be halted.

Cancer of the prostate is one of the most common forms of cancer afflicting males over the age of fifty. Huggins' discoveries in dogs led him to try to develop a form of treatment for humans. Working with his students Clarence V. Hodges and William W. Scott, Huggins published three papers in 1941 on the results of treating a group of patients with testosterone, estrogen, or surgery. Huggins found that testosterone, one of the male hormones, tended to promote the growth and spread of cancer. Of those patients treated with estrogen (a female hormone) or surgery (removal of the testes), four of twenty-one survived for more than twelve years. While developing this hormonal treatment of cancer, Huggins also introduced a useful clinical measurement of the activity of prostate cancer. Acid phosphatase is an enzyme that is normally secreted by the healthy prostate gland, and alkaline phosphatase is an enzyme secreted by osteoblasts, bone-forming cells. Huggins knew from the work of Alexander and Ethel Gutman that both of these enzymes are present in elevated levels in patients with prostate cancer which has spread (metastasized) to bone. He was therefore able to develop a blood test to measure the extent of the cancer and the effectiveness of his hormone or surgical therapies.

The hormonal treatment developed by Huggins and his coworkers rapidly became a common treatment for prostate cancer. In England, Sir Charles Dodds soon developed a synthetic female hormone similar to estrogen, called diethylstilbestrol, used in the clinical treatment of prostate cancer. Charles Huggins' work on prostate cancer led not only to the first nontoxic chemotherapy for cancer but also to important theoretical principles for medicine. Based on the clinical results he observed, Huggins suggested that cancers are not always autonomous and self-perpetuating, since his work showed that they could respond to external treatment; moreover, some cancers may actually require external stimuli (such as hormones) for continued growth. These principles were later used in the development of hormonal therapies for other types of cancer.

During the 1940's, Huggins, now a full professor at the University of Chicago, continued his studies of cancer. By studying chemicals in the urine, Huggins had observed that the levels of androgens were similar in men of the same age with or without prostatic cancer. After orchiectomy (removal of the testes), the production of androgens dropped dramatically, but then often rose again—to a level higher than that before surgery. Huggins deduced that the adrenal glands were somehow responding to lowered hormonal levels and were able to compensate by producing androgens on their own. These adrenal androgens were capable of encouraging the growth of prostate cancer, even in the absence of testes. Huggins then pioneered the first bilateral adrenalectomy (removal of both adrenal glands, which are located atop the kidneys). This surgery would prove more useful later, after the development of therapies to replace the other hormones, such as cortisone, produced by these glands.

In 1951, Huggins was appointed director of the Ben May Laboratory for Cancer Research, and, in addition to his administrative duties, he began to tackle the problem of breast cancer. In the late 1800's, Sir George Beatson had reported the retardation of breast cancer growth in women whose ovaries had been removed. Huggins and his students developed a treatment for breast cancer which involved the removal of both the ovaries (ovariectomy) and adrenal glands, supplemented by cortisone replacement therapy. Huggins' results in clinical trials showed improvement in 30 to 40 percent of patients with advanced, metastatic breast cancer.

The impact and value of Huggins' work had not gone unnoticed. He received more than twenty awards of international status between 1936 and 1966, including two gold medals from the American Medical Association (in 1936 and 1940), the American Cancer Society Award in 1953, the Borden Award of the Association of American Medical Colleges in 1955, and many others. He also received honorary degrees from many universities, including Yale, Acadia, Washington University, Leeds, Trinity, and Aberdeen, and he was named a fellow of the Royal College of Surgeons, Edinburgh, the Royal College of Surgeons (honorary), and the American College of Surgeons (honorary).

In the 1960's and early 1970's, Huggins concentrated more on problems of basic research, as opposed to clinical or applied research. In particular, he worked toward developing useful animal models for human breast cancer. He and his students were able to show that certain organic chemicals were able to induce mammary tumors rapidly in some strains of female rats. One chemical, 7,12-dimethyl-benz(a)anthracene (DMBA), produced tumors which were hormone dependent, thus imitating closely the behavior of similar tumors in humans. An added bonus for these studies was the finding that DMBA causes massive cell death in the adrenal glands of rats, thus making certain experiments in hormone reduction that much easier. Huggins and his students also used DMBA to induce and study leukemia in rats. He maintained his interest in research even while serving as chancellor of Acadia University from 1972 until his retirement in 1979.

On June 26, 1958, Charles Huggins delivered the tenth Macewen Memorial Lecture at the University of Glasgow. While discussing the achievements of Sir William Macewen, surgeon and teacher, he stated, "The deeds of man can be evaluated only in terms of the influence which they exert on others." By this criterion, Huggins' own deeds were truly impressive. The therapies he pioneered have alleviated the pain and suffering of thousands of cancer victims, and the students he taught have gone on to do good works of their own. Unfortunately, he did not achieve his dream of defeating cancer; even hormonal therapies have restricted effectiveness in many cases, resulting in only limited or temporary benefits. In understanding the cause of cancer, the work of his fellow Nobel Prize winner, Peyton Rous, may have more long-term impact. As a scientist, physician, and teacher, however, Charles Huggins is a worthy model for present and future generations to follow.

Bibliography

Primary

MEDICINE: "Studies on Prostatic Cancer I: Effect of Castration, Estrogen, and Androgen Injection on Serum Phosphatases in Metastatic Carcinoma of the Prostate," *Cancer Research*, vol. 1, 1941, pp. 293-297 (with Clarence V. Hodges); "Endocrine Methods of Treatment of Cancer of the Breast," *Journal of the National Cancer Institute*, vol. 15, 1954, pp. 1-25; *Frontiers of Mammary Cancer*, 1959; "Induction and Extinction of Mammary Cancer," *Science*, vol. 137, 1962, pp. 257-262; "Propositions in Hormonal Treatment of Advanced Cancers," *Journal of the American Medical Association*, vol. 192, 1965, p. 1141; *Experimental Leukemia and Mammary Cancer*, 1979.

Secondary

Cant, Gilbert. "Male Trouble." *The New York Times Magazine*, February 16, 1975, 14. This article, which runs over many pages, discusses the symptoms, anatomy, and incidence of prostate cancer as well as available treatments. Cant also discusses Huggins' work in using surgery and hormonal therapy to treat patients and how those treatments are still in use.

Crapo, Lawrence. *Hormones: The Messengers of Life*. New York: W. H. Freeman, 1985. This brief (176 pages) book is a useful and highly readable introduction to the normal roles of hormones in the human body. It also includes a bibliography, index, and many illustrations. Sex hormones are discussed in chapter 6, "It's a Girl."

Haddow, Alexander, et al., eds. *On Cancer and Hormones: Essays in Experimental Biology.* Chicago: University of Chicago Press, 1962. This book contains twenty-seven essays on different aspects of experimental biology and medicine dedicated to Charles Huggins as "one of the foremost leaders in contemporary experimental medicine on the occasion of his sixtieth birthday." Nine articles cover the nature or treatment of cancer; others stress the role of hormones in the induction and control of cancer.

Holleb, Arthur I., ed. *The American Cancer Society Cancer Book: Prevention, Detection, Diagnosis, Treatment, Rehabilitation, Cure*. Garden City, N.Y.: Doubleday, 1986. This large reference volume includes a glossary, index, and directory of resources for those interested in finding out more about cancer. Some chapters of interest include chapter 5, "Modern Cancer Therapy," chapter 17, "Breast Cancer," and chapter 29, "Cancer of the Male Reproductive System."

Lafond, Richard, ed. *Cancer: The Outlaw Cell*. 2d ed. Washington, D.C.: American Chemical Society, 1988. For those interested in research in cancer, this volume includes chapters written by twenty prominent researchers who attempt to discuss topics of research at a level accessible by nonscientists. The level of technicality varies from chapter to chapter, but a glossary, references, and colored illustrations help make this book an outstanding one.

Wissler, Robert W., Thomas L. Dao, and Sumner Wood, Jr., eds. *Endogenous Factors*

Influencing Host-Tumour Balance. Chicago: University of Chicago Press, 1967. This volume includes the papers presented at an international symposium on this subject held in Huggins' honor two days before the announcement of his Nobel Prize. Twenty-one technical articles (one of them by Huggins) are included, as well as tributes to Huggins by George Beadle, president of the university, and Paul Talalay, a former student.

Lisa A. Lambert

1967

Physiology or Medicine

Ragnar Granit, Sweden
Haldan Keffer Hartline, United States
George Wald, United States

Chemistry

Manfred Eigen, West Germany
Ronald G. W. Norrish, Great Britain
George Porter, Great Britain

Physics

Hans Albrecht Bethe, United States

Literature

Miguel Ángel Asturias, Guatemala

Peace

no award

RAGNAR GRANIT
1967

Born: Helsinge, Finland; October 30, 1900

Nationality: Swedish
Area of concentration: Neurophysiology

Granit used electrophysiological methods to demonstrate the presence of three kinds of color receptor elements in the retina and to show the importance of inhibition between nerve cells in retinal function and in the nervous system in general

The Award

Presentation

Ragnar Arthur Granit, Haldan Keffer Hartline, and George Wald were awarded the 1967 Nobel Prize in Physiology or Medicine. The three shared about $61,700 equally, and each received the Nobel medal and scroll, presented by King Gustav VI of Sweden. Carl Gustaf Bernhard, Granit's colleague at the Royal Caroline Institute, delivered the presentation address on December 10, 1967; he introduced the recipients and outlined their most important contributions.

Bernhard mentioned some of the history of neurophysiology important to Granit's work. He included Santiago Ramón y Cajal (the Nobel laureate in physiology or medicine for 1906), whose microscopic structural studies showed elaborate interconnections among the nerve cells of the retina; Frithiof Holmgren, who discovered the electroretinogram (ERG); and Edgar Douglas Adrian (Nobel laureate, 1932), who first recorded nerve impulses from a single nerve cell. He also spoke of the early theory of color vision developed by Thomas Young and Hermann von Helmholtz, which they based on experiments on perception. He contrasted their techniques with the electrophysiological methods possible since Adrian's contribution.

He said that Granit was being honored for his electrophysiological discovery of the elements responsible for color vision and for his demonstration and exploration of inhibition as part of the processing and integration of information that occurs in the retina. He further stated that Granit's work had given direction and stimulation to the field of visual physiology. He concluded by congratulating the three and asking them to receive the award from the king.

Nobel lecture

Granit's lecture, entitled "The Development of Retinal Neurophysiology," was delivered on December 12, 1967. Granit opened by commenting that he had not worked in retinal electrophysiology for about twenty years and that therefore his lecture would be retrospective. He spoke of the power of the electrophysiological methods that replaced the classical psychophysical approach to the eye prevalent in the 1920's. He gave Adrian credit for opening the door for the transition, but he traced the origin of the electrical analysis of the eye back sixty years to Holmgren's discovery of the electrical impulses initiated in the eye when it is exposed to light.

Granit traced his own interest in the retina to Ramón y Cajal's suggestion that, based on its structure, the retinal nervous network must act as a nervous center. He explained his work with the electroretinogram, which he had used to determine certain characteristics of the retina. He told of separating the electroretinogram into its electrical components and of observing changes between light-adapted and dark-adapted electroretinograms, which suggested that light and dark adaptation of the eye could not be entirely attributable to the direct photochemical action of light.

Granit then related his demonstration of inhibition in the retina, an experiment which he said gave him as much "delight" as any he ever carried out. He employed both Holmgren's electroretinogram and Adrian's technique of recording the activity of the optic nerve (the bundle of nerve-cell fibers carrying impulses from the eye to the brain). Hartline and, later, Granit developed more refined techniques that showed inhibition of many intensities within the retina. He went on to explain the importance of inhibition in the eye: It enhances contrast and thus improves the detection of form and movement. He pointed out that for many years, inhibition was "the theme" of work in visual electrophysiology.

He explained some work on rhodopsin, the chemical that absorbs light in the dark-adapted eye, then described his work on color vision. He shined lights of different wavelengths, or colors, on the retinas of many different vertebrates and, using microelectrodes, recorded the impulses produced in individual optic nerve-cell fibers. He demonstrated the individual retinal elements responsive to almost any color (wavelength) of light as well as elements which responded to a limited range of wavelengths. He explained his work with the cat retina and remarked how similar the cat retina is to the periphery of the human retina in regard to its elements.

Granit said that he had become frustrated with the lack of photochemical and psychophysical data in the field and had therefore moved on to other lines of research. He concluded by noting that a number of competent workers had moved into the field and stating that he felt no need to return.

Critical reception

The British science journal *Nature* welcomed the Nobel Committee's selection of Granit, Hartline, and Wald, saying that each had distinguished himself in a separate area of vision research, that each had stimulated research in many other laboratories, and that together they had converted vision research from a "narrow . . . specialism" to a growing field. Floyd Ratliff, in his description of Granit's and Hartline's work in *Science*, concluded by saying that the three had always been aware of the dependence of their work on that of others and had always shared credit generously. John Dowling, also writing in *Science*, concluded his description of Wald's work by saying that the vision research community was "exceedingly pleased" that the three were being honored with the prize.

Ratliff wrote that Granit's work "elucidated broad principles" of action and interaction in the nerve cells of the retina and optic nerve, that he was a true pioneer in visual physiology, and that his discoveries had "grown in basic significance in recent years." Finally, he stated that the "admirable" work that Granit had done after he left vision research demonstrated the broad importance of the work; inhibition is present in nerve networks throughout the body.

The true measure of Granit's work is best shown in the research that it stimulated and supported in subsequent years. The work of Stephen W. Kuffler and his associates is perhaps the most striking example. In the early 1950's Kuffler began working out the characteristics of the receptive fields of cat retinal nerve cells. His work involved extensive use of improved versions of the microelectrodes that Granit had developed as well as experimental techniques that Granit, Hartline, and others had refined. It was also based on the extensive information base that Granit had assimilated on the retina, its receptors and nerve cells, and their interactions in many species of animal.

In 1958, David H. Hubel and Torsten N. Wiesel joined Kuffler's laboratory to extend his work to the visual cortex, the part of the brain that receives information from the optic nerve and so, ultimately, from the retina. They mapped the organization of the visual cortex and explored the relationship between an infant's early visual experience and the development of the visual cortex. In 1981, Wiesel and Hubel were awarded the Nobel Prize for this work.

Biography

Ragnar Granit was born on October 30, 1900, in Helsinge, Finland, to Swedish parents. He was the first child of Arthur Wilhelm Granit and Albertina Helena Malmberg. His father was a forester. Granit was reared in Helsingfors, Finland, and attended the Swedish *Normallyceum* there. He participated in, and was decorated for his contribution to, Finland's 1918 War of Liberation. In 1919, he enrolled in Helsingfors University, from which he was graduated in 1923. He went on to receive an M.D. in 1927 from Helsingfors. His first degree was in experimental psychology, but an interest in vision encouraged him to get a medical degree and eventually to turn to physiology, which he thought would be a better base from which to approach the study of vision.

He spent part of 1928 in Charles Sherrington's laboratory at the University of Oxford. In 1929, he married Baroness Marguerite (Daisy) Emma Bruun. They have one son, Michael, an architect. In 1929-1931 he was a fellow in medical physics at the Johnson Foundation of the University of Pennsylvania, where he met Wald and Hartline. In 1932, he returned to Sherrington's laboratory under a Rockefeller Foundation Fellowship, which he held through 1933. He then returned to Helsingfors to teach physiology and perform research. He was a district physician during the Winter War with Russia in 1939.

In 1940, he moved to the Royal Caroline Institute of Stockholm, Sweden; he became director of the Institute of Neurophysiology there in 1945 and retired in July, 1967. Visiting professorships at the Rockefeller Institute and at Oxford interrupted his time at the Caroline Institute. After retirement, he was visiting professor at Düsseldorf (1974) and at the Max Planck Institute (1976). He has also remained active as a consultant.

Scientific Career

Early in the history of physiology, stimuli were thought to excite (stimulate) nerve cells to fire; receptors, such as the retina, were thought simply to record the pattern of some environmental stimulus—for example, the light pattern falling on the retina. When Granit began his work, Sherrington had established complex feedback systems involving inhibition as well as excitation in the control of the muscular movements in the body. Inhibition occurs when a nerve cell or environmental stimulus blocks (rather than stimulates) the firing of another nerve cell. Ramón y Cajal had shown that the structure of the retina was exceptionally complex. On the basis of this information, some neurophysiologists believed that the retina integrated and processed the information it collected before relaying it to the brain. The demonstration of integration and processing, however, had proved difficult. One event that should occur in the retina if it indeed processes information is inhibition.

Granit's first contribution was based on studies that were undertaken around 1930 on human subjects. He used flickering dots of light to illuminate the eye and used the flicker fusion frequency (the frequency at which the subject saw the flickering lights as steady lights) as a measure of retinal excitation. He interpreted some of the results of the experiments as demonstrating inhibition. These experiments led him to a more physiological approach, and he turned his attention to the electroretinogram.

An electroretinogram is produced by placing an electrode on the surface of the eye (on the cornea) and another on the skin of the subject, shining a light into the eye, and recording the electrical impulses produced. It is a record of the total electrical response of the retina, so it is not a very precise tool for studying the electrical activity of the eye. Granit and others used it, however, to generate some first principles of retinal activity.

Using certain chemicals and specified conditions, Granit was able to separate the electroretinogram into three components. One of these (called PI) developed slowly after the light was turned on, and it made the cornea electrically positive. The other two developed quickly when a light was turned on. One (PII) gave the cornea a positive charge that developed quickly, decreased slowly until the light was turned off, then dropped off more quickly. The other (PIII) resulted in the cornea becoming negative when the light was turned on, gradually becoming more negative while the light stayed on, and returning quickly to neutral when the light was turned off. Since all three occur at the same time, the electroretinogram depends on the relative sizes and timing of the three components.

One kind of electroretinogram becomes slightly negative when the light is turned on (because of the rapid initial response of PIII), swings strongly positive as PII overwhelms PIII, decreases in positive charge as PII becomes considerably less positive and PIII becomes slightly more negative, and may increase slightly as PI finally comes into play, depending on the balance between the three. The charge on the cornea remains positive until the light is turned off. When the light is turned off, the cornea becomes temporarily more positive because of the quick return of PIII from negative to near neutral. The entire electroretinogram then returns to neutral. Based on Granit's interpretation, the electroretinogram became an important tool both in research and in the diagnosis of clinical eye problems.

Granit hypothesized that the primary function of the electrical activity recorded in the electroretinogram is to trigger nerve impulses in the nerve cells that go to the brain. Fibers of these nerve cells pass out of the brain via the optic nerve. Certain fibers in the optic nerve carry impulses when a light is turned on, and others do so when the light is turned off. Granit thought that the PII component triggered the "on" response, and PIII the "off" response.

Granit used the electroretinogram to demonstrate that light could inhibit retinal cell activity as well as stimulate it. He noticed a change in the electroretinogram if a brief flash of light was introduced immediately after the light stimulus generating the electroretinogram was turned off. Without the flash, the cornea became more positive (as described above), but with the flash it became more negative. Granit reasoned that the flash blocked the "off" response of PIII. PII could not respond to the flash because it had not yet recovered from its response to the first light. Therefore, under these conditions, there should be no impulse in the optic nerve. Inhibition would then be demonstrated, because the flash of light is the only variable that could have blocked the transmission of the "off" signal.

Granit recorded the electrical activity of the optic nerve both with and without the brief flash of light. Without the flash, the normal "off" impulses were sent down the optic nerve. With the flash, impulses were not transmitted. Thus, light was shown to inhibit the initiation of a nerve impulse in the retina. Subsequently, Hartline, and then Granit, demonstrated more elaborate inhibition in the retina, showing inhibition of various types and intensities. Inhibition was established as a major mechanism of interaction and processing of visual information in the retina.

Granit also contributed to the understanding of the adaptation (adjustment) of the eye to different levels of light with his electroretinogram studies. Models at the time suggested that adaptation was mediated entirely by changes in the pigments (chemicals) responsible for absorption of the light. Using differences in the electroretinograms of light-adapted and dark-adapted eyes, Granit showed that nerve interactions are involved as well.

He used electroretinogram studies to initiate his work on color vision. Color vision is essentially the result of different responses to different wavelengths of light. Light of short wavelengths looks blue to the human eye, and that of long wavelengths looks red. Granit stimulated the retina with different wavelengths of light and recorded the electroretinograms. The results suggested that there are separate elements in the retina that absorb light of widely divergent wavelengths.

At about this time (1939), Granit and Gunnar Svaetichin devised and began using microelectrodes. These tiny wires enclosed in tiny glass tubes made it possible to record the impulse in a single nerve cell with minimal disruption of the eye or optic nerve. This is a much more precise window on the electrical activity of receptors and the nervous system than the electroretinogram or signals from entire nerves, such as the optic nerve, which contain many nerve fibers. Adrian's and Hartline's recordings from single nerve cells required dissection of the organ in which the nerve-cell fibers were found. The microelectrodes, on the other hand, could be inserted into the organ or nerve and placed next to a single nerve-cell fiber. Later, Svaetichin and others developed microelectrodes that could be placed inside single nerve cells or receptors. Hubel called microelectrodes the "single most important tool in the modern era of neurophysiology." Granit was a major contributor to their origin and early development.

With this new tool, Granit attacked the question of color vision. Using microelectrodes inserted into the optic nerve, he found two main types of fibers with respect to their responses to different wavelengths of light. Some responded to light of all visible wavelengths, with a maximum response to wavelengths around 560 nanometers. The maximum response shifted to wavelengths around 500 nanometers after the eye adapted to the dark.

The other type of response differed in detail among different animals. In all cases, there was one or more type of fiber that responded to a more narrow band of wavelengths. In the cat's eye, for example, some nerve fibers carried impulses when the retina was stimulated with blue light, but not if the stimulus was red or yellow light. The retina of the cat, like that of humans, is composed of two kinds of receptor cells (rods, responsible for vision in dim light, and cones, responsible for vision in bright light) and a complex set of interconnected nerve cells. Signals are initiated when light strikes the rods and cones and is passed on through the nerve-cell network to a set of retinal nerve cells called ganglion cells. Long fibers, called axons, extend from the ganglion cells and pass out of the eye toward the brain. All the axons from all the ganglion cells of one eye are gathered into a bundle as they leave the eye. That bundle is the optic nerve.

Granit's microelectrodes were detecting impulses in the ganglion cell axons of the optic nerve; these impulses originated in rods or cones. There are many more rods and cones in the retina than there are ganglion cells; therefore, most ganglion cells must receive signals from more than one receptor cell. This convergence of signals from several receptors onto one ganglion cell is effected through the maze of nerve cells between the receptors and the ganglion cells.

Granit hypothesized the following explanation. Cone cells are responsible for color vision as well as for vision in bright light. The ganglion cell axons (optic nerve fibers) that carried messages only when the appropriate narrow band of wavelengths was used to stimulate the eye carried signals from one kind of cone cell. Since there were three different signals of this type, there must be three kinds of cone cell.

The ganglion cell axons that carried impulses whatever the wavelength of the stimulating light were carrying signals from a mixture of cone cells. When taken together, the three narrow absorption bands spanned the visible spectrum. For example, the element that primarily absorbed blue light also absorbed violet and green light to a lesser extent. Therefore, if all three kinds of cone were in contact with a single ganglion cell through the nerve network, the ganglion cell would be stimulated by light of any wavelength. The shift of the absorption maximum for these ganglion cells (from 560 nanometers in bright light to 500 nanometers in dim light) was a result of a shift from cone vision to rod vision. Thus, these ganglion cells collected signals from rods as well as from the three cone types.

Granit had shown the existence of three color-responsive units in the retina that are widely divergent in the wavelengths to which they respond, thereby supporting the Young-Helmholz hypothesis for the mechanism of color vision. He had done this based on the impulses passing through ganglion cells, not on the basis of the characteristics of the rods and cones themselves. Later, Wald confirmed and extended these conclusions with his work on the chemistry of the rods and cones.

In the late 1940's, Granit shifted his research efforts from vision to the control of muscular action and movement. He continued to use the tools of electrophysiology—microelectrodes, for example—and to develop the ideas of inhibition and other interaction among nerve cells. These tools and concepts, which he had been instrumental in developing, proved to be of great value in general application throughout the nervous system.

Granit summarized his work and the work of his colleagues in a number of books. His work on the retina is summarized in *Sensory Mechanisms of the Retina* (1947) and in *The Eye*, volume 2 (1962). His later work is summarized in *The Basis of Motor Control* (1970). His Silliman lectures, *Receptors and Sensory Perception* (1955), published from lectures given at Yale University, deal with aspects of both areas of research, as does his more philosophical approach to the brain, *The Purposive Brain* (1977). His *Charles Scott Sherrington: An Appraisal* (1966) reviews the early history of neurophysiology.

Ragnar Granit discovered and developed principles upon which much of modern neuroscience is based. His role in establishing the important function of inhibition in the retina and exploring the mechanism of color vision are primary examples. He also played a key role in the development of the electroretinogram and microelectrodes, tools of great importance to neurophysiological research. The electroretinogram has also been important clinically as a means of diagnosing certain optical problems. Many important advances in understanding the nervous system, including the brain, have been based on principles and instrumentation that Granit played pivotal roles in developing.

Bibliography

Primary

PHYSIOLOGY: *Sensory Mechanisms of the Retina*, 1947; *Receptors and Sensory Perception*, 1955; "The Visual Pathway," in *The Eye*, edited by H. Davson, 1962; *Charles Scott Sherrington: An Appraisal*, 1966; *Muscular Afferents and Motor Control*, 1966; "The Development of Retinal Neurophysiology," *Science*, vol.

160, 1968, pp. 1192-1196; *The Basis of Motor Control*, 1970; *Mechanisms Regulating the Discharge of Motor Neurons*, 1972; *The Purposive Brain*, 1977.

Secondary

Dowling, John E. *The Retina: An Approachable Part of the Brain*. Cambridge, Mass.: Harvard University Press, 1987. Written for a general audience, this presents thorough coverage of the retina and its place in neuroscience. Covers the contributions of the three laureates. Explores the electroretinogram, Granit's contribution, and subsequent advances. A superb place to begin a study of the retina. Contains an appendix of basic ideas in neurobiology, as well as illustrations, a bibliography, and an index.

Evarts, Edward V. "Brain Mechanisms of Movement." *Scientific American* 241 (September, 1979): 164-179. For the general audience. It explains muscular movement and its control by feedback from the brain, the area in which Granit worked after abandoning vision. Some of Sherrington's ideas are covered, as are some of Granit's. Illustrations. The article contains a brief bibliography.

Hubel, David H. *Eye, Brain, and Vision*. New York: Scientific American Library, 1988. Traces Hubel and Torsten Wiesel's work with the visual cortex. They developed broad principles of brain organization and explored the relationship between visual development and early visual experience. It outlines the structure of the retina and visual cortex and gives examples of inhibition in the eye and brain. A fine introduction to neuroscience. Contains illustrations, a bibliography, and an index.

Kuffler, Stephen W. "Neurons in the Retina: Organization, Inhibition, and Excitation Problems." *Cold Spring Harbor Symposia on Quantitative Biology* 17 (1952): 281-292. Written for a scientific audience, but generally understandable. Presents a summary of Kuffler's work on the receptive fields in the cat's retina. Kuffler's work built on Granit's and acted as the base for Hubel and Wiesel's. Reference is made continually to Granit's (and Hartline's) work. Bibliography.

Kuffler, Stephen W., John G. Nichols, and A. Robert Martin. *From Neuron to Brain*. 2d ed. Sunderland, Mass.: Sinauer Associates, 1984. A summary of the nervous system's function written for the general audience. Covers the history of neuroscience, including the contributions of Granit (and Hartline); the bulk of the book is on the brain. Numerous examples of inhibition. Includes illustrations, an index, and a glossary. Bibliography.

Masland, Richard H. "The Functional Architecture of the Retina." *Scientific American* 255 (December, 1986): 102-111. For a general audience. Describes the expanding understanding of retinal structure as based on Granit's work. Gives several examples of inhibition in the eye. Illustrations; brief bibliography.

Ratliff, Floyd. "Nobel Prize: Three Named for Medicine, Physiology Award: Ragnar Granit." *Science* 158 (October 27, 1967): 469-471. Written for a scientific audience, but generally understandable. Presents a summary of Granit's life and work. Ratliff was a close colleague of Hartline and so was in touch with Granit's work for many years. He comments on the breadth of Granit's contributions and their fundamental nature. Excellent.

Carl W. Hoagstrom

1967

Physiology or Medicine

Ragnar Granit, Sweden
Haldan Keffer Hartline, United States
George Wald, United States

Chemistry

Manfred Eigen, West Germany
Ronald G. W. Norrish, Great Britain
George Porter, Great Britain

Physics

Hans Albrecht Bethe, United States

Literature

Miguel Ángel Asturias, Guatemala

Peace

no award

HALDAN KEFFER HARTLINE
1967

Born: Bloomsburg, Pennsylvania; December 22, 1903
Died: Fallston, Maryland; March 17, 1983
Nationality: American
Area of concentration: Neurophysiology of vision

Hartline determined the characteristics of the signals transmitted by optic nerve cells and established many of the principles of the ways in which visual information is processed in the retina; his discoveries are applicable to the function of receptors and the nervous system in general

The Award

Presentation

Haldan Keffer Hartline shared the 1967 Nobel Prize in Physiology or Medicine with George Wald and Ragnar Granit. The award was presented by King Gustav VI of Sweden and consisted of a gold medal, a scroll, and about $20,600 for each recipient. Carl Gustaf Bernhard of the Royal Caroline Medico-Surgical Institute delivered the presentation address on December 10, 1967.

Bernhard compared the function of the retina to Picasso's approach to painting, in which he painted a motif and then reworked it until it was dramatically different, though the original theme was still present. The retina works in a similar fashion, he stated. The pattern of light collected by the retinal receptors is processed and changed before being sent to the brain. The processing emphasizes the most important aspects of the light pattern.

Bernhard recalled some of the neurophysiological background on which the laureates built, including the work of previous Nobel recipients Santiago Ramón y Cajal (winner of the physiology or medicine prize in 1906), on the structure of the nerve net of the retina, and Edgar Douglas Adrian (winner of the award in 1932), on the functions of nerve cells.

Bernard emphasized Hartline's "elegant" and "refined" technique and his insightful choice of a research subject, the eye of the horseshoe crab (*Limulus polyphemus*), a primitive relative of spiders, scorpions, and ticks. He credited Hartline with establishing the nature of the signals traveling from the eye to the brain and the existence of elaborate processing of the signals in the retina itself. Finally, he pointed out the general importance of the principles that Hartline worked out to neural networks associated with sense organs.

Nobel lecture

On December 12, 1967, Hartline explained his work in a chronologically organized lecture entitled "Visual Receptors and Retinal Interaction"; he began by noting that Adrian's results had stimulated his early work. He explained several visual representations of the activity of a single optic nerve cell from a single receptor unit of the horseshoe crab's eye. He pointed out that the electrical signals in the nerve cell were not perfect representations of the light stimuli which triggered them. Therefore, he had concluded that the retina did not only receive light and relay signals, via nerves, to the brain, but also actually began the processes of integration and interpretation of the information in the signals.

Hartline told of his success in recording signals from single fibers of the frog optic nerve. Elaborate experimental systems for stimulating the receptor cells showed distinct interactions among the various retinal cells and strengthened the conclusion that the processing of the information gathered from the light signals must be initiated in the retina.

In an effort to understand the interactions in the retina, Hartline turned back to the horseshoe crab, reasoning that it would be easier to extract basic principles from this simpler system. The major interaction he found was inhibition, a process in which a light receptor sends signals not only to the brain but also to adjacent cells. The signals to neighboring cells suppress the number of signals they send to the brain. Hartline then explained a simplified experimental system in which an electrical stimulus was applied directly to a nerve cell (instead of light being applied to the receptor, which normally stimulates the nerve cell). Experiments uncovered additional characteristics of the impulse, including a delay in the initiation of inhibition and self-inhibition, in which an impulse retards the firing of subsequent impulses in the same nerve cell. He discussed how these and other factors would affect the nerve cells of the retina and ultimately the message being sent from the retina to the brain.

Despite all these interactions, he pointed out that the horseshoe crab retina and its interactions are very simple compared to the interactions in the retinas of more complex organisms; however, he explained that appropriate manipulation of light stimuli to horseshoe crab light receptors could elicit many of the responses he had found in the retina of frogs. He concluded by stating that the principles learned in the study of the horseshoe crab would be useful in the effort to understand the more complex systems of more advanced organisms.

Critical reception

The British science journal *Nature* reported the selection of Hartline, Granit, and Wald as a "welcome and imaginative step" and said that the three had "transformed" the study of the physiology of vision and stimulated considerable work by other investigators. In *Science*, John E. Dowling closed his comment on George Wald's selection by writing that the three "led and guided visual research for over thirty years" and that the members of that research community "owe them a great debt." *Time* reported that their research was a "remarkably sophisticated beginning" toward an understanding of the eye.

Floyd Ratliff, writing in *Science*, pointed out that Hartline (along with Granit) was instrumental in the early work which led to the development of modern experimental and clinical electroretinography, a widely used technique for analyzing electrical patterns of the eye. Hartline also refined Adrian's technique for measuring the impulses of single nerve cells and used it on the optic nerve. Microelectrodes, for insertion into single cells, were developed later by Granit and his colleagues; they were used extensively by Hartline in his later work.

Nature credited Hartline's studies of the horseshoe crab with providing "all kinds of object lessons" for understanding more complicated systems of vision. Ratliff also emphasized the value of Hartline's basic discoveries on the frog and horseshoe crab as models of the more complicated visual systems of higher organisms. Beyond his contribution to vision research, Hartline was recognized as having made important contributions to the understanding of the nervous system in general. The neural network of the retina was recognized as a potential model for other neural networks involved with other receptors in other parts of the nervous system. Hartline's quantitative approach to the description of such networks, describing them by using sets of mathematical equations, was also recognized as a potential model for the description of such networks.

The reception of Hartline's work can also be shown by its effect on subsequent research. Two examples from the 1980's suggest his influence in the field. Robert B. Barlow, Jr., and his colleagues learned that in addition to the retina of the horseshoe crab sending information to the brain, signals from the brain also stimulate a millionfold increase in the sensitivity of the retina at night. Barlow believes that his brain-eye feedback system may be an important model for the understanding of more complex brain-receptor feedback systems.

The second example demonstrates the breadth of the impact of Hartline's research. Many bats find their way in flight and catch their insect food by sending out high-frequency sounds and extracting information from the echoes of those sounds. Study of the response of the bat's ears to the echoes employs some of the same techniques developed and used by Hartline and other students of the retina, and the basic principles of neural organization in the bat ear are similar to those in the retina.

Biography

Haldan Keffer Hartline was born in Bloomsburg, Pennsylvania, on December 22, 1903. Hartline's father, Daniel, was a biologist at Bloomsburg State College. His mother's name was Harriet (née Keffer). He attended Lafayette College at Easton, Pennsylvania, from which he was graduated in 1923. He went to medical school at Johns Hopkins University and received his M.D. in 1927. He was already doing research on vision; believing that he needed a stronger physics background, he remained at Johns Hopkins on a National Research Council fellowship and studied physics. He received an Eldridge Reeves Johnson Traveling Fellowship and studied at the universities of Leipzig and Munich for the next two years.

In 1931, he moved to the University of Pennsylvania. He married Mary Elizabeth Kraus, a comparative psychologist, in 1936. They had three sons; all three became biologists. Except for a year at Cornell Medical College (1940-1941), he stayed at

Pennsylvania until 1949. At that time, he moved to Johns Hopkins, where he stayed until 1953. His last professional move was to Rockefeller University (then Rockefeller Institute for Medical Research) in New York. Floyd Ratliff joined him there in 1954, and the two headed an exceptionally productive laboratory for two decades. He retired in 1974.

Hartline enjoyed the outdoors. Among his favorite outdoor activities were hiking and climbing in the Rockies, flying an open-cockpit plane, and sailing. He sailed with Ragnar Granit on the Baltic Sea and with Detlev W. Bronk, who also made important contributions to the understanding of vision, on the Chesapeake Bay. Hartline died in Fallston, Maryland, on March 17, 1983.

Scientific Career

Hartline began his study of visual systems as an undergraduate, but his most important insights into the function of the retina began when he and Clarence H. Graham adapted Adrian's technique for recording the activity of a single nerve cell to the optic nerve of the horseshoe crab. The retina of each of the horseshoe crab's lateral eyes is made up of about a thousand light receptor units called ommatidia. Each of these consists of about thirteen cells, one of them a nerve cell called an eccentric cell. The ommatidium acts as a unit to gather light, which triggers the eccentric cell to send an impulse, or signal, along an extension of the cell called a nerve-cell fiber or axon. The fibers from the thousand eccentric cells in each lateral eye are gathered together in the optic nerve, which extends to the horseshoe crab's brain. In the brain, the fibers from the ommatidia separate and make contact with brain cells.

In the early 1930's, Graham and Hartline separated the fibers of the optic nerve from one another until they could record the electrical activity from a single fiber. As a result, they could record the signal initiated by light shining on a single ommatidium. The large size of the ommatidia and the small number of fibers made the dissection relatively easy. Theirs were the first recordings of single nerve cells from a visual receptor. They found, as had Adrian in nerve cells from other parts of the nervous system, that all the impulses sent down the fiber were identical. There was not a large impulse for a bright light and a small impulse for a dim light. Instead, intensity was coded by frequency: The brighter the light striking its ommatidium, the more impulses the fiber carried per second.

The ommatidia responded with high-frequency signals immediately after a light was turned on, then decreased the frequency to a steady state after the light had been on for a time. When a dim light was brightened, the frequency increased. Again the receptor "overshot," by sending high-frequency signals immediately, then settled back to a steady frequency—one higher than under the conditions of dim light but lower than the initial response to the brighter light. Hartline concluded that the receptor's basic response was to emphasize change.

Hartline and Graham also exposed ommatidia to various wavelengths of light (essentially light of different colors). They graphed the frequency of impulses generated in the eccentric cell from that ommatidium against the wavelength of light used. Years later, Wald separated the chemical that absorbs light from the ommatidia and measured the wavelengths it absorbs. This gave an absorption spectrum, a direct measure of the amount of light of each wavelength absorbed by the retina. The two spectra agreed almost perfectly, confirming the relationship between the pigment, the absorption of light, and the signal in the eccentric cell.

All the horseshoe crab ommatidia were essentially identical with respect to their response to light. When Hartline turned his attention to the frog retina and optic nerves, he found different kinds of receptors and more elaborate nerve cell connections in the retina. For example, several receptor cells contacted the same optic nerve fiber. All these receptor cells together made up the receptive field of that fiber. He again separated individual optic nerve fibers carrying impulses from the frog's eye to the brain, exposed the receptors to light, and recorded the impulses passing through the fibers. Some fibers carried impulses much like those of the horseshoe crab eccentric cells, but some carried impulses only for a short time after a light was turned on or brightened, others only briefly after a light was turned off or dimmed, and still others briefly after a light was turned on or off. These results demonstrated the presence of receptor groups, indicating a much more complex situation than that of the horseshoe crab.

Experiments involving a small spot of light or a tiny shadow moved over the frog retina indicated that the receptor complexes were not independent of one another. Within the receptive field of a fiber, the same light or shadow could stimulate (excite) or inhibit the firing of impulses in the fiber. Inhibitory responses could cancel the effect of excitatory responses on the fiber. Hartline concluded that there must be some kind of direct communication among cells in the retina, allowing both inhibitory and excitatory interactions.

Believing that a simpler retina would be a more tractable system in which to explore the interactions, Hartline returned to the horseshoe crab—essentially for the rest of his career. In the 1940's and 1950's, using the microelectrodes developed by Granit, Floyd Ratliff and Hartline found the "simple" retina to be more complex than anticipated. A simple experiment, first run in response to a somewhat serendipitous observation, demonstrated inhibition among the ommatidia of the eye. When an ommatidium was exposed to constant light and the light on surrounding ommatidia was increased, the frequency of signals in the eccentric cell of the first ommatidium decreased: The surrounding ommatidia inhibited the discharge of the first.

A number of other experiments established the following general pattern of inhibitory interactions. Bright light on an ommatidium results in greater inhibition of its neighbors than does dim light. The greater the number of surrounding ommatidia that are illuminated, the greater the inhibition in the surrounded ommatidium. The inhibitory power of a given ommatidium is limited to relatively close neighbors. Inhibition is reciprocal; each ommatidium inhibits its neighbors and is inhibited by them. The inhibition is mediated by branches from the nerve fiber of the eccentric cell carrying impulses to the brain. These branch off as the fiber leaves the eccentric cell and make contact with the fibers of adjacent eccentric cells. Unlike in the frog retina, there were no excitatory interactions found among the ommatidia of the horseshoe crab. The simpler retina confined its interactions to inhibition, although these inhibitory interactions themselves were quite complex.

With a simplified experimental system in which light on the ommatidium is replaced by direct electrical stimulation of eccentric cells, Hartline and his colleagues showed that the onset of inhibition is delayed. They also demonstrated complex changes in the signal of an eccentric cell caused by this delay. Further changes in the signal resulted from characteristic phenomena discovered earlier. These included delays in the "on" and "off" response of the cells, the emphasized on and off response of the cells, and the mutual inhibition between sending and surrounding cells.

Hartline proposed that the function of the interactions in the retina was to enhance contrast and thereby improve the organism's ability to detect environmental transitions and movement. For example, the mutual inhibition of neighboring ommatidia would enhance the border between a brightly illuminated area and one less brightly illuminated—even if there was very little difference. The more brightly illuminated receptor will inhibit its neighbor more than it will be inhibited by the poorly illuminated neighbor, resulting in an exaggeration of the difference. Similar interactions have been shown to play these same roles in the retinas of more advanced organisms.

While the horseshoe crab's retina was not as simple as Hartline expected it to be, he recognized that the retinal responses of more advanced organisms would be immeasurably more complex. At the same time, he recognized that the relatively simple system of the horseshoe crab retina might be usable for exploring some of the more complex responses of the vertebrate retina. By manipulating the pattern of light stimulation on a normal ommatidium, Ratliff and a colleague simulated the frog receptors that respond only to turning a light off and those which respond both when a light is turned on and when it is turned off.

Hartline produced a mathematical model of the basic inhibitory interactions between and among the receptors of the lateral eye using sets of simultaneous equations. Later, his research group employed linear systems analysis to model and simulate more complex interactions mathematically. He was one of the few physiologists of his generation to write his own computer programs and to use mathematics to simulate and analyze a physiological system. This procedure has since become a powerful tool in many areas of biology.

H. Keffer Hartline spent his entire career working on visual receptors, most of it working with an obscure, ancient, and primitive organism often regarded as a living fossil. From this superficially mundane context he has produced vital information on the function of visual receptors of all kinds, receptors in general, and the nervous system. He has contributed to the understanding of the nature of the signals in the nervous system, the response of visual receptors to light, and the elaborate processing of information that occurs in these receptors before they send any information to the brain. He explained how receptor-level processing results in enhanced recognition of contrast and thus of form and movement in an organism's environment. Many of the principles he established, found in neural networks in other parts of the nervous system, have led to greater understanding of more complex receptors and nervous systems, including those of humans.

Hartline was also instrumental in the development of much of the instrumentation of early optical science research; some of the principles involved led to the development of a clinical tool, the electroretinogram. He was a pioneer in the use of mathematical simulation in physiological research. He also introduced an experimental model, the retina of the horseshoe crab, which remained at the forefront of research into the function of the nervous system for more than fifty years. Finally, given the invaluable information that Hartline gathered from this simple creature and his emphasis on learning from comparative anatomy and physiology, he had provided an elegant argument for the potential value of, and so the need to conserve, all species.

Bibliography

Primary

PHYSIOLOGY: "The Discharge of Nerve Impulses from the Single Visual Sense Cell," *Cold Spring Harbor Symposia on Quantitative Biology*, vol. 3, 1935, pp. 245-249; "The Neural Mechanisms of Vision," *The Harvey Lectures: 1941-1942*, series 37, 1942, pp. 39-68; "The Peripheral Origin of Nervous Activity in the Visual System," *Cold Spring Harbor Symposia on Quantitive Biology*, vol. 17, 1952, pp. 125-141 (with Henry G. Wagner and Edward F. MacNichol, Jr.); "How Cells Receive Stimuli," *Scientific American*, vol. 205 (September, 1961), pp. 222-238 (with Floyd Ratliff and William H. Miller); "Inhibitory Interaction in the Retina and its Significance in Vision," in *Nervous Inhibition*, edited by Ernst Florey, 1961 (with Floyd Ratliff and William H. Miller); "The Dynamics of Lateral Inhibition in the Compound Eye of *Limulus*: I," in *The Functional Organization of the Compound Eye*, edited by Carl G. Bernhard, 1966 (with Floyd Ratliff and David Lange); "The Dynamics of Lateral Inhibition in the Compound Eye of *Limulus*: II," in *The Functional Organization of the Compound Eye*, edited by Carl G. Bernhard, 1966 (with David Lange and Floyd Ratliff); "Visual Receptors and Retinal Interaction," *Science*, vol. 164, 1969, pp. 270-278.

Secondary

Barlow, Robert B., Jr. "What the Brain Tells the Eye." *Scientific American* 262 (April, 1990): 90-95. Addressed to a general audience, this article describes the compound eye and ommatidia of the horseshoe crab (though Hartline's *Scientific American* article does so more carefully). More important, Barlow's article describes interaction between the brain and eye and shows how far the work initiated by, and the model system chosen by, Hartline have been taken. Excellent; contains good illustrations. Brief bibliography.

Kennedy, Donald. "Inhibition in Visual Systems." *Scientific American* 209 (July,

1963): 122-134. Explains several types of inhibition, including Hartline's work with the horseshoe crab and scallop. Excellent; accessible to the general reader. Includes diagrams and a brief bibliography.

Michael, Charles R. "Retinal Processing of Visual Images." *Scientific American* 220 (May, 1969): 104-114. For a general audience. A comparative study of the retinas of frogs, ground squirrels, cats, and monkeys, including Hartline's pioneering work with frogs. Supports Hartline's contention that comparative studies are of great value. Diagrams. Brief bibliography.

Milne, Lorus J., and Margery J. Milne. "Electrical Events in Vision." *Scientific American* 195 (December, 1956): 113-122. A history of the early work on visual responses, including Hartline and the horseshoe crab, that is accessible to the layperson. Good explanation, with diagrams, of the early systems for measuring electrical activity in the optic nerve cells. Brief bibliography.

Ratliff, Floyd. "Contour and Contrast." *Scientific American* 226 (June, 1972): 90-101. For a general audience. Explains clearly the mechanism by which inhibition enhances contrast and the value of contrast in visual and other contexts. Diagrams. Brief bibliography.

____________. "Nobel Prize: Three Named for Medicine, Physiology Award: Haldan Keffer Hartline." *Science* 158 (October 27, 1967): 471-473. Addressed to scientists, but generally understandable, this is an excellent summary of Hartline and his work. Ratliff had worked closely with Hartline for more than a decade. He comments on Hartline's choice of a system with which to work, describes his personality, and briefly outlines his most important work.

____________, ed. *Studies on Excitation and Inhibition in the Retina: A Collection of Papers from the Laboratories of H. Keffer Hartline*. New York: Rockefeller University Press, 1974. A collection of Hartline's most important papers. The forward by Hartline and the introductions to the five parts by Ratliff make up the most complete summary of Hartline's professional life and of the importance of his work. Contains an index and an extensive bibliography.

Carl W. Hoagstrom

1967

Physiology or Medicine

Ragnar Granit, Sweden
Haldan Keffer Hartline, United States
George Wald, United States

Chemistry

Manfred Eigen, West Germany
Ronald G. W. Norrish, Great Britain
George Porter, Great Britain

Physics

Hans Albrecht Bethe, United States

Literature

Miguel Ángel Asturias, Guatemala

Peace

no award

GEORGE WALD
1967

Born: New York, New York; November 18, 1906

Nationality: American
Area of concentration: Biochemistry of vision

Wald established the role of rhodopsin as the chemical responding to light in the rod cells of the retina, iodopsin as the responsive chemical in cones, and the specific effect of light on vitamin A aldehyde that initiates the visual response in both cases

The Award

Presentation

King Gustav VI presented the 1967 Nobel Prize for Physiology or Medicine to George Wald, Ragnar Granit, and Haldan Keffer Hartline on December 10, 1967. Carl Gustaf Bernhard of the Royal Caroline Medico-Surgical Institute introduced the recipients and the accomplishments for which the prize was given. The $61,700 prize was shared equally among the three. Each also received the traditional medal and scroll.

In his introduction, Bernhard traced some of the historic context on which Wald based his work, including the work of previous Nobel laureates Santiago Ramón y Cajal, who won the Nobel Prize in Physiology or Medicine in 1906 for his work on the nerve net of the retina, and Edgar D. Adrian, who won it in 1932, for his work on the responses of sensory cells. In addition, he mentioned the theories of color vision and perception proposed by Isaac Newton, Thomas Young, and Hermann von Helmholtz. He contrasted those theories with the experimental approach based on Adrian's research and used by Wald and his colleagues, in which electronic techniques are used to test responses of receptor cells directly. Adrian was in attendance at the presentation.

Bernhard also emphasized Wald's discovery and characterization of the role of retinal (vitamin A aldehyde) in the primary reaction of the eye to light. He explained the interaction between light and retinal, a yellowish substance derived from vitamin A that, in combination with certain proteins such as opsin, forms the visual pigments in the retina that are responsible for sight. Light causes a chemical change in the shape of the retinal, which causes a change in the association between opsin and retinal. This triggers the response in the cell. Bernhard also emphasized Wald's point that that is the entire effect of light—the rest of the response of the visual system could take place in the dark, noting that it is this reaction that takes place in vision receptors of all kinds in all species of animal that see.

Nobel lecture

On December 12, 1967, Wald began his lecture, "The Molecular Basis of Visual

Excitation," with a comment on experimentation. He then outlined the discovery of the chemical response of the eye to light. He became interested in the problem as a graduate student at Columbia University in the laboratory of Selig Hecht. After leaving Columbia, he worked in the laboratories of three winners of the Nobel Prize. With the help of Otto Warburg, who won the Nobel Prize in Physiology or Medicine in 1931, Wald was able to find vitamin A in the retina; in the laboratory of Paul Karrer, who won the Nobel Prize in Chemistry in 1937, Wald confirmed the presence of vitamin A; and in that of Otto Meyerhof, who won the Nobel Prize in Physiology or Medicine in 1922, Wald discovered retinal, which is the molecule actually changed when light is absorbed by the eye. Retinal is called the chromophore of the system because of its response to light.

Next he told of the discovery of rhodopsin, the visual pigment of the rods. Rods and cones are the cells that respond to light. The rhodopsin is a combination of retinal and a protein called opsin. He mentioned a number of scientists who made contributions that he used to determine the relationship among retinal, opsin and vitamin A. He then explained the chemistry of the visual response in all known systems.

Wald explained several of the techniques used in determining the effect of light on the retina and went into the chemistry of the visual pigment in some detail. He also discussed changes in the electrical potential of the rod cell membrane which are associated with the absorption of light.

The final topic of his talk was color vision. In this context, he discussed work which established the presence of three different kinds of cone cells in the retina of man and monkeys. Each cone responds to one of three different colors red, green, or blue. He described the technique used to determine the wavelengths, or colors, absorbed by individual cone cells, and the use of the technique to establish the cause of colorblindness as the lack of one kind of cone. Finally, he considered areas of the normal retina which are, or may be, colorblind. For example, the central part of the fovea has no blue cones and so cannot detect the color blue; other areas of the retina may be blind to certain other colors. He suggested that this system may be a good one in which to study the embryologic development of a complex system.

In the lecture, Wald summarized the knowledge of the molecular structure and mechanism of visual reception. He emphasized the unity of this structure and mechanism in all visual systems in the animal kingdom. He described the techniques used to establish the knowledge and suggested future uses for the techniques. He also suggested new directions for research on the visual pigments. He emphasized the important contributions of many investigators in unraveling the structure and function of the visual pigments and concluded with regret that he had to leave so many contributions unmentioned.

Critical reception

The selection of George Wald was favorably received. Writing in *Science* (October 27, 1967), John E. Dowling said that Wald deserved the award whether it was given for one outstanding contribution or for a long-term series of achievements. He listed the major contribution as the discovery of the role of vitamin A in vision and generated a long list of other studies by which Wald contributed to further understanding of the chemistry of vision in rods and in cones. He further stated that no one had contributed more to this field than Wald.

Wald's work was also widely recognized as going beyond the chemistry of vision in its scope. Here are some examples. The *Science News* article on the 1967 Nobel Prize credited him with participation in the conversion of biology from a "cellular to a molecular science." Understanding the means by which the eye responds to light contributed to the understanding of receptor mechanisms in general. Vitamin A was among the first vitamins, and was the first fat-soluble vitamin whose function was understood. The chemical reaction sequence of the rods was recognized as a potential model for understanding other such systems, that in the mitochondrion (the part of the cell that produces energy for use in the cell), for example. The work with rod-and-cone opsins led to a better understanding of the genetics of colorblindness and of genetics in general. These and other areas of scientific work were seen to benefit from Wald's discovery and elucidation of the chemical mechanism of vision.

Wald, Hartline, and Granit were also recognized as having stimulated an enormous amount of work in other laboratories. This is another measure of the impact of their work. In *Nature*, the article reporting the 1967 prize gave the three credit for transforming the physiology of vision from a "narrow and introspective specialism into a rapidly growing field of interest."

The propriety of all these contentions is supported by publications in the field of vision chemistry in the late 1980's, twenty years after the Nobel presentation and fifty years after Wald discovered the role of vitamin A in rods. Lubert Stryer and his colleagues have worked out the rest of the chemical reaction sequence that takes place in rods in response to absorption of light. They have shown that the sequence is very similar to that by which many hormones exert their effect on cells. Hormones are the chemical messengers of the body that, together with the nervous system, direct and control bodily activities. Vision, cellular chemical reaction sequences, and hormonal control systems are all better understood because of this work, an outgrowth of Wald's pioneering efforts.

Jeremy Nathans, David S. Hogness, and their colleagues have further explored the opsin genes of rods and cones and shown them to be a family of related genes. As a result of their work, based on Wald's earlier demonstration of the visual pigments in the rods and in the three kinds of cones, the genetics of color vision, mechanisms of genetic mutation and families of related genes are all better understood. The *Nature* article also said that Wald's work "posed as many questions as it answered." The two examples given above demonstrate the important results to which those questions have led.

Biography

George Wald was born in New York, New York, November 18, 1906. His father was Isaac Wald and his mother Ernestine (Rosenmann) Wald. He attended Washington Square College of New York University, from which he was graduated in 1927. He went on to Columbia University, where he obtained his Ph.D. in 1932. At Columbia, he worked with Selig Hecht, who had a great influence on him.

Wald spent parts of 1932 and 1933 in the laboratories of Otto Warburg in Germany, Paul Karrer in Switzerland, and Otto Meyerhof in Germany as a National Research Council Fellow. He moved to the University of Chicago for the second year of the fellowship and then, in 1934, took a position at Harvard. He spent the rest of his career there, retiring in 1977.

He has been married twice, and has two children from each marriage. Michael and David were born to Frances Kingsley, his first wife, and Elijah and Deborah to Ruth Hubbard, his second wife, with whom he has collaborated on a number of papers.

Wald is an art collector and his interests in this area include primitive art. He has also been an active opponent of the Vietnam War, nuclear weapons, and chemical and biological weapons. He has lectured and written in opposition to war in general and to these especially dangerous weapons in particular.

Scientific Career

Wald's career has been centered on the single subject of the chemistry of vision. He began this quest with Selig Hecht at Columbia and credits Hecht with an influence in his life far beyond that of introducing him to his life's work. He expressed that influence in the following terms: "I saw too little of him after leaving his laboratory but I felt his presence always. What I did or said or wrote was, in a sense, always addressed to him."

When he left Columbia, little was known of the chemistry of visual perception. It was known that the retina, a thin layer of cells lining the eye, is the part of the eye responsible for the detection of light, and that nerve impulses travel from the retina to the brain, where the pattern of light on the retina is interpreted. The retina was known to be made up of a network of nerve cells and a layer of receptor cells. The receptor cells were known to be of two kinds: rods for vision in dim light and recording colorless images, and cones, which respond only to bright light and also record color.

Hecht had proposed a model of the action of light on the receptor cell. He suggested that the visual pigment is a chemical which separated into two parts when it absorbs light. This separation triggered the receptor cell to initiate the nerve impulse. The cell put the two parts of the visual pigment back together in preparation for another encounter with light. Wald left Columbia determined to identify the chemicals of the visual system and to explain their reaction with light.

In the year he spent in Europe in the laboratories of Warburg, Karrer, and Meyerhof, Wald identified vitamin A in the retina. He also established that a derivative of vitamin A was an intermediate in the response of the rod cell to light. In recognition of their function in the retina, vitamin A is called retinol and the intermediate derivative is called retinal. Retinal is also called the chromophore of the system.

After moving to Harvard and using information from work done by Kühne and Ewald around 1880, Wald concluded that rhodopsin, a combination of retinal and a protein called opsin, was the visual pigment. Based on his own work and that of others, Wald eventually explained the chemistry of the visual response in rod cells by determining the relationship between them, opsin, rhodopsin, and retinal.

Having established the identity and basic function of the visual pigment of the rod, Wald and other workers looked to see how common the system works in nature. He and a number of colleagues found that all the terrestrial (land) organisms and marine (salt water) fishes tested have rhodopsin as a visual pigment. Freshwater fishes have a different, but exceptionally similar, pigment system. Wald called the visual pigment in these fishes porphyropsin. The chromophore of the porphyropsin system differs from retinal only in the presence of a double bond in place of one of retinal's single bonds. Because two hydrogens are lost in formation of the double bond, and because the bond occurs at the number three carbon in the molecule, this chromophore of fresh water fishes is called 3-dehydroretinal. Amphibians, which metamorphose from freshwater tadpoles to terrestrial adults, and fish, which migrate from fresh water to salt water or salt water to fresh water to spawn, change their visual systems appropriately.

To further characterize the natural occurrence of the visual pigment system and to develop an understanding of color vision, Wald and other investigators began the exploration of the visual system of cones. Wald, his longtime associate Paul Brown, and Edward F. MacNichol and his associates at The Johns Hopkins University established the presence of three different kinds of cone in the human retina. Each cone absorbs a different band of wavelength, and so a different color of light. One absorbs blue light, another green light, and the third red light.

Each kind of cone responds to light in the same way the rods do. The visual pigment in cones, however, differs from rhodopsin, and is called iodopsin. The first iodopsin was isolated and characterized by Wald. The chromophore of all three types of cone was found to be 11-*cis* retinal, so the differences in color absorbed was assumed to lie in the different opsins. Freshwater fish and some other freshwater organisms were shown to have a different visual pigment. Ragnar Granit, who shared the Nobel Prize with Wald in 1967, contributed to that observation by discovering a pigment called cyanopsin; the difference between it and iodopsin parallels the difference between rhodopsin and porphyropsin in rods. The chromophore in these freshwater organisms is 3-dehydroretinal, and the opsins are similar to those of iodopsin.

In light of the new understanding of color vision, Wald turned his attention to colorblindness. He found that a simple mechanism was the cause: A colorblind person is generally lacking one of the three types of cone. He hypothesized that the genetic mechanism for colorblindness involved a change in the gene for the opsin such that one or more of the subunits in the opsin molecule itself was changed. The changed opsin could no longer bind to the appropriate retinal; therefore, that particular type of visual pigment could not be formed and that cone type could not occur in the retina. Wald and his colleagues thus contributed to the chemistry of vision in a number of important ways.

Wald also used the generalizations he discovered in vision chemistry, as well as those of other aspects of the chemistry of life, to develop a hypothesis of the nature of life and the universe. To do so, he combined the observation of the widespread use of virtually identical photoreceptor systems in unrelated organisms, such as vertebrates (mammals, birds, reptiles, amphibians, and fish), arthropods (crayfish and insects, for example), and mollusks (squid and octopus, for example), with observations of other complex reaction sequences in living things. For example, all photosynthetic organisms use similar chemicals for the capture of light energy. Photosynthesis is the process by which plants make food from sunlight and atmospheric carbon dioxide. From these and other observations, Wald concluded that given the conditions under which the earth was formed and has evolved, the development of life on earth was inevitable.

Wald presents his scientific and his philosophical thoughts with exceptional clarity, whether speaking or writing. As a result of this and of his dedication to teaching, he was considered to be one of Harvard's best teachers. Most scientists of his stature are not involved in teaching freshmen, but he taught a popular introductory biology course for much of his career. This interest and excellence in teaching may be another influence of Selig Hecht, whom Wald considered to be a great teacher as well as scientist. Wald has also written summaries of his work and articles on his cosmic hypothesis that are readily understood by the nonspecialist.

George Wald spent his entire scientific career studying the chemistry of vision, but his influence reached into many other fields. His most important contribution, the discovery and characterization of the role of vitamin A in vision, was also the first description of the function of a fat-soluble vitamin and one of the first descriptions of the function of any vitamin.

Wald worked out the first steps in the transformation of light into an electrical signal and proposed that the chemical reaction sequence that followed might be similar to reaction sequences in complex cellular responses to other signals in the body. Lubert Stryer and his colleagues have completed an outline of the chemical reaction sequence in rod cells and have shown that a parallel sequence of events occurs in certain cells when they respond to hormones.

Wald and his colleagues contributed to the understanding of the mechanism and genetics of color vision and colorblindness. Jeremy Nathans and his colleagues have carefully compared the cone iodopsins to one another and to rhodopsin. They have also located the genes that code for these proteins and studied their relationships, including the changes (mutations) that bring about various forms of colorblindness. These studies, ultimately based on Wald's work, have not only enhanced understanding of color vision and colorblindness, but also of general protein structure and function, gene arrangement on chromosomes, genetic exchange between chromosomes, and other genetic phenomena as well.

These three examples suggest how far-reaching George Wald's contributions as a scientist have been. His commitment to teaching and to presenting his scientific work, his philosophical positions, and his concern for the planet may be as important and as far reaching as the work pertaining to the physiology of sight.

Bibliography

Primary

PHYSIOLOGY: "Eye and Camera," *Scientific American*, vol. 183 (August, 1950), pp. 32-41; "Defective Color Vision and its Inheritance," *Proceedings of the National Academy of Sciences*, vol. 55, 1966, pp. 1347-1363; "Molecular Basis of Visual Excitation," *Science*, vol. 161, 1968, pp. 230-239; "The Molecular Basis of Human Vision," in *Biology and the Physical Sciences*, edited by Samuel Devons, 1969; "The Chemistry of Vision," in *International Encyclopaedia of Food and Nutrition*, 1970; "Visual Pigments and Photoreceptors: Review and Outlook," *Experimental Eye Research*, vol. 18, 1974, pp. 333-343.

BIOLOGY: "The Origin of Life," *Scientific American*, vol. 191 (August, 1954), pp. 44-53; "Innovation in Biology" *Scientific American*, vol. 199 (September, 1958), pp. 100-113; "Life and Light," *Scientific American*, vol. 201 (October, 1959), pp. 92-108; "Fitness in the Universe: Choices and Necessities," *Origins of Life*, vol. 5, 1974, pp. 7-27.

Secondary

Dowling, John E. "Nobel Prize: Three Named for Medicine, Physiology Award: George Wald." *Science* 158 (October 27, 1967): 468-469. Written for the scientifically literate. Dowling outlines Wald's life and the accomplishments for which Wald was awarded the Nobel Prize. He also comments on his teaching, his art collecting, and his feeling for Selig Hecht and Paul Brown. Excellent.

"George Wald." *The New Yorker*, April 16, 1966, 42-44. For a general audience. An interview in which Wald discusses his "biophilosophy." Its greatest value might be that it gives a journalist's impression of George Wald. An interesting account.

MacNichol, Edward F. "Three-Pigment Color Vision." *Scientific American* 211 (December, 1964): 48-56. Writing for a general audience. MacNichol describes the methods used by his group to demonstrate that color vision is the result of three different pigments segregated into different kinds of cones. Brown and Wald made the same discoveries independently. The history leading up to the discovery is also outlined, and includes contributions from all 1967 prize recipients.

Nathans, Jeremy. "The Genes for Color Vision." *Scientific American* 260 (February, 1989): 42-49. Written for a general audience. Nathans outlines the development of knowledge of color vision in which Wald played an important part, and the methods used and results obtained when he and David Hogness compared the opsins of the different cones with one another and with the opsin from rods. He also describes their methods for finding and studying the genes that code for these opsins. Excellent. Brief bibliography.

"Nobel Prizes for Vision." *Nature* 216 (October 28, 1967): 324. A brief article written for a general audience. This is the premiere British science journal's comment on the 1967 Nobel Prize. It remarks on Wald's ability to express thoughts clearly and the potentially broad impact of his work. Short but excellent.

Stryer, Lubert. "The Molecules of Visual Excitation." *Scientific American* 257 (July, 1987): 42-50. Written for a general audience. Stryer traces the discovery of the chemical reaction sequence that results in an impulse in a rod cell. The elaboration of this reaction sequence began with Wald's description of the effect of light on rhodopsin. Stryer shows that the reaction cascade in the rod is very similar to that in cells under the influence of certain hormones. This well written account contains a brief bibliography.

Thomsen, Dietrick E. "A Knowing Universe Seeking to be Known." *Science News* 123 (February 19, 1983): 124. A brief article written for a general audience. Thomsen reports on a speech Wald gave in which he spoke of consciousness and cosmology and the problems science has in dealing with them. He outlines some of the amazing aspects of the earth and universe in terms of supporting life, then briefly explores the conflict between Wald's view of consciousness and the more materialistic (or mechanistic) view. Short but interesting.

Carl W. Hoagstrom

1968

Physiology or Medicine

Robert Holley, United States
Har Gobind Khorana, United States
Marshall W. Nirenberg, United States

Chemistry

Lars Onsager, Norway and United States

Physics

Luis W. Alvarez, United States

Literature

Yasunari Kawabata, Japan

Peace

René Cassin, France

ROBERT W. HOLLEY
1968

Born: Urbana, Illinois; January 28, 1922

Nationality: American
Area of concentration: Biochemistry of nucleic acids

Holley determined the sequence of nucleotides in the alanine transfer RNA and showed that this type of RNA was capable of reading the codon for alanine in messenger RNA. He also demonstrated the presence of unusual nucleotides in transfer RNA that were not found in other types of RNA

The Award

Presentation

Professor Peter Reichard, a member of the Staff of Professors of the Royal Caroline Medico-Surgical Institute, introduced to the Royal Swedish Academy of Sciences Robert W. Holley, Har Gobind Khorana, and Marshall W. Nirenberg on December 10, 1968, by briefly describing their research and its importance.

Reichard began by mentioning some of the outstanding achievements of the past in genetics and nucleic acid research. Friedrich Miescher, a Swiss physician, is given credit for the isolation of nucleic acids from cell nuclei in 1868. Gregor Mendel, a Czech monk, reasoned from his research with peas that traits were controlled by units of inheritance now called genes. Oswald Avery, in the United States, had demonstrated by 1944 that deoxyribonucleic acid (DNA) was the hereditary information rather than protein. He transformed bacteria unable to synthesize capsules by giving them DNA purified from encapsulated bacteria. The transformed bacteria produced capsules.

The discoveries by the 1968 Nobel Prize recipients rank with the great achievements of the past, Reichard stated. Marshall Nirenberg and Har Gobind Khorana, in the early 1960's, were able to deduce the genetic code. Nirenberg chemically synthesized messenger ribonucleic acid (mRNA) strands that were composed of a single base and used these to synthesize proteins in a test tube. The proteins that were made consisted of a single amino acid. It was found, for example, that an mRNA that was composed only of uracil bases coded for a protein made only of phenylalanine bases. Similarly, it was found that all-guanine, all-cytosine, or all-adenine mRNAs coded for protein made only of glycine, proline, or lysine, respectively. By using mRNA synthesized with alternating bases, Khorana was able to determine the codons for a number of other amino acids. These types of experiments allowed Nirenberg and Khorana to deduce all sixty-one condons that direct the incorporation of amino acids.

Robert Holley, over a period of nine years, had purified and sequenced alanine transfer RNA (tRNA) and showed that it had the correct anticodon to read alanine codons in mRNA. Holley's determination of a tRNA structure also led to the discovery of a number of chemically altered nucleotides and of the secondary structure for the tRNA known as the cloverleaf form.

Nobel lecture

On December 12, 1968, Robert W. Holley delivered his Nobel lecture, entitled "Alanine Transfer RNA." In his lecture, Holley explained how he had purified and sequenced the bases in alanine tRNA, a project beginning in 1956 that required more than nine years to complete. In the late 1950's, it was known that amino acids were activated when they chemically reacted with the nucleotide adenosine monophosphate (AMP) and that activated amino acids formed covalent bonds with low-molecular-weight RNAs called transfer RNAs. Each of the different amino acids appeared to bind at the end of its own tRNA. To demonstrate conclusively that there were tRNAs specific for each type of amino acid and that these were able to read the genetic code in the messenger RNA (mRNA), scientists needed to purify tRNA, determine the nucleotide sequences of tRNAs, and discover the genetic code. It took four years to develop a procedure to fractionate the almost identical classes of tRNA extracted from yeast. A 1962 paper in the *Journal of Biological Chemistry* showed how Holley's laboratory had separated alanine, valine, histidine, and tyrosine tRNAs. Alanine tRNA, because of its apparent purity, was chosen to be sequenced.

The experimental approach to determining the sequence of seventy-seven nucleotides in alanine tRNA was to cleave the tRNA into small fragments, identify the order of nucleotides in the fragments, and then reconstruct the entire nucleotide sequence. A number of enzymes that cut RNA in specific ways were used to fragment the tRNA. Pancreatic ribonuclease cleaved the tRNA next to uracil- and cytosine-containing nucleotides, giving fragments ending in a uracil or cytosine. A certain ribonuclease designated T1 cleaved tRNA, producing fragments ending in guanine nucleotides. Subsequently, the fragments were separated by chromatography using diethylaminoethyl cellulose columns. Each of the fragments was then individually hydrolyzed with alkali into separate nucleotides, and the separate nucleotides were identified by their electrophoretic properties. All dinucleotide fragments could be easily identified using this procedure. Ribonuclease T1 at 0 degrees Celsius was used to break the tRNA molecule into two halves. These halves were separated and then treated with pancreatic ribonuclease or ribonuclease T1. This procedure allowed the fragments to be separated into one of two halves of the tRNA.

Snake venom phosphodiesterase was used to digest partially fragments larger than dinucleotides. The minifragments that resulted were separated, and then each minifragment was hydrolyzed to its constituent nucleotides and the nucleotides were separated by electrophoresis. Missing nucleotides associated with each minifragment could be easily determined, indicating the nucleotide sequence of the minifragment. Determination of the structures for all the fragments required more than two years of work. The presence of modified nucleotides and unique sequences helped in determining the order of fragments.

The nucleotide sequence suggested a number of secondary structures for the tRNA that had the anticodon unpaired and consequently able to interact with the appropriate codon in messenger RNA. One arrangement of the tRNA molecule was a cloverleaf arrangement. All of the tRNA sequences that have been determined since 1965 have the same type of base-pairing arrangement and form a cloverleaf structure. In all tRNAs, the anticodon sequence was found at about the same position in the middle of an unpaired looped region.

Holley's purification and analysis of alanine tRNA demonstrated the presence of an anticodon capable of "reading" at least one of the alanine codons. This discovery provided more evidence that tRNAs were actually involved in reading the genetic code. The nucleotide sequence of alanine tRNA was the first complete nucleotide sequence for any natural nucleic acid. In addition, the tRNA sequence indicated what the sequence of nucleotides in the gene for alanine tRNA might be.

Critical reception

Holley's work provided important evidence confirming that the genetic code of messenger RNA (mRNA) was read by a group of small RNA molecules called transfer RNA (tRNA). He and his colleagues, over a nine-year period, developed techniques for purifying and sequencing the different tRNA molecules. Holley's work showed that at least one type of tRNA, the alanine tRNA, could form a hydrogen bond with the correct codon in mRNA. Holley also demonstrated the presence of unusual nucleotides in tRNA that were not found in ribosomal RNA (rRNA) or mRNA.

The science editor for the British journal *Nature* in an October 26, 1968, announcement of the Nobel Prizes described Holley's work as an "outstanding achievement." Determining the nucleotide base sequence of alanine transfer RNA from yeast allowed scientists to see the characteristics of the "two specific recognition sites, one for the specific amino acid and the other for the codon that specifies the amino acid." Although the alanine tRNA from yeast consisted of only seventy-seven nucleotides, its nucleotide determination required years of work. Holley spent four years developing methods for separating and purifying the alanine tRNA and then another five years finding ways to sequence the molecule and put together the pieces of the tRNA puzzle.

Time magazine of October 25, 1968, in an article announcing the 1968 Nobel Prize in Physiology or Medicine, referred to Nirenberg, Khorana, and Holley's discoveries in glowing terms. *Time*'s science editor wrote, "One of the greatest of man's scientific triumphs has been the discovery of the method by which the genes transmit and translate the message of heredity." Holley contributed to this triumph by working out the complete structure of a transfer RNA molecule and "demonstrating how it [the tRNA] attaches to a particular amino acid and brings it [the amino acid] to the growing protein chain at the proper time and place." In fact, Holley's achievements were not so broad. Holley showed that amino acids form bonds with tRNAs and chemically described the nucleotide sequence that resulted by identifying the attached amino acids. He also chemically described the anticodon, which consisted of inosine, guanine, and cytosine. Inosine is an unusual base that is made by removing an amine group from adenine. Inosine hydrogen bonds with cytosine in mRNA. Holley discovered the presence of seven unusual nucleotides in tRNA: inosine, methyl inosine, pseudouridine, dihydrouridine, ribothymidine, methyl guanosine, and dimethyl guanosine. He also proposed that the tRNA molecule bonded with itself and formed a secondary structure that resembled a cloverleaf. With this secondary structure, the anticodon was free to form a hydrogen bond with an appropriate codon.

Maxine F. Singer, writing for the October 25 issue of the journal *Science*, commented on the personalities of the 1968 Nobel Prize recipients with the following: "The achievements of Holley, Khorana, and Nirenberg show common attributes that set these men apart from the many. Their separate triumphs are a combination of elegant scientific insight and style with the courageous daring and determination of the frontiersman."

Biography

Robert Holley attended public schools in Illinois, California, and Idaho, graduating in 1938 from Urbana High School in Illinois. A major in chemistry at the University of Illinois led to an A.B. degree in 1942. He began graduate work in organic chemistry at Cornell University in Ithaca, New York, but his graduate work was interrupted by World War II. He received his Ph.D. in organic chemistry in 1947.

A year of postdoctoral work at Washington State University preceded Holley's appointment as assistant professor of organic chemistry at Cornell University in 1948. During a sabbatical in 1956 at the California Institute of Technology, Holley began some experiments designed to characterize the molecule that formed covalent bonds with activated amino acids. In 1957, he became a research chemist at the U.S. Plant, Soil and Nutrition Laboratory, a U.S. Department of Agriculture laboratory at Cornell University. Much of the research on transfer RNA that occupied nine years was done in this laboratory. The nucleotide sequence of alanine tRNA was completed at the end of 1964. Holley became professor of biochemistry in 1962 and then chairman and professor of biochemistry and molecular biology from 1964 to 1966.

Holley spent the 1966-1967 academic year at the Salk Institute for Biological Studies and the Scripps Clinic and Research Foundation in La Jolla, California, as a National Science Foundation senior postdoctoral fellow. Because of his characterization of tRNA, the nucleic acid that reads the genetic code, Holley shared the Nobel Prize in Physiology or Medicine with Nirenberg and Khorana in 1968. The same year, Holley went to work at the Salk Institute as a resident fellow, conducting research on the peptide hormones that stimulate or inhibit cell division.

Scientific Career

Robert Holley began his graduate work in organic chemistry at Cornell University in New York. From 1944 to 1946, he participated in the first chemical synthesis of penicillin. He completed his Ph.D. in organic chemistry in 1947. Chemists and biologists were stimulated to work on the details of DNA replication, RNA synthesis, and protein synthesis after James Watson and Francis Crick published their speculations on how DNA might replicate and control the synthesis of proteins. In the mid-1950's, Crick had proposed that there was an "adaptor molecule" for each amino acid that read the mRNA code. Caught up in the excitement of the Watson and Crick models, Holley carried out experiments to elucidate the process of protein synthesis. Near the end of his sabbatical at the California Institute of Technology, Holley began an investigation into the structure of transfer RNA, the molecule that covalently bonds with amino acids and that reads the genetic code. From 1956 to 1965, Holley purified alanine tRNA and then sequenced it. The sequence showed that the alanine tRNA had an anticodon that could form a hydrogen bond with one of the alanine codons. The anticodon was near the middle of the tRNA molecule. In addition, he demonstrated that the tRNA molecule had unusual nucleotides that were not found in other classes of RNA. Two of Holley's associates, Betty Keller and John Penswick, suggested that bases of the tRNA molecule would pair with each other and form a two-dimensional cloverleaf structure. The cloverleaf structure was shown by many other researchers to be the form that all tRNA molecules take as they fold into their three-dimensional forms. The anticodon was in an unpaired portion of the tRNA molecule. This was consistent with the idea that tRNA read the code.

A 1966-1967 sabbatical at the Salk Institute for Biological Studies began a new phase of Holley's career. Holley began to study some of the factors that controlled growth and proliferation in mammalian cells. Holley's research had been concerned with learning how peptide and steroid hormones regulate cell growth. One question to be answered was whether the relative concentrations of growth inhibitors and stimulators surrounding cells determined whether they proliferated. Cancerous cells are mutated cells that are stimulated to proliferate and are missing growth inhibitory substances. The various oncogene products, for example, are believed to stimulate proliferation, while the different tumor suppressor gene products are thought to be important in regulating and inhibiting proliferation.

A 1968 publication considered the peptide and steroid hormones influencing growth of mouse fibroblast cells in culture. Holley discovered that the concentration of hormones in serum determined the density to which the mouse cells could grow. Confluent cells that had stopped growing and appeared to be contact-inhibited would start growing again and pile on top of one another when given fresh serum. With various percentages of calf serum, cells would grow geometrically in density. If fresh serum frequently replaced old serum, cells could be grown to densities as high as 6×10^6 cells/dish. Cells became confluent at about 5×10^5 cells/dish. The fact that cell density depended upon the concentration of hormones and that contact inhibition could be overcome by increased concentrations of hormones was an important discovery. The overproduction of stimulatory hormones might be one of the factors responsible for uncontrolled proliferation of cells, one of the first steps in the development of cancer cells. Holley discovered that urine is an excellent source of stimulatory hormones. It was found that mouse cells transformed by viruses had greatly reduced requirements for the stimulatory hormones and did not demonstrate contact inhibition. He concluded that the exhaustion of essential stimulatory hormones present in serum was responsible for cessation of growth (contact inhibition) as the cells became crowded.

A paper in 1974 reported that nonproliferating mouse cells would initiate DNA synthesis upon the addition of fresh serum. The greater the concentration of serum, the more cells that would initiate DNA synthesis over a period of twenty-four hours. Fractionization of serum indicated that there were at least four serum factors that stimulate the initiation of DNA synthesis and that their effects are greater than the sum of the individual effects. Holley's lab discovered that the factors in serum that stimulate DNA synthesis can be replaced by a fibroblast growth factor (peptide hormone), insulin (peptide hormone), dexamethasone (steroid hormone), and an ammonium sulfate fraction (uncharacterized hormones) of serum. Except for the fibroblast growth factor, which stimulates as much as 35 percent, each of the other factors, when used alone, stimulates DNA synthesis less than 10 percent, compared to serum stimulation. Holley's work indicated that serum hormones are depleted during growth of mouse cells but can be replaced. It was also discovered that other types of cell lines have hormone requirements that differ from the mouse cell line that Holley's lab was investigating.

Holley's research broadened to include an African green monkey kidney epithelial cell line. Epithelial cells are important in the origin of most types of cancers. A 1977 paper summarized what was known about the role of serum factors in regulating epithelial cells. His lab found that both the growth rate and the final cell density of the cells increased with increasing serum concentrations. Epidermal growth factor was found in serum and was one of the factors that stimulated DNA synthesis and cell proliferation. The growth factor increased both the growth rate and the final cell density but did not completely replace serum. The cells had a low absolute requirement for serum. Quiescent epithelial cells would proliferate and grow into a "wound" in a confluent plate without the addition of fresh serum if there were some serum present in the medium; however, in the absence of old or new serum, the epithelial cells would not proliferate. The most significant discovery was that cells at low density bound more than ten times as much epidermal growth factor as cells at high density and, also, that much more of the hormone was internalized and degraded at high density. This finding explained why serum hormones were more effective on low-density cells and why more hormone is required to get high-density cells to proliferate. In addition, the findings suggested how the hormones are used up in culture. The differential binding of epidermal growth factor was the result of a difference in the number of receptor sites per cell. The binding sites were specific for epidermal growth factor, since other hormones did not compete with the epidermal growth factor for binding sites. In contrast to the epidermal growth factor receptors, receptors for some other hormones increased in number when the cell density increased or when the cells were starved for serum.

In Holley's 1977 paper, the effect of various concentrations of amino acids and sugars on epithelial cell proliferation was considered. It was shown that growth rate and maximum cell density are decreased approximately 50 percent when the concentration of sugars is decreased by 90 percent. Reducing a number of vitamins by 90 percent had no observable effect on the cell density. Decreasing twelve of the amino acids by 90 percent only reduced cell density by about 25 percent. Reducing individual amino acids by 90 percent decreased cell densities by only 10 percent; however, a 90 percent reduction of glutamine totally abolished "wound" healing in a confluent dish. These data indicated that low concentrations of nutrients, in particular low concentrations of sugars and glutamine, resulted in regulation that restricted growth. The cells were not only exhausting a nutrient necessary for growth; at high cell densities, glucose analogues and L-glutamine were taken up less effectively than at low cell densities.

Holley's lab reported in a 1978 paper that epithelial cells produced a peptide inhibitor that was very heat-sensitive and easily denatured by mechanical agitation. It turned out, however, that a growth stimulator was being activated by heating or shaking. The stimulator promoted an increase in DNA synthesis and cell density. In 1980, Holley reported the isolation of two real growth inhibitors from the culture medium used in the growth of African green monkey kidney epithelial cells. The peptide inhibitors were concentrated by ultrafiltration and then separated on acrylamide gel columns. The large and small inhibitory peptides decreased DNA synthesis by 80 percent and 60 percent, respectively, when used at a concentration of 10 nanograms per millimeter. These inhibitors were specific for monkey epithelial cells, as shown by the fact that they poorly inhibited other cell types, such as mouse fibroblasts, human fibroblasts, human epithelial cells, and rat epithelial cells. Pepsin, an enzyme that cleaves proteins, destroyed the two inhibitors. The inhibitors caused reversible arrest of growth in the G1 phase of the cell cycle. The discovery of growth inhibitors was important because they may be products of tumor suppressor genes that prevent cells from becoming cancerous.

A paper from Holley's lab in 1983 described the effects of both a growth inhibitor with a molecular weight of 24 kilodaltons from African green monkey cells and epidermal growth factor (EGF). They found that the growth inhibitor, by itself, blocked DNA synthesis and induced the synthesis of a secreted 48-kilodalton protein by a factor of ten. EGF, by itself, stimulated repeated DNA replications and induced the synthesis of three secreted proteins with molecular weights of 28, 59, and 61 kilodaltons, respectively. The increase in DNA synthesis resulting from EGF was opposed by the growth inhibitor; however, each hormone independently stimulated protein induction and secretion. No functions were associated with the secreted proteins.

A 1984 paper showed that the 24-kilodalton growth inhibitor prevented sodium ion (Na^+) accumulation, and this in turn stopped any increase in size and also any proliferation of monkey kidney epithelial cells. In many types of cells, sodium ion accumulation, opposed by the sodium-potassium ion pumps, is often associated with cell enlargement and cell proliferation. In a 1985 paper, Holley's lab demonstrated that hormones that induce an increase in cell size and mitosis in dishes showed only an increase in cell size in an animal. The growth inhibitory peptide blocked the mitogenic response to insulin and hydrocortisone in combination but not the increase in cell size, which could be induced by a single factor such as insulin, Prostaglandin E1, and hypertonic sodium chloride (NaCl). Another 1985 paper characterized the 24-kilodalton inhibitory protein isolated from the medium used to grow monkey epithelial cells. The peptide hormone was most effective against a mink epithelial cell line. As little as 0.05 nanogram per milliliter inhibited DNA synthesis by 50 percent, apparently because these cells had many hormone receptors on their surface. The 24-kilodalton growth inhibitor appeared to be very similar to transforming growth factor beta produced by human platelets.

In 1988, Holley's lab reported the entire nucleotide and amino acid sequence for one of the growth inhibitors produced by African green monkey kidney epithelial cells. The growth inhibitor was very active in arresting growth of a variety of cells in culture as well as in animals as shown by its inhibition of human mammary carcinoma in mice. The growth inhibitor was found to have 80 out of 112 amino acids in common with human transforming growth factor beta-1 (TGF-beta 1) from platelets; however, the entire amino acid sequence of human transforming growth factor beta-2 (TGF-beta 2) was identical to Holley's growth inhibitor. Holley proposed that these factors be called polyfunctional regulators of growth because of their inhibitory and stimulatory properties.

Holley's research after he received the 1968 Nobel Prize continued to be concerned with the various factors that control cell division. His discoveries have contributed to scientific knowledge about the factors that control cellular differentiation and proliferation. The factors that control differentiation and proliferation of cells are important in understanding how cells become cancerous. From 1969 to 1990, Holley was an American Cancer Society research professor of molecular biology at the Salk Institute for Biological Studies.

Bibliography

Primary

MOLECULAR BIOLOGY: "An Alanine-Dependent, Ribonuclease-Inhibited Conversion of AMP to ATP, and Its Possible Relationship to Protein Synthesis," *Journal of the American Chemical Society*, vol. 79, 1957, pp. 658-662.

CHEMISTRY: "Fractionation of Yeast Amino Acid-Acceptor Ribonucleic Acids by Countercurrent Distribution," *Journal of Biological Chemistry*, vol. 238, 1961, pp. 1117-1120 (with B. P. Doctor and Jean Apgar); "Chemistry of Amino Acid-Specific Ribonucleic Acids," *Cold Spring Harbor Symposia on Qualitative Biology*, vol. 28, 1963, pp. 117-121 (with Jean Apgar, George Everett, James Madison, Susan Merrill, and Ada Zamir); "A Growth Regulatory Factor That Can Both Inhibit and Stimulate Growth," *CIBA Foundation Symposium 116*, 1985, pp. 241-252 (with J. H. Baldwin, S. Greenfield, and R. Armour).

CELL PHYSIOLOGY: "Control of the Initiation of DNA Synthesis in 3T3 Cells: Serum Factors," *Proceedings of the National Academy of Sciences, U.S.A.*, vol. 71, 1974, pp. 2908-2911 (with Josephine Kiernan); "Density-Dependent Regulation of Growth of BSC-1 Cells in Cell Culture: Control of Growth by Low Molecular Weight Nutrients," *Proceedings of the National Academy of Sciences, U.S.A.*, vol. 75, 1978, pp. 339-341 (with R. Armour and J. H. Baldwin); "Purification of Kidney Epithelial Cell Growth Inhibitors," *Proceedings of the National Academy of Sciences, U.S.A.*, vol. 77, 1980, pp. 5989-5992 (with P. Bohlen et al.); "BSC-1 Growth Inhibitor Transforms a Mitogenic Stimulus into a Hypertrophic Stimulus for Renal Proximal Tubular Cells: Relationship to Na^+/H^+ Antiport Activity," *Proceedings of the National Academy of Sciences, U.S.A.*, vol. 82, 1985, 6163-6166 (with L. G. Fine, H. Nasri, and B. Badie-Dezfooly); "Amino Acid Sequence of the BSC-1 Cell Growth Inhibitor (Polyergin) Deduced from the Nucleotide Sequence of the cDNA," *Proceedings of the National Academy of Sciences, U.S.A.*, vol. 85, 1988, pp. 79-82 (with S. K. Hanks, R. Armour, et al.).

Secondary

Altman, Sidney, ed. *Transfer RNA*. Cambridge, Mass.: MIT Press, 1978. This book consists of ten review articles on tRNA. The book was intended as an introduction to the characteristics of tRNA. The first review is a history of tRNA and includes a summary of the scientists who contributed to the understanding of tRNA.

Celis, J. E., and J. D. Smith, eds. *Nonsense Mutations and tRNA Suppressors*. New York: Academic Press, 1979. This book consists of twenty review articles on the structure and role of tRNA. The articles are mainly concerned with how mutant tRNAs (suppressor tRNAs) translate the stop codons (nonsense codons) that normally are not translated and that terminate the polymerization of amino acids.

Judson, Horace Freeland. *The Eighth Day of Creation: The Makers of the Revolution in Biology*. New York: Simon & Schuster, 1979. An outline of Holley's work on tRNA is presented in the larger context of the research carried out by many other laboratories. This book is intended for general audiences and provides a very accurate history of molecular biology.

Lake, James A. "Aminoacyl-tRNA Binding at the Recognition Site Is the First Step of the Elongation Cycle of Protein Synthesis." *Proceedings of the National Academy of Sciences, U.S.A.* 74 (May, 1977): 1903-1907. This article describes how tRNA interacts with the ribosome and mRNA. A third site of interaction on the ribosome is postulated. This is worthwhile reading for those interested in how tRNA functions during protein synthesis. A general understanding of the mechanism of protein synthesis is required to understand this research paper.

Lengyel, Peter. "The Process of Translation: A Bird's-Eye View." In *Ribosomes*. Cold Spring Harbor, N.Y.: Cold Spring Harbor Laboratory, 1974. A worthwhile review article of protein synthesis with an excellent description of tRNAs and how they are involved. This article can be understood by general audiences.

Rich, Alexander, and Sung Hou Kim. "The Three-Dimensional Structure of Transfer RNA." *Scientific American* 238 (January, 1978): 52-62. This article, published ten years after Holley received the Nobel Prize, summarizes the role of tRNA in protein synthesis and what had been learned about the structure of tRNAs since 1968. The cloverleaf secondary structure is folded into an L-shaped molecule in which the anticodon (at the top) is 7.6 nanometers from the amino acid (at the end of the side arm). This paper should be easily comprehended by general audiences.

Schön, Astrid, Guido Drupp, Simon Gough, C. Gamini Kannangara, and Dieter Söll. "A New Role for Transfer RNA: A Chloroplast Transfer RNA Is a Cofactor in the Conversion of Glutamate to Delta-Aminolevulinic Acid." In *Molecular Biology of RNA: New Perspectives*, edited by Masayori Inouye and Bernard Dudock. New York: Academic Press, 1987. This paper is concerned with an unusual role that tRNA may have. It can function in metabolism as a coenzyme that donates amino acids. This is an informative paper on what tRNAs do in cells.

Walker, James. "A Transfer RNA Implicated in DNA Replication." In *Molecular Biology of RNA: New Perspectives*, edited by Masayori Inouye and Bernard Dudock. New York: Academic Press, 1987. The dnaY gene of the bacterium *Escherichia coli* codes for a rare arginine tRNA. The article is concerned with how the dnaY gene controls DNA replication. Does the gene bind, and so remove, a DNA replication inhibitor, or does it produce a product that acts directly or indirectly to stimulate DNA replication? Contains much information on tRNAs in cells.

Jaime S. Colomé

1968

Physiology or Medicine

Robert Holley, United States
Har Gobind Khorana, United States
Marshall W. Nirenberg, United States

Chemistry

Lars Onsager, Norway and United States

Physics

Luis W. Alvarez, United States

Literature

Yasunari Kawabata, Japan

Peace

René Cassin, France

HAR GOBIND KHORANA
1968

Born: Raipur, India (later West Pakistan); recorded as January 9, 1922

Nationality: American
Area of concentration: Biochemistry of nucleic acids

Khorana helped develop methods for investigating the structure of the nucleic acids and many of the techniques that allowed scientists to decipher the genetic code and show how RNA can specify the structure of proteins

The Award

Presentation

The presentation address was given on December 10, 1968, by the biochemist Peter Reichard of the Royal Caroline Institute, a member of the Nobel Committee for Physiology or Medicine. Reichard noted that in 1868, the Swiss physician Friedrich Miescher had isolated a new kind of compound from cell nuclei. Miescher called this new material nuclein; it later became known as nucleic acid. Only two years earlier, Gregor Mendel, a Czech monk, had worked out the laws of genetic inheritance. In the 1860's, the foundations of modern genetics—nucleic acids and Mendel's laws—had been discovered; however, since the connection between genes and nucleic acids remained unknown for many decades, research on nuclein was considered a rather obscure aspect of biochemistry until 1944, when experiments conducted by Oswald Avery suggested that genes are composed of nucleic acids. Avery's work is generally considered the foundation of modern molecular biology.

In trying to explain how nucleic acids could serve as the genetic code, scientists compare the building blocks that make up the gigantic molecules of nucleic acids to the letters of the alphabet. The letters of nucleic acid language could be arranged to spell out the many genes responsible for inherited traits. After Marshall W. Nirenberg introduced an ingenious and simple method of deciphering the genetic code, Khorana devised methods of synthesizing nucleic acids of known composition that were essential in arriving at a complete solution of the genetic code. This understanding of the genetic code and the way it functioned in protein synthesis provides the basis of understanding diseases which are, at least in part, determined by heredity.

Nobel lecture

On December 12, 1968, Khorana delivered his Nobel lecture, entitled "Nucleic Acid Synthesis in the Study of the Genetic Code." Khorana began by acknowledging the efforts of investigators in many scientific disciplines who had contributed to understanding the genetic code. Before discussing the work carried out in his own laboratory, he reviewed the main steps in the development of this subject. According to Khorana, a good starting point for biochemical genetics, the concept that genes make proteins, was the one gene, one enzyme hypothesis formulated by George W. Beadle and Edward L. Tatum in 1941. Another important insight was provided by the transformation experiments of Oswald Avery, Colin M. Macleod, and Maclyn McCarty. Further support for the hypothesis that nucleic acid was the genetic material of bacterial viruses was provided in 1952 by Alfred D. Hershey and Martha Chase. By the early 1950's, it was thus clear that genes were composed of nucleic acids and that nucleic acids directed protein synthesis. The pace of discovery quickened in the 1950's as investigators elucidated the fundamental chemical and biochemical nature of the nucleic acids.

When James D. Watson and Francis H. Crick proposed their elegant model for the structure of deoxyribonucleic acid (DNA), they focused intense interest on "the biological meaning" of the physical structure of this molecule. Scientists suggested that the linear sequence of nucleotides in DNA might specify the linear sequence of amino acids in proteins. A series of discoveries about the enzymes that are involved in the synthesis of DNA and ribonucleic acid (RNA) led to understanding of the way in which information stored in DNA is transcribed into a messenger RNA, which is then involved in the synthesis of protein. Credit for devising a direct experimental approach to the genetic code belonged to Johann H. Matthaei and Marshall W. Nirenberg, who showed that synthetic polynucleotides of known composition could be used as messengers for the synthesis of polypeptide chains in a defined in vitro (cell-free) protein-synthesizing system.

Khorana's research on the chemical structure of the nucleic acids began with the technically difficult problem of the chemical synthesis of oligonucleotides. By the early 1960's, Khorana had achieved success in developing methods for the synthesis of short chains of deoxyribopolynucleotides of known sequences which could then be used to decipher the codons, or "words," of the genetic code.

In his conclusion, Khorana admitted that some of the detailed aspects of the genetic code were still uncertain; however, he noted how satisfying it had been to have worked on such a significant problem and to have seen "complete agreement reached in regard to its general structure." No one individual or highly specialized approach could have deciphered the genetic code; it had taken evidence from various techniques, genetics, and biochemistry, and experiments conducted in many different model systems. Although much work remained at the chemical and biochemical level in order to clarify the nature of the protein-synthesizing system, the basic outlines of the problem were known: The relationship between the linear sequence of nucleotides in nucleic acids and the sequence of amino acids in proteins had been solved. Khorana ended his lecture by expressing the hope that this knowledge "would serve as a basis for further work in molecular and developmental biology."

Critical reception

When the 1968 Nobel Prize winners in Physiology or Medicine were announced, *Time* magazine (October 26, 1968) lauded the trio as the "code-breakers" who had revealed the secrets of the "spiral staircase of life." According to *Time*, the three new "U.S. Nobelmen" had provided a clearer understanding of the nature of life and had "brought closer the day when molecular biology will be able to correct genetic defects, control heredity, and perhaps even create life itself." In addition to honoring Har Gobind Khorana, the 1968 Nobel Prize recognized the work of Robert W. Holley and Marshall W. Nirenberg. Maxine Singer wrote in *Science* that the three laureates "together constitute a triplet of great sense." Scientists saw in the work of Khorana, Nirenberg, and Holley special attributes that marked them as outstanding researchers, constituting a "combination of elegant scientific insight and style with the courageous daring and determination of the frontiersman." *The New York Times* of October 17, 1968, reported that Khorana, Nirenberg, and Holley had "written the most exciting chapter in modern biology." *Science News* (October 26, 1968) predicted that the work of the 1968 Nobel laureates would serve as a model by which scientists would uncover the relationship between the "detailed structure of molecules and their biological functions." The implications of such knowledge were "endless" because an understanding of how cells are made could lead to manipulation of the genetic messages encoded in DNA. This might lead to "genetic surgery" with synthetic materials that could correct the genetic errors responsible for genetic disease or cancer; however, many journalists would probably agree with the statement in *The Nation* of November 9, 1968, that their readers would be more interested in the Nobel Prizes in Literature and Peace because "laymen frequently cannot appreciate the worth of creative scientists and physicians."

Instead of fading from the public eye after winning the Nobel Prize for basic research that seemed rather esoteric to laymen, two years later, Khorana captured even greater media attention. Khorana's announcement on June 2, 1970, of the synthesis of the first wholly artificial gene was hailed as one of the greatest scientific landmarks of molecular biology and the possible prelude to actual deliberate changes in the genetic material itself that could prove to be of great therapeutic value or that, in the wrong hands, could be very dangerous. According to *Time* magazine (June 15, 1970), this marked the first time that a gene had been created entirely from "off-the-shelf chemicals." The DNA molecule that Khorana synthesized was the gene coding for yeast alanine transfer RNA, whose sequence was known through the work of Robert Holley.

Described as modest and even shy, Khorana rarely gave press interviews. In discussing the popular fear of the potential dangers of science, however, Khorana told Victor Cohn of *The Washington Post* (June 8, 1970), "I do have a basic faith that survival of our civilization is not even going to be possible without proper use of science."

Biography

Har Gobind Khorana, the youngest of four sons and one daughter of Ganput Rai Khorana and Krishna (Devi) Khorana, was born in Raipur, a small village in the Punjab, which is now a part of West Pakistan. Khorana's birth date was recorded as

January 9, 1922, but the exact date of his birth is unknown. His father was a "patwari," a village agricultural taxation clerk for the British colonial government. His Hindu parents were poor but dedicated to education. They were practically the only literate family in Raipur. Khorana recalled receiving his first four years of schooling under a tree where the local teacher established his "classroom."

Khorana attended high school in Multan (now West Punjab), where he was especially influenced by Ratan Lal, one of his teachers. He received both the bachelor of science (1943) and the master's (1945) degrees, with honors, from Punjab University, Lahore, India. He described his supervisor, Mahan Singh, as a great teacher and skillful experimentalist. In 1945, a Government of India fellowship made it possible for him to continue his studies in England. He was awarded the Ph.D. degree by the University of Liverpool in 1948. Roger J. S. Beer, his dissertation supervisor, also served as Khorana's guide to Western culture. From 1948 to 1949, he worked as a postdoctoral fellow at the Federal Institute of Technology, Zurich, Switzerland, with Professor Vladimir Prelog, whom he remembered as a great scientist and human being. In his Nobel lecture, Khorana made a special effort to acknowledge how his association with Prelog had influenced his "thought and philosophy towards science, work and effort."

After a brief stay in India in 1949, Khorana returned to England to work with George W. Kenner and Alexander Todd at the University of Cambridge (1950-1952). During this period, he developed his interest in proteins and nucleic acids. At the invitation of Gordon M. Shrum, Khorana accepted a position in the organic chemistry section of the British Columbia Research Council, Vancouver, Canada (1952-1960). In 1959, Khorana received international recognition for the synthesis of coenzyme A, carried out in collaboration with John G. Moffatt.

In a moving tribute to his wife, Esther Elizabeth (née Sibler), Khorana said that their marriage in 1952 brought a sense of purpose into his life at a time when he felt "out of place everywhere and at home nowhere." They had three children, Julia Elizabeth, Emily Anne, and Dave Roy.

Khorana moved to the University of Wisconsin, Madison, Wisconsin, in 1960, to become codirector of the Institute for Enzyme Research and professor of biochemistry. In 1964, he was appointed to the university's most prestigious chair, the Conrad A. Elvehjem Professorship in the life sciences. In June, 1970, at a small symposium of biochemists, Khorana expressed his appreciation to the university for the fruitful decade he had spent there and announced that he would be leaving Wisconsin to become the Alfred P. Sloan Professor in the departments of biology and chemistry at the Massachusetts Institute of Technology in Cambridge, Massachusetts. He later told a colleague, "You stay intellectually alive longer if you change your environment every so often." From 1974 to 1980, he was Andrew D. White Professor-at-Large at Cornell University, Ithaca, New York. Khorana rarely took vacations; indeed, he once told an interviewer, "I work all the time, but then I guess we all do."

In 1966, Khorana was elected to the National Academy of Sciences. Khorana has won numerous honors and awards from many different nations, including the Merck Award from the Chemical Institute of Canada in 1958; the Dannie-Heinneman Preiz, Gottingen, Germany, 1967; the American Chemical Society Award for Creative Work in Synthetic Organic Chemistry, 1968; the Lasker Foundation Award for Basic Medical Research, 1968; the Padma Vibhushan Presidential Award, India, 1972; the Ellis Island Medal of Honor, 1986; National Medal of Science, 1987; and the Paul Kayser International Award of Merit in Retina Research, 1988. He holds honorary degrees from numerous universities, including Simon Fraser University, Vancouver, Canada; the University of Liverpool, England; the University of Punjab, India; the University of Delhi, India; Calcutta University, India; the University of Chicago; and the University of British Columbia, Vancouver, Canada.

Scientific Career

While the postdoctoral period Khorana spent with Vladimir Prelog molded his philosophical approach to scientific work, the period in which he worked with Kenner and Todd was of decisive value in establishing his interest in the chemistry of the proteins and nucleic acids. As a postdoctoral student in Prelog's laboratory, Khorana had accidentally come across references to a class of compounds called carbodimides in the German scientific literature. In 1953, Khorana and Sir Alexander Todd published their only coauthored paper; it appeared in the *Journal of the Chemical Society* and described the use of a novel phosphorylating reagent. Khorana found that these chemicals were very useful in dealing with previously intractable problems in the synthesis of nucleotides. Although Todd and his colleagues carried out extensive studies of methods for the synthesis of dinucleotides and coenzymes, it was Khorana who went on to extend these methods to the synthesis of polynucleotides.

During the early 1950's, Khorana became interested in the chemistry of biologically important phosphate esters. Many novel phosphate esters and nucleotide derivatives were being discovered during this period. Between 1956 and 1958, Khorana and his coworkers published a series of papers which established the fundamental new techniques of nucleotide chemistry. Their primary objective was to develop purely chemical methods of synthesizing oligonucleotides. Khorana and his coworkers investigated many aspects of nucleotide coenzymes and polynucleotide synthesis. In 1961, John Moffatt and Khorana succeeded in synthesizing coenzyme A, a factor needed for the activity of certain key metabolic enzymes.

In the spring of 1955, Khorana first learned about Severo Ochoa's discovery of the enzyme polynucleotide phosphorylase. Soon after, he met Arthur Kornberg, who described the first results of studies of the enzymatic synthesis of DNA. These discoveries immediately proved to be "electrifying" and instrumental in revolutionizing investigations of the nucleic acids. According to Khorana, the elucidation of the genetic code was a direct consequence of the discovery of polynucleotide phosphorylase. In a tribute to Severo Ochoa on his seventieth birthday, Khorana noted that progress in the research he had begun in the 1960's "hinged on the truly miraculous action" of DNA polymerase and DNA ligase on short-chain synthetic polynucleotides.

The 1968 Nobel Prize honored Holley, Khorana, and Nirenberg "for their interpretation of the genetic code and its function in protein synthesis." Nirenberg provided an ingenious method that initiated the highly creative period in which the genetic code was deciphered, but it was Khorana who conducted much of the final, technically sophisticated work. The chemical synthesis of polynucleotides (both the ribose and deoxyribose series) was largely the achievement of Khorana's laboratory. When Marshall W. Nirenberg and Philip Leder discovered the nitrocellulose binding technique, Khorana and his colleagues were able to extend the binding experiments by testing each of the sixty-four possible ribonucleotide triplets (codons). Having pioneered the synthetic approach to nucleic acid structure, Khorana and his coworkers replicated each of these possible triplets by synthesizing polynucleotides of known composition. Khorana also systematically devised the methods that led to the synthesis of large, well-defined nucleic acids.

By combining synthetic and enzymatic methods, many of the problems intrinsic in the chemical synthesis of polyribonucleotides were bypassed. Khorana's work provided unequivocal proof of codon assignments and defined some codons that had not been determined by other methods. Some triplets that did not seem to code for any particular amino acid were shown to serve as punctuation marks for initiating and terminating the polypeptide chain. Khorana's investigations also provided direct evidence concerning other attributes of the code, which had only been indirectly suggested by genetic experiments. For example, Khorana's work proved that three nucleotides specify an amino acid and provided proof as to the direction in which the information of the messenger RNA is read, demonstrating that punctuation between codons is unnecessary and that the code words cannot overlap. Construction of specific polyribonucleotides proved that the sequence of nucleotides in DNA specifies the sequence of amino acids in a protein by means of an RNA intermediary.

Summarizing the remarkable progress that had been made up to 1968 in polynucleotide synthesis and understanding the genetic code, Khorana remarked that the problem of the genetic code could be regarded as essentially solved, at least for *Escherichia coli*. The essential question was therefore what the direction of further work in the field of polynucleotide synthesis should be. Khorana suggested that areas of investigation for the immediate future include the punctuation marks on DNA, recognition of DNA by repressors, DNA-modifying enzymes, transcription enzymes such as RNA polymerase, and the problem of viral RNAs. More fundamental and obscure problems included the precise mechanism of genetic recombination and the control of DNA replication. His own untiring dedication to scientific research contributed much to the solution of many of these problems.

Once the genetic code had been elucidated, Khorana turned his attention to the question of the control elements in gene expression which were thought to lie between the genes. The question of gene expression might be solved by means of the synthesis of DNAs of known sequence that could be used in a new and general approach to the study of the relationships between gene structure and gene function and studies of DNA-protein interactions. In pursuit of the objective of understanding gene expression, Khorana's laboratory focused on the synthesis and sequencing of DNA. As in the case of the genetic code, success required sophisticated blending of organic synthetic methodologies with the use of special enzymes, such as polynucleotide ligase and polynucleotide kinase. Because of the importance of the class of ribonucleotides known as transfer RNA (tRNA) and the fact that Robert Holley's laboratory had succeeded in sequencing the major yeast alanine tRNA, Khorana made the decision to synthesize the DNA corresponding to the entire seventy-seven-nucleotide sequence.

Khorana's announcement on June 2, 1970, of the total synthesis of the first wholly artificial gene was hailed in the scientific community and the popular press as one of the greatest scientific landmarks of molecular biology and the possible prelude to the ability to manipulate the genetic material itself, resulting in, possibly, the development of new organisms (whether microscopic or mammal-sized) that could be of tremendous significance (for good or ill) to humankind. In reviewing this work, Khorana noted that the synthesis of yeast alanine tRNA had provided much insight into the problems of the laboratory synthesis of DNA. The next objective was the total synthesis of the structural gene for the precursor of a bacterial tyrosine suppressor transfer RNA. This goal was formulated in 1968 and achieved in 1976.

By 1976, with the availability of many new techniques, DNA sequencing was in high gear. At this point, Khorana anticipated that the use of the synthetic approach would be extended to many biologically interesting problems. Of primary interest would be the elucidation of the mechanisms of gene expression and the total laboratory synthesis of specific genes. In 1988, Khorana was awarded the Paul Kayser International Award of Merit in Retina Research for investigations of the chemistry and molecular biology of rhodopsin, the light-transducing pigment of the retina, and bacteriorhodopsin, a light-sensitive protein found in a bacterium. Using the tools of molecular biology that he had done so much to forge, Khorana synthesized the gene for bovine rhodopsin and studied its mechanisms of action and expression.

The methods and techniques pioneered by Har Gobind Khorana have led to fundamental insights into the genetic code and the mechanism of gene regulation. The remarkable progress of molecular biology since 1968 is, in large measure, the result of the achievements of Khorana and his coworkers.

Bibliography

Primary

BIOCHEMISTRY: "Studies on Phosphorylation: Part XI, The Reaction Between Carbodiimides and Acid Esters of Phosphoric Acid. A New Method for the Preparation of Pyrophosphates," *Journal of the Chemical Society*, vol. 465, 1953, pp. 2257-2260 (with A. R. Todd); "The Chemistry of Carbodiimides," *Chemical Reviews*, vol. 53, 1953, p. 145; *Some Recent Developments in the Chemistry of Phosphate Esters of Biological Interest*, 1961; "Preparation of Nucleotides and

Derivatives," *Methods in Enzymology*, vol. 6, 1963, pp. 645-670 (with M. Smith); "Enzymatic Synthesis of Deoxyribonucleic Acid. XVI. Oligomers as Templates and the Mechanism of Their Replication," *Proceedings of the National Academy of Sciences*, vol. 51, 1964, p. 315 (with Arthur Kornberg, LeRoy L. Bertsch, and John F. Jackson); "Nucleic Acids—Sequence Analysis," *Annual Reviews of Biochemistry*, vol. 35, 1966, p. 759 (with U. L. RajBhandary and A. Stuart); "Studies on Polynucleotides. LXVII. Initiation of Protein Synthesis in Vitro as Studied by Using Ribopolynucleotides with Repeating Nucleotide Sequences as Messengers," *Journal of Molecular Biology*, vol. 25, 1967, p. 275 (with H. P. Ghosh and D. Soll); "The Synthesis of Living Systems," *Chemical and Engineering News*, vol. 45, 1968, p. 144 (with K. Hofmann and S. Spiegelman); "Polynucleotide Synthesis and the Genetic Code," *The Harvey Lectures*, series 62, 1968, 79-105; "Total Synthesis of the Gene for an Alanine Transfer Ribonucleic Acid from Yeast," *Nature*, vol. 227, 1970, p. 27 (with K. L. Agarwal, H. Buchi, M. H. Caruthers, N. Gupta, K. Kleppe, A. Kumar, E. Ohtsuka, U. L. RajBhandary, J. H. van de Sande, V. Sgaramella, H. Weber, and T. Yamada); "Studies on Polynucleotides. CXXXI. Total Synthesis of the Structural Gene for the Precursor of a Tyrosine Suppressor Transfer RNA from *E. coli* (1)," *Journal of Biological Chemistry*, vol. 251, 1976, p. 565; "Total Synthesis of a Gene," *Science*, vol. 203, 1978, p. 614; "Studies on Bacteriorhodopsin and Rhodopsin," *Proceedings of the Retina Research Foundation Symposium*, vol. 1, 1988, pp. 62-89.

Secondary

Fruton, Joseph S. *Molecules and Life: Historical Essays on the Interplay of Chemistry and Biology*. New York: Wiley-Interscience, 1972. Although intended for a scientifically sophisticated audience, this well-written, lucid text is historical and general in approach. The history of the interplay between chemistry and biology since 1800 provides valuable insights into the background and context of Khorana's work. The sections entitled "The Nature of Proteins" and "From Nuclein to the Double Helix" are of special interest.

Judson, Horace Freeland. *The Eighth Day of Creation: The Makers of the Revolution in Biology*. New York: Simon & Schuster, 1979. A popular account of the development of molecular biology, largely based on interviews with the scientists involved in the study of proteins, nucleic acids, and the genetic code. The book was originally serialized in *The New Yorker* and is clearly written for general audiences.

Jukes, T. H. *Molecules and Evolution*. New York: Columbia University Press, 1966. A very readable exposition of the evidence available in the 1960's concerning theories of the evolution of the genetic code.

Kornberg, Arthur. *Enzymatic Synthesis of DNA*. New York: John Wiley & Sons, 1961. This interesting personal account of the early work in the field by one of the pioneers sheds light on one of the methodologies utilized by Khorana.

Olby, Robert. *The Path to the Double Helix*. Seattle: University of Washington Press,

1974. Although intended for a scientifically sophisticated audience, this well-written book contains much valuable information about the nucleic acids and the genetic code which should be accessible to general readers. It is one of the best historical studies of the discovery of the double helix.

Portugal, Franklin H., and Jack S. Cohen. *A Century of DNA*. Cambridge, Mass.: MIT Press, 1977. The book provides a comprehensive account of the history of studies of the structure and function of the nucleic acids from the discovery of nuclein in 1969 to the elucidation of the genetic code. The book provides the proper scholarly apparatus, but it is highly readable and should be of interest to general readers.

Reichard, Peter. *The Biosynthesis of Deoxyribose*. New York: John Wiley & Sons, 1967. This is an excellent, brief account of the experimental background of studies of the biosynthesis of mononucleotides by the biochemist who gave the presentation speech for Khorana's Nobel Prize.

Singer, Maxine F. "News and Comment: 1968 Nobel Laureate in Medicine or Physiology." *Science* 162 (1968): 433-436. Written as an analysis of the work of the three scientists who were awarded the Nobel Prize in Physiology or Medicine in 1968. This well-written tribute contains valuable information about Khorana's career and an analysis of the way his work related to that of his colaureates.

Singer, Maxine F., and P. Leder. "Messenger RNA: An Evaluation." *Annual Reviews in Biochemistry* 35 (1966): 195. A valuable review of the evidence available during the 1960's concerning the messenger hypothesis, ribosomes, and codons.

Zubay, Geoffrey, ed. *Papers in Biochemical Genetics*. New York: Holt, Rinehart and Winston, 1968. A valuable collection of articles revealing the state of biochemical genetics in the 1960's.

Lois N. Magner

1968

Physiology or Medicine
Robert Holley, United States
Har Gobind Khorana, United States
Marshall W. Nirenberg, United States

Chemistry
Lars Onsager, Norway and United States

Physics
Luis W. Alvarez, United States

Literature
Yasunari Kawabata, Japan

Peace
René Cassin, France

MARSHALL W. NIRENBERG
1968

Born: New York, New York; April 10, 1927

Nationality: American
Areas of concentration: Molecular biology and biochemical genetics

Nirenberg shared the Nobel Prize with two colleagues for their interpretation of the genetic code and the elucidation of its function in protein synthesis. Nirenberg's contribution involved the development of two techniques to decipher the code

The Award

Presentation

Professor Peter Reichard of the Royal Caroline Medico-Surgical Institute made the presentation address on December 10, 1968, on behalf of the Royal Swedish Academy of Sciences and His Majesty the King of Sweden. In his address, Reichard briefly presented historical background on genetics prior to the sophisticated genetic research that took place in the 1940's. It was in 1944 that a hereditable property was experimentally transferred and that deoxyribonucleic acid (DNA) was recognized as the genetic material containing the hereditary information (the genetic code). This work brought to life an area of research that had been considered dull and exclusive, and it began the field of science that has become known as molecular biology. This area of research became so active and important during the 1950's and 1960's that from 1958 to 1968, five Nobel Prizes in Physiology or Medicine were awarded for research in molecular biology.

Reichard went on to explain specifically why Nirenberg's research in molecular biology was so important, likening his work with the genetic code to the discovery of the Rosetta Stone used by archaeologists to decipher the Egyptian hieroglyphs. By using ribonucleic acid (RNA) segments of known nucleotide composition and by analyzing what kind of protein was produced by these RNA segments, it became possible to know which RNA nucleotides selected which amino acids to produce the protein. Because it enables the deciphering of DNA, RNA has been referred to as the genetic Rosetta Stone. In addition to this specific knowledge about the code, the process by which RNA uses genetic information from the DNA to synthesize proteins was better understood.

From the initial work begun by Nirenberg in 1960, enough research had been done by 1966 that many details of the genetic code and its role in protein synthesis were well established. Reichard concluded with a note on how much has been learned from this research and how much will continue to be learned from it about inheritance and about diseases in which heredity plays an important role.

Nobel lecture

Nirenberg's Nobel Prize lecture, entitled "The Genetic Code," delivered on December 12, 1968, was an overview of his research strategies and results, an analysis of the gene-protein code concept, a description of the chemical structure and sequence of the genetic code, and a description of the role and mechanism of the gene-protein translation. Nirenberg's research was based on the sophisticated genetic research that had begun in the 1940's. At that time, it was finally determined that DNA was the genetic material; research in the following decade produced the actual chemical structure of DNA. The one gene, one protein concept was also established, as was the relationship of RNA to protein synthesis and other related discoveries. In addition, new experimental methods were developed for use in the study of cellular activities during the 1940's and 1950's.

Nirenberg was able to tie all these individual bits of research together, and by improving upon the experimental methods recently developed at the time, he was able to develop his research. The two important research efforts made by Nirenberg in deciphering the genetic code are described in some detail. The first effort used a cell-free system whereby cellular material containing the needed ingredients to produce proteins was used. RNA of known composition was added to the system along with amino acids to produce the protein. The protein was then analyzed to determine its amino acid composition. While this technique provided information on which nucleotides translated to which amino acids, it did not provide information on the sequence of the nucleotides or of the amino acids. To determine this, another technique was used that involved an examination of the binding that takes place between the nucleotides and the amino acids at the ribosome.

In addition to the composition and sequence of RNA, information pertaining to messenger RNA, transfer RNA, protein synthesis, and heredity was determined by Nirenberg's research. Most important, the genetic code was deciphered, and the foundation was laid for research into genetics, genetic engineering, heredity, and heredity-based diseases.

Critical reception

Amid reports of the fighting in Vietnam, the racial tensions at home, the pending first landing on the moon, and the presidential election campaign, the announcement that the Nobel Prize in Physiology or Medicine had been awarded was reported with little fanfare in American newspapers, newsmagazines, and scientific journals. The news accounts tended simply to report the fact that the Nobel Prize had been awarded; they also sometimes provided a brief account of why they were awarded and provided brief biographies on each of the recipients.

To some extent, the announcement was overshadowed by other world events. Perhaps also, the work was of such importance that the awarding of the Nobel Prize for this particular research was expected, and therefore anticlimactic. Neither the research, nor the importance of the research, was disputed; however, *The New York Times* did mention that some scientists who initially heard Nirenberg's research presentation at the fifth International Congress of Biochemistry in Moscow (1961) believed that it was a fluke. Other accounts, such as those published in *Science*

(October 25, 1968), *Chemical and Engineering News* (October 21 and 28, 1968), *New Scientist* (October 24, 1968), *Nature* (October 26, 1968), *Time* magazine (October 25, 1968), *The New York Times* (October 17 and 20, 1968), and *The Times* of London (October 17 and December 11, 1968) stated that the research was significant and were content with only reporting the facts. While some biochemists questioned the research during the fifth congress, by the time Nirenberg presented his new research at the sixth International Congress of Biochemistry in New York (1964), the legitimacy and importance of his work had been established. By the time the Nobel Prize was awarded in 1968, the research was well established and the genetic code had been deciphered.

These research efforts were therefore apparently so well established and their importance so well recognized by 1968 that the Nobel Prize announcement was reported in a matter-or-fact way with little discussion or criticism by both the scientific journals and the popular magazines and newspapers. *Nature* confirmed this by stating that no one was in the least surprised by the Nobel Prize announcement, and *New Scientist* stated that the research was classical molecular biology. The articles did not point out any shortcomings of the research but did suggest the possible benefits that were foreseen even at that time, such as the advancement of molecular biology (which was a relatively young science at the time), the correcting of genetic defects, the study and control of heredity, the advancement of medical research, the rise of genetic engineering, and even the creation of life.

Biography

Marshall Warren Nirenberg, the son of Harry and Minerva Nirenberg, was born on April 10, 1927, in New York City. In 1939, when he was twelve, the family moved to Orlando, Florida. In 1945 he was graduated from high school and entered the University of Florida in Gainesville. Having an interest in zoology, he decided to study the subject while at the university; he had an assistantship in the department of biology from 1945 to 1948. He received his B.S. degree in zoology (with a minor in chemistry) in 1948 and began graduate work in the department of biology during 1949. From 1950 to 1951, he was a research associate in the nutrition laboratory, working in biochemistry with radioisotopes. He was also a member of the science honor societies Phi Eta Sigma and Phi Sigma. In 1952, he was graduated from the University of Florida with an M.S. degree in zoology. His M.S. thesis was entitled "The Caddis Flies of Alachua County, with Notes on Those of Florida."

The M.S. thesis was a systematic and ecological account of those insects and was a result of many years of zoological study; however, Nirenberg's experience at the nutrition laboratory awakened other interests that would overcome his zoological pursuits. Biochemistry and molecular biology were such new fields of science that they were not yet a part of the curriculum at the university. It was at the nutrition laboratory that Nirenberg first met biochemists and became interested in biochemical research. He moved to Ann Arbor, Michigan, in 1952 and entered the University of Michigan, where he held a teaching fellowship in the department of biological chemistry from 1952 to 1957. He received his Ph.D. in biochemistry in 1957. His Ph.D. dissertation was entitled "Hexose Uptake in Ascites Tumor Cells."

Nirenberg moved to Bethesda, Maryland, in 1957 and began his scientific career at the National Institutes of Health (NIH). In 1961, he married Perola Zaltzman, also a biochemist at NIH. He became a permanent staff member of the NIH in 1960 and began his biochemical genetics research that was to lead to the deciphering of the genetic code. For this research he has been awarded numerous awards, honorary degrees, and the Nobel Prize. He remained with the NIH, serving in various capacities and in the various institutes.

Scientific Career

Upon being graduated from the University of Michigan with a Ph.D. in 1957, Nirenberg moved to Bethesda, Maryland, and began his scientific career with a postdoctoral fellowship from the American Cancer Society at the National Institute of Arthritis and Metabolic Diseases of the National Institutes of Health (NIH). In 1959, he received another fellowship from the U.S. Public Health Service to study the biochemistry of the compounds controlling the synthesis of proteins. He then became a permanent NIH staff member in 1960, serving as a research biochemist in the metabolic enzyme section of the National Institute of Arthritis and Metabolic Diseases.

At this time, he was joined by Johann Heinrich Matthaei to work with cell-free systems to synthesize proteins using RNA. These are solutions of cellular material containing all the cellular ingredients necessary to synthesize proteins. By adding RNA with the genetic information necessary for this synthesis, researchers hoped to learn something about the process as well as the genetic code itself. Nirenberg had listed some two hundred experiments he felt needed to be done, and he began the laborious, systematic effort of conducting these experiments. Others were working with similar cell-free systems to study protein synthesis, but Nirenberg and Matthaei were appparently not in communication with such research efforts being conducted at Harvard University, the Massachusetts Institute of Technology, the California Institute of Technology, the University of Cambridge, or the Pasteur Institute. (Although not aware of the research in progress, they were familiar with the published research.) While this isolation, along with their inexperience in this field of research, may have been a hindrance to their progress, it allowed them to be appropriately innovative and experimentally unencumbered by the directions taken by other research groups.

It was not until May, 1961, that their research efforts began to be successful. In addition to being familiar with the published literature, Nirenberg did consult with scientists who he believed were familiar with particular segments of his research, and in May he spent four weeks consulting with Heinz Fraenkel-Conrat in Berkeley, California, on an experiment that he and Matthaei had conducted. This experiment, however, was to be overshadowed by another. While Nirenberg was in Berkeley, Matthaei continued with the series of experiments they had been pursuing, including the one using synthetic RNA (synthetic RNA of known composition) in the cell-free system. This experiment, using synthetic RNA with a multiple sequence of only one nucleotide, produced a protein with a multiple sequence of only one amino acid, thus providing the first "word" of the genetic code. Upon Nirenberg's return, this line of research was confirmed and expanded. It represented a significant step in that it made it possible to determine the composition of the coding—that is, which nucleotide in the RNA produced which amino acid in the protein. Its limitation was that it did not make it possible to determine the sequence of the nucleotides or of the amino acids when RNAs having more than one kind of nucleotide were used to make proteins of more than one amino acid; this was to come later.

The results of this research could have been presented that very summer at the Cold Spring Harbor Symposia, but Nirenberg's application to attend was rejected because he was unknown and unpublished. After additional work, the results of their ground-breaking research were published in two articles during the fall of 1961. At the same time, Nirenberg was able to present these results at the fifth International Congress of Biochemistry being held at Moscow in August, 1961. Yet because Nirenberg was relatively unknown and his newly published articles had not yet circulated, his presentation was assigned a fifteen-minute time slot during a small session in a classroom of the university. It was one of some four hundred papers being given that day. The paper, with the deceptive title "The Dependence of Cell-Free Protein Synthesis in *E. Coli* upon Naturally Occurring or Synthetic Template RNA," gave no indication that the genetic code had begun to be solved, and it attracted a very small audience.

In attendance were a few of the more influential biochemists of the day, one of whom was very much impressed by what was presented. Recognizing its significance, he went to Francis Crick, who had won an earlier Nobel Prize for determining the structure of DNA, and convinced him to allow Nirenberg to present his paper at the session chaired by Crick. Nirenberg presented his paper a second time to a much larger audience in the great hall of the university. It was the last paper of his last session, and Crick later wrote that it had electrified the audience (although a photograph taken of the audience showed several people who appeared to be asleep). There were others who believed that the important experiment upon which the research was based was really the control part of the experiment and that the successful results were accidental. Others even thought that the results were probably incorrect, regardless of whether they were accidental. Much of this feeling stemmed from the fact that Nirenberg was not known and that he was inexperienced in this type of research. It was expected that progress would have been made only at experienced, well-known laboratories. The NIH was not noted for conducting significant research at the time, and Nirenberg was not a "member of the club."

It nevertheless sent the biochemists scurrying back to their laboratories to renew their research with new vigor; Nirenberg himself did so as well. With Philip Leder and others, he began work on his second research technique, concentrating on the binding of RNA nucleotides with amino acids at the ribosome (a component of the cell that acts as a site for this binding) to determine the sequences of nucleotides that select the sequences of amino acids. Nirenberg was able to determine that three nucleotides were necessary to code for each amino acid and that a sequence of these trinucleotides was what determined the amino acid sequence of the protein. This technique was presented at the sixth International Congress of Biochemistry, held at New York City in the summer of 1964. The title of this paper was "Characteristics of the RNA Code."

By the time Nirenberg presented his continuing research at the Cold Spring Harbor Symposia of 1966, the encoded RNA instructions (the trinucleotides) for all twenty of the amino acids were known. The genetic code was finally deciphered. Three sets of trinucleotides had no amino acids assigned to them, but by 1967 it was known that these are nonsense codes whose function it is to signal the end of the amino acid chain. The structure of DNA and RNA, the code that allows the RNA to synthesize proteins, and the DNA-RNA-protein synthesis process had gone from being some of the greatest mysteries in biochemistry to being common textbook information in about twenty years. The genetic code itself was cracked in about six years.

Remaining at the NIH during this entire time, Nirenberg became chief of the Laboratory of Biochemical Genetics of the NIH in 1966. In 1965, he was awarded the National Medal of Science (from the National Science Foundation), and in 1968 he was awarded the Franklin Medal (from the Franklin Institute), the Priestley Medal (from the American Chemical Society), the Louisa Gross Horwitz Prize (from Columbia University), and the Nobel Prize in Physiology or Medicine. Nirenberg was also awarded honorary degrees from the University of Chicago, the University of Windsor, Yale University, Harvard University, George Washington University, and the Weizmann Institute (Israel).

Bibliography

Primary

CHEMISTRY: "The Dependence of Cell-Free Protein Synthesis in *E. coli* upon RNA Prepared from Ribosomes," *Biochemical and Biophysical Research Communications*, vol. 4, 1961, pp. 404-408 (with Heinrich Matthaei); "Characteristics and Stabilization of DNAase-Sensitive Protein Synthesis in *E. coli* Extracts," *Proceedings of the National Academy of Sciences, U.S.A.*, vol. 47, 1961, pp. 1580-1588 (with Heinrich Matthaei); "The Dependence of Cell-Free Protein Synthesis in *E. coli* upon Naturally Occurring or Synthetic Polyribonucleotides," *Proceedings of the National Academy of Sciences, U.S.A.*, vol. 47, 1961, pp. 1588-1602 (with Heinrich Matthaei); "The Dependence of Cell-Free Protein Synthesis in *E. coli* upon Naturally Occurring or Synthetic Template RNA," *Proceedings of the Fifth International Congress of Biochemistry*, vol. 1, 1962, pp. 184-189 (with Heinrich Matthaei); "Characteristics and Composition of RNA Coding Units," *Proceedings of the National Academy of Sciences, U.S.A.*, vol. 48, 1962, pp. 666-677 (with Heinrich Matthaei, Oliver Jones, and Robert Martin); "Qualitative Survey of RNA Codewords," *Proceedings of the National Academy of Sciences, U.S.A.*, vol. 48, 1962, pp. 2115-2123 (with Oliver Jones); "Ribonucleotide Composition of the Genetic Code," *Biochemical and Biophysical Research Communications*, vol. 6, 1962, pp. 410-414 (with Robert Martin, Heinrich Matthaei, and Oliver Jones); "On the Coding of Genetic Information," *Cold Spring Harbor Symposia on Quantitative Biology*, vol. 28, 1963, pp. 549-557 (with Oliver Jones, Philip Leder, B. Clark, W. Sly, and Sidney Pestka); "Approximation of Genetic Code via Cell-Free Protein Synthesis Directed by Template RNA," *Federation Proceedings*, vol. 22, 1963, pp. 55-61 (with Heinrich Matthaei, Oliver Jones, Robert Martin, and Samuel Barondes); "The Genetic Code: II," *Scientific American*, vol. 208 (3), 1963, pp. 80-94; "RNA Codewords and Protein Synthesis: The Effect of Trinucleotides upon the Binding of sRNA to Ribosomes," *Science*, vol. 145, 1964, pp. 1399-1407 (with Philip Leder); "RNA Codewords and Protein Synthesis: II. Nucleotide Sequence of a Valine RNA Codeword," *Proceedings of the National Academy of Sciences, U.S.A.*, vol. 52, 1964, pp. 420-427 (with Philip Leder); "RNA Codewords and Protein Synthesis: The Nucleotide Sequences of Multiple Codewords for Phenylalanine, Serine, Leucine, and Proline," *Science*, vol. 147, 1965, pp. 479-484 (with Merton Bernfield); "RNA Codewords and Protein Synthesis: VI. On the Nucleotide Sequences of Degenerate Codeword Sets for Isoleucine, Tyrosine, Asparagine, and Lysine," *Proceedings of the National Academy of Sciences, U.S.A.*, vol. 53, 1965, pp. 807-811 (with Joel Trupin, Fritz Rottman, Richard Brimacombe, Philip Leder, and Merton Bernfield); "RNA Codewords and Protein Synthesis: VII. On the General Nature of the RNA Code," *Proceedings of the National Academy of Sciences, U.S.A.*, vol. 53, 1965, pp. 1161-1168 (with Philip Leder, Merton Bernfield, Richard Brimacombe, Joel Trupin, Fritz Rottman, and C. O'Neal); "Protein Synthesis and the RNA Code," in *Harvey Lectures: 1963-1964*, 1965; "The RNA Code and Protein Synthesis," *Cold Spring Harbor Symposia on Quantitative Biology*, vol. 31, 1966, pp. 11-24 (with Thomas Caskey, Richard Brimacombe, D. Kellogg, et al.).

Secondary

Judson, Horace Freeland. *The Eighth Day of Creation: The Makers of the Revolution in Biology.* New York: Simon & Schuster, 1979. A detailed historical account of the discovery of DNA, RNA, and protein synthesis. The narrative is based on the published literature, numerous interviews, and the author's own knowledge of these individuals and their accomplishments. It contains an entire chapter on Nirenberg and his work.

Portugal, Franklin H., and Jack S. Cohen. *A Century of DNA: A History of the Discovery of the Structure and Function of the Genetic Substance*. Cambridge, Mass.: MIT Press, 1977. Although it concentrates on the discovery of DNA, this book includes a chapter on the genetic code and its discovery, including the work of Nirenberg.

Rothwell, Norman V. *Human Genetics*. Englewood Cliffs, N.J.: Prentice-Hall, 1977.

A textbook on genetics that does a better job of explaining the subject than most. It is surprisingly nontechnical, although it is difficult to explain this subject without being technical.

Szekely, Maria. *From DNA to Protein: The Transfer of Genetic Information*. New York: John Wiley & Sons, 1980. An account of DNA structure, DNA replication, RNA structure, RNA transcription, messenger RNA, transfer RNA, and protein synthesis. It provides a somewhat technical description of the entire process and discusses Nirenberg's work on the genetic code.

Watson, James D. *The Double Helix: A Personal Account of the Discovery of the Structure of DNA*. New York: Atheneum, 1968. A personal account of the events leading up to the discovery of the DNA structure and of the people involved. It provides a look at the way scientific work is sometimes carried out. It was not meant to be an objective history but was written as a subjective autobiographical contribution to a history that was, at the time, not yet written. Although it deals with the discovery of DNA several years before Nirenberg did his work, it has become a classic and reveals the kind of effort that occurs in this kind of work.

Vernon N. Kisling, Jr.

1969

Physiology or Medicine

Max Delbrück, Germany and United States
Alfred Day Hershey, United States
Salvador Edward Luria, Italy and United States

Chemistry

Derek H. R. Barton, Great Britain
Odd Hassel, Norway

Physics

Murray Gell-Mann, United States

Economic Sciences

Ragnar Frisch, Norway
Jan Tinbergen, The Netherlands

Literature

Samuel Beckett, Ireland

Peace

International Labour Organisation

MAX DELBRÜCK
1969

Born: Berlin, Germany; September 4, 1906
Died: Pasadena, California; March 9, 1981
Nationality: German; after 1945, American
Areas of concentration: Molecular biology, virology, and theoretical physics

Delbrück, with Salvadore Luria and Alfred Hershey, described the mechanism by which living cells are infected with viruses

The Award

Presentation

Professor Sven Gard of the Royal Caroline Medico-Surgical Institute delivered the presentation address for the Nobel Prize in Physiology or Medicine on December 10, 1969. Gard reviewed the vastness of the infestation of life by viruses. They are found in people, animals, plants, and microorganisms, and some even attack other viruses. It was Max Delbrück, working with the physician Salvador Luria and the biochemist Alfred Hershey, who showed how viruses multiply, Gard stated. Delbrück did his study with the utmost accuracy and used statistics to support the meaning of his observations.

A virus that attacks bacteria is called a bacteriophage. It has an outside covering of protein and an inner core of nucleic acid. A substance in the protein coat of the virus digests the cell wall of bacteria. The nucleic acid of the bacteriophage enters the bacterium; the protein coat remains in the outside environment and no longer has a role. The nucleic acid from the virus now regulates the chemical activities within the bacterium. Molecules of viral nucleic acid and viral proteins are formed. These are put together to form many viral particles. Within ten to fifteen minutes, more than a thousand viral particles (mature bacteriophages) are released from the now dead bacterium.

On some occasions a genetic error occurs. These mutations helped Delbrück, Hershey, and Luria to define further the molecular makeup of viruses. Since the same mechanisms occur in microorganisms and higher plants, as well as in animals and humans, Delbrück is one of the founders of molecular biology.

Nobel lecture

On Wednesday, December 10, 1969, Max Delbrück delivered his Nobel lecture, entitled "A Physicist's Renewed Look at Biology—Twenty Years Later." He attempted to show unity between the living and the nonliving world. Many physicists do not consider biology as part of their area, but recent knowledge in biochemistry indicates that "the break between the nonliving world might not be absolute."

In the late 1930's, a group of theoretical physicists in Berlin discussed biology at their physics meetings. The research of this Berlin group showed that the mutations in fruit flies, reported by the American geneticist Hermann J. Muller, were caused by negatively charged particles called ions. The idea that the gene could be a molecule was new. "Genes at that time were algebraic units" and were recombined from one generation to the next.

Delbrück believed that the study of genetics at the molecular level provided the proper way to reconcile some aspects of the living world with the "incorruptibility" of the physical world; however, questions arise concerning how other aspects of life, such as conscious logical thought, relate to the physical world. These areas in neurobiology, Delbrück rightly predicted, would be appealing to the next generation of researchers. Especially in neurobiology, researchers may easily underestimate what is unknown. Some of this necessary basic knowledge may come through research in transducer physiology, a study of the flow of information in the nervous system after a stimulus is received. Delbrück used a fungus, *Phycomyces*, which contains a structure sensitive to light, gravity, stretch, and maybe even odor. Other researchers have used other simple organisms, such as bacteria and insects, to obtain information that must be discovered before neurobiology can be understood successfully. The second hurdle in neurobiology is the lack of understanding of the meaning of "truth." Truth "must be excluded from objective language" and must be separate and prior to the system of provable truth. Science does not produce truth which does not already exist. There also exists the problem of understanding art and science. They differ in that a work of art remains a unique object, but the work of a scientist blends into the work of other scientists to produce culture. Art and science are alike in that the work of each is involvement in the world and provides an escape from the world.

Delbrück noted that the Nobel ceremonies exemplify the differences of art and science. He had looked forward to meeting the writer Samuel Beckett, but Beckett did not come to Sweden to receive his Nobel Prize in Literature. On the other hand, the scientists seem eager to discuss their achievements.

The appendix to Delbrück's Nobel lecture is a summary of understanding of the virus. Viruses are composed of molecules. The virus accomplishes its replication by using its host, but the virus controls its own replication: The genome, or deoxyribonucleic acid, of the virus replicates itself.

Critical reception

Max Delbrück's telephone at his home in Pasadena, California, rang at 5:25 A.M. local time on October 16, 1969. It was a reporter trying to interview him about his being awarded the Nobel Prize in Physiology or Medicine. Soon, the telegram from Stockholm arrived. There were many more telephone calls, photographers at breakfast, a midmorning press conference, and a celebration in the laboratory at California Institute of Technology (Caltech). About thirty years had passed since Delbrück, along with Hershey and Luria, had laid a firm foundation for molecular biology; however, their work was certainly not ignored. They had made no singular spectacular breakthrough, but *Time*, *Newsweek*, *Science*, and *Science News* noted that the research of Delbrück, Hershey, and Luria had provided a necessary basis for James Watson and Francis Crick's helical structure of deoxyribonucleic acid (DNA). Arthur Kornberg also provided the firm foundation of molecular biology by his identification of the enzyme, DNA polymerase, which lengthens the DNA molecule.

The New York Times of October 17, 1969, described the usefulness of the scientific work announced on October 16 for the Nobel Prize for 1969. Since we know the reproductive process of the virus, the article said, we can now interfere with this process and thereby control viral diseases. *Newsweek* on October 27, 1969, described the virus as an infectious gene and Delbrück's research as a road which has led to vaccines against polio, measles, rubella, and mumps. *The New York Times* quoted Edward L. Tatum, a former winner of the Nobel Prize, as saying, "The whole field of viral genetics research is indebted to both Drs. Delbrück and Luria."

In another section of *The New York Times* on October 17, Max Delbrück was described as a mentor to his students: Max is "our group conscience, goad, and sage." He won other prize money, $12,500 of which he donated to Amnesty International, an organization that helps political prisoners obtain freedom. An expression of Delbrück was used by *The New York Times* to summarize the tone of his person: "The pursuit of truth is a many-sided thing—science is one of them."

Although Delbrück, Hershey, and Luria usually worked independently, they always shared their scientific insights and mutual interests. *Science News* of October 25, 1969, described them as "the nucleus of what was called the Phage Group." What they shared most was the trait of total incorruptibility. Gunther Stent of Harvard Medical School, writing for the October 24, 1969, issue of *Science*, commented that "it is just this trait of their personalities that these three men managed to impose on an entire scientific discipline." It was Delbrück, however, who became a kind of Gandhi, a spiritual force without any temporal power, within this group; it was Delbrück who had the greatest influence. Stent also wrote that the award committee was to be congratulated for its wisdom in recognizing the contributions of these three men.

Biography

Max Delbrück was born on September 4, 1906. He was the seventh child of Lina (née Thiersch) and Hans Delbrück, professor of history at the University of Berlin. His maternal grandfather, Carl Thiersch, was the surgeon general of the allied armies in the Franco-Prussian War, and his great-grandfather was the world-famous chemist Justus von Liebig. Delbrück spent his early years in an intellectual, politically active family in an affluent suburban area of Berlin called Grunewald. Many university professors lived there, and Delbrück would steal cherries from the yard of Max Planck, discoverer of quantum theory. It was not science or religion, however, but needed social and political reforms, current affairs, and the dangers of excessive nationalism that were the usual topics of discussion. Later, Delbrück would avoid all political conversation.

After 1914, Delbrück experienced the sufferings related to war; then there was postwar inflation and revolution. In 1924, he finished high school and enrolled that summer at the university in Tübingen. Until 1930, he studied astronomy and physics. Religion was not a force in his life, even though Delbrück believed in God and was a Protestant. Music, including religious music, and poetry were important to him. He struggled much with the meaning of life. Three postdoctorals followed—in Bristol, England, Zurich, Switzerland, and Copenhagen, Denmark. In Denmark, Niels Bohr awakened in Delbrück an interest in biology. In 1937, Max Delbrück arrived in the United States, first working at the California Institute of Technology in virus research. In 1941, he married Mary Bruce. They had four children—two sets of twins. In 1945, Delbrück became a U.S. citizen.

In 1963, Delbrück had his first indications of heart problems. He walked as treatment, but in 1975 he was diagnosed as having advanced coronary disease. Later that same year, there was surgery for a detached retina. Routine X rays before bypass surgery scheduled in April, 1978, revealed bone cancer in his ribs. Chemotherapy and radiation treatments followed, and he also agreed to interferon treatments. He remained home during his final illness; the pain became unbearable on the last night. He died early in the morning on March 9, 1981, in the hospital in Pasadena, California. His wife was with him.

Scientific Career

A search for simple, basic, unifying reality summarizes the scientific career of Max Delbrück, and it led him from one area of science into another. In boyhood, Delbrück was exceptional with numbers, but astronomy was his first area of interest. Over his bed he hung a picture of Johannes Kepler, whose three laws of planetary motion were the beginning of modern astronomy. He had his own telescope on a balcony of his parents' home. In astronomy, Delbrück found a personal identity, as this was a field that none of his friends, relatives, or neighbors knew much about. At this time, Delbrück began a life-long friendship with the physical chemist Karl Friedrich Bonhoeffer, who later became the director of the Max Planck Institute for Physical Chemistry. Bonhoeffer helped Delbrück to see great value in the search for knowledge that occurs in science.

In 1924, Delbrück completed high school as class valedictorian. Preparing for his address, Delbrück searched his father's library for information on Kepler, and at the suggestion of a teacher also used the rare book collection at the university in Berlin. As Delbrück handled these three-hundred-year-old books, original editions of Kepler's works, he experienced the thrill of the use of original sources. This aspect of scholarship would always be a part of his professional life. In the summer of that year, Delbrück enrolled as a student at the university in Tübingen. His first professor, Hans Rosenberg, was teaching the newly developed field of astrophysics, which is the study of the various emissions of stars (rather than the position of stars in the sky). As more sophisticated physics was being introduced into astronomy at the University of Göttingen, Delbrück went there in 1926. His research in astronomy did not develop, however, and physics was becoming much more sensational, so Delbrück studied physics. His thesis was a study of why the covalent bonds (forces between two atoms) of lithium are much weaker than the covalent bonds between two hydrogen atoms. Delbrück published his first paper, "Ergänzung zur Gruppentheorie der Terme" (1928; supplement to the cluster theory of electrons) in the German journal *Zeitschrift für Physik* (periodical for physics).

In 1929, Delbrück was thrilled by an invitation to do research in England at Bristol University. He concentrated on learning English phonetically as well as working on his research. In 1930, he published "The Interaction of Inert Gases" in the *Proceedings of the Royal Society of London*. In December, 1929, Delbrück experienced a setback, as he failed his final oral examination at Göttingen. Everyone at Bristol University was puzzled and very kind. The following year, Delbrück was successful.

Delbrück wanted more in the area of theoretical physics. A fellowship from the Rockefeller Foundation made it possible for him to study at the Niels Bohr Institute in Copenhagen, Denmark, where he produced a paper with George Gamow in the area of nuclear physics. In Zurich, Switzerland, Delbrück worked with Wolfgang Pauli, who is known for the Pauli exclusion principle: No two electrons (negative particles in the atom) can occupy the same quantum (energy) state.

Physics is extremely mathematical, and Delbrück was more interested in ideas than in calculations. He was not at all pleased with the content of his first publication, in fact, because he thought it lacked substance. Delbrück hoped to arrive at a way in which he could explain biology, or life, through molecules. In 1936, Delbrück published "Cosmic Rays and the Origin of Species" in *Nature* and an article in German, "Strahlengenetische Versuche über sichtbare Mutationen und die Mutabilität einzelner Gene bein *Drosophila melanogaster*" (1936; assay for emitted genetic rays evident by visible mutations and the mutability of individual genes with *Drosophila melanogaster*) in an obscure German journal, *Zeitschrift Induktions Abstammung Vererbungslehre* (journal of induced alterations in inheritance). Both papers were written with Nicolai Timoféef-Ressovsky, a Russian who was interested in mutations caused by ultraviolet radiation. Delbrück would visit Timoféef-Ressovsky unofficially after the Nobel ceremony because of Timoféef's punishment for remaining in Berlin to do genetic research rather than returning to Russia. The genetic research done in Berlin became known to Erwin Schrödinger, who popularized Delbrück's ideas in his lectures. Many European physicists came to consider Delbrück's approach to studying the gene the correct one.

A second Rockefeller fellowship in 1937 brought Delbrück to the United States to study the influence of physical factors upon mutation. He spent a month at Cold Spring Harbor, New York. On his way West, he stopped in Columbia, Missouri, and met Louis Stadler, a *Drosophila* geneticist, and Barbara McClintock, who would receive a Nobel Prize in 1983 for her work with movable genes. Upon arriving at the California Institute of Technology (Caltech) in Pasadena, Delbrück became well acquainted with the work of Thomas Hunt Morgan. The fruit fly, *Drosophila melanogaster*, was the research organism. *Drosophila* had been used as a research tool in genetics for many years. Delbrück struggled to read the numerous articles; they all seemed immensely complicated. Delbrück also discovered the research of Emory Ellis, who was studying the viruses that attack bacteria. These viruses, called bacteriophages (or phages), seemed to Delbrück to be much less complicated than fruit flies. Delbrück began to call the phages the atoms of biology. In 1939, Delbrück and Ellis published a paper, "The Growth of Bacteriophage," in the *Journal of General Physiology.*

The Rockefeller fellowship was renewed, but only after some serious questioning of the appropriateness of a theoretical physicist doing research with viruses. Morgan praised Delbrück's work to the Rockefeller office. Ellis had to return to cancer research because of funding stipulations, but at least Delbrück could continue. He concentrated on the multiplication process of the phage particles and expected to find the solution to the genetic riddle of life, which he never did. He completed three papers using the "gadget of physics," Delbrück's special name for the viruses. These papers led to collaboration with others, especially Linus Pauling and Salvador Luria.

The political condition in Germany was such that Delbrück was not certain of a job in research. The Rockefeller Foundation found a job for Delbrück as instructor of physics at Vanderbilt University in Nashville, Tennessee; Rockefeller would provide Delbrück's full salary of $2,500 for the first year, and Vanderbilt would gradually assume the salary if Delbrück proved to be an acceptable staff member. As time passed, the Rockefeller Foundation would continue to fund much of Delbrück's research.

At a meeting of the American Association for the Advancement of Sciences in Philadelphia in December, 1940, Delbrück met Luria. They made plans to attend a symposium and spend the summer at Cold Spring Harbor, the place that would be the "watering hole" for molecular biologists. Both Luria and Delbrück were enamored of the bacteriophage. Their work would lead to their Nobel Prize and several joint publications.

Delbrück would publish one paper, "Bacterial Viruses and Sex" (1948), in *Scientific American* with his wife, Mary Bruce Delbrück. After they were married for a year, she wrote a report on a "new species," *Homo scientificus*, a delightful account of her career-oriented husband.

Alfred Hershey, who was doing some research with bacteriophages at Washington University in St. Louis, made a trip to Vanderbilt University to talk research with Delbrück. On a second visit, Hershey delivered a paper to the science faculty at Vanderbilt. Hershey invited Delbrück to St. Louis, and Delbrück arranged for Luria to travel with him in April, 1943. Hershey called this the first phage meeting; thus the trio that would share the 1969 Nobel Prize in Physiology or Medicine began their discussions; Delbrück and Hershey, however, would never publish a paper together.

Delbrück taught the first phage course at Cold Spring Harbor, New York, in August, 1945. After three years, he handed the course over to Mark Adams from New York University's College of Medicine, but Delbrück continued to be active as the leader in the developing phage group. Genetic findings exploded, and these led Delbrück to see that the virus was not the simple entity he had hoped. Funding and space were both problems at Vanderbilt University. When George Beadle invited Delbrück to return to Caltech in 1946, he accepted and held the position of professor of biology until his death. There were periods, though, in which Delbrück did spend some extended time in Germany helping to rebuild the German university system. He was titled a visiting professor in 1956 and an acting professor from 1961 to 1963 at Cologne University.

By February, 1953, Delbrück knew he must begin work with a different simple organism. He chose the fungus *Phycomyces* and hoped that its responses to light could not be explained in physical terms alone. The riddle of life was still uppermost in Delbrück's mind. In 1954, he returned to the university in Göttingen, Germany, to search the older literature on stimulus-reaction systems in biological material thoroughly. Before returning to Pasadena, California, he lectured on the reactions of the fungus *Phycomyces* at the Serum Institute in Copenhagen.

Delbrück would continue to study *Phycomyces* for the rest of his life. A geneticist from Spain, Enrique Cerda-Olmedo, injected much new life into the study of this organism and convinced Delbrück to look at the relationship between the genetics of the fungus and its behavior. When Delbrück became seventy years old, Caltech waived its retirement rule and asked Delbrück what he planned to research. Although he could see no great discovery on the horizon, Delbrück saw the need for much more work on the genetics of *Phycomyces*.

Toward the end of his life and career, Delbrück lectured and published a synthesis of his basic, global philosophical ideas, entitled "Mind from Matter?" One version was given at a Nobel conference at Gustavus Adolphus College in St. Peter, Minnesota, and published in *The Nature of Life* (1978), edited by William H. Heidcamp. Throughout his career, Delbrück tried to solve the riddle of life. Life fascinated him intensely, in its precious and transient nature. He considered life well worth being an object of study, even though his mind was trained to be a physicist. He helped break barriers between scientific disciplines, thereby giving molecular biology a sound foundation.

Bibliography

Primary

BIOLOGY: "Cosmic Rays and the Origin of Species," *Nature*, vol. 137, 1936, pp. 358-359 (with N. W. Timoféef-Ressovsky); "The Growth of Bacteriophage," *Journal of General Physiology*, vol. 22, 1939, pp. 365-384 (with Emory L. Ellis); "Radiation and the Hereditary Mechanism," *The American Naturalist*, vol. 74, 1940, pp. 350-362; "The Growth of Bacteriophage and Lysis of the Host," *Journal of General Physiology*, vol. 23, 1940, pp. 643-660; "Interference Between Bacterial Viruses: I, Interference Between Two Bacterial Viruses Acting upon the Same Host, and the Mechanism of Virus Growth," *Archives of Biochemistry*, vol. 1, 1942, pp. 111-141 (with S. E. Luria); "The Reproduction of Bacteriophage," *Journal of Bacteriology*, vol. 45, 1942, p. 74; "Electron Microscope Studies of Bacterial Viruses," *Journal of Bacteriology*, vol. 46, 1943, pp. 57-77 (with S. E. Luria and T. F. Anderson); "A Comparison of the Action of Sulfa-Drugs on the Growth of a Bacterial Virus and of Its Host," *Journal of Bacteriology*, vol. 46, 1943, pp. 574-575 (with S. E. Luria); "Induced Mutations in Bacterial Viruses," *Cold Spring Harbor Symposia on Quantitative Biology*, vol. 11, 1946, pp. 33-37 (with W. T. Bailey, Jr.); "On the Replication of Deoxyribonucleic Acid (DNA)," *Proceedings of the National Academy of Sciences, U.S.A.*, vol. 40, 1954, pp. 783-788; "Photoreactions in *Phycomyces*," *Journal of General Physiology*, vol. 42, 1959, pp. 677-695 (with R. Cohen); "Action and Transmission Spectra of *Phycomyces*," *Plant Physiology*, vol. 35, 1960, pp. 194-204 (with W. Shropshire, Jr.); "Photoreaction in *Phycomyces*: Responses to the Stimulation of Narrow Test Areas with Ultraviolet Light," *The Journal of General Physiology*, vol. 44, 1961, pp. 1177-1188 (with D. Varju); "Avoidance Response, House Response, and Wind Response of the Sporangiophore of *Phycomyces*," *The Journal of General Physiology*, vol. 66, 1975, pp. 67-95 (with R. J. Cohen, Y. N. Jan, and J. Matricon); "Meiosis in *Phycomyces*," *Proceedings of the National Academy of Sciences, U.S.A.*, vol. 72, 1975, pp. 4076-4080 (with Arturo P. Eslava and Maria Isabel Alvarez); "Replacement of Riboflavin by an Analogue in the Blue-Light Photoreceptor of *Phycomyces*," *Proceedings of the National Academy of Sciences, U.S.A.*, vol. 78, 1981, pp. 266-269 (with M. K. Otto, M. Jayaram, and R. M. Hamilton).

CHEMISTRY: "Statistical Fluctuation in Autocatalytic Reactions," *Journal of Chemical Physics*, vol. 8, 1940, pp. 120-124; "The Nature of Intermolecular Forces Operative in Biological Processes," *Science*, vol. 92, 1940, p. 77-79 (with Linus Pauling); "A Theory of Autocatalytic Synthesis of Polypeptides and Its Application to the Problem of Chromosome Reproduction," *Cold Spring Harbor Symposia on Quantitative Biology*, vol. 9, 1941, pp. 122-124; "Was Bose-Einstein Statistic Arrived at by Serendipity?" *Journal of Chemical Education*, vol. 57, 1980, pp. 467-470.

MATHEMATICS: "A Statistical Problem," *Journal of the Tennessee Academy of Science*, vol. 19, 1944, pp. 177-178; "Brownian Motion in Biological Membranes," *The Proceedings of the National Academy of Sciences, U.S.A.*, vol. 72, 1975, pp. 3111-3113 (with P. G. Saffman).

PHILOSOPHY: "Mind from Matter?" in *The Nature of Life*, edited by William H. Heidcamp, 1978.

Secondary

Brooks, Stewart M. *The World of the Viruses*. South Brunswick, N.J.: A. S. Barnes, 1970. This short book is a simple, good account of the variety of viruses that exist. Several photographs aid the reader in understanding the great variety of viruses. Much emphasis is placed upon disease-producing viruses, the symptoms of the disease, and how to combat it. At the end, there is an excellent bibliography of a wide range of references.

Curtis, Helena. *The Viruses*. Garden City, N.Y.: Natural History Press, 1965. This is a comprehensive, readable summary of basic knowledge in virology. Delbrück is referred to in eight different areas in this book. The photomicrographs help the reader to picture what is being stated. The book focuses upon viruses as causes of disease and as an object by which the nature of life can be better understood.

Engel, Leonard. *The New Genetics*. Garden City, N.Y.: Doubleday, 1967. This book begins with an introductory chapter on Arthur Kornberg's synthesis of deoxyribonucleic acid. A brief summary of classical genetics follows, and then the book moves into the chemical explanations of heredity. The research of Delbrück is discussed in two different sections. This book reads more like a story than a science book, even though the science is of excellent quality.

Fischer, Ernst Peter, and Carol Lipson. *Thinking About Science*. New York: W. W. Norton, 1988. This full-length book (334 pages) is the story of Delbrück's life by people who knew him well. This book was begun in conversations with Delbrück, especially after he decided not to complete the autobiography he had started. This biography is a delightful and very true account of a great scientist, the research at Cold Springs Harbor, and the rise of molecular biology.

Garber, Edward D., ed. *Genetic Perspectives in Biology and Medicine*. Chicago: University of Chicago Press, 1985. This is a collection of papers published elsewhere, grouped into five different aspects of genetics. Each paper has its list of references. Many were originally given as invited lectures for various occasions. Delbrück is not one of the authors, but he is mentioned in eight different places.

Keller, Evelyn Fox. *A Feeling for the Organism*. New York: W. H. Freeman, 1983. Even though the cover rightly suggests that the main focus of this paperback is on someone other than Delbrück, in one section, six pages do an excellent job of helping the reader understand Delbrück's accomplishments. The entire book gives much insight into the meaning of basic science research. It also is an excellent introduction to the area of molecular genetics.

Stanley, Wendell M., and Evans G. Valens. *Viruses and the Nature of Life*. New York: E. P. Dutton, 1961. This small book has a picture on almost every page to help the reader understand what a virus is, not only as an agent of disease but also as an aid in defining the chemicals and chemistry of life. Even though the six chapters are written by six senior staff members of the University of California Virus Laboratory in Berkeley, each chapter is nontechnical.

Rose A. Bast